Language Intervention Series
Volume VI

EARLY LANGUAGE:

Acquisition

and

Intervention

EARLY LANGUAGE: Acquisition and Intervention, edited by Richard L. Schiefelbusch, Ph.D., and Diane Bricker, Ph.D, is the sixth volume in the **Language Intervention Series**—Richard L. Schiefelbusch, series editor. Other volumes in this series include:

Published:
Volume I **BASES OF LANGUAGE INTERVENTION** edited by *Richard L. Schiefelbusch, Ph.D.*
Volume II **LANGUAGE INTERVENTION STRATEGIES** edited by *Richard L. Schiefelbusch, Ph.D.*
Volume III **LANGUAGE INTERVENTION FROM APE TO CHILD** edited by *Richard L. Schiefelbusch, Ph.D., and John H. Hollis, Ed.D.*
Volume IV **NONSPEECH LANGUAGE AND COMMUNICATION** **Analysis and Intervention** edited by *Richard L. Schiefelbusch, Ph.D.*
Volume V **EMERGING LANGUAGE IN AUTISTIC CHILDREN** by *Warren H. Fay, Ph.D. and Adriana Luce Schuler, M.A.*

In preparation:
DEVELOPMENTAL LANGUAGE INTERVENTION **Psycholinguistic Applications** edited by *Kenneth F. Ruder, Ph.D., and Michael D. Smith, Ph.D.*
COMMUNICATIVE COMPETENCE **Acquisition and Intervention** edited by *Richard L. Schiefelbusch, Ph.D. and Joanne Pickar, Ph.D.*

Language Intervention Series
Volume VI

EARLY LANGUAGE:

Acquisition

and

Intervention

Edited by

Richard L. Schiefelbusch, Ph.D.
University Professor
and
Director, Bureau of Child Research
University of Kansas
Lawrence, Kansas

and

Diane D. Bricker, Ph.D.
Center on Human Development
University of Oregon

Technical Editors
Marilyn Fischer
Robert Hoyt
Bureau of Child Research
University of Kansas

University Park Press
Baltimore

UNIVERSITY PARK PRESS
International Publishers in Science, Medicine, and Education
300 North Charles Street
Baltimore, Maryland 21201

Typeset by Maryland Composition Co.
Manufactured in the United States of America by The Maple Press Company

Library of Congress Cataloging in Publication Data
Main entry under title:

Early language.

   Papers from a conference held at Sturbridge, Mass.,
May 23–25, 1979.
   Includes index.
   1. Language acquisition—Congresses. 2. Language
arts (Preschool)—Congresses. 3. Child development—
Congresses. I. Schiefelbusch, Richard L. II. Bricker,
Diane. [DNLM: 1. Infant—Congresses. 2. Language
development—Congresses. WS 105.5.C E12 1979]
P118.E18   401'.9   81-4569
ISBN 0-8391-1618-7   AACR2

contributors

Julie Ahlsten-Taylor B.Ed., Dip. (Ed)
Grant MacEwan Community
  College
Mill Woods Campus
7319-29 Avenue
Edmonton, Alberta, Canada T5J 2P2

Donald M. Baer, Ph.D.
Department of Human Development
  and Family Life
University of Kansas
132 Haworth
Lawrence, Kansas 66045

Diane D. Bricker, Ph.D.
Center on Human Development
University of Oregon
901 E. 18th Street
Eugene, Oregon 97403

Dale Bull, M.A.
Center for Research in Human
  Development
Erindale College
Mississauga, Ontario
Canada L5L 1C6

Earl Butterfield, Ph.D.
Ralph L. Smith Mental Retardation
  Research Center
University of Kansas Medical
  Center
39th and Rainbow Boulevard
Kansas City, Kansas 66103

Laurel Carlson, M.A.
Center on Human Development
University of Oregon
901 East 18th Street
Eugene, Oregon 97403

Robin S. Chapman, Ph.D.
Department of Communicative
  Disorders
University of Wisconsin
1975 Willow Drive
Madison, Wisconsin 53706

Richard F. Cromer, Ph.D.
Medical Research Council
Developmental Psychology Unit
Drayton House, Gordon Street
London, England WCIH OAN

William Fowler, Ph.D.
Graduate School of Education
Harvard University
Roy E. Larson Hall, Appian Way
Cambridge, Massachusetts 02138

Howard Gardner, Ph.D.
Harvard Project Zero
316 Longfellow Hall
Harvard Graduate School of
  Education
13 Appian Way
Cambridge, Massachusetts 02138

Alex Hillyard, Ph.D.
Centre for the Study of Mental
  Retardation
University of Alberta
Edmonton, Alberta
Canada T6G 2G5

James Hogg, Ph.D.
Deputy Director
Hester Adrian Research Centre
The University
Manchester, England M13 9PL

Frances Degen Horowitz, Ph.D.
Vice Chancellor for Research
  Graduate Studies and Public
  Service
University of Kansas
214 Strong Hall
Lawrence, Kansas 66045

David Ingram, Ph.D.
Linguistics Department
University of British Columbia
Vancouver, British Columbia V6T
  1W5

Gerard M. Kysela, Ph.D.
Centre for the Study of Mental
  Retardation
Educational Psychology
University of Alberta
Edmonton, Alberta
Canada T6G 2G5

Linda McDonald, Ph.D
Glenrose Hospital
10230 111th Avenue
Edmonton, Alberta
Canada 5G0B6

Jon Miller, Ph.D.
Waisman Center on Mental
  Retardation and Human
  Development
University of Wisconsin
Madison, Wisconsin 53706

Craig Ramey, Ph.D.
Frank Porter Graham Child
  Developmental Center
University of North Carolina
Highway 54, Bypass West
Chapel Hill, North Carolina 27514

Richard L. Schiefelbusch, Ph.D.
Bureau of Child Research
University of Kansas
Lawrence, Kansas 66045

Bruce Schneider, Ph.D
Center for Research in Human
  Development
Erindale College
Mississauga, Ontario
Canada L5L 1C6

Howard C. Shane, Ph.D.
The Children's Hospital Medical
  Center
Developmental Evaluation Clinic
Hearing and Speech Division
Boston, Massachusetts 02155

Joseph W. Sullivan, Ph.D.
John F. Kennedy Child
  Development Center
University of Colorado Medical
  Center
4200 East Ninth
Denver, Colorado 80220

Evelyn Thoman, Ph.D.
Biobehavioral Sciences
The University of Connecticut
Box U-154
Storrs, Connecticut 06268

Sandra Trehub, Ph.D.
Center for Research in Human
  Development
Erindale College
Mississauga, Ontario
Canada L5L 1C6

Ina Uzgiris, Ph.D.
Department of Psychology
Clark University
Worcester, Massachusetts 01610

Dennie Wolf, Ph.D
Harvard Project Zero
316 Longfellow Hall
Harvard Graduate School of
  Education
13 Appian Way
Cambridge, Massachusetts 02138

preface

During the last 10 years, the human infant has become a major focus for scientific investigation. Psychologists, linguists, psycholinguists, speech pathologists, and educators have been expanding the boundaries of their respective disciplines to include the study of basic processes and structures of the human infant. More specialists from these disciplines seem to be persuaded that to focus on the occurrence and nature of early forms of cognitive, communicative, and affective behavior is a pertinent activity in its own right and is essential to the construction of a comprehensive epigenetic theory of development.

Whether caused by the expanded scientific interest in the infant or simply parallel to it, the development of educational intervention services for younger children has also occurred. The combination of results from descriptive investigations and intervention efforts has generated an amazing body of information. Although the knowledge base surrounding infants remains speculative in many areas (e.g., continuity) and has changed significantly in other areas (e.g., speech perception), a compendium of useful concepts, methods, and procedures are being rapidly gathered to assist in our understanding of infancy. This changing perspective is particularly evident in the area of language where the work conducted during the 1970s has produced results demanding significant reformulations in terms of our understanding of developmental processes and intervention.

The editors of this book believe this to be an opportune time to examine and synthesize the existing research; consequently, this volume has evolved into a transition statement. That is, the contributors have reviewed the field's past history as a basis for discussing the current focus of information gathering and intervention, which has suggested, in turn, new avenues for future exploration. We believe this volume offers a powerful synthesis of past experience and current knowledge that is blending into a productive reformulation of our concepts about early language development and intervention.

The editors have discussed the possibility of a book that focused on early language development and intervention for many years. The need for such a book has never been the question; rather the delay was dictated by our perceptions of the limitations in the research literature. We did not want to develop a book before its time. By the end of the 1970s a group of outstanding individuals had produced a critical core of information whose combined efforts make up the content of this book.

The mechanism we used to aid in the synthesis effort was a conference held at Sturbridge, Massachusetts, on May 23–25, 1979, which was supported by a grant from the Bureau of Education for the Handicapped. The plan of the conference involved the preparation and prior exchange of papers. The discussions that were held in the conference context were based upon in-depth analyses of the issues, including both the differences and congruences of opinion and procedure. After the conference, the papers were finalized and the summary papers were added to form an integrated proceedings statement. This final compendium reflects the productive efforts of a diverse group of language specialists.

The urgency of the issues addressed in this volume lead to the dedication of this book to all at-risk infants and their families. Our hope is that the next decade will signal a worldwide humanistic and scientific effort in behalf of infants and children at risk for communication problems because it is now

x   Preface

apparent that much can be done to facilitate an infant's development and well being.

A number of contributors to this project should be acknowledged. We would like especially to thank Dr. Edward Sontag and Dr. Nick Certo of the Office of Special Education (now at the University of Maryland) who encouraged the editors to plan and implement the Sturbridge Conference. Without the support of OSE neither the conference nor the book would have been possible. Also we should like to indicate our appreciation to Mr. Linton Vandiver, president of University Park Press, for his generous assistance during the conference and for his timely suggestions regarding the publication plans.

We thank Melissa Bowerman for cogent suggestions that were reflected throughout the conference even though she was unable to participate. Also our thanks to Dr. Harris Nober for advice regarding local arrangements, to Dr. Victor Denneberg for fascinating contributions to the discussion at Sturbridge, and to Dr. Richard Brinker for his enthusiasm and perceptive comments. Finally, we wish to thank Ms. Janet Hankin of University Park Press for her assistance during the entire publication effort.

The contributions of Ms. Marilyn Fischer have been varied and critical to the project at all stages. She has contributed generously to the final manuscript. Together with Mr. Robert Hoyt and Ms. Mary Beth Johnston, she has maintained the quality and the credibility of the continuing book series on language intervention.

The planning and execution of both the conference and this book have been exhilarating undertakings. We have attempted to capture not only the most pertinent and useful information currently available, but also the sense of our excitement about the future growth in our ability to understand and assist handicapped infants. We hope we have succeeded.

R. L. S.
D. D. B.

Introduction

This volume focuses on how infants learn a functional language. Language acquisition is complicated by individual differences and at-risk conditions. Most babies are well equipped to enter the world. They quickly learn to thrive and to use active tactics to secure their needs and to generate conditions of security and comfort. Infants apparently are able to do this because they are genetically endowed with appropriate energies, sensory perceptors, and responses, and because they likely encounter adults who respond actively and sensitively to them. Adults, especially mothers, also seem to be equipped genetically (Bell and Ainsworth, 1972) for bonding with the baby. This adult responding apparently provides much of the child's early sensory stimulation and the infant's sense of security and comfort. The importance of early infant/mother bonding has received increasing attention by those who develop plans for neonatal care. A neonate who receives sporadic or insufficient care may be in jeopardy; thus the issue of *risk* may be complicated by poor quality of care.

The ethology of neonatal life has been discussed by many specialists (Mahoney, 1975). The central premise of this work is that the infant is an active participant in the mother/infant reciprocal interaction (Ainsworth, 1973). The infant does not thrive in the absence of this reciprocal arrangement. Also it is becoming apparent that the infant often may not thrive if he or she is impaired, and consequently may not provide the essential evocative cues to the caregiver.

Thus, there are significant hazards and departures from the natural plan. These departures often are found in conditions of poverty and degradation where neither the health of the infant nor the morale of the mother is conducive to positive, enriched infant experiences. These departures are found in conditions where the infant is impaired and apparently does not evoke the positive, spontaneous mothering that is given to most newborns.

The infant may be at risk because of a variety of causal features, and the conditions that may maintain the early risk conditions are complex. The functional issue of infant stimulation induced by an affective relationship is usually considered to be basic to the child's well-being. During infancy, the sensitive responding of the mother/father caregivers can apparently improve developmental outcomes (Sameroff and Chandler, 1975). Under conditions of responsive attention, the infant seems to acquire a communication system that has considerable range and variety. The proto-action systems of the infant are developed in the play activities that are initiated by the adult and maintained and intensified by their mutuality.

The emergence of language is a natural developmental extension of the mutual communicative experiences between the daily caregiving events and contexts for alternations of attentive and expressive behavior. It is not surprising that first words are simply refined events

3

that mark the mutual designations that the adult-infant team has shared repeatedly. Probably the infant's maturing sensory perceptual capabilities are instinctively noted and responded to by the adult in the context of play. This sensitive alternation of responding behavior leads to new patterns of modeled activity as the two communicate. The further extensions of communicative activity take the form of more formally defined symbol functions. The parent participants seem to be generally alert and responsive to communicative changes in the infant. The range of imitations increase, and expansions are added to the instructions. More complex combinations of objects and actions are added to the language experiences (Bruner, 1974).

The question When language is deficient, how is it deficient? must be asked. It is not difficult to list a few logical explanations based upon diagnostic experiences and developmental observations, but such data and such speculations do not lead necessarily to a prevention of language delay. A better question might be: On the basis of what we know and what we have demonstrated, what are the most effective intervention strategies we can initiate to accelerate the development of language in infants at risk?

This volume provides critical information about developmental processes and functions of infant language development (Section I), about mother/child interaction during the first 2 years (Section II), about early symbolic acquisition (Section III), about decision and implementation procedures (Section IV), and about intervention issues and strategies (Section V). Each of these sections contributes important and essential information on the means for *early language intervention*. At the end of each section is a synthesis statement, which highlights the salient points presented in that section.

Language is an extremely important part of the young child's life for a number of reasons. First, language and communication issues are embedded in the infant's early perceptual and affective transactions with the caregivers who provide stimulation (Chapters 1–7). Second, early language is closely related to the infant's cognitive development, and as a reflection of that development, language provides a means for gauging the infant's competencies in social and cognitive domains (Chapters 8 and 9). Third, language provides the code system for the referential bases of symbolization, as well as the structure for syntactic elaboration and the pragmatic functions that extend into the infant's widening range of social relationships (Chapters 2, 3, 8, and 9). Fourth, the basic system of language allows for the extensive and intensive range of knowledge and functions that are essential for further learning and for assessment of progress (Chapter 11, 12, and 13). Fifth, the language system allows for the bridging to various modes and topographies of symbolization that the child subsequently must use in both social and educational pursuits—reading, writing, numbers, and logical thinking (Chapters 11, 12, and 13). Finally, because language has both formal and functional properties even at early stages of development, intervention strategies can be planned with mothers and other caregivers so that acquisition is accelerated and so that the strategies address prevention and remediation functions (Chapters 14, 15, 16, and 17).

These highlighted issues attribute a significant role to early language and, by implication, define language quite broadly. However, there are numerous reasons for doing so. We need not go exclusively to formal linguistic theory nor to the organized information available as a psychology of language for these reasons. We can simply look at language as children learn to use it to achieve their purposes. Language is a practical system of organized parts, functional consequences, and symbolic extensions. Both researchers and clinicians should advise and educate caregivers of the at-risk and handicapped child so that he or she has an early start in acquiring this most essential system.

REFERENCES

Ainsworth, M. D. 1973. The development of infant-mother attachment. *In* B. M. Caldwell and H. Riciutti (eds.), Review of Child Development Research. University of Chicago Press, Chicago.

Bell, S. M., and Ainsworth, M. D. 1972. Infant crying and maternal responsiveness. Child Dev. 43:1171–1190.

Bruner, J. S. 1974. From communication to language: A psychological perspective. Cognition, 3(3):255–287.

Mahoney, G. J. 1975. An ethological approach to delayed language acquisition. Am. J. Ment. Defic. 80:139–148.

Sameroff, A., and Chandler, M. 1975. Reproductive risk and continium of caretaking causality. *In* F. D. Horowitz (ed.), Review of Child Development Research. University of Chicago Press, Chicago.

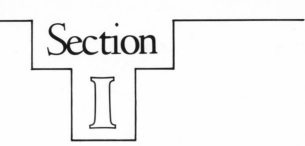

Developmental Processes and Functions

chapter

1

Infant Speech and Nonspeech Perception

A Review and Reevaluation

Sandra E. Trehub

Dale Bull

Bruce A. Schneider

Centre for Research in Human Development
Erindale College
University of Toronto
Mississauga, Ontario
Canada

contents

During the past decade, researchers have emphasized the similarities between the speech perception skills of infant and adult (Eimas et al., 1971; Eimas, 1974b, 1975b, 1978; Morse, 1974, 1978). As a result, they have fostered the view that age-related change is minimal in this domain. In this chapter it is argued that these similarities are of questionable significance and that there are differences that reveal an important role for development. Furthermore, it is argued that the traditional separation of infant speech and nonspeech research is unwarranted, and that the fundamental questions of infant speech perception may ultimately be reducible to general auditory issues. This review of speech and nonspeech findings is selective rather than exhaustive, emphasizing the aforementioned similarities and differences, their implications for development, and alternative research directions.

SPEECH STIMULI

Infants as Super-Discriminators

The claim regarding similarity, in its simplest form, is that infants can discriminate many, if not all, of the consonant (e.g., Eilers and Minifie, 1975; Eimas et al., 1971; Moffitt, 1971; Morse, 1972; Trehub and Rabinovitch, 1972) and vowel (Swoboda, Morse, and Leavitt, 1976; Trehub, 1973b) contrasts that are phonemically relevant in English. Not only are infants believed to make such discriminations but they are presumed to do so in a manner similar to that of adults. Thus, it has been argued that infants display categorical perception of voicing (Eimas, 1974b; Eimas et al., 1971)[1], place of articulation (Eimas, 1974a; Miller and Morse, 1976; Till, 1976), and liquid (Eimas, 1975a) contrasts. Moreover, infants, like adults, display continuous discrimination of vowels (Swoboda et al., 1976) as well as speech cues in a nonspeech context (Eimas, 1974a, 1975b). On the basis of this kind of evidence, infants are said to discriminate certain speech stimuli not only *auditorily* but also *phonetically* (Morse, 1978), that is, in a "linguistic mode." Infants' linguistic or phonetic perception is thought to reflect some innate knowledge of the adult phonetic categories (Eimas, 1978).

Preparation of this chapter and the authors' research reported herein was supported by grant MA 6239 from the Medical Research Council of Canada, grant 736-77/79 from the Ontario Mental Health Foundation, and grant A9956 from the Natural Sciences and Engineering Research Council of Canada.
[1] The perception of sounds is said to be categorical if discontinuities in discrimination are directly related to differences in identification, such that sounds labeled differently are highly discriminable whereas sounds reflecting comparable physical differences but labeled identically are not discriminable. On the other hand, perception is viewed as continuous when discrimination is not limited by the labeling or categorization of stimuli, such that many more stimuli can be discriminated than categorized (Mattingly, Liberman, Syndal, & Halwes, 1971).

In attempting to integrate infant categorical perception findings with theories of adult speech perception, Eimas (1975b) has rejected motor theory (Liberman, 1970; Liberman et al., 1967) and analysis-by-synthesis (Stevens and Halle, 1967; Stevens and House, 1972) approaches because they require excessive innate phonological knowledge. As an alternative to these accounts, he proposes the existence of linguistic feature detectors that are "especially tuned to restricted ranges of acoustic information that signal phonetic features" (p. 216), and that are operative shortly after birth. Evidence for these neurolinguistic mechanisms comes from a series of adult adaptation studies (Eimas and Corbit, 1973; Eimas, Cooper, and Corbit, 1973; Cooper, 1974) that revealed a post-adaptation shift in the locus of the identification boundaries. Eimas (1975b) argues that the presentation to infants of a particular speech signal excites the appropriate detector which, on the basis of repeated presentations of that signal, becomes adapted and generates reduced responding. If a second stimulus contains information that activates a different detector, this will result in increased responding. Thus, between-category stimuli are thought to stimulate different detectors as compared to within-category stimuli, which stimulate the same detector. Although this explanation is conceivably applicable to infant results obtained with techniques involving numerous stimulus presentations (e.g., the high-amplitude sucking technique), it is clearly inapplicable to other findings of infant discrimination, which have been obtained with as few as 20 stimulus repetitions (Miller and Morse, 1976; Till, 1976), a number insufficient to generate adult adaptation effects (Miller and Morse, 1979).

There is considerable dissent even with respect to the interpretation of adult adaptation data. Pisoni and Tash (1975) and Ades (1977) have proposed that auditory detectors replace the hypothesized phonetic detectors. Remez (1979), on the basis of adaptation effects obtained with a specially constructed speech-nonspeech continuum (vowel-buzz), has rejected both auditory and phonetic feature detectors, suggesting that the adaptation procedure reveals saturation effects but not detectors. "In studying adaptation using speech sounds, research has examined the mechanics of fatigue, not the process of speech perception" (p. 54). Elman (1979) has argued that adult adaptation effects are related to acquired cognitive processes as opposed to innate sensory mechanisms, with listeners merely redefining their phoneme categories after adaptation with an end-point stimulus. In short, the case for feature detectors is far from conclusive.

The categorical aspect of adult speech perception has assumed considerable importance in that it was thought to exemplify the uniquely human manner of perceiving speech compared to nonspeech stimuli (Liberman et al., 1967). Recent evidence has, however, eroded some of the "special" characteristics of human speech perception. For one thing, several studies with nonhuman species have revealed dramatic similarities in their processing of speech stimuli. For example, Morse and Snowdon (1975) found better between- than within-category discrimination of place contrasts by rhesus monkeys. In addition, it has been found that rhesus monkeys (Waters and Wilson, 1976) and chinchillas (Kuhl and Miller, 1975a) divide the voice-onset-time (VOT) continuum with a boundary at the approximate location of the English voiced-voiceless boundary. Kuhl (1978) has interpreted these findings as providing evidence for certain "natural" categories or perceptual discontinuities in speech stimuli that are related to the psychoacoustic abilities of mammals in general rather than to any phonetic abilities exclusive to human perceivers. Instead of the phylogenetic argument of Morse (1978) and Eimas (1978) that our perceptual capacities evolved to complement our phonetic abilities, Kuhl (1978) suggests the reverse, that these "natural" categories were ideal for inclusion in a human speech-sound repertoire, matched as they are to our auditory system. Given the fact that the auditory system must have predated speech production capabilities, it seems likely that evolving languages simply capitalized on the auditory propensities of prospective listeners.

Another problem with the supposedly distinctive manner of perceiving speech compared to nonspeech stimuli concerns several findings of categorical perception of certain nonspeech continua by adults (Burns and Ward, 1978; Cutting and Rosner, 1974; Miller et al., 1976; Pastore et al., 1977; Pisoni, 1977) as well as infants (Jusczyk et al., 1977). One proposed explanation of these findings relates to the processing of temporal order information in complex sounds, speech or nonspeech, that have two perceptually distinct components (Miller et al., 1976; Pisoni, 1977). When the onsets of these components are separated by an interval of less than 20–25 msec, the two components will be perceived as having simultaneous onsets; when separated by a greater interval, the components will be perceived as having successive onsets. Indeed, Pisoni notes that this temporal order phenomenon provides "still another example of how languages have exploited the general properties of sensory systems to represent phonetic distinctions" (p. 1360).

In addition to issues such as the uniqueness of categorical perception to human listeners or to speech continua, questions have been raised about the authenticity of the phenomenon itself. Macmillan, Kaplan, and Creelman (1977) have argued that the methods used for generating adult speech perception data yield biased estimates and, in fact, underestimates of sensitivity. Part of the problem is that there are only two response categories in the identification task. Macmillan et al. reanalyzed, with signal detection techniques, Cutting and Rosner's

(1974) identification and discrimination data for the syllables /ch/ and /sh/. They found discrimination to be 93% better than identification, notwithstanding the claim of categorical perception theorists that discrimination is no better than identification. Ades (1977) advanced a theoretical model based on Durlach and Braida's (1969) theory of intensity resolution that accounts for many of the classic differences between speech and nonspeech stimuli and between vowels and consonants. This model deals with differences between these stimuli "not by referring to how encoded they are, but in terms of a property of entire ensembles of stimuli—their range."

Finally, the absence of within-category discrimination has been linked to memory and coding constraints rather than to purely sensory constraints (Fujisaki and Kawashima, 1970; Pisoni and Lazarus, 1974). Indeed, when procedures that minimize memorial demands are used, adults successfully discriminate within-category stimuli (Carney and Widin, 1976; Carney, Widin, and Viemeister, 1977; Eilers, Wilson, and Moore, 1979; Pisoni and Lazarus, 1974; Sinnott et al., 1976). Infants tested with such procedures, however, failed to discriminate within-category stimuli from the VOT continuum (Eilers et al., 1979). Although Morse (1978) has suggested that language experience might result in a VOT category from that language becoming more categorical, the reverse seems more likely. This demonstrated "inferiority" of infants underlines the greater difficulty or perceptual subtlety associated with these within-category contrasts, a difficulty experienced, at least to some degree, by adults and by nonhuman species. This suggests either that the acoustic analyses of these continua have been inadequate or that our understanding of the mammalian auditory system is limited. Given the developmental course of these language-irrelevant (within-category) discriminations, it seems that explanations might be found in the realm of auditory abilities in general as opposed to speech perception skills in particular.

Although the status and significance of categorical perception remain unclear, the empirical evidence nevertheless preserves the notion of some infant-adult similarity, at least with respect to superior discrimination at the region of the phoneme boundary. However, the generalization that infants, like adults, can discriminate all phonemically relevant stimuli is simply untrue. For example, Eilers and Minifie (1975) failed to find discrimination of voicing with the fricative contrasts [sa] and [za] in 1- to 4-month-old infants. Eilers (1977) found that discrimination of these voicing contrasts in final position was dependent upon the availability of durational information, that is, [as] and [az] were discriminable only when the natural cue of differential vowel duration was present. It seems, then, that the discriminability of voicing and perhaps other phonemic contrasts may be dependent on context, a view at odds with the notion of neurophysiological detection mechanisms (Eimas, 1974b). Infants 3 to 8 months old have also failed to discriminate other fricative contrasts such as [f] and [θ] (Eilers, Wilson, and Moore, 1977), although it has been shown that exposure and training facilitate discrimination of these contrasts in 6-month-old infants (Holmberg, Morgan, and Kuhl, 1977). In the absence of specific training, however, improvement can be seen by 1 year of age (Eilers et al., 1977).

These discrimination failures by infants suggest that the speech perception system, short of being complete in early infancy, continues to develop throughout the first year of life and, perhaps, beyond. Eimas (1978) and Morse (1978) would counter that these studies were concerned with auditory rather than phonetic perception, the latter of which is independent of experience. In fact, both Eimas and Morse state explicitly that experience is unnecessary for infants' perception of the three major voicing categories: prevoiced, voiced, and voiceless stop consonants. In support of their view, they cite evidence of infants' ability to discriminate across both prevoiced-voiced and voiced-voiceless boundaries. However, Eilers et al. (1979) point out that of the numerous pairs of stimuli tested—stimuli that supposedly cross the prevoiced-voiced boundary[2]—only three revealed evidence of discrimination. Two of these instances (Lasky, Syndal-Lasky, and Klein, 1975; Streeter, 1976) involved infants from foreign language groups (Spanish, Kikuyu) that included a phonemic lead distinction; the third (Eimas, 1975b) involved English infants and a VOT difference of 80 msec. Compare this value with the 20 msec VOT differences in the Eimas et al. (1971) investigation of voiced-voiceless contrasts. On the other hand, Eilers et al. note that in all of the studies that tested the English voiced-voiceless boundary, evidence of discrimination was found whether the infants were from English backgrounds (Eilers et al., 1979; Eimas et al., 1971; Butterfield and Cairns, 1974) or from language groups in which the voiced-voiceless boundary is not phonemic (Syndal-Lasky et al., 1975; Streeter, 1976). This universal expertise at the English (voiced-voiceless) boundary coupled with limited proficiency at the foreign (prevoiced-voiced) boundary provides further evidence for general psychoacoustic abilities and against speech-specific phonetic abilities.

Part of the problem in evaluating the role of experience from these cross-language studies is that the crucial comparisons have generally been made across studies that were executed at different times and places and with varied methods. Eilers, Gavin, and Wilson (1979), in

---

[2] There is some dissent as to the precise location of the prevoiced-voiced boundary. See Eilers et al. (1979) for a discussion of this point.

a more definitive study on this issue, tested infants from English and Spanish environments in the same laboratory, under identical test conditions, with the English voiced-voiceless contrast and the Spanish prevoiced-voiced contrast, neither of which is phonemic in the language of the other. Interestingly, both groups of infants discriminated the stimuli that crossed the English boundary, but only the Spanish infants discriminated the stimuli that crossed the Spanish boundary. It seems likely, then, that some listening experience is indeed necessary for discrimination of the prevoiced-voiced distinction. The amount of such experience must be minimal, however, because Streeter's infants were only 2 months old, Lasky's 5 months old, and Eilers' 6 months old. (Eilers, Oller, and Gavin (1978) failed to find comparable effects of linguistic experience with stimuli differing along dimensions other than voicing.)

There is evidence to suggest that English adults also have difficulty with the prevoiced-voiced distinction (Abramson and Lisker, 1970). This makes one wonder why some language groups selected for their speech sound repertoire sounds that are not acoustically salient and that require linguistic experience for their discrimination. Eilers et al. (1979) make the interesting speculation that the synthesized lead stimuli used in these investigations may lack important cues that normally co-occur with VOT cues in natural speech. Thus, there may be some difficulty in generalizing from these laboratory studies with synthesized lead stimuli to real world abilities with natural prevoiced-voiced stimuli. If this is indeed the case, there may be cause for concern about the generalizability of speech perception research with infants and adults.

It is interesting that Morse (1978) and Eimas (1975a, 1978) do find some role for experience, albeit a limited one. On the basis of their view that infants can, without experience, discriminate prevoiced from voiced stimuli, and of Abramson and Lisker's (1970) negative evidence with English adults, they contend that linguistic experience involving disuse of the prevoiced-voiced category boundary operates to eliminate these discriminative abilities that were originally present. It has been shown, however, that these discriminative abilities most likely are absent in English infants. Moreover, there is evidence that the very same factors that have constrained adult within-category discrimination are operative in the adult voicing-lead research. Indeed, detection techniques that minimize memorial demands have yielded such evidence of adults' discrimination of synthesized lead cues (Carney et al., 1977; Eilers et al., 1979). In short, the developmental course of discrimination of these lead cues seems to be the reverse of that described by Eimas and Morse.

Although the evidence favors age-related improvement with respect to VOT and fricative discrimination, there is other evidence that supports the notion of developmental deterioration. Oriental adults, for example, have difficulty with the [r] − [l] distinction (Goto, 1971; Miyawaki et al., 1975), which is discriminable by infants (Eimas, 1975a). Moreover, English adults have difficulty with the Czech [z] − [ř] distinction, which is discriminable by infants (Trehub, 1976b). It should be noted, however, that infants in these studies were tested with very different procedures from those used with adults. (For a discussion of methodological issues related to infant-adult comparisons, see Trehub (1979).) In an attempt at greater comparability, Trehub (1978) tested infants and adults on these Czech stimuli under similar experimental conditions. The 7- to 8-month-old infants in this study showed evidence of discrimination but the English adults did not. This, then, represents the first unequivocal instance of infant perceptual "superiority" to adults. It is possible, of course, that these discriminations are accomplished with reference to distinctly different systems by language and nonlanguage users. Shvachkin (1973) has proposed a discontinuity between the "random, a-semantic" perceptions of the first year and the more orderly, semantically based perceptions of later years. One possible explanation is that the "a-semantic" perceptions involve a sensory code and the semantically based perceptions, a phonetic code. Although the phonetic code may be more efficient in the case of the highly overlearned categories of one's native language, it may, in fact, interfere with adults' perception of unfamiliar or foreign sounds (Trehub, 1979). Alternatively, or in addition, language-specific experience might provoke the ultimate loss of discriminative capacity with respect to nonfunctional phonetic distinctions (Trehub, 1976b), a point made inappropriately by Eimas (1978) and Morse (1978) with respect to voicing-lead distinctions.

The implications of these findings for a developmental theory of speech perception remain somewhat problematic because of the lead VOT instance of foreign speech discrimination in which infants are "inferior" and the Czech [z] − [ř] discrimination in which infants apparently are "superior." Further research with other foreign contrasts and at additional periods of the life span will help resolve this issue.

Infants as Super-Classifiers

There is another realm of proposed infant-adult similarity that is less abstract than the categorical perception issue. Kuhl and her associates (1976, 1978; Kuhl and Miller, 1975b) and Fodor et al. (1975) have argued that infants, like adults, can perceive or abstract similarities in speech stimuli despite variations in certain critical and noncritical acoustic dimensions. This phenomenon—termed *perceptual constancy* by Kuhl (1978), and *abstract phonetic invariance* by Morse (1978)— is seen as an important manifestation of linguistic processing. Kuhl and Miller (1975b) tested the ability of 1- to 4-month-old infants to discriminate the vowels [a] and [i] when the pitch contour was constant and when it was variable. The results indicated that infants could detect the vowel change in both contexts of constant or variable pitch contours. When infants were tested for their discrimination of the pitch contours, however, they succeeded when vowel color was constant but failed when vowel color was variable. On the basis of these findings, Kuhl and Miller argued that the segmental dimension of vowel color captured the infant's attention more readily than the suprasegmental and noncritical dimension of pitch contour. More recently, however, Kuhl and Hillenbrand (1979) demonstrated pitch contour discrimination in the context of vowel color and talker variation with 6-month-olds. Because different techniques were used with the two age groups, there is no basis for concluding that age-related changes are involved.

In another study that addressed the general question of phonetic invariance, Fodor et al. (1975) conditioned 3½- to 4½-month-old infants to respond to consonant-vowel syllables containing either the same or different initial consonants and varying vowels. They found more conditioned responses to the stimulus pairs with common initial consonants, suggesting that infants perceived the consonantal similarity across variable vowel contexts. Again, the substantially different technique in this study precludes direct comparisons with the investigations of Kuhl and her associates. In a further investigation along these lines, Kuhl (1976) demonstrated that 6-month-olds could discriminate vowel stimuli in the context of variable pitch contours and timbre differences resulting from synthesized male, female, and child voices. She argued that these infants were perceiving the abstract similarity between the vowels of male, female, and child talkers, an ability of obvious significance in the real world.

If infants are perceiving such similarities, on what basis are they doing so? In the task used by Kuhl with 6-month-olds, infants were trained to respond to a change in a repeating background stimulus. Initially, the pre-change and change stimuli were single tokens. Gradually, the variability in both stimulus sets was increased until the final set comprised six variations—three talkers with each of two pitch contours. During the course of training, infants presumably learned to extract the criterial differences between the two categories while ignoring the irrelevant changes in stimulation. It is likely that the critical differences are relational rather than absolute, but it is unclear whether specific phonetic as opposed to more general acoustic information is being extracted. Similar classification of speech stimuli across varying tokens by dogs (Baru, 1975) and chinchillas (Burdick and Miller, 1975; Kuhl and Miller, 1975a; Miller and Kuhl, 1976) suggests that the cues are probably acoustic rather than phonetic and that these cues are not as subtle to the listener as they seem to be to the psychologist or linguist.

What is also unclear, given Kuhl's protracted training procedure, which included training with the final test stimuli, is just how much training is in fact necessary for such performance. For the linguistically competent or knowledgeable adult listener, such categorization is obviously immediate and very likely accomplished on the basis of phonetic analysis, when this is relevant. On the other hand, if the linguistically naive listener could accomplish this kind of categorization with little or no training, this would imply that the cues are nonlinguistic and that these cues are perceptually prominent. Endman et al. (in preparation), using the same general technique as Kuhl (1976), trained 6-, 10-, and 13-month-old infants to respond to a segmental change ([pa], [mi]), and then tested them on a pitch change in the context of variable segmental cues ([pa], [pi], [pu]). All three age groups successfully discriminated the pitch change. Moreover, there were no differences between performance on this task and on another task involving a pitch change with single tokens. Because the discriminative cues in the training task were irrelevant to the test situation, it must be assumed that infants, during training, learned simply to respond to a change relative to the pre-change or background stimulation. In the test situation, perception of the change was immediate and automatic, even for the youngest infants, suggesting that the target dimension, pitch in this case, was indeed perceptually prominent. Thus, it seems that *learning* to recognize the essential differences is unnecessary, at least for stimuli such as these, and that the phenomenon is far broader than that originally envisioned by the term *abstract phonetic invariance*. Until more data on the discrimination of vowels, consonants, and suprasegmental features (in variable contexts) have been gathered, it will remain unclear whether the observed organization simply reflects the presence of prominent acoustic cues or whether some contribution is being made by knowledge, innate or learned, on the part of the perceiver.

Limitations of Infants

Infants' impressive performance with single-syllable stimuli has not been matched by their performance with multisyllabic stimuli. Trehub (1973a, 1976a) reported that infants 5 to 17 weeks old can discriminate voicing differences in the second syllable of two-syllable stimuli. This was found to be the case whether the contrastive syllable was preceded by a common vowel syllable or by a common consonant-vowel syllable. These findings are qualified, however, by the fact that such evidence was obtained only when the duration of individual syllables was approximately 500 msec but not when syllable durations were reduced to approximately 333 msec (Trehub, 1976a). Trehub has suggested that temporal processing constraints on the information processing capacities of young infants may be operative causing discriminative information from multisyllabic stimuli to be more readily extracted from stimuli presented at relatively slow rates. Support for this position emerges from her recent failure to demonstrate discrimination with comparable two-syllable stimuli (333 msec per syllable) with contrastive initial syllables and common second syllables (Trehub, in preparation). It should be noted, however, that the rapid rates of syllable presentation in these investigations are considerably slower than those of normal conversation.

Similar temporal processing constraints have been found with childhood aphasics with respect to both speech (Tallal and Piercy, 1974, 1975) and nonspeech (Tallal, 1976; Tallal and Piercy, 1973) stimuli. In the case of such developmental dysphasics, increasing the duration of transitions (Tallal and Piercy, 1975) or of interstimulus intervals (Tallal, 1976) has been found to facilitate performance.

The temporal constraints that have been proposed to account for the infant findings may be general, or instead, may be limited to a set of stimuli of which rapidly presented voicing contrasts in multisyllable contexts represent one instance. Evidence for the more limited interpretation comes from recent findings of infants' ability to discriminate second syllable differences in place of articulation (Jusczyk and Thompson, 1978; Jusczyk, Copan, and Thompson, 1977) when the contrastive syllables were as brief as 208 msec.

On the assumption that the findings of Trehub and of Jusczyk and his associates are replicable, it is not at all clear why VOT differences should pose greater difficulty than place-of-articulation differences, given comparable conditions of testing, in this case, the high-amplitude sucking paradigm. Nevertheless, there are some interesting parallels with heart rate findings. Although young infants' discrimination of place-of-articulation differences in initial position has been demonstrated with heart rate techniques (Miller and Morse, 1976; Till, 1976), evidence for discrimination of VOT differences in initial position with the same measures and age groups has been elusive (Roth and Morse, 1975; Miller and Hankes-Ruzicka, 1978). This finding is particularly puzzling because of the clear evidence of VOT discrimination with the high-amplitude sucking paradigm (Eimas et al., 1971; Trehub and Rabinovitch, 1972). What seems to be operative, then, is some constraint generated by an interaction between the nature of stimulation and the demands of the test situation. In the case of medial position contrasts and the high-amplitude sucking technique, this results in failure to discriminate VOT differences but success with place-of-articulation differences when syllable duration is 333 msec or less. In the case of initial position contrasts and heart rate measures, the result again is failure to discriminate VOT differences but success with place-of-articulation differences.

Although the limited research in this realm does not permit any definitive conclusions to be drawn, it does suggest that the temporal processing domain may provide fruitful avenues for future research. The manipulation of presentation rate should reveal general as well as stimulus-related processing limitations of the infant. Access to such processing limitations should advance our understanding of the relation between infant speech perception skills as seen in the laboratory and their application to real-world situations. In addition, it will be instructive to determine whether similar constraints are operative across speech and nonspeech domains.

Limitations of Techniques

Any discussion of the findings in infant speech perception is incomplete without some consideration of the different techniques that have been used to generate these data. Most of these techniques have been described elsewhere (Butterfield and Cairns, 1974; Eilers, 1978; Kuhl, 1978; Morse, 1974, 1978; Trehub, 1979), therefore, a brief description will suffice here. This discussion is concerned primarily with task demands and only secondarily with procedural details associated with these techniques.

The high-amplitude sucking (HAS) technique has been used extensively in infant speech perception research (e.g., Butterfield and Cairns, 1974; Eilers and Minifie, 1975; Eimas et al., 1971; Eimas, 1974a, 1975a; Jusczyk and Thompson, 1978; Morse, 1972; Streeter, 1976; Swoboda et al., 1976; Trehub, 1973a, b, 1976a, b; Trehub and Rabinovitch, 1972; Williams and Golenski, 1978). After a period of baseline sucking with no stimulus, infants are repeatedly presented with the same speech stimulus contingent upon their high-pressure or high-amplitude sucking. When infants meet a percentage criterion of sucking decrement, a contrasting sound is substituted for experimental infants, but comparison or control subjects receive no change in stimulation. Sensitivity to sound change is inferred from significant post-decrement differences between experimental and control subjects.

The contingency and subject-pacing aspects of the technique have been regarded as distinct advantages but they result in variable task demands from infant to infant. The frequently observed increase in infants' sucking following the introduction of response-contingent stimulation is thought to be attributable to the reinforcing properties of the speech stimulus, and the subsequent decrease in sucking, to the attenuation of these reinforcing properties (Eimas et al., 1971; Morse, 1974). Although there is some empirical support for the notion of conditioned response acquisition (Trehub and Chang, 1977), there is no evidence that the observed response decrement is other than incidental (Butterfield and Cairns, 1974). Nevertheless, this individualized criterion of sucking decrement, which cannot be presumed to reflect extinction, habituation, or other known processes, results in different infants having vastly different amounts of stimulus familiarization before the sound change. From a practical point of view, there is no procedural alternative within the framework of this technique because the potential increase in sucking to novel stimulation can only take place in the context of a prior decrease.

Other procedural details lead to further intersubject variability in task demands. The method of tabulating minute-by-minute sucking scores and the manner of introducing the sound change cause some infants to experience the change in the middle of a sucking burst. In this case, the infant receives the new stimulus within a second of hearing the familiar or old stimulus. For other infants, the stimulus change may occur in the pause between sucking bursts, which may cause the familiar and novel stimuli to be separated by as much as 30 or 40 seconds. It is obvious that the memorial demands in these two situations are not comparable. Indeed, Swoboda et al. (1978) found the rate of sucking in the first post-shift minute to be significantly related to the duration of the interval between familiar and novel stimuli, with discrimination deteriorating with longer intervals. There is no reason to expect that such differences would be confounded with experimental and control conditions and, in that sense, these variable demands do not discredit the results obtained with the HAS technique. They do, however, limit the productiveness of comparisons of HAS findings with those of other techniques and they suggest, as well, that infants' discrimination capacities are being underestimated with this technique.

The second most popular technique in infant speech perception research has been the heart rate (HR) habituation-dishabituation paradigm (Lasky et al., 1975; Leavitt et al., 1976; Miller and Morse, 1976; Miller, Morse, and Dorman, 1977; Moffitt, 1971). In the most common application of this technique, the infant is presented with a fixed number of familiarization or habituation trials with one stimulus, followed by test trials with a novel stimulus. Because the complete cycle of heart rate response and recovery takes several seconds (Jackson, Kantowitz, and Graham, 1971), a relatively long inter-trial interval (20–30 sec) has generally been used. Evidence for discrimination is provided by habituation to the familiarization stimulus followed by dishabituation or recovery of response to the novel stimulus.

It is obvious that the task demands of this heart rate technique differ considerably from those of the HAS technique. First, the test period in the HAS procedure is preceded by hundreds, perhaps thousands of presentations of the familiarization stimulus, compared with fewer than 100 presentations in the HR procedure. Thus, the possibility of sensory fatigue or feature adaptation (Eimas, 1974b, 1975b; Miller and Morse, 1979) is likely to differ, as is the opportunity for the development and refinement of appropriate schemes or engrams. Second, infants tested with the HAS procedure will, on the average, experience a shorter interval between the final familiarization stimulus and the first novel stimulus, compared with infants tested with the HR procedure.

Repeated failures to obtain discrimination when HR techniques were used with infants younger than 4 months of age (Berg, 1974; Leavitt et al., 1976; Miller et al., 1977) have led to an important modification that lessens memorial demands (Leavitt et al., 1976). This so-called *no-ITI paradigm* involves the presentation of several repetitions of the familiarization stimulus followed immediately by several repetitions of the novel stimulus, all of which are separated by equal but brief interstimulus intervals. This modified HR procedure has resulted in successful demonstrations of discrimination (Miller et al., 1977; Till, 1976), some with infants as young as 6 weeks of age (Leavitt et al., 1976). Nevertheless, the modified technique still seems to pose greater demands on the infant than does the HAS procedure, as evidenced by conflicting findings with these procedures when the identical stimuli are used with infants of the same age (Roth and Morse, 1975; Miller and Hankes-Ruzicka, 1978). Whether the occurrence of fewer repetitions in the familiarization period is responsible for these discrepant findings has not been determined.

A newer technique, which has been gaining in popularity, is the operant head-turning technique, VRISD (Visually Reinforced Infant Speech Discrimination), developed by Eilers et al. (1977, 1979). The technique has been used with infants 6 months old and older (Eilers et al., 1977, 1979; Endman et al., in preparation; Kuhl, 1977; Kuhl and Hillenbrand, 1979), and involves the reinforcement of head-turn responses to a change in background auditory stimulation. This background stimulation is continuously available and comprises a repeating stimulus with brief interstimulus intervals (approximately 1 sec) presented from a loudspeaker at the infant's side. When the infant is facing directly ahead, a test trial occurs during which a change in stimulus or comparable no-change interval is presented for 4–6 seconds. Correct responses are reinforced with the presentation of an animated toy. More frequent turns on change compared to no-change trials provide evidence of discrimination of the stimulus change.

In contrast to the HAS and HR techniques, the VRISD paradigm can generate individual as well as group data and thus provides an opportunity, as yet unused, for systematically examining individual differences. If such individual differences were identified, however, it is unclear what they would mean. Individuals with consistently deviant responsiveness in this test situation would likely require auditory assessment.

Some task demands seem to be minimized in the VRISD procedure, as compared with the HAS and HR paradigms. The infant has ample opportunity to hear the familiarization stimulus, which is continuously available from the moment he enters the testing environment. Moreover, because novel and familiar stimuli are separated by very brief intervals, the infant presumably compares sensory impressions of the new and old stimuli. In the case of the discrete-trial HR procedure or the HAS technique, the infant may be required to compare sense impressions of the new stimulus with stored representations of the old. Although the memorial demands of the VRISD paradigm make it ideal for use with very young infants, even newborns, the necessity of a reinforced head-turn or localization response to sound change effectively restricts its use to infants at least 5–6 months old (Moore, Wilson, and Thompson, 1976). Substitution of an alternative unconditioned response measure, perhaps heart rate, could provide the possibility of a downward extension in the testable age range.

The final technique in use was developed quite recently, thus, its application has been limited (Trehub, 1978). This technique involves habituation and dishabituation of the localization response to laterally presented stimuli, and is also restricted to infants at least 5 months old who can localize reliably. When infants are looking directly ahead, a trial, consisting of a train of identical stimuli, is presented on a loudspeaker at the infant's left or right, selected at random. During the period of stimulus presentation, the infant's first turn in either direction is scored as a response. Trials continue until the infant does not respond on a specified number of consecutive trials. Following this habituation criterion, experimental subjects receive a change in stimulus and control subjects continue to receive the same stimulus. Discrimination of the stimulus change is inferred from greater post-habituation responding by experimental subjects as compared with control subjects. The technique is far simpler to administer than any of the aforementioned procedures because an observable and readily tabulated response is used and no reinforcement is required. As with the HAS procedure, however, self-pacing results in a variable number of presentations, variable inter-trial intervals, and consequently, variable intervals between the familiar and novel stimuli.

The four techniques are applicable over somewhat different age ranges and thus differ in their suitability for developmental investigations. The HAS paradigm can and has been used from the neonatal period (Butterfield and Cairns, 1974) until about 4 months of age (Eimas et al., 1971; Trehub, 1973a, b, 1976a, b; Trehub and Rabinovitch, 1972). Although HR discrimination procedures can be used, in principle, throughout the life span, in practice, they have been most useful for infants between 3 and 5 months of age (e.g., Lasky et al., 1975; Moffitt, 1971). Younger infants have been tested with the no-ITI procedure but, as noted, the technique has failed to replicate some findings obtained with the HAS measure (Miller and Hankes-Ruzicka, 1978). With other infants, frequent body and limb movements increase the difficulty of obtaining reliable HR measurements. The technique has been used only infrequently for evaluating discrimination beyond infancy, and although it is potentially applicable to adults, its use has been somewhat problematic. For example, evidence of discrimination has been absent in some instances in which the stimuli were clearly discriminable (Brown et al., 1976).

Both procedures involving head turns cannot be used before 5 or 6 months of age and both can and have been adapted for use with adults (Eilers et al., 1979; Trehub, 1978). Substitution of age-appropriate reinforcers in the case of the VRISD procedure and modification of instructions in the case of the other localization procedure can potentially extend the applicability of these techniques to any age group. Thus, only these two techniques can provide an effective means of assessing discrimination over an extended age span.

On the basis of diverse task demands, comparisons involving different techniques at different ages are clearly unwarranted. The VRISD task seems to pose the fewest demands on infant and adult, and thus comes closest to evaluating the sensory competence of participant subjects. Indeed, it is with this and with similar techniques that adults have demonstrated within-category discrimination (e.g., Eilers et al., 1979).

Although the term *discrimination* is used in conjunction with any of the infant techniques, and with the standard adult techniques, it is quite likely that different processes are involved. Infant discrimination designs typically evaluate the ability to detect a stimulus change as evidenced by a response decrement or increment, whereas techniques used with children or adults generally assess discrimination by means of responses that necessarily engage higher order processes of considerable complexity (Trehub, 1979). The implications of this distinction are considerable. Infants' detection of speech differences can be considered as a prerequisite for language only in the most basic or general sense. Not only is the relation of such difference-detection ability to the production of phonemic distinctions unclear, but its relation to the perception of such distinctions is also unclear. Consider the sequence of phonemic speech perception proposed by Shvachkin (1973) or Garnica (1973) who have identified changes in the perception of consonantal and vocalic distinctions during the second year of life. Indeed, they note the nondiscrimination of many features apparently discriminated in early infancy. In contrast to the infant's task of simply detecting differences, the children in the Shvachkin and Garnica studies must distinguish between two objects on the basis of a sound difference in their labels. The child in such a language-like situation must first distinguish between the sounds, then remember them, and, finally, remember their association with referents. With respect to the nature of perceptual processes in the phonemic perception and difference-detection situations, Garnica makes a provocative observation: "The child must perceive the difference between, for example, /p/ and /b/ and not just between *p* and non-*p*" (p. 216).

NONSPEECH STIMULI

The perception of speech in infants should not be treated as a distinct mode of auditory processing but rather as one particular case of how the auditory system processes patterned acoustic signals of some complexity. Implicit in this position is the assumption that an understanding of the contribution of general auditory abilities to the discrimination and identification of acoustic patterns would resolve the ambiguity surrounding many, if not all, of the so-called special features of speech perception. In the literature on adult speech perception, this approach seems to be gaining in popularity. For example, Miller et al. (1976) argue that categorical perception "may be usefully approached in terms of psychophysical boundaries or thresholds for perceptual effects that are encountered as one component of a stimulus complex is changed relative to the remainder of the complex." Moreover, Pisoni (1977) accounts for adults' perception of voicing differences by invoking a general auditory constraint on our ability to process temporal order differences. Recent work on automatic speech recognition (Zwicker,

Terhardt, and Paulus, 1979) emphasizes the need for a "preprocessing" stage in speech perception in which the acoustic signal is characterized first with respect to essential auditory sensations such as loudness, pitch, and timbre before processing can proceed in a linguistic mode. As a final example, Ades (1977) uses the Durlach and Braida (1969) intensity discrimination model, which was developed with and intended for nonspeech stimuli, to account for many aspects of the perception of speech sounds.

If the perception of speech reflects certain facets of general auditory abilities, then age-related changes in these abilities will have direct consequences for the development of speech perception. For example, the ability to distinguish between certain speech patterns is dependent on the duration of individual components and the temporal relation of components of the patterned stimulus. Hence, changes in the ability to process temporal features of acoustic patterns will affect the developmental course of speech perception. Because the ability to resolve frequency and intensity differences must be involved in the discrimination of subtle linguistic cues, age-related changes in these skills will also have important implications for infant speech perception. Studies of frequency and intensity discrimination, however, are not readily interpretable without prior knowledge of age-related change in absolute sensitivity as a function of frequency. Finally, because arguments based on masking have been used to account for the categorical perception of speech (Miller et al., 1976; Pastore, 1979), and because speech in the real world is typically heard in a background of noise, developmental perspectives on auditory masking should provide theoretical and practical insights into the speech perception process. Unfortunately, current knowledge in these basic auditory domains is insufficient for an adequate account of infant speech perception in particular, or infant audition in general. Nevertheless, the following review includes what little is known about age-related changes in 1) the role of temporal and relational factors in pattern perception, 2) intensity discrimination, 3) frequency discrimination, 4) absolute sensitivity as a function of frequency, and 5) masking.

Much of our limited knowledge of general auditory abilities in infancy has come from studies that have used auditory stimuli incidentally to explore the development of affect (e.g., Wolff, 1963; Zelazo and Komer, 1971), cardiac orienting (e.g., Jackson et al., 1971; Porges, Arnold, and Forbes, 1973) or conditioning (e.g., Naito and Lipsitt, 1969; Watson, 1967). Although researchers in the field of infant auditory assessment (for reviews, see Cairns and Butterfield, 1975; Lloyd and Wilson, 1976; Wilson, 1978) have been directly concerned with hearing, their interest in rigorous psychoacoustic procedures has been subordinated to their primary objective of developing a means of screening infants conveniently and reliably for evidence of impaired hearing. As Wilson (1978) points out, the purposes of researchers and audiologists are frequently at odds. The researcher selects methods designed to elucidate general patterns of auditory development that are, for the most part, insensitive to the individual case. In contrast, the audiologist is specifically concerned with individuals, particularly those infants who fail to respond. These "discards" of psychological studies are the subjects of focus in clinical or audiological assessment situations. Moreover, sensitivity differences of 5, 10, or even 20 db as a function of experimental condition or age, although potentially important to theory construction and to the accumulation of normative data, are nevertheless inconsequential to the clinical focus of hearing loss. Despite these differences, it is clear that the ultimate interests of researchers and clinicians are related because it is doubtful that effective diagnostic instruments for infants and children can be constructed without knowledge of the normal developmental processes involved in hearing.

Hecox (1975), Rubel (1978), and Berg and Berg (1979) have organized somewhat broader contexts for the discussion of infant auditory functioning so that observations can be considered in relation to age-related changes in auditory structures or neurophysiological organization. Rubel notes, however, that there is a pressing need for more precise studies of auditory function so that the relations between structure and function can be delineated. Preliminary accounts of infant auditory function can be found in Eisenberg (1976) and Schneider, Trehub, and Bull (1979).

There are serious impediments to mapping the developmental course of audition. Most of the research effort has been concentrated on the neonate, with resultant gaps in knowledge beyond this period. Moreover, comparisons between studies are exceedingly difficult because of great diversity in the selection of response measures (e.g., auropalprebal reflex, Froding, 1960; Moro reflex or startle, Hardy, Dougherty, and Hardy, 1959; eye movement, Turkewitz et al., 1966; nonnutritive sucking, Eisele, Berry, and Shriner, 1975; head turning, Mendel, 1968; respiration rate, Steinschneider, 1968; skin resistance changes, Crowell et al., 1965; changes in general activity, Birns et al., 1965) and stimuli (e.g., cow mooing, Suzuki and Sato, 1961; squeak of a Micky Mouse toy, Miller, de Schweinitz, and Goestzinger, 1963; pulsed white noise, Hoversten and Moncur, 1969; square waves, Ashton, 1971; narrow-band noises, Ling, Ling, and Doehring, 1970; pure tones, Soderquist and Hoenigmann, 1973). Some of these response measures (e.g., nonnutritive sucking, general activity) are geared to a narrow age range and are, therefore, inappropriate for developmental investigations. Moreover, attempts to ascertain age-related improvements in auditory processing with certain physiological measures are problematic because of marked changes in these response systems during the period of early infancy (e.g., heart rate, Berg and Berg, 1979; skin conductance, Kaye, 1964). Although measures of response magnitude or response rate are frequently obtained, it is desirable to supplement this information with statements of responsiveness based on psychophysical measurement, that is, sensitivity (Hecox, 1975).

Temporal and Relational Determinants of Pattern Perception

In line with the general argument that speech perception is a "not so special" case of auditory perception, one should look to infants' perception of nonspeech patterns for important parallels. Unfortunately, however, there is little research in this area because most of the controlled investigations of infant audition have involved unpatterned or constant signals. Constant signals are characterized by fixed dimensions and have few natural analogues, as contrasted with patterned signals, which range in complexity from modulated tones to speech sounds. Eisenberg (1969) has suggested that constant and patterned signals evoke distinctive modes of responding in infants. Constant signals are effective principally in sleep states and they evoke nonspecific behavior such as changes in gross motor activity or startles, which are as readily evoked by non-auditory events. Furthermore, response magnitude is related to pre-stimulus arousal levels and exhibits homeostatic tendencies. In contrast, patterned signals are effective under both sleeping and waking states and are associated with specific behavioral responses such as selective body movement and responsive vocal activity (Eisenberg, 1976).

The few investigations of pattern perception involving nonspeech stimuli have concentrated on the processing of tonal sequences. Rearranging the order of a sequence of tones results in adults' perception of a novel pattern even when the frequencies and intensities of the component tones remain unaltered. Although there are several claims of infants' discrimination of the temporal order of sound sequences (Kinney and Kagan, 1976; McCall and Melson, 1970; Melson and McCall, 1970), these studies have suffered from design flaws in the sense that successful discrimination could have been accomplished solely on the basis of differences in the initial one or two tones. Moreover, Horowitz (1972) argued that infants do not process stimulus configurations as wholes. He suggests that in encountering a two-tone sequence, infants extract information about the first tone before and perhaps to the exclusion of the second tone. However, Chang and Trehub (1977a, b) demonstrated conclusively that 5-month-old infants can process six-tone sequences beyond the first two tones, and they have presented convincing evidence that infants process these patterns as wholes.

For adults, changing the temporal relations among elements of a tone sequence can result in the perception of an unfamiliar pattern. This demonstrates that the recognition of a familiar tonal pattern depends not only on the sequence of tones in the pattern but also on the duration of tones and intertone intervals. Initial demonstrations that infants could discriminate continuous versus pulsed tones (Berg, 1972; Clifton and Meyers, 1969) have been superseded by more sophisticated studies of temporal patterning. Chang and Trehub (1977b) assessed the ability of 5-month-old infants to discriminate between multi-tone patterns comprising identical component tones, but contrasting temporal arrangements of these tones. Following habituation of their cardiac response to a six-tone stimulus with 2, 4 grouping, infants dishabituated to the same tonal sequence with 4, 2 grouping. Allen et al. (1977) and Demany, McKenzie, and Vurpillot (1977) also reported discrimination of contrasting temporal groupings. One can, therefore, conclude that temporal patterning is a salient dimension for young infants.

Other infant research on temporal parameters of complex stimuli has been addressed more specifically to questions arising from the adult work on categorical perception. For example, Jusczyk et al. (1977) found infant categorical perception of sawtooth-wave stimuli differing in rise time, suggesting not only that categorical perception is not exclusive to speech stimuli but also that temporal factors may constitute one of the attributes underlying categorical perception. In a more direct test of the temporal order hypothesis (Pisoni, 1977; Miller et al., 1976), which links constraints on the perception of temporal order information to the categorical perception of voice onset time, Jusczyk et al. (1980) found infant discrimination of differences in the relative onset of two-component tones. Moreover, their results revealed three distinct perceptual categories that correspond to leading, simultaneous, and lagging events. Miller et al. (1976) and Pastore et al. (1977) suggested that the perception of these discontinuities is dependent on, among other things, the occurrence of changes in one component relative to other constant components of the stimulus complex. The contrasting finding of infant continuous discrimination of speech cues presented in isolation (Eimas, 1974a, 1975a) is consistent with the absence of a uniform context or reference pedestal against which judgments of simultaneity or successiveness can be made (Miller et al., 1976).

There is some indication that infants can also process frequency relations in auditory patterns. When a tonal sequence is transposed by a shift to different absolute frequencies, as long as the components remain invariant in relation to each other, adults perceive the shifted pattern as equivalent to the old pattern. This basic phenomenon underlies the recognition of melodies despite a shift in key (Dowling and Fujitani, 1971) as well as the recognition of speech across different speakers (Gibson, 1966). To investigate relational factors in the perception of melody, Chang and Trehub (1977a) habituated 5-month-olds to a sequence of six tones, then introduced either a transposition of the familiarized pattern, which altered the component tones but preserved the relation between tones, or a control pattern comprising the elements of the transposed pattern in scrambled order. Because infants, in both cases, received patterns with identical tonal elements, any differences in response would necessarily be attributable to the salience of relational information. Their results revealed no dishabituation or response recovery to the transposed pattern contrasted with dishabituation to the scrambled pattern. One can conclude, then, that infants responded to the transposed pattern on the basis of its similarity to the familiarization pattern. In other words, they recognized the familiar melody. Infants' recognition of transpositions implies that they are processing such patterns as integrated perceptual units and that they are perceiving such higher-order information in auditory patterns. It is clear, then, that infants' perception of relations is not exclusive to speech stimuli, as may be suggested by the work of Fodor et al. (1975) and Kuhl (1976, 1978), but that it represents instead, the usual mode of extracting information from patterned stimulation.

Intensity Discrimination

Several studies employing a variety of response measures have attempted to determine the relation between the intensity of the stimulus and the magnitude of the response both for neonates (Barnet and Goodwin, 1965, cortical evoked responses; Bartoshuk, 1964, heart rate; Bench et al., 1976a, behavioral activity) and for older infants (Bench et al., 1976b, behavioral activity; Berg, Berg, and Graham, 1971, heart rate; Soderquist and Hoenigmann, 1973, nonnutritive sucking). For example, Bartoshuk (1964) found that the relation between heart rate and sound intensity in neonates could be described by a power function.

These studies can, in principle, be used to determine the discriminability of two sounds differing in intensity. Bartoshuk (1964), for example, found that heart rate responses to 48, 62, and 77.5 dB stimuli were significantly different from each other. There is no indication, however, that this 14 dB difference represents an intensity-difference threshold, because no attempt was made to find the minimal intensity difference that could be discriminated. Similarly, evidence of intensity discrimination with habituation-dishabituation procedures (e.g., Bartoshuk, 1962; Bench, 1969a; Moffitt, 1973) has shed no light on the question of differential threshold because each investigation has generally been limited to two arbitrarily selected values.

It is clear, then, that infants can discriminate at least some differences in intensity but it is not at all clear how large these differences must be for discrimination to be evident. Exploring age-related changes in such difference limens is an important task for future research.

Frequency Discrimination

Several sweeping claims have been made about differential responsivity to stimulus frequency in neonates. Observations that neonates are differentially responsive to stimuli below 4000 Hz (Eisenberg et al., 1964), that they are more easily soothed by lower frequencies (Bench, 1969b; Birns et al., 1965), or that they exhibit greater behavioral and physiological responsivity to signals in the range of 125–250 Hz (Hutt et al., 1968; Lenard, von Bernuth, and Hutt, 1969; Weir, 1976) have been interpreted as being initial manifestations of complex psychological processes. Thus, it has been hypothesized that these patterns of frequency-dependent responding constitute evidence of neonatal precursors of adult affective responses to sounds (Eisenberg, 1976), "innate pitch discrimination or preference" (Bench, 1969b) or biological dispositions (attunement) to the carrier frequencies of speech (Eisenberg, 1976; Lenard et al., 1969).

Greater responsiveness to low or low-to-middle components of the adult audible spectrum seems to be a general feature of early auditory development in most animals (Rubel, 1978). For example, in mammals such as cats, rabbits, dogs, and mink, initial startle responses occur to lower frequency stimuli (Foss and Flottorp, 1974). Moreover, it has been suggested that the immature state of neuro-anatomical structures in human infants could result in the observed pattern of reduced high frequency responsivity (Hecox, 1975). In any case, the thesis that newborn auditory functioning reflects evolutionary specialization relevant to speech-like stimuli remains unevaluated. The effects of early aural experience are demonstrable in animal studies (Rubel, 1978) but have not been examined in human neonates. Because lower frequencies predominate in the intrauterine environment (Rubel, 1978), and because the attenuation of environmental sounds by the abdominal wall is greater as frequency increases (Bench, 1968; Walker, Grimwade, and Wood, 1971), experiential factors seem to warrant consideration, particularly with respect to infant soothing.

Regarding the discrimination of frequencies, early studies with neonates (Bartoshuk, 1962; Bridger, 1961; Bronshtein et al., 1958) had serious methodological limitations (see Jeffrey and Cohen, 1971; Morse, 1974; Trehub, 1973a). Although the findings of more recent neonatal studies have been conflicting, the magnitude of the frequency difference seems to be crucial, with successful demonstrations using more widely spaced frequencies (e.g., 500 versus 2000 Hz, Bench, 1969a; Stratton, 1970) than unsuccessful demonstrations (300 versus 700 Hz, Kittner and Lipsitt, 1976; 200 versus 500 Hz, Leventhal and Lipsitt, 1964).

Frequency discrimination has been repeatedly demonstrated in infants 1–4 months of age (Berg, 1972; Leavitt et al., 1976; Wormith, Pankhurst, and Moffitt, 1975), but there are no estimates of the smallest frequency change that is discriminable at any age during infancy or early childhood. Parametric investigations may reveal age-related changes that are comparable to the substantial "sharpening" of frequency discrimination shown by baby chicks during their first postnatal days (Rubel and Rosenthal, 1975). Some refinement in human infants' discrimination of frequency differences over the first several months of life has been noted (Kasatkin, 1969; Kasatkin and Levikova, 1935), but the limited research in this area has involved few subjects and relatively unsophisticated techniques.

The absence of information on differential intensity and frequency thresholds in infancy renders the negative evidence from studies of infant speech discrimination uninterpretable. Data relevant to the calculation of these thresholds could be obtained with the VRISD technique.

Absolute Sensitivity as a Function of Frequency

Several studies employing a variety of physiological and autonomic response measures indicate that neonatal thresholds are quite elevated with respect to adult thresholds (e.g., Rapin and Graziani, 1967; Schulman, 1973) and decline gradually throughout infancy and early childhood (Hecox, 1975; Schulman and Wade, 1970). In fact, one recent study found continuing improvement in auditory sensitivity up to 17 years of age (Roche et al., 1978). In line with the findings on suprathreshold responsivity, many studies have revealed greater sensitivity of the infant to low- as compared to high-frequency sounds (Eisele et al., 1972; Hoversten and Moncur, 1969; Hutt et al., 1968; Lenard et al., 1969; Weir, 1976). However, the crucial question of age-related changes in frequency-intensity relations has largely been ignored.

These authors have been gathering infant psychoacoustic data, particularly as it relates to frequency sensitivity. The procedure in use is a modification of the Visual Reinforcement Audiometry technique developed by Moore, Thompson, and Thompson (1975), which involves the reinforcement of localization responses to sound. During an experimental trial, a sound is presented on one of two speakers located 45 degrees to each side of the infant. The sound is initiated only when the child is looking directly ahead and is terminated only when a head turn (45 degrees or more) to either side has occurred. If the turn is in the direction of the sound, an animated toy (housed in a smoked glass enclosure above that speaker) is illuminated and activated for 4 seconds. If the turn is in the incorrect direction, there is a silent, 4-second-interval. The procedure, then, is a two-alternative forced-choice signal detection task. This contrasts with the Moore et al. (1975) procedure, which involves a single loudspeaker and a fixed response interval. To ensure that all of the infants can perform the task, they are first trained to a criterion of four successive correct responses at each of two suprathreshold levels. During the test session, four or five different intensity levels are presented five times each, the signals occurring randomly on the left or right speaker. At the conclu-

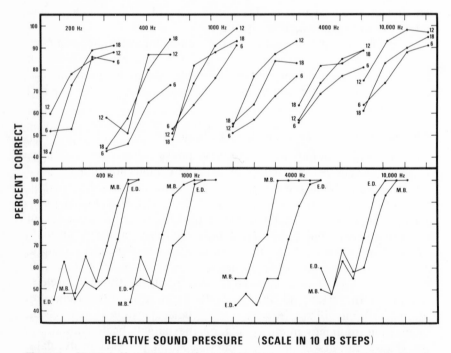

Figure 1.   Upper half: percentage of correct head turns as a function of decibel level of six test frequencies for infants 6, 12, 18 months old. Lower half: percentage of correct responses as a function of decibel level of four test frequencies for two adults. From Trehub et al. (1980).

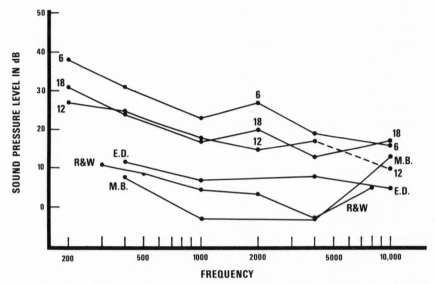

Figure 2.   Thresholds as a function of frequency for infants 6, 12, 18 months old and for two adults. Adult thresholds determined by Robinson and Whittle (1964) are also plotted. From Trehub et al. (1980).

sion of the first session there is a brief rest period before an abbreviated retraining and second test session are attempted.

In the first set of experiments (Trehub, Schneider, and Endman, 1980), 239 infants 6–18 months old were tested with one of the following pairs of octave-band noises: 200 and 2,000 Hz, 400 and 4,000 Hz; 1,000 and 10,000 Hz. Data were tabulated from all infants who completed at least one session. This resulted in 17–24 infants at each level of age (6, 12, 18 months old) and frequency. The upper half of Figure 1 shows the percentage of correct head turns as a function of the decibel level of the octave-band noises for the six different test frequencies, with each point being based on a minimum of 85 trials. It can be seen that as the intensity level increases, the percentage of correct responses also increases but never quite reaches 100%, even at the higher intensity levels. This is probably attributable to momentary lapses of attention to the task. The lower half of Figure 1 presents psychometric functions for two adults who were tested in a similar manner at frequencies of 400, 1,000, 4,000, and 10,000 Hz. Because each point of adult data is based on only 40 trials, these functions are more variable than the infant functions at the lower intensities.

Figure 2 plots the threshold values as a function of frequency for the three infant age groups. Three features of this graph should be noted. First, the threshold function for the 12- and 18-month-old groups seems to be fairly similar across the frequency range explored. Second, for the lower frequencies, the 6-month-old group seems to be approximately 5–8 dB less sensitive than the older groups. At the higher frequencies (4,000 and 10,000 Hz), however, there does not seem to be any significant difference between infant groups. Figure 2 also indicates threshold values for the two adult subjects, as well as thresholds determined by Robinson and Whittle (1964) in frontal-incidence conditions using a method of limits. It should be noted that the threshold functions are much flatter for the adult subjects than for the infants. At the lower frequencies, the differences between infant and adult thresholds are about 20–25 dB. For the higher frequencies, however, thresholds for the adults and infants are more nearly comparable.

Given the infant performance levels that were evident at the higher frequencies, it seemed reasonable to extend these findings to even higher frequencies. In a second study (Schneider, Trehub, and Bull 1980), 124 infants, 6–24 months old and 20 adults were tested with each of two half-octave bands of noise centered at 10,000 and 19,000 Hz. The final sample size at each level of age and frequency ranged from 20 to 31. At 10,000 Hz, the thresholds for the four infant groups were quite similar and were approximately 15 dB higher than the threshold for the adult group. At 19,000 Hz, however, the adult-infant differences were reduced considerably. In fact, thresholds for the 24-month-olds were equivalent to those of adults.

These two studies indicate that the disparity between infant and adult thresholds decreases as the frequency of the noise band increases until comparable thresholds are attained at 19,000 Hz. Thus, developmental changes in auditory sensitivity seem to be reflected largely in improvement at the lower frequencies. For frequencies below 4,000 Hz, improvement in sensitivity is evident at 12 months, although more substantial changes must occur sometime beyond infancy. The threshold differences between 6-month-olds and older infants (approximately 6 dB at the lower frequencies) seem similar to differences found by Wilson, Moore, and Thompson (1976) using a complex noise band (frequency undefined) and minor procedural differences.

The transformation of the Moore et al. (1975) technique into a two-alternative forced-choice signal detection task has the triple advantage of eliminating the need for control (no-stimulus) trials, minimizing concerns about response bias, and permitting the inclusion of infants who are slow to respond. Another advantage of this technique is the relatively modest attrition rate for infant subjects—about 25% at the youngest age level and 13% at the older age levels. In any case, support for the validity of the technique derives from the similarity of threshold functions between infants and adults at the higher frequencies, suggesting that the greater differences obtained at the lower frequencies are not merely attributable to the insensitivity of the technique.

The finding of adult-infant similarities at the high frequencies and substantial discrepancies at the low frequencies is inconsistent with earlier reports of greater infant-adult divergence at high rather than low frequencies (Eisele et al., 1975; Hutt et al., 1968; Lenard et al., 1969; Weir, 1976). A number of factors may be responsible for these conflicting findings. First, previous investigators used neonatal populations and typically employed physiological and autonomic indices of auditory sensitivity. Moreover, Schneider et al. (1979) have suggested that these physiological and autonomic measures may tap "attentional" thresholds rather than thresholds of hearing. Thus, two equally perceptible sounds may differ in their ability to evoke a physiological or autonomic response, depending on their "significance" (Bernstein, 1969; Bernstein, Taylor, and Weinstein, 1975) to the organism. For example, a sound that is above the threshold of hearing but is without "significance" might not elicit responses in an attentional or orienting system. If, however, responses to stimuli near the threshold of audibility are reinforced, as in the two-alternative VRA procedure, this would confer "significance" on these stimuli and, therefore, promote continued elicitation of responses. In short, it is argued here that the physiological, autonomic, and unreinforced behavioral measures reveal responsivity as opposed to sensitivity. The fact that thresholds obtained by these authors are as low or lower than those reported by other investigators is consistent with the view that the former are thresholds of detectability as opposed to attentional thresholds. Moreover, there is no necessity for the pattern of sensitivity to mirror that of responsivity. Indeed, it is interesting that the only other study of thresholds as a function of frequency that reinforced responses (Liden and Kankkunen, 1969) also obtained greater sensitivity at higher (4,000 Hz) than at lower (500 Hz) frequencies. There is no ready explanation, however, for the superior low-frequency responsivity that has been reported in the unreinforced context, and one can only speculate that certain natural "significance" factors, currently unknown, may be responsible for this effect.

Masking

Despite its direct relevance to the perception of speech, masking or the detection of signals in noise has not been studied in infants. In a preliminary investigation of the masking of a speech phrase by broad-spectrum noise (Trehub, Bull, and Schneider, 1981), one hundred eleven infants 6–24 months of age and 20 adults were tested. The two-alternative visual reinforcement procedure was modified by having both speakers carry the broad-band noise or masker. During a trial, a tape-recorded phrase, "Hi there," spoken by a female voice, was repeated until a head turn was observed. The phrase was 1 second long, and there was a 2-second pause between repetitions. The intensity of the signal was calibrated following the methods recommended by Kryter (1970) for speech sounds. Infants and adults were tested at two levels of background noise, 42 and 60 dBC. Thresholds for the speech signal were comparable across all four infant groups (6, 12, 18, 24 months) for both levels of masking noise. Increasing the masking noise from 42 to 60 dBC resulted in threshold shifts of approximately 14 dB for adults. These values are comparable to those found by Hawkins and Stevens (1950) for the masking of speech by noise in adults. A 10–12 dB difference in threshold, however, was found between adults and infants at both levels of background noise, that is, infants were 10 to 12 dB less sensitive than adults.

It is apparent that infants have greater difficulty than adults in detecting the presence of a speech signal in a background of noise, an impairment that has important implications for infant auditory performance in the real world. Unlike adult-infant threshold differences obtained in quiet, which are essentially irrelevant to most real world tasks, adult-infant differences in masked thresholds represent a serious practical impediment for infant subjects who required the speech signal to be more than ten times as intense (10 dB is an intensity ratio of 10:1) than that required by adults for signal detectability. Thus, in a moderately noisy environment, a signal that is easily perceived by an adult might be inaudible for an infant. These difficulties may be particularly relevant to the acquisition of linguistic skills. It is well known that context aids in the identification of spoken language in masking situations (Miller, Heise, and Lichten, 1951). The infant listener and language learner, however, is not afforded this rich context and thus, in certain listening environments, may not be able to disambiguate certain subtle acoustic cues.

Although the speech masking experiment suggests the presence of an impairment for infants, it does not provide sufficient information for specifying the nature and extent of this masking impairment. Because the signal was a complex auditory pattern, it is impossible to determine what aspect of the pattern was being detected. The use of a different phrase, for example, may lead either to larger or smaller adult-infant differences. On the basis of the threshold work in quiet (Trehub et al., 1980), it is known that threshold differences between adult and infant populations decrease with increasing frequency. If adult-infant differences in masking functions were to show the same pattern of convergence at the high frequencies, then adult-infant differences in the masking of speech would be expected to depend on the frequency components of the speech signal. For example, masked thresholds for complex speech sounds that are detected on the basis of their high-frequency components might be nearly equivalent for infants and adults, while other speech sounds with the same average intensity but less energy in the high-frequency region might show a substantial adult-infant difference. Hence, an understanding of the development of auditory masking will be facilitated by the initial use of simpler stimuli, so that the interaction between the extent of masking and the frequency of the masked signal can be determined. Preliminary efforts in this direction, which have involved the masking of octave-band noise by broad-band noise (Bull, Schneider, and Trehub, 1979), have been encouraging.

It is interesting to note that this masking paradigm could be used to study intensity discrimination in infants. As Miller (1947) indicated, increasing the intensity of a noise is functionally equivalent to adding noise to noise. In terms of the infant procedure, an increase in the intensity of the background noise on one of the two speakers would be expected to elicit head turning toward that speaker—a response that could be reinforced. By systematically varying the size of the intensity increment, a differential threshold for intensity could be determined. Should this procedure prove successful, it would be possible to ascertain, among other things, how differential sensitivity changes as a function of age.

Success at collecting masked thresholds with infants as young as 6 months of age suggests that other psychoacoustic issues can be investigated developmentally. For example, the notion of critical bands has been important in the analysis of many adult auditory phenomena. The critical band is a statement about the frequency-resolution capabilities of the auditory system; frequencies within this critical region can be said to interact with one another. As Scharf (1970) states, the "critical-band mechanism appears to discriminate between sound energy within a single critical band and energy outside the band, thus permitting the auditory system to treat subcritical stimuli alike with respect to threshold, masking, loudness and harmonic discrimination. The mechanism is analogous to a set of band-pass filters with variable center frequencies" (pp. 194–195). Although the critical band is generally discussed in the context of pure-tone masking, other methods of critical band estimation that would avoid the problems of testing infants with pure tones are available. For example, Gassler (1954) showed that the threshold for a narrow band of noise remains constant independent of its bandwidth, until the critical bandwidth is exceeded, at which point the threshold changes. Hence, infant thresholds of narrow-band noises of variable bandwidth can be compared. An estimate of the bandwidth at which these thresholds change should provide an estimate of the critical band. If critical band information can be collected in infants, it would provide a unifying concept applicable to many auditory phenomena throughout the life span.

CONCLUSION

It has been shown that infants are good but less than "super" discriminators of speech stimuli. It is readily acknowledged that they can discriminate many speech stimuli but the case for discrimination in a phonetic "linguistic mode" is not certain. The theoretical framework of speech perception as a unique process has been found wanting, at least so far as it applies to infants. Although it is possible that adults, on the basis of their extensive knowledge of language, do confer speech with special status, there is no clear evidence that infants do likewise with the meaningless sounds of their future language. This is not to discredit the claim absolutely and for all time, but to suggest that the onus is on its advocates to clearly prove rather than merely state their case. In short, there is no satisfactory developmental theory that can account for infant successes as well as failures to discriminate, and that can incorporate the limited information on age-related changes.

It has been suggested here that the speech/nonspeech dichotomy is counterproductive but there is, as yet, no conceptual framework with which to unify the research in both domains. Although some parallels in studies of patterned speech and nonspeech stimulation have tentatively been identified, it is clear that many of the crucial comparisons have not yet been attempted. The classic speech/nonspeech comparisons are exemplified by synthesized consonant-vowel syllables contrasted with formant transitions isolated from the same syllables (Eimas, 1974a, 1975a), a distinction that is commonly confounded with differences of duration, signal energy, and the presence or absence of a reference background or pedestal, which seems to be necessary for some categorical effects (Miller et al., 1976). The recent use of nonspeech stimuli, which avoids at least some of these confounds, has resulted in findings that are quite comparable to those with speech stimuli, both for adults (Cutting and Rosner, 1974; Miller et al., 1976; Pastore et al., 1977; Pisoni, 1977) and infants (Jusczyk et al., 1977; Jusczyk, et al., 1980).

Although threshold studies seem to be conceptually distant from investigations of patterned speech or nonspeech stimulation, they are nevertheless necessary for unequivocal interpretation of discrimination research which, in turn, is essential for the investigation of patterning. Researchers, in their attempt to structure infant investigations on adult theoretical foundations, have neglected the important fact that many of the basic dimensions of hearing are known for the adult but not the infant. Without knowledge of these basic processes and their developmental course, esoteric models will likely be invoked when simple accounts would suffice.

The abandonment of research in infant speech perception in favor of psychophysical investigations of frequency and intensity is not being advocated here; rather, the vigorous and rigorous pursuit of knowledge on all fronts is urged. The poverty of our knowledge base should direct us initially to the gathering of normative data across a broad age range. This will reveal the direction and rate of change in the acquisition of auditory skills. The availability of methodological tools (VRISD and modified VRA) that are applicable over most of the life span in both speech and nonspeech domains will facilitate the normative task. The real challenge, however, will be posed by attempts to delineate the organization and mechanisms that underlie the observed pattern of change.

ACKNOWLEDGMENTS

The authors are indebted to Neil Macmillan for his comments on an earlier version of this chapter.

REFERENCES

Abramson, A. S., and Lisker, L. 1970. Discriminability along the voicing continuum: Cross-language tests. Proceedings of the Sixth International Congress of Phonetic Sciences, Prague, 1967. Academia, Prague.

Ades, A. E. 1977. Vowels, consonants, speech, and nonspeech. Psychol. Rev. 84:524–530.

Allen, T. W., Walker, K., Symonds, L., and Marcell, M. 1977. Intrasensory and intersensory perception of temporal sequences during infancy. Dev. Psychol. 13:225–229.

Ashton, R. 1971. State and auditory reactivity of the human neonate. J. Exp. Child Psychol. 12;339–346.

Barnet, A. B., and Goodwin, A. M. 1965. Averaged evoked electroencephalographic responses to clicks in the human newborn. Electroencephalogr. Clin. Neurophysiol. 18:441–450.

Bartoshuk, A. K. 1962. Human neonatal cardiac acceleration to sound: Habituation and dishabituation. Percept. Mot. Skills 15:15–27.

Bartoshuk, A. K. 1964. Human neonatal cardiac responses to sound: A power function. Psychonomic Science. 1:151–152.

Baru, A. V. 1975. Discrimination of synthesized vowels [a] and [i] with varying parameters in dog. In G. Fant and M. A. A. Tatham (eds.), Auditory Analysis and Perception of Speech, pp. 91–101. Academic Press, New York.

Bench, J. 1968. Sound transmission to the human foetus through the maternal abdominal wall. J. Genet. Psychol. 113:85–87.

Bench, J. 1969(a). Audio-frequency and audio-intensity discrimination in the human neonate. Int. Audiol. 8:615–625.

Bench, J. 1969(b). Some effects of audio-frequency stimulation on the crying baby. J. Auditory Res. 9:122–128.

Bench, J., Collyer, Y., Mentz, L., and Wilson, I. 1976(a). Studies in infant behavioural audiometry. I. Neonates. Audiology. 15:85–105.

Bench, J., Collyer, Y., Mentz, L., and Wilson, I. 1976(b). Studies in infant behavioural audiometry. II. Six-week-old infants. Audiology. 15:302–314.

Berg, K. M., Berg, W. K., and Graham, F. K. 1971. Infant heart rate response as a function of stimulus and state. Psychophysiol. 8:30–44.

Berg, W. K. 1972. Habituation and dishabituation of cardiac responses in four-month-old, awake infants. J. Exp. Child Psychol. 14:92–107.

Berg, W. K. 1974. Cardiac orienting responses of 6- and 16-week-old infants. J. Exp. Child Psychol. 17:303–312.

Berg, W. K., and Berg, K. M. 1979. Psychophysiological development in infancy: State, sensory function, and attention. In J. D. Osofsky (ed.), Handbook of Infant Development, pp. 283–343. John Wiley, New York.

Bernstein, A. S. 1969. To what does the orienting response respond? Psychophysiology. 6:338–349.

Bernstein, A. S., Taylor, K. W., and Weinstein, E. 1975. The phasic electrodermal response as a differentiated complex reflecting stimulus significance. Psychophysiology. 12:158–169.

Birns, B., Blank, M., Bridger, W. H., and Escalona, S. K. 1965. Behavioral inhibition in neonates produced by auditory stimuli. Child Dev. 36:639–645.

Bridger, W. H. 1961. Sensory habituation and discrimination in the human neonate. Am. J. Psychiatry. 117:991–996.

Bronshtein, A. I., Antonova, T. G., Kamenetskaya, A. G., Luppova, N. N., and Sytova, V. A. 1958. On the development of the functions of analyzers in infants and some animals at the early state of ontogenesis. In Problems of Evolution of Physiological Functions, pp. 106–116. Moscow Academy of Science, Moscow. (U.S. Office of Technical Services translation 60-51066)

Brown, J. W., Morse, P. A., Leavitt, L. A., and Graham, F. K. 1966. Specific attentional effects reflected in the cardiac orienting response. Bull. Psychonomic Soc. 7:1–4.

Bull, D., Schneider, B. A., and Trehub, S. E. 1979. Infants' detection of an octave-band signal in a background of noise. Papers presented at meetings of the American Psychological Association, New York.

Burdick, C. K., and Miller, J. D. 1975. Speech perception by the chinchilla: Discrimination of sustained /a/ and /i/. J. Acoust. Soc. Am. 58:415–427.

Burns, E. M., and Ward, W. D. 1978. Categorical perception—phenomenon or epiphenomenon: Evidence from experiments in the perception of musical intervals. J. Acoust. Soc. Am. 63:456–468.

Butterfield, E. C., and Cairns, G. F. 1974. Discussion summary—infant reception research. In R. L. Schiefelbusch and L. L. Lloyd (eds.), Language Perspectives—Acquisition, Retardation, and Intervention, pp. 75–102. University Park Press, Baltimore.

Cairns, G. F., and Butterfield, E. C. 1975. Assessing infants' auditory functioning. In B. Z. Friedlander, G. M. Sterritt, and G. E. Kirk (eds.), Exceptional Infant, volume 3: Assessment and Intervention. Brunner/Mazel, New York.

Carney, A. E., and Widin, G. P. 1976. Acoustic discrimination within phonetic categories. J. Acoust. Soc. Am. 59(suppl. 1):S24 (Abstr.)

Carney, A. E., Widin, G. P., and Viemeister, N. F. 1977. Noncategorical perception of stop consonants differing in VOT. J. Acoust. Soc. Am. 62:961–970.

Chang, H.-W., and Trehub, S. E. 1977(a). Auditory processing of relational information by young infants. J. Exp. Child Psychol. 24:324–331.

Chang, H.-W., and Trehub, S. E. 1977(b). Infants' perception of temporal grouping in auditory patterns. Child Dev. 48:1666–1670.

Clifton, R. K., and Meyers, W. 1969. The heart-rate response of four-month-old infants to auditory stimuli. J. Exp. Child Psychol. 7:122–135.

Cooper, W. E. 1974. Adaptation of phonetic feature analyzers for place of articulation. J. Acoust. Soc. Am. 56:617–627.

Crowell, D. H., Davis, G. M., Chun, B. J., and Spellacy, F. J. 1965. Galvanic skin reflex in newborn humans. Science. 148:1108–1111.

Cutting, J. E., and Rosner, B. S. 1974. Categories and boundaries in speech and music. Perception and Psychophysics. 16:564–570.

Demany, L., McKenzie, B., and Vurpillot, E. 1977. Rhythm perception in early infancy. Nature. 266:718–719.

Dowling, W. J., and Fujitani, D. L. 1971. Contour, interval, and pitch recognition in memory for melodies. J. Acoust. Soc. Am. 49:524–531.

Durlach, N., and Braida, L. D. 1969. Intensity perception. I. Preliminary theory of intensity resolution. J. Acoust. Soc. Am. 46:372–383.

Eilers, R. E. 1977. Context-sensitive perception of naturally produced stop and fricative consonants by infants. J. Acoust. Soc. Am. 61:1321–1336.

Eilers, R. E., 1978. Infant speech perception: History and Mystery. Paper presented at NICHD Conference on Child Phonology, Bethesda, Md.

Eilers, R. E., Gavin, W. J. and Wilson, W. R. 1979. Linguistic experience and phonemic perception in infancy: A crosslinguistic study. Child Dev. 50:14–18.

Eilers, R. E., and Minifie, F. D. 1975. Fricative discrimination in early infancy. J. Speech Hear. Res. 18:158–167.

Eilers, R. E., Oller, D. k., and Gavin, W. J. 1978. A cross-linguistic study of infant speech perception. Paper presented at the Southeastern Conference on Human Development, Atlanta, Ga.

Eilers, R. E., Wilson, W. R., and Moore, J. M. 1977. Developmental changes in speech discrimination in infants. J. Speech Hear. Res. 20:766–780.

Eilers, R. E., Wilson, W. R., and Moore, J. M. 1979. Speech discrimination in the language-innocent and the language-wise: A study in the perception of voice onset time. J. Child Lang. 6:1–18.

Eimas, P. D. 1974(a). Auditory and linguistic processing of cues for place of articulation by infants. Perception and Psychophysics. 16:513–521.

Eimas, P. D. 1974(b). Linguistic processing of speech by young infants. In R. L. Schiefelbusch and L. L. Lloyd (eds.), Language Perspectives—Acquisition, Retardation, and Intervention, pp. 55–73. University Park Press, Baltimore.

Eimas, P. D. 1975(a). Auditory and phonetic coding of the cues for speech: Discrimination of the [r-1] distinction by young infants. Perception and Psychophysics. 18:341–347.

Eimas, P. D. 1975(b). Developmental studies of speech perception. In L. B. Cohen and P. Salapatek (eds.), Infant Perception: From Sensation to Cognition. Vol. II, pp. 193–231. Academic Press, New York.

Eimas, P. D. 1978. Developmental aspects of speech perception. In R. Held, H. W. Leibowitz, and H. L. Teuber (eds.), Handbook of Sensory Physiology, Vol. VIII, pp. 357–374. Springer-Verlag, Berlin.

Eimas, P. D., Cooper, W. E., and Corbit, J. D. 1973. Some properties of linguistic feature detectors. Perception and Psychophysics. 13:247–252.

Eimas, P. D., and Corbit, J. D. 1973. Selective adaptation of linguistic feature detectors. Cognitive Psychol. 4:99–109.

Eimas, P. D., Siqueland, E. R., Jusczyk, P., and Vigorito, J. 1971. Speech perception in infants. Science. 171:303–306.

Eisele, W. A., Berry, R. C., and Shriner, T. H. 1975. Infant sucking response patterns as a conjugate function of changes in the sound pressure level of auditory stimuli. J. Speech Hear. Res. 18:296–307.

Eisenberg, R. B. 1969. Auditory behavior in the human neonate: Functional properties of sound and their ontogenetic implications. Int. Audiology. 8:34–45.

Eisenberg, R. B. 1976. Auditory Competence in Early Life. University Park Press, Baltimore.

Eisenberg, R. B., Griffin, E. J., Coursin, D. B., and Hunter, M. A. 1964. Auditory behavior in the human neonate: A preliminary report. J. Speech Hear. Res. 7:245–269.

Elman, J. L. 1979. Perceptual origins of the phoneme boundary effect and selective adaptation to speech: A signal detection theory analysis. J. Acoust. Soc. Am. 65:190–207.

Endman, M., Trehub, S. E., and Thorpe, L. A. The discrimination of pitch changes in variable contexts by infants 6, 10, and 13 months of age. In preparation.

Fodor, J. A. Garrett, M. F., and Brill, S. L. 1975. Pi ka pu: The perception of speech sounds by pre-linguistic infants. Perception and Psychophysics. 18:74–78.

Foss, I., and Flottorp, G. 1974. A comparative study of the development of hearing and vision in various species commonly used in experiments. Acta Otolaryngol. 77:202–214.

Froding, C. A. 1960. Acoustic investigation of newborn infants. Acta Otolaryngol. 52:31–40.

Fujisaki, H., and Kawashima, T. 1970. Some experiments on speech perception and a model for the perceptual mechanisms. Annual Report of Engineering Research Institute. Faculty of Engineering, University of Tokyo, Tokyo, Japan. 29:207–214.

Garnica, O. I. 1973. The development of phonemic speech perception. In T. E. Moore (ed.), Cognitive Development and the Acquisition of Language, pp. 215–222. Academic Press, Inc., New York.

Gassler, G. 1954. Uber die Horschwelle fur Schallereignisse mit verscheiden brietem Frequenzspektrum. Acustica. 4:408–414.

Gibson, J. J. 1966. The Senses Considered as Perceptual Systems. Houghton Mifflin Company, Boston.

Goto, H. 1971. Auditory perception by normal Japanese adults of the sounds "L" and "R." Neuropsychologia. 9:317–323.

Hardy, J. B., Dougherty, A., and Hardy, W. G. 1959. Hearing responses and audiologic screening in infants. J. Pediatr. 55:382–390.

Hawkins, J. E., and Stevens, S. S. 1950. The masking of pure tones and of speech by white noise. J. Acoust. Soc. Am. 22:6–13.

Hecox, K. 1975. Electrophysiological correlates of human auditory development. In L. B. Cohen and P. Salapatek (eds.), Infant Perception: From Sensation to Cognition, Vol. II, pp. 151–191. Academic Press, Inc., New York.

Holmberg, T. L., Morgan, K. A., and Kuhl, P. A. 1977. Speech perception in early infancy: Discrimination of fricative consonants. J. Acoust. Soc. Am. 62(suppl. 1):S99. (Abstr.)

Horowitz, A. B. 1972. Habituation and memory: Infant cardiac responses to familiar and discrepant auditory stimuli. Child Dev. 43:43–53.

Hoversten, G. H., and Moncur, J. P. 1969. Stimuli and intensity factors in testing infants. J. Speech Hear. Res. 12:687–702.

Hutt, S. J., Hutt, C., Lenard, H. G., von Bernuth, H., and Muntjewerff, W. J. 1968. Auditory responsivity in the human neonate. Nature 218:888–890.

Jackson, J. C., Kantowitz, S. R., and Graham, F. K. Can newborns show cardiac orienting? Child Dev. 42:107–121.

Jeffrey, W. E., and Cohen, L. B. 1971. Habituation in the human infant. *In* H. W. Reese (ed.), Advances in Child Development and Behavior, Vol. 6, pp. 63–97. Academic Press, Inc., New York.

Jusczyk, P. W., Copan, H. C., and Thompson, E. J. 1977. Perception of glides in multisyllabic utterances in infants. Paper presented at 94th meeting of the Acoustical Society of America, Miami, Fla.

Jusczyk, P. W., Rosner, B. S., Cutting, J. E., Foard, C., and Smith, L. 1977. Categorical perception of nonspeech sounds by 2-month-old infants. Perception and Psychophysics. 25:50–54.

Jusczyk, P. W., and Thompson, E. J. 1978. Perception of a phonetic contrast in multisyllable utterances by 2-month-old infants. Perception and Psychophysics. 23:105–109.

Jusczyk, P. W., Pisoni, D. B. Walley, A. and Murrary, A. 1980. Discrimination of relative onset time of two-component tones by infants. J. Acoustic. Soc. Am. 67:262–270.

Kasatkin, N. I. 1969. The origin and development of conditioned reflexes in early childhood. *In* M. Cole and I. Maltzman (eds.), A Handbook of Contemporary Soviet Psychology, pp. 71–85. Basic Books, New York.

Kasatkin, N. I., and Levikova, A. M. 1935. On the development of early conditioned reflexes and differentiations of auditory stimuli in infants. J. Exp. Psychol. 18:1–19.

Kaye, H. 1964. Skin conductance in the human neonate. Child Dev. 35:1297–1305.

Kinney, D. K., and Kagan, J. 1976. Infant attention to auditory discrepancy. Child Dev. 47:155–164.

Kittner, S., and Lipsitt, L. P. 1976. Obstetric history and the heart-rate responses of newborns to sound. Dev. Med. Child Neurol. 18:460–470.

Kryter, K. D. 1970. The Effects of Noise on Man. Academic Press, Inc., New York.

Kuhl, P. K. 1976. Speech perception in early infancy: Perceptual constancy for vowel categories. J. Acoust. Soc. Am. 60(suppl. 1):S90. (Abstr.).

Kuhl, P. K. 1977. Speech perception in early infancy: Perceptual constancy for the vowel categories /a/ and /ɔ/. J. Acoust. Soc. Am. 61(suppl. 1):S39. (Abstr.).

Kuhl, P. K. 1978. Predispositions for the perception of speech-sound categories: A species-specific phenomenon? *In* F. D. Minifie and L. L. Lloyd (eds.), Communicative and Cognitive Abilities—Early Behavioral Assessment, pp. 229–255. University Park Press, Baltimore.

Kuhl, P. K., and Hillenbrand, J. 1979. Speech perception by young infants. Perceptual constancy for categories based on pitch contour. Paper presented at the meetings of the Society for Research in Child Development, March, San Francisco.

Kuhl, P. K., and Miller, J. D. 1975(a). Speech perception by the chinchilla: voiced-voiceless distinction in alveolar plosive consonants. Science 190:69–72.

Kuhl, P. K., and Miller, J. D. 1975(b). Speech perception in early infancy: Discrimination of speech-sound categories. J. Acoust. Soc. Am. 58(suppl. 1):S56. (Abstr.)

Lasky, R. E., Syrdal-Lasky, A., and Klein, R. E. 1975. VOT discrimination by four to six and a half month old infants from Spanish environments. J. Exp. Child Psychol. 20:215–225.

Leavitt, L. A., Brown, J. W., Morse, P. A., and Graham, F. K. 1976. Cardiac orienting and auditory discrimination in 6-week-old infants. Dev. Psychol. 12:514–523.

Lenard, H. G., von Bernuth, H., and Hutt, S. J. 1969. Acoustic evoked responses in newborn infants: The influence of pitch and complexity of the stimulus. Electroencephalogr. Clin. Neurophysiol. 27:121–127.

Leventhal, A. S., and Lipsitt, L. P. 1964. Adaptation, pitch discrimination, and sound localization in the neonate. Child Dev. 35:759–767.

Liberman, A. M. 1970. The grammars of speech and language. Cognitive Psychol. 1:301–323.

Liberman, A. M., Cooper, F. S., Shankweiler, D., and Studdert-Kennedy, M. 1967. Perception of the speech code. Psychol. Rev. 74:431–461.

Liden, G., and Kankkunen, A. 1969. Visual reinforcement audiometry. Arch. Otolaryngol. 89:87–94.

Ling, D., Ling, A. H., and Doehring, D. 1970. Stimulus, response and observer variables in the auditory screening of newborn infants. J. Speech Hear. Res. 13:9–18.

Lloyd, L. L., and Wilson, W. R. 1976. Recent developments in the behavioral assessment of the infant's response to auditory stimulation. In E. Loebell (ed.), XVIth International Congress of Logopedics and Phoniatrics. Karger, Basel.

Macmillan, N. A., Kaplan, H. L., and Creelman, C. D. 1977. The psychophysics of categorical perception. Psychol. Rev. 84:452–471.

Mattingly, I. G., Liberman, A. M., Syrdal, A. K., and Halwes, T. 1971. Discrimination in speech and nonspeech modes. Cognitive Psychol. 2:131–157.

McCall, R. B., and Melson, W. H. 1970. Amount of short-term familiarization and the response to auditory discrepancies. Child Dev. 41:861–869.

Melson, W. H., and McCall, R. B. 1970. Attentional responses of five-month girls to discrepant auditory stimuli. Child Dev. 41:1159–1171.

Mendel, M. I. 1968. Infant responses to recorded sounds. J. Speech Hear. Res. 11:811–816.

Miller, C. L., and Hankes-Ruzicka, E. 1978. A parametric investigation of the cardiac no-delay discrimination paradigm and voice-onset-time discrimination in infants. Research Status Report II, pp. 275–314. Infant Development Laboratory University of Wisconsin.

Miller, C. L., and Morse, P. A. 1976. The 'heart' of categorical speech discrimination in young infants. J. Speech Hear. Res. 17:578–589.

Miller, C. L., and Morse, P. A. 1979. Selective adaptation effects in infant speech perception paradigms. J. Acoust. Soc. Am. 65:789–798.

Miller, C. L., Morse, P. A., and Dorman M. F. 1977. Cardiac indices of infant speech perception: Orienting and burst discrimination. Q. J. Exp. Psychol. 29:533–545.

Miller, G. A. 1947. Sensitivity to changes in the intensity of white noise and its relation to masking and loudness. J. Acoust. Soc. Am. 19:609–619.

Miller, G. A., Heise, G. A., and Lichten, W. 1951. The intelligibility of speech as a function of the context of the test materials. J. Exp. Psychol. 41:329–335.

Miller, J., de Schweinitz, L., and Goestzinger, C. P. 1963. How infants three, four, and five months of age respond to sound. Except. Child. 30:149–154.

Miller, J. D., and Kuhl, P. K. 1976. Speech perception by the chinchilla: A progress report on syllable-initial voiced-plosive consonants. J. Acoust. Soc. Am. 59(Suppl. 1):S54. (Abstr.)

Miller, J. D., Wier, C. C., Pastore, R. E., Kelly, W. J., and Dooling, R. J. 1976. Discrimination and labeling of noise-buzz sequences with varying noise-lead times: An example of categorical perception. J. Acoust. Soc. Am. 60:410–417.

Miyawaki, K., Strange, W., Verbrugge, R., Liberman, A. M., Jenkins, J. J., and Fujimura, O. 1975. An effect of linguistic experience: The discrimination of [r] and [l] by native speakers of Japanese and English. Perception and Psychophysics. 18:331–340.

Moffitt, A. R. 1971. Consonant cue perception by twenty- to twenty-four-week-old infants. Child Dev. 42:717–731.

Moffitt, A. R. 1973. Intensity discrimination and cardiac reaction in young infants. Dev. Psychol. 8:357–359.

Moore, J. M., Thompson, G., and Thompson, M. 1975. Auditory localization of infants as a function of reinforcement conditions. J. Speech Hear. Res. 40:29–34.

Moore, J. M., Wilson, W. R., and Thompson, G. 1976. Visual reinforcement of head-turn responses in infants under twelve months of age. J. Speech Hear. Disord. 41:328–335.

Morse, P. A. 1972. The discrimination of speech and nonspeech stimuli in early infancy. J. Exp. Child Psychol. 14:477–492.

Morse, P. A. 1974. Infant speech perception: A preliminary model and review of the literature. In R. L. Schiefelbusch and L. L. Lloyd (eds.), Language Perspectives—Acquisition, Retardation, and Intervention, pp. 19–53. University Park Press, Baltimore.

Morse, P. A. 1978. Infant speech perception: Origins, processes and alpha centauri. In F. D. Minifie and L. L. Lloyd (eds.), Communicative and Cognitive Abilities—Early Behavioral Assessment, pp. 195–227. University Park Press, Baltimore.

Morse, P. A., and Snowdon, C. T. 1975. An investigation of categorical speech discrimination by rhesus monkeys. Perception and Psychophysics. 17:9–16.

Naito, T., and Lipsitt, L. P. 1969. Two attempts to condition eyelid responses in human infants. J. Exp. Child Psychol. 8:263–270.

Pastore, R. E. 1979. Possible psychoacoustic factors in speech perception. Unpublished manuscript, S.U.N.Y., Binghampton.

Pastore, R. E., Ahroon, W. A., Baffuto, K. J., Friedman, C., Puleo, J. S. and Fink, E. A. 1977. Common-factor model of categorical perception. J. Exp. Psychol. [Hum. Percept.] 3:686–696.

Pisoni, D. B. 1977. Identification and discrimination of the relative onset time of two-component tones: Implications for voicing perception in stops. J. Acoust. Soc. Am. 61:1352–1361.

Pisoni, D. B., and Lazarus, J. H. 1974 Categorical and noncategorical modes of speech perception along the voicing continuum. J. Acoust. Soc. Am. 55:328–333.

Pisoni, D. B., and Tash, J. 1975. Auditory property detectors and processing place features in stop consonants. Perception and Psychophysics. 18:401–408.

Porges, S. W., Arnold, W. R., and Forbes, E. J. 1973. Heart rate variability: An index of attentional responsivity in human newborns. Dev. Psychol. 8:85–92.

Rapin, I., and Graziani, L. J. 1967. Auditory-evoked responses in normal, brain-damaged, and deaf infants. Neurology. 17:881–894.

Remez, R. E. 1979. Adaptation of the category boundary between speech and nonspeech: A case against feature detectors. Cognitive Psychol. 11:38–57.

Robinson, D. W., and Whittle, L. S. 1964. The loudness of octave-bands of noise. Acustica. 14:24–35.

Roche, A. F., Siervogel, R. M., Himes, J. H., and Johnson, D. L. 1978. Longitudinal study of hearing in children: Baseline data concerning auditory thresholds, noise exposure, and biological factors. J. Acoust. Soc. Am. 64:1593–1601.

Roth, P. L., and Morse, P. A. 1975. An investigation of infant VOT discrimination using the cardiac OR. Research Status Report I, pp. 207–218. Infant Development Laboratory, University of Wisconsin.

Rubel, E. W. 1978. Ontogeny of structure and function in the vertebrate auditory system. In M. Jacobson (ed.), Handbook of Sensory Physiology, Vol. IX, Springer-Verlag, Berlin.

Rubel, E. W., and Rosenthal, M. H. 1975. The ontogeny of auditory frequency generalization in the chicken. J. Exp. Psychol.: Animal Behavior Process. 1:287–297.

Scharf, B. 1970. Critical bands. In J. V. Tobias (ed.), Foundations of Modern Auditory Theory, Vol. I, pp. 157–202. Academic Press, Inc., New York.

Schneider, B. A., Trehub, S. E., and Bull, D. 1980. High-frequency sensitivity in infants. Science 207:1003–1004.

Schneider, B. A., Trehub, S. E., and Bull, D. 1979. The development of basic auditory processes in infants. Can. J. Psychol. 33:306–319.

Schulman, C. A. 1973. Heart rate audiometry. Part I. An evaluation of heart rate response to auditory stimuli in newborn hearing screening. Neuropadiatrie. 4:362–374.

Schulman, C. A., and Wade, G. 1970. The use of heart rate in the audiological evaluation of nonverbal children. Part II. Clinical trials on an infant population. Neuropadiatrie. 2:197–205.

Shvachkin, N. K. 1973. The development of phonemic speech perception in early childhood. In C. Ferguson and D. Slobin (eds.), Studies of Child Language Development, pp. 91–127. Holt, Rinehart & Winston, Inc., New York.

Sinnott, J. M., Beecher, M. D. Moody, D. B. and Stebbins, W. C. 1976. Speech sound discrimination by humans and monkeys. J. Acoust. Soc. Am. 60:687–695.

Soderquist, D. R., and Hoenigmann, N. 1973. Infant responsivity to pure tone stimulation. J. Auditory Res. 13:321–327.

Steinschneider, A. 1968. Sound intensity and respiratory changes in the neonate. Psychosom. Med. 30:534–541.

Stevens, K. N., and Halle, M. 1967. Remarks on analysis by synthesis and distinctive features. *In* W. Wathen-Dunn (ed.), Models for the Perception of Speech and Visual Form, pp. 88–122. M.I.T. Press, Cambridge.

Stevens, K. N., and House, A. S. Speech perception. *In* J. Tobias (ed.), Foundations of Modern Auditory Theory, Vol. II, pp. 1–62. Academic Press, Inc., New York.

Stratton, P. M. 1970. The use of heart rate for the study of habituation in the neonate. Psychophysiology. 7:44–56.

Streeter, L. A. 1976. Language perception of 2-month-old infants shows effects of both innate mechanisms and experience. Nature. 259:39–41.

Suzuki, T., and Sato, I. 1961. Free field startle response audiometry, a quantitative method for determining hearing thresholds of infant children. Ann. Otol. Rhinol. Laryngol. 70:997–1007.

Swoboda, P. J., Kass, J., Morse, P. A., and Leavitt, L. A. 1978. Memory factors in vowel discrimination of normal and at-risk infants. Child Dev. 49:332–339.

Swoboda, P. J., Morse, P. A., and Leavitt, L. A. 1976. Continous vowel discrimination in normal and at-risk infants. Child Dev. 47:459–465.

Tallal, P. 1976. Rapid auditory processing in normal and disordered language development. J. Speech Hear. Res. 19:561–571.

Tallal, P., and Piercy, M. 1973. Developmental aphasia: Impaired rate of nonverbal processing as a function of sensory modality. Neuropsychologia. 11;389–398.

Tallal, P., and Piercy, M. 1974. Developmental aphasia: Rate of auditory processing and selective impairment of consonant perception. Neuropsychologia. 12:83–93.

Tallal, P., and Piercy, M. 1975. Developmental aphasia: The perception of brief vowels and extended stop consonants. Neuropsychologia. 13:69–74.

Till, J. 1976. Infants' discrimination of speech and nonspeech stimuli. Unpublished doctoral dissertation, University of Iowa, Iowa City.

Trehub, S. E. 1973(a). Auditory-linguistic sensitivity in infants. Unpublished doctoral dissertation, McGill University, Montreal, Quebec, Canada.

Trehub, S. E. 1973(b). Infants' sensitivity to vowel and tonal contrasts. Dev. Psychol. 9:91–96.

Trehub, S. E. 1976(a). Infants' discrimination of two-syllable stimuli: the role of temporal factors. Paper presented at meetings of the American Speech and Hearing Association, Houston.

Trehub, S. E. 1976(b). The discrimination of foreign speech contrasts by infants and adults. Child Dev. 47:466–472.

Trehub, S. E. 1978. More on infants' and adults' discrimination of Czech sounds. Paper presented at meetings of the American Speech and Hearing Association, November, San Francisco.

Trehub, S. E. 1979. Reflections on the development of speech perception. Can. J. Psychol. 33:368–381.

Trehub, S. E. Infants' discrimination of natural voicing contrasts in multisyllabic stimuli. In preparation.

Trehub, S. E., Bull, D., and Schneider, B. A. 1981. Infants' detection of speech in noise. J. Speech Hear. Res. In press.

Trehub, S. E., and Chang, H.-W. 1977. Speech as reinforcing stimulation for infants. Dev. Psychol. 13:170–171.

Trehub, S. E., and Rabinovitch, M. S. 1972. Auditory-linguistic sensitivity in early infancy. Dev. Psychol. 6:74–77.

Trehub, S. E., Schneider, B. A., and Endman, M. 1980. Developmental changes in infants' sensitivity to octave-band noises. J. Exp. Child Psychol. 29:282–293.

Turkewitz, G., Birch, H. G., Moreau, T., Levy, L., and Cornwell, A. C. 1966. Effect of intensity of auditory stimulation on directional eye movements in the human neonate. Animal Behavior. 14;93–101.

Walker, D., Grimwade, J., and Wood, C. 1971. Intrauterine noise: A component of the fetal environment. Am. J. Obstetrics and Gynecology. 109:91–95.

Waters, R. A., and Wilson, W. A., Jr. 1976. Speech perception by rhesus monkeys: The voicing distinction in synthesized labial and velar stop consonants. Perception and Psychophysics. 19:285–289.

Watson, J. S. 1967. Memory and contingency analysis in infant learning. Merril-Palmer Q. 13:55–76.

Weir, C. 1967. Auditory frequency sensitivity in the neonate: A signal detection analysis. J. Exp. Child Psychol. 21:219–225.

Williams, L., and Golenski, J. 1978. Infant speech sound discrimination: The effects of contingent versus noncontingent stimulus presentation. Child Dev. 49:213–217.

Wilson, W. R. 1978. Assessment of auditory abilities in infants. In F. D. Minifie and L. L. Lloyd (eds.), Communicative and Cognitive Abilities— Early Behavioral Assessment, pp. 37–59. University Park Press, Baltimore.

Wilson, W. R., Moore, J. M., and Thompson, G. 1976. Sound-field auditory thresholds of infants utilizing visual reinforcement audiometry. Paper presented at meetings of the American Speech and Hearing Association, Houston.

Wolff, P. H. 1963. Observations on the early development of smiling. In B. M. Foss (ed.), Determinants of Infant Behavior, Vol. II, pp. 113–138. Methuen, London.

Wormith, S. J., Pankhurst, D., and Moffitt, A. R. 1975. Frequency discrimination by young infants. Child Dev. 46:272–275.

Zelazo, P. R., and Komer, M. J. 1971. Infant smiling to nonsocial stimuli and the recognition hypothesis. Child Dev. 42:1327–1339.

Zwicker, E., Terhardt, E., and Paulus, E. 1979. Automatic speech recognition using psychoacoustic models. J. Acoust. Soc. Am. 65:487–498.

chapter 2

Reconceptualizing Language Acquisition and Cognitive Development

Richard F. Cromer

Medical Research Council
Developmental Psychology Unit
Drayton House
Gordon Street
London, England

At this point in the development of language intervention programs, it is important to take stock of the directions taken over the past few years by those working on the acquisition of language in normal, unimpaired children. The focus of this chapter is on the acquisition of the structure of language. Any intervention program that is intended truly to deal with "language" cannot confine itself merely to "communication." Understanding the development of grammar for language training programs was emphasized by Waryas and Stremel-Campbell (1978).

Although there has been a good deal of interesting work on the communicative and pragmatic aspects of language, our knowledge of the structure of language has barely increased, and those acquisition processes are still shrouded in mystery. There has been little progress in this area partly because many psychologists are confined by a number of conceptual prejudices that prevent the emergence of an adequate understanding not only of language acquisition but of cognitve development in general. This chapter suggests that the recent directions taken by language acquisition research, although valuable for the advancement of knowledge of important aspects of communication (and therefore of great interest to those designing language intervention programs), have nevertheless failed to fulfill their promise to explain adequately the acquisition of the linguistic structure of language. It is further suggested that at least two major reconceptualizations of development may be in order. The first part of this chapter reviews recent research directions in language acquisition with the aim of indicating the reasons such research has not solved the problem of the acquisition of language structure. In the remainder of the chapter, two reconceptualizations are suggested.

The first reconceptualization stresses the importance, for language acquisition, of internal factors in the child. Two frameworks are mentioned within this first reconceptualization—one stressing possibly innate factors and the other emphasizing the child's treatment of the language system as a conceptual puzzle space to be dealt with in its own right. Although these two frameworks are different, they are not incompatible. They share the feature of being critical of purely environmental/associationistic approaches to the acquisition of the structure of language. This section is introduced by a brief outline of how the mechanisms of growth and development can be reconceptualized to give a modified account of Piagetian mechanisms of development so that innate mechanisms can be considered more seriously. The fact that these concepts are stated in a Piagetian framework does not imply that they are limited to that theoretical position. In fact, it is preferable to see the suggestions that are offered as part of a broad "epigenetic" framework for development, but the ideas are stated in terms of Piagetian mechanisms because these are currently popular. The other framework—treating language as a structural system that is acquired—draws on the recent work by Karmiloff-Smith that analyzes in some detail how the child deals with particular structural subsystems of language.

The second reconceptualization deals with the content of cognitive stages. This reconceptualization asserts the need to look in more detail at the cognitive processes that comprise any putative stages. Some examples are given from recent research on language-disordered individuals to support the claim that to have effective intervention programs, there is no substitute for finding the true deficit. In a recent review of language intervention programs, Siegel and Spradlin (1978) reasoned that differential diagnosis and the discovery of specific underlying causes of language impairment would be important if it could be shown that these had significant consequences for the type of treatment and/or instructional programs undertaken. They concluded somewhat pessimistically, however, that given the present state of knowledge, the instructional task seemed to be identical regardless of whether the individual child was labeled autistic, brain-damaged, retarded, or congenitally aphasic. Although their conclusions are not unwarranted given present knowledge, the examples that are given of underlying deficits being uncovered by recent research will perhaps give a more optimistic outlook for the near future. The emphasis on the need to look at specific cognitive deficits in the various types of language-disordered individuals is related to the second reconceptualization. It is argued that mere correlations between broadly conceived Piagetian stages and various indices of language development are of little value for language intervention programs.

The concluding section presents recent advances in language acquisition that take into account what the child brings to the language acquisition process, and suggests some links to language intervention procedures.

RESEARCH DIRECTIONS THAT HAVE NOT FULFILLED EXPECTATIONS TO ADVANCE KNOWLEDGE OF THE ACQUISITION OF THE STRUCTURE OF LANGUAGE

This section discusses four topics, but they are not all strictly "research directions"; at least one of them is really only a theoretical orientation for research. It should be noted that the research mentioned below is not being criticized. Much of it is excellent in quality and has led to real advances in our broad understanding of communication. In every case, however, there has been a failure to shed any light on the processes involved in the acquisition of the structure of language. This is true despite the claims often made that only by understanding the broader aspects of language acquisition will the acquisition of linguistic structure be made clear. Such claims have so far proved empirically empty.

Research on Language Acquisition Strategies

In 1956, Bruner, Goodnow, and Austin introduced the notion of strategies for problem solving. They presented subjects with the task of acquiring concepts concerning features illustrated on specifically constructed cards. The cards had four attributes, each of which could take one of three values. For the attribute of shape, for example, the three values were a cross, a circle, and a square. Another attribute was number, for which there were either one, two, or three crosses, circles, or squares on a card. The cards, which varied in color, being either green, red, or black, were either borderless or had one- or two-line borders around the edge. The total array shown to the subject was 81 cards. A subject was first shown a positive instance of the concept the experimenter had in mind (e.g., all the cards with two figures). Then, the subject chose cards one at a time and the experimenter answered whether the chosen card was or was not a positive instance of the concept. The subject's goal was to discover the concept with the minimum number of choices. Bruner et al. inferred the use of particular strategies by the subjects from the pattern of decisions they made on successive cards. For example, a subject was said to have the strategy of "conservative focussing" if he or she found a positive instance of the concept, for example two red circles, and carefully changed attribute values one at a time to see whether this yielded a positive or negative instance. Thus, the subject might now choose a card with two *green* circles to see if color was part of the concept. Next, *three* red circles might be chosen to see if number was part of the concept. Subjects who used a strategy of "focus gambling" changed more than one attribute at a time in the hope of economy. Other subjects used various "scanning" strategies in contrast to the "focussing" strategies exemplified above. It should be noted that Bruner et al. took seriously the internally generated strategies of the subject—seeing the person as an active, goal-oriented organism—rather than relying on a notion of a passive subject impinged on by external stimulation. It is perhaps this aspect of their research that has excited researchers of language acquisition. At about the time Bruner et al. published their work on strategies, Chomsky (1959) attacked traditional theories of learning as being inadequate to explain the language acquisition process. Furthermore, a number of empirical studies indicated that the child is engaged in a very active process in acquiring language rather than passively responding to differential frequencies of language input, practice, and reinforcement (Bellugi-Klima, 1969; Brown, 1973; McNeill, 1970a, 1970b; Miller and McNeill, 1969). Against this background, the idea that children used particular internally generated strategies for acquiring language became very attractive.

There has been a good deal of research on the kinds of strategies that children are said to apply to language input. To give an indication of the type of research that has been successful in this area, a small sampling of experiments is mentioned here. A detailed account of a variety of strategies that have been investigated was given by Cromer, 1976b. It is argued, however, that the notion of "strategies" as used by most researchers of child language is quite different from that used by Bruner et al. Those strategies were the use of principles, consciously or unconsciously, to arrive at a given concept. By contrast, so-called language acquisition strategies are based on what the child does in a comprehension task. It will be shown that for this reason, such research has failed to solve the mystery of the acquisition of the structure of language.

One early strategy that young children use can be called the "probable event strategy." Strohner and Nelson (1974) tested children's comprehension of sentences by having 2- to 5-year-old children carry out actions with puppets and toys. It is often said that young children correctly interpret active sentences but have problems with the acquisition of passives. Strohner and Nelson, however, observed an interesting result with their youngest children—the 2- to 3-year olds. Given active sentences in which the actions were "improbable," the children would perform incorrectly. For example, given the sentence "The fence jumps the horse," the children in this age group would show the horse jumping over the fence, that is, they would interpret sentences referring to improbable events as if they referred to probable events. In contrast, the 5-year-olds, who used sentence word order for their interpretations, would show the "silly" action of the fence jumping over the horse. This interpretation occurred even though by age 5 the child knows much more about real world event probabilities than the younger children. Dewart (1979) showed that severely retarded children with a mean mental age (MA) of 3;2, matched for MA and on their understanding of single words with a group of normal children, relied more on a probable event strategy than the normal children.

Probability can even be affected by a short linguistic context. In another experiment, Dewart (1975) presented 20 normal subjects, ages 3;5 to 4;10, with passive voice sentences such as "The duck is bitten by the monkey." The child's task was to show the required action by means of hand puppets. First, children were tested on their knowledge of passive sentences with no context, like the above example. Then, they were tested on passive sentences that were preceded by a short phrase that provided either an appropriate or an inappropriate context. The appropriate context sentences were:

> Poor duck.   The duck is bitten by the monkey.
> Bad monkey.   The duck is bitten by the monkey.

The inappropriate context sentences were:

> Bad duck.   The duck is bitten by the monkey.
> Poor monkey.   The duck is bitten by the monkey.

For children who in the no-context condition demonstrated that they understood passive sentences, the contexts had no effect. But children who did not yet understand the passive, as revealed in the no-context condition, were very much influenced in their answers by the varying contexts. For example, for them, in the no-context condition the overall percentage of correct responses to passives was only 2%. It was similarly low (10%) for sentences with an inappropriate context. Correct performance for passive sentences preceded by an appropriate context, however, rose to 37%. It seems then, that a short linguistic context that bears on the appropriateness or likelihood of the action can affect the performance of children in this comprehension task. This appropriateness mainly affects those children who do not know how to interpret passive sentences correctly. It has little effect on children who have adequate syntactic knowledge. This is similar to Strohner and Nelson's finding that 5-year-olds were not misled by improbable active sentences into incorrect interpretations, whereas 2- to 3-year-old children were. Children who do not yet know the structures of the language comprehend in terms of appropriateness and probability; by contrast, older children with adequate syntactic knowledge are enabled by that knowledge to talk and comprehend nonsense.

Clark (1973a) showed that children often have very specific strategies for interpreting linguistic information. In her study, she was interested in the comprehension of "in," "on," and "under" by 70 children, ages 1;6 to 5;0. The subject's task was to place various toy animals in, on, or under six reference points of three types: a box on its side and a tunnel, a dump truck and a crib, and a table and a bridge. Three contrasts can be illustrated. The placement of a toy with reference to a box on its side allows either "in" or "on" to be tested. The dump truck tests for comprehension of the contrast "in" and "under." And for the bridge, "on" and "under" can be contrasted. The child placed 24 items—eight for each of the three prepositions.

For the youngest age group, mean age 1 ; 9, the results showed virtually total comprehension of "in" (94% correct replies), the beginnings of the comprehension of "on" (61% correct), and no comprehension of "under" (4% correct). Other experimenters might have concluded that children had acquired the meaning of "in," were in the midst of acquiring "on," and had no knowledge of the word "under." But Clark showed that such results can be deceptive and that another interpretation was more likely. If these youngest children used two very specific strategies, the same results would be obtained. One strategy is "If the reference point is a container, put the toy *in* it." The other strategy, which is used only if the objects do not allow the first strategy, is "If the reference point has a horizontal surface, put the toy *on* it." These two strategies give the same results as those mentioned above. Whenever the box or tunnel was used, children put the toy "in," regardless of whether the instructions were for "in" or "on." Similarly, for the dump truck and crib, all toys were put "in," regardless of whether the experimenter had said "in" or "under." This first strategy, then, gave 100% correct for "in" and 0% correct for "on" and "under." The second strategy, which comes into play with the table and bridge, results in the child putting toys "on" those objects, whether the instruction was for "on" or for "under." Thus, over all three contrasts, "under" still remains with no correct responses, but "on," with 100% correct in this third contrast, combined with 0% correct when contrasted with "in," was responded to correctly 50% of the time.

The materials that are used in the experiment can help to determine the strategy that the child uses. Wilcox and Palermo (1975) claim that by using a new set of toys, they can obtain results quite different from Clark's. The children in their experiment were divided into three age groups, with mean ages of 1 ; 9, 2 ; 3 and 2 ; 9. They also tested the comprehension of "in," "on," and "under," but with different materials. For example, where Clark had used toy animals for the children to place on the reference points, Wilcox and Palermo used a variety of materials so as to manipulate the probability or improbability of the relationships. Thus, by giving the child a toy bridge and a toy boat, they tested both what they called congruent sentences ("Put the boat under the bridge") and incongruent sentences ("Put the boat on the bridge"). Using a dump truck and a plastic piece of road, they could construct congruent sentences ("Put the road under the truck") or incongruent ones ("Put the road in the truck"). The results of this experiment showed that many children now treated "in" as if it meant "under" or "on," and "on" as if it meant "under"—just the opposite of what Clark had found. According to Wilcox and Palermo, this occurred because children put objects in the most congruent (probable) relationship. This was true, however, only for the two older groups, mean age 2;3 and 2;9. In other words, these 2- to 3-year-olds performed the way 2- and 3-year-olds did in Strohner and Nelson's experiment: they followed a probable event strategy. In contrast, the youngest children in Wilcox and Palermo's study, mean age 1;9, actually performed better on the incongruent (improbable) sentences. Wilcox and Palermo claim that this is because the youngest children tended to make the easiest motor response. It should be noted, then, that the findings are not really contradictory to Clark's at all. The group in her experiment, which used the two placement strategies, were also mean age 1;9. Whereas Clark interprets the results in terms of very specific strategies, Wilcox and Palermo hypothesize a more general principle based on ease of motor activity. It is easier for very young children to put the road "in" the truck than to put it "under" the truck.

There are other experiments that have shown that children of varying ages are affected in their answers by motor response patterns. Huttenlocher and Strauss (1968) showed that 9- and 10-year-old children, given instructions to make an array of blocks with the red block on top of the green block, perform differentially depending on which block they are holding and which is stationary. The sentence is easier if the child is holding the red block than if he or she is holding the green one. Similar effects have been observed for performance on passive sentences (Huttenlocher, Eisenberg, and Strauss, 1968). Dewart (1975) extended these findings to younger children, ages 4, 5, and 6. Children who did not yet know the passive sentence structure as measured in a preliminary condition used a strategy of showing the toy held in their hand (the "mobile" toy) to be the actor in the test sentence. Children who already knew passive sentences performed correctly and were not affected by which toy was held in their hand.

The strategies discussed above depend on such variables as real world knowledge of likely events, rules for the placement of objects, and the ease of motor movements in doing so. There are also a number of strategies that children use, however, that depend more directly on the structure of the linguistic input. One of these has to do with self-embedded sentences. It has often been noted that the processing of sentences like "The rat that the cat that the dog that the cow tossed worried killed ate the malt" is difficult. Grammatical rules allow such sentences, and with fewer embeddings such structures become understandable ("The rat that the cat killed ate the malt"). It might seem that there is difficulty with multiply-embedded structures because of memory limitations on processing (Miller, 1962; Miller and Chomsky,

1963). Bever (1970), however, noticed that some self-embedded sentences are easier than others that even have the same number of embeddings. One difficult type is exemplified in the sentence "The dog the cat was scratching was yelping." Broken down into constituents this sentence would be:

The dog	the cat	was scratching	was yelping
NP1	NP2	VP1	VP2

The main sentence is made up of NP1 + VP2: "The dog was yelping." Into this sentence is embedded NP2 + VP1: "The cat was scratching," which is reduced from "The cat was scratching the dog." The first NP, the dog, serves two different functions: it is the subject of the matrix sentence ("The dog was yelping"), but it is also the object of the embedded sentence ("The cat was scratching the dog"). This double function of NP1 is said to cause the difficulty. Bever claims that it is hard to perceive a unit as having two positions on the same classificatory dimension.

Sheldon (1974) studied an analogous problem with relative clauses. Take, for example, the sentence, "The dog that jumps over the pig bumps into the lion," In this sentence, it is the dog that jumps over the pig and the dog that bumps into the lion. In both instances "dog" serves a subject function, or as Sheldon put it, there is parallel function in the two clauses. In contrast, take the sentence, "The horse that the lion bumps into jumps over the giraffe." In this sentence the lion bumps into the horse and the horse jumps over the giraffe. "Horse" is the object of the first clause but the subject of the second. There has been a role change from the first to the second clause, and Sheldon calls this *nonparallel function*. When 33 children, ages 3;8 to 5;5, carried out the actions to these and similar sentences with toy animals, they performed significantly better on those with parallel function than on those with nonparallel function. (It should be noted that more recent experiments on relative clauses by deVilliers et al. (1979) challenge Sheldon's interpretation of these results.)

Maratsos (1973b) studied some structures that share the parallel/nonparallel contrast. In the sentence "John hit Harry and then Sarah hit him," uttered with normal stress, "him" refers to "Harry." Notice that "him" is the object of the second clause, and refers to "Harry," the object of the first clause. If, however, the sentence is uttered with contrastive stress on the word "him," the interpretation changes so that "him" now refers to "John." In contrastive stress, then, "him," the *object* of the second clause, refers to "John," the *subject* of the first clause. Contrastive stress causes a change of role relationships. The same phenomenon occurs with subject positions as well. In "John hit Harry and then he hit Sarah," "he," the subject of the second clause, refers to "John," the subject of the first clause. But with contrastive stress on "he," that *subject* of the second clause is made to refer to "Harry," the *object* of the first clause. Maratsos tried such sentences on 106 3-, 4-, and 5-year-olds. All of the children were correct on the unstressed forms. When sentences were uttered with contrastive stress, performance improved with age and language ability (as measured by an imitation task). The least mature group treated the stressed pronouns just like the unstressed ones. Maratsos concluded that children use a general heuristic strategy for sentence comprehension: change the grammatical and semantic roles as little as possible.

The sentences that cause trouble because they have constituents that serve a double function (Bever) or a nonparallel function (Sheldon), or that require role change (Maratsos), are related by a common factor. It is interesting to speculate that children use the strategies they do because of the effects of a broader cognitive principle. In Piagetian terms, only "operational" children are able to deal with entities serving more than one function simultaneously. For example, in conservation experiments, operational children know that the water not only is higher in the tall, narrow glass, but that at the same time, it is narrower (compensation). In seriation experiments, again, only operational stage children are able to conceptualize that one and the same stick is at the same time both longer than the preceding and shorter than the succeeding sticks. Experimental attempts have tried to relate sentence interpretation strategies to the action strategies children use in playing with objects and in constructing models with blocks, boards, nuts, and bolts (Greenfield, Nelson, and Saltzman, 1972; Goodson and Greenfield, 1975).

Probably the most researched strategy that children use in sentence comprehension in English is one based on word order. Bever, Mehler, and Valian (1968) noticed that children pass through several stages in their comprehension of passive sentences. In one of the stages, which occurs at about age 4, children's performance actually declines from what is observed at earlier ages. This is because of the use of a strategy of interpreting noun-verb-noun sequences as actor-action-object. Strohner and Nelson (1974), in the experiment mentioned above, also found that although the youngest children used the probable event strategy, 4-year-olds used a word order strategy. Dewart (1975) found that 4-year-olds used this strategy across a variety of sentence types including not only passive structures, but double-object constructions (with both a direct and indirect object), instrumental constructions, and cleft sentences. In fact, the strategy can more accurately be referred to as the "first-noun-is-actor" strategy (where actor merely refers to the thing the child moves), because many of these sentences did not have noun-verb-noun sequences, nor were the semantics always realized as actor-action-object. (See Slobin, 1978, however, for claims that this strategy applies only to noun-verb-noun sentences in English.)

There has been a good deal of research on other strategies; however, it was claimed that this is a research direction that has not advanced our knowledge of the acquisition of the structure of language. Considering the experimental findings that have been cited here, how can this be? The real question is, does a strategy for comprehension allow learning to occur, and if so, how? If one examines the situations in which strategies are observed, a notable fact becomes apparent: they are used by children who do not yet know how to handle particular linguistic structures. Indeed, that is why we know that a child uses a strategy at all. If he performed on each sentence in the comprehension task as an adult would, we would say that he has acquired the structure and there would be no need to speak of strategies. This becomes clearer if one reexamines the Dewart experiments mentioned above. In her studies, she carefully carried out pretests on the structures she manipulated in the experimental conditions. Children who could perform correctly, for example, on passives in the no-context condition were not influenced by appropriate and inappropriate contexts in the experiment proper. In contrast, it was precisely those children who did not yet know how to interpret passive sentences who adopted strategies in the experimental situation. Indeed, many of these children used strategies in the no-context condition as well, for example by using a word order strategy. In the experimental condition, these were the same children who were influenced by context and who adopted a new strategy across trials—performing in accordance with the experimentally manipulated variables. Similarly, in the Strohner and Nelson experiment, children who were confident of their structural knowledge of the language correctly showed a fence jumping over a horse. Only the youngest children used the strategy of interpreting sentences by the probability of the event in the real world. This was true for all the other situations as well. It was only those children who did not yet have adequate knowledge of the semantic or syntactic structures examined who based their interpretations on the ease of the motor movements to be made, placement rules for containers or horizontal surfaces, and ordering rules such as treating the first noun as the thing to be moved. Strategies, then, are merely ways of answering the psycholinguist's questions or interpreting sentences in the real world when the structure of these sentences is not yet understood, and the child does not know what else to do. They do not explain how the child *acquires* those structures. By whatever means the child acquires the structures of his or her language, the comprehension strategies used cannot, by definition, provide insight into that process.

Research on Parent-Child Interaction

One of the more interesting developments over the past few years has been the close analysis of parent-child interaction. Because the child's exposure to the linguistic system in the first few years consists primarily of the speech of the parent, it certainly seems that the features of that system will be important in determining the child's language growth. Several questions are posed in this section: what is special about this language input? Why is it used by parents? What effects does it have?

One of the criticisms of the early studies of the growth of structure in child language was that it left meaning and communicative intent unexplored. Researchers began to make a more detailed analysis of the relationship between the mother and the child, and they especially focused on the prelinguistic communication (Bates, 1976; Bruner, 1974/75, 1975). Much time is devoted in the mother-child relationship to the development, in Bruner's words, of joint activity and joint attention. Language is seen as an instrument for regulating this activity, for example, by ensuring joint reference. It was also noted that much of the mother's activity was shaped by the child. This is in contrast to the more purely empiricist view that the child's actions are primarily shaped by external experience. The issues raised by studies of the communicative interactions are important for those dealing with language intervention programs. Nevertheless, when the question of how the acquisition of the structure of language is to be explained, the answer is unclear. Developing cognitive processes, meaning, communicative intent, and the like are examined in the next section. Here, the speech of parents to infants is examined to see what effects it does and does not have.

The Special Characteristics of Baby Talk   In the early 1960's it was assumed that the input the child was exposed to was, like speech of adults to one another, filled with pauses, hesitations, and false starts. It was thought to constitute a degenerate signal from which to extract the syntactic regularities of the linguistic system. The ability of the child to master the system in only a few years was seen as even more remarkable given the characteristics of this input. People began to question, however, whether the speech to children was really as ill-informed as had been believed. After a good deal of observational study, much of it cross-cultural in nature, it is now established that adults speak to infants and young children in ways that are markedly different from the ways they talk to other adults. Brown (1977) noted that there are over 100 features that can be detailed for "baby talk," or "motherese," as some researchers call it. Baby talk is a special register in which adults speak to infants and young children (Ferguson, 1977). An excellent collection of original research articles on this topic can be found in Snow and Ferguson (1977). Sachs (1977) found that adults use a higher fundamental pitch when speaking to young children. In addition, special intonational patterns are used as well as special rhythmic patterning. Certain sounds are more commonly used—for example, initial stop consonants, especially the voiced forms. Garnica (1977) also noted the use of higher pitch and such features as the assignment of more than one primary stress to short and simple sentences, the prolongation of certain content words, and the use of rising sentence-final pitch terminals in sentences in which the adult grammatical form would call for a falling pitch. Cross (1975, 1977) called attention to such discourse features as the self-imitations and self-repetitions by the mother. In addition, there are several structural features that have been observed. Wills (1977) noted the use of third person forms for both the "sender" and "receiver" of the message (e.g., "Where are Mommy's eyes?" "Did Adam eat it?"), replacement of a singular "sender" and "receiver" with a plural form (e.g., "Let's get you some mittens, huh?" "We'll put some music on, wait, wait, wait"), and the deletion of independent pronouns from the surface structure of declarative sentences (e.g., "Got that duck on ya now," "Shouldn't talk with your mouth full"). Other structural features of baby talk include low mean utterance length, less use of long utterances (Cross, 1977), and low semantic complexity (Cross, 1977; Snow, 1977). These are only a few examples of the kinds of features noted in the special baby talk register.

Why Is Baby Talk Used? Before discussing why baby talk is used by parents, it is interesting to note some other uses of baby talk, or at least of registers resembling it. Brown (1977) pointed out that baby talk is found in speech addressed not only to infants but also to animals, to foreigners, and between lovers. It is usually thought that the use of a simplified register is to ensure communication. This can hardly be the case with the use of the register with domestic animals and between lovers. There are several other possible uses for the register. For example, as used in speaking to animals, or by the 4-year-old to the 2-year-old, or by nurses to patients, the use of the register may be to assert power or status (Gopnik, personal communication). Brown (1977) suggests that these are different registers, and that baby talk is more specific in that it is created by a specific conjunction of two main components. One of these deals with the dimension of communication-clarification; the other is an expressive-affective dimension. The registers used with animals or with lovers do not contain both of these components.

Why parents use baby talk as a special register to infants or young children is an interesting question. Brown (1977) pointed out that in response to this query parents often answer that they are teaching the child to speak, but Brown questions this assumption. He gives evidence (e.g., from Cross, 1977; Garnica, 1977) that the real aim is not to teach but to communicate. The parent uses the various features of the register not with a tutorial purpose but to control attention, improve intelligibility, and to specify that those particular utterances are directed to the child. These are significant aids to learning. Many of the functions of baby talk are important in the design of intervention programs for the language-handicapped, although some of the principles such as the need for clarity and control of attention are obvious and have always been employed. A close study of spontaneous "motherese," however, will be useful in revealing a number of techniques that serve less obvious functions that can be used in such programs.

What Effect Does Baby Talk Have? In addition to discussing the specific effects baby talk may have on the language learning of the child, it is useful to ask what effects the mother-child interaction studies have had on our notions of language acquisition in general. It is possible to put the question in a stronger form. The parent-child interaction studies are referred to here under the heading of research directions that have not fulfilled expectations to advance knowledge of the acquisition of the structure of language. In what way have they not done so? Underlying most of the research is an assumption that the child is acquiring what the environment has to offer. Chomsky (1967) argued that children acquired their language system on the basis of a restricted amount of evidence—evidence that was moreover of a degraded sort, consisting largely of utterances that break grammatical rules in that they are made up of false starts, disconnected phrases, and other deviations. The mother-child interaction studies have shown that the speech the child is receiving is a far less degraded sample than Chomsky and others had hitherto believed. This has been taken by some as evidence that there is no innate component to the language acquisition process, or that at the very least, innate mechanisms should be de-emphasized (Brown, 1977; Garnica, 1977). Such conclusions, however, are unwarranted. To show that the input signal to many children is far clearer than had been assumed in no way explains how the grammatical structures that the child uses are developed. Even those mother-child interaction researchers who conclude that the child is an active participant and indeed the participant who shapes the interaction (e.g., Bruner, 1974/75, 1975; Gleason, 1977; Seitz and Stewart, 1975)—as opposed to the older behaviorist view of a passive child almost totally influenced by environmental input—do not extend those notions to the linguistic structure of language itself. It is asserted in this section that what is known about children's use of grammatical structures is not incompatible with a strong internal component. A close analysis of the structural acquisitions of the child reveals that there is not a close fit between the nature of the structures that the mother uses and those that the child is producing. One important experimental study makes this especially clear and is therefore reviewed here in some detail.

Newport, Gleitman, and Gleitman (1977) analyzed the motherese directed by 15 mothers to their young daughters. The children were in three groups: ages 12–15 months, 18–21 months, and 24–27 months. They were visited twice for 2½ hour sessions, held 6 months apart. Both the mother's and the child's utterances were coded on a variety of features. The mother's speech was coded in terms of well formedness, sentence length, structural complexity (as determined by the number of sentence-nodes per utterance and derivational length), sentence type, intelligibility, and expansions. Child measures included mean length of utterance (MLU), the frequency and length of noun phrases and verb phrases, and the use of various inflections (marking of plurals, modals, and tenses). Newport et al. found that there is a pattern (which they called motherese) that incorporates many devices that aid in clarity. For example, the utterances to the young children were significantly shorter than those to other adults (mean MLU of 4.24 to children compared to 11.94 to other adults). The utterances also were highly intelligible (only 4% of utterances to children were unanalyzable because of mumbles and slurs, compared to 9% in speech to other adults) and well formed (only 1 utterance of 1,500 spoken to the children was disfluent; in speech to other adults there was a 5% disfluency rate). Most utterances to both children and adults were bona fide grammatical sentences (60% of those to children, and 58% to other adults)—the rest were primarily well formed isolated phrases. These results showed that the mothers' speech is indeed shorter and clearer than had been supposed. However, Newport et al. also pointed out that the sentences of motherese were not structurally simpler in terms of other important aspects. The canonical structure of English sentences is the active declarative sentence of the form subject-verb-object. Although 87% of sentences to other adults were of this type, in motherese only 30% were. There was also a wider range of sentence types to children than to adults. To children, 18% of the utterances were imperatives and 44% were questions. Newport et al. also found that derivational complexity is significantly higher in speech to children than in speech to other adults. This measure is suspect however and indeed open to an interpretation that so-called derivationally complex sentences are in fact psycholinguistically easier than less derivationally complex ones. In any event, it is the case that motherese in general is a simpler form of the adult language because it is shorter and has fewer sentence-nodes. This is reflected in the rare use of sentences involving embedding and conjunctions. Even this latter finding, however, is seen in terms of a move toward brevity and not in terms of syntactic simplicity. This interpretation is supported by the fact that there was no correlation between the number of sentence-nodes used by the mother and the child's age or with any of the measures of the child's syntactic sophistication.

Newport et al. concluded that motherese is not a special register for teaching language structure. They claimed that one can envisage three basic principles for teaching a language to a beginner: 1) use the canonical sentences of the new language first, 2) introduce one new construction at a time, 3) move from simple to complex sentences over time. Newport et al. pointed out that none of these holds for motherese. For example, canonical declaratives actually increase over time, and the range of sentence types used by the mother narrows as the child grows older. The increases in MLU and a number of sentence-nodes are not statistically significant. As Newport et al. concluded, ". . . there is no compelling evidence in our data that mothers tune their syntactic complexity to the growing competence of their children through this crucial age of syntax acquisition, the period from one to two and a half years" (pp. 123–124). This is not to say that motherese has no effects on the acquisition of certain aspects of language (this is discussed in detail on page 70, where the positive effects found by Newport et al. are examined). At this point, it is worth noting, however, that Newport et al. are making two major claims. First, motherese is not a register designed for teaching the syntax of language. Others (e.g., Brown, 1977) have reached a similar conclusion. As Newport et al. stated, motherese arises in order to communicate with a cognitively and linguistically naive child in the here-and-now. It is a style designed to get the child to do something now. It does not to teach him structure. Second, Newport et al. accept that the child, in addition to being affected by the communication setting, possesses language-specific mental structures, that is, hypotheses for evaluating incoming linguistic data. The usual assumption of studies of adult speech styles directed to children is that the carefully structured input determines the child's acquisition. In contrast, Newport et al. concluded that "nativist assumptions are left intact by a close look at motherese—they neither gain nor lose plausibility" (p. 123). It is possible to go further than what Newport et al. suggest by looking at what the child is producing in conjunction with the motherese he or she is receiving as input.

The data from the first serious language acquisition studies of the 1960s revealed one important feature: the child actively organized the structure of his or her productions in ways that did not match the structure of what he heard others saying. The productions were not "telegraphic"—merely shortened forms of the adult input—as had at first been postulated. Consequently, it was claimed that imitation was not the method the child used to acquire the structures of his or her language. There are numerous examples demonstrating that children produce utterances that are structurally ordered in ways quite different from the input (e.g., Bellugi-Klima, 1969; Brown and Bellugi, 1964; reviewed in Cromer, 1970, 1980). When young children produce negative utterances by prefixing "no" or "not" to affirmative sentences, as in "No wipe finger" and "Not fit," they are not simply associatively picking up adult language forms or imitating the adults around them, no matter how short and clear the sentences are that are directed at them. Bellugi's analysis (Bellugi-Klima, 1969) of the development of self-reference by the child, which attempts to specify the rules by which the child first uses his or her own name and then "I" or "me" dependent initially on sentence position rules and later on rules of grammatical structure, shows that the changes over time are not related to the use of these terms in the mother's speech. A clear example of the lack of correspondence between the adult input and the child's utterances comes from Bellugi's careful analysis of the child's use of auxiliaries. For example, at first, the child always produced the full, uncontracted form of "will," thus producing utterances that sounded very precise: "We will put it here," "It will go away." In contrast, the mother almost invariably used the contracted form, " 'll," leading to inputs to the child of numerous forms like "He'll," "You'll," "It'll," "That'll," (as in "It'll hurt you," "That'll be enough"). The mother only used the complete form of "will" in interrogatives, as in "Will it be fun?" "Will you finish it?" As Bellugi pointed out, the child must have organized the forms "will" and " 'll" into a single system leading to the production of forms by the child that differ from the adult input in significant ways.

Although these are only a few examples, close analysis of child language data shows that this is the rule, not the exception. Children construct their own productive rule systems. They constantly produce utterances and sentence forms that do not match the adult model. Of all the recent studies on mother-child interaction, not one mentions this basic and important fact—clear findings from the 1960s that to date no strictly empiricist theory has adequately explained. This neglect of basic observations is primarily attributable to the conceptual prejudice of most psychologists to consider only concepts that show direct association with environmental input. The mother-child interaction studies have not explained or accounted for the acquisition of linguistic structure. This is clearly pointed out in the Newport et al. study in which the attempt was made to relate specific features of input to specific features of child production.

The type of studies reviewed in this section are often referred to as studies of mother-child *interaction*. Indeed, some researchers have emphasized the interactiveness of the process and are thus thought to be in advance of those conceptions that saw the child as passively receiving environmental input. But the "interactiveness" is ignored when the question of the *structure* of language arises. Some psychologists even allow the child to have innate capacities and/or innate schemata to deal with behavioral exchanges between the self and others. By fiat, however, the child is not allowed to have innate capacities for the organization of language. Part of the reason for this is the continued misinterpretation of the nativist issue in terms of an either/or situation. It is mistakenly assumed that if a theory allows for an innate component, environmental influences have only a moderate or little or no part to play in development. Such a belief is misconceived, and a truly interactive theory is advanced as part of the first of the reconceptualizations presented in this chapter. It is helpful, however, to continue examining the Newport et al. study to clarify these issues and to show that the structure of the input does play an important part in the acquisition process.

Newport et al. studied the relations between the maternal speech styles and language acquisition by carrying out a series of correlations between differences in those styles and the child's language growth rate when both the child's age and the initial level of linguistic achievement had been partialled out. They found that certain aspects of the mother's speech did have an effect on some aspects of the child's learning. This is, while many properties of motherese had no effect on the child's language growth, some aspects did exert an influence. They claimed that this was true only for what they called language specific structures, that is, the surface morphology and syntactic elements that vary between languages. Even these, however, only had an effect through what they called the filter of the child's selective attention to portions of the speech stream. Newport et al. claimed that the child has a means for restricting and organizing the flow of incoming linguistic data. He or she filters out some kinds of input and selectively listens for others. (This notion of filtering is referred to on page 124, where some suggested links to language intervention programs are considered.) According to Newport et al., then, learning does respond to narrowly specified features of the environment, even though "it is contingent on what the children are disposed to notice in that environment, on their strategies of listening and the hypotheses they are prepared to entertain" (p. 131). Newport et al. then considered what aspects of the child's language were affected by the input. The number of auxiliaries used by the child correlated positively both with the mother's use of yes/no questions and the number of her expansions. The number of nominal inflections (e.g., formation of plurals on nouns) was positively correlated with the mother's use of deixis (use of "this" and "that" as in "That's a dog"). The growth of a number of language features, however, was not sensitive to individual differences in motherese styles. Thus, the number of verbs per utterance or the number of noun phrases per utterance were dependent on cognitive and linguistic maturity—not on specific aspects of environmental input.

Newport et al. claimed that what is and is not affected by maternal speech style are very different aspects of language. The universal aspects of language structure and content are basically unaffected by differences in motherese. This supports the view of a semi-autonomous unfolding of language capabilities in the child. In contrast, those features that are specific to the surface features of different languages are the ones on which motherese exerts an influence (although even these are subject to a filtering system noted above). These findings are similar to differences recently observed in the written language samples by aphasic children and congenitally profoundly deaf children (Cromer, 1978a, 1978b). The aphasic children evidenced problems with basics of linguistic structure. In contrast, the deaf children used structural relationships that the aphasic children seemed incapable of using, but made many "surface" grammatical errors such as inconsistent use of plural inflections, and possessives (see pages 117–119).

The studies of parent-child language and interactions have made an important contribution to our knowledge of the growth of communication processes. They have not, however, provided a solution to the problem of how children acquire the structures of their language. The Newport et al. study, in contrast, does succeed in showing how a reconceptualized viewpoint, incorporating in a truly interactive manner what the child brings to bear on the process, can contribute not only to a better understanding of how language acquisition occurs but how language intervention programs can use those principles. Most studies of baby talk fail to explain the acquisition of structure because of a primarily environmentalist viewpoint and the implicit empiricist assumptions made about the mind of the child when acquisition of linguistic structure is considered.

Semantically Based Theories

Many recent reviews and discussions of language acquisition criticize child language research in the 1960s for concentrating on syntax and neglecting the field of semantics. This was certainly true, and a great deal of research effort has been invested in righting this imbalance (e.g., Bowerman, 1976; Clark, 1973b; Donaldson and Balfour, 1968; Klatzky, Clark, and Macken, 1973; Maratsos, 1973a; Nelson, 1973; Nelson and Bonvillian, 1973; Wales and Campbell, 1970). Although most researchers were clear about what aspects of the child's developing language system they were studying, psychologists with more general interests frequently misunderstood and confused such notions as semantics, thought, and syntax. A good example of this is the use made by psychologists of "case grammar" theory from linguistics.

Case grammar (Fillmore, 1968) incorporated features of meaning into the syntax. That is, it was suggested that "case" categories should appear in the base component of the grammar. According to Fillmore, grammatical concepts such as "subject" and "object" are constituents only of the surface structure of some but possibly not all languages. What was important in the new view was the underlying case assignment that relied on the covert meaning of sentence relations. For example, in English, the subject of a sentence may express a variety of case functions. In "John opened the door," "John" is an agent, but in "The key opened the door," "key" is an instrument, not an agent. In other sentences the subject serves other functions. In "John received a gift," "John" is a recipient, in "John received a blow on the head," "John" is a patient; and in "Chicago is windy," "Chicago" functions as a location. Case grammatical conceptions, then, express some aspects of meaning not found in the linguistic constituents "subject" and "object." In contrast, these latter terms express a different level of generalization. As in the examples above, the "subject" of a sentence can serve various case functions. But "grammatical subject" is a linguistically relevant constituent in that speakers use these constituents in a number of transformations or changes independently of their particular case functions. Psychologists proposed that case grammar might better capture the essence of young children's utterances. Bowerman (1973) demonstrated that very young children's grammars were more adequately described using case grammar terminology during the initial phases of language acquisition. But she also noted that at some point in development, it was necessary to invoke grammatical notions such as "subject" and "object" to account for the more purely syntactic relations that were observed.

Although case grammar is itself a linguistic theory—and one which virtually no linguist still accepts as an adequate description of language—many psychologists have taken case notions as if they were identical to nonlinguistic concepts, equating them with more general "meanings" or "intentions" of the speaker. To clarify this problem, and also to relate it to language intervention, the interpretations of some recent research findings should be examined. In the past few years, there have been a number of attempts to teach nonhuman primates to use "language" or at least to "communicate." The distinction between these terms is crucial for the argument of this section. In one successful venture of great interest and importance, Premack (1969; Premack and Premack, 1972) used plastic shapes backed with metal that a chimpanzee, Sarah, could manipulate and place on a magnetic board. Each plastic abstract shape was associated with a particular stimulus. Although Premack used reinforcement techniques to gradually shape the chimpanzee's behavior, he did not claim that this was the way in which language functions were acquired by human beings. He was interested in investigating whether language functions similar to those found in humans could be established in another species. Premack had a good deal of success. Sarah acquired the basic communication units that he taught including what he termed the names for objects, verbs that described various actions, modifiers, questions, and negations. Some of these consisted of the judgment and communication of complex concepts. Not only did Sarah learn symbols for "yes," "no," "same," and "different," but she combined these in understanding and answering questions. For example, given the symbol for:

$$(X) \qquad \text{(same as)} \qquad (X) \quad (?)$$

she would answer with the symbol for "yes," She would similarly answer "yes" to:

$$(X) \quad \text{(not)} \qquad \text{(same as)} \qquad (Y) \quad (?)$$

Given the symbolic strings:

$$(X) \quad \text{(not)} \qquad \text{(same as)} \qquad (X) \qquad (?)$$
$$(X) \qquad \qquad \text{(same as)} \qquad (Y) \qquad (?)$$

she would answer "no" to both. Premack taught Sarah communication structures built from simple structures to more complex ones. For example, Sarah was first taught simple messages with symbols corresponding to "Sarah insert banana pail" and "Sarah insert apple dish." After Sarah could understand both messages separately, as gauged by her being able to carry out the appropriate actions, Premack then combined them. Thus, he progressively introduced the more condensed instructions, "Sarah insert banana pail insert apple dish" and "Sarah insert banana pail apple dish," in which the second uses of "Sarah" and "insert" were eliminated. Again, Sarah was able to perform appropriately on these more complex tasks. These are amazing feats, and research of this type makes more probable the exciting prospect of being able to communicate with other species in a direct fashion. In the context of the problem of the acquisition of the structure of human language, however, and in terms of intervention programs with language-handicapped individuals, it is important to make the conceptual distinctions mentioned above.

On the basis of Premack's results (and those of other researchers, e.g., Gardner and Gardner, 1969, 1975; Rumbaugh, 1977; Rumbaugh and Gill, 1976), some psychologists have concluded that chimpanzees have been able to learn "language." The actual results of these studies have now been the subject of strong criticism (e.g., Sebeok & Umiker-Sebeok, 1980; Seidenberg & Petitto, 1979; Terrace, 1979). Even if the claims that have been made for communicative abilities in nonhuman primates were true, however, there is little evidence that the production of these primates would be correctly characterized by claiming that these constitute subject-verb-object strings. Cromer (1978a) argued caution must be used in making such interpretations. The terms *subject*, *verb*, and *object* are terms for linguistic constituents, and although they often express the meanings "actor," "action," and "acted upon," they need not do so, as the examples from case grammar indicated. The former linguistic terms are not identical to the latter specific conceptual meanings. Perhaps the systems acquired by chimpanzees are communication systems encoding the linkages of meanings rather than of linguistic elements. If this is true, then chimpanzee messages may be more accurately described in terms such as *actor-action-acted upon* rather than in terms such as *subject-verb-object*, which imply a different level of linguistic generalization that human children have been observed to eventually build upon (Bowerman, 1973).

This distinction between meaning and the linguistic structures in which meaning is encoded is important to language intervention programs. It is possible, for example, that in some types of aphasia, certain conceptual meanings may be preserved while the more purely linguistic structures in which these meanings are usually encoded break down. On a suggestion by Dr. Hermelin, Hughes (1972, 1974/1975) carried out a study to see if children with developmental or early acquired aphasia could acquire the type of communication system that Premack used. The four children she studied were of average or above average intelligence as measured by nonverbal tests. They were unable to comprehend and to produce normal language, and this was true either from birth or from an early age despite the fact that no known brain trauma had occurred. The children were trained individually in 30-minute sessions twice a week for about 9 weeks, using materials similar to those used by Premack—plastic symbols backed with metal that could be placed on a magnetic board. Hughes reported that the aphasic children rapidly acquired all of the functions she taught. These included the names for objects and persons, names for attributes of these objects, actions such as "give" and "point to," negatives, and questions. Despite an inability to comprehend or use normal linguistic forms—and this was not merely because of auditory modality defects (see Cromer, 1978a)—these aspasic children acquired a fairly sophisticated communication system without much difficulty.

Glass, Gazzaniga, and Premack (1973) reported similar findings with adult aphasics. Seven patients with global aphasia resulting from cerebral vascular accidents were trained in the use of cut-out paper symbols varying in color, size, and shape. These symbols were arranged on a table in a set left-right direction. Glass et al. found that with an average of 1 month's training, all seven patients acquired same/ different and interrogative constructions. In addition, two of the patients learned simple sentences consisting of what were described as "subject-verb-direct object" strings, to a level of accuracy of about 80%. There was evidence that the other five patients also would have progressed to the same level had training continued, but for administrative reasons (e.g., patients being discharged from the hospital) this was not possible. Glass et al. concluded that global aphasics may not suffer a cognitive impairment as severe as their linguistic impairment; globally aphasic patients are capable of sophisticated and abstract symbolic thought despite severe language deficits.

The demonstration by Hughes and by Glass et al. that developmentally aphasic children and globally aphasic adults can acquire abstract plastic symbol systems despite known language disability is evidence that these systems, although encoding some of the functions that language encodes, are nevertheless not really the same as *linguistic* systems. Conceptual distinctions like these, which psychologists have blurred, are important if one tries to improve the language abilities of language-handicapped individuals, and not just their communication abilities.

A similar confusion of meanings and language is found when psychologists have considered another movement within linguistic theory—generative semantics (see, e.g., Lakoff, 1971; McCawley, 1971a, b, 1973; and a collection of reprinted articles edited by Seuren, 1974). An earlier version of Chomsky's particular formulation of transformational grammar (Chomsky, 1965) was criticized for its neglect of the semantic component of the grammar. This earlier version is sometimes referred to as "standard theory." As a reaction to these criticisms, which showed inadequacies in the theory for dealing with various sentences, two types of theories were developed. One of these was a modified version of the earlier Chomskian theory, and is referred to as "extended standard theory" (Chomsky, 1972; Jackendoff, 1972). It still emphasized the autonomy of the syntactic component of the grammar. Although more attention was given to the semantic component and its interaction with the syntax, this semantic component was nevertheless conceived of as a set of interpretation rules that acted on or were applied to the syntax. The followers of that theory, therefore, also came to be called "interpretive semanticists." The followers of the other theory were called "generative semanticists." They believed that the meaning component itself is important in the generation of sentence structures and cannot be separated from them. Indeed, it was claimed that syntactic phenomena could not be explained without reference to semantic factors. In other words, the claim by the generative semanticists was that the semantic and syntactic components of grammar are inextricably entwined. To capture these essential differences, this broad school of thought was also called "semantic syntax" in contrast to the "autonomous syntax" of Chomskian theory (Seuren, 1974).

Although linguistic theory has progressed from these positions— the Chomskian tradition now embraces "trace" theory (Chomsky, 1975), and the theory of "generative semantics" is said to have collapsed about 1975 (Newmeyer, 1980)—it should be noted that these two main positions, the extended theory or interpretive semantics and the generative semantics theory, were both reactions to the inadequacies of the earlier Chomskian viewpoint. More importantly, both theories were concerned with specifically linguistic entities. The issue between them was the exact placement of the semantic component in the grammar. The term *semantics* is a linguistic term that refers not to meaning, but to meaning-in-language. It is in no way identical to "thoughts," "concepts," or "meanings." Many psychologists have been confused about this, and have even drawn on the arguments used by linguists of the generative semantics school as support for a relatively anti-linguistic view. This confusion still exists although Bloom (1973) called attention to this misinterpretation. Bloom argued that the semantic versus the syntactive basis for grammar is not an important issue for psychologists unless the differences in formal theory lead to different predictions about cognitive and behavioral aspects of language use. She also claimed that the important distinction for those studying child language was not within linguistic categories (syntactic and semantic) but between linguistic categories on the one hand and cognitive categories on the other.

Psychologists tend to view semantic theories as if they were identical to "cognitive" theories. (The reasons that such theories have not explained the acquisition of the structure of language is discussed in the next section.) Obviously, there is a close relationship between *meaning* (in the broad sense), *semantics*, and *syntax*. Schlesinger (1977) tried to formulate a theoretical position that would relate a speaker's intentions to his or her production of utterances, but there is still little direct evidence concerning how such systems actually work. One of the most interesting recent works on this problem is that by Carey (1978). It is especially valuable because it is one of the only experimental papers in which the distinctions between the conceptual system, the semantic system, and the syntactic system are made clear. She was concerned with the acquisition of the meaning of particular lexical items. By the age of 6, the average child has acquired the meaning of some 14,000 words. As Carey put it, assuming that such learning begins in earnest at age 18 months, the child learns an average of nine new words per day, or one per waking hour. After the age of 2, conscious drill on words—for example, by parents pointing and naming referents—is not typical; therefore, the child learns most of those 14,000 words by hearing other people use them in normal contexts. In order to study this acquisition and the means used to accomplish it, Carey experimentally introduced a "new" word, "chromium" (an actual color name), for olive-colored objects, in natural situations in a nursery school atmosphere. The 14 3- and 4-year-olds originally applied either the label "green" or "brown" to the olive color when they were asked to name the color of various objects at the beginning of the study. The ways the children changed their concepts over the months of the study were the focus of the investigation. Carey developed a theory in which children engage in "fast mapping," which allows them to hold onto fragile new entries in their lexicon while the meanings are built up. She also criticized a simple "missing features" hypothesis in which a child merely fills in those lexical features that are not yet part of the representation. The details of her arguments are relevant for those interested in the growth of lexical knowledge. What is pertinent for this review is that Carey clarified some of the distinctions that most psychologists currently gloss over. Most important is the differentiation of the conceptual domain from the lexical domain. The conceptual domain is the mental representation by which one describes or understands the world or one's own actions. The lexical domain is the structured set of words that encodes aspects of the conceptual domain. As Carey put it, in terms of colors, there are many things that we know about colors that are not captured in the structure of the color lexicon. Indeed, each domain has its own identity and structure. According to Carey, in the child there can be development within each domain separately before any mapping of one domain onto the other occurs. To illustrate this point she noted that preverbal infants, and even animals, have knowledge of the conceptual/perceptual domain of color. This point can also be illustrated by Rosch's study of the Dani of Indonesian New Guinea whose language has only two color words, "mili" and "mola." According to Rosch (1977), the Dani evidence knowledge of the same focal colors as other groups despite the lack of individual lexical entries for them. In contrast, regarding the lexical domain Carey noted that individuals who are blind can learn a great deal of the structure of the lexical domain of color without ever mapping it onto perceived colors. She also cited Bartlett (1978), who demonstrated that children can list the names of color hues in response to questions such as "Do you know any colors? What color is this?" before they know how to map those color terms correctly onto the conceptual/perceptual domain.

It is possible, then, to have concepts without any corresponding lexical or semantic encoding (as in the examples of young children, animals and of groups with a limited vocabulary of color); and it is possible to possess certain aspects of lexical and semantic knowledge without the corresponding perceptual experiences or conceptual knowledge. Semantics is not the same as meaning. Carey studied both aspects by observing how children restructured their lexicon to find the right place for the word "chromium," and how they restructured their conceptual domain by learning that olive was not included in green or brown but had its own name. Her experiments make it clear why it is important to make the distinction between semantics and conceptual meanings even though they interact during development.

Cognitively Based Theories

Despite recent work on semantics by the psychologists mentioned above, the interest of more broad-based, mainstream psychologists has been not so much in the development of semantic theory, but in theories relating conceptual knowledge and language. These theories have taken two major forms: theories concerning the development of specific aspects of conceptual knowledge and their consequent effect on language acquisition; and theories concerning the development of the structures of thought (usually Piagetian) and their effect on the language acquisition process. The two approaches are somewhat similar and are not always distinct in practice. For example, theories that propose that specific concepts must develop before the child encodes them in language, even by imitation, may themselves be based on the assumption that such concepts can only develop when the child is capable of certain cognitive operations. There are many studies and reviews of cognitive theories of language acquisition (e.g., Beilin, 1975; Cromer, 1974, 1976a, 1979; Macnamara, 1972; Moore, 1973); therefore, they will not be examined in detail here. A few examples can illustrate what a cognitive theory of language acquisition would claim.

In a study of the development of reference to time in language (Cromer, 1968), it was observed that certain aspects of language acquisition were dependent on prior development of particular concepts. The two children were Adam and Sarah of Roger Brown's study (Brown, 1973). In looking at their development of reference to various aspects of time, two contrasting methods were used. In one, the child's intention was judged from situational cues and from context. For example, the child would be credited with referring to some aspect of time, even if this was encoded inadequately or incorrectly from the adult grammatical point of view. What the child seemed to be attempting to express was contrasted with the data from the second method— examining the linguistic form and context of the utterance. It was found that children did not attempt to produce certain linguistic forms until after the point in their development when they were making use of the *concepts* that those forms encoded. This was true for a variety of temporal features. One of these was reference to hypothetical situations. True hypotheticalness of predicating a future event on the basis of another event also in the future, as in "If it rains (future) I will take an umbrella (later future)," developed from earlier uses of pretending. Another was "relevance," or the ability of the speaker to note the importance of a referred-to-event to the time indicated by his or her utterance. This is usually encoded in English by use of the perfect tense: "The lamp has fallen" usually indicates that the lamp is still in a fallen position at the time of the utterance or is in a state effected by its fall, whereas "The lamp fell" merely indicates that the lamp fell at some time in the past but does not imply anything about the current state of the lamp. Another type of time reference was "timelessness," in which the speaker refers to an event that normally occurs in some timed context but in such a way as to lift it out of any particular situation and to so imbue it with a timeless quality. This is not the same as descriptions, which are usually references to things in the present. Rather, the timeless quality as expressed by one of the children in the utterance "Playing a banjo is good exercise for your thumb," is what is intended here.

When these and other time reference categories were explored, it was found that children began to use the concepts shortly before using the linguistic forms in which they were usually encoded by adults. Furthermore, it was demonstrated that many of the forms had been used by adults in the child's presence, sometimes for years, before the child began to use them productively. This was true not only for linguistic forms, but for specific lexical items as well. For example, it was only after age 4 that the children began to use words like "always," "sometimes," and "never" productively—and they began to use these only when they began to express "timelessness" by other formal means.

There is a great deal of evidence that can be cited in support of the view that conceptual understandings precede the acquisition of linguistic forms used to encode them. Slobin (1966) postulated that the late emergence of the hypothetical form in children who speak Russian, a language in which the hypothetical is exceedingly simple grammatically, is attributable to conceptual difficulty. Brown (1973) cited examples of children making reference to the concept of possession (e.g., "Mommy nose," "Daddy nose") before they acquired the "'s" inflection by which it is commonly encoded. (Bloom (1970) gave similar evidence from three other children.) Brown (1973) also noted that the first verb inflections that children acquired during Stage I of language acquisition encoded the concepts they seemed to be trying to encode when they used only the generic unmarked form of the verb. That is, given the situation and context, adults interpreted the child's verbal meaning in one of four ways: 1) as an imperative, as in "Get book"; 2) as a reference to immediate past, as in "Book drop"; 3) as a form of intention or predication, as in "Mommy read" (pronounced reed) in a context where she was about to do so; and 4) as an expression of present temporary duration, as in "Fish swim" where an adult would use the progressive form "The fish is swimming." During Stage I, the children modified the verb in three ways. One of these was to begin marking the past with -ed or with an irregular allomorph (e.g., "It dropped," "It fell"). A second way the verb was modified was to use it with a semi-auxiliary such as "wanna" and "gonna" in utterances such as "I wanna go" and "It's gonna fall." The third modification was that the child used a primitive progressive form—producing the -ing but omitting the copula verb (e.g., "Fish swimming"). What is interesting is that these first three modifications of the verb form encode three of the four meanings that the child was credited by adults with trying to express before he acquired the ability to do so in the adult way. For the fourth meaning, the imperative, Brown noted that although there is no special imperative form in English, it is just at this age that the children started to use the word "please."

These are a few examples illustrating the kinds of observations that support the position that specific aspects of conceptual knowledge have an effect on language acquisition. The examples of time reference also illustrate the second type of theory concerning the effect of cognitive variables on language. Some of the more complex types of temporal reference, such as true hypotheticalness, relevance, and timelessness, were observed to emerge more or less together in the child and at similar points in development in the different children. It was hypothesized (Cromer, 1968, 1974) that this emergence at about the age of 4 could be accounted for by a more broadly based stage-related development of the ability to decenter. The lessening of "egocentrism" allows one to move from one's own viewpoint as a speaker and to place oneself at other perspectives and at other points on the time continuum. This enables the speaker to use true hypotheticals (predicating a later future on an earlier future), relevance (relating events of other times to the time indicated by the utterance), and timelessness (the ability to stand outside of the actual order of events in time). This is an example, then, of using a Piagetian notion of cognitive development to explain the emergence of several concepts concerned with understanding time. More direct uses of Piagetian stages to account for aspects of language development have included theories about both what sensorimotor intelligence allows, and later, what operational thinking makes possible (e.g., Edwards, 1973; Morehead and Morehead, 1974; Piaget and Inhelder, 1969a; Sinclair, 1970, 1971; Sinclair-de-Zwart, 1969, 1973).

These two cognitively-based theories can be termed the "Conceptual Underpinnings of Language Theory" and the "Cognitive Operations Theory of Language Acquisition and Use." Although they both have some very interesting things to say about language acquisition, they both have dangers. The first theory is flawed, and the second is usually (but not necessarily) interpreted in a way that does not explain language acquisition. It is useful to examine the theories separately.

Conceptual Underpinnings of Language Theory   One problem with the theory that language depends on the formation of prior concepts is that despite the demonstrated conceptual influence in some areas, not all of what is encoded in language is necessarily dependent on prior conceptual knowledge. The examples above from Carey (1978) illustrated that some aspects of the lexicon in children were developed independently of conceptual knowledge. Thus, children knew when color terms were required in discourse, but not how to relate these to the perceptual/conceptual domain of color. A similar finding was reported in a different context by Blank and Allen (1976). They noticed that children used "why" before they comprehended its meaning. Furthermore, it was noted that at first children only used "why" for verbal stimuli and never to ask about nonverbal events. According to Blank and Allen, the early use of "why" by the child is not with the adult sense of the word, but represents the child's search to determine the meaning of "why."

Curtiss, Fromkin, and Yamada (1978) presented some evidence that there is no link between syntactic and morphological ability and what they call general cognition. They studied six mentally retarded individuals, ages 6 to 9. A seventh subject was Genie, age 20, who was isolated from language input throughout her childhood. They were compared to a control group of 74 normal children, ages 2 to 6. The subjects in the experimental group were seen once a week for 20 to 45 minutes, for a period of 10 months. The control group was seen two or three times a week for 2 months. The language recorded was the spontaneous conversation between the child and the experimenter. Tests for various aspects of comprehension of language were also administered. These included studies of word order, uses of "before" and "after," complex modifications, negation, disjunction, tense and aspect, verb pluralization, and Wh-questions. The children were also given tests of nonlanguage mental abilities. These included a variety of tests of memory, perception, construction tasks, copying, drawing, tests of Piagetian skills (classification, conservation, etc.), and conceptual sequencing. Their spontaneous play was also noted for evidence of symbolic activities. In the matrices of correlations among the various measures, it was noted that expressive *semantics* correlated with a number of nonlanguage tasks including conservation ability, conceptual sequencing, drawing ability and spatial operations. Expressive *syntax*, the measure of structural complexity of language use, however, correlated only with auditory short term memory. This means that memory constrains the length and complexity of utterances in child language, but conceptual, and even broader Piagetian cognitive abilities, are not related to structural measures of language. Curtiss et al. contrasted two extreme cases in their sample. Genie's expressive syntax was lower than all of her scores on the other measures. It was her semantic ability that was most comparable to her cognitive level. Indeed, her level of performance on Piagetian tasks fell within the 6- to 12-year-old range, indicating that she was in the stage of concrete operations, but her expressive language ability was barely above the

2-year level. Thus, even operational cognitive structures, and the concepts they allow are not sufficient to account for grammatical development. It might be said, then, that such operations are therefore necessary but not sufficient for language acquisition and development. But the analysis of another child in their sample raises doubts even on this point. This child's profile revealed that expressive syntax was high, as was his auditory short-term memory, but his scores on nonlanguage tasks were very low as was the measure of his expressive semantic ability. As Curtiss et al. put it, this child was able to acquire a highly complex grammar while possessing only limited conceptual abilities in other spheres. He had complex syntactic and morphological structures, but his language often lacked appropriate semantic reference and many of his utterances were semantically anomalous. He demonstrated the structural use of Wh-words, but had trouble distinguishing one Wh-form from another. He produced all the English tense and aspect verb forms and the auxiliaries, but did not use them appropriately. His syntax was highly complex and his morphology was normal, but his utterances were often semantically irregular. Lenneberg (1967; see also Lenneberg, Nichols, and Rosenberger, 1964) similarly found that intelligence was not highly related to language development. It seems then, that conceptual knowledge and language are separate systems and can develop independently.

A second problem with the theory that language depends on the formation of prior concepts, is that even in some conceptual areas where this seems to be true, nothing is explained about the ability to encode those concepts in language. As noted above, developmentally aphasic children, and indeed adults suffering from traumatic aphasia, have concepts that they cannot encode into linguistic structures. This is seen most clearly in those studies that showed that they could learn the symbolic concepts of the communication system that Premack designed even when their language abilities were impaired. The so-called "weak form of the cognition hypothesis" (Cromer, 1974) was put forward precisely because of the inability of nonlinguistic, purely cognitive theories to explain the acquisition of the structure of language:

> Our cognitive abilities at different stages of development make certain meanings *available* for expression. But, in addition, we must also possess certain specifically linguistic capabilities in order to come to express these meanings in language, and these linguistic capabilities may indeed be lacking in other species or in certain pathological conditions (p. 246).

This basic criticism of purely conceptual or cognitive approaches to language acquisition was illustrated by Slobin (1978) in what he calls the "waiting room metaphor." In this metaphor there is a box, or "waiting room," for each linguistic form. The entrance to this room is an underlying notion or concept. The entry key is thus cognitive development that results in discerning the existence of a given notion. The problems to be solved in the waiting room are both semantic and morphologico-syntactic. That is, the semantic problem is the necessity to figure out just what aspects of the particular conceptual notion are encoded in the language. The morphologico-syntactic problem involves determining what linguistic means are used for that encoding. The solution will take various amounts of time and effort depending on linguistic features, and the exit from the waiting room is accomplished by the appropriate linguistic form.

The basic problem with some conceptual theories of language acquisition, then, was the notion that once the child had the concepts, there was nothing more to explain. All the child had to do was to see how these concepts that he or she was now capable of forming were encoded in everyday language. The trap was the old purely associationistic view of language acquisition—this time an association between the concept and its encoding by adults. Clear input signals such as baby talk or motherese were seen as solving the remaining obstacle to the theory by removing the problem of the child having to form associations between his intentions and signals replete with hesitations, false starts, and the like. As pointed out earlier, the productive utterances by normal children in their natural environment is at variance with such a theory. One of the frameworks for the first reconceptualization proposed in the next section suggests the important part linguistic factors play in the acquisition of the structure of language.

Cognitive Operations Theory of Language Acquisition and Use   Theoretical approaches that concentrate on cognitive operations are less concerned with the specific concepts made possible by such operations, and concentrate instead on the operations themselves and the direct effects they might have on the language acquisition process. For example, sensorimotor schemata are said to account for corresponding linguistic abilities observed in language acquisition (Piaget and Inhelder, 1969a). That is, a number of sensorimotor schemata are said to account for specific linguistic abilities. The child's ability to order things both spatially and temporally has its linguistic equivalent in the concatenation of linguistic elements. The child's ability to classify actions—using whole categories of objects for the same action, and applying an entire category of action schemata to one object—is observed in the linguistic realm as the ability to categorize linguistic elements into major categories like noun phrase and verb phrase. The ability to relate objects and actions to one another provides the basis for the functional grammatical relations "subject of" and "object of." The ability to embed action schemata into one another is the same operation that allows phrase markers to be inserted into other phrase markers in language behavior.

Experimental techniques have been devised to demonstrate action structures in behavior and problem solving that are formally parallel to the grammatical structures of language (Goodson and Greenfield, 1975; Greenfield, 1978; Greenfield et al., 1972). At the same time, there has been an unfortunate trend in recent research to do mere correlational studies between measures of cognitive capacity and language ability. Theories of cognitive operations as the foundation of language development are often claimed to be supported by demonstrated positive correlations between measures of behavior in these two domains. The usual assumption is that if one has a particular cognitive ability, it is manifested both in nonlinguistic actions and in linguistic structure. But the criticisms of the previous sections hold here as well. Curtiss et al., by analyzing individual cases, gave examples that counter this view. They found children who had operational ability but who lacked the grammatical structures these are supposedly paralleled by; and they found children who had complex grammatical structures who lacked the cognitive abilities that are supposed to make the use of such structures possible. In addition, cognitive operations theories suffer from the other problem mentioned in the previous section. Just as having concepts does not explain how these concepts come to be encoded in language, so, too, having the ability to perform particular cognitive operations fails to explain how those operations come to be used in linguistic structures.

There is, however, another way to view cognitive operations. One of the problems in Piaget's approach to language has been to treat it as only one factor of the symbolic function as a whole. Language was not really viewed as different in kind from other symbolic factors such as deferred imitation, mental imagery, symbolic games, and drawing. Of course, language was seen as especially important, and the advantages it confers and the developments it allows have been discussed in some detail (Piaget and Inhelder, 1969b). Nevertheless, it was still considered part of the overall symbolic function, although a very important part. It is possible, however, to take a slightly different view. If language itself is seen as constituting a complex body of knowledge that must be discovered on its own terms (Slobin, 1978) in addition to being a part of the symbolic function, then it is possible to apply Piagetian notions concerning the child's acquisition of any system to the acquisition of the language system itself. The other framework for the first reconceptualization proposed in the next section draws on the work of Karmiloff-Smith (1977a,b, 1978, 1979a,b). Her experimentally based work demonstrates the advantages of viewing the child as an active organism with internally generated procedures and operations addressing himself to the linguistic system as a problem space to be solved.

There has been another effect of cognitive operations theories and the general upsurge of interest in Piagetian stages as applied to language acquisition. Many researchers have shown an increasing tendency merely to accept the broad Piagetian periods as they have been theoretically presented and to treat these as explanatory of all correlated behaviors. For example, children are given tests designed to measure their stage-related abilities, and on the basis of these measurements they are classified as being preoperational or concrete operational, or occasionally substages of these. These stage-grouped children are also compared on their language abilities. On the basis of such correlational studies, claims are then made that the achievement of this or that broad developmental stage is a necessary prerequisite for the acquisition of particular features of language. Quite apart from the logical flaws in such arguments, this is not a very useful procedure for advancing the kind of knowledge needed for language intervention programs with the linguistically handicapped. The second reconceptualization presented in this chapter is concerned with the necessity to look in more detail at exactly what cognitive processes make up the stages of growth and development.

THE BASIC ASSUMPTION BLOCKING REAL PROGRESS

In the previous section, four directions in recent research were reviewed. The claim was made that in some sense they have failed to provide insight into the nature of the acquisition of the structure of language. To what is this failure attributable? The shortcoming of the first research direction is slightly different from the others. Most of the research on language acquisition strategies has actually revealed what children do in interpreting certain structures when they do not yet have the linguistic competence to comprehend these structures in the adult manner. It was claimed that the strategies used did not really show how children acquired that competence. In fact, it would be more accurate to say that most of the research on children's strategies has been on strategies for *processing* language, and that very little is known about strategies children use for *acquiring* language. Nelson (1973), who originally pointed out this distinction, characterized acquisition strategies as methods for adding new elements to the original repertoire. There has been some work done on such strategies, and it is referred to as part of the argument for the first reconceptualization. It should be noted that strategies for acquisition, insofar as they go beyond the more traditional theories of acquiring any new information, presuppose an important contribution from the child, and one that may be specifically linguistic (the first framework) or at least composed of general cognitive principles for solving problems by members of the human species (the second framework).

The other three research areas, in contrast, fail to provide an understanding of the acquisition of the structure of language for a different reason. Work in those areas has often been characterized by the assumption of an empiricist theory of mind, which gives no place for specifically linguistic internal procedures. With the exception of the Newport et al. study, the parent-child interaction research has proceeded as if the child merely matched his or her productions to the input signal—which was shown to be clearer than had been supposed. Few attempts have been made to analyze the linguistic patterns used by both participants in the fine-grained manner necessary to demonstrate an empiricist claim, and the fact that child language productions do not match that input has been virtually ignored. Research on semantic theory is not reviewed in this chapter, but the misinterpretation that many psychologists make of semantic theories in linguistics by confusing them with psychological theories of concepts was noted. Such errors are further promulgated by the misappropriation of the term *semantics* from linguistic theory to a variety of theoretical notions in psychology.

One prominent example of this terminological misuse is found in so-called semantic memory theories, most of which are concerned solely with concepts and not at all with semantics. True semantic theories were not evaluated. The criticisms in that section pertained to the confusion of terms. It was in the discussion of cognitively based theories that inadequacies were discussed. The review of conceptual and cognitive theories pointed out how these theories do not account for the acquisition of linguistic structure. The reason is the same as that claimed for the failure of the parent-child studies: the naive assumption that once certain cognitive properties (either concepts or operations) have developed, they will be encoded in linguistic structure. There is an implied associationistic assumption. Children associate the ideas they wish to encode with the linguistic structures they hear in the environment around them. The inadequacies of such theories for language acquisition have been pointed out since the 1960s (e.g., Bellugi, 1967, 1971; Bever, Fodor, and Weksel, 1965a,b; Brown et al., 1969; Ervin-Tripp, 1966; McNeill, 1966, 1970a,b; Miller and McNeill, 1969; Sachs, 1971; and Slobin, 1971a,b, 1973). Empirical research on the utterances children actually produce while acquiring language supports these anti-associationist claims. Yet the real challenge of these findings has been for the most part systematically ignored.

The kind of theoretical reconceptualization that is needed to encourage research in the acquisition of the structure of language to proceed along useful lines is not limited merely to language. The same reconceptualization is needed if the development of broad areas of cognition is to be understood. Since the publication of Neisser's *Cognitive Psychology* (1967), it has been popular for an increasing number of psychologists to assume "a constantly *active* organism that searches, filters, selectively acts on, reorganizes, and creates information" (Reynolds and Flagg, 1977). In spite of these protestations, a great deal of research on the development of cognitive processes, like much of the work on language acquisition, in reality assumes a much more externally oriented approach than is either professed theoretically or is warranted by the evidence. A good example of this is the explosion of research into the development of conservation ability by 6-year-old children. Piaget's demonstration that young, preoperational children believe that the amount of liquid changes with the shape of the container was intended to illustrate the inability of the child at that stage of thinking to perform particular operations. Thus, a child who answers that there is more juice in the tall, narrow container than in a container identical to the one from which it has just been poured, is considered a nonconserving child. The child's answers, but more importantly, the child's methods of reasoning, are taken as evidence of preoperational thinking: he or she is unable to compensate the two dimensions. Note that what is important for the Piagetian view is not the child's answer. Indeed, there are tasks for which preoperational children almost always give correct answers (for the "wrong" reasons), although most adults give incorrect answers. In problems concerning area, for example, changing the layout but not the overall length of the perimeter so as to transform a square into a rectangular shape leads children to claim that the area (the space that "cows can graze over") is less, as it actually is, while adults "conserve" and incorrectly claim that the amount of grass to graze over must be the same; what is lost in one dimension is made up by the other. Adults use compensation, and are led to the wrong answer. In other words, tasks, like the typical conservation problems, were intended to show evidence of the limits of children's thinking when their thought structures could be characterized in particular ways. Whether Piaget is right or wrong over the particular descriptions of those structures (or even whether children's thinking can in fact be characterized by stage-like thought structures) is an empirical question that can be settled by observational and experimental research. What is at issue here is the approach that was taken to these problems by researchers mainly in America and Great Britain.

Although Piaget was "translated," his intentions and theoretical orientations were not. Psychologists in English-speaking countries have been concerned much more with a purely externally oriented approach to development. What followed were scores of studies purporting to show that preoperational children could be taught conservation by various techniques. (The number of articles that share this orientation in child development journals is too numerous to list. The interested reader can refer to collections of reprinted research articles that come under headings such as "training research," as is found, for example, in Siegel and Hooper, 1968). This was, of course, not Piaget's point. More important, such training-oriented research misses the real significance for development that Piaget had observed. Piaget's equilibration process, which is made up of assimilation and accommodation (this is discussed in the next section), considers what the child brings to any problem-solving task. In contrast, the question as to how the structures of thought are acquired are often ignored in training research, which is primarily concerned with external influences.

The claim being made here is that research that is founded on the theoretical assumption that what is crucially important for development is found almost exclusively in external influences will be unable to explain development adequately. This is true for the acquisition of the structure of language, and it is true for cognitive development in general. The usual rationale for such research is that if it can be demonstrated that children can be taught particular concepts, such as conversation, then it follows that all children must be acquiring these and similar concepts from environmental input. Not only is such a claim illogical, it is not empirically supported. In order to show this clearly, it is useful to quote the results from an early training experiment. Smedslund (1961) demonstrated that he could train a number of nonconserving children to acquire the concept of the conservation of substance and weight. Smedslund reasoned that if children were truly acquiring the concept of conservation on the basis of learning theory, it ought to be extinguishable, and this should be true whether the concept was acquired in the laboratory or in natural life. In contrast, Piaget's equilibration theory predicts that a genuine principle of conservation would be practically impossible to extinguish because it is thought to reflect an inner logical necessity. Smedslund pretested 5- to 7-year-old children on the conservation of weight. He was thereby enabled to see which children were natural conservers. The nonconservers were those who showed no trace of conservation. These non-conservers were then given training sessions. Eleven children were successfully trained to become conservers. They then undertook a series of extinction trials that were also administered to thirteen children who had been found to be natural conservers. The extinction trials were carried out by cheating the child. That is, when the plasticine was deformed into other shapes, pieces were inconspicuously taken away so that the two objects would not balance. The results were very interesting. Of the children who were taught to conserve, none showed any resistance to the extinction trials. Smedslund reported that they showed little surprise and rapidly switched back to nonconservation answers supported by explanations referring to the perceptual appearance of the objects. By contrast, almost half of the natural conservers maintained conservation in the face of apparent nonconservation, and this was evidenced in statements such as "I think you have taken away some of the clay!" and "We must have lost some clay on the floor." Smedslund concluded that children who had acquired a notion of conservation in the training sessions had learned only a relatively arbitrary empirical law. As he put it, they were not very shocked or surprised when the law was falsified, and they rapidly modified their answers and explanations. This contrasted with the resistance shown by many of the natural conservers.

This experiment has often been quoted as showing that trained conservers differ from those acquiring conservation naturally. Since that time, many experimenters have attempted more comprehensive training techniques or have disputed some of the specific details of Smedslund's procedures. But to do so—and even to demonstrate the existence of a tutorial program on conservation that is resistant to extinction—is to miss a much more crucial point. That some concept can be trained, and truly acquired, in no way explains how a concept is nevertheless acquired by children who have not undergone such training procedures. The usual empiricist assumption (and it should be noted that it is merely a theoretical assumption) is that if children can be trained in a particular concept, then other, untrained children are similarly acquiring that concept but by less direct means of environmental input. There is something in Smedslund's study, however, that has never been discussed. If it is assumed that children become conservers because of incidental environmental learning, and this process can be accelerated by direct tuition and environmental demonstrations of the concept, then another prediction is necessary. In Smedslund's study, the so-called extinction trials constituted direct tuition and environmentally supported demonstrations that conservation of weight in fact does not hold true in the world. By any reasonable learning theory, then, we would have to suppose that these children were made into nonconservers, and it must be assumed that they remain so because the normal environment offers only very indirect, incidental learning to the contrary. Although no proper follow-up has been made, it is doubtful that we would find these 11 Swedish young adults now in their mid-20s to be nonconservers—or even that they were delayed in their acquisition of operational thinking. There have been experiments that indicate that some aspects of development can be accelerated by tuition, but such techniques in no way *explain* that development, especially in those who have not had the benefit of that tuition, or as in the case just cited, of children who were directly trained in incorrect concepts.

THE FIRST RECONCEPTUALIZATION: INTERNAL FACTORS

The current emphasis on purely empiricist theories is as inadequate as are purely rationalist theories. What is needed is a reconceptualization of development that stresses the interaction of inner determinants and environmental factors.

The First Framework: An Epigenetic-Interactionist Viewpoint

What is here called an epigenetic-interactionist viewpoint is really nothing more than the assertion that there is inherent in the human species a number of unfolding developmental phenomena, some of which may be specifically linguistic, that interact with environmental variables. Such a position does not claim that children are born in possession of particular structures, but that structures are built up from an interaction of innate potential with environmental factors. There is a sense in which Piaget's genetic epistemology can be viewed in these terms although Piaget would disagree with the nativist component of such a view. In the Piagetian system, the structures of thought are said to develop through a process of assimilation and accommodation. Assimilation is the process of incorporating elements in the environment into the structure of the organism. These external elements are said to be assimilated to the system. In the process of assimilation, however, the organism is also undergoing modification. This modification is termed accommodation. Accommodation, then, is the modification of assimilatory schemata or structures by the elements that are assimilated.

Seiler (1979) attempted to employ Piaget's equilibratory system to notions of differentiation as a model of cognitive development. In doing so, he emphasized the relationship between assimilatory and accommodatory processes and innate and environmental variables. Seiler equated what he calls "pure" assimilation with predetermined

aspects of behavior. "Pure" accommodation, in contrast, is environmentally determined. But, of course, there is no such thing as "pure"
assimilation and accommodation. As Seiler put it, the linkage of the
two concepts dissolves the contradiction. Environmental objects do
not enforce the accommodation that children "endure." Rather, the
children themselves accommodate their structures while acting. Assimilation and accommodation are both actions of the developing child.
As Seiler stated, "Development is not suffered, but done." But at the
same time, development depends on the structures that determine the
actions. The activity of the organism is constructive. Development is
therefore seen as the active formation of new structures through modification and integration of existing ones.

The view that developmental growth depends on internal processes in interaction with the environment is certainly not new. The
problem for understanding the acquisition of the structure of language
is that most research assumes a rather strong empiricist/environmen-
talist orientation, as was indicated in preceding sections. Very little
research proceeds from the assumption of the possibility of specific
innate factors. This is partly because the term *innate* is usually mis-
interpreted as being in total contrast to environmental influences on
development. It is therefore necessary to take a closer look at what
"innateness" could possibly mean in terms of language acquisition,
and in what ways research could provide useful ideas concerning how
to implement intervention and remedial programs.

Interpretations of Innateness   The usual reaction by psychologists
and educators to the suggestion of innate components for any behavior
is to reject the notion out of hand. That there should be any innate
component to the acquisition of language seems especially absurd in
view of the necessity to acquire the specific structures of the language
to which one is exposed. Such rejection usually represents the mistaken
view, however, that innate and environmental factors are opposite
poles. There is, in addition, the assumption that positing innate aspects
of behavior is a way of cloaking one's ignorance of environmental
factors that at present are unknown. Because any discussion of innateness often becomes obscured by these and other misunderstandings, it is necessary to present the epigenetic-interactionist viewpoint
in some detail. One way to do this is to give an example of theory and
findings in the field of perception.

Until only recently, it was usual to encounter almost totally empiricist theories of perception in textbooks of psychology. For example,
depth perception was said to depend on the development of a number
of cues. One of these is interposition or superposition of objects in
which one learns that if one object seems superimposed on another,

the interrupted object seems to be further away. Another set of cues include learned features of perspective such as linear perspective (where parallel lines seem to converge in the distance), decreasing size with distance, height in the horizontal plane, and gradients of texture. Still other cues include the acquired knowledge with experience of the muscular feelings accompanying accommodation and convergence of the eyes. It was seen as somewhat of a breakthrough when the experiment by Gibson and Walk (1960) demonstrated that young infants seemed to have the knowledge of depth perception by as young as 6 months of age. They tested 36 infants between 6 and 14 months of age on a "visual cliff" that consisted of a large sheet of heavy glass, one side of which was several feet over a patterned floor (the deep side) or flush against it (the shallow side). The mother called to the child from both sides in turn. Almost all of the infants crawled off the shallow side, but refused to do so for the deep side. Even this demonstration was criticized because the infants were already 6 months old, and a great deal of perceptual learning had already taken place. It has also been demonstrated, however, that chickens, goats, lambs, and kittens, would venture out over the shallow side but not the deep side of the visual cliff as soon as they were able to walk—which in some cases was less than 24 hours after birth. Other aspects of perception, which had formerly been believed to be learned, have now been shown to be either innate or at least present at very early ages. For example, Bower (1966) showed that infants as young as 2 months of age possess size constancy. Having trained a baby to respond to a 30-cm cube, he then presented it both with a cube three times the size but farther away so that the retinal size was identical, and with the original 30-cm cube at varying distances. It was found that the baby primarily responded to the original stimulus in spite of distance and retinal size changes, and not to objects of the same retinal size.

The experiments on depth perception and size constancy have to do with functional properties of vision. Of course, psychologists have always accepted that certain physiological structures are prerequisite for vision. No one would argue that humans can, by mere experience, learn to "see" ultraviolet rays, although such stimuli can, of course, be experienced by conversion through mechanical means to stimuli that can be perceived. Experiments on properties of receptor cells in the visual cortex, however, have not only provided evidence of inborn detectors of a very specific nature, but have led to some discoveries that illustrate the interaction between innate and environmental factors in development. Hubel and Wiesel (1959) found that cells in the visual cortex of cats showed the greatest amount of activity to stimuli that were lines of a certain width located in a particular plane in the visual field. It seems that there are inborn receptors for horizontal and vertical lines. Some of the innate detectors are species-specific. For example, frogs have visual cells that respond to certain types of movement—a kind of "bug detector" as it has been called.

The finding that cats have inborn receptors for horizontal and vertical stimuli has led to further research on how such cells develop functionally, and it is here that a good example of environmental interaction has been observed. Blakemore and Cooper (1970) raised kittens in either a vertical or horizontal striped environment. After more than 5 months of this visual experience, it was observed that the adult neurons were all responding within 45 degrees of the expected orientation. Hirsch and Spinelli (1971) similarly found that kittens raised seeing only vertical or horizontal lines—one set to each eye in special goggles—developed monocular receptive fields that had the orientation of the experience of the eye to which they were connected. Blakemore (1974) concluded on the basis of these and other similar results that binocularity is innate, but that it can be modified by experience. Furthermore, early visual experience can modify the orientation of cell receptivity selectively. Blakemore noted that the human visual system is also subject to the same types of inborn/environmental interaction. He cited evidence that humans who grow up with severe astigmatism of a type that weakens the contrast of patterns of one orientation are left with *meridional amblyopia* (reduced acuity for the orientation that was originally out of focus). This cannot be rectified by eyeglass correction of the eye's optics. It has also been found that humans have higher resolution acuity for vertical and horizontal patterns than for diagonal ones. Blakemore speculated that this may be because of the predominance of rectilinear orientations in Western urban environments. It seems then, that inborn biological structures that are genetically determined are very much affected by environmental experience. Such environmental effects are within limits however. Cells responding to linear orientation can be made to react to specific orientations in accordance with environmental experience, but those same calls do not respond to other aspects of visual input.

Regarding the possibility of certain innate mechanisms for language acquisition, it is best to be quite clear. The proposal being advocated here is not an acceptance of the nativist position for language acquisition, although that may seem to be the case from this section. Rather, the claim being made is: 1) that it is dogmatic and unscientific to dismiss such claims; 2) that even where nativist claims are not explicitly rejected, much research proceeds without a true appreciation of internally generated factors; 3) that purely environmental (empiricist) theories have so far proved to be inadequate to account for the acquisition of the structure of language; and 4) that it is possible to conceive of theories of development that place a greater emphasis on epigenetic-interactionist principles and that take species-specific structures and functions into account. Furthermore, this view is especially important for intervention programs dealing with language disorders in that in the most obvious case, the impairment of specific biological structures determines not only the basic cause of the problem but gives clues as to techniques of remediation. No one pretends that someone who is congenitally deaf is not deaf. Similarly, it is important to determine whether other structural and functional properties that underlie language as we know it are impaired in certain groups. One major objection to studying innate factors—that finding something to be innate is to take a very pessimistic view for remediation—can be reversed; indeed, the opposite can be concluded. For purposes of effective intervention, it is obvious that if it is known at the biological structural level what the impairments are, there is a far better chance of undertaking appropriate remediation procedures. This is equally true if the deficits are of functional or organizational properties rather than physiological ones. The notion of physiological deficits is fairly easy to comprehend. In discussing the possibility of a nativist position for language acquisition, however, the importance of innate functional and organizational properties of language must be considered. One way this has been done has been by appeal to language universals.

Universals That May Be Innate   It is somewhat dangerous to use the phrase that one way to study possibly innate organizational properties of language is to look at linguistic universals. The whole appeal to universals has often been misunderstood. It should be made quite clear at the outset that no competent psycholinguist has made the claim that because certain aspects of language are found universally they must be innate. To do so is illogical because it is equally possible that certain things that are found universally arise through similarities of environment. A circular mandala need not be an innate symbol as Jung (1959) and others have claimed. All peoples share the important experience of a circular-appearing sun and moon. The argument by Chomsky (1965, 1968) for innateness was based on very different considerations. These included the arbitrariness of certain types of rules and constraints on the structure of language, the regularity of onset of language acquisition, the ease and rapidity of that acquisition, the fixed sequence of typical primitive language forms representing broadly similar approaches to language across children (in spite of more specific individual differences in that acquisition), and the observation that the unfolding of the sequence of acquisitions is not greatly affected by practice and reinforcement variables nor even by large variations of intelligence except in cases of severe retardation.

In other words, language was claimed to reflect a number of innate properties. Because these properties are innate, they are found universally. Thus, the search for linguistic universals was not to offer evidence of innateness; that is illogical, as was pointed out above. Rather, the search has been to discover what specific aspects of language reflect the inborn, species-specific human linguistic ability. What are some of these universals?

There are two approaches to this problem. One is to claim that specific linguistic rules or rule types are somehow inborn. The second is to claim that certain procedures or operating principles are brought to bear by human individuals on language input. Catlin (1978) pointed out that claims of the first type constitute a preformationist rather than an epigenetic view of innate factors. According to Catlin, Chomsky's position seems to be of this preformationist type. This contrasts with Lenneberg's position (1967), which is compatible with epigenetic theories. Chomsky claimed that the child has a set of specifically linguistic inborn structural properties and constraints that are applied to linguistic input. According to his view, there is a genetically determined universal grammar that permits a range of possible realizations. Individual experience acts only to specify the particular grammar and performance system within the range of possible grammars allowed by universal grammar.

When psychologists looked for clues in the linguistic literature as to what constituted particular linguistic universals, they found little that could help them in designing specific experimental tests of these claims. Most of the linguistic universals that are posited are not couched in absolute terms. For example, Slobin (1978) pointed out that in a long review of word order types in languages of the world, Greenberg (1966) did not make the absolutist claims that psychologists have attributed to him. Rather, his study focuses on statistical tabulations of dominant order types in conjunction with co-occurring linguistic features. In other words, universal linguistic features and constraints only operate within certain structural environments. It has nevertheless been possible to isolate a few instances that seemed to lend themselves to observational and experimental attempts to study whether children acquiring language behave in ways that would be predicted on this basis. McNeill, Yukawa, and McNeill (1971), for example, provided some data from Japanese children indicating that children expected the language input to match observed universals. The universal in question concerned direct and indirect objects. Many languages provide case markings for these forms. In some languages, only one of the forms is marked. It had been noticed that if a language marks only one form, it is always the oblique or secondary form that is marked—in this example the indirect object. In Japanese, both forms are marked. McNeill et al. reasoned, however, that if Japanese children who had not yet fully acquired the system were presented with slightly deviant sentences with only one form marked, they would expect it to be the indirect object in accordance with the universal. This can be made clearer with an Anglicized example. In Japanese, the post-particle "ni" marks the indirect object, and "o" marks the direct object; this contrasts with English in which word order plays an important part instead. Thus, a sentence something like "Turtle-ni fish-o give" would be identical to "Fish-o turtle-ni give," that is, Give the fish (direct object) to the turtle (indirect object). In contrast, in English, word order would affect the interpretation as in sentences like "Show the baby the cat" and "Show the cat the baby." McNeill et al. presented sentences to Japanese children in which only one of the two forms was marked. Although they are deviant sentences, they are interpretable by adults because one of the two forms still retains its marking. What was observed with the children, however, was that some of them performed in accordance with the expectation based on linguistic universals. They actually performed better when only the indirect object was marked than when both direct and indirect objects were marked appropriately, as is done by adult Japanese. They did the poorest when only the direct object was marked, treating it as the indirect object. The results suggested that children made use of innate tendencies that matched this linguistic universal. Attempts to see whether speakers of other languages share these universal expectations, however, have failed. Cromer (1975) presented 6- to 8-year-olds with a language game in which they had to learn which animal to push or to give to another on the basis of post-particle markings. Children in one group received sentences with the direct object marked; children in the other group heard sentences with marked indirect objects. After each trial they were shown which animal should have pushed the other, and trials continued until they had learned the "secret language." The experiment was designed so that both groups received word orders such that the correct answer to the very first trial violated English word order for acting on the sentences in the game. The expectation was that if children are acting in accordance with the linguistic universal, the children in the marked-indirect object group should learn the secret language in fewer trials and with fewer errors than children in the direct object group. This did not occur; there were no observed differences between the two groups, and this was true even when the children were subdivided according to their knowledge of the adult English word order rules for structures of this type. This one experimental test of children's expectations matching a particular structural universal in language has given negative results. There are, of course, possible drawbacks in this study concerning the nature of the particular linguistic universal chosen for investigation, the age of the children (perhaps being beyond an age when they might make use of expectations based on universal grammar), interactions with the particular grammar of English that does not make use of this type of case marking, etc. Other studies should be designed to investigate the claim that children make use of innate properties of universal grammar in the acquisition of the language to which they are exposed. Unfortunately, the most common reaction to Chomsky's preformationist claims has been to deny them dogmatically without adequate empirical investigation.

There is another approach to the study of possibly innate factors that is based more directly on Lenneberg's epigenetic view on what might be innate than on Chomsky's preformationist view. One such approach looks at the kinds of procedures that children bring to bear on language production. These procedures or operating principles may constitute true language *acquisition* strategies as opposed to the language *processing* strategies reviewed above. Some recent studies in this area have yielded encouraging results.

Slobin (1978), whose "waiting room" analogy was mentioned above, believes that language acquisition cannot be explained without understanding the connection between cognitive development and specific linguistic encoding. He argued that prelinguistic cognitive and social development obviously prepares the child for the acquisition of his or her native language, but those developments do not give the key to the particular categories and structures of the language. Linguistic expression is not in a one-to-one correspondence with thought. The child has to learn which possible notions receive formal marking in his or her language and how to form these notions in producing an utterance. To illustrate this point, Slobin gave the example of the English sentence, "Daddy gave me the ball." This sentence has four essential categories—actor, action, recipient, object. One of these, "gave," is marked for past. There is an additional notion of definite/indefinite contrast encoded in the word "the." To express this same thought, the German sentence would be "Der Vater gab mir den Ball." Slobin pointed out that the notions that the German speaker must encode, in addition to the four essential semantic categories, are:

Der: definite, singular, masculine, subject
gab: past, third person, singular
den: definite, singular, masculine, object

These notions change yet again and/or appear in different combinations in the examples Slobin gave of the same sentence in Hebrew, Turkish, Kaluli, Tagalog, etc. Furthermore, as he pointed out, still other languages require the speaker to encode, for example, the shape of the object and considerations such as whether the action took place recently. In other words, as Slobin showed, there is a large gap between a communicative intention and the semantic structure that contains the notions that must be mapped onto the grammatical utterance in a particular language. Each language, then, presents the child with a different problem in terms of discovering the notions that have to be encoded and the means of encoding them. Slobin posed the question directly by asking what kinds of linguistic structures might facilitate language acquisition. This is seen in terms of the operating principles like those given in Slobin (1973). They include, for example, the principle that underlying semantic relations should be marked overtly and clearly; and the principle that postponed markers (suffixes and postpositions) are more salient than preposed markers (prefixes and prepositions). Although Slobin presents these principles in terms of the structures of the language the child is acquiring, his view is compatible with a view that focuses on the procedures the child brings to bear on the acquisition of such strutures. The ease or difficulty with which particular features of language are acquired presupposes internal (and possibly innate) factors favoring some types of structures over others in terms of ease or speed of acquisition.

Slobin (1978) reported the results from his Berkeley Cross-Linguistic Acquisition Project, in which the acquisition by children of four languages was investigated—English, Italian, Serbo-Croatian, and Turkish. These languages contrast in certain basic ways. For example, Turkish and Serbo-Croatian are inflectional languages in that, unlike English, the greater portion of syntactic contrasts involves modification of word stem forms. These two languages themselves contrast in that Turkish is a pure inflectional system with maximal freedom of word order. It is an agglutinating language in which words are typically composed of sequences of morphs (word parts) with each morph representing one morpheme or meaning unit. Turkish is often cited as an example of an agglutinating language that approximates very closely to the "ideal" type (Lyons, 1968). Serbo-Croatian is a fusional language whose words are not readily segmentable into morphs. It relies on a mixture of both word order and inflections. In contrast to these two inflectional languages, English is considered an analytic or "isolating" language. Fixed word order is one of the main ways grammatical relations are encoded. Of the languages studied, English has the most fixed word order, Italian has more flexibility as does Serbo-Croatian, and Turkish has the maximum freedom of word order.

For each of the four languages 48 children were studied. These samples were composed of six children at each of eight age levels that were set at 4-month intervals between the ages of 2;0 and 4;4. Each child was studied intensively for a total of 15–20 hours in a 10-day period. A battery of linguistic and nonlinguistic tasks was administered. Language production, both free and elicited, was studied, as was language comprehension. Specific investigations were made of the agent/patient relation, causatives (which are reported in more detail in Ammon and Slobin, 1979), locatives, and the understanding of before/after. The basic finding was that the languages patterned differently according to the task. For example, for causatives, the two inflectional languages were superior; for before/after, Turkish was the easiest for the children; for locatives, Turkish and Italian were in the lead. The conclusion was that the child's acquisition of the means of encoding particular relations was influenced by the types of linguistic structures involved. In addition, there was something about Turkish that made these structures especially easy to discover. Turkish uses a stock of regular particles for expressing single elements of meaning. These particles demonstrate word harmony and exist without irregular forms. In the findings, there was no support for the use of word order strategies or for the notion that certain word orders are more natural than others. In languages in which word order plays an important role (English, Italian), sensitivity to word order was not found initially; it was not observed until the children were between 2;8 and 3;0. It is interesting to note in this regard Slobin's claim that word-order languages impose a greater burden on short term memory and this may account for the later emergence of word-order strategies in sentence comprehension.

For Serbo-Croatian, the child must learn an interaction of both inflections and word order. When an inflectional contrast is not available to distinguish certain grammatical relations, then a particular word order is used. Slobin claimed that the inflectional system of Serbo-Croatian, being fusional rather than agglutinating, lacks the clarity of the Turkish system. In Serbo-Croatian, there are interactions of case with number, gender, and animacy, and there are many irregular forms. Some of the case forms are homonyms. There are no unique markers for number, case, or gender. As Slobin put it, it is a challenge to theories of language acquisition that such confused systems are learned at all in the first few years of life.

There are other aspects of the acquisition of these four languages that Slobin noted. When it comes to aspects of language that are typically acquired late—for example, instances where surface forms are very different from their underlying representations—languages like Turkish that seem to have an advantage in early acquisition, are at a disadvantage. Relative clauses in Turkish may be difficult because unlike Indo-European languages, such clauses do not look like surface sentences. In languages in which relative clauses do have such a resemblance, normal sentence-processing strategies with minimal adaptations can be used to interpret them. Slobin concluded that languages may not differ considerably in the overall ease of their acquisition. Advantages in morphology are compensated for by disadvantages in syntax and vice versa.

Slobin's work shows the importance of considering the particular linguistic features of the language to be acquired. As he put it, the child behaves as if he expects to find a certain consistency in the linguistic system. The child interprets new and deviant forms on the basis of rules or strategies that he has already established from earlier input. Beyond this internal aspect, however, Slobin speculated that perhaps children only attempt to interpret sentence structures that fit their notions of language. Although Slobin did not commit himself on the point, some of these acquisition strategies or operating principles could conceivably reflect innate organizational principles that may be specifically evolved for dealing with language structure. In whichever manner this is viewed, his overall approach is significant because he takes serious consideration of the internal aspects that the child brings to bear on the very specific system of language structure.

Linguistic Specificity of Possibly Innate Processes   If the child brings to bear on language acquisition certain processes that may possibly be innate, the question arises as to whether such processes are specifically linguistic or whether they merely represent broader cognitive procedures that may be applicable to the acquisition of other structures of knowledge. The processes studied by Karmiloff-Smith, which are discussed below as part of the second framework for viewing internal factors, seem to be the same processes the child uses in approaching any problem space. The contrasting view, that some processes may be specifically linguistic, has met with a good deal of scepticism.

It is true of course that language as a human communication system depended evolutionarily on the anatomical and physical features of the human species. The issue of what is meant by "specifically linguistic" is therefore very complex. Obviously, an impairment of any of those other systems on which language depends will result in an impairment of language. These can include defects of anatomical structures that impair the speech mechanism—but these are considered as speech problems and not as language impairments as such. Other physical structures, however, may be crucial for true language functioning. These may include such systems as auditory processing, auditory storage, abilities to deal with interruption, abilities to process hierarchically ordered materials, and long-term memory, among others. If one can isolate impairments in one or another of these systems in various language disordered groups, there will be important implications for intervention programs.

There is also the question of whether there are some specifically linguistic principles that are innate. Chomsky concluded that there are. It is difficult to specify whether the types of operating principles that Slobin proposed (1973) are purely linguistic or whether they represent somewhat broader cognitive approaches to the language system. Although little is known about the psychological reality of possibly innate linguistic processes, there is no logical *a priori* reason for dismissing the possibility of their existence. Certainly the observation of widespread constraints on certain linguistic structures across wide divergences in language (see, e.g., Keenan and Comrie, 1977) points to the existence of some mysterious and unexplained natural phenomena; empiricist theorists have been unable, when not unwilling, to account for their existence.

Uniqueness of the Human Species   Of all the arguments against the possibility of innate linguistic principles, the charge (e.g., Linden, 1975) that those who propose such principles are attempting to hold onto a vestige of human uniqueness in an anthropocentric sense must surely rank as one of the most illogical. To argue for species-specificity of a particular behavior in no way implies holding such a viewpoint. It would be as absurd to claim that the discovery of innate releasing mechanisms in greylag geese or in sticklebacks implies an attempt to defend their uniqueness in the quasi-religious sense of which proponents of species-specific language behavior in humans are accused. Indeed, to believe that human beings somehow do *not* share with other animal species various types of innate mechanisms is more akin to arguing for a human soul. That the issue has been raised is because of the interest in teaching "language" to closely related species. These studies are interesting and important; indeed, the techniques on which they provide information may give valuable clues to *methods* for intervention with persons who have impaired language abilities.

There are two points about these studies that should be clarified. First, so far it has not been possible to demonstrate the acquisition in other species of a linguistic system as distinct from a system of meanings and/or communication. Second, and more importantly, even if it is eventually demonstrated that other species can be taught linguistic structures, this would in no way address the problem concerning how children acquire language in the ways that they do nor would it account for the universal existence of particular linguistic structures, principles, and constraints in human languages. The argument that any positive results of teaching language to other species would falsify the claims of an innate component of language in human beings is illogical. It is possible to train a pigeon to react aggressively to a red patch. Such training does not invalidate the fact that robins do so as the result of innate releasing mechanisms (Lack, 1943; a good review of literature on innate releasing mechanisms can be found in Eibl-Eibesfeldt, 1970). Limber (1977) made the same point: "Some may interpret the achievements of . . . trained apes as disproving Chomsky's hypothesis. Presumably, such individuals would also consider the successful training of a dog to move about on hind legs as evidence against the hypothesis that humans are genetically predisposed to walk" (p. 292, footnote).

In summary, the overall claim that is being made here is not that certain aspects of language acquisition are necessarily innate. But problems do arise concerning why only certain types of linguistic procedures and constraints, and not others that are logically possible, are found universally in particular language environments; why children acquiring language evidence a regularity of onset, ease, and rapidity of acquisition, and sequences of acquisitions not greatly affected by practice, reinforcement, and wide variations in intelligence; and why children acquiring different languages seem to make use of particular operating principles and not others during that acquisition. In addition, one must also consider the continued failure to explain the acquisition of the structure of language by purely empiricist theories despite some 15 or more years of intensive research into this issue. If the continual misunderstandings and misinterpretations of what constitutes an epigenetic-interactionist viewpoint can be cleared away, it may be possible to consider in an unbiased fashion the biological underpinnings that exist for language acquisition. The continued dogmatic rejection of such a viewpoint is unwarranted in the face of empirical evidence, and is in fact detrimental to the development of effective intervention programs.

The Second Framework:
Language as a Specific Structural System To Be Acquired

There is another approach to language acquisition that focuses on the child's contribution. It is that of viewing language as a structural system to be acquired, and one that children will approach in ways not unlike the manner in which they approach other conceptual tasks. This is the view proposed by Karmiloff-Smith (1977a, 1977b, 1978, 1979a, 1979b). She believed the reasons usually offered to explain why children begin to use new linguistic devices were inadequate. The new linguistic forms used by children are not just due to communicative pressure. As has been pointed out by many researchers, the child is understood most of the time anyway even when he is using forms quite different from the adult model. Furthermore, the child is not progressively accommodating to the linguistic input that he or she hears—a point made clear by all of the careful observational studies of child language acquisition in the 1960s. Karmiloff-Smith offered evidence that the reason the child uses new forms is quite different: it is because of a metalinguistic push to deal with the structured language system. When children first begin to use particular forms, they do so primarily for themselves, not for communication purposes. According to Karmiloff-Smith, there is an attempt by the children to get a grip on the linguistic system. The children are trying to come to terms with their own budding organizational activities, language, and all of their environment.

In one of her experiments, Karmiloff-Smith (1978) studied the acquisition and use of gender distinctions by French-speaking children. She first noted that there is no foolproof way to predict gender on conceptual grounds. Furthermore, although prediction of the correct gender is often possible from word endings, there are many exceptions. The only foolproof strategy is to use grammatical gender, that is, to use as definitive the gender of the article, and then to make adjectives, past participles, and pronouns agree with that gender. Karmiloff-Smith wanted to know what acquisition strategies children used for gender. To do this, she carried out a set of experiments on 339 monolingual French children, ages, 3;2 to 12;5. To test knowledge of gender agreement, she used 30 nonsense words that were assigned to pairs of identical but differently colored pictures. The nonsense words had either typically masculine, typically feminine, or neutral word endings. For example, the nonsense word "bicron" had a masculine ending; "bravaise" had a feminine ending; a word like "fediste" is audibly typical of neither gender. Note that the color word pronunciation depends on the gender of the noun with which it is used. The masculine and feminine forms for "white" in French are "blanc" and "blanche."

The child was asked questions about the different nonsense words. He was confronted with five types of problems. In one, the article and the noun were consistent as in "un bicron" and "une bravaise." In another type, the article and noun endings were inconsistent. In a third problem, no article gender was provided, as in "deux bicrons" and "deux bravaises." In a fourth type of problem, the sex of the pictured person was inconsistent with the noun ending and no gender marked article was provided. The child had to give spontaneous responses containing the definite article ("le"/"la"), the nonsense noun, and an adjective of color (e.g., "blanc"/"blanche"). In a fifth task, the child was asked to create names for pictures of imaginary people of both sexes. The questions used forms in which gender was not audibly marked, as in "Ça", "quel/quelle x?" and "Ça c'est quoi?" Karmiloff-Smith reported that the results from these tasks showed that the youngest children used a very powerful implicit system of phonological rules based on the consistency of phonological changes of the word endings. They did not use syntactic clues (gender of the article) nor semantic clues (the sex of the person in the drawing) to determine gender agreement. She also noted that young children even made errors on frequently used words such as "la maison," whose masculine ending but feminine article are inconsistent with regard to phonological rules. The young children responded, "la maison vert" using the masculine form of the French word for green, to make it agree phonologically with the masculine noun ending, even though the article shows it to be feminine. Older children, however, took syntactic and semantic cues into consideration and changed the suffixes so that they agreed with the definite article or with the sex. They spontaneously changed "une bicron" into "la bicronne." In some cases they simply avoided pronouncing the suffix by using only the definite article and the agreeing adjective, as in "la grise" (the grey one) instead of "la bicron grise" (where "bicron" would have needed to be changed into "bicronne").

In this experiment, the use by the youngest French-speaking children of a predominantly phonological strategy, and thus one which is specifically linguistic, has been demonstrated for the system of gender. Karmiloff-Smith's paper discusses the intricacies of this system and how it interacts with other aspects of the language system—for example, how older children go on to use the phonological rules for more extended syntactic cohesion, as in the use of gender endings to govern anaphora and lexical concord. In this short review of her findings on phonological rules for gender, one does some injustice to the complexity of her arguments, and the interested reader should refer directly to her writings. In the context of the issues raised in this chapter, her work is cited with the more specific aim of giving an example of how one can take account more directly of the kinds of strategies the child brings to bear on language acquisition and how some of these may be specifically linguistic. Karmiloff-Smith noted that the phonological strategy used by French-speaking children on the gender system is input-dependent. In German, the noun endings are not good clues to formal gender and German-speaking children may use quite different strategies in acquiring that system. Furthermore, other aspects of French may depend to a greater extent on semantic, syntactic, or pragmatic procedures.

These results can be interpreted by others in a variety of ways. One possibility is to view the phonological strategy as reflecting some kind of innate language-specific procedure used in conjunction with environmental language input of particular types. In that sense, this work could have as well been reviewed in the previous section on the epigenetic-interactionist viewpoint. It should be noted that Slobin's work, although reviewed in that section, could have been summarized here as research that takes account of language as a specific structural system. The placement in this review of the results of Slobin's and Karmiloff-Smith's studies is merely intended to illustrate one or another of the viewpoints being presented and is not meant in any way to imply that these researchers see their work in the light of those viewpoints. Both of these researchers would, however, agree as to the importance of considering the internal factors that the child brings to bear on language acquisition, regardless of how such processes are seen to arise; both would find an empiricist theory of purely external input inadequate; and both would view the linguistic system as an organized structural entity to be understood and acquired.

Karmiloff-Smith (1977b, 1978) also showed the kinds of strategies children use in an attempt to separate linguistic functions that overlap. She found that the child tries to keep separate two meanings normally represented by a single reference element so that he can consolidate the two meanings independently. The child actually creates forms that are ungrammatical from the adult point of view in order to accomplish this separation. For example, in French, *une voiture* means both "a car" and "one car." When the child wants to specify "*one*," he will often produce *une de voiture*, a form which is slightly ungrammatical in adult French except in some dialects where it is used for emphatic contrast—which was not the case with these children. Children similarly distinguish the determiner and descriptive functions of adjectives. Thus, when describing a red crayon, they will correctly say *Je prends le crayon rouge*. But in a task requiring the determiner function, they produce *Je prends le rouge de crayon*, which again is slightly ungrammatical in adult French.

Another example of keeping distinct meanings encoded by separate forms can be seen in the child's use of même ("same"). Karmiloff-Smith pointed out that "same" has two meanings: *same kind*, as in "Jane is wearing the same dress as Mary," and *same one*, as in "Jane is wearing the same dress as yesterday." In comprehension tasks, Karmiloff-Smith (1977b) found that children interpreted "the same x" as "another x with the same attributes" and not "one and the same x." The child was given various objects. Some were identical, some were of the same class but differed in color, and others were of the same class but differed in several ways. Also included were objects that were the only members of their class available in the experiment. Forty-seven children between the ages of 2;10 and 7;11 were tested by the Genevan method of changing items, asking the child questions, etc. Not only did the youngest children treat "the same x" as "another x with the same attributes" (= another one) but they understood the word "another" for the contrast case (= another kind); they would refuse to carry out a task on "another x" unless the objects differed in some way. It is interesting to note that older children (age 6 to 7 years) created a slightly ungrammatical form to express "the same kind." They avoided using the economic and correct J'ai la même ("I have the same") and produced such utterances as J'ai *une de même de* vaches chez moi ("I've got *one of the same of* cows") or la *même de* vache, which were ungrammatical in the context in which they were used (Karmiloff-Smith, 1978).

In addition to creating ungrammatical forms, children also make use of what Karmiloff-Smith calls the "overmarking" of forms. That is, they add redundant markers for clarity—and again they seem to do this for themselves and not to aid communication (Karmiloff-Smith, 1977a, 1979b). Thus, children will not place the burden of anaphoric reference on articles and pronouns in contrasts where ambiguity of reference might occur. Instead of saying "The girl pushed a dog and then the boy pushed *it*," they will make utterances like "The girl pushed a dog and then *also* the boy *re*-pushed *again the same* dog." Karmiloff-Smith (1979b) also showed that such overmarking is not necessarily limited to approaches to language. In an ingenious memory task in which children had to recall a very long series of T-maze-type choices, the same types of overmarking were observed. The interest in the task was not in the child's learning of the choice points. Rather, the memory aids the child used were studied. The path was drawn on a long roll of brown wrapping paper. As the next choice came into view by unrolling the wrapping paper, the earlier choices disappeared as the other end of the paper was being re-rolled. When it was demonstrated to the child how difficult it would be to remember all the choice points, he was given pencils and paper and told he could make what notes he wanted in order to trace the path correctly later. At first the child would overmark in his notes, and even during the course of the experiment would simplify his system by dropping redundant features in later notes. For example, for a particular choice point, he might first draw a forked path with an arrow indicating the correct side to take and a cross blocking the incorrect path. Later, he might drop the blocking cross, and merely show the arrow along the correct choice of the two paths. Eventually, he might no longer draw the entire fork in the path, but merely that part going up in the correct direction.

Karmiloff-Smith argued that some of the strategies or principles that children bring to bear on language acquisition, then, are not necessarily specific to language. They are procedures for attempting to cope with any system or task. What is emphasized is the child's contribution to the acquisition process. No stand is necessarily taken as to how these internal processes arise. It is possible to interpret her results as showing some procedures that may be purely linguistic. Others are strategies that the child might apply to any problem space. But in an important extension of such an approach, Karmiloff-Smith emphasized that language is to be viewed as a structural system and not merely as a collection of auditory stimuli, nor as merely one of several aspects of a general symbolic function. Her own theories are more complex than is evident here. For example, the relation between language and cognitive processes is seen in terms of a constructive interaction, and Karmiloff-Smith (1978) presented evidence that some advances in language acquisition also provoke other cognitive changes.

It has been asserted that a reconceptualization concerning development is necessary in which internal factors within the child are taken into more serious consideration. Although this was emphasized as regards the acquisition of the structure of language in the theoretical positions of the 1960s and was supported by the observational studies of children acquiring language, much of the research in the past few years has drifted back to an approach that can be described as being based on assumptions of an empiricist theory of mind as regards language. Although the child is likely to be seen as a more active participant in general cognitive development, that same active structuring is ignored when studying the acquisition of the specific structural system of language. Two frameworks have been proposed within which to emphasize the importance of internal factors on that acquisition—one advocating an epigenetic-interactionist view and the other advocating that language be understood as a specific structural system to be acquired. The second reconceptualization is different and concerns the content of cognitive stages.

THE SECOND RECONCEPTUALIZATION: SPECIFIC DEFICITS

Recently, a number of controversies have developed over the specific aspects of some of Piaget's developmental periods. One of these controversies pertains to the ability to make a transitive inference of the type that if $A > B$, and $B > C$, then $A > C$. According to Piaget, such an inference should not be possible until the child has reached the stage of concrete operational thinking, which occurs at about the age of 6 or 7 (Piaget and Inhelder, 1956; Piaget, Inhelder, and Szeminska, 1960). Bryant and Trabasso (1971), however, challenged this view and claimed that children could indeed form transitive inferences if it could be ensured that they could recall the premise information at the time of making the transitive inference. In their experiment, they used five sticks in order to eliminate a labeling strategy—that is, learning to label particular sticks "large" or "small." Children were over-trained on the specific comparisons. Each adjacent pair had to be learned to a stringent criterion. When this was done, 4-year-old children were found to be able to make the correct judgments of relative size on the non-adjacent sticks that had not been specifically contrasted. In other words, it was claimed that they could now make correct transitive inferences. If this is true, then it would challenge the assumption in Piaget's theory that a certain type of logical structure is not attained until operational thinking is possible, as seen in a variety of other tasks. Smedslund (1963, 1965), however, had previously rejected a memory interpretation of the Bryant and Trabasso type when he reported that some of the children he tested sometimes were unable to make the transitive judgment even when they were able to recall the specific comparisons immediately before the test on the transitive relation. More recently, Halford and Galloway (1977) specifically tested for memory of the shown comparisons after the transitive inference. Of 163 children, ages 4½ to 9 years, 107 did not make the transitive inference. Of these, however, only 20 were unable to remember the comparisons; 87 remembered both comparisons but still failed to make the transitive inference. It has also been argued that success in the Bryant and Trabasso task may be attributable to other factors, and that the children had not really made inferences of the Piagetian type. Riley and Trabasso (1974) came to this conclusion. They claimed that if by operational transitivity is meant the coordination of the members of the premises by way of a middle term at the time of testing, then the young children they have tested do not use operational transitivity. They present a process model of how the transitive judgments are made by these children, but also assert that their results and those of Bryant and Trabasso (1971) are irrelevant as far as Piaget's theory is concerned. Whether this is so or not, the point can be made that at the very least, transitivity judgments cannot be correctly made until the child has developed a sufficient memory span to recall the initial comparisons. A certain memory span is at least necessary for certain aspects of operational thinking to occur, and whether it is sufficient, as Bryant and Trabasso had originally claimed, is another issue.

However they are interpreted, the Bryant and Trabasso results suggest that it may be wiser to consider more specific aspects of cognitive functioning rather than merely to rely on broad Piagetian stages. Those broad developmental periods such as the sensorimotor and concrete operational stages were a very valuable and useful way of describing the child and of making sense of the way the child approached very disparate aspects of the world. There has been a tendency, however, for research on the relationship between language acquisition and cognitive functioning to focus only on such broad stages, often using correlational techniques. These studies are not very useful for language intervention programs. Instead of concentrating on the macro level of broad developmental stages (if they do indeed exist), a more useful approach would be to concentrate on the micro-level processes that contribute to making such intellectual accomplishments possible.

Memory

One of the specific processes that might be impaired in some language-disordered groups is short-term memory. That short-term auditory memory plays a role in verbal comprehension has been demonstrated in a variety of experiments. For example, Conrad (1972) presented evidence supportive of the notion that verbal stimuli pass into an auditory short-term store in order for various operations to be performed to extract meaning. Rapin and Wilson (1978) noted that lesions involving the supramarginal and angular gyri of the left parietal lobe have been found to interfere with short-term verbal acoustic memory, thus producing amnestic aphasia (Geschwind, 1967; Warrington, Logue, and Pratt, 1971). There has been speculation that short-term memory impairment may be responsible for the language disorders of some children. Menyuk (1964, 1969) studied a group of children, ages 3;0 to 5;11, who were described as using infantile language. Menyuk found that their language was in fact deviant and not merely infantile or delayed. In conjunction with some imitation tasks that she gave, she concluded that the differences were possibly attributable to a short-term memory impairment. Leonard (1979) challenged this view. He claimed that the manner in which she made her statistical comparisons of spontaneous speech with a younger normal group was unusual, and that the comparison even at a descriptive level showed that only two structures out of 33 that were examined were used by one group but not the other. Leonard argued that the language structures used by language-disordered children are not different from those used by normal children but are merely *like* those used by younger normal children. In his own study of nine language-impaired children, ages 4;10 to 5;10, who were compared to nine normal children of the same ages (Leonard,

1972), he found that the two groups differed not in absolute terms (one group using a structure that was never evidenced in the other group), but that they did differ in terms of the frequency of use of particular structures.

The observation that one or another language-disordered group does not differ absolutely in the use of structures found in younger normal children does not invalidate the claim that they are not necessarily behaving like normal children. To look at the language structures that are or are not used only in themselves is to take a rather narrow view of what can be learned from such studies. Structures that are rarely or never used by language-disordered groups but are used by normal children or adults may give clues as to the nature of underlying deficits. Furthermore, as noted above, Menyuk's conclusion concerning a memory deficit was based not only on the examination of spontaneous language. She also gave the language-disordered group a sentence imitation task that was administered to younger, normal children as well. This sentence repetition task revealed significant differences between the groups. The normal children made use of sentence structure and were able to repeat some sequences that would have exceeded their memory span as measured by traditional methods. In the imitation task, repetitions were constrained by syntactic structure and not by sentence length as such. The correlation between sentence length and inability to repeat sentences was only 0.04, that is, at chance level. The imitations by the language-disordered group showed rather different results. For these children, the correlation between sentence length and inability to imitate was 0.53. In addition, the kinds of errors that were observed differed from those made by the normal children. The normal children made errors and omissions that consisted primarily of modifications of transformational structure. In contrast, the omissions that were made by the language-disordered children were almost invariably from the first part of the sentence. The last thing heard was more frequently recalled, which seems to indicate a short-term memory deficit. Short-term memory even for utterances as short as three to five morphemes in length seemed to be impaired. Menyuk speculated that if these children were able to keep in memory no more than two or three morphemes, they would be unable to carry out a deepening linguistic analysis on the language input. This would result in producing utterances that would be impoverished and limited. Such utterances would not be qualitatively different from those used by younger, normal children who also have a limited short-term memory span. Such a hypothesis would not be at variance with Leonard's findings. However, Menyuk also suggested, however, that such a short term memory limitation would result in qualitatively different utterances because they would be based in some cases on different hypotheses and rules concerning language. Menyuk (1978) summarized work on language-disordered children as showing that the intentions of sentences (to command, declare, negate, and question) are preserved as are the main relations (actor, action, and object). She also noted that these children preserve the syntactic rule of word order to express those relations. They do not, however, preserve certain transformational modifications. Lee (1966) provided evidence that a language-disordered child that she studied did not produce some types of utterances even at the two-word level that is found in normal children. Bloom (1967; see also Leonard, 1979) raised some doubts concerning Lee's findings particularly because the language samples of the two groups were obtained in a different manner. In any case, because the differences observed were at the two-word level, short-term memory was not implicated, and the deficit was attributed to other factors.

Graham (1968, 1974; Graham and Gulliford, 1968) presented a memory limitation hypothesis to account for language observed in educationally subnormal children. Repetition and comprehension scores on various sentence types increased regularly with short-term memory as measured by the repetition of random words and digits. By relating the notion of short-term memory to the amount of computation required by sentences of various structural types, Graham concluded that the children in his study were unable to process sentences that made demands on short-term memory and that were beyond their capacity.

Processing Deficits in Autistic Children

In discussing Menyuk's work, it was noted that normal children made use of sentence structure in the repetition task that she administered, but that her language-disordered group was more greatly affected by sentence length than by sentence structure and a memory impairment was therefore hypothesized. Similarly, most subnormal children have extremely short memory spans. This is not true of autistic children who are also subnormal (O'Connor and Frith, 1973). But nonautistic subnormal children have been observed to increase the amount of information they can process by making use of sentence structure, whereas autistic children do not do so to the same degree. Hermelin and O'Connor (1967) compared 12 subnormal autistic children with 12 severely subnormal nonautistic children matched on the basis of their immediate memory span for digits and on scores from the Peabody Picture Vocabulary Test. The task was to repeat words that were arranged either randomly or in sentences. The results showed that although the severely subnormal nonautistic children performed significantly better with sentences than with random sequences, no significant difference was found for the autistic children.

Frith (see Aurnhammer-Frith, 1969) compared 16 autistic children with 16 normal children on a similar task. The autistic group included only those children who had some speech. Their chronological age was 11;6. They were compared with a normal group (mean chronological age of 4;3) that was matched on digit span. The two groups were of comparable mental age as measured on the Peabody Picture Vocabulary Test. The results showed that although both groups benefited from grammatical structure and performed better for sentences than for words arranged randomly, the normal children benefited significantly more than the autistic group did. It was as if the autistic group was impaired in the ability to deal with sentence structure as compared with the normal children. This result is especially interesting when one recalls that the two groups were prematched for digit span performance. Fyffe and Prior (1978) replicated this finding.

There have been other studies that have shown that autistic children may be suffering from specific language or communication deficits. Ricks (1972, 1975) found differences in the early cries of autistic children, subnormal nonautistic children, and normal children. The autistic children were 3 to 5 years old, as were the matched nonautistic, subnormal children. The normal children were 8 to 12 months old. Different types of cries were obtained from the children in standardized situations designed to elicit messages of frustration, request, greeting, and pleased surprise. These cries were tape recorded and test tapes were made by splicing the four cries of four children onto a single tape, resulting in 16 cries on each tape. These tapes were played to six parents of normal children and six parents of autistic children. Parents of normal children heard tapes of the four cries of their own child, the four cries of two other normal English babies, and the four cries of one baby being raised by non-English-speaking parents. The cries were spliced onto the tapes in random order. Parents of an autistic child heard the cries of their own child, two other autistic children, and one nonautistic retarded child of the same age. The parents' task was to identify and label the meaning of all 16 cries and to identify their own child. In addition, parents of normal children were also asked to identify the non-English child; parents of autistic children had to identify the nonautistic subnormal child. Finally, all of the parents were presented with the request sounds of six babies and had to pick out their own child from among these. The results showed that parents of normal children could easily identify all 16 messages including those of the non-English baby although they could not identify which child was the non-English one. To their surprise, they were unable to pick out the cries of their own baby. It seems that the cries of normal children have a marked similarity and these signals seem to be independent of language background. The results from the autistic group were quite different. The parents of autistic children could only identify the idiosyncratic messages of their own child and the cries of the nonautistic retarded child. They could not identify the messages of the other two autistic children. Furthermore, they could easily identify their own child. Retarded children who are not autistic seem to have normal cries that can be identified by adults. But autistic children have their own idiosyncratic and distinctive cries that can only be identified by adults familiar with them; they do not share the vocabulary of intonated signals used by normal and even subnormal children.

Because of their language impairment, autistic children have often been confused with or compared to developmentally aphasic children. Bartak, Rutter, and Cox (1975; see also Bartak and Rutter, 1975), however, provided evidence that the two groups can be reliably differentiated. They present entirely different kinds of language impairment. For example, autistic children show significantly greater *I-you* pronoun reversal, echolalia, stereotyped utterances, and inappropriate remarks than do aphasic children.

Deficits in Developmentally Aphasic Children

Short-Term Storage Deficit   A number of recent reviews of possible deficits in childhood aphasia are available in Wyke (1978) Benton, (1978) Cromer (1978a) Menyuk (1978) and Rapin and Wilson (1978). One such deficit is that of an impairment of short term storage of the type mentioned above. Eisenson (1968) speculated that the aphasic child's storage system for speech signals may be defective. Stark, Poppen, and May (1967) studied eight aphasic children, of mean age 8 ; 3, on a task that involved pressing keys with pictures on them in the same order as the order in which the items were auditorially presented by the experimenter. Five of the eight aphasics performed very poorly on this task. Furthermore, most of their errors occurred on the item in the first position. Verbal stress put on this item led to an improvement of their scores. Although Stark et al. concluded that the results were evidence for a sequencing disability, they can also be interpreted as showing an impaired auditory memory.

Rosenthal and Eisenson (1970) presented short speech sounds either singly or in pairs to aphasic and normal children. The child's task was to put the paired sounds in temporal order. The time taken to do this was compared with the time taken for the same task with nonspeech sounds. Both normal and aphasic children could identify the sounds presented singly. The aphasic children, however, did poorly when they had to report the order of two sounds that were presented in close temporal proximity. Rosenthal and Eisenson took this as evidence that the aphasic children they studied were suffering from an auditory storage deficit. The auditory trace that could be identified when presented on its own could not be retained long enough to allow a perceptual analysis of temporal order.

Rate of Auditory Processing Deficit Tallal and Piercy (1973a, 1973b, 1974, 1975, 1978) conducted a series of studies on the processing of temporal order by aphasic children. They found that when the rate of presentation of auditory signals is too great, the child is unable to analyze their order. A deficit that affects the rate of auditory processing may even cause difficulty in discriminating particular speech sounds. Tallal and Piercy (1974) indeed found that aphasic children had difficulty in discriminating between stop consonants that have rapidly changing spectra provided by the 2nd and 3rd formant transitions—in the range of about 50 msec. They had no trouble, however, in discriminating vowels that have steady state frequencies that remain constant over the entire length of the stimulus—approximately 250 msec. In a later experiment, Tallal and Piercy (1975) showed that aphasic children similarly could not discriminate specially synthesized vowel-vowel syllables in which the discriminable information occurred in the first 43 msec, but they could distinguish consonant-vowel syllables in which the transitional period of each stimulus was increased from 43 to 95 msec. In other words, it was not some specific feature of the stimuli (steady state versus transitional features) that caused difficulty for the aphasic children. They had no trouble distinguishing syllables when the discriminable components were of long (95 msec) durations regardless of whether they were transitional in nature, but they could not discriminate syllables of either type when the discriminable components were brief (43 msec). Tallal and Piercy concluded that the language deficit in aphasic children is due to an inability to process rapidly occurring acoustic information.

Sequencing Deficit The idea that some adult aphasics may be suffering from a kind of temporal disorientation or temporal order deficit has been discussed for some time (e.g., Critchley, 1953; Hughlings-Jackson, 1888). Hirsh (1959) emphasized the importance of a central temporal sequencing ability for making sense of auditory input and language. Monsees (1961) speculated that the basic disability in aphasic children was a central disorder involving the perception of temporal sequences. In adult aphasics, Efron (1963) observed that the ability to say which of two sounds came first was seriously impaired unless the sounds were separated by a gap of over 500 msec. Because normal speech sound segments occur at the rate of every 80 msec, such a deficit could prevent the processing of normal speech because the order of phonemes could not be sorted out. That such sequencing may be important at the phoneme level is supported by a study by Sheehan, Aseltine, and Edwards (1973). They found that the comprehension of adult aphasics could be aided by the insertion of silent intervals between phonemes. These same patients were not aided by the insertion of silent intervals between words.

Lowe and Campbell (1965) studied eight children classified as "aphasoid," who were between 7 and 14 years old. They were compared to a matched group of normal speaking children. Two types of tasks were studied. In succession tasks, the time required by the child in order for him or her to hear two auditory signals as separate signals was measured. In temporal ordering tasks, what is measured is the slightly longer time needed for the child to say which of the two signals occurred first. On succession tasks, the two groups did not statistically differ from each other. But on the temporal ordering task, there were large differences. The aphasoid children required an average of 357 msec to separate the two signals. This compared to only 36 msec required by the normal children. Lowe and Campbell concluded that a temporal order deficit may be the major factor causing language difficulties in these children.

Other researchers also observed a sequencing deficit in aphasic children. Some of these have claimed that the deficit is not limited to the auditory modality. Withrow (1964) studied immediate memory for visual stimuli that were presented sequentially to aphasic, deaf, and normally hearing children. The deaf and the aphasic children performed significantly worse than the normal children. Poppen et al. (1969) had six aphasic children (ages 5 ; 8 to 9 ; 3) press three frosted panels in the same order as they saw them lighted. Although they performed better on this visual task than on auditory sequencing tasks, they still performed poorly, achieving only a 75% success rate. These authors also gave the children five different types of sequencing tasks. The Kendall coefficient of concordance for these tasks was 0.71. They concluded that there is a general sequencing ability and that aphasic children are deficient in that ability.

Although there has been much interest in the possibility of a sequencing deficit in aphasic children, there are some problems with such a theory. Efron (1963), whose results on aphasic adults were cited above, found a curious anomaly in his study. The subjects who showed the poorest performance on his temporal ordering task were patients with expressive aphasia, and those patients with receptive difficulties had little trouble with auditory sequencing. This is the opposite of what would be expected. That is, Efron found that the expressive aphasics who needed so large an interval between auditory stimuli in order to sequence them correctly, nevertheless understood normal speech, even though this comes at the rate of one phoneme per 80 msec. Efron later noted (in Millikan and Darley, 1967) that he found no significant correlation between the severity of the aphasia and the degree of difficulty aphasic patients have with sequencing. Some of his patients who were profoundly aphasic scored near normal on sequencing tasks. An even stranger finding is that a number of patients who he described as "hopeless" on auditory sequencing tasks could understand speech reasonably well.

Rosenthal (1972), whose findings implicating an auditory storage deficit were mentioned above, similarly had problems concerning how his results can explain the language behavior of the children. All of the older children who were subjects in his experiments possessed usable language in spite of the fact that most of them evidenced impaired auditory processing abilities.

There are other problems for a sequencing deficit theory of aphasia in children. If the sequencing disability is purely or primarily in the auditory modality—for example, caused by a more basic problem in rate of auditory processing and thus at the level of the phoneme—one would expect aphasic children to exhibit jumbled words, not disordered syntax. Furthermore, if the deficit was specifically auditory, these children would be expected to acquire language easily by lip reading, or to acquire written language through the visual modality. This, however, does not seem to be the case.

Leonard (1979) pointed out that the nature of the speech used by language-impaired children suggests that auditory processing and sequencing deficits are a corollary to and not a cause of the language difficulties. He noted that if such theories were truly causal, the children should evidence some degree of word order reversals in their syntax. But instead, the syntactic problems they have take the same form as those of younger normal children, that is, the deletion of elements that are obligatory in adult syntax. It should also be noted that sequencing difficulties have often been found in deaf children, but no one would claim that such deficits are the "cause" of their deafness. Furthermore, O'Connor and Hermelin (1973a, 1973b) showed that the lack of auditory input does not prevent deaf children from being able to appreciate temporal order, but it makes them unlikely to use that mode of ordering. For tasks in which various strategies can be used, deaf children were found to prefer spatial left-to-right orderings rather than temporal first-to-last ones. But this was shown to be an elective strategy. In experiments in which they were instructed to retain only temporally ordered information they were able to do so. In children with developmental aphasia, a temporal order disability has sometimes been observed, but it remains to be shown whether this is an elective strategy. In any case, the notion that a temporal ordering or sequencing disability causes the language impairment in these children needs to be further scrutinized.

Hierarchical Planning Deficit   In some cases it may be possible to analyze the types of sentence structures being produced by language-disordered children in an attempt to uncover a more basic deficit. Such an approach has been taken with a very special group of aphasic children (Cromer, 1978a, 1978b). There is a rare aphasic syndrome that has been referred to in the literature as "acquired aphasia with convulsive disorder in children" (Landau and Kleffner, 1957; McKinney and McGreal, 1974; Van Harskamp, Van Dongen, and Loonen, 1978; Worster-Drought, 1971). Children who are described by this syndrome, either from birth or from a very early age, have neither comprehended nor produced language. As Landau and Kleffner (1957) described it, "For most of these children the deficit seems to be congenital, since they have failed to acquire the ability to use speech or language normally. Some of them, however, have acquired the ability to use language in an apparently normal fashion and have subsequently lost it" (p. 523). Most of these children have an associated convulsive disorder and EEG abnormalities (McKinney and McGreal, 1974). The etiology of the syndrome is unknown. The special group of ten aphasics with a median age of 13 ; 6 that Cromer studied seem to fit this basic pattern. Deafness, mental deficiency, motor disability, and severe personality disorder could be excluded as the cause of their language difficulty. The nonverbal IQs of the children as assessed by the Collins-Drever Test were in the normal range with a median of 99.5. Most of these children could produce and comprehend single words that seemed to be semantically correct in the sense of being appropriate to the situation. The children were bright and interested and gave the appearance of being frustrated by their lack of communicative ability. Although they had been taught to read and write, they were still handicapped in these abilities.

In order to study the grammatical constructions they used, a standardized situation was devised. The children were presented with a nonverbal story enacted by hand puppets. After viewing the puppet show, they wrote a description of what they saw. The story was designed to elicit a range of grammatical devices. For example, two characters of one of the types of animals were used in order to stimulate the use of plurals in later descriptions (e.g., "two ducks") and to force a differentiation of the characters by the use of adjectives and other descriptive devices (e.g., "the duck with the little eyes"/"the duck with the big eyes") when these characters differed in their motivation in the story. Themes in the story were repeated in order to try to elicit various adverbial expressions such as "at first" and "again." Materials such as low wide containers and tall narrow ones were used in order to encourage the use of more complex descriptions.

Of the ten children, the two youngest merely drew pictures. Two produced written samples that were so severely disordered that a grammatical analysis has not yet been attempted. The remaining six samples were compared with the writings of six deaf children with a median age of about 10;6, who viewed the same show and similarly wrote free descriptions of what they had seen. Both groups of children wrote about the same number of words per sentence. Despite this overall similarity, significant differences were observed when the sentences were broken down into phrase structure categories such as noun phrases, verb phrases, adverbial phrases. The deaf had a significantly greater mean number of categories per sentence (4.51) than the aphasic children (3.73). The number of different verb types used was also significantly greater in the deaf than in the aphasic children's writings. But the two groups were most different when the types of sentences they wrote were examined in a different way. The sentences of the deaf were more complex in that they attempted to combine units using devices such as embedding some constituents within others, and in general using processes that involved the interruption of simple sequences. The aphasics, in contrast, used very few such structures. Of all of the sentences written by deaf children, 35.9% included one or more embedded or conjoined structures. In contrast, only 12% of the sentences of the aphasic children evidenced such embedding and conjoining. When the aphasic children did use what could be classified as embedded structures, the second verb was always omitted. Furthermore, the aphasic writings differed significantly from those of the deaf in that the aphasic children never produced sentences that involved more than one embedding or conjoining. Of the sentences written by the deaf, 10.9% did so.

It should be noted that a child was credited with attempting a structure even if he or she made grammatical errors. The sentences of the deaf were not correct by adult standards. Their grasp of various grammatical devices was inconsistent and limited; they made many errors on all sorts of surface features such as the inflections and suffixes indicating possession, plurality, tense markers and the like. The aphasic children seemed to make fewer errors, but this was because they attempted less. They confined themselves to fairly simple forms. This was not thought to be attributable to differences in educational methods used with the two groups because other groups of aphasic and language-disordered children in the same residential school as the aphasic group in this study, and thus learning by the same instructional methods, did not evidence this lack of embedding and interrupted structures when they undertook the same task.

Whether the structures used by the aphasic children are qualitatively different from the structures used by younger normal children is a difficult question. The two severely disordered samples that were not analyzed are certainly unlike the writings of younger children. But the writings of the six aphasic children that were analyzed could be viewed in such terms. The question that arises, however, is not whether the outputs of two groups look similar but whether anything can be inferred about an underlying deficit from the structures that are lacking. The writings of this particular aphasic group seem to reflect an inability to plan or program sentences that incorporate hierarchical structuring in the sense that the production of some parts is postponed during the performance of other parts. The writing of somewhat younger deaf children did not show such a deficit. The utterances of normal speaking children as young as age 3 contain features that have been described as requiring this type of hierarchical planning ability.

Evidence that these aphasic children may have a hierarchical planning deficit comes from another source. It has often been observed that developmentally aphasic children have an almost uniformly poor sense of rhythm (Griffiths, 1972). They often cannot march in time or clap to the rhythm in music. Kracke (1975) found that aphasic children performed significantly poorer on tasks of identifying rhythmic sequences than did either normal or profoundly deaf children. This was true even when the rhythms were presented to the child in the tactile instead of the auditory modality by applying the rhythms to the child's fingertips with a vibrating disc. It is often assumed that rhythms are merely a sequential concatenation of beats. Martin (1972) challenged this assumption. He claimed that the view of rhythm as consisting merely of periodic, repetitive behavior is misconceived. Such a series of sequential elements would have no structured internal organization. The alternative, for which Martin presented a strong case, sees rhythm as being composed of hierarchically structured units in which the change of any one element alters the interrelationships of all the elements to one another. Altering one rhythmic element does not merely affect its relationship to the immediate preceding and succeeding units; the whole rhythmic structure is affected.

Just as a hierarchical planning or structuring ability is said to underlie the appreciation of rhythm, so such an ability is said to be necessary to describe normal language. Lashley (1951) asserted that associative chain explanations are unable to account for a variety of behaviors including rhythmic activity, motor movements, piano playing, typing, speech, and language. He claimed that theories that attempted to account for grammatical form in terms of the associative linkages of words in a sentence would overlook the essential structure of sentences. Such theories would also be unable to account for the processes by which sentences are produced or understood. Most modern linguistic theories since Chomsky (1965), regardless of their competing claims as to specific details, assign an important place to processes of embedding and interruption that would be difficult to account for in terms of simple temporal sequences. The alternative is that processes that are not themselves sequential underlie the sequential output of surface strings. The suggestion by Cromer (1978a, 1978b) is that the causal or at least associated condition found in the special group of developmentally aphasic children with convulsive disorder is some form of hierarchical planning disability. Such a deficit prevents them from dealing adequately with rhythm and makes the structure of normal language difficult.

In order to test this disability more directly, a task was devised in which a child had to copy a two-dimensional drawing of a "tree structure" and to build a replica with constructional straws of a three-dimensional mobile that was hierarchically ordered (Cromer, 1978c). The task was based on that designed by Greenfield and Schneider (1977) in a developmental study of normal children. (See Figure 1.) The mere inability of a child to succeed on such a task would not be indicative of the child's underlying deficits. If it can be shown, however, that these children can copy the drawing or build the model in one way (requiring only sequential behavior) but not in another (requiring a hierarchical planning ability) then one is on firmer grounds for making claims about the nature of their deficit. The children were allowed to draw their copy or build the model by whatever method they chose. One basic method that can be employed is to start at the bottom of one side of the figure and to place succeeding elements in a sequential or chain-like way up that side of the figure, across the top and down the other side. The other basic method is a hierarchical plan that consists of beginning with the midpoint at the top and adding the symmetrical units alternatively on the left and right sides until the structure was complete. When the child completed the task using the spontaneous method, the experimenter demonstrated the use of the opposite strategy and the child was again asked to do the task using this alternative method. Each of the drawings and the constructions was separately scored in terms of interruptedness in the placing of the elements. Twelve aphasic children, median age 12;6, were compared with eight congenitally profoundly deaf children, median age 10;0. The

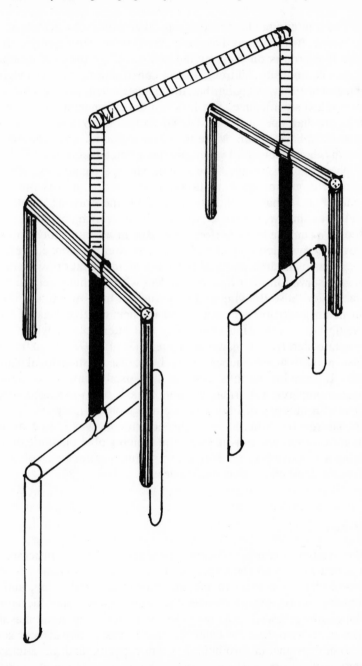

Figure 1.   An illustration of the model children were asked to build. (This is not the drawing the children were asked to copy. In the drawing task, children copied a flat, symmetrical, two-dimensional drawing of this structure.)

child's best interruptedness score was taken from two attempts at each of the tasks. It was found that these scores were significantly different for the two groups on the copying task (7.38 for the deaf group and 4.42 for the aphasic children). In the construction task, although the deaf mean of 10.0 was higher than the aphasic mean, 7.0, this difference did not reach significance. The task is a developmental one, however, and the median age of the deaf children was 2½ years younger than that of the aphasic group. More recently, a group of deaf children was tested in which each child was individually matched to the children in the aphasic group by age. The results show a significant difference between the groups on both tasks. Furthermore, it was noted that several of the aphasic children could copy the drawing or build the model when they were allowed to do so by their own chain-sequencing method. When made to perform the task in an interrupted manner, however, they failed to succeed. There is some evidence, then, that some aphasic children may suffer from a hierarchical ordering deficit. This is observed in their inability to deal with rhythm, their poor performance on these drawing and construction tasks when asked to do them in an interrupted manner, and in their relative lack of use of linguistic structures using embedding and interruption, which would necessitate hierarchical planning. Semenza et al. (1978) found that adult aphasic patients also evidenced what they call a constructional planning defect. In copying various designs they used primarily an analytic strategy compared to normal and non-aphasic brain-damaged subjects who used a mixture of both analytic and global strategies. This lack of global constructions by the aphasic patients was linked by these authors to modern linguistic theory in which global planning of utterances is necessary because language structure cannot be accounted for by a mere chain-like, sequential process.

SUMMARY

In this section, a number of hypotheses about impaired processes are mentioned as well as the experimental procedures designed to study them. Studies of deficits in memory, linguistic processing, auditory processing, phonological processing, sequencing, and hierarchical planning are reviewed. This list of possible deficits is not exhaustive. Others have proposed, for example, that language impairment can be due to limitations of production span capacity and to attentional deficits.

It is noted that the so-called reconceptualization urged in this section is not a reconceptualization at all. Those doing research on language disorders have always been aware of the need to be specific about the kinds of deficits that may exist in one or another group of language-disordered individuals. Some recent work on normal language development, however, has focused exclusively on broad Piagetian stages in an attempt to explicate the relationship between cognitive development and language acquisition. It is argued in this section that such a broad-based approach is not valuable especially for those concerned with language disorders. Furthermore, the grouping of children in a broad category such as developmental aphasia for purposes of intervention programs is equally poor. It has been difficult in the past to tie intervention programs to specific disorders. Although this is still true, some suggestions are offered in the next section to indicate how to begin that difficult task.

Implications for Intervention

Two reconceptualizations are suggested in this chapter. What are the implications for language intervention programs that these reconceptualizations suggest? In a recent review of semantic and syntactic development, Bowerman (1978) suggested the basic necessity of viewing the child as an active participant in the language acquisition process. It is argued in the first part of this chapter that recent research has not always done this. The underlying but not stated assumption that has emerged shows a reversion to studies that are at base extensions of purely empiricist theories, at least where the structure of language is concerned. One way to take account of the linguistic processes that children bring to bear on language acquisition is to see if some of the operating principles suggested by Slobin can be incorporated into the procedures used by intervention programs. A good example of the direct but unconscious exploitation of such procedures by mothers was found in the study by Newport et al. (1977). Although they found that what they described as universal aspects of language structure were not sensitive to individual differences in styles of "motherese," certain specific individual properties of language were indeed responsive to environmental input. The number of auxiliaries that the child used was correlated with the mother's use of expansions and her use of yes/no questions. The latter is especially interesting in that yes/no questions require the auxiliary to be moved to sentence initial position (e.g., "*Can* you do it?", "*Will* it be fun?") This position may be more salient for young children, and easier to process. It may be, then, that aspects of the input play an important part when they fit in with the child's processing strategies. The kinds of operating principles suggested by Slobin, and methods children bring to bear on language acquisition that have been noted by Karmiloff-Smith serve to indicate the kinds of principles that can play a role in specific language development. Newport et al. also noted a number of features of "motherese" that were positively correlated with the child's vocabulary development. These include deixis (using words that point out and identify a referent, as with "this," "that," "here," "there") and exact imitations with expansions. Deixis was also correlated with the child's use of nominal inflections (mainly plurals). Partial imitations with expansions by the mother were positively correlated with every measure of the child's linguistic sophistication. It is also interesting to note that the mother's self-repetition was negatively correlated to many of the measures of the child's sophistication in language. Nelson (1973) similarly found a negative correlation between the rate of language acquisition and the mother's efforts to control and direct the child. These findings should give pause to any language intervention programs that do not take sufficient account of what the child brings to the situation.

Newport et al. concluded that maternal speech does exert an influence on the child's language acquisition, but only on structures specific to the individual language. These are such aspects as surface morphology and the syntactic elements that vary between languages. More importantly, they noted that even these are only influenced through the filter of the child's selective attention to portions of the speech stream. In their study they found these to be basically utterance-initial positions and items whose referents were clear. They concluded, in other words, that learning does respond to narrowly specified features of the environment, but it is still contingent on what children are disposed to notice in that environment, on their strategies of listening, and on the hypotheses they are prepared to entertain. Particular aspects of the mother's style interact with the child's processing biases for language and this can lead to differential rates of acquisition. This matches the epigenetic-interactionist viewpoint presented in this chapter.

The second reconceptualization emphasized the need to examine specific deficits in language-disorderd children. One immediate problem that must be faced in intervention programs is whether to undertake procedures designed to aid in communication or whether to concentrate on language. It was pointed out above that the two are not identical. It may be that if irreversible deficits of a kind crucial for language are discovered, intervention procedures may be better directed to the establishment of more broadly based communication systems. The importance of language, however, both for communication with the majority of the people in the community and for internal processes of thought and development suggests that such a step should be taken only with some reluctance and after careful consideration of all the issues involved. In any case, language intervention programs are the concern of this chapter, not communication programs. In this regard, the discovery of the existence of specific impairments requires that attempts be made to structure the input material or instructional methods to make use of unimpaired processes. An example of the discovery of specific impairments and their implication for remedial programs comes from work on dyslexia.

Studies of adult aphasic patients with acquired reading difficulties have given a good deal of insight into the various processes that can be used in that skill. Marshall and Newcombe (1973, 1977) classified patients according to the method they used for reading on the basis of the errors they made in a task requiring them to read single words without context. Two basic methods were described. One was the use of a phonemic route in which the word is converted into a sound before it is interpreted. The other is a direct semantic route in which the meaning of a word is recovered directly from its visual appearance. Shallice and Warrington (1975) reported in detail a patient who showed impairment of the phonemic route and whose grapheme-semantic route (i.e., visual route) was relatively unimpaired. Patterson and Marcel (1977) tested this notion with two patients exhibiting a similar impairment. They found that although the patients could *repeat* non-words, they could not *read* them. Furthermore, they gave these patients a lexical decision task in which the requirement was to make a judgment as to whether the presented stimulus was a real word. Normal subjects are usually slower in making such judgments when the presented stimuli are nonwords that sound like real words when pronounced (e.g., "caik"). Their two patients, in contrast, did not show such an effect. It seems that they too suffer from a grapheme-phoneme impairment.

Snowling (1980) studied a group of dyslexic children who were substantially behind their peers in reading ability but whose low reading scores could not be attributed to low intelligence. Eighteen such children with a mean chronological age of 12 ; 1 and mean IQ of 106 were matched for reading age with 36 normal readers, whose mean age was 9 ; 5 and whose mean IQ was 105. The task was to make a same/different judgment for pronounceable nonsense words presented either auditorially or visually. The four conditions consisted of auditory or visual presentation of the first word coupled with either auditory or visual presentation of the word to be judged as the same or different from the first. The results showed that both groups did well on the auditory-auditory task, thus showing that the dyslexic children had no problems with auditory discrimination. There was a significant difference in performance, however, on the visual-auditory task (the condition most like real reading), with the dyslexic group scoring poorly. Snowling concluded that dyslexic readers perform in a qualitatively different manner from other readers, for it should be recalled that they were matched to the normals in terms of reading age. As Snowling put it, they are not just the low end of a normal distribution of readers; they have difficulties in visual-sound decoding. These children develop strategies to read whole words and this leads to a considerable sight vocabulary. But they have difficulty in decoding unfamiliar words. The dyslexic children in her sample, then, evidence a specific impairment in grapheme-phoneme translation.

Jorm (1979) reviewed evidence also leading to the conclusion that developmental dyslexics have difficulty with a phonological route to meaning, although he attempts to explain this in terms of a short-term memory deficit. Whatever the true reason for their grapheme-phoneme impairment, Jorm offered some suggestions for remediation programs. He argued that because dyslexics can access words visually but have difficulties in using the phonological route, methods of instruction should capitalize on their intact system. He suggested that the look-say method may be more effective for this group of children than phonic methods that try to teach grapheme-phoneme correspondences. The value of a phonic method is that it allows one to access the meaning of unfamiliar and novel words. But the designers of remediation programs are left with a dilemma. Does one teach to the strength, as Jorm seems to suggest, or does one teach to the weakness in the hopes of improving a poorly functioning system but one which has advantages for the individual?

Other issues arise as well. Teaching to the weakness results in the experience of failure. There may be important motivational reasons for avoiding such failure. Cooper and Griffiths (1978) made a similar point in regard to educational programs for aphasic children. They noted that the language failure of such children is not due to a linguistically deprived environment. Therefore, language enrichment and stimulation should not be the sole means of treatment. They point out that children who are subjected to stimulation and demands beyond their abilities may react with disorganized, disturbed or withdrawn behavior.

Cooper and Griffiths (1978) suggested that, from an educational point of view, children should be identified in terms of their disabilities and impairments. Once these have been ascertained, children whose handicaps are amenable to the same teaching approach should be grouped together. They gave an example of five types of groups of aphasic children that they found valuable to differentiate in terms of educational considerations.

It is clear that a child is not a passive entity to be subjected to one intervention program or another based on broad learning principles and the assumption that all children, and even all animals, learn in one and the same way. For language intervention programs, the general features, predispositions, procedures, and operating principles that human beings bring to bear on the language acquisition process need to be considered. Some of these procedures may be specifically linguistic. The individual child must also be examined for specific disabilities and impairments affecting language acquisition. The conjunction of the two reconceptualizations outlined in this chapter may help to encourage a reconceptualization of intervention.

REFERENCES

Ammon, M. S. and Slobin, D. I. 1979. A cross-linguistic study of the processing of causative sentences. Cognition. 7:3–17.

Aurnhammer-Frith, U. 1969. Emphasis and meaning in recall in normal and autistic children. Lang. Speech. 12:29–38.

Bartak, L., and Rutter, M. 1975. Language and cognition in autistic and 'dysphasic' children. *In* N. O'Connor (ed.), Language, Cognitive Deficits, and Retardation, pp. 193–202. Butterworths, London.

Bartak, L., Rutter, M., and Cox, A. 1975. A comparative study of infantile autism and specific developmental receptive language disorder. I: The children. Br. J. Psychiatry. 126:127–145.

Bartlett, E. J. The acquisition of the meaning of colour terms: A study of lexical development. *In* R. N. Campbell and P. T. Smith (eds.), Recent Advances in the Psychology of Language: Language Development and Mother-Child Interaction. pp. 89–108. Plenum Press, New York.

Bates, E. 1976. Language and Context: The Acquisition of Pragmatics. Academic Press, New York.

Beilin, H. 1975. Studies in the Cognitive Basis of Language Development. Academic Press, New York.

Bellugi, U. 1967. The acquisition of the system of negation in children's speech. Unpublished doctoral dissertation. Harvard University.

Bellugi, U. 1971. Simplification in children's language. *In* R. Huxley and E. Ingram (eds.), Language Acquisition: Models and Methods, pp. 95–119. Academic Press, New York.

Bellugi-Klima, U. 1969. Language acquisition. Paper presented at the Wenner-Gren Foundation for Anthropological Research in the Symposium on Cognitive Studies and Artificial Intelligence Research, Chicago.

Benton, A. 1978. The cognitive functioning of children with developmental dysphasia. *In* M. A. Wyke (ed.), Developmental Dysphasia, pp. 43–62. Academic Press, Inc. London and New York.

Bever, T. G. 1970. The cognitive basis for linguistic structures. *In* J. R. Hayes (ed.), Cognition and the Development of Language, pp. 279–362. John Wiley & Sons, Inc., New York.

Bever, T. G., Fodor, J. A., and Weksel, W. 1965a. Is linguistics empirical? Psychological Review, 72:493–500.

Bever, T. G., Fodor, J. A., and Weksel, W. 1965b. Theoretical notes on the acquisition of syntax: A critique of "context generalization." Psychol. Rev. 72:467–482.

Bever, T. G., Mehler, J. E., and Valian, V. V. 1968. Linguistic capacity of very young children. Mimeographed paper.

Blakemore, C. 1974. Developmental factors in the formation of feature extracting neurons. In F. O. Schmitt and F. G. Worden (eds.), The Neurosciences: Third Study Program, pp. 105–113. MIT Press, Cambridge. Mass.

Blakemore, C., and Cooper, G. F. 1970. Development of the brain depends on the visual environment. Nature. 228:477–478.

Blank, M., and Allen, D. A. 1976. Understanding "why": Its significance in early intelligence. In Michael Lewis (ed.), Origins of Intelligence: Infancy and Early Childhood, pp. 259–278. John Wiley & Sons, Inc., New York.

Bloom, L. 1967. A comment on Lee's "Developmental sentence scoring: A method for comparing normal and deviant syntactic development." J. Speech Hear. Disord. 32:294–296.

Bloom, L. 1970. Language Development: Form and Function in Emerging Grammars. MIT Press, Cambridge, Mass.

Bloom, L. 1973. One Word at a Time. Mouton, The Hague.

Bower, T. G. R. 1966. Slant perception and shape constancy in infants. Science. 151:832–834.

Bowerman, M. 1973. Early Syntactic Development. Cambridge University Press, Cambridge.

Bowerman, M. 1976. Semantic factors in the acquisition of rules for word use and sentence construction. In D. M. Morehead, and A. E. Morehead (eds.), Normal and Deficient Child Language, pp. 99–179. University Park Press, Baltimore.

Bowerman, M. 1977. The acquisition of word meaning: An investigation of some current concepts. In P. N. Johnson-Laird and P. C. Wason (eds.), Thinking: Readings in Cognitive Science, pp. 239–253. Cambridge University Press, Cambridge.

Bowerman, M. 1978. Semantic and syntactic development: A review of what, when, and how in language acquisition. In R. L. Schiefelbusch (ed.), Bases of Language Intervention, pp. 98–189. University Park Press, Baltimore.

Brown, R. 1973. A First Language. Harvard University Press, Cambridge, Mass.

Brown, R. 1977. Introduction. In C. E. Snow and C. A. Ferguson (eds.), Talking to Children: Language Input and Acquisition, pp. 1–27. Cambridge University Press, Cambridge.

Brown, R., and Bellugi, U. 1964. Three processes in the child's acquisition of syntax. Harvard Education. Rev. 34:133–151.

Brown, R., Cazden, C., and Bellugi-Klima, U. 1969. The child's grammar from I to III. In J. P. Hill (ed.), Minnesota Symposia on Child Psychology, pp. 28–73. Vol. 2. The University of Minnesota Press, Minneapolis.

Bruner, J. S. 1974/5. From communication to language—A psychological perspective. Cognition. 3:225–287.

Bruner, J. S. 1975. The ontogenesis of speech acts. J. Child Lang. 2:1–19.

Bruner, J. S., Goodnow, J. J., and Austin, G. A. 1956. A Study of Thinking. John Wiley & Sons, Inc., N.Y.

Bryant, P. E., and Trabasso, T. 1971. Transitive inferences and memory in young children. Nature. 232:456–458.

Carey, S. 1978. The child as word learner. In M. Halle, J. Bresnan, and G. A. Miller (eds.), Linguistic Theory and Psychological Reality, pp. 264–293. MIT Press, Cambridge, Mass.

Catlin, J. 1978. Discussion of the chapters by Stolzenberg and Chomsky. In G. A. Miller and E. Lenneberg (eds.), Psychology and Biology of Language and Thought, pp. 271–280. Academic Press, Inc. New York.

Chomsky, N. 1959. A review of B. F. Skinner's Verbal Behaviour. Language, 35:26–58.

Chomsky, N. 1965. Aspects of the Theory of Syntax. MIT Press, Cambridge, Mass.

Chomsky, N. 1967. The formal nature of language. In E. H. Lenneberg, Biological Foundations of Language, pp. 397–442. John Wiley & Sons, Inc., New York.

Chomsky, N. 1968. Language and Mind. Harcourt Brace Jovanovich, Inc. New York.

Chomsky, N. 1972. Studies on Semantics in Generative Grammar. Mouton, The Hague.

Chomsky, N. 1975. Reflections on Language. Pantheon Books, New York.

Clark, Eve V. 1973a. Non-linguistic strategies and the acquisition of word meanings. Cognition. 2:161–182.

Clark, E. V. 1973b. What's in a word? On the child's acquisition of semantics in his first language. In T. E. Moore (ed.), Cognitive Development and the Acquisition of Language, pp. 65–110. Academic Press, Inc., New York.

Conrad, R. 1972. The developmental role of vocalizing in short-term memory. J. Verbal Learn. Verbal Behav. 11:521–533.

Cooper, J. M., and Griffiths, P. 1978. Treatment and prognosis. In M. A. Wyke (ed.), Developmental Dysphasia, pp. 159–176. Academic Press, Inc., London & New York.

Critchley, M. 1953. The Parietal Lobes. Edward Arnold & Co., London.

Cromer, R. F. 1968. The development of temporal reference during the acquisition of language. Unpublished doctoral dissertation, Harvard University, Cambridge, Mass.

Cromer, R. F. 1970. In defense of the empirical method: A reply to Broadbent concerning psycholinguistics. Bull. Br. Psychol. Soc. 23:271–279.

Cromer, R. F. 1974. The development of language and cognition: The cognition hypothesis. In B. Foss (ed.), New Perspectives in Child Development, pp. 184–252. Penguin Books, Ltd. Harmondsworth, Middlesex.

Cromer, R. F. 1975. An experimental investigation of a putative linguistic universal: Marking and the indirect object. J. Exp. Child Psychol. 20:73–80.

Cromer R. F. 1976a. The cognitive hypothesis of language acquisition and its implications for child language deficiency. In D. M. Morehead, and A. E. Morehead (eds.), Normal and Deficient Child Language, pp. 283–333. University Park Press, Baltimore.

Cromer, R. F. 1976b. Developmental strategies for language. In V. Hamilton, and M. D. Vernon (eds.), The Development of Cognitive Processes, pp. 305–358. Academic Press, London and New York.

Cromer, R. F. 1978a. The basis of childhood dysphasia: A linguistic approach. In M. A. Wyke (ed.), Developmental Dysphasia, pp. 85–134. Academic Press, Inc., New York.

Cromer, R. F. 1978b. Hierarchical disability in the syntax of aphasic children. Int. J. Behav. Dev. 1:391–402.

Cromer, R. F. 1978c. Hierarchical ordering disability and aphasic children. Paper presented at the First International Congress for the Study of Child Language, August 7–12, Tokyo.

Cromer, R. F. 1979. The strengths of the weak form of the cognition hypothesis for language acquisition. In V. Lee (ed.), Language Development, pp. 102–130. Croom Helm, London.

Cromer, R. F. 1980. Normal language development: Recent progress. In L.

A. Hersov, M. Berger, and A. R. Nicol (eds.), Language and Language Disorders in Childhood, pp. 1–21. Pergamon Press Oxford.

Cross, T. G. 1975. Some relationships between motherese and linguistic level in accelerated children, Papers and Reports on Child Language Development, pp. 117–135, No. 10. Stanford University,

Cross, T. G. 1977. Mothers' speech adjustments. The contributions of selected child listener variables. In C. E. Snow and C. A. Ferguson (eds.), Talking to Children: Language Input and Acquisition, pp. 151–188. Cambridge University Press, Cambridge.

Curtiss, S., Fromkin, V., and Yamada, J. E. 1978. The independence of language as a cognitive system. Paper presented at the First International Congress for the Study of Child Language, August 7–12 Tokyo.

deVilliers, J. G., Tager Flusberg, H. B., Hakuta, K., and Cohen, M. 1979. Children's comprehensions of relative clauses. J. Psycholinguist. Res. 8;499–518.

Dewart, M. H. 1975. A psychological investigation of sentence comprehension by children. Unpublished doctoral dissertation, University College, London.

Dewart, M. H. 1979. Language comprehension processes of mentally retarded children. Am. J. Ment. Defic. 84:177–183.

Donaldson, M., and Balfour, G. 1968. Less is more: A study of language comprehension in children. Br. J. Psychol. 59:461–472.

Edwards, D. 1973. Sensory-motor intelligence and semantic relations in early childhood grammar. Cognition. 2:395–434.

Efron, R. 1963. Temporal perception, aphasia, and déjà vu. Brain. 86:403–424.

Eibl-Eibesfeldt, I. 1970. Ethology: The Biology of Behaviour. Holt, Rinehart, & Winston, Inc., New York.

Eisenson, J. 1968. Developmental aphasia: A speculative view with therapeutic implications. J. Speech Hear. Disord. 33:3–13.

Ervin-Tripp, S. 1966. Language development. In M. Hoffman and L. Hoffman (eds.), Review of Child Development Research, pp. 55–105, Vol. 2. University of Michigan Press, Ann Arbor, Mi.

Ferguson, C. A. 1977. Baby talk as a simplified register. In C. E. Snow, and C. A. Ferguson (eds.), Talking to children: Language Input and Acquisition, pp. 206–235. Cambridge University Press, Cambridge.

Fillmore, C. J. 1968. The case for case. In E. Bach, and R. T. Harms (eds.), Universals in Linguistic Theory, pp. 1–88. Holt, Rinehart & Winston, Inc., New York.

Fyffe, C. and Prior, M. 1978. Evidence for language recoding in autistic, retarded and normal children: A re-examination. Br. J. Psychol. 69:393–402.

Gardner, B. T., and Gardner, R. A. 1975. Evidence for sentence constituents in the early utterances of child and chimpanzee. J. Exp. Psychol. [Gen] 104:244–267.

Gardner, R. A., and Gardner, B. T. 1969. Teaching sign language to a chimpanzee. Science. 165:664–672.

Garnica, O. K. 1977. Some prosodic and paralinguistic features of speech to young children. In C. E. Snow, and C. A. Ferguson (eds.), Talking to Children: Language Input and Acquisition, pp. 63–88. Cambridge University Press, Cambridge.

Geschwind, N. 1967. The varieties of naming errors. Cortex. 3:97–112.

Gibson, E. J., and Walk, R. D. 1960. The "visual cliff". Sci. Am. Vol. 202, no. 4, 64–71.

Glass, A. V., Gazzaniga, M. S., and Premack, D. 1973. Artificial language training in global aphasics. Neuropsychologia. 11:95–103.

Gleason, J. B. 1977. Talking to children: Some notes on feedback. *In* C. E. Snow, and C. A. Ferguson (eds.), Talking to Children: Language Input and Acquisition, pp. 199–205. Cambridge University Press, Cambridge.

Goodson, B. D., and Greenfield, P. M. 1975. The search for structural principles in children's manipulative play: A parallel with linguistic development. Child Dev. 46:734–746.

Graham, N. C. 1968. Short term memory and syntactic structure in educationally subnormal children. Lang. Speech. 11:209–219.

Graham, N. C. 1974. Response strategies in the partial comprehension of sentences. Lang. Speech. 17:205–221.

Graham, N. C., and Gulliford, R. A. 1968. A psychological approach to the language deficiencies of educationally subnormal children. Educ. Rev. 20:136–145.

Greenberg, J. H. 1966. Language universals. *In* T. A. Sebeok (ed.), Current Trends in Linguistics, pp. 61–112, Vol. III. Mouton, The Hague.

Greenfield, P. M. 1978. Structural parallels between language and action in development. *In* A. Lock (ed.), Action, Gesture, and Symbol: The Emergence of Language, pp. 415–445. Academic Press, London and New York.

Greenfield, P. M., Nelson, K. and Saltzman, E. 1972. The development of rulebound strategies for manipulating seriated cups: A parallel between action and grammar. Cognitive Psychol. 3:291–310.

Greenfield, P. M., and Schneider, L. 1977. Building a tree structure: The development of hierarchical complexity and interrupted strategies in children's construction activity. Dev. Psychol. 13:299–313.

Griffiths, P. 1972. Developmental Aphasia: An Introduction. Invalid Children's Aid Association, London.

Halford, G. and Galloway, W. 1977. Children who fail to make transitive inferences can remember comparisons. Aust. J. Psychol. 29:1–5.

Hermelin, B., and O'Connor, N. 1967. Remembering of words by psychotic and subnormal children. Br. J. Psychol. 58:213–218.

Hirsch, H. V. B., and Spinelli, D. N. 1971. Modification of the distribution of receptive field orientation in cats by selective visual exposure during development. Exp. Brain Res. 12:509–527.

Hirsh, I. J. 1959. Auditory perception of temporal order. J. Acoust. Soc. Am. 31:759–767.

Hubel, D. H., and Wiesel, T. N. 1959. Receptive fields of single neurones in the cat's striate cortex. J. Physiol. 148:574–591.

Hughes, J. 1972. Language and communication: Acquisition of a non-vocal "language" by previously languageless children. Unpublished Bachelor of Technology thesis, Brunel University, London.

Hughes, J. 1974/5. Acquisition of a non-vocal "language" by aphasic children. Cognition. 3:41–55.

Hughlings-Jackson, J. 1888. On a particular variety of epilepsy ("intellectual aura"), one case with symptoms of organic brain disease. Brain, 11:179–207.

Huttenlocker, J., Eisenberg, K., and Strauss, S. 1968. Comprehension: Relation between perceived actor and logical subject. J. Verbal Learn. Verbal Behav. 7:527–530.

Huttenlocher, J., and Strauss, S. 1968. Comprehension and a statement's relation to the situation it describes. J. Verbal Learn. Verbal Behav. 7:300–304.

Jackendoff, R. S. 1972. Semantic Interpretation in Generative Grammar. MIT Press, Cambridge, Mass.

Jorm, A. F. 1979. The cognitive and neurological basis of developmental dyslexia: A theoretical framework and review. Cognition. 7:19–33.

Jung, C. G. 1959. The Archetypes and the Collective Unconscious. Bollingen Series XX: The collected works of C. G. Jung, Vol. 9, Part I. Pantheon Books, New York.

Karmiloff-Smith, A. 1977a. The child's construction of a system of plurifunctional markers. In M. Bullowa (chair), Language Development. Symposium presented at the biennial conference of the International Society for the Study of Behavioural Development, September, Pavia, Italy.

Karmiloff-Smith, A. 1977b. More about the same: Children's understanding of post-particles. J. Child Lang. 4:377–394.

Karmiloff-Smith, A. 1978. The interplay between syntax, semantics, and phonology in language acquisition processes. In R. N. Campbell, and P. T. Smith (eds.), Recent Advances in the Psychology of Language: Language Development and Mother-Child Interaction, pp. 1–23. Plenum Publishing Corp., New York.

Karmiloff-Smith, A. 1979a. A Functional Approach to Child Language: A Study of Determiners and Reference. Cambridge University Press, Cambridge.

Karmiloff-Smith, A. 1979b. Paper presented at the Child Language Seminar, April 2, Reading, England.

Keenan, E. L., and Comrie, B. 1977. Noun phrase accessibility and universal grammar. Linguistic Inquiry. 8:63–99.

Klatzky, R. L., Clark, E. V., and Macken, M. 1973. Asymmetries in the acquisition of polar adjectives: Linguistic or conceptual? J. Exp. Child Psychol. 16:32–46.

Kracke, I. 1975. Perception of rhythmic sequences by receptive aphasic and deaf children. Br. J. Disord. Commun. 10:43–51.

Lack, D. 1943. The Life of the Robin. Cambridge University Press, London.

Lakoff, G. 1971. Presupposition and relative well-formedness, pp. 329–340. In D. D. Steinberg, and L. A. Jakobovits (eds.), Semantics. Cambridge University Press, Cambridge.

Landau, W. M., and Kleffner, F. R. 1957. Syndrome of acquired aphasia with convulsive disorder in children. Neurology. 7:523–530.

Lashley, K. S. 1951. The problem of serial order in behaviour. In L. A. Jeffress (ed.), Cerebral Mechanisms in Behaviour, pp. 112–136. John Wiley & Sons, Inc., New York.

Lee, L. L. 1966. Developmental sentence types: A method for comparing normal and deviant syntactic development. J. Speech Hear. Disord. 31:311–330.

Lenneberg, E. 1967. Biological Foundations of Language. John Wiley & Sons, Inc., New York.

Lenneberg, E. H., Nichols, I. A., and Rosenberger, E. F. 1964. Primitive stages of language development in mongolism, In. D. McK. Rioch and E. A. Weinstein (eds.), Disorders of Communication, pp. 119–137. (Research publications of the Association for Research in Nervous and Mental Disease, Vol. XLII). Williams & Wilkins, Co., Baltimore.

Leonard, L. B. 1972. What is deviant language? J. Speech Hear. Disord. 37:427–446.

Leonard, L. B. 1979. Language impairment in children. Merrill-Palmer Q. 25:205–232.

Limber, J. 1977. Language in child and chimp? Am. Psychol. 32:280–295.

Linden, E. 1975. Apes, Men, and Language. Dutton, New York.

Lowe, A. D., and Campbell, R. A. 1965. Temporal discrimination in aphasoid and normal children. J. Speech Hear. Res. 8:313–314.

Lyons, J. 1968. Introduction to Theoretical Linguistics. Cambridge University Press, Cambridge.

Macnamara, J. 1972. Cognitive basis of language learning in infants. Psychol. Rev. 79:1–13.

Maratsos, M. P. 1973a. Decrease in the understanding of the word "Big" in preschool children. Child Dev. 44:747–752.

Maratsos, M. P. 1973b. The effects of stress on the understanding of pronominal co-reference in children. J. Psycholinguist. Res. 2:1–8.

Marshall, J. C., and Newcombe, F. 1973. Patterns of paralexia: A psycholinguistic approach. J. Psycholinguist. Res. 2:175–199.

Marshall, J. C., and Newcombe, F. 1977. Variability and constraint in acquired dyslexia. In H. Whitaker, and H. A. Whitaker (eds.), Studies in Neurolinguistics, pp. 257–286, Vol. 3. Academic Press, Inc. New York.

Martin, J. G. 1972. Rhythmic (hierarchical) versus serial structure in speech and other behaviour. Psychol. Rev. 79:487–509.

McCawley, J. D. 1971a. Meaning and the description of languages. In J. F. Rosenberg, and C. Travis (eds.), Readings in the Philosophy of Language, pp. 533–548. Prentice-Hall, Englewood Cliffs, N.J.

McCawley, J. D. 1971b. Where do noun phrases come from? In D. D. Steinberg and L. A. Jakobovitz (eds.), Semantics, pp. 217–231. Cambridge University Press, London.

McCawley, J. D. 1973. A review of Noam A. Chomsky, Studies on semantics in generative grammar. Paper reproduced by the Indiana University Linguistics Club, Bloomington, Ind.

McKinney, W., and McGreal, D. A. 1974. An aphasic syndrome in children. Can. Med. Assoc. J. 110:637–639.

McNeill, D. 1966. Developmental psycholinguistics. In F. Smith, and G. A. Miller (eds.), The Genesis of Language, pp. 15–84. MIT Press, Cambridge, Mass.

McNeill, D. 1970a. The Acquisition of Language. Harper & Row, New York.

McNeill, D. 1970b. The development of language. In P. H. Mussen (ed.), Carmichael's Manual of Child Psychology, pp. 1061–1161, Vol. I. John Wiley & Sons, Inc. New York.

McNeill, D., Yukawa, R., and McNeill, N. B. 1971. The acquisition of direct and indirect objects in Japanese. Child Dev. 42:237–249.

Menyuk, P. 1964. Comparison of grammar of children with functionally deviant and normal speech. J. Speech Hear. Res. 7:109–121.

Menyuk, P. 1969. Sentences Children Use. MIT Press, Cambridge, Mass.

Menyuk, P. 1978. Linguistic problems in children with developmental dysphasia. In M. A. Wyke (ed.), Developmental Dysphasia, pp. 135–158. Academic Press, Inc. London & New York.

Miller, G. A. 1962. Some psychological studies of grammar. Am Psychol. 17:748–762.

Miller, G. A., and Chomsky, N. 1963. Finitary models of language users. In R. D. Luce, R. R. Bush, and E. Galanter (eds.), Handbook of Mathematical Psychology pp. 419–491, Vol. II. John Wiley & Sons, Inc., New York.

Miller, G. A., and McNeill, D. 1969. Psycholinguistics. *In* G. Lindzey and E. Aronson (eds.), The Handbook of Social Psychology, 2nd Ed. pp. 666–794. Vol. 3. Addison-Wesley Publishing Company Reading, Mass.

Millikan, C. H., and Darley, F. L. (eds.), 1967. Brain Mechanisms Underlying Speech and Language. Grune & Stratton, New York and London.

Monsees, E. K. 1961. Aphasia in children. J. Speech Hear. Disord. 26:83–86.

Moore, T. E. (ed.) 1973. Cognitive Development and the Acquisition of Language. Academic Press, New York.

Morehead, D. M., and Morehead, A. 1974. From signal to sign: A Piagetian view of thought and language during the first two years. *In* R. L. Schiefelbusch, and L. L. Lloyd (eds.), Language Perspectives—Acquisition, Retardation, and Intervention, pp. 153–190. University Park Press, Baltimore.

Neisser, U. 1967. Cognitive Psychol. Appleton-Century-Crofts, New York.

Nelson, K. 1973. Structure and strategy in learning to talk. Monographs of the Society for Research in Child Development, 38 (Nos. 1–2, Serial No. 149).

Nelson, K., and Bonvillian, J. 1973. Concepts and words in the 18-month-old: Acquiring concept names under controlled conditions. Cognition. 2:435–450.

Newmeyer, F. 1980. Linguistic Theory in America. Academic Press, New York.

Newport, E. L., Gleitman, H., and Gleitman, L. R. 1977. Mother, I'd rather do it myself: Some effects and non-effects of maternal speech style. *In* C. E. Snow, and C. A. Ferguson (eds.), Talking to Children: Language Input and Acquisition, pp. 109–149. Cambridge University Press, Cambridge.

O'Connor N., and Frith, U. 1973. Cognitive development and the concept of set. *In* A. Prangishvili (ed.), Psychological Investigations: A Commemorative Volume Dedicated to the 85th Anniversary of the Birth of D. Uznadze, pp. 296–300. Metsniereba, Tbilisi, U.S.S.R.

O'Connor, N., and Hermelin, B. 1973a. Short-term memory for the order of pictures and syllables by deaf and hearing children. Neuropsychologia. 11:437–442.

O'Connor, N., and Hermelin, B. M. 1973b. The spatial or temporal organization of short-term memory. Q. J. Exp. Psychol. 25:335–343.

Patterson, K. E., and Marcel, A. J. 1977. Aphasia, dyslexia and the phonological coding of written words. Q. J. Exp. Psychol. 29:307–318.

Piaget, J., and Inhelder, B. 1956. The Child's Conception of Space. Routledge & Kegan Paul Ltd., London. (Originally published in 1948).

Piaget, J., Inhelder, B., and Szeminska, A. 1960. The Child's Conception of Geometry, Basic Books, Inc., New York.

Piaget, J., and Inhelder, B. 1969a. The gaps in empiricism. *In* Arthur Koestler, and J. R. Smythies (eds.), Beyond Reductionism, pp. 118–160. Hutchinson, & Co. London.

Piaget, J., and Inhelder, B. 1969b. The Psychology of the Child. Routledge & Kegan Paul Ltd., London. (Originally published in 1966).

Poppen, R., Stark, J., Eisenson, J., Forrest, T., and Wertheim, G. 1969. Visual sequencing performance of aphasic children. J. Speech Hear. Res. 12:288–300.

Premack, D. 1969. A functional analysis of language. Invited address before the American Psychological Association, Washington, D.C.

Premack, A. J., and Premack, D. 1972. Teaching language to an ape. Sci. Am. 227 (4):92–99.

Rapin, I., and Wilson, B. C. 1978. Children with developmental language disability: Neurological aspects and assessment. *In* M. A. Wyke (ed.), Developmental Dysphasia, pp. 13–41. Academic Press, Inc., London and New York.

Reynolds, A. G., and Flagg, P. W. 1977. Cognitive Psychology. Winthrop Publishers, Cambridge, Mass.

Ricks, D. M. 1972. The beginnings of vocal communication in infants and autistic children. Unpublished doctorate of medicine thesis, University of London.

Ricks, D. M. 1975. Vocal communication in pre-verbal normal and autistic children. *In* N. O'Connor (ed.), Language, Cognitive Deficits, and Retardation, pp. 75–80. Butterworths, London.

Riley, C. A., and Trabasso, T. 1974. Comparatives, logical structures, and encoding in a transitive inference task. J. Exp. Child Psychol. 17:187–203.

Rosch, E. 1977. Linguistic realitivity. *In* P. N. Johnson-Laird, and P. C. Wason (eds.) Thinking: Readings in Cognitive Science, pp. 501–519. Cambridge University Press, Cambridge.

Rosenthal, W. S. 1972. Auditory and linguistic interaction in developmental aphasia: Evidence from two studies of auditory processing. *In* Papers and Reports on Child Language Development. Special issue: Language disorders in children (D. Ingram, Ed.), No. 4, 19–34.

Rosenthal, W. S., and Eisenson, J. 1970. Auditory temporal order in aphasic children as a function of selected stimulus features. Paper delivered at the 46th annual convention of the American Speech and Hearing Association, November, New York.

Rumbaugh, D. M. (ed.), 1977. Language Learning by a Chimpanzee: The LANA Project. Academic Press, Inc., New York.

Rumbaugh, D. M., and Gill, T. V. 1976. The mastery of language-type skills by the chimpanzee (Pan). *In* S. R. Harnad, H. D. Steklis, and J. Lancaster (eds.), Origins and Evolution of Language and Speech. Annals of the New York Academy of Sciences. 280:562–578.

Sachs, J. 1971. The status of developmental studies of language. *In* J. Eliot (ed.), Human Development and Cognitive Processes, pp. 381–394. Holt, Rinehart, & Winston, New York.

Sachs, J. 1977. The adaptive significance of linguistic input to prelinguistic infants. In C. E. Snow and C. A. Ferguson (eds.), Talking to Children: Language Input and Acquisition, pp. 51–61. Cambridge University Press, Cambridge.

Schlesinger, I. M. 1977. Production and Comprehension of Utterances. Lawrence Erlbaum, Hillsdale, N.J.

Sebeok, T. A., and Umiker-Sebeok, D. J. (eds.), 1980. Speaking of Apes: A Critical Anthology of Two-Way Communication with Man. Plenum, New York.

Seidenberg, M. S., and Petitto, L. A. 1979. Signing behavior in apes: a critical review. Cognition. 7:177–215.

Seiler, T. B. 1979. Cognitive differentiation as a model of development and its application to a theory of personality. Arch. Psychol. 47:151–164.

Seitz, S., and Stewart, C. 1975. Imitations and expansions: Some developmental aspects of mother-child communications. Dev. Psychol. 11:763–768.

Semenza, C., Denes, G., D'Urso, V., Romano, O., and Montorsi, T. 1978. Analytic and global strategies in copying designs by unilaterally brain-damaged patients. Cortex. 14:404–410.

Seuren, P. A. M. (ed.). 1974. Semantic Syntax. Oxford University Press, London.

Shallice, T., and Warrington, E. K. 1975. Word recognition in a phonemic dyslexic patient. Q. J. Exp. Psychol. 27:187–199.

Sheehan, J. G., Aseltine, S., and Edwards, A. E. 1973. Aphasic comprehension of time spacing. J. Speech Hear. Res. 16:650–657.

Sheldon, A. 1974. The role of parallel function in the acquisition of relative clauses in English. J. Verbal Learn. Verbal Behav. 13:272–281.

Siegel, G. M., and Spradlin, J. E. 1978. Programming for language and communication therapy. In R. L. Schiefelbusch (ed.), Language Intervention Strategies, pp. 357–398. University Park Press, Baltimore.

Siegel, I. E., and Hooper, F. H. 1968. Logical thinking in children. Holt, Rinehart & Winston, New York.

Sinclair, H. 1970. The transition from sensory-motor behaviour to symbolic activity. Interchange. 1:119–126.

Sinclair, H. 1971. Sensorimotor action patterns as a condition for the acquisition of syntax. In R. Huxley and E. Ingram (eds.), Language Acquisition: Models and Methods, pp. 121–130. Academic Press, London and New York.

Sinclair-de-Zwart, H. 1969. Developmental psycholinguistics. In D. Elkind and J. H. Flavell (eds.), Studies in Cognitive Development, pp. 315–336. Oxford University Press, New York.

Sinclair-de-Zwart, H. 1973. Language acquisition and cognitive development. In T. E. Moore (ed.), Cognitive Development and the Acquisition of Language, pp. 9–25. Academic Press, Inc. New York.

Slobin, D. I. 1966. The acquisition of Russian as a native language. In F. Smith, and G. A. Miller (eds.), The Genesis of Language, pp. 129–148. MIT Press, Cambridge, Mass.

Slobin, D. I. (ed.), 1971a. The Ontogenesis of Grammar: A Theoretical Symposium. Academic Press, New York.

Slobin, D. I. 1971b. Psycholinguistics. Scott, Foresman, & Co. Glenview.

Slobin, D. I. 1973. Cognitive prerequisites for the development of grammar. In C. A. Ferguson, and D. I. Slobin (eds.), Studies of Child Language Development, pp. 175–208. Holt, Rinehart, & Winston, New York.

Slobin, D. I. 1978. Universal and particular in the acquisition of language. Paper presented at the workshop-conference, "Language acquisition: State of the art," May 19–22, University of Pennsylvania.

Smedslund, J. 1961. The acquisition of conservation of substance and weight in children: III. Extinction of conservation of weight acquired "normally" and by means of empirical controls on a balance. Scand. J. Psychol. 2:85–87.

Smedslund, J. 1963. Development of concrete transitivity of length in children. Child Dev. 34:389–405.

Smedslund, J. 1965. The development of transitivity of length: A comment on Braine's reply. Child Dev. 36:577–580.

Snow, C. E. 1977. Mothers' speech research: From input to interaction. In C. E. Snow, and C. A. Ferguson (eds.), Talking to Children: Language Input and Acquisition, pp. 31–49. Cambridge University Press, Cambridge.

Snow, C. E., and Ferguson, C. A. (eds.). 1977. Talking to Children: Language Input and Acquisition. Cambridge University Press, Cambridge.

Snowling, M. J. 1980. The development of grapheme-phoneme correspondence in normal and dyslexic readers. J. Exp. Child Psychol. 29:294–305.

Stark, J., Poppen, R., and May, M. Z. 1967. Effects of the alterations of prosodic features on the sequencing performance of aphasic children. J. Speech Hear. Res. 10:849–855.

Strohner, H., and Nelson, K. E. 1974. The young child's development of sentence comprehension: Influence of event probability, nonverbal context, syntactic form, and strategies. Child Dev. 45:567–576.

Tallal, P., and Piercy, M. 1973a. Defects of non-verbal auditory perception in children with developmental aphasia. Nature. 241:468–469.

Tallal, P., and Piercy, M. 1973b. Developmental aphasia: Impaired rate of non-verbal processing as a function of sensory modality. Neuropsychologia. 11:389–398.

Tallal, P., and Piercy, M. 1974. Developmental aphasia: Rate of auditory processing and selective impairment of consonant perception. Neuropsychologia. 12:83–93.

Tallal, P., and Piercy, M. 1975. Developmental aphasia: The perception of brief vowels and extended stop consonants. Neuropsychologia. 13:69–74.

Tallal, P., and Piercy, M. 1978. Defects of auditory perception in children with developmental dysphasia. In M. A. Wyke (ed.), Developmental Dysphasia. pp. 63–84. Academic Press, Inc. London and New York.

Terrace, H. S. 1979. Nim: A Chimpanzee who Learned Sign Language. Alfred A. Knopf, Inc. New York.

Van Harskamp, F., Van Dongen, H. R. and Loonen, M. C. B. 1978. Acquired aphasia with convulsive disorders in children: A case study with a seven-year follow-up. Brain and Lang. 6:141–148.

Wales, R., and Campbell, R. 1970. On the development of comparison and the comparison of development. In G. B. Flores D. Arcais and W. J. Levelt (eds.), Advances in psycholinguistics, pp. 373–396. North Holland Publishing Company, Amsterdam.

Warrington, E. K., Logue, V., and Pratt, R. T. C. 1971. The anatomical localization of selective impairment of auditory verbal short-term memory. Neuropsychologia. 9:377–387.

Waryas, C. L., and Stremel-Campbell, K. 1978. Grammatical training for the language-delayed child. In R. L. Schiefelbusch (ed.), Language Intervention Strategies, pp. 145–192. University Park Press, Baltimore.

Wilcox, S., and Palermo, D. S. 1975. 'In', 'on', and 'under' revisited. Cognition. 3:245–254.

Wills, D. D. 1977. Participant deixis in English and baby talk. In C. E. Snow, and C. A. Ferguson (eds.), Talking to Children: Language Input and Acquisition, pp. 271–295. Cambridge University Press, Cambridge.

Withrow, F. B. Jr. 1964. Immediate recall by aphasic, deaf, and normal children for visual forms presented simultaneously or sequentially. Asha. 6:386.

Worster-Drought, C. 1971. An unusual form of acquired aphasia in children. Dev. Med. Child Neurol. 13:563–571.

Wyke, Maria A. (ed.), 1978. Developmental Dysphasia. Academic Press, Inc. London and New York.

chapter 3

Experience in the Social Context

Imitation and Play

Ina C. Uzgiris

Department of Psychology
Clark University
Worcester, Massachusetts

contents

It is of both theoretical and practical interest to understand how experience is interwoven in the construction of competence. Theoretically, if interchanges with the environment are assumed to have a significant part in the development of competence, it becomes important to specify how various aspects of the environment attain salience, contribute to the activities of the individual, and enter into changing the individual's very means for interacting with the world. It should be clear that this does not deny the centrality of the individual's role in shaping such interchanges. Practically, when it is thought desirable to intervene for the benefit of a young child, it becomes necessary to decide how to alter the child's environment and, concomitantly, to affect the child's experience in a productive direction. Yet the specific links that join a pattern of experience to aspects of the environment, on the one hand, and to the individual's competence, on the other, have been difficult to unravel.

THE ROLE OF EXPERIENCE

The role of experience in development has been addressed from two divergent perspectives. The first perspective is associated with differential psychology; it focuses on the role of experience in yielding relatively stable individual differences in various psychological characteristics such as intellectual ability, linguistic competence, or social disposition. From this perspective, experience is important to the extent that experiential differences can be shown to be predictably related to differences between individuals in such characteristics. Individual variation constitutes the main concern, and understanding of the nature of the characteristic in question remains a secondary concern. The second perspective is associated with developmental psychology; the role of experience is discussed in regard to sequential change in the nature of some characteristic with development. From this perspective, experience is important insofar as it supports the construction of progressively more advanced forms of that characteristic. The terms *interaction* or *transaction* have been attached to models of development in order to emphasize the essential role attributed to experience. Nevertheless, the focus is on the overall developmental sequence, with individual variation viewed as perturbation of a basic pattern.

The two perspectives have tended toward divergent emphases in describing psychological functioning. Concern with individual differences has highlighted the content and dynamics of individual functioning. In contrast, delineation of overall developmental sequences has been attained by greater weighting of the formal, structural aspects of functioning.

In recent years, there have been several attempts to bridge these two perspectives. In discussing methodological approaches to the study of development, Wohlwill (1973) introduced the notion of developmental function. He suggested this notion to describe the modal pattern of change in a behavioral characteristic with age, to be stated as some mathematical function. Once the developmental function for some characteristic was described, the study of individual differences could be pursued by investigating the effects on different parameters of that function of any factor distinguishing groups of individuals, including specific patterns of experience. With a similar aim, McCall, Eichorn, and Hogarty (1977) examined longitudinal data on mental test performance of children during the first 5 years of life. They suggested that changes in the stability of individual differences correlate with inflection points or discontinuities in the developmental function. Presumably, experience might exert a greater influence at these transition phases than at other periods, affecting developmental progress as well as differentiation between individuals within a group. Research into cognitive styles (e.g., Kogan, 1976; Fowler, 1977) has also tried to delineate modes of functioning that might consistently characterize individuals across developmental levels.

Despite these efforts, a connection between the differential and developmental perspectives remains more a goal than a reality. The efforts have foundered on the difficulty of integrating specificity with general structural descriptions of levels of functioning. Delineated patterns of individual functioning rapidly become ordered hierarchically and take on characteristics of a developmental sequence, and individual variations within developmental sequences tend to translate into differential rates of progress along a single sequence. In a complex hierarchical model of development, the possibility of alternate paths to integration at each next higher level seems viable (Uzgiris, 1976), but has not been sufficiently pursued. This chapter concentrates on the role of experience in supporting progress along a modal developmental sequence.

Piaget's Views

It is precisely at this juncture that Piaget's developmental theory, which has been enormously influential in the past two decades, provides relatively little guidance. Piaget includes experience among the four factors he names to account for development (together with maturation, equilibration, and social transmission), but the role that experience has in the formation of cognitive structures in his theory is ultimately uncertain (e.g., see Rotman, 1977). On the one hand, interactions with the world provide knowledge about reality, most clearly evident in the types of knowledge termed *figurative*. On the other hand, the basic operations of thought are said to derive from the coordinations of an individual's actions during such interactions and from their integrations forged as a result of self-regulation. Piaget considered operative knowledge to be more fundamental than figurative, and reflective abstraction to transcend simple abstraction from objects embodied in schemes or concepts. Thus, although he claimed that the structures of intelligence are not innate but are constructed, Piaget left unspecified the extent to which individual experience in a particular milieu can exert any effect (except to provide resistance or help) on cognitive organization at each developmental level. At the level of the epistemic subject (the level at which Piaget presents his theoretical account of development), the substitutability between different patterns of experience may be so great that this question becomes intractable. The notion of horizontal decalage recognizes the tangible role that reality has in extension of understanding over it, but only in terms of ease of such extension for groups of individuals. Any substantive relationships between patterns of experience and cognitive functioning remain indefinite.

Furthermore, Piaget's discussion of the factor of experience is conducted mostly from the standpoint of an isolated individual. Although he has consistently acknowledged the social context of human existence in his enumeration of factors that affect development, social and cultural variables are given second place to general coordinations resulting from the factor of self-regulation. Ultimately, self-regulation has primacy because social and cultural institutions are the creations of individuals. Piaget did not see unique implications in the fact that they are creations of individuals acting jointly.

> So the important question is not how to assess the respective merits of individual and group . . . but to see the logic in solitary reflection as in cooperation, and to see the errors and follies both in collective opinion and in individual conscience. Whatever Tarde may say, there are not two kinds of logic, one for the group and the other for the individual; there is only one way of coordinating actions A and B according to relationships of inclusion and order, whether such actions be those of different individuals A and B or of the same individual (who did not invent them singlehanded, because he is part of society as a whole). Thus cognitive regulations or operations are the same in a single brain or in a system of cooperations (Piaget, 1971, pp. 368–369).

When discussing the role of experience, he generally focused on the child's solitary interactions with the world of objects. Although experience leading to the construction of knowledge about the world is distinguished from experience leading to the construction of knowledge about one's actions in it—an important distinction—the social world is not considered a realm for distinct actions, yielding distinct experience in both of the above categories. It may be useful to consider the two types of experience delineated by Piaget (physical and logico-mathematical) with respect to both the physical and the social world.

Piaget's relative denial of social experience may have encouraged a partition: the use of Piagetian theory in studies of the construction of understanding of reality composed of things and the use of some other theory in studies concerned with growth of social relations. The assumption seems to be frequently made that actions with objects contribute most to understanding of physical reality while interactions with people support social development. But this may be a faulty partition. Especially in infancy, but also in other periods, the domain of social experience interpenetrates that of physical experience. For infants, many interactions with things take place in the context of interactions with people. Moreover, the infant's world of objects is essentially a man-made world. Those objects not only possess certain characteristics as physical objects, but also particular meaning as cultural objects. Thus, the infant's experience is social in two senses: in the sense that the infant participates in interactions with persons and in the sense that the infant acts on objects that have cultural significance.

Extrapolating from the overall character of Piaget's theory, one would posit that the infant's first understandings of reality would be global and only come to be particularized with respect to persons or things in the course of development. Knowledge of the self, of interpersonal relations, and of social institutions would be constructed gradually and increasingly differentiated from knowledge of things, their properties, and their effects on one another.

Vygotsky's Views

Although sharing a basic developmental orientation with Piaget, Vygotsky's historical-cultural approach to development differentiates the special role of social experience in human development. His rejection of both the innatist and the empiricist approaches was similar to Piaget's:

> We have found that sign operations appear as a result of a complex and prolonged process subject to all the basic laws of psychological evolution. This means that sign-using activity in children is neither simply invented or passed down by adults; rather it arises from something that is originally not a sign operation and becomes one only after a series of qualitative transformations. Each of these transformations provides the conditions for the next stage and is itself conditioned by the preceding one; thus, transformations are linked like stages of a single process, and are historical in nature (Vygotsky, 1978, pp. 45–46).

However, Vygotsky went on to emphasize the special significance of sociocultural experiences made available to the human child through exposure to tools and human speech.

Within a general process of development, two qualitatively different lines of development, differing in origin, can be distinguished: the elementary processes, which are of biological origin, on the one hand, and the higher psychological functions, of socio-cultural origin, on the other. The history of child behavior is born from the interweaving of these two lines (Vygotsky, 1978, p. 46).

In Vygotsky's view, the coordinations of actions giving rise to experience involved in the construction of operations and cognitive structures are first achieved in joint activity with another person, who already is a member of a sociocultural group.

The path from object to child and from child to object passes through another person. This complex human structure is the product of a developmental process deeply rooted in the links between individual and social history (Vygotsky, 1978, p. 30).

Or to repeat his oft-quoted statement:

Every function in the child's cultural development appears twice: first, on the social level, and later, on the individual level; first, between people (interpsychological) and then inside the child (intrapsychological) (Vygotsky, 1978, p. 57).

Vygotsky's writings emphasize the emergence of the sociocultural meaning of the world for the child and the fundamental significance of social reality in the organization of human psychological functioning. His description of how an infant's unsuccessful attempt to reach and grasp an object may become a pointing gesture as a result of the meaning given to the action by another person prefigures the recent systematic studies of the development of gestural communication in infancy (e.g., in Lock, 1978; in Schaffer, 1977). Yet Vygotsky saw the infant as entering the social community gradually, helped in large measure by the vistas opened through language. An even stronger emphasis on the significance of interpersonal experience in human development is found among a group of British researchers investigating the emergence of communication.

Communication in Infancy

The thinking of philosophers (e.g., Macmurray, 1961; Habermas, 1972) who emphasize the primacy of personal relatedness for typically human understanding underpins the views of the British group that includes the Newsons, Richards, Trevarthen, Schaffer, and others. Trevarthen presented the most radical formulation of their position (Trevarthen and Hubley, 1978). He proposed that the human infant possesses three distinct modes of action appropriate for 1) knowing and using objects, 2) communicating with other persons, and 3) for self-direction or reflection. All these modes of action and experience exist as biological predispositions, but become differentiated and developed with experience. In contrast to others, Trevarthen prefers to emphasize the innate roots of intersubjectivity and a biological timetable for development:

> We would describe the mother's acts we have seen as adaptations to the infant's changing play, and this in turn reflects the infant's changing understanding of her mother as a person. This is not to deny that what a mother does may be essential for the infant to expand his knowledge at an optimal rate. If she acts with spontaneity and freedom in responding, she cannot help creating a series of demonstrations fitted to the infant's cognitive and interactive schemata and stimulating to their growth. Helpful play appears to be her natural response to the infant's communicative personality and it can take many particular forms (1978, pp. 212–213).

Intersubjectivity, or directedness toward action with others as conscious and intending subjects, is assumed to be characteristic of humans at birth, but undergoes development from primary to secondary intersubjectivity and, through coordination with praxic intentions, to cooperative activity (Hubley and Trevarthen, 1979). The changes are said to be initiated not by the adults, but by changes in the infant's intentions. Consequently, Trevarthen stated:

> We believe the same developments will be found in all human societies, but think it likely, too, that cultural differences will take root at this stage of infancy (1978, p. 214).

Trevarthen viewed his position as distinct from both Piaget's conception of the infant as an isolated mind constructing knowledge and from Mead's (1934) conception of the infant as coming to know the self as a result of participation in a social system. For Trevarthen, the infant is an active partner in intersubjective exchanges from birth on.

Others have expressed views placing less weight on the biological predispositions of the infant and more on the responsive actions of the adult partner. Newson stated:

> What is being argued here is that, whenever he is in the presence of another human being, the actions of a baby are not just being automatically reflected back to him in terms of their physical consequences. Instead they are being processed through a subjective filter of human interpretation, according to which some, *but only some*, of his actions are judged to have coherence and relevance in human terms—either as movements born of intentions, or as communications (or potential communications) addressed to another socially aware individual: subjectively filtered and then reflected back. It is thus only because mothers impute meaning to "behaviors" elicited from infants that these eventually do come to constitute meaningful actions so far as the child himself is concerned. Actions achieve this status to the extent that they are capable of being used as communication gestures which he knows how to produce, on cue, in the context of a social exchange between himself and someone else. In a real sense, therefore, gestures only acquire their significance insofar as they can be utilized as currency within social dialogues (1978, p. 37).

The importance of experience arranged for by an adult partner, in line with Vygotsky's proposals, also was stressed by Clark:

> A mother, then, will take the grasping and reaching movements of a neonate, movements which are not yet related to the physical world, interpret them as evidence for intelligible intentions from her cultural standpoint and by manipulating the environment *construct* the action that the movements imply. Having performed these actions with mother's assistance the child has been shown a relation between his body and the world. Thus he can now intend to do this thing, having done it before, though he may be unable to achieve a successful completion of his intention without assistance (1978, p. 237).

Because language rapidly becomes the dominant means for human communication, most of the research conducted by the British group has focused on the emergence of language within the larger context of human communication. In this larger context, interactions between the child and an adult partner that normally are viewed as "play activities" seem to have special significance. These play activities include imitations, ritualized games, as well as pretend actions. The next two sections of this chapter examine changes in imitation and play activities during infancy with the goal of relating experience in these contexts to both cognitive and communicative development.

IMITATION IN INFANCY

The phenomenon of imitation has been of enduring interest to those concerned with human development because it captures the intermeshing of the individual and the world with which the individual interacts. It seems to be a choice means for influence from the social world, but is not a simple or automatic process. Although there has been interest in whether the capacity to imitate is present at birth (e.g., Parton, 1976), the nature of changes in imitation with development seem to be of greater theoretical importance. Both Baldwin (1895) and Guillaume (1971) recognized development in imitation during infancy and related it to changes in the child's understanding of the self as agent and of others as individuals like the self. Piaget (1962) built on their ideas and related development in imitation to the general course of development in sensorimotor intelligence (Uzgiris, 1979).

For Piaget, imitation represents the accommodatory pole of adaptation and exemplifies the highly visible part of a process that relates to imagery, representation, and figurative knowledge in general. Yet, being an aspect of the functioning of intelligence, it also involves some assimilatory schemes; thus, it is always bound by the intellectual level of the individual. Although an integral part of intellectual functioning, it is not a privileged means for ensuring developmental progress. Because Piaget's stages in the development of imitation during infancy remain a reference point for much of current research, they are outlined in Table 1.

The system of stages delineated by Piaget seems to involve two main dimensions: the familiarity of the modeled act and the ease with which accommodation to it takes place. Thus, at the second stage, there is imitation only to the extent that the act modeled is both familiar to the infant and already in progress at that time; accommodation is present in that the child's activity is modulated by the presence of the model. At the third stage, there is greater accommodation to the model in that the child systematically imitates the familiar act selected by the model, but not a novel act. At the fourth stage, imitation of novel acts may be observed, but it is achieved through a drawn out process of gradual approximation. The fifth stage is marked by greater facility in accommodation and, at the sixth stage, accommodation may take place internally and become manifest at a later time. Thus, for Piaget, development in imitation rests on progress in cognitive understanding as well as on increasing differentiation of the processes of assimilation and accommodation.

Evidence supporting, in general terms, Piaget's description of the developmental sequence is found in current studies, but specific points of disagreement also are evident. Because familiarity is a dimension difficult to specify, there have been some attempts to equate stages in the development of imitation with imitation of particular acts, although such a procedure, strictly speaking, is contrary to Piaget's approach. Precise data on imitation during the first 2 years of life are still quite scant.

The first point of disagreement concerns imitation during the first month of life. Piaget claimed that there would be hardly any imitation in the first few months; true imitation, that is, imitation as clearly differentiated accommodation, was posited only at the fourth stage.

Table 1.   Piaget's stages in the development of imitation

Stage	Approximate age	Description
1	Birth–1 month	Preparation through reflex actions
2	1–4 months	Sporadic imitation: a. mutual imitation (adult joins child) b. sporadic imitation of familiar acts
3	4–8 months	Systematic imitation of familiar acts
4	8–12 months	Imitation of familiar acts on nonvisible parts of the body and some new models
5	12–18 months	Systematic imitation of new models
6	18–24 months	Representative imitation (includes deferred imitation)

Recent studies indicate that imitation of some facial movements (tongue protrusion, mouth opening), finger movements, and hand movements may occur in the first few weeks of life (Dunkeld, 1977; Maratos, 1973; Meltzoff and Moore, 1977; Jacobson and Kagan, 1978), but probably declines a few months later. The question arises whether such results constitute a fundamental challenge to Piaget's conception of development in imitation. Such movements are highly familiar to young infants in that they are frequently practiced by them, therefore, it might be possible to assimilate these observations to Stage 2 or Stage 3 imitation of familiar acts. Moreover, other studies have questioned the replicability of these findings (Hamm, Russell, and Koepke, 1979; Hayes and Watson, 1979) or their interpretation as imitation (Jacobson and Kagan, 1978; Waite, 1979). Nevertheless, these studies indicate a need for further research on imitation in the earliest months of life because under some conditions, a match in the behavior of an infant and an adult seems to take place.

There have been relatively few studies investigating imitation during the remainder of the first year of life and the beginning of the second. The existing data support a general increase in imitation with age and some selectivity in the types of acts most readily imitated at different age periods, but the validity of Piaget's emphasis on the familiarity/novelty dimension is difficult to evaluate because most investigators have not specifically attempted to use it in their studies.

The few reports of imitation before eight months of age consist largely of simple hand or arm movements (Maratos, 1973; Pawlby, 1977; Uzgiris, 1972) such as banging, waving, clapping, and finger motions, or highly practiced acts with toys, such as shaking (Killen and Uzgiris, 1979). Vocal imitations largely consist of single sounds (Uzgiris, 1972) or expressive vocalizations such as coughs, sighs, and laughs (Pawlby, 1977). Entry into Stage 4 at around eight months would be expected to produce a change in the types of acts imitated, but the presence of such a transition has not been adequately assessed. An increase in imitation of acts involving manipulation of toys and of speech sounds around eight months has been observed (Pawlby, 1977) as well as the appearance of imitation of socially meaningful manipulation of toy objects (Killen and Uzgiris, 1979). It might be possible to consider some of these manipulations novel for the infant, but the investigators have emphasized other interpretations.

A transition around 12 months of age has been more clearly shown. Around the beginning of the second year, imitations of acts that require recognition of the specific characteristics of an object, such as stirring in a cup, driving a toy car, and ringing a bell or acts that require specific manipulations of several objects increase (Abravanel, Levan-Goldschmidt, and Stevenson, 1976; Killen and Uzgiris, 1979; McCall, Parke, and Kavanaugh, 1977; Rodgon and Kurdek, 1977), as do imitations of repetitive sound combinations that make up the first nonconventional words (Rodgon and Kurdek, 1977; Uzgiris, 1972). There is also some support for a change in the quality of imitation toward the end of the second year of life (Killen and Uzgiris, 1979; McCall et al., 1977); accommodation to any model is more facile so that both different and inappropriate acts with an object are imitated and imitation of conventional words becomes prevalent (Rodgon and Kurdek, 1977; Uzgiris, 1972). Deferred imitation has not been assessed except in the McCall et al. (1977) study, where it was observed with some frequency only around age 2.

These empirical studies are more supportive of Piaget's proposal that imitation is related to the child's ability to understand the action of the model than to his specific characterization of stages in imitation development. As an accommodatory act, imitation should be most evident when the infant possesses assimilatory schemes relevant to the observed act but is not yet capable of assimilating the act immediately. Thus, the acts that are most readily imitated would be expected to change as the child's understanding changes. Not only would complex acts come to be imitated, but imitation of relatively simple acts might decline. In this view, the most salient feature of the imitation exchange is the child's understanding of the act being modeled; the model and the imitative context remain secondary. It is a view in keeping with Piaget's overall perspective of the individual constructing his or her own understanding. This view, however, may capture only one function of imitation.

Because imitation most frequently takes place as an exchange between two persons, it may also function as a means of communicating that an encounter, a connection, between them exists. Such a function for imitation is suggested by observations of social interactions between infants and their mothers rather than by the more constrained studies of imitation ability.

Studies of mother-infant interaction at two or three months of age report some instances of imitation of the mother's facial or arm movements by the infant; however, the matching of the infant's expressions, moods, and vocalizations by the mother seems to be much more frequent (Papousek and Papousek, 1977; Trevarthen, 1977). Trevarthen emphasized this observation to support his view of the baby as an initiator in interpersonal exchanges. Regardless of which partner is responsible for the match in the exchange, the similarity attained can be noted by both. An observation made by Waite and Lewis (1979) is interesting in this regard. In a study including neonates and 3-month-old infants, they found that a fair proportion of facial and hand movements made by the mothers were matched by their infant. The mothers had the impression that their infants were imitating them. When the video records were examined, however, it was found that the various acts were performed with similar frequency to the "correct" model as to the others. The impression of imitation was sustained by ignoring the occurrence of acts when they did not match the one being modeled. This might suggest that attainment of an imitative response is very salient for the mother. In turn, the infant seems to find imitations by the mother also salient, indicated by smiles to such imitations (Papousek and Papousek, 1977). The point suggested by these observations is that an instance of imitation can epitomize the presence of mutuality; to do something that has just been done by the other is to know something not only about the act but also about the similarity between oneself and the other. Imitations during the neonatal period can be interpreted not only as evidence of innate intersubjectivity, but also as instances of the construction of a sharing on the interpersonal plane (largely as a result of the mother's actions) before its occurrence intrapersonally, in keeping with Vygotsky's and Newson's views.

This social function of imitation seems to be evident at other periods in development as well. The period corresponding to Piaget's fourth stage has been found to be a time for many new achievements; with respect to imitation, it is a time when object-directed acts are increasingly imitated. Trevarthen and Hubley (1978) identified this period with appearance of coordination between the intent to do and an intent to communicate with another. Cooperative actions are said to grow out of this coordination. The imitation with objects observed during this period can be interpreted as a sharing of understanding with respect to the intention to act on a particular object. Pawlby (1977) observed that between 6 and 12 months, imitation by infants of their mothers increased, but mothers also continued to imitate their infants, particularly in manipulation of objects, supporting the interpretation that imitation might be serving a communicative function. A similar pattern has been reported for interactions between young siblings in the home (Dunn and Kendrick, 1979). When the younger siblings were 8 months old, the majority of imitative interactions consisted of the older child imitating the younger; when the younger children were 14 months old, the ratio was reversed for motor actions and/or object manipulations. In addition, quite a few episodes of co-action accompanied by positive affect were observed, suggesting that imitation or joint execution of actions may have a communicative function in sibling interactions as well. Similarly, the observed increase in imitation of acts that have social meaning past 1 year of age may be interpreted as a sharing of understanding of the function of the object with a partner in a social encounter. Such an interpretation helps account for the findings of comparable imitation of "real" acts such as drinking from a cup and "play" acts such as driving a toy car (Killen and Uzgiris, 1979).

The changes in imitation that occur around 18 months of age also may be related to changes in understanding of the interpersonal situation. First, there is an increase in imitation of most types of acts. Second, infants readily imitate acts with substitute objects and various pretend activities. It is possible to interpret imitation as sharing of understanding of the imitation activity itself rather than of any specific act. It is as if the act of imitation indicates understanding that the point of the interaction is to reply with a comparable act. This interpretation is supported by informal observation of instances where the infant "turns the tables" and models something for the adult to imitate.

The communicative function of imitation clearly contrasts with imitation occurring when an act is not completely understood. In the latter case, imitation functions to reduce the disequilibrium, or uncertainty, created by the observation of the model and, when successful, might be expected to increase cognitive understanding. In contrast, in the case of social interactions, the acts that are imitated are usually ones that are well known to the infant. If there is accommodation, it is to the other person rather than to the act. Recognition of these two different functions of imitation might be useful in thinking about the role of imitation in language. In children's early language, there are recorded instances of imitation that seem to fit the case of incomplete understanding. In other instances, however, imitation seems to serve as a device to continue the conversation. Once the child has some linguistic proficiency, sharing of understanding can be accomplished better through other than imitative means. To the extent that imitation continues to serve a communicative function, it is probably contained in gestural, rhythmic, and expressive acts. Nevertheless, the role of imitation in creating the context of mutuality within which language as a means of communication can develop may be worth closer examination.

PLAY IN INFANCY

Although play intuitively seems easy to recognize, it has proved difficult to define precisely. Much of the literature on play concerns the content or the dynamics of play activities (Millar, 1968), although recently the structure of play has also received attention (Garvey, 1977). There is very little material on play during infancy in non-Western cultures, particularly from a perspective concerned with the structure rather than the content of playful activities. Piaget (1962) discussed development in play in relation to the functioning of intelligence .and considered it to represent the assimilatory pole of adaptation. He examined play in infancy largely to trace the evolution of the symbol, however, and hardly touched on many other aspects of play development. Recent studies of play focus mainly on the emergence of symbolic play and on inception of play with peers. In order to facilitate comparison with development in imitation, Piaget's description of play at each of the six stages of sensorimotor intelligence is presented in Table 2.

Piaget viewed play as derived from generalizing assimilation when effort to adapt to any new elements appearing as a result of the generalization is either not necessary or is suspended. Development consists in the progressive dissociation of actions from their usual adaptive contexts and greater facility in creating new combinations of actions. Again, development is described from the standpoint of the individual child without specific reference to the social environment. Piaget suggested that ritualized repetition of actions out of their usual context is an early form of play and may be viewed as self-imitation, but he did not suggest any direct link between imitation of others and play until the end of the sensorimotor period.

Piaget's distinction between adaptive activity aimed toward mastery and play activity with a minimal accommodatory component has been reflected in the distinction between exploration and play made

Table 2.   Piaget's stages in the development of play

Stage	Approximate age	Description
1	Birth–1 month	Occurrence of play is indefinite
2	1–4 months	Ludic continuation of circular reactions, distinguishable by accompanying positive affect
3	4–8 months	Continuation of secondary circular reactions once they are fully understood, distinguishable by the attitude of the child
4	8–12 months	Repetition of child's activities out of their usual context or combination of activities known to the child without an extrinsic goal
5	12–18 months	Ritualized repetition of new combinations of activities, which include both familiar acts taken out of their usual context and adventitious new acts
6	18–24 months	Symbolic play, created by repetition of activities out of their usual context and in relation to inadequate objects

in the research literature (Hutt, 1970; McCall, 1974). This distinction, however, has not been consistently applied in studies conducted in a laboratory setting unfamiliar to the child and with toys that are also relatively novel. Any activity fitting certain content categories (e.g., banging, shaking, moving toy objects around) usually is termed *play*.

Systematic changes in infant's actions toward objects during the first 2 years have been documented (Uzgiris, 1967; Uzgiris and Hunt, 1975); appearance of actions differentiated in terms of the particular characteristics of objects around the transition to Stage 4 and of socially appropriate actions on objects toward the end of the first year may be taken as indications of emergence of ritualization. In a longitudinal study of play with objects by infants between 8½ and 11½ months of age, McCall (1974) also noted changes in play behaviors with age. He reported that with age, infants spent increasingly more time with objects that offered more varied feedback and performed more manipulations accompanied by visual regard as well as a greater number of actions appropriate to each particular object. Although almost no appropriate actions were shown at 8½ months, almost half the children in the sample showed actions such as holding a toy telephone to the ear by 11½ months of age. Repetition of actions produced during exploration of the toys also increased with age. It is interesting to note that the number of looks to mother while the infant was contacting a toy also increased over the 3-month period. These observations are, in general, consistent with the developmental sequence proposed by Piaget.

A greater number of studies have examined play in the second year of life. Fenson et al. (1976) observed play with a tea set by infants 7, 9, 13, and 20 months of age. The most frequent action by the 7-month-olds was to bang the objects; the 9-month-olds engaged in acts involving more than one object, but the combinations usually did not consist of appropriate use of the toys. By 13 months, the most frequent activity was an appropriate relating of two or more objects, but symbolic acts (e.g., drinking, pouring, stirring) were seen with considerable frequency only at 20 months. These results are consistent with other studies reporting that actions recognizing the social function of an object may be observed around 1 year of age, but symbolic play (the combining of an inadequate object with an activity taken out of context) does not become frequent until the middle of the second year of life (Bates et al., 1977; Inhelder et al., 1972; Lowe, 1975). Studies have also confirmed that pretend actions in which the self remains the agent are seen earlier than such actions for a substitute agent such as a doll (Lowe, 1975; Watson and Fischer, 1977). Planned use of substitute objects occurs still later (Nicolich, 1977).

In contrast to these studies of play directed toward objects, a number of recent studies observed joint activities between the mother and her infant that may or may not involve objects; they also may be viewed as play. Episodes of social interaction between infants and adult partners in the earliest months of life have been considered play as well as opportunities for communication (e.g., Stern, 1974). The repetitive character of the actions of both partners, systematic variations in tempo, and the synchronization between the two partners give these interactions a structure resembling that characteristic of later interpersonal games.

The earliest joint activities with objects seem to revolve around the adult presenting an object and facilitating its taking by the child. From such beginnings evolve the "give and take" games that have been observed by several investigators (Bruner, 1977; Clark, 1978; Gray, 1978). The full pattern of exchanging objects seems to progress from the adult helping the child take an object, to the adult complying with the child's request for an object, to the child's giving up an object requested by the adult, to the child's offering objects to the adult with an expectation of acceptance. The full exchange structure seems to be worked out between approximately 5 and 11 months of age (Clark, 1978). Although the investigators who conducted these studies emphasized the emergence of communicative gestures out of these repetitive activities, the element of ritual present in their repetition suggests that they might be treated as interpersonal play.

Games having a script that comes to be known by both participants also have been described. A prime example of such a game is peek-a-boo (Bruner and Sherwood, 1976), although various other games unique to individual dyads have been studied (Newson and Pawlby, 1972; Ratner and Bruner, 1978; Trevarthen and Hubley, 1978). The most notable features of these games are an invariant basic structure, often marked by vocalizations by the adult partner, a gradual shift of the agent role from the adult to the child, a gradual introduction of acceptable variants on the basic structure, and a reduction of segment-marking as well as a compression in time of the game as its basic structure comes to be known by both participants. Bruner (1975, 1977) discussed these games as opportunities to gain experience with basic rule structures that are also fundamental to language. They include not only the categories of agent, recipient, object of action, but also generate reversibility, recursiveness, and so on. These games have been considered as instances of a ritualized dialogue in which nonlinguistic acts such as vocalizations, gestures, affective expressions make up the medium of exchange into which linguistic tokens come to be inserted (Ninio and Bruner, 1978). In contrast, Trevarthen emphasized the aspect of cooperation and responsiveness to the partner's intentions in these games, preferring to view the emergence of language as less directly dependent on the experience gained in such contexts. Whatever the significance eventually given to these joint ritualized games, the reported studies make it clear that infants engage in a great deal of structured play with adults before they demonstrate symbolic transformations in their own play. This suggests that a good portion of the activities from which the child would be expected to abstract relations and regularities occurs with reference to other persons. If symbolic play activities were studied in contexts that permitted free interaction with significant adults, it might be found that it also occurs in the larger framework of sharing one's interests and plans with another. It may be recalled that McCall (1974) found a consistent increase of visual contacting of mother during play with a toy even among children under 1 year of age. A high incidence of "showing" also has been found in observations of play in which a parent is present as an observer (e.g., Bates et al., 1977).

It is impressive how well the evolution of these joint games fits the pattern suggested by Vygotsky (1978). The adult partner acts to help make an outcome possible that the child would not be able to accomplish (or might not even conceive) alone. At the inception of requesting, the adult interprets a glance, a movement, an outstretched hand as a request and supplies some object. At the inception of offering, the adult places an outstretched hand under the object the child is holding and waits. At the beginning of peek-a-boo, the adult both hides her face and unmasks it when the child acknowledges the mask in any way. As the child begins to roll toys, the adult utilizes every opportunity to roll one back and to create a dyadic activity. It does seem that a whole range of relations are first constructed interpersonally, and only subsequently come to govern the actions of the child acting alone. Bruner (1975) remarked on this aspect of mother-child interactions in discussing skill development and termed the facilitatory actions of the adult *scaffolding*. It seems that this interpersonal sphere of experience is worthy of further investigation.

Two other types of play activities deserve mention. First, infants engage in vocal activities that can readily be considered play, but these have been studied only minimally. Some repetitive vocal exchanges between young infants and their mothers have been recorded (Newson and Pawlby, 1972) as well as some monologues of older children (e.g., Weir, 1962), but, more generally, vocalizations accompanying mutual games have been noted as occurring, but have not been specified. The structure of such vocal exchanges might be interesting to study. Second, infants' play with peers is only beginning to be investigated. There is an increment in such play over the second year of life and instances of showing, offering, taking a toy, and coordinated play with a single focus have all been observed (Eckerman, Whatley, and Kutz, 1975; Mueller, 1979). Although many of the play interactions with peers involve objects, purely social sequences with peers also have been recorded (Eckerman and Whatley, 1977; Jacobson, 1979) as well as with siblings (Dunn and Kendrick, 1979). Because peers are unlikely to act so as to support the achievement of outcomes not attainable by each child individually, a comparison of the structure of games characteristic of mother-child interactions with those found in peer interactions would illuminate the role of adult facilitation in development.

Social play constitutes a considerable part of the infant's experience. It has been studied mainly as an elemental communication situation within which gesture, symbol, and language emerge. It is difficult to conceive that it would not link to intellectual progress generally.

EXPERIENCE IN IMITATION AND PLAY AND DEVELOPMENT

The main objective of this juxtaposition of findings concerning development in imitation and play during the first 2 years of life is to raise the question of what role a child's experience in activities with others has in cognitive and linguistic development. Because of the nature of the evidence, it is impossible to argue that specific kinds of experience are necessary for the achievement of particular competencies. In fact, data on early development imply that there is a great deal of experiential substitutability; experience in many different contexts seems adequate to support construction of equivalent means for knowing and manipulating the world. This should not imply that experience as such is not necessary. The challenge is to understand the configurations of adequate experiential alternatives and the constraints created when the developing child is in some way organically or functionally impaired. Although an impairment is likely to reduce the opportunity for certain kinds of experience, it is not obvious that the way to foster development of a child with an impairment is to attempt to fill them in. Some alternative experience might be as adequate and more congenial. Consequently, one task is to describe the process of cognitive and linguistic development with sufficient thoroughness so as to appreciate the alternative routes and strategies that children may follow.

This discussion of development in imitation and play is meant to show that experience gained in these contexts will vary with developmental level. Therefore, the importance of experience in these contexts for a complex competence such as language also has to be considered with regard to developmental level. Even if patterns of interaction having certain structural properties are found to be realized in the context of play or imitation regularly before their manifestation in language, the relationship between these formally similar realizations would not be clear. The various interpretations that can be given to occurrence of such sequentially linked structures across different domains are discussed by Bates et al. (1979). Nevertheless, knowledge of such typical sequences adds a dimension to the portrayal of human development.

Regarding language, the imitative interaction has been considered mostly an avenue for acquisition of lexical items. Whether it can be progressive and productive for other aspects of linguistic development is debated (e.g., Bloom, Hood, and Lightbown, 1974; Moerk and Moerk, 1979), and there is little agreement on what constitutes an imitation. If imitation may serve the two functions discussed above, it may be useful to consider the two types of resulting instances of imitation separately.

The literature on early language contains some evidence for both types of imitations. Several studies reported that at the beginning of multiword utterances, children seem to produce phrases that have been acquired as wholes. For example, Ferrier (1978) reported multiword utterances by her 21-month-old daughter that were clearly derived from phrases addressed to her: "/ə/ peel it xx like" as a demand to peel her own apple was derived from offers of "I'll peel it if you like," or, "Wheresa Mummy sho?" included "wheresa" taken over as one unit from questions addressed to her. Similarly, Ingram (Chapter 8, this volume) described a child who was producing many multiword utterances quite early, but a number of them seemed to be stock phrases acquired through imitation. A case of an older child whose language included a whole repertoire of stock conversations is described by Blank, Gessner, and Esposito (1979). It is interesting that this child's language was acquired in quite specific play contexts and expressed meanings appropriate to those contexts; however, an analysis of the interchanges from the perspective of communication revealed that a large percentage of his utterances, when produced in response to a partner's utterance, even in the play context did not meet the communication demand of the prior utterance. The parents also reported that the child had not participated in any of the early social games such as peek-a-boo. Although this child is clearly unusual, his case raises the question of how children manage to analyze, understand, and use productively such imitated phrases. It is tempting to speculate that the larger communication framework within which language usually emerges facilitates analysis and comprehension.

A study of interactions that involved an offer from the caregiver to the child documents how redundancy between context, gesture, and verbal statement facilitates the transition to understanding of purely verbal communications (Zukow, Reilley, and Greenfield, in press). Moreover, Bretherton and Bates (1979) provided a number of examples of similar redundancy in the child's own early productions. Playful routines between the caregiver and child may present a good opportunity for the child to comprehend the structure of routinely employed phrases because the ongoing interaction is already understood at the nonverbal level and because both partners are likely to use nonverbal and verbal checks to ensure communication. Selective imitation may actually be one type of check on communication and, thus, have a role in the transition to productive use of new linguistic forms. Keenan (1977) documented the use of imitation (or repetition) by a set of twins as a communication check; they repeated utterances to indicate their understanding and sought repetition from others to verify that they were understood. Her discussion of communication checks to ensure shared knowledge is similar to the proposed communicative function for imitation discussed in this chapter.

Imitation and play, when regarded as activities strongly tied to the social domain, link the child's experience in interaction with others to cognitive development. The centrality of the concept of self in the organization of knowledge during infancy has been emphasized recently by Lewis and Brooks-Gunn (1979). Parallels between development in these domains based on recent research are highlighted in Table 3, which suggests that consciousness of self, coordination with others, and knowledge of one's exchanges with the world of both objects and people have a developmental course originating in early infancy. It seems that there are basically three stances that one may take to their interrelation in development.

The first stance might be attributed to Piaget. It would claim that the construction of the child's understanding of the world proceeds in steps as the child's actions adapt to reality and coordinate into more coherent and stable systems. Experience in various contexts serves as aliment for the child's intellect. In turn, development in intelligence permits the child to act differently in, and consequently, to come to understand better, the different contexts. Experience in specific contexts (e.g., with physical objects versus persons) might be thought to become more important as the child's understanding becomes more differentiated and adapted. Cognitive level, however, would be the fundamental determiner of activities in all contexts. From this perspective, the sensorimotor stage level would be taken as the base for activities that would be expected in imitation, play, or other situations.

Table 3. Summary of significant changes in cognition, imitation, and play

Piaget's stage	Characterization	Organization of Actions	Imitation	Play	Knowledge of self
2 (1–4 mos.)	Primary circular reactions	Simple unitary actions	Matching of facial expressions, hand movements, more frequently by mother than infant	Dyadic mother-infant play without objects	
3 (4–8 mos.)	Secondary circular reactions	Simple unitary actions with some attention to outcome	Simple familiar acts such as banging; single sounds or vocalizations	"Infant reaches, mother gives" games	Contingency to own actions noted (e.g., in a mirror, by caregiver)
4 (8–12 mos.)	Means-ends differentiation	Differentiated actions organized into sequences; relations of succession, inversion, inclusion possible	Speech sounds; simple manipulations of toys; a few socially appropriate acts on objects	Object play involves combination of two objects; games with a script (peek-a-boo) increasingly mastered	Relations between positions of self and objects noted and used
5 (12–18 mos.)	Tertiary circular reactions	Action sequences regulated by differentiated feedback; relations inherent in reality reflected in the organization of actions	Socially appropriate actions on objects; sequences of actions; sound combinations	Play recognizes social function of objects; child takes over active agent role in mutual games; child takes direction from adult in mutual play	Differentiated behaviors directed toward active image (e.g., video) of self and of other
6 (18–24 mos.)	Mental invention	Anticipatory regulation of actions; relations inherent in reality can be represented	Imitation of inappropriate actions on objects; increase in imitation of different types of acts; imitation of "words"	Symbolic play; coordinated play with peers	Knowledge of one's specific features, name

Shields expressed the fundamental objection to this position this way:

> Piaget once said that children learn about persons as they learn about things. If he meant by this that they form representational schemes both of other persons and of their interactions with them and that these schemes assimilate new instances and accommodate and elaborate as new experiences cease to fit the previous structure, then he is certainly right. The question then arises as to the logical nature of these schemes for he surely cannot mean that they are of exactly the same logical kind as those which govern encounters with the spatio/temporal world. The constancy of objects in space can be stretched to cover constancy of identity of persons which is a necessary preliminary for the development of specific attachments; but what of reversibility which, according to Piaget, originates in the grouping of spatial displacements which allows the child to back track and make detours by compensating movements in one direction by moving in another? Time, and human action in it, is irreversible and what has gone before is retained and reconstructed only in the minds of persons. Likewise, what is to come is unfolded in human intentions (1978, p. 536).

The above quote suggests the second stance, which seems to be the one taken by Trevarthen (Trevarthen and Hubley, 1978). It claims that interpersonal actions and interpersonal understanding is fundamentally different from understanding of objects. Intersubjective knowledge is separate from both objective and subjective knowledge. Consequently, levels of understanding by the child derived from observations of actions with objects cannot be considered determative of the child's actions with persons; both need to be studied as such. Any parallelisms found between the two types of understandings might be attributed to a biological plan for development. This stance would not deny that these separate types of knowledge would come to coordinate as reflection on one's knowledge and understanding developed. In fact, humans do treat other persons as objects for certain purposes. Nevertheless, in infancy, these separate types of knowledge would certainly not depend one on the other.

The second stance has considerable appeal. Yet, a third stance that would not posit such fundamental separation between development in intersubjective and objective understanding is proposed here. Greater attention and greater weight must be given to the child's experiences with persons and the social world than Piaget's statements imply, but not to the extent of losing sight of the underlying structuration of children's actions and the roots of fundamental thought operations inherent in them. Thus, the proposed stance consists of two hypotheses.

First, there may be considerable substitutability in the child's experiences with the world of persons and objects. Persons are also objects and experience gained with persons in certain activities may be comparable to that gained with objects. By adapting their own actions to infants, adults might make themselves less like persons in certain respects. Thus, particularly in early infancy, experience with both persons and objects might serve to support basic cognitive development. The aspects of experience most appropriate at this time might be to a considerable extent available in both contexts (Uzgiris, 1977). Rather than asserting that one aspect of understanding is fundamental, a reciprocal support model would be assumed. That is, understanding from one realm when applied in the other would create perturbations and spur new adaptations which, in turn, when applied in the first realm would act in a similar way. For example, having had one's acts mirrored in the face and actions of another, one may differentiate the outcomes of one's actions better than having merely experienced contingencies, but having differentiated means and ends, one may be in a position to come to appreciate the structure of games with reversible roles. It does seem possible to have a hierarchical model of development without resorting to a biological plan to account for its orderliness.

Second, the experience unique to interactions with persons might generate structures essential for human types of interaction with the object world. In particular, experiences gained in the context of imitation and play may teach generativity of action structures and the value of mirroring a puzzling event. Both of these operations combined with activities directed toward the object world may eventuate in what we recognize as investigation and creativity.

SUMMARY

The current acceptance of an interactionist approach to the study of human development imparts added significance to the concept of experience because this concept expresses the merging of an individual's initiatives with environmental opportunities during activity. But experience is a difficult variable to study because an individual's experience has to be inferred from activity observed in specific situations. It cannot be determined by an assessment of the individual's characteristics or by an evaluation of the environmental circumstances taken separately, and an accepted vocabulary to speak of them jointly is lacking. Thus, one necessary task is to devise a systematic way to describe experience (particularly an infant's or a young child's experience) that would focus on the dimensions of experience rather than on the specifics of observed activity. Furthermore, given some persisting set of environmental conditions, different patterns of experience may be expected to characterize individuals at different stages in development because developmental progress both relies on and is reflected in experience. Another task, then, is to delineate the patterns of experience central to each stage in development, particularly if intervention aimed at modifying children's experience is to be contemplated. Ultimately, a direct focus on experience may also facilitate dealing with the theoretical issue of the precise nature of the link between experience and developmental progress.

In the literature on development in infancy, when the variable of experience has been considered, categories typically used to identify domains of functioning have been also applied to experience. As activities have been called cognitive, linguistic, social, play, or learning, so has experience. Such practice has encouraged the study of the effects of social experience on sociality and of linguistic experience on development in language or, more often, of the effects of social experience on cognitive development or of play experience on development in language. Although studies conceived in these terms have provided some interesting data, it seems that it might be useful to cleave experience in different ways. Similar dimensions may characterize experience in different contexts of activity. The experience of control over events, of mutual exchange, of coordination of actions toward a common goal, of the nonliteral treatment of reality may occur while a child is engaged in many activities. These dimensions of experience may relate strongly to developmental progress; however, the existence of such relations would be difficult to demonstrate through the study of one specific type of activity. Only an examination of experience across a number of specific activities may reveal the alternative contexts for similar experiences at a given level of development.

A distinction between experience in relation to the physical world and experience in relation to the social world has become accepted. It seems evident that interactions with physical objects and with persons have a different configuration in experience. For infants, however, this distinction may be much less clear. Infants and young children exist in a relation with others; persons usually mediate their interactions with the physical world. It is persons who arrange the life situation of the infant, engage the infant in joint activity toward selected objects, demonstrate the possibilities of action on new objects, and capitalize on the behavior of the infant to guide him or her toward activities that have meaning in the culture. The impression of the presence of a distinct realm of experience in relation to physical objects is sustained only by the practice of taking the individual infant as the unit for study. When a slightly broader focus is adopted, it can be seen that most of the activities of infants (including exploration and play with objects) take place in a social context. For example, studies of cognitive development in infancy have been described as dealing with achievements related to the world of objects and have been criticized in this respect.

In fact, these achievements are attained and are demonstrated in the context of interaction with others. During the early years, the physical and the social world seem to intertwine much more closely than has been assumed.

The goal of this discussion of the activities of imitation and play is to exemplify that a social context is implicit for most activities of infants and young children, even when it is not directly acknowledged. Although usually imitation and play are studied separately, they both can be observed within the spontaneous interactions of young children with adults. In games, repetition of the action of the partner is often an acceptable way to take one's turn. The modeling of different acts for the partner to imitate can constitute a game. There is evidence that with development, parallel transformations take place in both play and imitation. The imitative interaction may be particularly suited for introducing new action goals for the child. The playful interaction may be particularly suited for encouraging the child to construct variants of well-known routines. In both, however, mutual understanding of the interchange has to be established by the participants. The repetition of an act may be one means for communicating understanding through action; doing one's part in a routine may be another. Viewed in this fashion, neither the activity of imitation nor of play as such seems necessary for language development. But the experience of communicating with another about a shared world may constitute a necessary framework for language to emerge.

Language is a unique and highly adapted means for coordinating one's activities with others in society. Mastery of a language infuses the social context into even the most personal activities. Initially, however, some of the functions served by language seem to be accomplished through other means in the interactions between an infant and an adult partner. A better understanding of these early means for communicating through action may facilitate understanding of the emergence of language as well as its use in later years.

REFERENCES

Abravanel, E., Levan-Goldschmidt, E., and Stevenson, M. B. 1976. Action imitation: the early phase of infancy. Child Dev. 47:1032–1044.

Baldwin, J. M. 1895. Mental Development in the Child and the Race. Macmillan and Co. New York.

Bates, E., Benigni, L., Bretherton, I., Camaioni, L., and Volterra, V. 1977. From gesture to the first word. In M. Lewis, and L. Rosenblum (eds.), Interaction, Conversation and the Development of Language, pp. 247–307. John Wiley, & Sons, Inc. New York.

Bates, E., Benigni, L., Bretherton, I., Camaioni, L., and Volterra, V. 1979. The Emergence of Symbols: Cognition and Communication in Infancy. Academic Press, Inc. New York.

Blank, M., Gessner, M., and Esposito, A. 1979. Language without communication: A case study. J. Child Lang. 6:329–352.

Bloom, L., Hood, L., and Lightbown, P. 1974. Imitation in language development: If, when, and why. Cognitive Psychol. 6:380–420.

Bretherton, I., and Bates, E. 1979. The emergence of intentional communication. In I. C. Uzgiris (ed.), New Directions for Child Development, No. 4: Social Interaction and Communication During Infancy, pp. 81–100. Jossey-Bass, San Francisco.

Bruner, J. S. 1975. The ontogenesis of speech acts. J. Child Lang. 2:1–19.

Bruner, J. S. 1977. Early social interaction and language acquisition. In H. R. Schaffer (ed.), Studies in Mother-Infant Interaction, pp. 271–289. Academic Press, New York.

Bruner, J. S., and Sherwood, V. 1976. Peek-a-boo and the learning of rule structures. In J. Bruner, A. Jolly, and K. Sylva (eds.), Play—Its Role in Development and Evolution, pp. 277–285. Basic Books, New York.

Clark, R. A. 1978. The transition from action to gesture. In A. Lock (ed.), Action, Gesture and Symbol, pp. 231–257. Academic Press, Inc. New York.

Dunkeld, J. 1977. The development of imitation in infancy. Doctoral dissertation, University of Edinburgh. Personal communication.

Dunn, J., and Kendrick, C. 1979. Interaction between young siblings in the context of family relationships. In M. Lewis, and L. A. Rosenblum (eds.), The Child and its Family, pp. 143–168. Plenum Publishing Corp. New York.

Eckerman, C. O., Whatley, J. L., and Kutz, S. L. 1975. Growth of social play with peers during the second year of life. Dev. Psychol. 11:42–49.

Eckerman, C. O., and Whatley, J. L. 1977. Toys and social interaction between infant peers. Child Dev. 48:1645–1656.

Fenson, L., Kagan, J., Kearsley, R. B., and Zelazo, R. 1976. The developmental progression of manipulative play in the first two years. Child Dev. 47:232–236.

Ferrier, L. 1978. Word, context and imitation. In A. Lock (ed.), Action, Gesture and Symbol, pp. 471–483. Academic Press, Inc. New York.

Fowler, W. 1977. Sequence and styles in cognitive development. In I. C. Uzgiris, and F. Weizmann (eds.), The Structuring of Experience, pp. 265–295. Plenum Publishing Corp. New York.

Garvey, C. 1977. Play. Harvard University Press, Cambridge, Mass.

Gray, H. 1978. Learning to take an object from mother. In A. Lock (ed.), Action, Gesture and Symbol, pp. 159–182. Academic Press, Inc. New York.

Guillaume, P. 1971. Imitation in Children. University of Chicago Press, Chicago. (Originally published in 1926.)

Habermas, J. 1972. Knowledge and Human Interests. Heinemann, London.

Hamm, M., Russell, M., and Koepke, J. 1979. Neonatal imitation? Paper presented at the SRCD meetings, March, San Francisco.

Hayes, L. A., and Watson, J. S. 1979. Neonatal imitation: Fact or artifact? Paper presented at the SRCD meetings, March, San Francisco.

Hubley, P., and Trevarthen, C. 1979. Sharing a task in infancy. In I. C. Uzgiris (ed.), New Directions for Child Development, No. 4: Social Interaction and Communication during Infancy, pp. 57–80. Jossey-Bass, San Francisco.

Hutt, C. 1970. Specific and diversive exploration. In H. W. Reese, and L. P. Lipsitt (eds.), Advances in Child Development and Behavior, pp. 119–180. Vol. 5. Academic Press, New York.

Inhelder, B., Lezine, I., Sinclair, H., and Stambak, M. 1972. Le debut de la fonction symbolique. 'The appearance of symbolic function.' Arch. Psychol. 41:187–243.

Jacobson, J. L. 1979. The role of inanimate objects in early peer interaction. Paper presented at SRCD meetings, March. San Francisco.

Jacobson, S. W., and Kagan, J. 1978. Released responses in early infancy. Paper presented at the International Conference on Infant Studies, March, Providence, R.I.

Keenan, E. O. 1977. Making it last: Repetition in children's discourse. In S. Ervin-Tripp, and C. Mitchell-Kernan (eds.), Child Discourse, pp. 125–138. Academic Press, New York.

Killen, M., and Uzgiris, I. C. 1979. Imitation of actions with objects: The role of social meaning. Unpublished manuscript.

Kogan, N. 1976. Cognitive Styles in Infancy and Early Childhood. John Wiley, & Sons, Inc. New York.

Lewis, M., and Brooks-Gunn, J. 1979. Social Cognition and the Acquisition of Self. Academic Press, New York.

Lock, A. (ed.) 1978. Action, Gesture and Symbol. Academic Press, Inc. New York.

Lowe, M. 1975. Trends in the development of representational play in infants from one to three years. J. Child Psychol. Psychiatry. 16:33–47.

Macmurray, J. 1961. Persons in Relation. Faber and Faber, Ltd. London.

McCall, R. B. 1974. Exploratory manipulation and play in the human infant. Monographs of the Society for Research in Child Development. 39, No. 2 (Serial No. 155). Published by the University of Chicago Press, Chicago, Ill. for the Society for Research in Child Development.

McCall, R. B., Eichorn, D. H., and Hogarty, P. S. 1977. Transitions in early mental development. Monographs of the Society for Research in Child Development. 42, No. 3 (Serial No. 171). Published by the University of Chicago Press, Chicago, Ill. for the Society for Research in Child Development.

McCall, R. B., Parke, R. D., and Kavanaugh, R. D. 1977. Imitation of live and televised models by children 1–3 years of age. Monographs of the Society for Research in Child Development, 42, No. 5 (Serial No. 173). Published by the University of Chicago Press, Chicago, Ill. for the Society for Research in Child Development.

Maratos, O. 1973. The origin and development of imitation in the first six months of life. Paper presented at the British Psychological Association annual meeting, Liverpool.

Mead, G. H. 1934. Mind, Self and Society. University of Chicago Press, Chicago.

Meltzoff, A. N., and Moore, M. K. 1977. Imitation of facial and manual gestures by human neonates. Science. 198:75–78.

Millar, S. 1968. The Psychology of Play. Penguin Books, New York.

Moerk, E., and Moerk, C. 1979. Quotations, imitations, and generalizations. Int. J. Behav. Dev. 2;43–72.

Mueller, E. 1979. (Toddlers and toys) = (An autonomous social system). In M. Lewis, and L. A. Rosenblum (eds.) The Child and its Family. Plenum Publishing Corp. New York.

Newson, J. 1978. Dialogue and development. In A. Lock (ed.), Action, Gesture and Symbol. Academic Press, Inc. New York.

Newson, J., and Pawlby, S. 1972. Imitation and pre-verbal communication. Nottingham University, Unpublished paper.

Nicolich, L. McC. 1977. Beyond sensorimotor intelligence: Assessment of symbolic maturity through analysis of pretend play. Merrill-Palmer Q. 23:89–99.

Ninio, A., and Bruner, J. 1978. The achievement and antecedents of labelling. J. Child Lang. 5:1–15.

Papousek, H., and Papousek, M. 1977. Mothering and the cognitive headstart: Psycho-biological considerations. In H. R. Schaffer (ed.), Studies in Mother-Infant Interaction, Academic Press, Inc. New York.

Parton, D. A. 1976. Learning to imitate in infancy. Child Dev. 47:14–31.

Pawlby, S. J. 1977. Imitative interaction. In H. R. Schaffer (ed.), Studies in Mother-Infant Interaction. Academic Press, Inc. New York.

Piaget, J. 1962. Play, Dreams and Imitation in Childhood. Norton, New York

Piaget, J. 1971. Biology and Knowledge. University of Chicago Press, Chicago.

Ratner, N., and Bruner, J. 1978. Games, social exchange, and the acquisition of language. J. Child Lang. 5:391–401.

Rodgon, M. M., and Kurdek, L. A. 1977. Vocal and gestural imitation in 8-, 14-, and 20-month-old children. J. Genetic Psychol. 131:115–123.

Ross, H. S. and Kay, D. A. 1980. The origins of social games. In K. H. Rubin (ed.), New Directions for Child Development, pp. 17–31. No. 9: Children's Play. Jossey-Bass, San Francisco.

Rotman, B. 1977. Jean Piaget: Psychologist of the Real. Cornell University Press, New York.

Schaffer, H. R. (ed.), 1977. Studies in Mother-Infant Interaction. Academic Press, Inc. New York.

Shields, M. M. 1978. The child as psychologist. In A. Lock (ed.), Action, Gesture and Symbol, pp. 529–556. Academic Press, Inc. New York.

Stern, D. N. 1974. Mother and infant at play. In M. Lewis, and L. Rosenblum (eds.), The Effect of the Infant on its Caregiver, pp. 187–213. John Wiley, & Sons New York.

Trevarthen, C. 1977. Descriptive analyses of infant communicative behaviour, pp. 227–270. In H. R. Schaffer (ed.), Studies in Mother-Infant Interaction. Academic Press, Inc. New York.

Trevarthen, C., and Hubley, P. 1978. Secondary intersubjectivity: Confidence, confiding, and acts of meaning in the first year. In A. Lock (ed.), Action, Gesture and Symbol, pp. 183–229. Academic Press, Inc. New York.

Uzgiris, I. C. 1967. Ordinality in the development of schemas for relating to objects. In J. Hellmuth (ed.), The Exceptional Infant, Vol. 1. Special Child Publications, pp. 315–334. Seattle.

Uzgiris, I. C. 1972. Patterns of vocal and gestural imitation in infants. In F. J. Monks, W. W. Hartup, and J. de Witt (eds.), Determinants of Behavioral Development, pp. 467–471. Academic Press, Inc. New York.

Uzgiris, I. C. 1976. Infant development from a Piagetian approach. Merrill-Palmer Q. 22:3–10.

Uzgiris, I. C. 1977. Plasticity and structure. In I. C. Uzgiris, and F. Weizmann (eds.), pp. 89–113. The Structuring of Experience. Plenum, Publishing Corp. New York.

Uzgiris, I. C. 1979. Die Mannigfaltigkeit der Imitation in der frühen Kindheit. 'The many faces of imitation in early childhood.' In L. Montada (ed.), Brennpunkte der Entwicklungspsychologie. Verlag W. Kohlhammer, Stuttgart.

Uzgiris, I. C., and Hunt, J. McV. 1975. Assessment in Infancy. University of Illinois Press, Urbana, Ill.

Vygotsky, L. S. 1978. Mind in Society. Harvard University Press, Cambridge, Mass.

Waite, L. H. 1979. Early imitation with several models. Paper presented at the Society for Research in Child Development meetings, March, San Francisco.

Waite, L. H., and Lewis, M. 1979. Early imitation. Unpublished manuscript.

Watson, M. W., and Fischer, K. W. 1977. A developmental sequence of agent use in late infancy. Child Dev. 48:828–836.

Weir, R. 1962. Language in the Crib. Mouton, Hague.

Wohlwill, J. F. 1973. The Study of Behavioral Development. Academic Press, Inc. New York.

Zukow, P. G., Reilley, J., and Greenfield, P. M. Making the absent present: Facilitating the transition from sensorimotor to linguistic communication. *In* K. Nelson (ed.), Children's Language, Vol. 3. Gardner Press. New York. In Press.

chapter

4

Some Theoretical Considerations in the Design of Language Intervention Programs

Summary Chapter

Earl C. Butterfield

Department of Pediatrics
University of Kansas Medical Center
Kansas City, Kansas

Richard L. Schiefelbusch

Bureau of Child Research
University of Kansas
Lawrence, Kansas

contents

The purpose of the conference whose proceedings are reported in this book was to air the best thoughts of basic and applied scientists about how to design and implement intervention programs to facilitate language development in developmentally delayed children. The conferees accepted the practical and socially important goal of developing a prescription for effective language training for infants and small children; but they knew in advance that, even in aggregate, their knowledge of the relevant areas of science was not up to task. The functional goal of the conferees was to foster the *improvement* of early language intervention programs (however they could). If science cannot yet fulfill all of our hopes for it, it should at least help us do better.

Basic science can improve intervention programming in two ways. It can create new understandings of normal speech, language, and hearing functioning, and it can yield techniques to diagnose and treat abnormal functioning. Because the primary purpose of basic behavioral research is to create new understandings of normal functioning, it will at any time be more likely to do this than to create techniques for diagnosing and treating abnormal functioning. A practical yield of diagnostic and treatment techniques is likely to result from basic research only when understanding of a type of behavior is relatively complete and when investigators deliberately attempt to extend new understandings to abnormal behavior. Neither of these conditions has been met in the study of speech perception, discussed by Trehub and her colleagues (see Chapter 1), the study of child language, discussed by Cromer (see Chapter 2), or the study of social development, discussed by Uzgiris (see Chapter 3). The value of considering these fields in relation to language intervention programming lies in the possibility that they have created insights from which new approaches to teaching language can be derived. Accordingly, the conferees looked to the papers by Trehub, Cromer, and Uzgiris for theoretical and conceptual inspiration, not for how-to-do-it prescriptions.

INFANT SPEECH PERCEPTION

Innate and constitutional factors are important in the development of speech and language. Sometimes constitutional factors limit experience, as when congenital deafness causes severe speech impairment. Perhaps children who have normal hearing nevertheless suffer speech and language impairments because of experiential limits resulting from inadequate perception of speech that they hear perfectly well. That possibility is the reason for considering at this conference what is known about speech perception and its development. The question is whether language intervention programmers should try to improve children's speech perception by promoting skills needed to extract phonetic and linguistic information from speech in order to prevent speech and language problems.

The prevailing view of speech perception and its development grew from research demonstrating that very young infants perceive speech as well as adults. This research also demonstrated that adults perceive speech differently from how they perceive other auditory stimuli. This research promoted the prevailing view that innate constitutional factors determine how persons perceive speech. According to this view, language interventionists should not waste their time trying to promote speech perception in order to prevent language disorders.

Trehub effectively challenges this view, thereby providing reasons for interveners to consider the possibility of promoting perceptual skills. She cites diverse data to show that speech is probably not perceived differently from other auditory signals. The data come from comparative studies of lower primates' "categorical" discrimination of synthetic speech signals, studies of adults' "categorical" perception of nonspeech signals, and developmental studies of infants' discrimination of various speech and nonspeech sounds. The conclusion is inescapable: speech is not perceived as uniquely as it is usually purported to be. Speech is probably not perceived uniquely at all. Trehub also cites data to show that speech perception does develop. This introduces the possibility that the considerable body of theory about the development of visual perception will apply to the development of speech perception. According to the prevailing view, visual theory is irrelevant to speech phenomena. By challenging the prevailing view, Trehub provides theoretical and conceptual hope that intervention programs may one day include instruction in speech perception skills.

Partly because of the hegemony of the prevailing view of speech perception, studies of infants' psychoacoustic capacities are seldom undertaken. Yet, if speech is perceived as other auditory signals, it is essential to understand infants' psychoacoustic capabilities and their development in order to build adequate conceptions of how to influence speech perception. Fortunately, the psychoacoustic capabilities of adults have been studied extensively, and the technical problems of stimulus manufacture and scaling are far less formidable in the realm of psychoacoustics than in the realm of speech perception. Unfortunately, considerable methodological work needs to be done before sound comparisons can be made among infants and older persons. Trehub documents the differences among techniques used to study auditory functions of infants and older people, and she gives reasons to believe that the technical differences will influence conclusions about psychoacoustic capabilities. Nevertheless, procedural progress is being made, and it seems not too unrealistic to anticipate the collection of data that will allow sounder decisions about whether to include perceptual instruction in language training programs. For now, it is enough to have the conceptual and theoretical justification to seek the data, and Trehub has justified that neatly in her contribution to this conference.

CHILD LANGUAGE—ACQUISITION OF STRUCTURE

Cromer takes the position that little progress has been made in recent years in understanding the way children acquire the structure of language. He acknowledges the importance given to communication and the rules of functional use in language intervention programs, but argues that the formal structure of language should be taught and that one must understand "internal factors"—the cognitive processes that serve the development of syntax and semantics. He laments that the recent work on language intervention has not "fulfilled expectations" in advancing knowledge of internal (epigenetic) factors. He speculates that there has been a conceptual prejudice against innateness theories. In particular, there has been a reluctance to accept as a premise for research the notion that children have a species-specific capability for perceiving, acquiring, and using the universals of language. He argues that research data will remain empirically slanted and inadequate unless this reluctance is overcome. To illustrate his point, Cromer focuses on the work of Newport, Gleitman, and Gleitman (1977), which shows that motherese does not provide a program of instruction tailored to the child's limits, but rather presents complex, fully "grammatical" language from which the child must somehow extract rules. Cromer argues that empiricists, by which he means language programmers, ignore these data and persist in behavioral stimulation with no sound theoretical rationale. Cromer urges the consideration of two reconceptualizations in order to balance the emphasis in the direction of the standard theory of syntax acquisition.

A *first reconceptualization* is to emphasize the uniqueness of the human species (child) for acquiring language. He characterizes this uniqueness as "a number of unfolding developmental phenomena, some of which may be specifically linguistic, that interact with environmental variables." His position is not that children are born with particular structures, but that structures are built from an interaction of innate potential with environmental factors. Cromer takes the epigenetic position that innate and environmental factors interact, thereby endorsing a centrist point of view on the nature-nurture controversy. He takes as his mission, however, the balancing of the two functions in favor of nature. He feels that psychologists have skewed their language research in favor of environmental influences, and he is trying to balance the picture.

He draws his arguments from research on infant perception, language universals, and the connection between cognitive development and linguistic encoding. In regard to the latter, he concludes that children do not acquire thought and linguistic rules in a one-to-one correspondence. In other words, prelinguistic cognition does not give a child particular categories and structures for his language. Cromer raises the possibility that some linguistic principles are innate, thus agreeing with Chomsky that there are innate proclivities and inborn language processes.

A second reconceptualization is presented in terms of *specific deficits*. Cromer examines a number of studies of impaired processes—that is, deficits in memory, linguistic processing, auditory processing, phonological processing, sequencing, and hierarchical planning. He raises several intriguing issues, especially in regard to memory, rate of auditory processing, and hierarchical planning. He urges the consideration of specific, individualized assessments for language impaired children so that interventions can be tailored to the child's deficits. This approach is contrasted with use of broad deficit categories—that is, aphasia, autism, dyslexia, etc.—or a global stage of cognitive development. Because children are obviously active learners, and one child is different from another, care should be taken to remain sensitive to each child's weaknesses and strengths when selecting intervention strategies. Cromer assumes that close attention to specific deficits will help interventionists to individualize their approaches.

His proposed method is to discover deficits in a child's processing, and then to repair the direct effects of the deficits by specific skill training. This approach is not used in the United States as often now as it was 15 years ago. A problem with the procedure is that even after the deficient skill has been taught, it may not generalize beyond the training setting. Also, it is difficult to demonstrate that the newly taught skill combines with other skills to effect language acquisition. The contrastive rationales used in other chapters on intervention call for assessments of language structures and functions, and then targeting of the skills to be taught, either formally or informally. The issue is the teaching of skills assumed to undergird language development on the one hand (Cromer), or on the other (interveners), the teaching of functional language features that the child will actively use.

For instance, Bricker and Carlson (Chapter 15, this volume) emphasize that language development is integrally related to concomitantly developing cognitive and affective systems. They urged that environmental contexts and complex interactive feedback networks should be used by language interventionists. Ramey, Sparling, and Wasik (Chapter 14, this volume) use parental caregiving contexts as settings for intervention. They assume that mothers can provide appropriate environmental stimulation. Fowler (Chapter 16, this volume) also uses early stimulation as a means for promoting language acquisition. Kysela et al. (Chapter 11, this volume) emphasize the importance of an instructional environment. Cromer acknowledges the prominence of these approaches but is nonetheless convinced that the long-term language acquisition and intervention goals are best served by close attention to epigenetic features.

SOCIAL EXPERIENCE

Language intervention programs are exercises in social engineering. Even though special physical environs may be provided, the emphasis in intervention is on interaction between infants and specially responding adults. It is as if the guiding hypothesis is that specialized social experience will promote greater linguistic and cognitive growth than at-risk infants and children would otherwise achieve. The paradox, which Uzgiris addresses directly, is that Piagetian theory gives primacy to experience with the physical world and indeed denies the importance of social experience as a determinant of cognitive growth. Uzgiris's chapter contributes an extremely important conceptual inspiration for language interveners, by analyzing Piagetian theory (1962, 1972) and contrasting it with the ideas of Vygotsky (1978) and such British theorists as Trevarthen (1978), thereby providing a sweeping theoretical justification for using social interaction to promote mental development.

Although language programmers have not often taken inspiration from Piaget, they have used imitation as a teaching device. Piaget's is a highly developed theory of imitation, and that theory has been the impetus for much developmental research. Uzgiris masterfully summarizes Piaget's view of imitation and the points of disagreement with that view raised by recent research (especially recent research with neonates); and she highlights gaps in our empirical knowledge about imitation, especially our ignorance of its characteristics during the bulk of the first year of life. Using imitation as a vehicle for her considerations of the role of social experience certainly creates close contact between her analysis and the practice of language intervention. This should increase the chances of further elaborating the theoretical rationale for the use of imitation. Focusing on play should have an analagous effect because the social interactions by which infants are taught must often take the form of play.

Uzgiris's contribution to the theory of language intervention is to increase the likelihood that such rich views as those of Piaget, Trevarthen, and Vygotsky will be brought to bear in the design of intervention procedures.

DISCUSSION

Cromer's assumptions about innate and constitutional (epigenetic) factors are in general agreement with the prevailing view of speech perception. Both positions are based on research that seems to show that the infant possesses a special capacity to relate to speech and language events. Cromer's assumptions are advanced to explain why infants can extract rule features from complex speech events. Likewise, the prevailing view of speech perception contends that innate constitutional factors determine how children perceive speech. Trehub considers this position of innateness in speech perception but rejects most of it. In somewhat the same way, Uzgiris, in Chapter 3, presents experience as a principal part of the explanation for early language aptitudes. These divergent positions in regard to the relevant importance of constitutional or innate factors, on the one hand, and experiential features on the other, provide an intriguing design for analyzing all three chapters in this section.

Chapters 2 and 3 also differ in their analyses of Piaget's contributions to the acquisition of language. Although Cromer and Uzgiris make extensive reference to Piaget, they deliver substantially different messages. Cromer points out that Piaget's cognitive stages do not explain the infant's ability to extract language rules. Also, Piaget's cognitive theory does not provide a basis for a theory of syntax—prelinguistic cognition does not give children particular categories and structures for their language. In this sense, Piaget's developmental cognitive theory fails to explain children's aptitudes as language learners.

Uzgiris examines Piagetian theory of social development. She observes that social and cultural variables are given second place to general coordinations resulting from self-regulation. When discussing the role of experience, Piaget generally focuses on the child's solitary interactions with the world of objects. This position differs from Vygotsky's view of the origin of cognitive structures. According to Vygotsky, cognitive structures are achieved in joint activity with persons who are already members of a sociocultural group. This agrees with Thoman's and Chapman's discussions of mother/child interaction and protoaction behavior of preverbal children during play. Also, Uzgiris provides an intriguing account of imitation and play in infancy. In combination, these chapters extend the early acquisitional picture beyond the epigenetic—transactional perspective.

It is difficult to evaluate Cromer's effort to put internal factors and specific deficits into perspective, both for acquisition and intervention. He has succeeded in assessing and synthesizing a great amount of relevant and useful information. Along the way he urges us to look more closely at the structure of language and at the way it is actively acquired. He also offers an approach to children with specific processing deficits, although he is not operationally clear how this information can be used to plan refined and specific interventions.

Perhaps Cromer's primary contribution to this discussion is to establish a rationale for more research on the acquisition of language structure. This research effort should test the premise that innate aptitudes produce rule-governed language under conditions of limited stimulation. It is equally important, however, to continue to test the premise that enriched environmental arrangements can successfully stimulate the development of functional language.

REFERENCES

Newport, E. L., Gleitman, H., and Gleitman, L. R. 1977. I'd rather do it myself: Some effects and non-effects of maternal speech style. *In* C. E. Snow and C. A. Ferguson (eds.), Talking to Children: Language Input and Acquisition, pp. 109–149. Cambridge University Press, Cambridge.
Piaget, J. 1962. Play, Dreams and Imitation in Childhood. W & W Norton Co., Inc., New York.
Piaget, J. 1971. Biology and Knowledge. University of Chicago Press, Chicago.
Trevarthen, C. 1978. Descriptive analysis of infant communicative behavior. *In* H. R. Schaffer (ed.), Studies in Mother-Infant Interaction. Academic Press, New York.
Vygotsky, L. S. 1978. Mind in Society. Harvard University Press, Cambridge, Mass.

Section II

Mother–Child Interaction

chapter

5

Affective Communication as the Prelude and Context for Language Learning

Evelyn B. Thoman

Department of Biobehavioral Sciences
University of Connecticut
Storrs, Connecticut

contents

Language is one of man's most complex expressions of cognitive functioning. Thus the study of the precursors of language development has generally been carried out within the framework expressed by Bruner (1975a) "... whoever studies prelinguistic precursors of language must commit himself to the 'cognitive hypothesis.'" This chapter is concerned with the precursors of language development, and the perspective presented diverges dramatically from the cognitive hypothesis. The basic notions developed are: 1) that *affect* is more appropriate as the major organizing concept for the infant's earliest communication experiences; and 2) assuming that affective forms of communication precede, influence, and subsequently become integrated with linguistic (i.e., cognitive) communication, disruption of early social-affective relations may be a prelude to later emotional and language disorders. The objectives of this chapter are to provide biological and behavioral evidence for these views and to indicate the implications of this perspective for the study of the infant's earliest communicative behaviors.

MODELS FOR THE STUDY OF PRELINGUISTIC COMMUNICATION

Cognition has been the overriding emphasis in the study of the infant's prelinguistic social interactions. The child acquires strategies for enlisting aid and achieving ends in the course of joint activities through the priming experiences of early mother-infant interactions. From these experiences, the child acquires expectations and conceptualizations about people and the environment that later provide the basis for grammar. Thus, cognitive development prior to the use of speech is considered to be the major source of continuity between prespeech communication and language (Bruner, 1978).

This rationale, derived from the cognitive hypothesis, has encouraged research designed to explore how, during the period before the child is capable of language, interactions with the mother and father, grandparents, peers, etc. provide the child with a working model of the world. Bruner (1975b) stated, "whatever view one takes of research on language acquisition proper . . . one must still come to terms with the role or significance of the child's prespeech communication system." Numerous studies have explored the child's acquisition of concepts and schemas within the context of social relationships. These studies are important because they focus on events that may serve as precursors of language in babies as young as 6 months old. The recognition that significant experiences are occurring this early has had a major impact on the study of early development.

Social interaction and its influence on cognitive function has been extended even earlier in recent research: 3 months seems to be the magical age because of the appearance of the social smile. The smile is of great interest because it can communicate to the world—and especially to the research observer—something about what the baby "knows." From the smile, the observer can infer recognition of a familiar person, objects, or a significant event. It can even signal the infant's pleasure in accomplishment of a challenging task (Papousek and Papousek, 1975; Watson, 1979). Thus, the expression of pleasure at 3 months of age is a clue to cognitive competence and provides a research handle to the study of the beginnings of the infant's capacity for communication. The trend toward an interest in the emergence of cognitive competence at earlier and earlier ages is clearly associated with a major interest in the relevance of this competence for later and more complex cognitive functioning, including language.

Studies of social interaction in infants even younger than 3 months old have also been concerned with cognitive implications. A common dependent variable for the effects of early interaction is later mental development of the infant.

Not all researchers in early infancy, especially those concerned with early social interaction, are committed to the cognitive hypothesis. An alternative framework—which can be called the organismic hypothesis—is characterized by the objective of identifying the nature of the socioemotional processes by which mother and infant adapt to each other. Their mutual adaptation is viewed as being achieved through a continuous feedback system resulting in mutual modification of behaviors. Thus, the nature of this feedback system is basically that of a communication system.

It would not be reasonable to presume that this earliest communication is in any way intentional in nature—certainly, not on the part of the infant, and much of it is not even on the part of the mother. Thus, it would also not be reasonable to expect that a cognitive or a sequential, linguistic model would be completely applicable for analysis and understanding of communication during the earliest weeks of life. On this point, we agree with Chomsky (1967)! Rather, communication of the newborn with the mother or caretaker primarily takes the form of interdigitation of behavioral rhythms of the two partners, with variations in the state of each partner and variation in intensity of expression of these states as basic elements. This mutual adaptation, or communication, is biologically determined; it is based on interactive capabilities of the newborn organism that have derived from the evolutionary process; and it is a critical form of early adaptation that assures the infant's survival. The newborn infant's needs must be met before the infant can "know" the existence of these needs or how they might be met by the external world. The mother's involvement *must* be integrated with the infant's ongoing status expression. From these notions, the term *organismic hypothesis* is derived for referring to these characteristics of the mother-and-infant communication, which can be studied from the time of birth.

Such a hypothesis clearly does not preclude concomitant cognitive development. Cognitions are undoubtedly accruing from experiential events occurring from birth, and thus integration of affect and cognition begins at this early time. Their integration is evident in studies of the infant's earliest learning. For example, Butterfield has shown that 2-day-old infants can learn to suck in a specific burst-pause pattern to hear a preferred auditory stimulus (Cairns and Butterfield, 1975). Research including the study of learning at 3 days of age in infant rats was done by Thoman, Wetzel, and Levine (1968) and in infant humans by Thoman, Korner, and Beason-Williams (1977). In each of these cases, preferences or approaches were expressed in terms of acquired behaviors. These and other studies, which are referred to below, reveal not only learning capabilities in neonatal organisms, but also the presence and potency of evaluations that occur without prior learning or experience (Bowlby, 1969). Although behavioral modifications may be occurring from the beginning of life, these cannot be learned rapidly enough to assure survival at this immature stage of life. Breland and Breland (1966) reached the same conclusion:

> If we study even the externally visible behaviors of the incredible number of species in the animal world . . . we can see that most organisms enter the world prepared to cope with it . . . learning is not one of nature's most prevalent ways of guaranteeing the preservation and reproduction of the individual or the species . . . (p. 40).

Given the acceptance of an initial mutual exchange that can best be described as affective in nature and that functions as a communication system, the following sections concern some major issues raised by this position. Then, a summary of our longitudinal project is presented, with illustrative data. The Connecticut Longitudinal Study involves intensive observations of the earliest interactive behaviors of mothers and infants, with the objective of exploring the nature of their earliest adaptive process—their first communication network.

CAN THE NEWBORN INFANT BE A PARTNER IN COMMUNICATION

A major theme in research in infancy over the past several decades has been the competence of the newborn: the infant's capacity to perceive, to respond, to learn, and to adapt to the early social environment. The newborn is no longer perceived as a passive recipient of maternal ministrations, but an active participant in the social milieu from the first day of life. Yet the capacity for communication is still seriously questioned:

The baby's initial contributions to (the) diadic process consists mainly of nonspecific crying (Eveloff, 1977, p. 1897).

. . . communication waits the development of the child's systematic use of expressive behaviors (Mayo and La France, 1978, p. 214).

. . . non-verbal communication is already working in *three-year*-olds (italics added) (Jones, 1977, p. 277).

When mothers were asked to communicate with infants of one week (in the laboratory), they were essentially being asked to communicate with beings commonly thought 'nonintentional.' Our mothers were faced with the problem of communicating with infants who . . . were . . . unresponsive . . . (Brazelton, Koslowski, and Main, 1974, p. 68).

In human ontogeny, the earliest behavior with even a marginal claim to the label 'communicative' is the global cry of the neonate . . . (Lamendella, 1977, p. 191).

This chapter's perspective is clearly a contrary one, namely that the newborn infant is not only an adapting but a communicating organism from the time of birth. There is now a vast literature depicting the perceptual, responsive, and learning capabilities of the newborn. After describing newly discovered adaptive capabilities of the newborn, the numerous studies in the past two decades concluded with a statement that from the time of birth the infant is an active, not a passive, participant in his or her social environment. It is now accepted that the newborn infant is biologically designed for survival in a social context. Therefore, the infant is, of necessity, a "born communicator."

Within this view, communication may have characteristics unique to this stage of development that require special explanatory principles differing from those designed to model exchanges occurring later. The nature of this communication and its implication for cognitive development and the acquisition of language has hardly been explored.

The proposal that early social skills should be viewed as a communicative capability may be clarified by considering the various interpretations of the term *communication*.

CRITERIA FOR APPLYING THE TERM *COMMUNICATION*

There are different definitions and criteria for communication, and an explicit definition is not presented here. There are some distinctions, however, that are relevant to the possible application of the term *communication* to the interactive behaviors of the newborn infant.

One distinction is between an extremely restrictive definition of communication—that the term only applies to those situations in which culturally acquired codes are exchanged between persons—and a broader definition that is not so loose as to lose any meaning. Clearly, the extremely restrictive definition precludes any further discussion of communication in early infancy. The vast literature on animal communication, however, provides a potent argument for the heuristic value of a broader definition.

Another consideration is whether communication, even though nonverbal, must be propositional in nature (i.e., gestures that are learned substitutes of codes, or words). Most research in nonverbal communication is concerned with the use of gestures as an intentional transmission of a propositional message. This concern is exemplified even at the animal level by the work of Thorpe (1972), who considered the extent to which communication in various species of animals possess the design features of human language. Again, the human infant cannot qualify as a communicator within such a framework. Within his formal framework, Chomsky (1979) would agree with this conclusion. Furthermore, he would also dismiss the application of linguistic models to animals. There is "no striking similarity between animal (or infant) communication systems and human language" (Chomsky, 1967, p. 73).

Some researchers require both intention *and* transmission of propositional messages as necessary constituents of communication. This perspective requires intention, cognitive schemas, and a formalized code system. A different perspective is needed to account for the exchanges among animals and between young infants and their parents. This perspective would provide a distinction between affective and cognitive components of communication, including language. With these restrictions, as well as those already mentioned, the denial of communicative ability to the infant would only be appropriate.

SEPARATION OF AFFECTIVE AND PROPOSITIONAL COMPONENTS OF COMMUNICATION

Language has affective and propositional components. Many researchers have separated the cognitive and affective aspects of communication. If it is reasonable to separate cognitive and affective processes conceptually and functionally, it is also reasonable to propose that the developmental course of cognitive processing may not parallel that for affective processing, even though the two may seem inseparably integrated. Furthermore, it is also reasonable to propose that communication need not await the cognitive competence required for propositional schemas.

Monrad-Krohn (1947, 1963) examined the cognitive and affective aspects of language. He found speech to be comprised of 1) vocabulary, 2) grammar, and 3) prosody. Prosody is the melodic line produced by the variations of pitch, rhythm, and stress of pronunciation that bestow both semantic and emotional meaning to speech. Then he partitioned prosody into four additional categories: 1) intrinsic prosody, 2) intellectual prosody, 3) emotional prosody, which conveys anger, pleasure, fear, sorrow, etc., and 4) inarticulate prosody, characterized by grunts and nonlinguistic sounds. The first two forms of prosody are cognitively determined and culturally derived and they are intimately involved in propositional speech, whereas emotional and inarticulate prosody represent the affective aspects of speech. The integration of both propositional and affective components of speech generate the full spectrum of language.

This conceptual separation of cognitive and affective expression may seem artificial. Recent evidence, however, supports this separation on the biological level. Ross and Mesulam (1979) described two adult patients who lost the ability to impart affective qualities to their speech after lesions developed in the right hemisphere. These patients only spoke in a monotone, and did not exhibit gestures that were appropriate to the implied emotional message in the words they uttered. One of these patients, who was a teacher and mother, reported serious difficulties in controlling her class and her own children as well because she had no capacity to communicate the degree of urgency in her messages. Brain scans in each of these patients revealed lesions in the right hemisphere which were symmetrical to Broca's area in the left hemisphere. Their findings indicated that the anatomical organization of cortex areas subserving affective speech in the right hemisphere is similar to the organization of the cortical areas subserving propositional speech in the left hemisphere.

In keeping with the notion that the right hemisphere has a special function in the modulation of emotional behavior, Ross and Mesulam concluded that the right hemisphere is responsible for prosody, the coloring, melody, and cadence of speech, along with emotional gesturing. Thus, the central neural processing of propositional and affective aspects of speech apparently is lateralized in adults.

Neurological evidence for the separation of these two constituents of speech in adults supports the suggestion offered here that these two components of communication may develop at different times and at different rates early in life. Thus, the affective component may take precedence and prevail during the neonatal period. Evidence in this regard comes from the study of brain lateralization in newborn infants. Using simple nonspeech stimuli, Wada (1977) demonstrated hemispheric asymmetries in neonates. These findings support Wada's interpretation that, even at this young age, the right hemisphere is more able to process stimuli that are not easily identifiable or referable. "These capabilities would not be based on language and hence would be expected to develop independently and possibly before speech'' (p. 377).

Although perception is firmly linked to cognition in the older infant (Decarie, 1978), Stechler and Carpenter (1967) point to attention as an affective expression in the newborn. They concluded that sensory-affective intelligence develops before sensorimotor intelligence and that the earliest feedback relationships are affected through this sensory-affective system.

Lamendella (1977) reported specific neurological evidence. He reviewed the literature on the role of the limbic system in social and communicative behavior and discusses the evolution of the limbic system and its development in human ontogeny. He pointed out that over and above intentional nonverbal communication schemata, there are still other forms of nonpropositional multimodal behavior patterns that communicate. Both are products of neural elements "other than the neocortical structures on which neurolinguists have focused their attention" (p. 159). The level of brain activity likely to be responsible for the bulk of nonpropositional human communication is the *limbic system*. This network of cortical and subcortical structures has more often been thought of only in relation to regulation of emotion and motivation, but in fact its range of functional responsibilities is quite large and includes major segments of social and communicative behavior. Man shares these structures homologously with other mammals, and for nonhuman primates the limbic system comprises the level of neural activity that controls behavior patterns for interacting with others in the environment. "Furthermore, the majority of the limbic functions acquired by the child remain part of the adult communication repertoire as a neural behavioral framework into which linguistic communication is imbedded" (p. 159).

In view of the behavioral and neural evidence, it is reasonable to consider affect and cognition as separable processes, and to postulate the earlier expression of affect during development. Thus, it may not be sufficient to consider affective expression of the infant, such as smiling, as having implication primarily for cognition (propositional) communication. The smiles of the infant may be of greater significance because they express *affect*, and because they communicate affect to the mother. The infant's expressive behaviors elicit affective responses from the mother and participate in the ongoing feedback relationship that is necessary to assure the infant's survival.

From this reasoning it can be concluded that the earliest communication system is primarily an affective one—the behaviors of mother and infant are integrated through the expression, reception, and reaction to affective behaviors of each member of the dyad.

THE INFANT'S SIDE OF THE AFFECTIVE COMMUNICATION SYSTEM

Anyone who has spent time watching newborns is aware that their faces are highly expressive. Some forms of that expression are: smiles, frowns, grimaces, looks of bewilderment, mouth puckering, tongue protrusion, sucking and other forms of mouthing, bright eyes, dull eyes, and eyes shut tightly during crying. Motor movements are equally expressive and range from small and slow displacement of the limbs to very large, rounded movements of the limbs and trunk, movements that involve a great deal of twitching, jerky or tremulous motion, and larger movements including stretching, writhing, and head turning. Each baby has an individual repertoire of these behaviors as they are combined during states of sleep and wakefulness (Thoman, 1975a, 1975b, Thoman, Korner and Kraemer, 1976). Likewise, each baby exhibits patterns of movements in an individual fashion in response to external stimulation. Associated with the wide range of motor patterns is the range of behavioral states that the baby exhibits over time—alertness, drowsing, dazing, sleep-wake transition, and the sleeping states including quiet sleep, active sleep, and active-quiet transition sleep (Wolff, 1966; Thoman, 1975a).

The infant's states and motility reflect ongoing changes in attention and affective status (Stechler and Carpenter, 1967), even though they may not reflect specific affective states as we know them in the adult. When expressions of the newborn infant, however, *are* analogous to ones seen in the adult, such as excitement, distress, quiet wonder, surprise, or bewilderment, it is clear that researchers generally do not accept these expressions at "face" value.

". . . Crying is the only clear affect expression during the first 2 months. The infant is either crying or 'contented' " (Emde, Gainsbauer, and Harmon, 1976). This view is tied to the position that the infant does not have the capacity to experience or express "specific" emotions until cognitive development has provided schemas about which the baby can have emotions, thus the emphasis on the appearance of the social smile (Stroufe, 1977). Lewis, Brooks, and Haviland (1978) provided an extreme statement of this position: the infant does not experience affect until the latter part of the first year when it is possible to have a notion of self-consciousness. Thus, there is a general conviction that cognitive development is the fundamental process that permits the emergence of affect.

These convictions about the lack of affective competence of the newborn infant are consistent with the views cited above with respect to the infant's early lack of capacity for communication. Both views reflect the assumption that cognitive capabilities are fundamental to the potential of the infant for either experiencing or expressing affect or for being engaged in the communicative process.

This chapter suggests that the requisites should be reversed, that is, that affect is fundamental for the development of cognition, and their integration in this sequence permits the acquisition of culturally determined expressions of affect and other learned codes for communication.

A promising note is offered by some naturalistic observations of infants. Wolff (1966, 1973) spent as much as 32 hours per week watching individual babies in their homes. He noted a wide range of facial expressions, some of which may be very fleeting. He has avoided interpreting these expressions, however, as the antecedents to later expression of specific emotions.

The macro-level studies of infants' facial expressiveness by Oster (1977, 1978) are more relevant. She emphasized the maturity of the facial muscular system at birth and that their action is not random. Rather, according to Oster, patterns of movements occur in predictable combinations and sequences and constitute the very earliest expression of affect in infants.

Bennett (1971) described the "pursing of the lips of the newborn with the accompanying head thrusts, along with head and extremity movements during social engagements, and he says these have a similarity to 'gaping in birds'" as described by Tinbergen (1951).

Burke (1977) described sucking rate and swallowing activity as forms of "pleasure" responses. Likewise, Lipsitt (1979) described the sucking patterns of newborn infants as an expression of "the pleasures and annoyances of infants." These studies suggest that careful, ethological observations will reveal very subtle cues given by babies that reflect emotional responsiveness to external events, and these cues may serve in an important way in the communicative relation with the mother. A vast area of research is open for exploration.

THE MOTHER'S SIDE OF THE COMMUNICATION SYSTEM

The infant's affective messages range from highly explicit ones, such as frowns and grimaces, to highly amorphous expressions as when the infant seems puzzled. Although researchers may express uncertainty about the validity of these expressions, the behaviors of parents leave no doubt about *their* interpretations. Oster (1978) reported that a mother will note a fleeting smile as short as 0.5 seconds. Brazelton, Koslowski, and Main (1974) described mothers' responses to infants in the laboratory even when the infants seem to be most unresponsive: "mothers . . . are unwilling or unable to deal with neonatal behaviors as though they are meaningless or unintentional. Instead, they endow the smallest movement with highly personal meaning and react to them affectively. They insist on joining in and enlarging on even the least possible interactive behaviors through imitation" (p. 68).

There are two possible interpretations: 1) babies emit a wide range of very subtle cues to their emotions, to which parents respond, or 2) the mobile but indefinite expressions of infants lend themselves to being responded to interpretively by an enthusiastic parent. These are not mutually exclusive alternatives.

IMPLICATIONS OF AN AFFECT MODEL FOR EARLY COMMUNICATION

The newborn infant's behaviors are not random; they are organized patterns of movements, of states of attentiveness, and preferences. These complex behaviors dovetail with those of the mother as they achieve mutual engagements. The nature and content of these exchanges and their significance for subsequent communications, including language, has yet to be explored.

The bases for characterizing mother-infant interaction as communication that is primarily affective in nature are: 1) each partner exhibits a range of expressive, affective behaviors; and 2) these behaviors constitute a feedback system that produces a "coupling" of mother and infant behaviors. The baby's behaviors must constitute more than just a "sign" to be interpreted by the mother; and the mother's behaviors must be more than a simple stimulus that elicits reflexive behaviors from the infant. The behaviors of both must actually participate in an ongoing exchange that leads to the mutual modification of behaviors of each member of the dyad.

Behavioral and biological evidence has been presented to support an affective communication model for this early interaction. The suggestion is that the early affective communication precedes and provides the context for the development of cognitive capabilities and verbal communication. The Connecticut Longitudinal Study provided some insights into the nature of the earliest mutual feedback and mutual modification in the mother-infant system.

MOTHER-INFANT INTERACTION STUDIED AS A COMMUNICATION SYSTEM

The guiding theoretical model for the Connecticut Longitudinal Study is that of general systems theory (Thoman, Becker, and Freese, 1978;

Thoman et al., 1979). The basic characteristic of mother-infant inter-action that qualifies it for systems modeling is the ongoing reciprocal feedback. Within this perspective, even though it is necessary to iden-tify some behaviors as mother behaviors and some as infant behaviors, all behaviors of each member of the dyad are regarded as character-istics of the mother-infant relationship or system. For example, even when an infant is alone in the crib and asleep, the nature of the sleep may be a function of the interaction between mother and baby during the waking periods (Sander et al., 1979; Thoman, unpublished).

The system's perspective is consistent with the perspective of the mother-infant relationship as a communicative system. Communica-tion during the early weeks is not directly analogous to that which occurs in a linguistic exchange. That is, whereas a focus on turn-taking by members of the dyad may be appropriate for a vocal dialogue be-tween mother and child, the *co-occurrence* of behaviors of both mother and infant may be more relevant for the early prelinguistic commu-nication. This is an important point for an affective interpretation of the earliest communication in the mother-infant system. For example, while the mother is holding the baby and adjusting his position in relation to her own body, she may be looking at, smiling and talking to the infant. Simultaneously, the baby may be exhibiting a variety of facial expressions, or body movements that contour the baby's body to the mother's, or even vocalizing as well. To analyze these ongoing interlacing behaviors into sequences by an elicitor and respondent simply does not match with the reality of these events. The overall patterning of co-occurring behaviors is the essence of this interaction.

Mother-infant interaction is an organized system with its own rhythm and flow. Hedonic, rather than cognitive, factors must be the major determinants of the complex behavior patterning, and mutual adaptation is the optimal outcome.

This view of the earliest communication reflects our knowledge of the evolutionary process and the biological competence of the new-born. The newborn adapts to survive in interaction with a caregiver. The infant must maintain the mother's interest, and the mother must maintain the infant's attention. This mutuality may seem to be very ephemeral during the early weeks, but its importance should not be underestimated.

In the Connecticut Longitudinal Study, the subtleties of this early interaction were explored by observing mothers and babies under very natural circumstances and by recording behavioral actions of both mother and baby. This approach permitted analyses based on the pat-terning of co-occurrence of behaviors that reflect their communicative system.

The Connecticut Longitudinal Study

In this study, beginning on the day after the infant's birth and continuing through the first 5 weeks, intensive observations were made by code-recording the occurrence of any of 75 mother or infant behaviors during each successive 10-second epoch throughout a 7-hour period. All observations were made without interfering with the family's usual routine and without any interventions. A full 7-hour day enabled the investigators to record the mother-infant interaction in the variety of circumstances under which it typically occurs—feedings, caregiving activities, baby naps, periods of intermittent social interaction, and periods when the mother may be focused on housework despite auditory cues from the infant.

Generally, the behaviors recorded in the home during these early weeks provided information on the infant's behavioral states, including sleep states and state-related behaviors, respiration during sleep, and the infant's responses to maternal stimulation. They also provide information on the mother's proximity to the baby as well as behaviors directed toward the baby including her visual attention, tactile stimulation and vocalization. From 32 hours of observation during the first 5 weeks after birth, over a million pieces of data were obtained on each mother-infant pair during the first five weeks of the infant's life. These observations have produced the largest extant data bank based on the naturally occurring behaviors of mothers and babies from birth through the early weeks of life.

Follow-up assessments and observations are made of the babies through 1 year of age, and development assessment is made at 3 years. Contact is maintained with all children in this ongoing project, and follow-up assessments are being planned for subjects who will soon be 6 years old.

This very brief description of the project indicates the intensity of study during the early weeks of the infants' lives. Details of the methodology are described elsewhere (Thoman et al., 1978; Thoman et al., 1979). The data permit analysis and description for each mother and baby for depicting the orchestration of behaviors that are involved in their mutual adaptation during the early weeks of life.

Selection of Interactive Variables

Combinations of infant, mother, or mother-and-infant behaviors that are intuitively meaningful were chosen for the study. Examples of these behavior combinations are:

1. The baby is awake while the mother is holding or carrying the baby
2. The baby's eyes are closed while the mother is holding or carrying the baby

3. The baby is awake while the mother is holding or carrying the baby, but not engaged in any caregiving activity (social interaction)
4. The mother is patting or caressing or moving or rocking the baby while they are engaged in social interaction (stimulation and social interaction)
5. The mother is looking at the baby while they are engaged in social interaction (looking and social interaction), including en face and vis-à-vis.

Such patterns are categories in a taxonomic system of mother-infant interaction. For example, the category name given to item 3 above is *social interaction* because the mother and the baby are together while the baby is awake but they are not engaged in any of the caregiving activities including feeding, changing or bathing the baby. Their togetherness is more specific than that stated in category 2. Even greater specificity is indicated in categories 4 and 5, which indicate the nature of the ongoing stimulation or attention by the mother while she and the baby are together. Social interaction requires that the baby be awake, not just that the mother is holding the baby without caregiving. Mothers may spend a great deal of time holding their infants and even stimulating them while their eyes are closed. Although the nature of labels or category names are somewhat arbitrary, the nature of the interaction is depicted by the labels that are given. For example, the category *Caretaking* includes feeding, changing or bathing the baby.

It is possible to determine the percent of each 7-hour observation day devoted to these behavior patterns in each mother-infant pair. In order to illustrate the usefulness of this approach, three of the relationship variables listed above, 3, 4, and 5, will be used to characterize two mother-infant pairs.

Reliability of Relationship Variables

An analysis of variance for repeated measures was used to determine the lower-bounds reliability coefficient for the three variables for the first 20 subjects in the longitudinal study over weeks two, three, four, and five. The r_{tt} for each variable is presented in Table 1.

These reliability levels indicate stability of ranks for the babies in the group over the four weeks. There were no trends over weeks on any of the measures, therefore measures of the three variables indicate stability over weeks as well. Thus, these variables can reliably describe the behaviors of individual mother-infant pairs.

Behavior Patterns of Two Mother-Infant Pairs

Data for two mother-infant pairs are presented because they were characterized by markedly contrasting patterns of social interaction

Table 1. Lower bounds reliability coefficient
for measures of interactive patterns over
weeks 2, 3, 4, and 5

	R_{tt}
Social interaction	0.73
Stimulation and social interaction	0.68
Looking and social interaction	0.75

during the early weeks of life. Table 2 shows the mean percent of the total observation time that the social interaction patterns were present.

Table 2 indicates that both of these subject-pairs deviated from the group mean, with Pair 139 being markedly higher and Pair 161 being markedly lower on each variable. In fact, on all of these measures, both pairs deviate from the group mean beyond the 95% confidence limits, as determined by the standard error of measurement.

If periods of social interaction between mother and baby can be considered periods of communication, it is clear that there was far less opportunity for communication in Pair 161. It is even possible to suggest that baby 161 was socially deprived. This suggestion is supported by the fact that the two babies did not differ significantly from each other, nor from the group mean, with respect to the amount of time spent in caregiving activities. Caregiving would be the only other period when mother and baby would be together.

Follow-up Observations at 1 Year of Age

These two babies were among ten that were observed at 1 year of age. For 2 hours on 3 successive weeks, mother and baby behaviors were recorded every 10 seconds using the same observational procedures as those described for the early weeks. The 2 hours were periods when the babies were awake, but not during feeding or other major caregiving activities.

Over the 6 hours of observation, Baby 139 cried a total of 6 minutes. During the same observational time, Baby 161 cried for 51 minutes. The average crying time for the total group of ten babies was 25 minutes. Once again, these two infants represent extremes: no baby

Table 2. Mean number of minutes spent in interactive patterns over weeks 2, 3, 4, and 5

	X_{Group} (SEMeas)	X_{161}	X_{139}
Social interaction	43.7 (9.7)	26.5	57.5
Stimulation and social interaction	35.3 (8.8)	18.5	49.6
Looking and social interaction	41.6 (8.0)	23.1	52.9

cried less than baby 139; and no other baby cried more than Baby 161. The dramatic difference in affective expression of these two infants does not reflect a linear relationship to early expression of affect (namely crying). During the first 5 weeks, Baby 161 cried less than the average for the group; and Baby 139 cried more than average, a reversal of rank compared to 1 year. Thus, fussing and crying during the early weeks was not the antecedent to fussing and crying at 1 year. Social-affective interactions may have been the more significant factor in the developmental course for these two babies.

This interpretation is strengthened by the developmental assessment results at 12 months. On the Bayley Scales, Baby 139 had a mental developmental quotient of 112, and Baby 161 had a mental developmental quotient of 74. Even more relevant, on the Language Subscale, Baby 161 scored lower than any of the 18 (out of the 20) babies that were given the Bayley Scales at 12 months. Thus, the early deviant pattern of social interaction was the prelude to deviancy in affective, intellectual, and communication deviancy at 1 year of age in this baby.

The picture is more complex than was possible to present here. Many more variables were examined for this mother-infant pair, and overall the results are consistent with a social deprivation interpretation (Thoman, 1979). The data illustrate the potential of intensive observations of naturally occurring interactive events for indicating the quality of the earliest interchange. This approach examines the relationships between early events and later characteristics of the child and the mother-child interaction. The relationships over time may not be linear ones, nor need they be the same for each mother-infant pair. This is the rationale for the in-depth description of individual mothers and infants. One pair was selective for communication was so restricted and the outcome at 1 year was so clear in terms of affective and communication deviancy.

The picture of this pair was painted with broad strokes of the brush—the data are summed over 4 weekly observations. The patterns are formed, however, from more than 10,000 epochs recorded for each baby. The patterning of social interaction is formed from those epochs when an opportunity for communication was present but not pressing, that is, when the mother was attending to her child without focusing on physical needs. The affective nature of these interaction periods is assumed rather than specifically demonstrated by these data. This assumption is based on the arguments already given for the affective nature of early interaction, the period when sensory-affective processes are preeminent for the infant (Stechler and Carpenter, 1976; Izard, 1978).

SUMMARY AND CONCLUSION

Both biological and behavioral evidence are presented here to support the position that *affect* can more appropriately be considered as the major organizing concept for the infant's earliest communication experiences. Through the evolutionary process, the newborn infant is designed to adapt to and participate in a social environment; and the mother's and infant's modes of expression and responding in the social situation can best be depicted as affective rather than cognitive. The success of this original communication network is critical for the infant's survival—which is largely dependent on the infant engaging the mother's attention and involvement in the caretaking of a responsive and comprehensible offspring. In this sense, the infant is a "born communicator."

In recent years there has been a growing interest in the affective development of children; however, this interest has generally focused on babies 2 months old or older, when affective measures can be indicative of cognitive competence. The suggestion posed here is that researchers should be asking questions that may lead to an understanding of cognitive development initially as an expression of organismic affect rather than affect developing as an expression of cognitive processing. Greater understanding will need to come from intensive descriptions of the naturally occurring events involved in mutual attention, mutual responsiveness, mutual entrainment, and mutual modification of mother and infant behaviors from the time of birth. Description of the circumstances that facilitate mutuality in affect and the circumstances of abnormalities in this early adaptation process should provide insights into the etiology of communicative disorders that are more obvious at a later age.

The prevailing emphasis on cognition in early development may be a natural outcome in a culture that places a heavy value on cognitive development and cognitive experiences. But there is clearly more to development than the unfolding of cognition.

REFERENCES

Bennett, S. 1971. Infant-caretaker interactions. J. Am. Acad. Child Psychiatry. 10:2.

Bowlby, J. 1969. Attachment and Loss, Vol. 1. Hogarth Press, London.

Brazelton, T. B., Koslowski, B., and Main, M. 1974. The origins of reciprocity: The early mother-infant interaction. *In* M. Lewis and L. Rosenblum (eds.), The Effect of the Infant on Its Caregiver. pp. 49–76. J. Wiley & Sons, Inc., New York.

Breland, K., and Breland, M. 1961. The misbehavior of organisms. Am. Psychol. 16:681–684.

Bruner, J. S. 1975a. From communication to language—A psychological perspective. Cognition, 3(3):255–287.

Bruner, J. S. 1975b. The ontogenesis of speech activities. J. Child Lang. 2:1–19.

Bruner, J. 1978. Learning how to do things with words. In J. S. Bruner and A. Garton (eds.), Human Growth and Development. Clarendon Press, Oxford, England.

Bugental, D. E. 1974. Interpretations of naturally occurring discrepancies between words and intonation: Modes of inconsistency resolution. J. Soc. Psychol. 1:125–133.

Burke, M. 1977. Swallowing and the organization of sucking in the human newborn. Child Dev. 18: 523–531.

Cairns, G. F., and Butterfield, E. C. 1975. Assessing infants' auditory functioning. In Exceptional Infant 3: Assessment and Intervention, pp. 84–108. Brunner/Mazel, New York.

Chomsky, N. 1971. On interpreting the world. Cambridge Review. 92, 77–93.

Chomsky, N. 1967. The general properties of language. In F. L. Darley (ed.), Brain Mechanisms, Speech and Language. Grune & Stratton, New York.

Decarie, T. G. 1978. Affective development and cognition in a Piagetian context. In M. Lewis and L. A. Rosenblum (eds.), The Development of Affect, pp. 183–204. Plenum Publishing Corp., New York.

Emde, R. N., T. G. Gainsbauer, and R. J. Harmon. 1976. Emotional expression in infancy: A biobehavioral study. Psychol. Issues. Monograph 37. International University Press, New York.

Eveloff, H. H. 1971. Some cognitive and affective aspects of early language development. Child Dev. 42:1895–1907.

Grant, E. C. 1968. An ethological description of non-verbal behaviour during interviews. Br. J. Med. Psychol. 41:177–183.

Izard, C. E. 1978. On the ontogenesis of emotions and emotion—Cognition relationships in infancy. In M. Lewis and L. A. Rosenblum (eds.), The Development of Affect. Plenum Publishing Corp., New York.

Jones, O. H. M. 1977. Mother-child communication with pre-linguistic Down's syndrome and normal infants. In H. R. Schaffer (ed.), Studies in Mother-Infant Interaction. Academic Press, New York.

Lamendella, J. T. 1977. The limbic system in human communication. In H. Whitaker and H. A. Whitaker (eds.), Studies in Neurolinguistics. Academic Press, New York, 3:157–222.

Lewis, M., Brooks, J., and Haviland, J. 1978. Hearts and faces: A study in the measurement of emotion. In M. Lewis and L. Rosenblum (eds.), The Development of Affect. Plenum Publishing Corp., New York.

Lipsitt, L. P. 1979. The pleasures and annoyances of infants: Approach and avoidance behavior of babies. In E. B. Thoman (ed.), Origins of the Infant's Social Responsiveness. Lawrence Erlbaum Assoc., Hillsdale, N.J.

Mayo, C., and LaFrance, M. On the acquisition of nonverbal communication: A review. Merrill-Palmer Quarterly, 24.

Monrad-Krohn, G. H. 1947. Dysprosody or altered "melody of language." Brain, 70:405–415.

Monrad-Krohn, G. H. 1963. The third element of speech: Prosody and its disorders. In L. Halpern (ed.), Problems of Dynamic Neurology, pp. 107–117. Hebrew University Press, Jerusalem.

Oster, H. 1978. Facial expression and affect development. In M. Lewis and L. A. Rosenblum (eds.), The Development of Affect, pp. 43–75. Plenum Publishing Corp., New York.

Oster, H., and Ekman, P. 1977. Facial behavior in child development. Minnesota Symposia on Child Psychology, Vol. 2, Lawrence Erlbaum Assoc., Hillsdale, N.J.

Papousek, H., and Papousek, M. 1975. Cognitive aspects of preverbal social interaction between human infants and adults. *In* M. O'Connor (ed.), Parent-Infant Interaction. pp. 241–269. Elsevier-North Holland, New York.

Ross, E. D., and Mesulam, M. M. 1979. Dominant language functions of the *right* hemisphere: Prosody and emotional gesturing. Arch. Neurol. 36:144–148.

Sander, L., Stechler, G., Burns, P., and Lee, A. 1979. Changes in infant and caregiver variables over the first two months. *In* E. B. Thoman (ed.), Origins of the Infant's Social Responsiveness, pp. 305–448. Lawrence Erlbaum Assoc., Hillsdale, N.J.

Stechler, G., and Carpenter, G. 1967. A viewpoint on early affective development. *In* J. Hellmuth (ed.), Exceptional Infant. Brunner/Mazel, New York.

Stroufe, L. A. 1977. Wariness of strangers and the study of infant development. Child Dev. 48(3):731–746.

Thoman, E. B. 1975a. Early development of sleeping behaviors in infants. *In* N. R. Ellis (ed.), Aberrant Development in Infancy: Human and Animal Studies, pp. 123–138. John Wiley & Sons, New York.

Thoman, E. B. 1975b. Sleep and wake behaviors in neonates; consistencies and consequences. Merrill-Palmer Quarterly, 21:295–314.

Thoman, E. B. 1981. Early communication as the prelude to later adaptive behaviors. *In* M. J. Begab, H. Garber, and H. C. Haywood (eds.), Prevention of Retarded Development in Psychosocially Disadvantaged Children. University Park Press, Baltimore.

Thoman, E. B., Wetzel, A., and Levine, S. 1968. Learning in the neonatal rat. Animal Behavior, 16:54–57.

Thoman, E. B., Acebo, C., Dreyer, C. A., Becker, P. T., and Freese, M. P. 1979. Individuality in the interactive process. *In* E. B. Thoman (ed.), Origins of the Infant's Social Responsiveness, pp. 305–338. Lawrence Erlbaum Assoc., Hillsdale, N.J.

Thoman, E. B., Becker, P. T., and Freese, M. P. 1978. Individual patterns of mother-infant interaction. *In* G. P. Sackett (ed.), Application of Observational/Ethological Methods To the Study of Mental Retardation. University Park Press, Baltimore.

Thoman, E. B., Korner, A. F., and Beason-Williams, L. 1977. Modification of responsiveness to maternal vocalization in the neonate. Child Dev. 48:563–569.

Thoman, E. B., Korner, A. F., and Kraemer, H. C. 1976. Individual consistency in behavioral states in neonates. Dev. Psychobiol. 9:271–283.

Thorpe, W. H. 1972. Duetting and antiphonal song in birds: Its extent and significance. Behavior, 18, Monograph.

Tinbergen, N. 1951. The Study of Instinct. Oxford University Press, London.

Wada, J. A. 1977. Pre-language and fundamental asymmetry of the infant brain. Ann. N.Y. Acad. Sci. 299:370–379.

Watson, J. S. 1979. Perception of contingency as a determinant of social responsiveness. *In* E. B. Thoman (ed.), Origins of the Infant's Social Responsiveness. Lawrence Erlbaum Assoc., Hillsdale, N.J.

Wolff, P. 1966. The causes, controls and organization of behavior in the newborn. Psychol. Issues, 17, Monograph.

Wolff, P. H. 1973. The organization of behavior in the first three months of life. Res. Publ. Assoc. Res. Nerv. and Ment. Dis., 51:132–153.

chapter

6

Mother–Child Interaction in the Second Year of Life

Its Role in Language Development

Robin S. Chapman

University of Wisconsin–Madison
Madison, Wisconsin

This chapter focuses primarily on the linguistic aspect of mother-child interaction in the second year of life, and more specifically on linguistic input to the child. The stable and changing characteristics of the mother's speech to the language-learning child are reviewed with respect to phonology, syntax, semantics, and pragmatics.

The causes of the mother's speech modifications and the consequences for the child are discussed: why is the mother altering her speech, and which of her alterations play causal roles in the child's acquisition? The answers suggested are necessarily speculative; other writers (e.g., Sachs, 1977; Snow, 1977a; DePaulo and Bonvillian, 1978) have carried out similar speculation. The emphasis throughout, however, is to take the point of view of the child.

In particular, it is argued that limited comprehension skills play an important role in determining what information the child takes from input, and that perceptual processing characteristics may further constrain what the child learns (Trehub, this volume). The episodic and interactive nature of mother-child language exchanges (Thoman, this volume) and the restrictions of social (Uzgiris, this volume) and cognitive skill (Cromer, this volume) are additional factors that must be taken into account in predicting whether input is effective.

A significant body of research demonstrates that mothers alter their speech from adult conversational patterns when talking to language-learning children. (See, for example the excellent reviews by Snow, 1977a, and Rondal, 1978.) These changes are phonological, syntactic, semantic, and pragmatic; they may number in the hundreds. There is evidence for a distinctive, simplified baby talk register that is in part continuously adjusted to child characteristics. The description of mother's speech is discussed in both its broadly and finely-tuned aspects. Phonological, syntactic, semantic, and pragmatic aspects are considered in turn. The possible causes—and consequences—of the mother's speech adjustments are discussed at the end of each section.

PHONOLOGY

Segmental Characteristics

When we say that a mother speaks baby talk to her child we most often mean that she *sounds* different: *Is da pwetty pwetty baby seeping? Does its wittle tum tums hurt?* This bit of talk to a baby includes phonological simplifications—*seeping* for *sleeping*; sound substitutions—*w* for *l*; and reduplications—*pwetty-pwetty* (Ferguson, 1964).

Not all American mothers make these particular segmental phonological changes in their speech. Many prospective mothers swear that they will never talk baby talk to their kids. They mean that they will not make the kind of sound changes in the preceding example.

They don't mean that they will speak to their 2-year-old as they speak to each other. They are as likely as the preceding mother to say things like *Oh, the pretty baby's sleeping, Does its little tummy hurt?* retaining prosodic characteristics and words typical of mother's speech to children.

Prosodic Characteristics

Mothers' speech to children is likely to contain a number of prosodic characteristics different from their speech to adults or to 5-year-olds. Among these are exaggerated pitch, intensity, duration, and stress; slower rate; and syntactically related pause distributions.

Higher Fundamental Frequency The pitch of mothers' voices talking to 2-year-olds is higher (267 Hz fundamental frequency, on the average) than the pitch for mothers talking to 5-year-olds or adults (200 Hz, on the average) (Remick, 1976; Garnica, 1977). These measures reflect the rate of opening and closing of the vocal folds.

Greater Frequency Range Speech frequencies to 2-year-olds range much higher than speech to older children and adults (Ferguson, 1964; Garnica, 1977). The low-pitched end of the range is typically similar, but in talking to 2-year-olds, mothers may range up two octaves in their speech sounds, rather than one-half to one octave (Garnica, 1977). The effect, described perceptually, is one of greatly exaggerated intonation contour.

Occasional Whispering Marked intensity shifts have been reported in mothers' instructions to their 2-year-olds, including whispering (Garnica, 1977).

Longer Duration of Content Words in Commands In telling their 2-year-olds to *Push in the red piece* or *Take out the green piece*, mothers took longer to say the verbs and color terms than they do in talking to adults (Garnica, 1977).

Two Primary Stresses in Sentences Calling for One In telling 2-year-olds to *Push in the red piece*, for example, mothers frequently stress more than one element of the sentence (Garnica, 1977).

Slower Rate Broen (1972) reported that mothers speak at a slower rate to 2-year-olds than to older children. Whether this effect is achieved primarily through slower rate within utterances or between them is unclear from Broen's study. Mothers talk to 2-year-olds at rates of approximately 75 words per minute—or two to three utterances for every one of the child's (Cross, 1977).

In a study of forty-eight 10- to 21-month-olds, the children and their mothers averaged a combined total of 20.3 utterances per minute (Miller et al., in prep), with no developmental changes observed. Studies of older children in conversation with mothers suggest some later increase in utterance rate. For example, Retherford, Schwartz, and

Chapman (in press) found their mother-child pairs talking more at 25 months (26.3 utterances per minute) than at 21 months. These findings, taken together with the pause data reported below, suggest that a slower rate of talking is achieved in part through fewer utterances and more between-utterance pause time.

Pauses at Utterance Boundaries In adult conversation, pauses come at different places in the utterance as the speaker searches for a word or idea. One cannot use pauses in adult conversation to predict sentence boundaries. When adults speak to 2-year-olds, however, there are almost always pauses after each sentence or single word remark— and only there (Broen, 1972). (A "pause" was defined in this study as a break in speaking of more than 260 milliseconds.)

In the study of forty-eight 10- to 21-month-old children (Miller et al., in prep), it was found that pauses longer than 2 seconds in mother-child conversation occurred at a rate of about 3.6 per minute. Approximately 18% of the dyad's utterances were followed by silence of more than 2 seconds duration. There were no consistent developmental changes. Either young children take very little time to respond, or they are left little time by their conversational partners.

High Intelligibility Intelligibility of mothers is typically high— nearby 100% for mothers talking to 12- to 27-month-olds, in contrast to 91% in the same mothers' conversing with adults (Newport, Gleitman, and Gleitman, 1977).

Children, in contrast, exhibit variation in intelligibility. Some part of this arises from variation in recording techniques and in transcriber familiarity with the child's phonological system and lexicon; another part from maturation of the speech motor control mechanism (Netsell, in press). With videotaped context provided, transcribers found an average of 85% of 2-year-olds' utterances intelligible; the percent varied from 72% to 97% at 25 months (Retherford et al., in press).

Causes and Consequences of Phonological Changes

Brown (1977) suggested that two dimensions underlie the phonological (and other) shifts in adult speech to young children: the *affective* and the *communicative*. By observing when similar changes in speech are made to other objects of affection (pets, plants, lovers) or to other individuals with limited communication skills (foreigners; the hearing impaired), one may parcel out which of the two dimensions more importantly governs that linguistic characteristic. The segmental phonological changes, although they reflect child processes, seem to vary primarily with the affective dimension.

Prosodic characteristics, in contrast, seem to reflect the mother's effort to gain and keep her child's attention. Taken together, the higher frequency and exaggerated contour, intensity, duration, and stress make speech addressed to the child perceptibly different—and more salient—than speech addressed to others. The vowel duration and utterance stress differences, in particular, may arise simply because the mother is timing her speech to the child's accompanying actions. Finally, the slower rate, presence of pause boundaries, and higher intelligibility may reflect her wish to make herself understood or the simpler production requirements of simple, repetitive content. Increased intelligibility could, alternatively, be a product of the increased predictability of content for the listener.

The consequences, for the child, may be to alert him to the fact that this is speech intended for him; and to make the processing of speech easier.

SYNTAX

Complexity Measures

Mothers' utterances to 2-year-olds are shorter, simpler, and more frequently well formed than speech to older children and adults, as indicated by several measures.

Utterance Length   Utterances to children are shorter than those to older children or adults both in number of words or morphemes per utterances (Snow, 1972, Phillips, 1973) and in preverb length (Snow, 1972; Broen, 1972; Phillips, 1973; Cross, 1977). Average preverb length in mothers' speech to 1 ; 7 to 2 ; 8 year-olds was 1.63 morphemes (Cross, 1977), reflecting the simplicity of the subject noun phrase in particular.

Mothers' mean length of utterance (MLU) varies with the conversational context (Snow, 1972). It is shortest, typically, in free play; longer in book reading, task explanation or narrative contexts.

In the 3-to-18 month period there is little evidence of change in mothers' MLU with age (Phillips, 1973; Longhurst and Stepanich, 1975; Snow, 1977b). Mothers begin using short sentences well before their children are using words, and the use seems related to the use of a conversational model in talking to the child (Snow, 1977b) or to the mothers' beliefs that the children can understand them (Bingham, 1971).

Several studies show a significant correlation between mother's and child's MLU from 18 months on (Seitz and Stewart, 1975; Cross, 1977), even with age partialled out. Examination of average utterance lengths for mothers and children engaged in free play (see Table 1) suggests that the mother's speech averages about 2.4 morphemes longer than her child's during the 12–27 month period. Cross (1978) reported little variation in the individual differences between mother

Table 1. Mean utterance lengths in mother-child speech samples obtained in free play and difference between mother and child MLU

Study	Date	Measure	Child age	Number dyads	Mother MLU	Child MLU	Difference
Nelson	1973	WORD	1;1	18	3.24	1.00	2.24
Newport et al.	1977	M = WORD C = MORPH	1;0–2;3	15	4.24	1.65	2.59
Retherford et al.	in prep	MORPH	1;9	6	4.24	1.32	2.92
Glanzer and Dodd	1975	MORPH	1;10	6	3.53	1.46	2.07
Seitz and Stewart	1975	WORD	1;11	9	3.62	1.37	2.25
Rondal	1978	MORPH	1;11	1	4.24	1.27	2.97
Cross	1977	MORPH	1;7–2;8	16	4.80	2.20	2.60
Chapman and Kohn	1978	MORPH	2;0	8	3.64	1.58	1.94
Retherford et al.	in prep	MORPH	2;1	6	4.61	1.91	2.70
Glanzer and Dodd	1975	MORPH	2;1	6	4.03	2.21	1.82
Rondal	1978	MORPH	2;3	7	4.64	1.96	2.68
Glanzer and Dodd	1975	MORPH	2;5	6	4.24	2.95	1.29
Rondal	1978	MORPH	2;6	7	4.84	2.88	1.96
Chapman and Kohn	1978	MORPH	2;8	10	4.20	2.46	1.70
Chapman and Kohn	1978	MORPH	3;5	7	4.80	3.01	1.80
Wanska	Unpub	MORPH	3;5	20	4.73	3.73	1.00
Wanska	Unpub	MORPH	4;8	20	5.14	4.29	0.85
Wanska	Unpub	MORPH	6;1	20	5.32	4.28	1.04

and child utterance length—the range was only 1.8 to 3.3 for her 1;7- to 2;8-year-olds. We can expect mothers' MLUs to be 2 to 3 morphemes longer than their children's, then, in the latter half of the second year.

For older children, both mother and child MLU increase (Longhurst and Stepanich, 1975; Miller and Chapman, in press), but the difference decreases. The average difference is 1.7 morphemes for 2;5- to 3;5-year-olds and 1.4 words for 4;8-year-olds.

Sentence Types Data on the grammatical forms of mothers' utterances to 1- to 2-year-olds are summarized in Table 2. These distributions are markedly different from those found in adult conversation, which is 80 to 90% declarative in form (Broen, 1972; Newport et al., 1977; Cross, 1977).

Table 2.   Distribution of grammatical sentence types in mothers' speech to language-learning children, ages 1;0 to 3;0

Sentence Type	Newport et al., 1977 1;0–2;3 15	Broen, 1972 1;6–2;2 10	Cross, 1977 1;7–2;8 16	Rondal, 1978 1;11 (Mean age) 7	Rondal, 1978 2;3 (Mean age) 7	Rondal, 1978 2;6 (Mean age) 7	Longhurst and Stepanich, 1975 1;0 12	2;0 12	3;0 12
Imperative	18%	24.3%	7.4%	16%	13%	9%	44.0	41.2	41.5
Question	44%	36.9%	33.4%	49%	41%	45%			
WH	15%	8.6%	15.4%	25%	18%	27%	13.2	13.1	21.0
YN-Question	21%	27.8%	18.2%	24%	22%	17%	20.8	25.3	19.9
Deictic	8%								
Declarative*	30%	30.4%	33.6%*	24%	33%	32%	1.0	2.9	.6

* Including deictic statements

The proportion of total questions remains fairly constant over 1 to 3 years (Longhurst and Stepanich, 1975), ranging in these middle Socioeconomic Status (SES) samples from 36% to 49% of the mother's total utterances. The kind of question asked shifts between 2 and 3 years, from a predominance of yes/no questions to an equal number of yes/no and WH-questions (Longhurst and Stepanich, 1975). Imperative types decrease over the 2-to-3 year period (Savić, 1975; Rondal, 1978).

Questioning rates must, of course, begin to drop at some point. Savić (1975) reported a decrease in question forms relative to declaratives, beginning at 30 months, in a longitudinal study of Serbo-Croation parents' input to twins.

Grammatical Complexity Mothers' utterances are undeniably shorter, on the average, to language-learning children than to adults. Whether they are grammatically simpler, as these length indices could indicate, has been disputed. Newport et al. (1977) pointed out that many of the constructions that mothers use more frequently to children than to adults—yes/no and Wh-questions in particular—might be viewed as linguistically more complex than the simple declarative sentences predominating in adult conversation.

Embedded and conjoined sentences with multipropositional content, in contrast, are infrequent in mothers' speech to 12- to 27-month-olds, comprising approximately 3% of the sample (Newport et al., 1977). Retherford et al., (in press) reported that 10% of mothers' speech to 21-month-olds is complex.

Grammaticality The majority of utterances addressed to language-learning children are syntactically well formed (60% in the 12- to 27-month-olds studied by Newport et al., 1977; 70% in the 2-year-olds studied by Broen, 1972).

The ungrammatical exceptions are usually of three types (Broen, 1972; Newport et al., 1977): single word utterances (10%–17%); deleted beginnings to yes/no questions (6%–15%); and partial repetitions of the mother's speech. These ungrammatical instances, then, deviate from rules of grammaticality in minimal ways.

Dysfluency Dysfluencies, including broken sentences, false starts, *ums* and *ers*, almost never occur. Newport et al. (1977) found fewer than 0.1% dysfluencies in the mothers' speech to 12- to 27-month-olds; Broen found less than 1% in speech to 2-year-olds. A typical value in adult conversation might be 10%, one to two orders of magnitude greater.

Syntactic Changes: Causes and Consequences

The speech of the mother to the young child is shorter, simpler, and more grammatical than speech to adults. The longitudinal studies of length changes suggest that mother's speech is fine-tuned to a level approximately 2 to 3 morphemes longer than the child's productive speech in the age range beyond 18 months. Comprehension status is a rarely investigated alternative to which the mother may be adjusting her speech. Furrow, Nelson, and Benedict's (1979) study of seven children at 1;6 months and 1.0 MLU showed mother MLU to vary with children's rate of comprehension development.

The child's linguistic comprehension skills cannot account for all the early characteristics of the mother's syntax, however, because these characteristics emerge at 7 months, prior to word comprehension (Snow, 1977b). Snow suggested that the mother's adoption of a conversational model with simple content, based in part on the child's limited activities, is responsible. Alternatively or additionally, the child's apparent comprehension skills or responsiveness in context may serve to bring about the modification.

Distributions of sentence types, in contrast to length indices of grammatical complexity, include high proportions of sentences viewed as syntactically more complex by linguistic metrics (Newport et al., 1977). Furthermore, complex sentences, although infrequent, constitute a not negligible portion of mother's speech to children at the two-word period (Retherford et al., in press).

Taken together, these facts suggest that the mother is not directly simplifying her syntax, but rather, that syntactic simplification (or obfuscation) is itself a product of other changes; for example, in the content of the mother's utterances, the reasons for which she speaks, and the child's ability to respond appropriately in context. Sentence type distributions, for example, are likely to reflect the mother's attempt to get the child to perform or to participate in conversation.

Whatever the causes, the consequence for children is that they, unlike adults, are confronted by short, often simple grammatical models of the language they must learn. Many students of child language believe that the simple well formed structure of the mother's input plays a critical role in the child's ability to learn language rapidly.

Furrow et al. (1979), for example, reported that differences in mothers' MLUs at 1;6, when their children had MLUs of 1.0, were correlated with differences in child MLUs at 2;3. This finding indeed suggests that shorter mother utterances facilitate syntactic acquisition in the child.

Syntactic Aspects the Child Comprehends

On the basis of what we know about the 1- to 2-year-old's comprehension, the mother's syntactic simplifications or complications are mainly irrelevant. The child's limited linguistic comprehension skill would willy-nilly reduce the amount of input to deal with. There is little evidence that the child from age 1 to 2 attends to syntactic cues, and no evidence that the child attends to meaning differences signaled by word order (see Chapman, 1978, for a review), so that the apparent complexity of imperative and question sentence types is irrelevant from his or her point of view.

Comprehension skills of 1- to 2-year-olds, taken from a study by Miller et al. (1980), are presented in Table 3. The children begin by demonstrating comprehension only for one lexical item in an utterance. Comprehension of people or object words signaled by looking preceded comprehension of action verbs signaled by compliance. Comprehension of words for objects in the visual field preceded comprehension of objects outside the immediate surroundings. The transition to comprehension of two lexical items in the utterance occurred in the 16-to-21 month period; only one child in the entire sample of 48 indicated comprehension of any instance of agent-action-object utterance.

Other work (Huttenlocher, 1974; Wetstone and Friedlander, 1973; Benedict, 1978; Shatz, 1978) makes clear that children in the second year of life interpret pragmatic intent of the utterances on the basis of the situation and semantic intent on the basis of situation plus lexical cues. Word order plays no role (deVilliers and deVilliers, 1973; Chapman and Miller, 1975; Chapman and Kohn, 1978)—nor, apparently, do the inflectional niceties of English sentence construction. (When

Table 3.   Percentage of children in each age group passing a comprehension task at least once**

Comprehension task	Age group (months) and number of Ss				
	10–12 12	13–15 12	16–18 12	19–21 12	Ss (n – 48)
Person name	100%	100%	92%	92%	96%
Object name	42%	100%	100%	100%	85%
Action verb	8%	33%	75%	83%	50%
Possessor-Possession	0%	8%	42%	83%	33%
Absent person or object	0%	17%	33%	67%	29%
Action-object	0%	8%	42%	67%	29%
Agent*-action	0%	0%	8%	58%	17%
Agent*-action-object	0%	0%	0%	8%	2%
Average percentage passing	18.7%	33.2%	49.0%	69.8%	

From Miller, Chapman, Branston, and Reichle, 1980.

* Other than child.

** Differences between entries are significant ($p < 0.05$) by Tukey's post-hoc HSD Test if they exceed: 25.7 for task by age entries; 15.2 for age averages; and 19.0 for task averages.

inflections, rather than word order, mark case categories, comprehension in 2-year-olds is reported (Slobin, 1979; Schieffelin, 1979).

Rather, what the child understands—and what he or she talks about—seems to emerge from the episodic contexts of recurring mother-child interactions. This point is discussed in the next section. Here, the moral that is important to draw from the comprehension data is that *the mother's language input from 1 to 2 years may be chiefly important for its lexical, rather than its syntactic characteristics.* To the extent that a mother's utterances contain fewer words, the child may have a somewhat higher probability of associating the right words with the right aspect of context. The benefit comes not from syntactic simplification, but from the reduction in number of words; and it would additionally depend on the mother's skill in encoding just that aspect of the immediate situation to which the child was attending. The child's problem in learning to understand the mother's input during this year is one of discovering the referents of the mother's words and learning how those referents interact in situations. The problem of discovering syntactic cues to meaning is at least a year away.

SEMANTICS

Semantics: Vocabulary

Diversity   The words used by mothers in speaking to their 2-year-olds are less diverse than those used in conversation with older children or adults (Broen, 1972; Phillips, 1973; Rondal, 1978). Mothers' type-token ratios (TTR) are summarized in Table 4. The changes between 18 and 28 months in Phillip's study, and those between 23 and 27 months in Rondal's study, are significant. By 30 months, child and mother TTRs are similar (0.47 versus 0.49) (Rondal, 1978). In Long-hurst and Stephanich's (1975) study, however, changes in the Carroll

Table 4.   Type-token ratios in mothers' speech to children

Study	Age (in months)	n	TTR, Mother to child
Phillips 1973	8	10	0.31
Phillips 1973	18	10	0.34
Broen 1972	21	10	0.53
Rondal 1978	23	7	0.44
Rondal 1978	27	7	0.49
Phillips 1973	28	10	0.41
Rondal 1978	30	7	0.49

TTR in mother's speech (3.97 to 1-year-olds; 4.26 to 2-year-olds; 4.61 to 3-year-olds) were not significant, but the greater variability of 1-year-olds may have contributed to this fact. (The Carroll TTR measure divides the number of different words by the square root of twice the number of tokens, rather than by the number of tokens, as in the TTR.) Vocabulary diversity would seem to be a property of mother's speech to children that is finely tuned to the child's vocabulary changes or comprehension skill in the second year of life.

Frequency   The different vocabulary used by the mother over the 1-to-3 year period is consistently high frequency: from 80% to 84% of her words are in the most frequent 1,000 of the Thorndike-Lorge list (1944) (Longhurst and Stepanich, 1975). No change is seen in this measure with child age.

Concreteness   Mothers' speech to children in the second year of life contains more concrete words, and fewer abstract ones, than those used in conversation with adults (Phillips, 1973).

Form Class   The number of modifiers—adjectives or adverbs—per utterance in the mother's speech increases from 23 to 27 months: from 0.55 to 0.68 per utterance (Rondal, 1978).

There are currently few data on changes in noun versus verb vocabulary in mother's speech over the second year of the child's life. Such data would be particularly interesting in assessing the questions of whether the mother's vocabulary is tuned to the child's productive vocabulary, and whether shifts in the mother's vocabulary use precede shifts in child use. The relevant change reported in the 1- to 2-year-olds' productive language is the shift from an earlier high proportion of nouns to a more equal distribution of nouns and verbs (Goldin-Meadow, Seligman, and Gelman, 1976); there is some evidence for a similar developmental shift in comprehension (Miller et al., 1980).

Furrow et al. (1979), in a study of 7 dyads at 1;6 and again at 2;3, found a drop in the frequency of nouns per 100 utterances over the period, but little change in verb use. These children were too old, however, for the shifts of interest to be expected.

Pronoun Use   Pronoun use differs from that found in adult conversations. Second person *you* is more common in speech to 2-year-olds (Snow, 1972; Sachs and Devin, 1976) than to adults. Furthermore, the child listener is also often referred to in the third person (*Did Adam eat it?*) (Wills, 1977), a use atypical in adult conversation. At points where a first person singular pronoun would be used in adult conversation, mothers talking to children often substitute the third person (*Where are mommy's eyes?*) or, less frequently, the plural first person (*We'll put some on. Let's have it*) or nothing at all (*Gonna get you*) (Wills, 1977).

Wh-Question Words   The Wh-questions asked of 1- to 2-year-olds are restricted in content (Brown, Cazden, and Bellugi, 1969; Savić, 1975; Buium, 1976) primarily to forms that will appear earlier in comprehension or production in the child. Frequency of use, as well as order of appearance in parental speech, is correlated with later order of emergence in child speech. For example, *where, what,* and *who* questions are among the earliest and most frequent questions addressed to the twins studied by Savić (1975) in their second year. Relative frequency of Wh-adverbial questions addressed to Adam, Eve, and Sarah at Brown's Stage II, from high to low, was *where, why, how,* and *when*; this rank order matched the proportion of appropriate answers from the children at Stage V (Brown et al., 1969).

Referential Versus Expressive Vocabularies   Nelson (1973) proposed stylistic differences in children's first 50-word vocabularies in the proportion of general nominals (as opposed to nouns referring uniquely to an individual). She classified children with more than 50% general nominals in their vocabularies as *referential*, the others as *expressive*. (The distribution is apparently a unimodal one, however.) Nelson reported that referential children seem to acquire vocabulary faster, but that mothers who are accepting of their child's language forms and uses, whatever the child's style, facilitate acquisition.

Early Vocabulary Acquisition: Causes and Consequences

The mother's vocabulary in speaking to the language-learning child is less diverse, more concrete, and high frequency, with developmental shifts in some form classes. A less diverse set of Wh-questions is asked younger children. These characteristics most probably reflect the restricted topics of mother-child conversation.

What we do not know are the causes and consequences of these shifts: is the mother following the child's lead in terms of the child's activity? The child's comprehension? The child's produced utterances, which she then expands? Do mothers differ in the vocabulary they model to children, and is there a consequence of this difference? Is frequency of use by the mother related to order of emergence in children's vocabularies?

The vocabulary development of American children themselves in the second year of life can be briefly summarized by saying that it begins slowly, accelerates exponentially, changes developmentally in that verbs emerge later than nouns, and exhibits individual variation in the proportion of early words that are not nouns. The first word understood or produced typically emerges at 10 months (Pierce, 1974); the first 50 words have typically been acquired by 19 months (Nelson,

1973). Early Wh-questions are routine in form and restricted in content: *What's that? Where (X) go? What he do?* (Brown et al., 1969).

Early vocabularies show striking similarities in their content: what children talk about is similar and selective relative to the range of objects, activities, and words in their environment. People, pets, and objects that children can act upon or that move, disappear, reappear or change are principle sources of children's words (Nelson, 1973; Bloom, 1973; Volterra et al., 1979). What they talk about in the 10- to 19-month period is also strikingly restricted in frequency of use and, to an unknown degree, in the contexts of use and comprehension. Contextual support seems to be necessary to early comprehension of object and people names; it may also be required for comprehension of all morphemes in the early period.

How do we account for these facts? What is our model of early vocabulary acquisition? What role does the mother's interaction with her child play in the process? We have no fully satisfactory account, of course. It is instructive to begin, however, by considering how two generalized versions of current semantic models provide such an account.

Semantic models have typically posed the infant's problem in learning early words as one of noting the consistency between instances of the object and instances of the word in the mother's speech (e.g., Huttenlocher, 1974). There have been two different views of the causal relation underlying this task. At one extreme, the way in which words grouped objects in a particular language has been thought to determine the structure of the child's concepts or object groupings (Brown, 1957). At the other, it has been argued that conceptual groupings of objects are given naturally in the child's perception (Rosch, 1973) or through the child's actions upon objects (Nelson, 1974). Some objects may be better exemplars of the category than others. These two views (of which there are many subcategories) have different consequences for the way in which one would expect early vocabulary to develop.

Word-Object Learning Paradigm   If one believes that object names determine conceptual groupings, then the problem is to provide frequent pairing of the word and its full range of object exemplars. Within the labeling paradigm, number of sets consistently and frequently labeled would be the determinant of referential vocabulary size.

For example, a frequency of input view might account for the semantic facts of the child's Wh-question acquisition: mothers' uses of particular Wh-questions begin months or years before the children's lexical comprehension or use of the forms, and order of acquisition seems to reflect in part mother's frequency of use (Brown, 1973). Savić

(1975), however, pointed out that the two twins that she studied received exactly the same parental input—they were usually together and addressed jointly—but showed somewhat differing ages of first use for all but *why* questions. (Ironically, Wh-questions, even if their acquisition could be predicted by frequency of input, are not very satisfactorily conceptualized in a word-referent paradigm. Nor is it then obvious why there should be developmental shifts in the content of the mother's questions.)

A simple frequency explanation fails to take into account the rate at which vocabulary learning must take place in the child's life—eight new words a day, on the average, in the preschool years (Miller, 1978). This statistic suggests that only a few instances can be necessary for acquisition. Carey and Bartlett (1978) demonstrated this conclusion experimentally for color terms in older preschoolers; substantial learning can occur given only three widely spaced instances. But if only a few occurrences are necessary for learning, then only the most infrequently modeled inputs should show "frequency" effects—most lexical elements in mother's input would occur frequently enough so that frequency would not be a limiting factor in vocabulary selection.

The view of the child as a young Ebbinghaus, and the mother as a memory drum diligently drilling the way in which language maps the world, is then incomplete in several ways. It fails to provide accounts of 1) how the child segments out the recurring morpheme from the stream of speech; 2) why the child pairs the morpheme with the object, rather than some property of the object or some aspect of the interaction with it; 3) why rate of vocabulary acquisition changes so dramatically; 4) why there is such selectivity among words and children in early word content; and 5) why there are content shifts developmentally. These are problems whether the paradigm is applied narrowly to the learning of object names or broadly to all lexical categories.

The view does predict that the most underextension should be observed for recently acquired words; that no true overextension should occur unless modeled, and that individual variation in the size of referential vocabulary acquisition should arise as a function of consistency and frequency of labeling in input.

Word-Natural Category Paradigm A more recent view of the child's problem of vocabulary acquisition has been to assume that the conceptual content, or natural grouping of objects, arises out of nonverbal aspects of experience or the perceptual structure of the child. The child links the word not with the particular referential object present but with the conceptual category of which it is a member. The consistency and frequency of the mother's input would still play an influential role in rate of vocabulary acquisition, but the existence of the natural category and the status of the object as an exemplar of the category (i.e., its prototypicality) would also play significant roles in what the child learned and how the term was extended.

This view of the mother as a judicious tutor holding up the best examples to her young Plato also has its limitations. Several problems that the preceding model did not solve are not solved here, either, but shifted into the domain of cognitive development for explanation. These include the problems of explaining the selectivity and commonality of early word content and of explaining the development shift in content. Like the preceding model, this account is incomplete in specifying how the child segments out the recurring morpheme from the stream of speech, in accounting for the changing rate of vocabulary acquisition, and in explaining why the child pairs the morpheme with the object rather than some other aspect of the situation.

This account does not predict underextension of early uses unless the conceptual categories themselves are initially restricted. Individual differences in children's early referential vocabularies could be accounted for in the same way as in the preceding model: mothers differ either in the frequency or consistency with which they make use of the opportunities to label objects.

Consequences of Abstracting the Word-Referent Relation From Context What concerns us here, in a discussion of the role of mother-child interaction in lexical acquisition, are the common shortcomings of both views: the problems of accounting for segmentation of input; identification of the referent (be it object, action, attribute, or whatever) and accounting for the marked changes in frequency of talking and content of talking, both in the sense of noun-verb shifts and semantic role shifts.

These problems arise from two sources. The first is a failure to make explicit predictions about how the child processes input. How does the child segment the stream of speech that he hears? The second is the problem of divorcing lexical acquisition from acquisition contexts. The episodic structure of early learning is ignored; the problem is not placed in its proper situational context of mother-child dialogue in familiar routine.

The Segmentation Problem Brown (1973) defined the segmentation problem confronted by the child early in his consideration of child language acquisition, but there has been little direct experimentation on the topic. How does the child segment out of the speech stream the morpheme-size recurring units?

A part of the answer to that problem became evident in Broen's (1972) work on mothers' speech to language-learning children. She found that pauses in the mother's speech were located always and only at utterance boundaries and that 15% to 20% of the mothers' speech to 2-year-olds consisted of single words. Shipley, Smith, and Gleitman (1969) found that children at the one-word stage attended to objects mentioned most frequently when the word was uttered alone rather than embedded in a context.

These findings serve to redefine the child's segmentation problem; the segmentation at the utterance level is acoustically given in the speech addressed to him or her. What we must now ask is what the child retains of an utterance long enough to relate it to a situation. We know from the early comprehension data that children in the first months of language acquisition do not give evidence of comprehending more than one morphemic unit of an utterance at a time. Single word utterances may play a uniquely important role in shaping early vocabulary. It is possible that recency and syllabic stress play roles in determining which piece of the utterance remains in memory long enough to learn its meaning. Certainly the cross-cultural data on older children suggested that post-positions are easier to learn than prepositions (Slobin, 1973) and that suffixes are easier to learn than prefixes (Kuczaj, 1979).

Experimental Evidence for the Role of Word Position in the Utterance   Blasdell and Jensen (1970) found that both sentence stress and word position could produce significant effects on the elicited imitation of nonsense-word sentences by 28- to 39-month-olds, with primary stressed items and final position best. Eilers (1975) also found that words in final position were correctly imitated more frequently than all words by children 18 to 36 months old in an elicited imitation task. Slobin and Welsh (1971) reported that it was common for 2-year-olds to reproduce the last word first in imitating sentences upon request. Thus, there is direct evidence of the role that word position may play in making a phonological segment more likely to be retained (and, hence, allowing the child to link it to the situation). Morse, Younger, and Goodsitt (in preparation) are currently investigating the role of syllable position on 7-month-old infants' head-turning responses.

Similar perceptual factors, then, may operate at the utterance level for the child just learning to talk. Pay attention to the ends of utterances. This would mean that only a subset of input, consisting of single words and final stressed syllable in an utterance, would have a high probability of appearing early in children's vocabularies.

Two data sources were examined for indirect confirmation of this prediction. One was Nelson's (1973) data on the first 50 words in children's vocabularies. (Compare, in Table 5, the non-object words emerging in the first 10 words with words emerging in the last 10 words

Table 5. The emergence of non-object words blocked by
time of vocabulary entry in 8 children studied
longitudinally (13–24 months)

Words occurring more than once	Number of children for whom use was reported at each vocabulary level			
	Words 1–10	Words 11–30	Words 31–50	Total 1–50
Hi (there)	4	3	0	7
hot	1	5	1	7
yes	1	3	1	5
no	2	2	1	5
(bye) bye	2	3	0	5
up	0	2	2	4
go	0	3	0	3
see	1	2	0	3
thank you	1	2	0	3
all gone	0	2	1	3
more	0	2	1	3
please	0	2	1	3
sit	1	1	1	3
here	1	0	1	2
there	1	1	0	2
dirt (y)	1	0	1	2
cuckoo	0	0	2	2
bow-bow	1	0	1	2
cold	0	0	2	2
down	0	1	1	2
night-night	0	2	0	2
outside	0	1	1	2
eat	0	2	0	2
want	0	1	1	2
in	0	0	2	2

Constructed from data in Appendix A, Nelson, (1973).

for probable occurrence as one-word utterances or in utterance final
position.)

In Table 6 are summarized data from mothers' diaries for 45 children ages 10 to 21 months (Chapman, Klee, and Miller, in preparation).
The diaries were recorded over the course of a day in which three to
four activities were recorded for 15–20 minutes each: bathing, diapering, grooming, feeding, or other activity of mother's choice. Children's
uses of all non-noun words associated with action in those reports are
summarized in Table 6 in terms of the number of children using that
form in at least one action context. What is important to note about
the table for present purposes is that all the early-appearing words

Table 6.   The emergence of action verbs and action words reported in
mothers' 1-day diaries

| | Number of children in each age group for whom use was reported | | | |
Word	10–12 months $N = 10$	13–15 months $N = 11$	16–18 months $N = 12$	19–21 months $N = 12$
all-done	1	1	1	5
no	0	3	6	5
uh-oh (oops)	0	3	7	2
more	0	2	3	7
up	0	2	2	4
down	0	2	2	2
night-night	0	2	2	2
(bye) bye	0	1	5	2
see (lookit)	0	1	3	3
here	0	1	2	0
I-do-it	0	1	0	2
out (side)	0	0	3	3
all gone	0	0	2	1
there	0	0	1	1
put on	0	0	1	0
eat	0	0	1	3
kiss	0	0	1	1
go	0	0	0	4
get	0	0	0	3
have	0	0	0	2
fall (boom)	0	0	0	2
drop	0	0	0	1
kick	0	0	0	1
hold	0	0	0	1
tinkle	0	0	0	1
dry	0	0	0	1
need	0	0	0	1
watch	0	0	0	1
enough	0	0	0	1
sit down	0	0	0	1
read	0	0	0	1
bark	0	0	0	1
Total number types	1	11	16	31
Mean number types/child	0.08	1.6	2.75	5.2

Based on Chapman et al., in preparation.

associated with action context could have occurred as a single word
utterance or in utterance-final position, and that all the late appearing
words, which are, incidentally, mostly verbs, are unlikely to have done
so. (The same is true for the 10- to 13-month lexicons reported by
Volterra et al., 1979.)

This argument is indirect. It could be countered by an alternative interpretation that the semantic notions being encoded in the child's early and late vocabulary were distinctly different, with the later vocabulary reflecting concepts that were later to emerge. This indeed is one current interpretation of the later appearance of action words. What is suggested here is an alternative interpretation: that most verbs (and many other parts of speech), by virtue of their failure to occur singly or in utterance final position, are less accessible perceptually to the child.

Cross-linguistic comparisons should offer a test of this hypothesis. In languages in which mothers' speech includes frequent utterances with verbs (or any other morpheme category infrequent in the one-word speech of English-speaking children) in utterance final position, or as frequent one-word utterances, the content of early words should differ from those of the English-speaking child, reflecting the differential accessibility of input in the contrasting languages.

The Role of Context in Lexical Acquisition

Bruner (1975a; 1975b; 1978) and his colleagues (Ninio and Bruner, 1978; Ratner and Bruner, 1978) have been instrumental in showing the detailed ways in which mother-child joint interaction provides specific context in which language and language use can be learned.

They stress the role of the mother in "scaffolding," that is, supporting and extending the child's behavior in routines. For example, a book-reading activity was analyzed in videotapes of free mother-child play made every 2 to 3 weeks from 8 to 18 months for a single child (Ninio and Bruner, 1978). Pure pointing, the gestural form of nomination, had first arisen in this context, so it seemed a useful one in which to trace the child's later labeling of objects. Analyses of full free play sessions between 10;0 and 1;5 showed that 76% of the instances in which the mother labeled objects consisted of a picture; 17% for objects at a distance; and only 7% for objects being manipulated by the child.

This labeling activity took place in the context of a structured interaction sequence involving repeated use of four restricted sets of utterances by the mother: a request for attention (most frequently *Look*), a *what* question (most frequently *what's that?*), a Label (most frequently the Label alone and stressed, otherwise in utterance final position) and feedback (most frequently *yes*).

The cycle of interaction with the child is illustrated by the following example. The child was age 1;1 (Ninio and Bruner, 1978, p. 6):

Mother: Look!
Child: (Touches picture)
Mother: What are those?

Child: (Vocalizes and smiles)
Mother: Yes, they are rabbits.
Child: (Vocalizes, smiles, and looks up at mother)
Mother: (Laughs) Yes, rabbit.

Every dialogue cycle contained at least one utterance type. Every cycle was initiated with one of the first three types. The order, if more than one was present, was almost invariant: *look* preceded *what*, which preceded a Label. Label and feedback frequently occurred together; when they were separate, Label occurred first. Thus, the child is participating in an interaction where not only the referents are familiar, but also the game; both the mother's input and his responses are parts of a familiar and unvarying interaction sequence.

The mother solved the problem of what aspect of the picture to label by giving common names of whole objects 89% of the time. She made clear use of her detailed knowledge of the child's lexicon in choosing what to ask: what the child had seen and heard labeled before, what he understood, and what he had said.

The child, in turn, became increasingly active in his participation in the book-reading game, progressing from at least one active response (vocalization, gesture, smile, eye contact with mother, or search for specific object) 50% of the time at age 0;8 to 100% of the time at age 1;6. These active turns increasingly included vocalization: 0% at 8 months, 30% to 90% from 1;0 to 1;2; and 90% to 100% between 1;2 and 1;6. Increasingly, these vocalizations became recognizable labels, beginning at 1;2 and reaching 50% of vocalizations at 1;6.

When feedback effects were examined in this specified interaction format, several important facts emerged: 1) once the child could produce easily recognizable words, the mother corrected all incorrect labels; 2) the mother reinforced, that is, confirmed, the child's correct label at least once in the cycle 80% of the time, through idealized imitation, *yes*, and laughter, singly or together.

The effect of correction was to correct, not to suppress the words used incorrectly by the child; they were as likely to reoccur used correctly, as correctly used words.

The child's provision of a Label is most probable if the cycle is initiated by the child (0.49), or a *what's that* mother question (0.37) than when it begins with *Look* (0.20) or the mother's Label (0.10). Thus, simple modeling by the mother does not lead to child imitation.

The mother's contributions to the child's process of lexical acquisition, from Ninio and Bruner's (1978) viewpoint, are far more extensive than the simple association paradigms outlined earlier would suggest. The mother is historian, gamesleader, and informant as she and the child play together at one structured version of the game of language acquisition.

Semantics: Utterance Content

Recent studies (Snow, 1977a; Rondal, 1978; Schwartz, 1978; Retherford et al., in press) have examined not only the mothers' vocabulary and syntax in speaking to their children, but also the semantic roles played by words in the mothers' utterances and the ways in which these roles are combined (semantic relations).

Roles Permitted by Verb Types Rondal analyzed mothers' speech to 2-year-olds using Chafe's (1970) semantic categorization scheme for verb types in utterances (Tables 7 and 8). This scheme distinguishes basic verb properties (state, process, action) and the associated roles that they require or permit to co-occur in the utterance (e.g., locative; instrument; benefactive).

Rondal's analysis indicates that mothers talk about states, or static relationships, a little more frequently than they talk about processes or actions: 42% versus 37% of their utterances, averaged over time. The frequencies with which verbs require or are associated with the semantic roles of locative, experiencer, benefactive (including recipient), and instrument in Rondal's data are, respectively, 21%, 15%, 6%, and 1%. The semantic categories reported to be infrequent in children's speech (Brown, 1973) seem to be infrequent in the mother's speech as well. This conclusion is also borne out by studies of the semantic roles or relations actually present in mothers' utterances.

Semantic Relations and Roles Snow (1977a), analyzing the speech of Dutch-speaking mothers to 11 children ages 23 to 35 months, found that 76% of their multiterm utterances could be accounted for by the two- to four-term semantic relational categories reported by Brown (1973) to be prevalent in the speech of children putting two words together. (See Table 9.) Two-term utterances expressing stative relationships (entity-locative, possessor-possession, entity-attribute, demonstrative-entity) comprise 51% of the mothers' utterances, a figure a little higher than Rondal's findings would predict. The inclusion of a book-reading task by Snow, however, probably increased the proportion of stative *What's that?* questions compared to free play samples. (Her figure differs from the comparable category analyzed for free play by Retherford et al., (in press).)

An important aspect of Snow's (1977a) findings was the lack of change in proportion of prevalent relations in the mothers' speech across conversations with children in Brown's linguistics stages I through IV. The mother's speech, one might infer, was not finely tuned to the child in this regard. No comparable data on the children's semantic relations, however, were available.

This comparison is available in a recently completed study by Retherford et al. (in press), who analyzed the semantic and syntactic

Table 7. Distribution of semantic verb-types in mothers' speech ($N = 7$ each group)

Verb type	Example (Chafe, 1970)	Age MLU	1;11 1.27	2;3 1.96	2;6 2.88
State	The wood is dry		27%	23%	21%
State-experiential	Tom wanted a drink		6	7	7
State-benefactive	Tom has the tickets		2	3	3
State-locative	The knife is in the box		10	10	8
Process	The wood dried		2	2	4*
Action	Harriet sang		4	3	5
Process-action	Michael dried the wood		5	6	9
Process-experiential and action-experiential	Tom saw a snake Harry showed Tom the snake		7	9	8
Process-benefactive, action-benefactive, and process-action-benefactive	Tom found the tickets Mary sang for Tom Mary sent Tom the tickets		4	5	2
Process-instrumental, action-instrumental, and process-action-instrumental	The door opened with a key He jumped with a pole Tom opened the door with a key		1	0	1
State-completable and action-completable	The candy costs ten cents Mary sang a song		13	10	11
Process-locative, action-locative, and process-action-locative	Tom fell off the chair Tom sat in the chair Tom threw the knife into the box		7	16	13*
Nominations			10	3	2*
Residual verb types			2	4	5*

Adapted from Rondal. 1978, pp. 231–232.

* $p < 0.05$ for language level effect in one-way ANOVA.

Table 8. Distribution of semantic verb-types in children's speech ($N = 7$ each group)

VERB TYPE	AGE: MLU:	1;11 1.27	2;3 1.46	2;6 2.88
1. State		21%	20%	26%
2. State-experiential		4	4	6*
3. State-benefactive		0	2	4*
4. State-locative		7	14	10
5. Process		1	2	3
6. Action		1	4	3
7. Process-action		4	6	7*
8. Process-experiential and action-experiential		3	4	9*
9. Process-benefactive, action-benefactive, and process-action-benefactive		0	1	3
10. Process-instrumental, action-instrumental, and process-action-instrumental		0	0	1*
11. State-completable and action-completable		5	7	10
12. Process-locative, action-locative, and process-action-locative		2	13	9*
13. (Nominations)		53	24	7*
14. Residual verb types		0	0	2*

Adapted from Rondal, 1978, pp. 223–224.
* $p < 0.05$ for language level effect in one-way ANOVA

roles coded in six mothers' speech in relation to the roles by which the children's speech could be coded. (See Table 10.) Speech samples were taken from children at an average age of 21 months and again at 25 months.

Approximately 17% of the mothers' utterances fell into conversational device categories; 10% into complex sentences; 6% into routines, and 3% into simple utterances not codable by the semantic categories. The remaining 64% of their utterances could be coded by 21 semantic and syntactic role categories, ignoring grammatically obligatory information and auxiliary verb content.

Mothers showed a stable speech style with no significant differences in categories from 21 to 25 months. The categories that predominated in the coding of these single and multiterm utterances were those eight roles prevalent in the Stage I multiterm speech of children summarized by Brown (1973)—agent, action, object of action, demonstrative, locative, entity, possessor, attribution—and the categories of state and adverbial. Excluding single-term entity categories, approximately 78% of the roles coded for the mothers fell into Brown's eight

Table 9.   Prevalent semantic relations in Dutch mothers' speaking to 2-year-olds during free play and book reading[a]

	Average percent of multiterm utterances
Two-term relations	
Agent-action	11.4
Action-object	2.8
Action-locative	1.6
Entity-locative	11.1
Possessor-possessed	3.9
Entity-attribute	12.1
Demonstrative-entity	23.1
Other semantic relations	2.6
Three-term relations	
Agent-action-object	4.1
Agent-action-locative	3.1
Agent-object-locative	.2
Action-object-locative	1.7
Other semantic relations	3.9
Four-term relations	
Agent-action-object-locative	1.3
Other semantic relations	1.8
Unanalyzable	15.9
Total prevalent semantic relations	76.3

Adapted from Snow, 1977a, p. 45.

[a] Multiterm utterances of mothers speaking Dutch with their 23- to 35-month-old daughters, 2 studied twice, provide the data base. Wh-questions were included in the coding; tense, time, and manner adverbials, copular, modal, and catenative verbs, prepositions, articles, and apparently, semantic relations expanding noun phrases were ignored.

prevalent categories. The analogous figures for children were 64% and 70% at mean ages 21 and 25 months.

Children showed one apparent change in the pattern of semantic roles used. The frequency of action, agent, and object categories increased significantly. The increase in the latter two, which were coded only for multiterm utterances, may simply reflect the increased frequency of multiterm speech. But increase in action verbs may be a replicable phenomenon. Rondal (1978) also reported significant increases in the category over the same period.

Frequency of use of categories, then, was fairly stable in children as well as mothers. When categories were similar in their high or low frequency of use by the pair in 21-month conversation, the probability was 0.80 that they would continue to be so for both at the 25-month sample. (High frequency was defined as being above the median frequency of use by the speaker at the time; low as at or below the median.) When individual mothers and children differed in their high versus low frequency use of a category at time 1, however, the probability was substantial that someone would change at time 2 (see Table 11), 0.69 to 0.61 on the average. In these cases one can ask *who* changed. The answer is that the child did so much more frequently than the mother.

Mothers and children increased significantly over time in the proportion of categories used at least once by both. (See Table 12.) The increase comes about through an increase in the categories used by the children. Only once in the entire set of categories and children did a child use a category not coded in the mother's speech at that time.

Table 10.   Semantic and syntactic roles in mother's and children's speech during free play as percentages of total instances, averaged across 6 dyads

Category	Age 21 months		Age 25 months	
	Child	Mother	Child	Mother
*Action	10.8	16.8	16.9	19.3
Entity (1 term)	34.3	3.1	14.6	1.0
*Entity (multiterm)	11.4	16.2	11.4	10.4
*Locative	8.7	8.8	10.2	8.6
Negation	7.2	3.0	8.1	2.9
Grammatical morphemes	5.3		7.8	
*Agent (multiterm)	2.4	10.0	6.7	12.6
*Object of action (multiterm)	0.8	7.4	5.0	10.8
*Demonstrative	2.6	8.4	4.5	6.2
Recurrence	0.6	1.0	3.6	1.7
*Attribute	3.6	5.0	3.0	5.1
*Possessor	1.6	4.2	2.1	3.6
Adverb	1.4	4.6	2.1	6.5
Quantifier	2.2	1.6	1.2	2.4
State	2.3	4.0	1.1	3.3
Experiencer	3.5	3.4	0.8	2.7
Recipient	0.0	0.7	0.4	1.3
Beneficiary	0.0	0.1	0.2	0.2
Name	0.0	0.2	0.2	0.1
Created object	0.0	1.2	0.1	1.2
Comitative	1.1	0.2	0.1	0.1
Instrument	0.0	0.2	0.0	0.1
Total percent	99.8	100.1	100.1	100.1
Total instances	166.0	721.7	254.2	806.3

Adapted from Retherford et al., in press.

* Included in Brown's (1973) list of prevalent semantic relations.

Table 11.   Average conditional probabilities of time 2 category frequencies (high or low) in mother and child, given time 1 category frequencies in each

Who changes at T2?	Neither		Child		Mother		Both	
Time 1: M-C	M-C	Time 2	M-C	Time 2	M-C	Time 2	M-C	Time 2
H-H	H-H	0.79	H-L	0.13	L-H	0.06	L-L	0.02
H-L	H-L	0.31	H-H	0.48	L-L	0.22	L-H	0.00
L-H	L-H	0.39	L-L	0.49	L-H	0.04	H-L	0.08
L-L	L-L	0.80	L-H	0.11	H-L	0.04	H-H	0.06

From Retherford et al., in press.

When the ways that mother and children combined roles in multiterm utterances were examined, it was apparent that the mothers provided a wide and stable variety of simple sentence models: from 98 to 129 different two-, three-, and four-term patterns in the two half-hours of talking at 21 and 25 months (Schwartz, 1978). The children used fewer different combinations: from 10 to 48 at 25 months. The average percentage of child combinations at 25 months that were present in the mothers' speech at the same time or 4 months earlier are given in Table 13. The average percentages of mother combinations used by the children at 25 months are given in Table 14. What these figures show is that mothers model many more patterns than children use, and that children use some patterns that are not directly observed in the mothers' speech in our samples. This is increasingly true for longer combinations, suggesting that children may not only be selective in the models they copy but also creative in the utterances they construct.

Semantic Roles and Relations: Causes and Consequences

Mothers provide models of a wide range of semantic roles and short combinations; their speech seems rather stable in this aspect. Children, in contrast, show a developmental progression in the use of roles over the second year of life (Greenfield and Smith, 1976). These uses may be rather more idiosyncratic and contextually bound than the category coding reveals (Braine, 1976). The important point here is that mothers

Table 12.   Percent of 17 semantic and syntactic categories used by either mother or child that both use, at two times[a]

Ages	A	B	C	D	E	F	Mean percent	S.D.
19–24 mo.	64.7%	57.1%	56.3%	66.7%	57.1%	62.5%	60.7%	4.48
24–28 mo.	62.5%	86.7%	85.7%	73.3%	57.1%	92.9%	76.4%	14.42

[a] Unpublished data from Retherford et al. (in press). Categories coded only for multiterm utterances are collapsed for these figures.

Table 13.   Mean percent of six children's combinations at 24–28 months in mothers' speech at the same or earlier time

Children's combinations	Average percent present in mothers' speech (%)
2 Term	83.2 ($N = 6$)
3 Term	85.7 ($N = 6$)
4 Term	61.1 ($N = 3$)
5 Term-plus	50.0 ($N = 2$)

Based on Schwartz, 1978.

are not finely tuned to their children with respect to semantic roles when their speech is generally assessed, although the roles and relations used frequently include those that the child is acquiring. The child comes to look more like the mother, rather than the reverse.

Moreover, similar distributions of semantic roles are observed in the speech of mothers talking to hearing-impaired children of cognitively and chronologically more advanced levels (3½ years) who are at an early Stage I level of oral language comprehension and production (Chapman et al., 1978).

If the mother does not fine-tune her speech in this respect to changing aspects of the child (comprehension, production, cognitive level), what does determine her adjustment? The most likely explanation seems to come from topic restrictions to the immediate, here-and-now context: the mother is talking about the immediate situation. This adjustment may arise in recognition of the topics of interest to the child, in continuation of the child's initiated topic, or in recognition of the child's need for situational support in order to understand input. The three interpretations lead to somewhat different predictions about

Table 14.   Mean percent of mothers' combinations at either time present in six children's 24–28-month speech

Mothers' combinations	Average percent present in new combinations (%)
2 Term	31.3 ($N = 6$)
3 Term	14.9 ($N = 6$)
4 Term	6.6 ($N = 3$)
5 Term	4.1 ($N = 2$)

Based on Schwartz, 1978.

other occasions on which the mother will limit topics similarly. When appropriate adult conversational controls are run, perhaps the same semantic roles are frequent in adult-adult interaction when the topic is restricted to ongoing activity. (The combinations will of course be more complex.)

PRAGMATICS

Communicative Intents of Mothers' Speech to Children

Speech Act Distribution   There are relatively few studies of the reasons for which mothers talk to their children. Folger and Chapman (1978) reported the distribution of speech acts in six mothers talking to 21-month-old children during free play and lunch, using a category system modified from Dore (1977). These results are summarized in Table 15. The functional categories reinforce the pragmatic picture suggested by the distributional data on syntactic sentence type: requests for information are most frequent, followed by statements and descriptions and requests for action.

Utterances With Possible Teaching Functions   Moerk (1975) categorized mother's speech to preschoolers for functions that he believes may play a language teaching role. These are summarized in Table 16. About 28% of the mother's utterances fall into these categories. The corresponding child uses of language are given in Table 17. The changes seen over time seem to reflect changes in the mother-child activities and discussion about events removed in time and space.

Table 15.   Distribution of 4,489 mothers' speech acts to their six children during free play and lunch settings (children ages 1;7–2;1, mean age 1;9)[a]

Speech act	Average percentage (%)	Range (%)
Request for information	37.2	(31.4–44.2)
Request for action	14.9	(10.1–17.4)
Statements	16.2	(10.0–23.2)
Descriptions	13.0	(10.3–15.4)
Conversational devices	9.7	(6.4–15.1)
Repetitions	2.7	(1.4–3.6)
Elicited imitation	0.7	(0.3–1.0)
Performative play	1.2	(0.1–2.9)
Request for permission	0.2	(0.0–0.4)
Other	3.1	(0.3–7.8)

[a] Adapted from Table 2, p. 32, Folger and Chapman, 1978.

Table 16. Moerk's (1975) categories of mothers' language use in mother-child conversation (20 children ages 1;9 to 5;0)

Mother category	Mean percent of total utterances (S.D.) (%)	Direction of change with increase in child MLU
Models from picture book	5.02 (6.68)	Decrease (r = −0.61)
Describes object or event	5.41 (3.86)	No change
Describes own acts	1.03 (1.04)	No change
Describes child's acts	1.30 (1.32)	Decrease (r = −0.44)
Gives corrective feedback	4.18 (4.83)	Decrease (r = −0.61)
Answers a question	5.17 (6.73)	Increase then decrease
Guides child's action	2.60 (2.58)	No change
Gives explanation	3.54 (2.54)	No change

Requests for Action   Rondal's (1978) data on requests for action suggest that the proportion in the mother's speech is dropping as the child moves from the second into the third year of life. (See Table 18.) Additions to the mother's request, including inquiries as to the child's willingness to carry out the action or giving a justification for the request, almost double over the 23- to 30-month period.

Differences in mothers' rate of requesting action, or "manding," then, cannot be interpreted unless the children are matched for cognitive level. Indeed, mothers address fewer directives to 3-month-olds, and more to 6- to 9-month-olds, than they do to 2-year-olds (Masur, Holzman, and Ferrier, 1977).

These data make clear that requests for action do not increase simply as a function of increased capacity for compliance through

Table 17. Moerk's (1975) categories of child language use in mother-child integration (20 children ages 1;9 to 5;0).

Child category	Mean percent of total utterances (S.D.) (%)	Direction of change with increasing MLU
Imitates	5.54 (6.99)	Decrease (r = −0.61)
Asks a question	9.62 (6.88)	Increase and then decrease
Expresses a need	10.81 (5.97)	No change
Answers a question	16.98 (9.02)	Increase and then decrease
Encodes from picture book	8.34 (11.39)	Decrease (r = −0.61)
Describes object or event	6.36 (3.67)	No change
Describes own acts	3.07 (2.17)	No change
Describes past experience	2.71 (2.41)	Increase (r = 0.57)
Describes own plans	3.43 (2.88)	Increase (r = 0.60)

Table 18.   Changes in percent requests for action and adjuncts in mothers' speech to children

Child age MLU	23 months 1.27	27 months 1.96	30 months 3.07
Request for actions	19%	13%	10%
Percent of requests with adjuncts	12%	19%	22%

Adapted from Rondal, 1978, pp. 233. ($N = 7$, each group).

intentional action, a greater repertoire of actions, or improved comprehension skill. Shatz (1978) showed that 2-year-olds interpret utterances as requests for action when the situation makes it appropriate to do so regardless of the utterance's grammatical form. Thus, the child's compliance in context is often good. Requests for action and attention are frequently made for activities the child is already carrying out (Chapman et al., in preparation); accompanying gestural cueing reduces the comprehension requirements further. Mothers repeat a request for attending to objects before compliance more frequently to 10- to 12-month-olds than to 19- to 21-month-olds (Chapman et al., in preparation). These findings suggest that the higher frequency of directives at the beginning of the second year may reflect the child's relative lack of comprehension, despite the increased repertoire of actions.

Requests for Information   Requests for information are frequent in speech addressed to children, and question forms are even more frequent. Sachs and Devin (1977) analyzed the functions of question forms in children role-playing mothers; these are summarized below.

Seeking information about external world
Seeking information about internal states
Requesting goods
Requesting services or prohibiting actions
Requesting permission
Instruction (eliciting answer to something the speaker already knows)
Seeking approval or confirmation
Seeking clarification
Attention getting

The children, as mothers, were more likely to address real informational requests to the 2-year-old about internal states, and to seek new information about the external world from older children (Sachs and Devin, 1976).

Pragmatics: Discourse Relations

When the relation of one utterance to another is examined, repetition on the mother's part and imitation on the child's part are frequently found in conversations of mothers with 2-year-olds and decrease as the child grows older.

Self-Repetitions   The mother's repetition of herself, either exactly or in partial paraphrase, is frequent in her speech to young children. Benedict (1975) found that 43% of mothers' speech to 10- to 14-month-olds was self-repetitions. Self-repetitions account for about a quarter of mothers' utterances to 2-year-olds. Kobashigawa (1969) reported 34%; Newport et al. (1977) reported an average of 23% for speech to 12- to 27-month-olds; and Cross (1977), an average of 28% for 19- to 32-month-olds. Maternal repetitions were negatively correlated with age in the latter two studies. Message content, then, is redundant to the 2-year-olds.

Causes and Consequences of Self-Repetition   The mother's frequent repetition of herself (Kobashigawa, 1969), particularly in imperative buildups and breakdowns (Broen, 1972) or in replacement sequences (Braine, 1971) has been singled out as a device that may play a causal role in acquisition in two ways. First, investigators have asked if the probability of understanding the mother increases with self-repetition or paraphrase (Benedict, 1975; Newport et al., 1977). Second, the relationships between full and partial utterance repetitions have been thought to reveal to the child the constituent organization of the sentence (Braine, 1971; Broen, 1972).

The first question has been investigated by looking at the probability that the child complies on successive mother repetitions in free play. Although the cumulative probability of compliance increases across trials for children in the second year (Benedict, 1975, 1978; Newport et al., 1977), the conditional probability of complying on a trial, given that the child failed to comply on the previous trial, is constant (Newport et al., 1977). The mother's repetition of her request does not alter the basic probability of her child's complying with it, then. That is, repetitions do not seem to serve a teaching function, although they do serve to get the child to do something.

The second role advocated for mothers' self-repetitions—that of displaying the structural organization of sentences across successive utterances—would seem highly unlikely for children with the limited comprehension skills of the 1- to 3-year-old period. Such pattern practice drills are far more likely to be helpful to school-age children and adults who can memorize the successive utterances and interpretations.

Finally, the fact that repetitions decrease with increasing child age suggests that such patterned illustrations in the mother's speech will not normally play a role in the acquisition of language at all.

As to why mothers speaking to young children should be so redundant, two explanations can be offered. The first arises from Snow's finding (1977b) that mothers adopt a conversational model well before their children can participate. Under these circumstances, repeating oneself is an easy way to keep the conversation going.

The second explanation, which is not antithetical to the first, is that mothers repeat in an attempt to get children to comply. With repetition, the cumulative probability of the child's compliance increases. As the child's lexical and pragmatic comprehension skills increase, the unconditional probability of compliance increases and the mother's need to repeat decreases.

Corrections of Children's Speech   Brown (1973) reported that explicit corrections of Adam, Eve, and Sarah's utterances in the third year were infrequent. Corrections were made, moreover, not to correct pronunciation or grammar, but to correct the truth-value of an utterance. In older children, social unacceptability also becomes an occasion for correction (Berko-Gleason, 1973).

Ninio and Bruner's (1978) analysis of the child's use of labeling in the book-reading task similarly indicates that the mother corrects for truth-value of the label rather than mispronunciations or unintelligible vocalizations. Ninio and Bruner found, however, that corrections occur very consistently when mislabelings occur; furthermore, the corrections seemed to be effective. It is the child's semantic errors, then, that are infrequent, rather than the mother's corrections.

Compliance and Confirmation as Reinforcement   Brown (1973) concluded that reinforcement played little role in the child's acquisition of language because explicit approval of the child's utterances (*that's right; good*) was infrequent.

There are other events, however, more likely to be reinforcing to the sensorimotor Stage V or Stage VI child than being told that he or she said something correctly. These include bringing about the desired pragmatic effect—initiating the game, getting the object, getting the mother's attention—and getting feedback that the message has been understood. Thus, the mother's compliance and confirmation rates may be better indicators of the reinforcing values of communicating for the child in the 1- to 2-year-period. They may also prove to be better indicators of individual differences in mothers that are associated with differential rates of language acquisition.

Experimental Demonstrations of the Effects of Modeling   Nelson and Bonvillian (1974) reported that labeling of toys increased 18-month-olds' use of modeled names. Hovell, Schumaker, and Sherman (1978) demonstrated significant effects of modeling plus nondifferential praise on 2-year-olds' spontaneous use of color and size adjective-noun combinations in a picture book routine, although not in nontrained conversational contexts.

Mothers' Expansions of Children's Utterances   Expansions are defined as the repetition of the other speaker's utterances with added words. From that point, definitions vary. For some, only function words can be added. No new content words are allowed if the instance is to count as an expansion (Cazden, 1965). Other investigators allow content word additions (e.g., Folger and Chapman, 1978). The looser criterion is more typical of studies of mother's speech to children in the one-word period or early Stage I of word combinations, where grammatically obligatory content words are frequently missing. Finally, some investigators also relax order constraints (e.g., Cross, 1977).

Expansions of the child's speech in the sense of Cross's definition are frequent in mother's speech to children ages 19 to 36 months, in Brown's Stages I through III. Even when order variation is excluded by the definition, expansion of children's speech in early Stage I, about 21 months, is frequent (Seitz and Stewart, 1975; Folger and Chapman, 1978), although it drops off afterward. As many as 20% to 30% of the mothers' utterances may be expansions of the child. Because mothers at these stages typically talk more than the children, the corresponding percentage of child utterances that are expanded by the mother may be twice as high. Why should expansion be so frequent in speech to the young child? One part of the answer emerges when one remembers that expansions or repetitions are defined by formal similarity rather than pragmatic intent. If one considers the reasons for speaking that might be realized in expansions or repetitions of the other person's utterance, as Keenan (1977) has done, it becomes apparent that mothers' expansions could—and surely do—arise for diverse communicative purposes. Below, for example, is a list of reasons for which Keenan's 3-year-old twins repeated each other; a similar set of purposes could be identified for expansions.

To comment attitudinally
To agree with
To self-inform
To query
To answer requests for information appropriately
To imitate when specifically requested to do so
To make counterclaims

To make claims matching those of previous speaker
To greet back
To reverse the direction (roles) of an order or request for information
To request clarification of an utterance

Cross studied a large number of semantic, syntactic, and pragmatic characteristics of mothers speaking to children ages 19 to 36 months with MLUs between 1.5 and 3.5 ($N = 16$). Eight of the children were linguistically accelerated compared with the other eight; the two groups were of matched MLUs but differed in age by approximately 6 months. Only a few of Cross's (1978) measures differentiated the mothers of these two groups. The differentiating measures included the mother's rate of expansion (in which all of the child's words were repeated) and the mother's rate of extension (in which some of the child words were repeated and new content added). These rates were higher for the younger, and hence linguistically accelerated, group. Mothers who more frequently expanded and extended their children's utterances were more likely to have linguistically accelerated children.

Experimental Confirmation of the Role of Expansions in Language Acquisition   Schumaker (1976) found that mothers' expansions of their 2-year-olds' picture labels with phrases (e.g., *See* dog, *See the* dog, *Here is the* dog in successive conditions) resulted in the increased spontaneous use of each phrase, including use with novel words. Hovell et al. (1978) found that expansions plus nondifferentiated praise had a greater effect than modeling plus praise on children's spontaneous use of adjectives in the training routine. Some instances of generalization to conversations outside the routine were noted by mother.

That expansions contingent on child utterances can play a causal role in the acquisition of semantic relations at the linguistic Stage I level has been demonstrated by Branston (1979) for five developmentally delayed children. Briefly, Branston trained student teachers to expand the children's utterances for one specific semantic relational target not present in the child's spontaneous repertoire (e.g., action-object, entity-locative, etc.) although constituents of the target structure were present. To elicit constituents of the target structure so that expansions could be delivered, student teachers engaged the children in activities exemplifying the basic semantic roles of the target structure while modeling constituents and asking questions answerable with constituents of the target structure. Production of a constituent by a child was immediately expanded into the target structure.

Following 4 weeks of 20 minutes per day of intervention, there was a significant increase in the frequency of both spontaneous and imitated production of target structures over the pre-intervention control condition frequencies. Thus, Branston obtained experimental evidence that expansions in conjunction with structured activities were effective in increasing the production of target semantic structures for developmentally delayed children at linguistic Stage I.

The accelerating effects of expansion could come about through at least three rather different mechanisms. On one view, expansions may be important primarily for their frequent pragmatic effect of confirming for the child that he has been understood. If so, repetition for the same purpose should be an equally effective motivational device.

A second reason for the accelerating effects of expansions may be that they serve as optimal models of how one or more elements should be added to an utterance already produced by the child. Whether this contribution is primarily to syntactic production or to comprehension, and hence indirectly to production, we do not know; and indeed, both could happen.

A third way in which mothers' expansions may be related to accelerated syntactic production is through their general pragmatic effect of continuing the child's topic. On this view, mothers' topic extensions should also be related to accelerated production—and they are. Here the effect is presumably mediated by semantic considerations. The mother's meaning, other things being equal, may be more easily discovered—or more useful for communicative purposes—for topics the child has chosen to raise than for topics introduced by the mother.

The three ways in which expansions may prove important are not necessarily mutually exclusive. Confirming communicative intent, modeling small additions to a child's production within the communicative context and allowing the child to control conversational topics may all prove to play important causal roles in acquisition.

Children's Imitations of Mothers' Utterances   Bloom et al. (1974) demonstrated that frequency of imitating the mother varies with individual children: from 6% to 42% of their six Stage I children's utterances were imitations. Furthermore, children's imitation rates decrease with age beyond 24 months (Moerk, 1975; Seitz and Stewart, 1975; Bloom, Rocissano, and Hood, 1976). Dore (1975) reported imitators to be frequent in the one-word stage.

For those children who do imitate, little overall difference in grammatical level between imitated and spontaneous utterances is observed (Ervin, 1964). In finer-grained analyses of the semantic relation, word, structure, or bound morpheme that is imitated, however, a different picture emerges. Bloom et al. (1974) reported that their imitative children were significantly more likely to imitate semantic relations or words that they were just in the process of acquiring in their spontaneous speech, rather than either familiar or entirely novel items. Ramer

(1976) confirmed the selective character of imitation. Analyzing the imitations of children with MLUs between 1 and 2, Ramer found that the majority (63%–75%) of imitations, for every child, were lexically progressive. That is, the words imitated had occurred spontaneously fewer than 5 times in prior production. This was true both for children who imitated frequently and for those who imitated infrequently. Coggins and Morrison (1979) found the same thing in four Down's syndrome children at Stage I.

Moerk (1977) found the imitations of 2 children between 24 and 30 months to be associated with words, phrase structures or grammatical morphemes that the child was just acquiring; often, within the same session, the child would shift from imitative to spontaneous use.

Folger and Chapman (1978), in examining the pragmatic contexts in which 21-month-old children imitate, found that imitation rates varied relatively little as a function of the different parental speech acts. Rather, the children were most likely to imitate repetitions or expansions of their own utterances. (See Table 19.) This finding conforms to Ninio and Bruner's finding (1978) that their child was unlikely to label following mother's model labels. Rather, children are likely to imitate above base-rate levels only when they are the originators of the topic and the utterance being expanded or repeated. Thus, it was the frequency of parental expansion that made the difference between children who were imitators or non-imitators in the Folger and Chapman study.

This finding suggests a reinterpretation of Bloom et al.'s (1974) distinction between imitators and non-imitators. Indeed, this may be a dimension of individual difference, but the difference may reside in different expansion rates among mothers, rather than imitation rates

Table 19.   Mean percentage of parental speech acts imitated by six children with parent expansions as a separate category[a]

Parent's utterance	Average (%) imitated	Range (%)
Imitative expansion	32	10–46
Exact repetition	22	0–53
Descriptions	9	0–14
Statements	5	0–11
Requests for information	8	2–18
Requests for action	4	1–12
Conversational devices	2	0–4

[a] Adapted from Table 4, p. 33, Folger and Chapman, 1978.

of children. The selective aspect of children's imitations, in contrast, seem to be common to all children.

The causal role that imitation plays in acquisition, if any, is not so clear from these data. Spontaneous imitation may be an epiphenomenon of the acquisition process: a behavior accompanying the acquisition phase, but not necessary or sufficient for it (Snyder-McLean and McLean, 1978). Snyder-McLean and McLean suggest that spontaneous imitations may be useful for the rehearsal of specific speech motor acts in association with appropriate referential contexts.

Clark (1977) observed that spontaneous imitations can occur for forms that children fail to comprehend fully, can be more grammatically advanced than usual, and may contain distortions or veridically copied elements due to mechanical reasons rather than the child's own rule system. She also argues that imitation may aid the learning of fragments not yet generated by the child's rule system, and that perception of such fragments (and ultimately, comprehension) may thereby be facilitated. In production, the fragments may be used in juxtapositions that lead to discovery of alternative forms or in unanalyzed padding of sentences, resulting in the appearance of more complex and idiosyncratic child grammars than may actually be the case.

Whitehurst and Vasta (1975) proposed, in contrast to Clark, that imitation allows newly understood syntactic structures to be introduced to the production mode: that comprehended forms are introduced to production via imitation. This argument is wrong if by "comprehension" they mean ability to use the syntactic cue alone as the clue to meaning; if, in contrast, they mean comprehension in context, their proposal is similar to that of Snyder-McLean and McLean.

Topic Initiation and Continuation in Discourse   The mother takes her topics principally from the immediate situation (73% of her utterances in Cross's 1977 study of input to 16 children ages 19 to 36 months). The topics are far more likely to concern child events (48% of the mother's utterances in Cross's study) than mother events (16%), and least likely to concern activities of third parties (9%). The last finding may simply reflect the fact that only the two parties were present most of the time, a consistent characteristic of the situations in which mother-child speech has been studied, although not a consistent reflection of the situations in which children must learn language.

That the mother talks about the child's activities more frequently than her own, and about the immediate situation more frequently than events remote in time and space, are important facts about mothers' speech to 2-year-olds. Because the language-learning child must construct pragmatic and semantic role aspects of meaning from the interaction, rather than from the mother's language, these topical restrictions are a great aid to him or her in puzzling out the mother's meanings.

Cross's (1978) data, interpreted from the point of view of topic, would suggest that the mothers who continue their children's topics more frequently in their speech may accelerate their children's acquisition. Alternatively, we may be looking at an effect of the children's cognitive acceleration. Perhaps the more frequent topic continuation in the speech of the mothers talking to the linguistically advanced children reflects an increased capacity for topic initiation by these children that is linked to their advanced cognitive status. We cannot choose between these possibilities without information on the cognitive status of the two groups of children. We do not know whether to view the difference in mothers' input as a consequence of the child's cognitive status or a cause of the linguistic status.

Bloom et al. (1976) make clear that the topic continuation skills of the Stage I and Stage II child are limited. (See Table 20.) When topic continuation does occur, it is achieved chiefly through imitation by the 2-year-old. Only in the older, linguistically advanced Stage V children (see Table 21) is new information being contributed to the topic with any frequency. The way in which turntaking and topic continuation skills emerge in the 1- to 2-year-old child is a topic of current study (Miller et al., in press).

Mother's Initiation of Topics Remote in Time   Sachs (1979) provided a particularly clear documentation of an instance in which the mother may contribute to the child's semantic development through the topics she initiates, rather than continues. Although talk about events remote in past time (*earlier past*) from the immediate situation is rare in mothers' speech to young children, Sachs found that it did occur in a longitudinal study of her daughter from 20 to 29 months. The proportion of mother's utterances referring to *earlier past*, rather than an immediate *past* event, increased in frequency at the same rate as the child's—except that mother's use of *earlier past* began two months

Table 20.   Average distribution of topic continuations in child utterances immediately following adult speech ($N = 4$)[a]

Utterances immediately following adult speech	Mean age	21 months	25 months	36 months
	Mean MLU	1.26	2.60	3.98
Same topics, something new		0.21	0.33	0.46
Same topic, nothing new		0.18	0.06	0.02
Different topic		0.31	0.20	0.16
Total		0.70	0.59	0.64

Computed from Bloom et al., 1976.

[a] 400 utterances for each child at each stage are included in the consecutive samples.

Table 21.   Average distribution of topic related discourse $(N = 4)^a$

Categories of topic related discourse	Mean age Mean MLU	21 months 1.26	25 months 2.60	36 months 3.98
Yes/No only answers		0.11	0.29	0.26
Expansion		0.33	0.37	0.51
Alternative		0.05	0.10	0.08
Imitation		0.47	0.16	0.05

Computed from Bloom et al., 1976.

^{a} Categories occurring less than 10% of the time in any sample are omitted. These include social routines, recoding of the adult utterance, and explanation in which new topics are introduced following continuation of the old topic. Note that topic-continuing Wh-questions did not appear in children's speech until Stage V.

before the child's, which began at 25 months. In the 5 months prior, the few child utterances containing past references were to the im-mediate *past*. When reference to the *earlier past* began in the child, it was almost exclusively in response to continuing topics introduced by the mother.

In Sachs' (1979) case then, these input topics were not adapted to semantic content that the child was already expressing, a fine-tuning proposal made by van der Geest (1977) and Snow (1977a). Indeed, examples at 22 months suggest they were not adapted to semantic content the child could comprehend either (Cross, 1977):

Mother: Did you go on the slide?
Naomi: Go slide. (p. 152, Sachs, 1979)

Sachs proposed that the purpose for the mother's early and infrequent initiations of the *earlier past* topics was simply to probe whether the child could respond appropriately. A similar argument could be made for the Wh-questions asked before the child has acquired the ability to ask (or probably, to answer) them. Once the child began to answer appropriately, frequency of reference to earlier past topics increased in the mother, with a concomitant increase in responsive production by the child. Thus, the initial probes permitted the mother to fine-tune further frequency increases.

Sachs argued that the probes may have had the effect, for the child, of demonstrating the semantic mapping between syntactic forms (already used by the child to express immediate past) and *earlier past*: that is, of teaching the child to refer to events that occurred in earlier time. The timing of the probes was crucial; they involved syntactic forms that the child was already producing frequently in marking im-mediate past.

Mother's Wh-questions might also be expected to play a similar role in Wh-question acquisition. Encouraged by behavior or vocabulary suggesting that the child may be able to answer (e.g., counting words; a time marker such as *now* or *yestermorning*), mothers may begin to probe the relevant question domain with some frequency and increase their frequency as children began to answer appropriately. Indeed, they may teach question/answer routines as the first instances of appropriate responding on the child's part.

Children's Comprehension of Mother Discourse Functions   Scherer and Coggins (in preparation) analyzed the relation of four child behaviors to antecedent discourse functions in the mothers' speech: asserting, clarifying an utterance, acknowledging an utterance, and carrying out an action. Four dyads were studied; the children were in Brown's Stage I. All four of these behaviors were significantly more likely to occur when preceded by particular discourse acts in the mothers' speech. Respectively, these were requests for information, requests for clarification, requests for acknowledgments, and requests for action. Thus, there is evidence that children recognize the discourse obligations that these four speech acts impose, at least in the course of naturalistic interactions incorporating contextual cues at Stage I.

Pragmatics: Variations in Mothers' Input?

Ecological Validity of the Free Play Samples?   Most findings previously reviewed come from interactions in which a high socioeconomic status (SES) mother was instructed to play with the child as usual. Such interactions typically yield high speaking rates for mother and child, and an intent on the mother's part to elicit performance from the child that is evident in pragmatic analyses. Graves and Glick (1978) demonstrated that the rates of talking in the observed free play situation are twice that found in the unobserved waiting room situation. Relative distributions of utterance types seem similar in the two situations, but there does seem to be an increase in the observed condition in utterances whose intent is to show off the child's knowledge—test questions, for example.

SES Effects?   Tulkin and Kagan (1972) found similar nonverbal mother behaviors in middle class and working class mothers of 10-month-old daughters, but significantly less frequent verbal behaviors directed to the infant by the working class mothers. They attributed this decreased frequency to the less frequent belief in working class mothers that their infants were capable of communicating.

Clarke-Stewart (1973), who observed for an entire day low SES infants in their homes, provided an account of home activity contrasting sharply with the interaction patterns reported in free play samples of high SES children. Infants and mothers were together a large proportion of the time. At 9 to 13 months, infants spent 84% of their waking time in the same room as their mothers (56% to 99%); 53% of the time within arm's reach. At 16 to 17 months, the average decreased to 77% (38%–97%); 45% within arm's reach.

Interaction of any kind with the infant, however, occurred less frequently—36% of the time that he or she was awake, on the average. The mother talked to the child 25% of the infant's waking time on the average (4% to 72% range); and played with the infant 4% of the time (0% to 27%). Affectionate behavior (5%) and stimulation with toys (5%) were also infrequent. Mother's verbal stimulation was the single variable most highly related to the children's competence—particularly to their language level at 17 months, in Clarke-Stewart's study.

Snow, Arlman-Rupp, Hassing, Jobse, Joosten, and Vorster (1976) examined the syntactic and pragmatic characteristics of Dutch mothers from three different social classes speaking to their 18- to 34-month-olds. Amount of talking was not analyzed. The working class mothers used less substantive deixis and more modal verbs, and more imperatives than middle and academic middle-class mothers. The latter two groups used more than twice as many expansions and repetitions of the children's utterances.

Newport et al. (1977) reported fewer imperatives and more substantive deixis to be associated with greater linguistic growth across a 6-month period; Cross (1977) found expansion rates to be higher in mothers of linguistically accelerated children.

Individual Differences? Controlled studies are not available to show whether the SES differences reflect different cultural styles, demands on the mother's time that are associated with SES level, or in the case of Clarke-Stewart's study, differences between normal, daily interaction patterns and those to be found when play is requested. Whatever the causes, they would seem to result in marked individual differences, rather than similarities, in the proportion of time that these low SES mothers talk to their children. There are correlated individual differences in the children's language skill, despite the general low SES status of her sample. The extremely low frequencies of talking and joint play to be found in some mothers of the Clarke-Stewart sample seem to rule out an explanation of the mother's reduced input based simply on the child's language level. Even prelinguistic higher SES children seem to receive a substantial amount of linguistic input (e.g., Cohen and Beckwith, 1976; Snow, 1977b). Given Fowler's (Chapter 16, this volume) experimental demonstration of the effects of increased maternal language stimulation on language acquisition in middle class children in this same period, it seems clear that substantial numbers of low SES children may be acquiring language slower than high SES children simply because of reduced opportunity for verbal interaction.

CONCLUSION

Effect of Limited Comprehension Skill: A Lexical Role for Input   The problem of learning language, from the child's perspective, is the chiefly nonlinguistic one of learning what to expect and what to do in interactive contexts. Only limited lexical content in the mother's speech seems to play a linguistic role in this process. Meaning may be particularly likely to be associated with lexical content in single word utterances or utterance final position.

Making Input Contingent on Child Behavior   The factors likely to enhance the child's ultimate comprehension and use of a lexical item in a perceptually salient position within the utterance include the following: 1) the immediate presence of the referent or event to which the child is attending; 2) the salience of the referent for the child; 3) use by the mother in a conversational routine; 4) lexical expansion of the child's utterance; 5) semantic extension (commenting) of the child's topic. If one of the operating principles for the child is "Pay attention to the ends of utterances," the most important operating principle for the mother seems to be "Pay attention to what the child is doing and saying."

The mother's important roles, from the child's perspective, are to create order in his or her social and experiential world and to respond consistently to communicative attempts. Input seems to play a demonstrable role in the 2-year-olds' language acquisition when it is specifically contingent on the child's initiated actions and utterances. It is the linguistically responsive environment, rather than the linguistically stimulating one, that should accelerate language acquisition in the 1- to 2-year-old.

REFERENCES

Benedict, H. 1975. The role of repetition in early language comprehension. Paper presented at the Society for Research in Child Development Biennial Meeting, Denver, April.
Benedict, H. 1978. Language comprehension in 9–15 month old children. *In* R. Campbell and P. Smith (eds.) Recent Advances in the Psychology of Language: Language Development and Mother-Child Interaction, pp. 57–70. Plenum Publishing Corp. New York.
Berko-Gleason, J. 1973. Code switching in children's language. *In* T. E. Moore

Mother-Child Interaction in the Second Year of Life 245

(ed.), Cognitive Development and the Acquisition of Language, pp. 159–168. Academic Press, Inc. New York.

Bingham, N. E. 1971. Maternal speech to pre-linguistic infants: Differences related to maternal judgments of infant language competence. Unpublished paper. Cornell University, Ithaca, N.Y.

Blasdell, R., and Jensen, P. 1970. Stress and word position as determinants of imitation in first language learners. J. Speech Hear. Res. 13:193–202.

Bloom, L. 1973. One Word at a Time. Mouton. The Hague.

Bloom, L., Hood, L., and Lightbown, P. 1974. Imitation in language development: If, when and why. Cognitive Psychol. 6:380–420.

Bloom, L., Rocissano, L., and Hood, L. 1976. Adult-child discourse: Developmental interaction between information processing and linguistic knowledge. Cognitive Psychol. 8:521–552.

Braine, M. D. S. 1971. The acquisition of language in infant and child. In C. Reed (ed.), The Learning of Language, pp. 7–96. Appleton-Century-Crofts, New York.

Braine, M. D. S. 1976. Children's first word combinations. Monographs of the Society for Research in Child Development, 41 (Serial No. 164). The University of Chicago Press, Chicago, Ill.

Branston, M. E. 1979. The effect of increased expansions on the acquisition of semantic structures in young developmentally delayed children: A training study. Unpublished doctoral dissertation. University of Wisconsin-Madison.

Broen, P. A. 1972. The verbal environment of the language-learning child. American Speech and Hearing Association Monograph. No. 17, American Speech and Hearing Assoc., Washington, D.C.

Brown, R. 1957. Words and Things. Free Press, Glencoe, Ill.

Brown, R. 1973. A First Language: The Early Stages. Harvard University Press, Cambridge, Mass.

Brown, R. 1977. Introduction, In C. Snow and C. Ferguson (eds.), Talking to Children: Language Input and Acquisition, pp. 1–30. Cambridge University Press, Cambridge

Brown, R., Cazden, C., and Bellugi, U. 1968. The child's grammar from I to III. In J. Hill (ed.), Minnesota Symposia on Child Psychology, pp. 28–73, Vol. 2. University of Minnesota Press, Minneapolis.

Bruner, J. 1975a. From communication to language—A psychological perspective, Cognition. 3:255–287.

Bruner, J. S. 1975b. The ontogenesis of speech acts. J. Child Lang. 2:1–19.

Bruner, J. 1978. On prelinguistic prerequisites of speech. In R. N. Campbell and P. T. Smith, Recent Advances in the Psychology of Language, pp. 199–214, Vol. 4a. Plenum Publishing Corp. New York.

Buium, N. 1976. Interrogative types in parental speech to language-learning children: a linguistic universal? J. Psycholinguist. Res. 5:135–147.

Carey, S., and Bartlett, E. 1978. Acquiring a single new word. Paper presented to the Tenth Child Language Research Forum, April, Stanford University, Stanford, Ca.

Cazden, C. 1965. Environmental assistance to the child's acquisition of grammar. Unpublished doctoral dissertation, Harvard University, Cambridge, Mass.

Chapman, R. S. 1978. Comprehension strategies in children. In J. F. Kavanagh and W. Strange (eds.), Speech and Language in the Laboratory, School, and Clinic, pp. 308–327. MIT Press, Cambridge, Mass.

Chapman, R. S., Hayes, D. M., Retherford, K. S., and Hayes, C. S. 1978. Early stages of language acquisition in hearing impaired children: What mothers and children talk about. Paper presented to A. G. Bell Association Convention, June, St. Louis, Mo.

Chapman, R. S., Klee, T., and Miller, J. F. Children's comprehension of requests for attention and action in context: pragmatic development and mothers' input. In preparation.

Chapman, R. S., and Kohn, L. L. 1978. Comprehension strategies in two and three year olds: Animate agents or probable events? J. Speech Hear. Res. 21:746–761.

Chapman, R. S., and Miller, J. F. 1975. Word order in early two and three word utterances: Does production precede comprehension? J. Speech Hear. Res. 18:355–371.

Clark, R. 1977. What's the use of imitation? J. Child Lang. 4:341–358.

Clarke-Stewart, K. A. 1973. Interactions between mothers and their young children: Characteristics and Consequences. Monographs of the Society for Research in Child Development. 38 (6–7, Serial No. 153). The University of Chicago Press, Chicago, Ill.

Coggins, T. E., and Morrison, J. A. 1979. Spontaneous imitations of Down's Syndrome Children: A lexical analysis. Unpublished manuscript, University of Washington, Seattle.

Cohen, S., and Beckwith, L. 1976. Maternal language in infancy. Dev. Psychol. 12:371–372.

Cross, T. G. 1977. Mothers' speech adjustments: The contribution of selected child listener variables. In C. E. Snow and C. A. Ferguson (eds.), Talking to Children, pp. 151–183. Cambridge University Press, Cambridge.

Cross, T. 1978. Mothers' speech and its association with rate of syntactic acquisition in young children. In N. Waterson and C. Snow (eds.), The Development of Communication, pp. 199–216. John Wiley & Sons, Inc., New York.

DePaulo, B., and Bonvillian, J. 1978. The effect on language development of the special characteristics of speech addressed to children. J. Psycholinguist. Res. 7:189–211.

deVilliers, J., and deVilliers, P. 1973. Development of the use of word order in comprehension. J. Psycholinguist. Res. 2:331–342.

Dore, J. 1977. Children's illocutionary acts. In R. Freedle (ed.), Discourse Relations: Comprehension and Production, pp. 227–244. Lawrence Erlbaum Associates, Hillsdale, N.J.

Eilers, R. E. 1975. Suprasegmental and grammatical control over telegraphic speech in young children. J. Psycholinguist. Res. 4:277–289.

Ervin, S. 1964. Imitation and structural change in children's language. In E. H. Lenneberg (ed.), New Directions in the Study of Language, pp. 163–189. MIT Press, Cambridge, Mass.

Ferguson, C. A. 1964. Baby talk in six languages. Am. Anthropology. 66:103–114.

Folger, J. P., and Chapman, R. S. 1978. A pragmatic analysis of spontaneous imitations. J. Child Lang. 5:25–38.

Furrow, D., Nelson, K., and Benedict, H. 1979. Mothers' speech to children and syntactic development: Some simple relationships. J. Child Lang. 6:423–442.

Garnica, O. K. 1977. Some prosodic and paralinguistic features of speech to young children. *In* C. E. Snow and C. A. Ferguson, Talking to Children, pp. 63–68. Cambridge University Press, Cambridge.

Glanzer, P., and Dodd, D. 1975. Developmental Changes in the language spoken to children. Paper presented at the biennial meeting of the Society for Research in Child Development, Denver.

Goldin-Meadow, S., Seligman, M., and Gelman, R. 1976. Language in the two-year-old. Cognition. 4:189–202.

Graves, Z. R., and Glick, J. 1978. The effect of context on mother-child interaction: A progress report. Q. Newsletter Institute Comparative Human Dev. 2:41–46.

Greenfield, P., and Smith, J. 1976. The Structure of Communication in Early Language Development. Academic Press, Inc. New York.

Hovell, M. F., Schumaker, J. B., and Sherman, J. A. 1978. A comparison of parents' models and expansions in promoting children's acquisition of adjectives. J. Exp. Child Psychol. 25:41–57.

Huttenlocher, J. 1974. The origins of language comprehension. *In* R. L. Solso (ed.), Theories of Cognitive Psychology, pp. 331–368. Lawrence Erlbaum Associates, Potomac, Md.

Keenan, E. O. 1977. Making it last: Repetition in children's discourse. *In* S. Ervin-Tripp and C. Mitchell-Kernan, Child Discourse, pp. 125–138. Academic Press, Inc. New York.

Kobashigawa, B. 1969. Repetitions in a mother's speech to her child. Working paper No. 14, Language-Behavior Research Laboratory, University of California, Berkeley.

Kuczaj, S. 1979. Evidence for a language learning strategy: On the relative case of acquisition of prefixes and suffixes. Child Dev. 50:1–13.

Longhurst, T., and Stepanich, L. 1975. Mothers' speech addressed to one-, two-, and three-year-old normal children. Child Study J. 5:3–11.

Masur, Holzman, and Ferrier, 1977.

Miller, G. 1978. Lexical Semantics. *In* J. Kavanagh and W. Strange (eds.), Speech and Language in the Laboratory, School, and Clinic, pp. 394–428. MIT Press, Cambridge, Mass.

Miller, J. F., and Chapman, R. S. The relation between age and mean length of utterance in morphemes. J. Speech Hear. Res. In press.

Miller, J. F., Chapman, R. S., MacKenzie, H. and Bedrosian, J. The development of discourse skills in the second year of life: Turn-taking, topic initiation, and topic continuation. In preparation.

Miller, J. F., Chapman, R. S., Branston, M., and Reichle, J. 1980. Language comprehension in sensorimotor stages 5 and 6. J. Speech Hear. Res. 23:243–260.

Moerk, E. 1975. Verbal interactions between children and their mothers during the preschool years. Dev. Psychol. 11:788–795.

Moerk, E. 1977. Processes and products of imitation: Additional evidence that imitation is progressive. J. Psycholinguist. Res. 6:187–202.

Morse, P., Younger, B., and Goodsitt, J. Infants' recognition of speech sounds in complex contexts. In preparation.

Nelson, K. 1973. Structure and strategy in learning to talk. Society for Research in Child Development Monograph No. 141, The University of Chicago Press, Chicago, Ill.

Nelson, K. 1974. Concept, word and sentence: Interrelations in acquisition and development. Psychol. Rev. 81:267–285.

Nelson, K. E., and Bonvillian, J. D. 1974. Concepts and words in the 18-month-old: Acquiring concept names under controlled conditions. Cognition. 4:435–450.

Netsell, R. The acquisition of speech motor control: A perspective with directions for research. In R. Stark (ed.), Language Behavior in Infancy and Early Childhood, Johnson and Johnson Co. In press.

Newport, E., Gleitman, H., and Gleitman, C. 1977. Mother, I'd rather do it myself: Some effects and non-effects of maternal speech style. In C. E. Snow and C. Ferguson, (eds.), Talking to Children. Cambridge University Press, Cambridge.

Ninio, A., and Bruner, J. 1978. The achievement and antecedents of labeling. J. Child Lang. 5:1–16.

Pierce, J. E. 1974. A study of 750 Portland, Oregon children during the first year. Papers and Reports on Child Language Development. 8:19–25. Stanford University, Stanford, Conn.

Phillips, J. R. 1973. Syntax and vocabulary of mother's speech to young children: Age and sex comparisons. Child Dev. 44:192–195.

Ramer, A. L. H. 1976. The function of imitation in child language. J. Speech Hear. Res. 19:700–717.

Ratner, N., and Bruner, J. 1978. Games, social exchange, and the acquisition of language. J. Child Lang. 5:391–402.

Remick, H. 1976. Maternal speech to children during language acquisition. In W. von Raffler-Engel and Y. Lebrun (eds.), Baby Talk and Infant Speech, pp. 223–233. Swets & Zeitlinger B. V. Amsterdam.

Retherford, K. S., Schwartz, B. C., and Chapman, R. S. Semantic roles and residual grammatical categories in mother and child speech: Who tunes into whom? J. Child Lang. In press.

Rondal, J. 1978. Maternal speech to normal and Down's syndrome children matched for mean utterance length. In C. E. Meyers (ed.), Quality of Life in Severely and Profoundly Mentally Retarded People: Research Foundations For Improvement, pp. 193–265. American Association on Mental Deficiency, Washington, D.C.

Rosch, E. 1973. On the internal structure of perceptual and semantic categories. In T. E. Moore (ed.), Cognitive Development and the Acquisition of Language, pp. 111–144. Academic Press, Inc. New York.

Sachs, J. 1977. The adaptive significance of linguistic input to prelinguistic infants. In C. Snow and C. Ferguson (eds.), Talking to Children, pp. 51–62. Cambridge University Press, Cambridge.

Sachs, J. 1979. Topic selection in parent-child discourse. Discourse Processes. 2:145–153.

Sachs, J., and Devin, J. 1976. Young children's use of age appropriate speech styles in social interaction and role-playing. J. Child Lang. 3:81–98.

Sachs, J., and Truswell, L. 1978. Comprehension of two-word instructions by children in the one-word stage. J. Child Lang. 5:17–24.

Savić, S. 1975. Aspects of adult-child communication: The problem of question acquisition. J. Child Lang. 2:251–260.

Scherer, N., and Coggins, T. Contingent responses to adult-initiated requests in the dialogue of stage I children. In preparation.

Schieffelin, B. 1979. A developmental study of word order and case marking in an ergative language. Papers and Reports on Child Language Development. 17:30–40.

Schumaker, J. B. 1976. Mothers' expansions: Their characteristics and effects on child language. Unpublished doctoral dissertation, University of Kansas, Lawrence, Kan.

Schwartz, B. C. 1978. Mother and child use of specific semantic combinations over time. Unpublished masters' thesis, University of Wisconsin, Madison, Wis.

Seitz, S., and Stewart, C. 1975. Expanding on expansions and related aspects of mother-child communication. Dev. Psychol. 11:763–769.

Shatz, M. 1978. Children's comprehension of their mother's question-directives. J. Child Lang. 5:39–46.

Shatz, M., and Graves, Z. 1976. The role of maternal gesturing in language acquisition: Do actions speak louder than words? Paper presented at Boston University Conference on Language Development, October, Boston, Mass.

Shipley, E., Smith, C., and Gleitman, L. 1969. A Study on the acquisition of language: Free responses to commands. Language. 45:322–342.

Slobin, D. I. 1968. Imitation and grammatical development in children. In N. S. Endler, L. R. Boulter, and H. Osser (eds.), Contemporary Issues in Developmental Psychology, pp. 437–443. Holt, Rinehart, and Winston, New York.

Slobin, D. I. 1973. Cognitive prerequisites for the development of grammar. In C. A. Ferguson and D. I. Slobin (eds.), Studies of Child Language Development, pp. 175–208. Holt, Rinehart and Winston, New York.

Slobin, D. 1979. The role of language in language acquisition. Borchers Lecture, April 26, University of Wisconsin-Madison,

Slobin, D. I., and Welsh, C. A. 1971. Elicited imitation as a research tool in developmental psycholinguistics. In C. S. Lavatelli (ed.), Language Training in Early Childhood Education, pp. 170–185. University of Illinois Press, Champaign. Urbana, Ill.

Snow, C. E. 1972. Mother's speech to children learning language. Child Dev. 43:549–565.

Snow, C. 1977a. Mothers' speech research: From input to interaction. In C. Snow and C. Ferguson (eds.), Talking to Children, pp. 31–51. Cambridge University Press, Cambridge.

Snow, C. 1977b. The development of conversation between mothers and babies. J. Child Lang. 4:1–22.

Snow, C. E., Arlman-Rupp, A., Hassing, Y., Jobse, J., Joosten, J., and Vorster, J. 1976. Mothers' speech in three social classes. J. Psycholinguist. Res. 5:1–20.

Snyder-McLean, L. K., and McLean, J. E. 1978. Verbal information gathering strategies: The child's use of language to acquire language. J. Speech Hear. Disord. 43:306–325.

Tulkin, S. R., and Kagan, J. 1972. Mother-child interaction in the first year of life. Child Dev. 43:31–41.

van der Geest, T. 1977. Some interactional aspects of language acquisition. In C. Snow and C. Ferguson (eds.), Talking to Children, pp. 89–108. Cambridge University Press, Cambridge.

Volterra, V., Bates, E., Benigni, L., Bretherton, I., and Camaioni, L. 1979. First words in language and action: A qualitative look. In E. Bates, The Emergence of Symbols: Communication and Cognition in Infancy. Academic Press, Inc. New York.

Wetstone, H., and Friedlander, B. 1973. The effect of word order on young children's responses to simple questions and commands. Child Dev. 44:734–740.

Whitehurst, G. J., and Vasta, R. 1975. Is language acquired through imitation? J. Psycholinguist. Res. 4:37–59.

Wills, D. D. 1977. Participant deixis in English and baby talk. *In* C. E. Snow and C. A. Ferguson (eds.), Talking to Children, pp. 271–296. Cambridge University Press, Cambridge.

chapter 7

Mother–Child Interaction Issues

Summary Chapter

Frances Degen Horowitz

Joseph W. Sullivan

Infant Research Laboratories
Department of Human Development and Family Life
University of Kansas
Lawrence, Kansas

It has been claimed that language acquisition in humans is "over-determined" in the sense that, with the exception of the presence of the physical ability to process auditory stimuli, no single factor or determinant is critical to language acquisition. There are likely many different avenues and strategies available to the language learning organism that facilitate and foster language acquisition. This point of view gains increasing credence as we study the child in a language environment in the first few years of life. Chapman's main claim that we ought to think of the environment as being responsive to the language learner rather than as characterizing the environment mainly in terms of its stimulative functions is well taken. Although there is a considerable body of evidence to indicate that mothers and other caregivers offer special language tuition in the form of modified speech called motherese, the discussion that followed Chapman's presentation stressed a number of issues that might serve to caution our over-interpretation of existing data as guides for intervention strategies where language acquisition has not proceeded normally.

Chapman's work and data focus on the language-learning child in the second year of life. Thoman pointed out that the mother-infant dyad in the second year of life already has a history of interaction and we would add that a considerable amount of acquisition has probably already occurred during the first year of life on the receptive side of language. In fact, the strategies of interaction during the first year of life and the nature of language stimuli that maintain and attract infant attention may provide us with important clues to understanding what is going on in the second year of life and beyond. Two additional points merit emphasis. Several conference participants noted that motherese only describes that language input that is aimed directly at the child but that a great deal of the child's language environment may not involve speech directed to the child. In many ways the young infant is, in the first year of life, bathed in a language environment that is flowing about him or her with only segments of it directed at the infant and/or modified for the interactive episodes. As an adult, one has only to participate in a dinner party conversation where a second language that you understand only partially is being spoken in order to realize how much "learning" of that language can occur even when the language is not directly aimed at you. Although an analogy between first and second language learning is not fully warranted, as Roger Brown has taught us, there are aspects of second language learning that may help us become sensitive to the broad range of opportunities for language learning that occur in a complex naturally flowing environment.

Another point raised by several of the conference participants in discussion of Chapman's paper was that one must be careful about generalizing from the knowledge of normal acquisition to the specification of strategies for intervention. It is not necessarily the case that the conditions that are responsible for normal language learning will function in a similar fashion when attempting to correct delayed or disordered language. Cromer pointed out that the language-disordered child may lack sufficient internal strategies for coping with linguistic input. One may wish to consider how those limited strategies might best provide the clue for proper intervention techniques. It may not be the case that more or slower input will be effective; rather, it may be that entirely different kinds of input strategies will be necessary. Such a point of view highlights the importance of the simultaneous study of both normal and disordered acquisition in both normal and abnormal populations. Ultimately, only the combined information from diverse research efforts will provide the clues as to what kinds of interventions with what kinds of populations will be most successful.

Dennenberg cautioned that it is important not to expect straight line predictions from one kind of input to one kind of output and not to expect necessarily short-term effects of intervention. Both of these points are extremely pertinent to our considerations. If, in fact, in the normal organism, language acquisition is overdetermined it is quite possible that for both normal and different children environmental input and responsiveness function in multiple and complex ways. For example, reinforcing vocalization rate in the first year of life may not necessarily result in increased verbal behavior in the second year of life but rather in increased discriminative use of verbal behavior for communicative purposes in the second or later years of life. Motherese may serve to model some suprasegmental features of language, or it may serve mainly as a means of attracting the infant's attention.

The demonstration of latent effects of intervention programs in the area of early education is further evidence that the absence of short-term follow-up effects may not mean that there will be no long-term effects. It has become clear that the effects of intervention may be found immediately after an intervention, and may disappear subsequently, only to reappear with effects that were not directly programmed in the intervention. Thoman made the comment that it is important not to pinpoint intervention strategies too specifically in the hopes of targeting a particular outcome. In the area of language intervention it may be particularly important to utilize a variety of techniques to maximize an array of outcome effects.

In her paper, Thoman stressed that the communication between the mother and the infant is an ongoing, cue-giving feedback and mutual modification system for which the normal infant is biologically prepared. She suggested that affect is the organizing concept for this communication in that it precedes, influences, and becomes integrated with cognitive communication. Thoman also proposed that early disruption of the social-affective interaction may be a prelude to later affective and communicative disorders. Her thesis is an intriguing one but one for which there is not a great deal of data. This is partly because our measurement abilities in the area of affect are quite limited. Most of the effort at measurement has been directed to cognitive behavior. Yet, it is in the affective domain that many parents identify problems and data reported by Bob Emde about Down's syndrome infants is supportive. Emde and his colleagues noted that Down's Syndrome infants show flatter affect and thus provide fewer discriminative cues to the caregiver.

Wolf and Gardner, in chapter 9, acknowledged the importance of affect but questioned whether, ultimately, in the content of a communicative interaction one was not dealing with cognitive content. Thus, they question whether the stress on an affective base for communicative behavior was not "begging the question." Other conference participants also raised questions concerning the role of affect in communication, and Trehub suggested that affect might provide the context for communication but was not synonymous with communication itself. But Thoman and Dennenberg argued that it was important to keep affective and cognitive domains separate conceptually. Dennenberg mentioned that Harlow's monkeys were cognitively intact but affectively disordered.

The question of whether it is meaningful to retain a dichotomy between cognition and affect is an important one, and it is probably the case that we do not yet have the data base to provide us with the definitive answer. It is possible that the distinction between the two classes is less important for the normal infant than for the handicapped or impaired infant. If a handicapped infant has delayed cognitive development, a caregiver may receive more cues from the infant's affective behavior and thus may be able to be more appropriately responsive. Learning to read the affective cues may be an important skill to teach parents of handicapped infants. Furthermore, it is possible that handicapped or impaired infants who progress slower developmentally stay at given levels of development for longer periods of time thus, possibly, satiating or "boring" the parent. The result may be less responsive feedback from the parent and a breakdown in the communicative context. By teaching parents to read affective cues, which may be more continuously variable and thus provide more interesting feedback to the parents, we might find that we can keep parents responding at a higher rate to the infant's behavior. Schiefelbusch observed that affective states may prove to be useful for activating parental responsiveness.

It is obvious, from the papers presented by Chapman and by Thoman and from the discussion that ensued, that the caregiver-infant interaction, particularly the mother-infant interaction, is the central

context for the development of communicative skills and ultimately
language acquisition. How much of the functional variables are embedded in the direct interactive process, the modification of maternal
speech, the responsiveness of the mother or caregiver to the infant's
verbal and other behaviors is still to be determined. It is also clear that
although we need to understand the normal processes between normal
infants and parents, these processes may or may not be abbrogated in
the dyadic interactions with impaired or handicapped infants. Furthermore, these processes may or may not provide the clues for effective interventional strategies. The process of language acquisition
is very complex, probably overdetermined, and probably amendable
to a variety of intervention strategies. Given our current knowledge
about language acquisition and intervention, our best bets are probably
placed upon multiple strategies that both mimic and differ from the
normal processes as we know them.

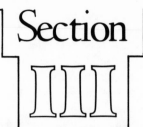

Section III

Early Symbolic Acquisition

chapter 8

The Transition from Early Symbols to Syntax

David Ingram

Department of Linguistics
University of British Columbia
Vancouver, B.C.
Canada

When langauge acquisition research was renewed and augmented in the early 1960s, there was a period of active investigation into syntactic acquisition. The classic early studies (c.f., Brown and Fraser, 1964; Miller and Ervin, 1964; Braine, 1963) examined early word combinations, using basic linguistic constructs concerning segmentation, co-occurence, and productivity to develop some initial hypotheses about the first categories and rules of children's grammars. This interest was inspired no doubt by similarly high levels of activity in linguistic theory because of Chomsky's theory of transformational grammar. Sinclair (1978) concluded that "almost all interesting studies of child language based either on experimental or observational data of recent years have been concerned with syntax (p. 150)."

ISSUES: FROM SYMBOLS TO SYNTAX

In subsequent years, there has been a transition from the study of syntax to early symbols. This shift of emphasis is well known and easy to document: a concern for semantic rather than syntactic characterizations of early word combinations (Bloom, 1970; Schlesinger, 1971; Bowerman, 1973; Brown, 1973); an examination of single-word utterances for evidence of these semantic interpretations (Ingram, 1971; Bloom, 1973; Greenfield and Smith, 1976); a shift from semantic to pragmatic descriptions of early single-word speech (Bates, Camaioni, and Volterra, 1975; Dore, 1975; Halliday, 1975); general investigations of cognitive precursors in the sensorimotor period (e.g., object permanence, symbolic play) for the use and meaning of early vocalizations (Bates et al., 1977; Ingram, 1978a; Nelson and Bonvillian, 1978); the search for biological explanations for the evolution of symbolization and language (Bates, 1978). The focus of research is evident from the nature of most recent books on language acquisition, most notably Lock (1978) and Nelson (1978).

The current interest in early symbolization has led to a rediscovery of Piaget's classic book on this topic *La Formation du Symbole* (1962). This interest also has added new observational data (e.g., Braunwald, 1978), closer examinations of the implications of Piaget's claims on the relation of cognition and language (e.g., Bates et al., 1977, Ingram, 1978), and experimental investigations into the predictions of this theory for both normal children (e.g., Corrigan, 1978; Nicolich and Raph, 1978; Bates et al., in press) and those with language delay (Synder, 1976; Cook, Dale, and Goldstein, 1978; Miller, 1978). There are at least *two* fundamental issues examined in this research. One concerns the causal relations between specific sensorimotor and linguistic structures, for example, the demonstration that certain linguistic developments (e.g., multiword utterances) may be the direct result of specific cognitive milestones (e.g., symbolic play). The second issue concerns the nature of linguistic structures themselves. Is there autonomous syntax, as argued frequently by Chomsky (1975), with its own unique properties? or can these be reduced either to cognitive structures or common logical structures that underlie both cognition and language (c.f., Beilin, 1975)?

The general effect of all of this research and speculation has been a widespread diminution of interest in syntax. The consequences of this can be seen in various ways. Studies of single-word and early multiword speech have provided insight into the meaning of these early utterances and subsequently into what young children know about the world. Few new facts about how syntax develops have been provided though. One reason for this is the assumption that there is no syntax at this stage, but rather cognitive structures, natural categories, and semantic rules of a universal kind. Also, the attempt to eliminate purely syntactic universals and determine language-external explanations for syntax in functional terms, that is, as it is used in the communicative context (Bates, 1978), leads to research disproving rather than proving patterns of early syntax. It is possible that we now know more about the emergence of symbols than the nature of syntactic structures in early vocalizations.

This chapter focuses on the transition from the first symbols to early syntactic patterns by examining the two issues mentioned earlier on cognitive prerequisites and the nature of linguistic structures. First, some results are presented from a preliminary study demonstrating that syntactic development may occur during the sensorimotor period, and that the nature of early syntactic processing may not be easily reduced to some specific cognitive precursor. Next, the syntactic analysis of these data indicates that refinements in the methodology of writing grammars for children are necessary for providing information about the nature of the young child's grammatical structures. The current evidence, however, indicates a certain degree of autonomy. It is concluded that 1) although certain cognitive milestones seem necessary for the onset of intentional communication, the issue is not as clear in regard to syntactic structures because structures may occur at divergent points after the onset of symbolization; and 2) we need to explore more carefully the nature of the child's early syntactic rules and categories before comparisons to cognitive structures are possible.

Cognitive Prerequisites and Language Development

The first issue concerns the possibility that certain cognitive prerequisites are necessary for the onset of language. For Piaget, language is part of a general semiotic function that emerges after the sensori-

motor period; for example, "articulate language makes its appearance
. . . at the end of the sensorimotor period, with what have been called
'one-word utterances'" (Piaget and Inhelder, 1969, p. 85). Recently,
diverse studies have examined this issue in detail and have contributed
insights into the issues at stake, despite differences in their approaches.
Although Inhelder et al. (1972) found that the achievement of object
permanence preceded symbolic behavior, others have been more cautious in concluding a direct relation between these two (c.f., Corrigan,
1978, Bates et al., in press). One of the most ambitious experimental
studies to date on this topic (Bates et al., in press) concludes that tool
use, imitation, and preverbal communication are correlated with the
onset of symbols. These results are similar to results obtained by Ingram (1978a) using a very different observational methodology that
was more in line with Piaget's original approach. Both studies, however, are cautious about concluding a causal relation. Bates (1978)
suggested that they are homologous structures, that is they are similar
because of shared genetic characteristics. She stated "Presumably at
some point in history these three capacities must have reached some
new, threshold level that permitted a qualitatively different kind of
interaction, leading to symbols inside and outside communication (p.
K16)." Also, Bates emphasized that these three aspects may move
independently toward thresholds until all three are met, a point at
which symbol formation may occur. Miller (1978) reported similar findings within the experimental paradigm on the correlational relation
between these behaviors.

Cognitive Precursors to Syntactic Development

A more specific issue concerns the cognitive precursors to syntactic
development, that is, the onset of multiword utterances. Piaget suggested that representational ability is necessary. This view is supported
by Sinclair (1978) and Bloom (1973) who argued against assigning relational interpretations to single-word speech. To date, the data reporting cognitive and linguistic milestones support this interpretation
to the extent that children who reach the representational stage are
still in the holophrastic stage also (c.f., Ingram, 1978a). If so, this
supports claims cognitive structures influence syntactic structures in
that the unidirectionality of their developmental patterns could be
interpreted as indicating a causal relation (Bates, 1978).

Experimental examination of these issues across many subjects
allows for statistical analyses and generalizable conclusions. The disadvantages (Ingram, 1978a) concern the range of each child's behavior
being studied and the depth of linguistic analysis. Usually, the language

measures are gross ones of mean length of utterance (MLU) and the size of lexicon, which are in most cases satisfactory in that multiword speech has not yet begun.

A Study Relating the Onset of Syntax to Cognitive Advances

Both Bates et al. (1975) and Ingram (1978a) have found, for example, that the first words appear in sensorimotor stage 5, and that rapid vocabulary growth and the onset of multiword utterances do not occur until later in Stage 6 and representation. The study described below, however, reports longitudinal data which indicate that syntax may appear earlier than previous studies suggested. The interpretation of these results raises questions about precursors to syntax and the nature of syntactic structures.

Subjects

Two girls (K and P) and one boy (D) were observed longitudinally from the middle of their first year of life to the middle of the second. (See Table 1.) The families of the children all lived within two blocks of each other in a white middle-class neighborhood in Vancouver, B.C.; the parents knew one another but did not normally socialize together. The mothers of the two girls were unemployed and provided full-time care for them. D's mother pursued a profession outside the house but took off the first year and 3 months of his life to provide full-time care. K was a first-born child of older parents who were very concerned about providing an enriched environment for her. K's mother spent a great deal of time alone with her child and spoke frequently to her. She was interested in her child developing language early and insisted on "hello's," "goodbye's," and "thank you's" from an early age. K's language environment could be described as highly verbal, with a restricted code in the sense of Bernstein (1964). The other two children

Table 1.　Information on birth order, sex, age, number of visits, and language on three children observed longitudinally

Birth order	Child	Sex	Age at 1st visit	Number of visits	Age at last visit	Size of lexicon at last visit	MLU at last visit[d]
first	K	Female	0;7(7)	19	1;7(17)	93 words[b]	2.35
second	D	Male	0;9(19)[a]	21	1;7(19)	26 words[c]	1.00
second	P	Female	0;10(9)	16	1;7(29)	25 words[c]	1.13

[a] Diary notes are available from birth.
[b] Based on words used in last language sample.
[c] Based on last language sample and diary notes.
[d] Tapes are available for both K and D beyond this but they are not included in the analysis.

were both second-born with sisters who were 5 years older. Neither mother consciously attempted to expedite their child's language development and each used a style that could be described as expressive (c.f., Nelson, 1973). Although both P and D spent several daytime hours alone with their mothers, they also were frequently around other children because they had older siblings. K and P's fathers were out of the home most of the child's waking hours and spent little time with their child. D's father (the author) was around more frequently and was actively involved in early child care. None of the children had any expressive language at the onset of the study and all three seemed to be developing normally. Their development during and since the study has continued to be normal.

Materials

Cognitive development was assessed by observing the child's behavior in spontaneous and experimentally altered conditions, and followed through Piaget's six sensorimotor stages. A checklist of prominent sensorimotor behaviors, based on Piaget's three books on this period, was compiled (see Appendix in Ingram, 1978) and used to follow each child's progress. A collection of various toys and objects was brought to each session for this purpose. Although these objects varied during the study, each child saw more or less the same ones. The objects included: a jar and buttons, pennies, a variety of small figures of people and animals, two squeeze toys, a stop watch on a chain, a collection of colored blocks, a plastic spindle with colored rings for stacking, a plastic ball with different shaped holes for placing blocks, a horn, a harmonica, a mirror, a musical ball, a rubberball, plastic sticks, a doll, and children's books. The books were also used to see how well the children could label a variety of pictorially represented objects.

Procedure

At the onset, a schedule was set for each child to be visited every 2 weeks for approximately 30 minutes. This was occasionally interrupted because of illness, vacations, etc., but a regular series of visits was maintained over the year (see Table 1). Three experimenters collected data. Two experimenters were present at the session. One was responsible for taking contextual notes on the child's behavior and the experimental conditions presented. The other was responsible for the primary interaction with the child. At the start of the session, the mother was informally interviewed on the child's progress since the last visit. At the same time, the other experimenter would begin to play with the child. Then, a series of predetermined tasks were presented to the child. In the early sessions, this would often consist of simply placing some toys before her. Once the child was involved with some activity and object, skills such as object permanence and displacement of objects were tested. The tone of the sessions was generally relaxed and the experimenter usually waited to let the child shape the direction of activity. It was usually possible to achieve most of the predetermined tasks following this format by the end of the session. When the children began to show signs of productive language, sessions were audio-taped in their entirety. By 10 months of age, all three children were regularly recorded.

Every week or two, the three experimenters met to discuss the previous sessions. These meetings included a report on the mother's interview, a discussion on what the child did and said, and a discussion on what should be done in the next visit. A notebook was kept on each child based on these meetings. If there was not unanimous agreement that a child had achieved a particular cognitive stage, testing would continue, even though there might have been a high success rate. Although impressionistic, it was found that there was a point where visitors were quite confident a level had been reached. Audio-tapes were transcribed as soon after a session as possible which, unfortunately, was sometimes weeks later. Because contextual notes were available, however, and phonetic transcriptions were made of all child utterances, interpretations were assigned to most of the children's utterances.

Analysis

The cognitive behaviors of the children at each session were assigned to one of Piaget's six sensorimotor stages (Ingram, 1978a). Basically, it was assumed that a sensorimotor stage is achieved only when a cluster of behaviors representing that stage co-occur, not by the appearance of isolated behaviors. This procedure was used with Piaget's original data (c.f., Ingram, 1978a) and found to be a useful observationally oriented alternative to the experimental paradigm (Uzgiris and Hunt, 1975) for placing children into sensorimotor stages. Once a child's sensorimotor stages were assigned, the linguistic ability of the child was examined from the session notes, parental reports, and language transcriptions for each sensorimotor stage.

Results

Tables 2, 3, and 4 present the results for P, D, and K, respectively. The results from P and D are similar to each other and also to results found in Ingram (1978a). Both children started using a few words in Stage 5 (less than a dozen each), but more gradual acquisition of vocabulary awaits Stage 6. Even when two or more months into Stage

6, both children only used around 25 words and only P seemed on the verge of using multiword utterances. K, however, showed a different profile. By the end of Stage 4, she began using a few words that were heavily bound to context, for example *ta* when handing objects, and names of animals if they were pictures in a particular book her mother always read to her. In the middle of Stage 5, at only 1;0(3) she already had a vocabulary of over 30 words, which seemed to increase every day. The first multiword utterances appeared in late Stage 5 and developed rapidly, reaching an MLU of 2.42 by age 1;6(12), only 2 months into dominant Stage 6 behaviors. Even allowing for the variability inherent in the method used for determining sensorimotor stages, K was clearly months ahead of the other two children linguistically. Her cognitive development can be exemplified by presenting in more detail K's behavior during the session at 1;0(26). Motorically she was slow; at this age she was only crawling. During most of the session, she simply sat in the middle of the floor. The first toy presented was the plastic spindle with colored rings of different diameters stacked

Table 2.   Linguistic observations on P and the sensorimotor stage of their appearance

Stage	Age	Linguistic observation
Stage 4	0;10(9)	Vocalized frequently and seemed aware of adult speech. Says [tætæ], [dædæ], no clear understanding of specific words.
	0;10(30)	Mother reports child says "tata" when handing an object, and has "mama" when wants something. Will put arms out when adult says "up."
	0;11(3)	Words are "dada" for *daddy*, "ta" for handing objects, "mama," "bye-bye," and "da" for *dog*.
Late 4, early 5	0;11(27)	Child will kiss mother on cheek if latter says "kiss." Uses tone variations on vocalizations for communication.
	1;0(13)	"Daddy" is clearly used. "Wowo" is used for *doggie*. Will imitate "hi" and "baby."
Stage 5	1;1(3)	Understands "no," will hand toy if adult says "ta." Says "doggie."
	1;2(1)	When wants toy, will point to object and vocalize. Will say "hi" and "okay."
	1;2(15)	Said "hi" when mother came into room, and later said "bye-bye."
	1;3(12)	No noticeable gains in language; says "uppy" to get up.

Table 2.   (Continued)

Stage	Age	Linguistic observation
Late 5, early 6	1;5(1)	Has about a dozen words. "Tina" for *Christina* (her sister), "mommy," "daddy," "boat," "up," "bellybutton," "bye-bye," "juice," "shoes," "boom," "night-night," "there," "ah" when finishing something. Mother reports comprehension has increased a great deal, e.g., will respond to "go get teddy," "go to bathtub," "get off." When heard "bye-bye" she went to her room and got her coat.
	1;5(18)	Mother remarks that most of what she says is uncomprehensible, yet it seems to be meaningful. Vocabulary is beginning to increase; says "no," "dirty," "mine," "ball," "ouchie," "bottle," ([ba]). Understands "sit down," "come here," "come in to eat," "go potty."
Stage 6	1;6(29)	Some of new words are "cookie," "allgone," "ball," "baby," "that," "pretty," "boat," "out," "doll," "hello," "shoe," "book." Beginning to put two words together, but most utterances are holophrastic.
	1;7(29)	Not many new words, but more combinations: "Theresa _____," "where's _____," "_____allgone." Use of some stereotyped phrases.

on it. K eventually managed to remove them all, but was unable to replace more than two correctly. She preferred to hand them back and forth to the experimenter, saying *tata* each time this took place (a vocalization that frequently accompanied giving and taking). Later, when playing with nested cups, two became stuck; she handed these to the experimenter in expectation that they would be repaired, an act of Stage 5 causality. Her stacking ability was restricted to two objects or blocks at once, which would be immediately knocked down. When handed a jar of beads, she managed to remove the lid, but still would not dump the container to get the contents. Up to this stage she had not yet succeeded at finding an object that had been invisibly displaced. This was tested several times during this session with a button she had been playing with, all without success. It was not until 1;4(8) that she succeeded once or twice, although there was reliability disagreement. Finally, at 1;5(2) she had three consecutive successes. The general evaluation of the session at 1;0(26) was that she was still Stage 5 with

Table 3.   Linguistic observations on D and the sensorimotor stage of their occurrence

Stage	Age	Linguistic observation
Stage 4	0;9(19)	Seems to understand "no." Will stop what he is doing and look at adult. This has been noted repeatedly. Babbling is increasing. Common patterns [dædæ], [bæbæ].
	0;10(4)	Babbles during play, more guttural sounds. Sighs when picked up.
	0;10(22)	Shows nondeictic pointing when he sees object of interest. Says "mama" a lot, often in distress, "dada" is also common.
Late 4, early 5	0;11(8)	Imitates "mama," "dada." Does not imitate gestures except clapping. No words, but has expressive vocalizations.
Stage 5	1;0(4)	No words. Babbles "mama," "mami," "dædæ," "dædi," "nænæ," nasal "m-m" often when hungry. Still seems to understand "no," perhaps also "sit down."
	1;0(7)	When father said "hi" to him, he said "hi" back, and smiled.
	1;1(20)	Until recently, "dædæ," "dædi" were favorite babblings. Now uses "mami" more often. Seems to use it to mean "I want something," particularly food. Uses segments and intonation as if in conversation.
	1;2(16)	Babbles "dudi" as if model was "Judy," his mother's name.
Late 5	1;3(17)	"ha ([ā]) has become used as a greeting consistently. Said it today to passing children and then laughed. Some characteristic babblings are "ninina," "dudi," "danu" (Daniel?), "dadi," "mami." None are used consistently in context.
Late 5, early 6	1;5(6)	Says "hi" in three contexts 1) when he first sees you; 2) when playing on telephone; 3) in games of peekaboo. Said "mami" when needed help 1) to open locket; 2) to pull string toy. "hm?" said as if imitating adults. Hands objects as he says it. "de" (Dave?) as if referring to father.
		"i:," "u:" nonreferential, uses as if practicing vowels. Babbled sentences—sound like sentences with adult intonation, for last couple of weeks. Only comprehends "Daniel" and "no" it seems.

Table 3. (*Continued*)

Stage	Age	Linguistic observation
Early 6	1;5(19)	Will imitate his own babbled words, e.g., "dædi," "dada," "dodo," "dudu," "mami," "mama," "bubu," "i-u," "u-i," "didu." Likes to make nonsense conversation. Current words: "mami" I need help "nænæ" *banana* (two times) "gugi" *cookie* "dodo" *bottle, blanket* "ai" *hi* when greeting ?"no" practicing this, no clear meaning "*m*" creaky nasal, when really wants object.
	1;6(11)	More examples of symbolic play. Current words "coat" ([goʔ]) clearly said when he sees his coat. "Cookie" ([gugi]) with great phonetic variation. "Banana" ([nænæ]) clearly a word, reached for banana on fridge. ʔ"shoe" ([gu] [du]) varies phonetically. "Bye-bye" ([baba]) waves hand, only when people leave the house. "Mami" = "I want" "hi" ([ai]) said when people enter house. "Bottle"([babu]). "Apple" ([æpo], [æʔo]), latter is more common. When hungry mostly says "mamama." Some common babblings are "i-a-u," "bæbæ," "bibu," "bubu." Comprehension is not good. Seems to know "kiss"—will close lips and kiss, "no," "hot," "cookie," "banana," "shoe," "bye-bye," "hi," "truck"?
	1;6(25)	New words each day, on verge of rapid development. Words said tonight: "milk" ([naʔ], [maʔ]). Recently "hat" ([æʔ]), "ball" ([baʔ]), "there" (dɛə]), "yeah" ([dᴸpʰ], [jᴸpʰ]), "no."Words from 1;6(11) still occur. Common words are "cookie," "shoe," "Judith" ([dugɛt], [gugᴸtˑ]), "coat" ([goʔ]). Today he said "egg" ([eᴸ]), only once. "Blanket," "bottle" ([baba]), "banana." He stopped saying "apple".
	1;7(1)	Most common utterance is [dudi]. When changed he will say [bupi] "poopy." Says "thankyou" — phonetically imprecise, high pitched. "Dog" ([u::], [gɔki], [gɔgi]).
Stage 6	1;7(14)	Most common words in daily speech are: "banana" [nænæ] "blanket" [dudu] —understands the word "blanket"

Table 3. (*Continued*)

Stage	Age	Linguistic observation
		"bottle" [babu]
		"coat" [goʔ]
		"hat" [aʔ] [ak]
		"hi" [ai]
		"cookie" [gɛgi]
		"bye-bye" [baba]
		"shoe" [du]
		"no" [noʊ]
		"thankyou" [gege] (high pitch)
		[mami] "I want"
		"baby" [bebe]
		"dog" [gɔgi] [u::]
		Some recent new words are:
		"milk" [maʊ]
		"pants" [bubipæ]
		"there" [dɛəˀ]
		"here" [iə]
		"get up" [didæ ʔ]
		"give back" [bābā] —a created word
		Today said "sock" ([hak]). Does not babble
		"Judith" anymore. No longer says "apple,"
		"cereal," "car," "truck," "ball," "yeah,"
		"egg."

a rather large vocabulary. The other two children had only two words between them at this comparable period.

K's advanced language is exemplified by looking at the session at 1;5(2) when she first succeeded at a single invisible displacement. The experimenter (E) and K were seated on the floor, and E planned to hide the watch that K was playing with by putting it under a plastic cup and leaving the watch behind E's back. The following interaction took place (contextual remarks are in parentheses):

K	Experimenter
(playing with a watch) huh?	Look at this K. (a cup)
	Can I have it?
	K, give me the watch.
can give me cup?	
	Alright here. (holds out cup to K)
	Put in cup.
(K puts watch into cup)	
want the cup?	
(E moves cup behind back, leaves watch, shows empty cup to K) where it go?	
	Where'd it go?

Table 4.   Linguistic observations on K and the sensorimotor stage of their occurrence

Stage	Age	Linguistic observation
Stage 3	0;7(7)	Did not engage in vocalization.
	0;7(28)	Practically no sounds made at all.
Late 3, early 4	0;8(21)	When mother said "hi," K said [ha]. Imitated [dada], [baba], [mama], [nænæ]. "Ta" was imitated as [da]. Imitated clapping and "bye-bye." Child seemed to understand "apple," "dolly," "book."
Stage 4	0;9(4)	Said "bye-bye" and waved hand when heard "bye-bye" on tape. Not an active vocalizer when playing. Mother tried to show she understood "apple," "doll," "book." Negative results.
	0;9(18)	Does pattycake, "bye-bye," "ta." Mother interprets everything K says as one adult word. Mother reports K has 12 words "dada," "mama," "nænæ," etc. also "duck," "car." M: "What do bunnies do?" K: [ha]
	0;10(2)	Waves when hears "bye-bye." If you say "ta," will hand object to you, and says "ta" at same time. Mother says K has new word "flower."
	0;10(22)	Mother reads book to K three times a day. Words on tape were "duck," "coat," "car," "woof." Imitated "boat," "bus," "boy," "squirrel."
Late 4, early 5	0;11(6)	Words on tape: "toe," "boy," "book," "cat," "woo," "duck," "peep," "birdie," "moo moo."
Early 5	0;11(20)	When K wants something, she will grasp it with hands and say "ta." Said "apple" ([apu]) and took Patricia's apple (said "ta" first) Mother says she can combine words. Words on tape: "hi," "ball," "ta," "heh?" "cookie," "there," "cat," "car," "boy," "cow," "duckies," "book," "hop," "horse."
Stage 5	1;0(3)	Mother says she has different names for six different relatives. Mother says her multiword utterances are: "empty bottle," "mama lunch," "daddy's books," "daddy working," "King boys," "Daniel's crying." No evidence for this on tape.
	1;0(26)	Active language production begins. Words on tape: "cookie" "mami"

Table 4. (*Continued*)

Stage	Age	Linguistic observation
		"Uncle Ben" "huh?"
		"wowwow" "Norway"
		"ooh" "Daniel"
		"yeah" "tata"
		"hi" "oh!"
		"up" "have it"
		"birdie" "two"
		"counting" "take this"
		"I'm-doing" "bunny"
		"horse" "squirrel"
		"car" "meow"
		"ball" "in there"
		"this" "get it"
		"honk" "cow"
		"book" "ticktock"
		"donkey" "cuckoobird" (34 words)
	1;1(10)	Mother gave us list of 56 words K knows. Language sample shows 17 multiword utterances produced spontaneously, but they seem to be learned phrases. e.g., "how are " "baby's crying" "read this" "who's that"
Late 5	1;2(15)	Similar to last session
	1;3(2)	MLU = 1.18 Noticeable increase in spontaneous and imitated phrases, e.g.,

Spontaneous phrases	Imitated phrases
"there's a meow"	"put them all in"
"change the baby"	"put all jar"
"drop it down"	"another one"
"there it is"	"you comb my hair"
"take off"	"dump them out"
"there's a die"	"there it go"

Stage	Age	Linguistic observation
Early 6	1;4(8)	MLU = 1.30 Relational patterns are beginning to emerge, e.g.,

Action

"get a toy?"	"hold the toy?"
"get it?"	"hold that"
"get it there?"	"play toy"

Locative Action

"put in the cup"	"put it down"
"put in the jar"	"get in the box"
"get it off"	"take it off"

Table 4.   (*Continued*)

Stage	Age	Linguistic observation	
		"get in jar"	"put it in"
Stage 6	1;5(2)	MLU = 1.54	
	1;5(20)	MLU = 1.99	
		Some utterances	
		"I want money"	"want some more money?"
		"want this one"	"wanna take it off?"
		"want cars?"	"want put that on?"
		"want book?"	"I wanna go see Sheebo"
	1;6(12)	MLU = 2.42	
	1;7(17)	MLU = 2.35	

hide it?
hide it?
                    (K goes behind E to find watch)
                    Aha! You found it didn't you?
                    You found it.

K also succeeded when the experimenter used her hand instead of the cup.

Data from other studies mentioned earlier indicate that children usually have very little language, only a few words and certainly no syntax, when they first succeed at this task. The data from D is typical in this regard. His first successes were during session 1;5(6) when he found the hidden object placed behind E's back, then under a blanket, then in a teapot. Here is a sample of his language during this session (D's utterances are given in phonetics because most are babbling at this stage):

<u>D</u>   <u>Experimenters (1, 2)</u>

(D is vocalizing, most of which do not seem meaningful. D plays with his blanket while E1 and E2 get ready for task. D places blanket over head)

                    E1: What do you have the blanket over your head for?
                    E2: Hey, D, hey D, where are ya?
(no verbal response)
                    E1: D, you think you're funny, look at this, D.

(E1 places object under cup and moves it behind his back, leaving object there. D looks at cup)

                    E2: Hm.
                    E1: Let's do it again, D, see?

(E1 repeats task, D looks at cup, then retrieves object behind E1's back)

E1:   Way to go.

[wɪː]
[hɪə]
[hʌdɪwɪ]
[hae]

E1:   Let's do it again, see? D lookit.

[wə: boʊn]

(D ignores E1, then successfully finds object again)

E1:   Hm, are you doing that D, are you
        doing the ole invisible
        displacement?

Unlike K, D had only a small vocabulary and no sentences at this stage, and many of his vocalizations were babbling or sounds of excitement. Yet, his ability to seek the hidden object was comparable to that of K, only he could not ask the adult where it had gone and if he had hidden it.

DISCUSSION

The results above support studies like Bates et al.(in press) and (Ingram 1978a) that the Stage 5 ability to use new instruments as means to ends, intentional nonverbal communication, and some ability to communicate are related to the onset of language. Indeed, they seem to be necessary precursors to the rudimentary forms of language that occur at this stage.

Two other predictions about the form of language during the sensorimotor period, however, are not so readily substantiated. One concerns the nature of the child's early symbols. Piaget (1946) argued that the first words appear in Stage 6, and that they represent symbols more than signs, that is, they are fleeting and highly personal to the child's momentary experience. In analyzing Piaget's own data, Ingram (1978) I noted that even for his own children these forms actually appeared in Stage 5. For K, Stage 5 showed a more stable and growing number of words than predicted by studies to date. It seemed that the pairing of auditory schema (or words) to real world contexts in a consistent fashion was possible before other forms of symbolic ability (e.g., symbolic play) had yet occurred. Recent experimental research with 20 children by Cook et al. (1978) also found little evidence for a relation between early language development and the onset of symbolic play. In examining K's situation, the contributing factor seemed to be the very repetitive use of language by the mother in highly constrained and well delineated contexts. In other words, K always seemed to know what to say and when to say it.

The second unsubstantiated prediction is that the onset of syntax (or multiword utterances) requires the attainment of representational ability at the end of the sensorimotor period. K was clearly using longer utterances and apparently productive patterns months before she had reached that point of cognitive development. This fact raises serious doubts about claims concerning the relation of syntactic structures to cognitive structures (a point to be returned to later), and raises questions about the causes of K's precocious syntactic behavior and whether her syntactic rules differ from those of children who begin at a later cognitive stage. The one factor that was evident to all who observed K and suggests further investigation is the fact that K was a very good imitator. She could repeat spontaneously quite well and did so often in the early sessions. There were several uses of learned phrases in the first sentences that indicate longer-term memory for delayed uses. The results indicate that claims about the precursors to syntax need to await more careful examination of data such as that from K. The next sections examine some of these data and discuss their implications for the description of syntax.

SOME ASPECTS OF K'S LANGUAGE

During the visits to K's home, it became clear to the observers that K's language environment and interaction was different from that of the other two children. One aspect was that K from very early on would participate in very structured discourse routines. Perhaps the most striking example of this took place during the session at 1;0(26) (when phonetic transcription is given, one interpretation is provided immediately beneath within parentheses):

<u>K</u>

[akʰaba]
(Uncle Ben)

    (E does not understand that K has just said "Uncle Ben" and looks to mother (M))
    M: Uncle Ben (whispered to E)
    E: Uncle Ben's? (whispered to M)
    M: Uh huh. Ask her where he is.
        (to E)
    E: Where's Uncle Ben?

huh?
[i:wei]
(Norway)

    M: Norway. (an explanation to E)

[ni:wei]
(Norway)

> E: What's that? (to M)
> M: Norway. (to E)
> E: Norway?
> M: Yeah, that's where he is.

[jae]
(yeah)

Here, K knows she can talk about Uncle Ben and can respond to the question "Where is he?" even though she has no idea about Norway or where it is. This presumably is a routine practiced often by K and her mother that allowed them to have miniature conversations.

This dialogue also contains another example of one of K's discourse devices, this being the use of "huh?" which occurred frequently in all the early sessions, most commonly after Wh-questions. The session at 1;2(15), for example, contains 61 instances of "huh?" that would either be followed by a response as above (when she knew what to say) or simply used as a verbal response to maintain interaction. She would often interject other responses between her "huh?'s." Here is a sample dialogue at 1;2(15):

K	Experimenter
huh?	What are those? (buttons in a jar)
huh?	What are those?
	What are they?
huh?	
huh?	
(pause)	
huh?	
tata please (3 times)	
	Can't you get them out?
huh?	
huh?	
	You do it.
huh?	

Although "huh?" made it possible to respond to adult speech, K had other routines that allowed for the initiation of discourse. These could be quite specific, as in the "Uncle Ben" example, or more general by using interactional terms in the sense of Halliday (1975). The most frequent around this time was "ooh!" when presented with toys, "hi" as a greeting, and "tata" when handing items back and forth. In the session at 1;0(26) "tata" occurred 85 times. Here is a typical conversation from 1;0(26) that shows several turns with just a few words exchanged:

K		Experimenter
tata		
tata	(hands object to E)	
tata	(hands object to E)	Thank you.
		Thank you.
oooh!		
tata		Ta, ta.
		Thank you.
tata		
	(drops toy)	
oh		
tata	(hands object to E)	
		Thank you.
oooh!	(playing with toys)	
		M: Put'em on.
		M: Don't do that.
hi		
		E: Hi.

These conversational routines allowed for a lot of linguistic interaction, which in turn allowed opportunities for learning new words and
phrases.

Although these examples are all single word utterances, K's language also began to show the use of stereotyped phrases, that is,
sentences in which little evidence exists to suggest that the child is
aware that they are divisible into words. At 1;1(10), for example, when
her speech was essentially holophrastic, she produced the utterances
"how are you?" "can't have this," "let's play something else." These
seemed to evolve from the interaction of her ability to converse and
to imitate spontaneously. Here is an example of her imitative behavior
at 1;0(26) with the words "brand new":

K	Experimenter
	Have you ever seen one of those?
this?	
	Brand new one.
[ae nu:]	
(brand new)	Brand new.
[n:u]	
(new)	
	Can you repeat that?
	Brand new.
	That's amazing. (to E2)
[ən:u]	
(brand new)	
tata	
[hʌn::u]	
(brand new)	
tata	
tata	

Here she even interspersed the newly imitated form into her use of "tata."

A closer look at K's spontaneous imitation reveals that its use is quite specific. Imitation was frequent during the later part of the holophrastic period when stereotyped phrases appeared and it dropped out once syntactic utterances were common. Some data on this, using the criteria for imitation in Bloom et al. (1974) is presented in Table 5. The data show that imitation was quite frequent during the period from 1;0(26) to 1;3(2) when the first multiword utterances occurred. This is consistent with Piaget's claim that imitation in Stage 5 can be directly attributed to models that are not part of the child's spontaneous behavior.

These summary data suggest that multiword utterances and early syntax may appear before truly representational ability and symbolic play, and that the onset of such utterances is closely tied to contextually predictable uses and imitation. Sinclair's suggestion (1978) that syntax may evolve from operations such as spatial arrangements and stacking were not borne out by these data. At 1;3(2), for instance, K was still barely able to stack more than two blocks and yet was well on her way toward developing multiword utterances. D meanwhile, was the most capable at stacking and arranging blocks and yet was the slowest at developing multiword patterns. To use Bates' (1978) terminology, the

Table 5. Summary of stages of linguistic production for K from 0;10(22) to 1;7(29) and her rate of imitiation

Age	MLU	Total tokens	Proportion (no.) of intelligible tokens	Number of syntactic types (spontaneous)	Proportion of imitated types
Holophrastic Sessions					
0;10(22)	1.00	53	0.36 (19)	0	0.57 (4/7)
0;11(6)	1.00	39	0.41 (16)	0	0.00 (0/10)
0;11(20)	1.00	103	0.47 (49)	0	0.16 (3/19)
1;0(3)	1.00	32	0.41 (13)	0	0.22 (2/9)
Onset of multiword utterances					
1;0(26)	1.01	358	0.85 (305)	5	0.50 (20/50)
1;1(10)	1.06	220	0.74 (163)	17	0.26 (7/27)
1;2(15)	1.00	199	0.88 (176)	5	0.23 (7/30)
1;3(2)	1.18	129	0.80 (103)	13	0.24 (13/55)
Growth of multiword utterances					
1;4(8)	1.20	591	0.89 (526)	78	0.09 (12/138)
1;5(2)	1.54	148	0.82 (122)	26	0.00 (0/55)
1;5(20)	1.99	439	0.87 (381)	114	0.06 (10/156)
1;6(12)	2.42	179	0.86 (154)	80	0.04 (5/129)
1;7(17)	2.35	378	0.86 (324)	140	0.06 (10/187)

similarities between patterns of displacement and those of syntax are structural analogies, that is, they are similar because of constraints on the nature of things rather than because of any direct relation between them.

STRUCTURAL FEATURES OF EARLY SYNTAX

In addition to looking for causal prerequisites to multiword speech, it is also important to examine the nature of the early rules used by children. This aspect has been most closely studied, and the current view is that early word combinations are produced by semantic rules (c.f., Bowerman, 1973; Brown, 1973) such as Agent + Action, Action + Object, etc. The claim is that the child has acquired a group of linguistic signs, for example, *boy, hit,* and has learned to order these to express certain semantic or conceptual ideas. Although the relations themselves are thought to be universal (e.g., Brown, 1973), children vary the ones they use most frequently (Braine, 1976). This perspective lends itself to an interpretation that there is nothing particularly syntactic occurring at this stage of acquisition.

Ingram (1979) discussed a number of difficulties with this point of view, based on research that analyzed K's syntactic development. The concerns are related to the issue of "productivity," that is, determining when a child has actually produced an utterance by using a linguistic rule. Once productivity is more carefully defined, there are particular syntactic processes at work from the onset of sentences.

Most studies analyzing the grammatical structure of children's first multiword utterances have made certain assumptions that have gone unchallenged until recently. These assumptions can be explicitly enumerated as the following purported linguistic universals:

1. The structure dependence of rules
2. Universal grammatical relations
3. Universal grammatical categories
4. Grammatical rules are:
   a) analytic
   b) productive

The structure dependence of rules, a point discussed at some length in Chomsky (1975), claims that all rules by nature will refer to linguistic categories, for examples, noun, noun phrase, agent, etc., dependent on one's theory. In terms of child language, the assumption means that the child will group symbols or signs into categories for the purpose of rule formation. Although earlier accounts claimed that the universal relations and categories were syntactic (e.g., McNeill, 1966), the common view now among those in language acquisition is that they are semantic (e.g., Bloom, 1973), and their source is the child's cognitive structures. Finally, rules are thought to be "analytic" in that they put these general categories together. For example, Agent + Action, and "productive" in that they may create new utterances because potentially all "Agent" words can combine with any "Action" word although vagaries of performance limit all possibilities.

Braine (1976) was one of the first to question some of these assumptions by attempting to restrict what can be considered to be a productive or rule-based utterance. Bloom, Lightbown, and Hood (1975) suggested that five instances of a pattern are sufficient to consider a pattern to exist. Braine increased the number to six and added conditions of positional consistency and evidence for novel productions (although the latter is never operationalized). The results of these restrictions are fewer purported rules, and rules that may be lexically based, e.g., *eat* plus things that can be eaten (c.f., also Ervin-Tripp, 1977, for a similar lexically-based grammar). Also, Braine criticized certain semantic categories such as "Object" as lacking semantic consistency (c.f., discussion of "Agent" in Ingram 1979). The child may have several available cognitive categories, and needs to determine for the individual language how these are encoded (Schlesinger, 1977, provided an excellent discussion of this interaction). The above assumptions are misleading in the early stages and there is a need to focus more carefully on how categories, relations and rules develop. The data from K suggest some ways that these aspects of language are developed. Peters (1977) noted a child who did not just learn single words and how to put them together (analytic development), but instead learned entire sentences as unanalyzed wholes (synthetic development). As already mentioned, K learned whole phrases early and so seemed to be synthetic in her acquisition. Rather than stockpile a lexicon of phrases, however, K began to take the phrases apart as if to find their constituent structure (c.f., Ingram, 1979 for details). For example, at 1;5(20) K knew the phrase "want take it off for you?" which she used as a request to be allowed to turn the tape recorder off. Below are eight forms this utterance took in that context during the session at 1;5(20). The utterance numbers are also provided to show how these were spread across the session:

				Utterance number
1.	want?			25
2.	want	it off?		24
3.		take it off?		199
4.	want take it off?			10, 11, 13, 22, 23, 431
5.	wanna take it off?			252, 428
6.	want	it off for you?		374
7.	want take it off for you?			12
8.	wanna take it off for you?			430

Similar development occurred with various other phrases, one of which was "want put it on for you?" These were part of a sample that still contained primarily single- and two-word utterances. The rule for this particular request was:

Request

$$S \rightarrow \text{want} \begin{bmatrix} \text{put} \begin{Bmatrix} \text{it} \\ \text{that one} \end{Bmatrix} \begin{Bmatrix} \text{on} \\ \text{off} \end{Bmatrix} \\ \text{take} \quad \text{it} \end{bmatrix} \text{for you?}$$

Over several sessions, these rules would become more general as words freed themselves from other words and began to co-occur more. Also, categories began to be constructed, such as pronoun, which developed out of rules like the one above. K did not bring ready made rules and categories to the task of language learning but discovered them through active manipulation of utterances. The process she used focused on the composition of utterances and can be summarized as follows:

Determine the phonetically distinct sequences in strings of utterances
Observe the co-occurrence of certain words with certain other words,
     along with positional constraints
Develop categories of words that share co-occurrence and positional
     properties
Develop rules that state which categories can go with other categories,
     and which cannot

Although K's language was semantic in that she talked about what she knew about the world, her focus in multiword acquisition was on aspects that have come to be known as syntactic (i.e., sequencing and co-occurrence). The rules were formulated across so-called semantic boundaries.

It is, of course, possible to say that K was unique in her development of syntax. Ramer (1976) noted two styles of syntactic acquisition that are relevant to this explanation. She found that the boys in her study were less productive in their rules, somewhat like K in the early stages, and the girls showed highly productive combinations. One initial discrepancy with K's data is that unlike the boys, K was learning language quite rapidly, a fact that was still true when she was revisited at the age of 2;6. The real issue that K's language raises, however, is the question of productivity. For K, there was only a gradual transition from the condition of "no rule" to "general rules," and this can only be effectively demonstrated by refining a great deal of the procedures for determining a "productive" utterance. Once done, other children's grammars resemble K's more than one would have originally believed.

This point can be demonstrated by examining the following data from Bloom et al. (1975) for Gia at age 1;8:

MLU 1.34

Action Pattern

turned on light	ka push uh carriage
ride Gumbo	ride dis
ride da fish	eat piece
	read uh book

According to the authors, these utterances are produced by a semantic-syntactic rule that combines actions with objects, because at least five such utterances occur. It is difficult to see how anyone can say anything about the nature of a child's rules by simply counting utterances. The only information that such a criterion provides is a picture of the kinds of things a child may like to talk about, and subsequently about the nature of the child's cognition (with all its subsequent problems of interpretation, c.f., Howe, 1976). In order to compare the language of K with children such as Gia, a more stringent criteria for productivity needs to be developed to see if their rule systems are similar.

Ingram (1979) provided a first attempt to develop in some detail criteria for productivity based on decisions about co-occurrence and precedence. Two notions, which are crucial to such criteria, are explored in that study: whether a child has *analytic* knowledge of an utterance, that is, that there are separate parts or words, and whether it is *productive*, that is, produced by rule. The former can exist without the latter, although studies to date have not tried to separate the two. To determine if an utterance like "ride Gumbo" is analytic, it needs to be established if the words in it are lexically free, that is, if they occur in isolation or in other utterances with a consistent meaning. In the above example, "ride" occurs in other utterances, but there is no evidence in this limited data to say that "Gumbo" is lexically free. Neither word in the utterance "eat piece," for example, has evidence for analyticity in these data. For productivity, it needs to be established if the words are grammatically free, that is, if they occur more than once in a particular grammatical role. Here "ride" occurs in three sentences with an object and thus can be considered grammatically free to take objects. None of the object words, however, show grammatical freedom in this sense. These criteria divide utterances into different levels in terms of the amount of lexical and grammatical freedom in their words.

With this establishment of some stringent criteria for productivity, it is possible to propose with some confidence rules that have psychological reality. The rules in K's data, taken from Ingram (1979), show that the syntactic rules transcend the semantic relations currently in vogue and that syntax rules are not simply reflections of cognitive patterns. The generalization from K's data to other children needs to await syntactic analyses of the type discussed here, but the direction of similar research by others (e.g., Braine, 1976, Ervin-Tripp, 1977) indicates comparable patterns of development.

CONCLUSION

This chapter relates the onset of syntax to the cognitive advances made by young children during the latter part of the sensorimotor period. Research into this question is important because causal relations can provide insight into the developmental origins of language. A variety of data shows that syntax normally occurs at the end of this period with the onset of representational ability and symbolic play, and several investigators have concluded that syntax is interrelated. Data are presented from one child, that indicate that syntax may appear earlier, and that syntactic processes of organization emerged once the child retained and produced longer vocalizations. Cognitive limitations seemed to restrict the use and content of language, but not its syntactic processing. It is suggested that the child evidenced specific syntactic mechanisms for the development of a grammar, and that analyses from other children may yield similar results once syntactic grammars are written (with linguistic criteria for co-occurrence and precedence) to replace current approaches based only on semantic taxonomy.

ACKNOWLEDGMENTS

I would like to extend my appreciation to Judith Ingram and Werner Neufeld for their assistance in the collection of the data reported in this chapter. We had originally hoped to produce a report on it to be entitled "A longitudinal study of language development during the sensorimotor period," but time has taken our interests in other directions. Their insightful comments on the behavior of the children observed have been very helpful to me in coming to an understanding of the early emergence of syntax.

REFERENCES

Bates, E. 1978. Functionalism and the biology of language. Papers and Reports on Child Language Development, Stanford University. 15:K1–K26.

Bates, E., Camaioni, L., and Volterra, V. 1975. The acquisition of performatives prior to speech. Merrill-Palmer Quarterly. 21:205–226.

Bates, E., Benigni, L., Bretherton, I., Camaioni, L., and Volterra, V. 1977. From gesture to first word: On cognitive and social prerequisites. *In* M.

Lewis and L. Rosenblum (eds.), Interaction, Conversation, and the Development of Language. pp. 247–307. John Wiley & Sons, New York.

Bates, E., Benigni, L., Bretherton, I., Camaioni, L., and Volterra, V. The emergence of symbols. Academic Press. New York. In press.

Beilin, H. 1975. Studies on the Cognitive Basis of Language Development. Academic Press, New York.

Bellugi, U., and R. Brown (eds.). 1964. The acquisition of language. Monographs of the Society for Research in Child Development. Vol. 29.

Bernstein, B. 1964. Elaborated and restricted codes: Their social origins and some consequences. Am. Anthropol. 66:55–69.

Bloom, L. 1970. Language Development: Form and Function in Emerging Grammars. M.I.T. Press, Cambridge, Mass.

Bloom, L. 1973. One Word at a Time: The Use of Single Word Utterances before Syntax. Mouton, The Hague.

Bloom, L., Lightbown, P., and Hood, L. 1974. Imitation in language development: If, when and why. Cognitive Psychology. 6:380–442.

Bloom, L., Lightbown, P., and Hood, L. 1975. Structure and variation in child language. Monographs of the Society for Research in Child Development. Vol. 40. (Serial no. 160).

Bowerman, M. 1973. Early Syntactic Development: A Cross-linguistic Study with Special Reference to Finnish. Cambridge University Press, London.

Braine, M. 1963. The ontogeny of English phrase structure: The first phase. Language. 39:3–13.

Braine, M. 1976. Children's first word combinations. Monographs of the Society for Research in Child Development. 41(1). (Serial no. 164)

Braunwald, S. 1978. Context, word and meaning: Towards a communicational analysis of lexical acquisition. In A. Lock (ed.), Action, Gesture, and Symbol: The Emergence of Language, pp. 485–527, Academic Press, Inc., New York.

Brown, R. 1973. A First Language: The Early Stages. Harvard University Press, Cambridge, Mass.

Brown, R. and Fraser, C. 1964. The acquisition of syntax. In U. Bellugi and R. Brown (eds.), Acquisition of Language. SRCD Monograph. Serial 92 Vol. 29(1) pp. 43–79.

Chomsky, N. 1975. Reflections on Language. Pantheon, New York.

Cook, N., Dale, P., and Goldstein, H. 1978. Pragmatics and symbolic play: A study in language and cognitive development. Paper presented at the First International Congress for the Study of Child Language. Tokyo, Japan.

Corrigan, R. 1978. Language development as related to stage 6 object permanence development. J. Child Lang. 5:173–189.

Dore, J. 1975. Holophrases, speech acts and language universals. J. Child Lang. 2:21–39.

Ervin-Tripp, S. 1977. From conversation to syntax. Papers and Reports on Child Language Development, Stanford University. 13:K1–K21.

Greenfield, P., and Smith, J. 1976. The Structure of Communication in Early Language Development. Academic Press, New York.

Halliday, M. A. K. 1975. Learning How to Mean: Explorations in the Development of Language. Edward Arnold, London.

Howe, C. 1976. The meaning of two-word utterances in the speech of young children. J. Child Lang. 3:29–47.

Ingram, D. 1971. Transitivity in child language. Language. 47:888–910.

Ingram, D. 1978. Sensori-motor intelligence and language development. *In* A. Lock (ed.), Action, Gesture, and Symbol: The Emergence of Language, pp. 261–290, Academic Press, New York.

Ingram, D. 1978a. Piaget's data: A chronological record of Jacqueline, Lucienne and Laurent. Mimeo, University of British Columbia.

Ingram, D. 1979. The psychological reality of grammatical rules in children's language. Paper presented at the University of Washington.

Inhelder, B., Lezine, I., Sinclair, H., and Stambak, M. 1972. Les debuts de la fonction symbolique. *Archives de Psychologie*. 41:187–243.

Lock, A. (ed.). 1978. Action, Gesture and Symbol: The Emergence of Language. Academic Press, London.

McNeill, D. 1966. Developmental psycholinguistics. *In* F. Smith and G. Miller (eds.), The Genesis of Language: A Psycholinguistic Approach, pp. 15–84, M.I.T. Press, Cambridge, Mass.

Miller, J. 1978. Identifying language disorders in retarded children. School Psychol. Digest. 7:27–44.

Miller, W., and Ervin, S. 1964. The development of grammar in child language. *In* U. Bellugi and R. Brown (eds.), Acquisition of Language. SRCD Monograph. Serial 92 Vol. 29(1) pp. 9–34.

Nelson, Ka. 1973. Structure and strategy in learning to talk. Monographs of the Society for Research in Child Development. Vol. 38. (Serial no. 149).

Nelson, Ke. (ed.). 1978. Children's Language. Vol 1. Gardner Press, New York.

Nelson, Ke., and Bonvillian, J. 1978. Early language development: Conceptual growth and related processes between 2 and 4½ years of age. *In* Ke. Nelson (ed.), Children's Language, Vol. 1. Gardner Press, New York. pp. 467–556.

Nicholich, L. and Raph, J. 1978. Imitative language and symbolic maturity in the single-word period. J. Psycholinguist. Res. 7:401–417.

Peters, A. 1977. Language learning strategies. Language. 53:560–573.

Piaget, J. 1962. *La formation du symbole chez l'enfant*. Neuchatel: Delachaux et Niestle, 1946. Published in English under the title Play, Dreams and Imitation in Childhood. W. W. Norton Co., New York.

Piaget, J., and Inhelder, B. 1964. The Psychology of the Child. Basic Books, New York.

Ramer, A. 1976. Syntactic styles in emerging language. J. Child Lang. 3:49–62.

Schlesinger, I. M. 1971. Production of utterances and language acquisition. *In* D. Slobin (ed.), The Ontogenesis of Grammar. Academic Press, New York.

Schlesinger, I. M. 1977. The role of cognitive development and linguistic input in language acquisition. J. Child Lang. 4:153–169.

Sinclair, H. 1978. The transition from sensory-motor behavior to symbolic activity. Interchange 1970, 1:119–126. Page citations from reprint in L. Bloom (ed.). Readings in Language Development, pp. 149–160, John Wiley, New York.

Synder, L. 1976. The early presuppositions and performatives of normal and language disabled children. Papers and Reports on Child Language Development. 12:221–229.

Uzgiris, I. and Hunt, J. McV. 1975. Assessment in Infancy. University of Illinois Press, Urbana-Champaign.

chapter
9

On the Structure of
Early Symbolization

Dennie Wolf

Howard Gardner

Harvard Project Zero
Harvard Graduate School of Education
Cambridge, Massachusetts

Ask any psychologist what the "most human," "best," or "most typical" of our symbol systems is and the answer will be "language." We all recognize this as a "good" and maybe the only "right" answer, and one made correct by the universality of language across cultures, its obvious range from simple names to metaphors, the way a generation of researchers has picked out the rules that structure not just the framework of grammar but also meaning, diction, and dialect-use. In fact, we may be so aware of language's elegant structure and its capacity to encode a range and subtlety of meanings that we often assume not just that all language is symbolic, but that all symbolization is linguistic. Bruner, discussing the capacity for representing experience, speaks of enactive and perceptually grounded representations and commented, "Finally, there is representation in words and language. Its hallmark is that it is symbolic in nature (Bruner, 1965, p. 11)." Even if we suspect that the foundations or realizations of symbolic capacities exist outside the specifically linguistic contexts of talking, listening, or writing, we commonly validate our intuitions by extending the metaphor of language-use to these behaviors. Consequently, we hear of the "dialogue structure" of early communication (Bruner, 1975) or that representational gestures are "manual names" (Bates, 1979).

Language is the most common and possibly the most critical symbol system children use. Distilling symbolization down to language-use, however, may yield a narrow picture of human symbolic capacities. For the moment, let us define symbolization as the capacity not only to recall but to *render* experience into externally observable forms (typically called symbols or signifiers, which refer to, without being taken as synonymous with, what they signify (Bates, et al., 1979; Werner and Kaplan, 1963). Abiding by this definition, both everyday observation and normative studies of development (Bayley, 1969; Gesell, 1940; McCarthy, 1970) make it clear that, between ages 1 and 7, gesture, drawing, block-building, number, and music seem to be symbolic forms. In the past, however, the obvious co-existence of these other forms has not seriously challenged the language-centered view of symbolization. First, whereas language is so strikingly a translation of experience into conventional forms, activities like symbolic play or drawing have been viewed as less "translated" and thus, less advanced, because they "imitate" or resemble the experience or objects to which they refer (Peirce, 1932; Piaget, 1962). Second, (and possibly as an artifact of a language-centered view of symbolization), we have rarely studied and consequently been doubtful about the existence of identifiable analogues to "vocabulary" and "grammar" within activities like drawing, gesture, or music. Finally, it has been a frequent

The research described in this chapter was supported by the Carnegie Foundation, the Spencer Foundation, and the National Institute of Education (G-78-0031).

assumption that symbolic capacities are "of a piece"—that forms like gesture or drawing develop according to principles no different from those which guide the appearance and growth of language (Piaget, 1962; Werner and Kaplan, 1963).

The reasons to break with these assumptions are increasing. It is clear on philosophical (Goodman, 1968), historical (Gombrich, 1960) and psychological grounds (Golomb, 1974; Goodnow, 1977; Smith, 1980) that the distinction between arbitrary and iconic forms of symbolization may not hold. Although it is clear that drawings and gestures will not exhibit vocabulary or grammar except in some metaphorical sense, the set of elements and the rules that govern either the construction of graphic signifiers or the combinations within larger gestural statements are becoming more sharply delineated (Freeman and Janikoun, 1972; Goldin-Meadow and Feldman, 1975; Goodnow, 1977). Moreover, the assumption that symbolization is a uniform capacity across language and any other symbol-systems is seriously questionable. For example, what people remember from filmed and read presentations of the same materials differs significantly (Kelly and Meringoff, 1979; Meringoff, in press; Salomon, 1979). Finally, children in their own behavior offer provocative, ample evidence of both the fully symbolic and, if not the language-independent, at least the language-distinct nature of their capacity to render rather than simply re-enact what they experience:

> J, a six-year-old, is seated on the floor engaged in a game in which she is given the problem of "remembering by writing down" a series of rhythms that are presented to her by an experimenter:

> E: Here is the next one. It's a tricky one, so listen carefully. E plays a four-beat rhythm (one beat-two beats-one beat).
> (J: Listens then plays it back correctly on the drum.)
> E: Good. Now let's see you write that down so we know how to play it again later.
> (J: Plays it on the drum again. Then she draws it out with a marker on a sheet of paper. She draws four small circles, from left to right across the bottom of the sheet, first one, then a pause in the air, then two more drawn one right after the other, then a pause in the air, and finally one more circle.)
> E: Tell me how that goes.
> (J: "Reads" the rhythm back simply as four even beats, "One, two, three, four.")
> E: Listen, here it is again. E plays the rhythm over.
> J: Oh, I see, like this . . . (This time she goes back to her drawing, making one circle, then a space, then two closely grouped circles, another space and then one final circle.)
> (J: Plays it back on the drum and sees still another possibility. She goes back to her most recent drawing of the rhythm and draws an enclosure around the closely spaced second and third beats and then a

larger enclosure around the total array. Holding her drawing in one hand and the drumstick in the other, she beats out the rhythm once more.)

Clearly, saying something like "One, then two together, then one more" is just one of many ways to remember what is heard.

In the remainder of this chapter, early language activity is inserted into a broader view of symbolic development. As a means to that end the transition from planned action to early sentences is examined alongside contemporary events in other symbol systems. In examining the fuller range of symbolic acquisitions in this period, we are attempting to pick out what is shared *across* the range of developments within symbolization. The objective is to determine whether there is an underlying pattern or structure to this first phase of symbolization, which is broader than language acquisition. The effort entails trying to view early language as one among a range of symbolic capacities. It also entails viewing the mechanisms of symbolic development broadly conceived as potentially superordinate to, rather than synonymous with, the means to language acquisition. In the end, by knowing language against the background of other symbol systems, its peculiar developmental history and its particular genius may be understood much more clearly.

To appreciate this particular view of symbolization, it is essential to lay out the pattern of facts within symbolic development to which any model of symbolic development must be responsive. Subsequently, it is critical to discuss existing explanations of symbolic growth. Particularly important is the contrast between the Piagetian description of the shared nonsymbolic origins for changes in symbolic capacities and a complementary picture that stresses how symbolization results from the combined mastery of diverse physical materials (media) and from the highly specific rules that underlie particular symbol systems (e.g., language, number, drawing). Insights and difficulties within each of these views provide the beginnings of an outline for an alternative, or at least supplementary, model of early symbolic development.

BASIC FACTS OF SYMBOLIC DEVELOPMENT

Frequently, humans are distinguished from other primates on the basis of symbol use. Yet knowledge about symbolization as a process in its own right is slight. Either symbolic capacities have been subsumed as part of general intelligence (McCarthy, 1970), taken to be structures largely reflective of cultural meanings (Douglas, 1975; Levi-Strauss, 1957, 1962), or have been seen as vehicles for personal expression (Freud, 1927, 1938, 1955; Kris, 1952; Kubie, 1971; Winnicott, 1971).

When interest has turned to symbolization per se, three basic findings emerge.

The first finding concerns the changing quality of symbolic forms. It is most familiar in Peirce's (1932) and Piaget's (1962) distinction between indices (parts of actions or objects that signal the presence of a larger whole, as a voice indicates a person's presence), symbols (personally motivated and descriptive forms like children's onomatopoetic words or adult dream images), and signs (arbitrary, socially-shared forms like mature language or numbers). The second findings focus attention on the types of symbolic forms, pointing out the fundamentally distinct understandings or "grammars" that are necessary for adequate performance within diverse symbol systems (Arnheim, 1974; Gardner et al., 1974; Golomb, 1974; Ives et al., 1979; Shotwell et al., 1979). There is a third equally important, but theoretically less prominent set of findings about symbolic development. These findings concern the patterns of acquisition across symbolic skills within early development. Simply put: language appears in the second year; between three and four the capacity to "make things" like drawings and spatial models surfaces. At approximately school-age, children begin to master the alphabet and the numerical systems. If this commonsense sequence is filled out with research findings, an even more detailed picture emerges. In the second year, gesture and symbolic play also occur as symbolic forms, although it is the semantic rather than the transformational bases for sentences that is acquired. (Bates, 1976; Bates et al., 1979; Bloom, 1970, 1973; Brown, 1973; Fenson et al., 1976; Fillmore, 1968; Miller et al., 1978; Nicolich, 1975). Between ages 3 and 4, children can not only draw and build but can make extensive use of the physical properties of objects in a range of symbolic tasks like metaphor and primitive forms of measurement (Golomb, 1974; Kellogg, 1968; Luquet, 1917; Piaget, 1965; Smith, 1972; Winner et al., 1979). Between ages 5 and 7, it is not simply command of numbers and letters that appears, but rather a range of highly systematized symbolic forms that also includes musical scales, maps, and diagrams (Barrett, 1965; Biemillier, 1970; Feldman, 1971; Karmiloff-Smith, 1979; Read, 1970; Saxe, 1979; Shotwell, 1979).

EXISTING MODELS OF SYMBOLIC DEVELOPMENT

In current research only two of these points concerning symbolic development—the observation of the growing abstractness of all symbolic forms across time and the observation of the eventual diversity of individual symbolic skills—are used. Each of these observations derives from and speaks for a particular view of the nature of symbolic development. It is the Piagetian model for symbolic development that underlies the earlier observation that all symbolic capacities, whether language, drawing, or number use, undergo a similar and developmentally coordinated progression from the highly concrete index, to the personally motivated sign, and finally to the conventional symbol. Such a model necessarily regards as less than critical the differences in physical characteristics, rule systems and patterns of acquisitions characterizing different symbolic forms. In place of any emphasis on the internal diversity of symbolic activities, the Piagetian model underscores the changes in the basic nature of thought that are likely to have significant reverberations *across* symbolic conduct (Furth, 1969; Piaget, 1962).

The complement to the Piagetian approach is one that stresses the tremendous internal diversity of symbol use, particularly as it derives from physically or culturally grounded differences in the way particular media are used in the service of individual symbol systems or symbolic tasks (e.g., how writing, spoken language, or gesture may emphasize different aspects of the same story). This model views as essential precisely those characteristics of symbolic forms that are minimized within the Piagetian model—chiefly the distinctive physical possibilities inherent in different material (e.g., words occur sequentially, lines are two dimensional, blocks have volume) and the distinctive rules that govern the conventional symbol systems using these raw materials (e.g., the necessity for lines and blocks to depict volume in different ways). Within this second view, symbolization is seen as the result of the separate development of at least potentially independent symbolic skills. That is, given that language and drawing start out with radically different physical materials and will eventually elaborate quite distinct means for referring to actions, the past, or mood, there is considerable reason to predict independent developmental trajectories for the two skills.

Intuitively, each of these models captures some of the essentials of the process of symbolization. The Piagetian model, for instance, speaks to our sense that a dramatic revolution in thought divides the essentially motoric and perceptual world of infants from the world of the 2-year-old in which symbolization makes it possible to remember and invent alternatives to the "here-and-now." The medium-centered model answers to our impression of the eventual diversity of a symbolic function that can include algebra, landscape painting, poetry, even models for symbolic development. Nevertheless, a model for symbolic development has to answer to more than individual impressions. With reference to the models under discussion, perhaps the major question concerns the extent to which either model can adequately map not an aspect but the course of symbolic development.

Nonsymbolic Origins of Symbolic Development: The Case of the Semiotic Function

Where Piaget and his colleagues have turned their attention to the symbolization process, their emphasis has fallen on the nonsymbolic or cognitive foundations that permit either the initial appearance of or the subsequent changes within symbol-use. Perhaps their most articulate work in this area concerns the appearance of symbolic capacities. Piaget and others have documented the transitions from pragmatic or sensorimotor intelligence to symbolically guided activity, which occurs in the second year. Within Piagetian theory this transition is marked by the appearance of the ability to represent experience internally. This ability, often termed the *semiotic function*, manifests itself in several new phenomena: *mental symbols* (chiefly, deferred imitations of events and persons, the preservation of an object's existence despite its disappearance from the perceptual field, problem-solving behaviors indicative of planning or anticipation); symbolic play, and initial forms of language use (Inhelder et al., 1971; Lezine, 1973; Piaget, 1954; 1962). Past the onset of the semiotic function, the essential developments within symbolization are: 1) the increasing dissociation of the signifier from the signified—for instance, the ability to use words to refer to absent rather than present objects and to comment on rather than demand, and 2) the increasingly social-conventional, as opposed to personal, nature of meanings (Furth, 1969; Piaget, 1962). These changes are envisaged as affecting virtually any form of symbolic activity. The timing of such changes derives from changes in the structure of logical thought (e.g., the onset of preoperational or concrete-operational abilities) rather than from the process of symbol formation— the use of either particular physical materials like lines, sounds, or clay or the individual rule systems like mapping, language or modeling, into which experience is being encoded.

Research into symbolization has raised some serious questions for the Piagetian concept of symbolization based largely on shifts in the nature of logical thought. These questions become quite clear in examining the case of the earliest, and perhaps the most significant, of the changes Piaget proposes for symbolization: the onset of the semiotic function during the second year. To begin with, studies of development in infancy fail to show the inter-correlated onset of different types of behavior thought to signal the onset of a unified capacity to employ mental symbols. There are both serious precursors to object permanence as early as 5 months (Bower, 1974) and a demonstrated *lack* of co-occurrence of later forms of object permanence, anticipations in problem-solving, deferred imitations, symbolic play, and language (Corrigan, 1979; Uzgiris and Hunt, 1975). If patterns of skill development in late infancy are closely examined, a revised pattern appears in which certain problem-solving skills (e.g., sophisticated searches for absent objects, anticipations and planning in problem-solving) co-occur at a typically earlier time than a second cluster of skills that includes deferred imitation, depictive gesture, symbolic play, and early language (Bates, 1976; Bates et al., 1979; Corrigan, 1978, 1979; Miller et al., 1978). What this suggests is that the original conception of the semiotic function may break down into two rather separate developmental capacities: representation and symbolization. Representation, the ability to reconstruct or recall information to guide behavior, seems to occur earlier and gives rise to a number of phenomena: object permanence, anticipations in problem-solving, and stored knowledge of space. Symbolization is a process that is different from this ability to remember and to guide behavior via an internal image or plan; it is the ability to convert such information into observable forms that refer to, rather than simply guide, experience. Unlike representation, symbolization calls for the translation of knowledge or experience into both physical materials (sounds, lines) and particular rule systems (language, drawing).

The second revision relates to whether symbolization should be considered a psychologically unified capacity. It is mentioned above that when children first exhibit rich productive capacities in gesture, speech, and play, they show no sustained evidence of the prototypical forms of symbolization in drawing, construction, or number (Forman, 1979; Goodnow, 1977; Saxe, 1979; Smith, 1972; Wagner and Walters, in press). What this suggests is that symbolization may not consist simply in the growing abstraction and socialization available across all symbolic forms. Furthermore, it is apparent that only selected abilities *within* a particular symbol system become available at a given time, for instance, the above mentioned way in which drawing precedes map-making and case grammars precede transformational grammars in language. In light of findings that basic shifts in cognition do not fully account for the complexity of symbolic development, it is important to examine a second model for symbolic growth, one which is predicated on the study of particular media and rule systems.

Distinct Symbol Systems: The Endpoint of Symbolization

An alternative to the Piagetian model for symbolic development has developed from research into the interaction between media, symbol systems, and the cognitive processes underlying representational development (Gardner, 1973; 1979; Gardner et al., 1974; Salomon, 1979.) Originating in the study of the mature use of different symbolic skills (Arnheim, 1974; Chomsky, 1957, 1965), semiotics and philosophy (Goodman, 1968), this view of symbolization proceeds from the basic premise that the knowledge required to encode an experience in a particular symbolic form (e.g., language) will differ radically from the knowledge prerequisite to capturing that same experience in a different medium (e.g., drawing). This difference derives from two sources: the differences in the sheer physical possibilities of the two media and the differences in the rule systems or "grammars" that are applied to each of these media. In other words, not only do symbols differ in the particular physical materials from which they are made, but the way in which the rules within symbol systems structure meaning also differs and affects which aspects of experience come to the fore and which are "lost in translation" into a given medium. To illustrate the effects of physical materials, consider the effect of being offered clay or blocks as the raw material out of which to fashion the representation of a particular terrain. To illustrate just one consequence, the manner in which elevation was symbolized might differ significantly: the blocks could only approximate smooth curves and slopes, whereas the use of clay might demand a condensation in the scale of the model, given the difficulty of building up large masses of clay. As a result, the block model representation emphasizes the representation of height but cannot provide information regarding slope. These "compromises" in the representation of elevation exist even though the two physical materials are being used in the service of the same symbol system, three-dimensional construction. Similar differences in the information coming to the foreground occur when the physical material is held constant but used in the service of different symbol systems. Imagine the differences in information where clay is used as the raw material for the graphic symbolization of a terrain as compared with its use in a constructional rendition of the same landscape. In the graphic format, height might be represented via contour lines made of clay; in the construction, height would be represented via mass and volume. The contour lines, like the blocks, can represent a series of fixed points, but can only approximate mass. By underscoring the prominence of materials and symbol systems in shaping what meanings can be effectively encoded, this view offers an important extension of the Piagetian model for an internally undifferentiated symbolic function that operates uniformly across media and symbol systems. This second view of symbolization raises the possibility that symbolic development might consist of acquiring a succession of rather different understandings about encoding experience into different physical materials and symbol systems.

Some serious difficulties exist, however, within such an approach to a model for symbolic development. One possible prediction from such a model is that within a given medium or symbol system, representational operations should be psychologically similar and therefore should progress at the same or a similar pace across a range of contents. On the contrary, it is becoming clear that any particular physical material (e.g., lines) being used in the service of a particular symbol system (graphic representation) can be employed in a number of different, but nevertheless symbolic, formats at different ages. To be more specific, children as young as 3 can use drawn lines to represent the path or motion qualities of a moving object (Smith, 1972); at 4, children can draw simple pictures of objects (Golomb, 1974; Goodnow, 1977; Kellogg, 1968; Smith, 1972); but it is not until they reach school age that children can make maps and diagrams that are distinct from pictures (Feldman, 1971; Karmiloff-Smith, 1979). Similarly, within language, sentence formation and metaphoric production occur and develop on distinct rather than shared time schemes, presumably because sentences and metaphors take up on the referential possibilities of language in quite different ways (Winner, 1979).

A second difficulty stems from the complementary prediction that where raw materials and symbol systems differ, symbolic operations should differ in the onset, pace, and manner of their development. The more we study early symbolization, however, the clearer it becomes that symbolic development can be characterized as taking place in the previously mentioned bursts or clusters—for instance, at approximately 18 months, gesture, language, and symbolic play appear despite the dramatic differences in the physical materials and symbol systems involved.

A final point can be made based on a lesson from the study of early language: the simple fact that a child uses the materials or even some of the forms characteristic of an adult symbol system in no way implies that the rules for encoding meaning coincide with the adult's. The distance between early semantic grammars and later syntactical knowledge is considerable (Bowerman, 1973; Fillmore, 1968). Not only may children hold variants of the rule structures guiding adult performances within a particular symbol system, they may fail to distinguish effectively between symbol systems. For a considerable period, children do not distinguish between two- and three-dimensional forms of symbolization. They often treat a piece of paper as if it was a model for the object drawn, drawing the back side of the object on the reverse side of the paper or drawing the belt on a figure so that it encircles the front, sides and back of the paper (Wolf, 1980). These findings suggest that symbol systems as adults practice them are a final result of, more than a causative factor within, symbolic development. This last point, taken with the ones above, raises important questions concerning the adequacy of an account of symbolic development in which individual media and symbol systems are viewed as determining the sequence of acquisitions.

Considerations for an Alternative
Model of Early Symbolic Development

Conceptual Obligations   The foregoing analysis of models of symbolic development points out the conceptual obligations for any alternative model. Two such obligations emerge from the critique of Piaget's semiotic funtion model. First, it is crucial to distinguish between the nonsymbolic prerequisites to symbolization (e.g., the capacity for internal representation) and the ability to "translate" experience into externally observable forms that abide by the limitations of particular physical materials (media) and particular rules for structuring meaning (symbol systems). Second, a model for symbolic development must acknowledge the complex, rather than unified, nature of this development, notably the fact that symbolic growth occurs at different rates depending on whether language, drawing or number is at issue. But, as the examination of the media and systems approach shows, a simple succession of acquiring one then another symbol system is equally unsatisfactory. Two more complicated sets of facts require accommodation: 1) children acquire a series of distinct symbolic skills *within* larger symbol systems (e.g., motion paths, pictures, maps in graphic representation), and 2) symbolic development is characterized by clusters of symbolic acquisitions that spread across a range of media and symbol systems.

Developmental Obligations   There is a gap in our understanding of symbolic development. On the one hand, we have, in Piaget's work on the semiotic function, a model for the nonsymbolic origins for symbolization. As a complement to this knowledge about the underpinnings of symbolic behavior, something is known about what it is like for mature users to operate productively within the limits of particular media and symbol systems. Considerably less is known about what lies *between* the foundations and the mastery of particular symbolic grammars like language or pictorial representation. It is particularly critical to fill this blank because developmental evidence indicates that, during this intervening period, symbolic abilities are not simply or steadily drawing closer to adult capacities. As in the case of the progression from semantic to syntactic grammars, symbolic development within particular domains may be more a matter of transformations than steady approximations. The previous analysis of the Piagetian model pointed out that it may be inadequate to think of the onset of symbol use as occurring virtually "at once" across the range of children's symbolic capacities. It may be similarly crude to think in terms of the onset of symbolization with a particularly symbolic domain.

The point is worth illustrating. The same horizontal line can refer to or signify the same content, "road," on several quite different grounds: by reproducing the typical forward motion of vehicles along a road; by picturing a likeness of its curves and contour; by offering a scale reduction of its extent that is indifferent to the details of width and curves. In much the same way, the units of language, single words, can capture meaning on different grounds—there is the enactive, mimetic naming of early speech (Piaget, 1962; Werner and Kaplan, 1963); conventional referential labels; metaphoric usage where conceptual and physical similarities are allowed to undercut usual labels, turning fog into cats and lovers into "stiff twain compasses." (Wagner et al., 1979, Winner, 1979). These examples show the possibility that individual symbol systems like language and drawing may be grounded first in one approach to encoding meaning and then in another. Put differently, symbolic activity with particular materials (e.g., words, lines, gestures) may be structured and then restructured according to a succession of distinct understandings about how meaning can be encoded before full competence in a range of specific symbol systems emerges (e.g., language, pictorial representation, American Sign Language). A comprehensive model of early symbolic development would have, as its major outstanding obligation, the specification of the understandings that lie between the cognitive foundations to symbol use and the eventual mastery of these specific symbol systems.

One approach to constructing an alternative model is taking a novel point of view on what Piagetian and symbol-system approaches have to say regarding early symbolization. Piaget, observing what he took to be the concurrent emergence of a range of representational and symbolic skills, posited that this temporal clustering of diverse acquisitions resulted from the onset of a single underlying conceptual structure, the semiotic function. If this notion of underlying structures is applied to the full range of abilities picked out by the study of symbol systems, the "naturally occurring" points could be defined within symbolic development where acquisitions in a range of materials and rule-systems cluster together temporally. Having identified such clusters, we can then ask, "What underlying understanding about symbol use would permit the concurrent emergence of this particular set of symbolic skills?'' Eventually, an examination of the hypothesized sequence of structures would provide at least the outline of a new model for each symbolic development.

Based on a re-examination of existing knowledge about the initial and final forms of symbolization, established developmental findings, and new data from a longitudinal study, a model for symbolic development outlining such a sequence of structures underlying the pattern of symbolic acquisitions is proposed here. The model stresses two essential points. The first is to insist on the length and significance of the period between the nonsymbolic foundation for symbolic activity and the appearance of conventional grammars. During this period, the mature forms of particular symbol systems are actively constructed from a number of sources: the physical characteristics of the materials involved; cognitive understandings about physical and psychological realities; models of mature practice; *and* a changing knowledge of how meaning can be encoded. The second point is to suggest that a developmentally ordered series of distinct understandings about how symbolic forms can encode meaning emerges during the period between the ages of 1 and 7. Each of these distinct understandings, termed *encoding structures*, represents a fundamental insight into the ways in which symbolic forms can be made to capture, preserve, invent, and communicate information. To offer an analogy, these encoding structures are to the process of symbolization what particular logical operations are to stages within the development of logical thought. The advent of a particular encoding structure provides the essential capacities and issues for a particular period in symbolic development in much the same way that the advent of transitivity operations structures or ''flavors'' the abilities and difficulties typical of concrete operational thought (Inhelder and Piaget, 1958).

The remainder of the chapter describes the particular encoding structure that provides the basis or integrity for the earliest period of symbolic development, the time between late infancy and the emergence of early language, gesture, and play symbols. The particular structure in question is termed *role-structuring*; it refers to the capacity to use earlier pragmatically derived understandings of the roles that persons and objects assume in events as a fundamental template or ground upon which to base symbolic representations of experience. It is suggested that role-structuring provides the scaffolding for the role-based or case grammars that underlie early sentences; the ability to dramatize situations in play, and possibly, the nature of other contemporary symbolic performances, such as early attempts at motion-based representations in drawing and enactively grounded metaphors. As it is discussed here, role-structuring is conceived as the first in a series of distinguishably different modes for grounding symbolic activity. It is the subsequent appearance of different encoding structures that lends symbolic development its particular contours and eventual diversity.[1]

FINDINGS ON THE STRUCTURES OF EARLY SYMBOLIZATION

The Early Symbolization Study at Project Zero

During the past several years, researchers at Harvard Project Zero have attempted to build a more detailed and complex model of symbolic development. The primary goal has been to secure an adequate description of the developmental processes that link the cognitive prerequisites of recall and planning abilities that characterize late infancy with the symbolic fluency suggested by the 6-year-old who speaks, draws, counts, and reads. The emphasis is on the development of an integrated model for the early acquisitions within symbolic competence which is, nevertheless, sensitive to the diversity of that accomplishment.

The primary vehicle for this work has been a longitudinal study of nine first-born children.[2] The children were visited on a regular basis from their first birthday to the onset of schooling in order to secure detailed information about their symbolic growth in seven different domains: language (particularly storytelling and metaphor), drawing, construction out of three-dimensional materials (particularly clay and blocks), number, music, bodily expression (dance and gesture) and symbolic play (the use of objects, language and action to act out familiar or imagined sequences). In addition to monitoring their progress in these media, members of the research team also administered standard cognitive and linguistic measures. Both the observation of spontaneous play and parent diaries supplied insight into naturally occurring symbolic behaviors. Finally, as a means of supplementing and checking the major outlines of the information gained in the intensive work, a

---

[1] In previous presentations of this work, slightly different terms have been used (Shotwell, Wolf, and Gardner, 1979). Originally the term *central symbolic skill* was used where we refer to *encoding structures*. This change·was made to sharpen the contrast between what we call representation and symbolization; symbolization requires encoding experience into observable forms like gesture or language. In earlier work, a broader term *event-structuring*, was used in place of the current term, *role-structuring*. The former term no longer seems precise enough because it implies that the fundamental understandings being discussed concern entire events rather than the structures of roles within events.

[2] The longitudinal study population includes two cohorts of children: an older group of five subjects begun at approximately 1 year of age, and currently age 6 as well as a second group of subjects begun at age 1 and currently age 4. Between ages 1 and 3 the children were seen weekly, between 3 and 6 they are seen twice a month.

group of 75 subjects, ranging in age from 2 to 5, have been seen performing the same tasks, within a cross-sectional study.

Previous Research Related to Role Structuring

A reading of existing research on cognitive development during the second year suggests the pragmatic origins for a first encoding structure. There is considerable evidence that during this period young children are learning to break up whole events by analyzing them into their constituent elements. In both object-based and interpersonal instances of tool-use (Bates, 1976; Piaget, 1954), children between 9 and 13 months learn to "dissolve" the attainment of a difficult goal into its components. What appears, based on this analysis, is a set of enactive schemes for coordinating the parts within a whole situation: the child (as the agent) acts (by pointing, reaching, vocalizing) on a parent or a tool (as an instrument or means) in order to get the toys or crackers (as the object or goal). Parallel development in children's understanding of situational "roles" occurs in the realm of more purely social interchanges. At about age 1½, children drop their highly stylized and unilateral participation in game-exchanges, showing a new flexibility that permits them to play from the vantage point of any of the game's roles (e.g., children go from only being able to play the well-rehearsed role of the hider to being able to play the part of either the hider or seeker in peek-a-boo (Bruner and Sherwood, 1976). In a contemporary advance, this same role flexibility appears in symbolic play in two forms. First, children dramatically replay familiar scenes in which they trade roles with other familiar persons. A child may imitate his father vacuuming by shooing the father (who is made to play the child) out of the way with a wheeled toy, saying "Out of way . . . vacuum coming . . . pick up, pick up" (Piaget, 1962; Wolf, 1978). Second, children animate dolls with the figure acting out scenes in which the child or familiar others are typically agents (Watson and Fischer, 1977; Wolf, 1978). Toward the end of the second year these latter role-play abilities advance still another level; using small replicas, children can play out several roles (e.g., doll can be handled so as to speak and act the parts of a parent and child, a monster and a victim c.f., Rubin and Wolf, 1979). This capacity to maintain the distinctiveness of multiple roles is evident in children's ability to handle clearly their role as the "manager" of a toy figure apart from the figure's role as the agent or supposed performer of the action (Wolf, 1978; Scarlett and Wolf, 1979).

The crystallizing knowledge concerns the parts that various actors or objects can play relative to a central action. In the early examples of tool use and games, this knowledge remains implicit and pragmatic. At the later end of the second year, however, this pragmatic knowledge is used to structure re-presentations of familiar experience. The nature of the earliest clearly symbolic performances confirms the significance of role-structure knowledge. What is acquired in early sentences is the ability to encode semantic cases into the word orders characteristic of a particular natural language. (Bloom 1970; 1973; Bowerman, 1973; Brown, 1973; Fillmore, 1968). As concepts, semantic cases are, simply put, categories of situational roles—agent, object, instrument. It is proposed here that the emergence of a first "encoding structure" may rest on the crystallization of understandings latent in tool use and social interaction into a set of concepts about roles. These concepts, called role structures, provide a critical entry first into the re-presentation of experience in symbolic play and then into the more rigorous and conventional grammar of language.

In the next section, the discussion of this initial encoding structure is extended by presenting findings from a longitudinal study that confirm the translation of pragmatic to symbolic role-structures occurring in the second year. These role-structures provide an essential cognitive "template" for a first approach to encoding meaning. The use of this template yields, not system specific conventional grammars, but a set of grounds for representation that children apply across symbol systems. The application of role-structure knowledge to the media of action and speech yields symbolic play and semantic or case-grammars. The application of these same concepts to other representational tasks yield what may be less effective results, for instance, metaphors and drawings that are situationally rather than linguistically or graphically grounded.

Longitudinal Findings on the Emergence of Role-Structures

As a means of testing the hypothesized centrality of role-structure knowledge within the symbol systems emerging in the second year, data from the four youngest longitudinal subjects were analyzed with attention to the emergence of three developmentally ordered capacities: 1) the ability to parse a single event into the multiple situational roles that compose it and put this analysis to effective pragmatic use; 2) the ability to treat situations as frameworks and roles as categories. This second level ability becomes evident in children's increased grasp of forms of interchange like conversation and games and their willingness to rotate new instances or persons through various situational roles, and 3) the ability to capture this knowledge in generative, rule-governed, medium appropriate ways. In language, this last level is exemplified in the appearance of a semantic or case grammar. In symbolic play, the ability was defined as the capacity to represent two distinct pretense roles, either two separate characters or the ability to turn a toy prop into an "independent agent" while the child maintains the stance of the operator or "stage-manager." In the period between 12 and 24 months, children's performances were examined in several areas: social interaction, formal and invented games, dramatic play with others, spontaneous and elicited symbolic play with toys, and spontaneous language. A summary of the tasks used to elicit responses is presented in Tables 1 and 2 in the Appendix, pages 320–321.

Determining the accuracy of such a hypothesis with a small longitudinal sample was no simple matter. The process of developing an answer began with a proposed set of steps leading from pragmatic use to the symbolic application of role-structure knowledge within each of the monitored domains. Pairs of trained scorers applied the proposed scaling to a subset of the observations of spontaneous and elicited performances for each child. The observations were scored blind, with scorers obtaining a 0.82 level of reliability across domains scored. Subsequently, finer steps for acquisition within each of the domains were constructed. These separate lines of developmental acquisitions (e.g., social interaction, games, play, and language) were aligned with one another, yielding the cross-domain synchronies discussed below and outlined in Table 3 in the Appendix, pages 322–326.

Results from this analysis suggested a three-stage transition from the pragmatic control of several situational roles to the ability to encode these roles symbolically. Briefly summarized, children in Stage I, ending roughly at 13 months, are able to coordinate several practical roles effectively; for instance, as agents they can use another person as a means (in the situational role of "instrument") to help them secure some distant or difficult end (in the role of "object"). Consider the following observation[3]:

> J, at 13 months, wants a banana down from the top of the refrigerator. Knowing that he will need an intermediary, he crosses the room and yanks on his father, pointing and vocalizing toward the fruit, checking back to his father's line of gaze and expression to make sure that he has connected. His father shakes his head and refuses, saying that it is almost time for dinner. J fusses but then goes on playing.

In this period, however, neither games, symbolic play nor language is marked by a similar ability to parse a whole situation into its parts. Game-playing is little more than the repetition of familiar or favorite bits of action. Symbolic play consists of inserting familiar objects into routines typically associated with them (e.g., putting an empty cup to the mouth, a brush to the hair) (Lowe, 1975; Nicolich, 1975). Lan-

---

[3] The observations presented throughout this section are taken from the observational records of a single subject to preserve the longitudinal flavor and integrity of the study.

guage is uninflected by this practical understanding of how several actors and objects are organized into an event. At most, the single words which appear only imply such relations through the apt use of content (e.g., a child can signal the larger meaning "I want Daddy to pick me up" by throwing out his arms toward his father and calling, "Up") (Greenfield and Smith, 1976).

In an interim period between 14 and 20 months, this practical grasp of situational roles evolves toward a symbolic encoding of roles. The defining characteristics of this period (Stage II in Table 3) is the appearance of role concepts that permit the separation of a situational role from particular role-takers and the near-symbolic capacity to rotate a range of actors through the same role. In social interaction children show a new distance on roles, coming to handle them as frameworks for behavior, or stances within situations, through which any number of actors may rotate. Children become adept at playing the part of both the question-asker and the question-answerer in conversation (Halliday, 1975). They also become adept at inventing and carrying out simple two-sided games. They even manage to play very simple, familiar games from various vantage points—being either the hider or the seeker in peek-a-boo (Bruner and Sherwood, 1976). These activities signal a separation between roles and role-takers: the same person can take on a variety of situational roles and the same role can be filled by a variety of persons. Children in the early months of Stage II could be said to possess "role *concepts*" based on this new flexibility.

> J, at 18 months, invents a game. It consists of taking off his father's glasses and putting them on himself. He wants to play a second round where his father is the taker, so he points to his father, saying "You, Daddy" and juts his face toward his father. His father catches on and grabs back his glasses. J makes the jutting face at his father, to get him to repeat just what J had looked like as the "victim" a moment before. The game continues, with much trading back and forth of roles, until J turns and notices the observer's glasses and initiates the game with her.

In the second strand of this same development, visible in symbolic play with people, the earliest symbolic renditions of situational roles appear. At the outset of Stage II, behaviors almost "hover" between pragmatic (e.g., nonsymbolic) interactions and the symbolization of roles, as in what follows:

> J, at 14 months, watches as his mother vacuums his room. After watching a moment, he burrows in his toy box and produces a long-handled pushtoy that he grabs onto and shoves along before him, poking into crevices and under furniture much as his mother had done shortly before.

> J, at 14 months, sees his father shake a dust mop out of the window. Later that same day, J finds a broom in the closet and drags it out. He

pulls it to the window where his father had shaken out the mop and tries to push it up. When he has no luck, he goes off in search of his father, who hangs onto him, as J tries shaking the broom out the window.

At this juncture, children seem more nearly to repeat, or at most, to condense, roles, without attempting to construct a symbolic form that is distinct from and capable of standing for those roles.

During Stage II there are only inklings of this future construction of symbols for situational roles:

At 14 months, J has been playing in his room. There he finds his jack-in-the-box sitting on the table with a block resting on its lid. He cranks the handle and the jack pops up, sending the block flying off behind a shelf. J wants the amazing event to happen again, but he has lost the block. He runs to the kitchen, calling out for his father. He pulls his father back into the room and points behind the shelf, saying something like "There, there." His father has a hard time understanding and tries several guesses, pulling out first one favorite book and then another. J, somewhat exasperated, at last takes his father's hand in his own, places them both on top of the jack, makes a kind of explosive noise and moves his and his father's hand in an arc toward the shelf. J then reaches his own hand down behind the shelf, making somewhat conventionalized effort sounds to signal that he is reaching for something. All the while he looks back and forth between the back of the shelf and his father, saying something like "block."

In the instance of the block situation just reported, the child uses both his own and his father's hands to assume the role originally occupied by the block. This capacity to do more than share roles across persons develops throughout the course of Stage II. Perhaps it is more clearly visible in children's increasing ability to use toys in action sequences typically performed by people:

At 18 months J had a bad cold. He hated to blow his nose and resisted taking cough medicine. If, however, an adult would reach down a red wooden horse from a shelf and make it blow its nose and take medicine first, then J would also agree to submit. The same was true if the adult would perform these actions on J's big doll, "Baby." At about the same time, J became interested in making "Baby" wear snow boots, mittens, and a hat just as he (J) had to.

Although there is increased evidence for symbolization of the actors and actions within situations, behaviors like those reported above fall short of the later-to-emerge ability to signify an interrelated set of situational roles. In neither of the reported instances does the child struggle with the problem of constructing several distinct symbols that will permit one situational role to be distinguished from another. Nor does the child attempt to coordinate such symbols according to some rule system that might encode the relations between situational roles.

For instance, the child does not or cannot capture the relation between the agent (self or father) and the object (the escaped block).

The final phase, (Stage III in Table 3) occurs between 20 and 24 months and is marked by the concurrent emergence of the ability to encode symbolically a coordinated set of distinct roles in both language and symbolic play. It is in this period that children progress to play sequences in which the actions of a range of actors are distinguished symbolically. This is probably most evident in their ability to maintain an effective distinction between their role as the "operator" behind the agent-like behavior of small figures (Watson and Fischer, 1977; Wolf, 1978) and their ability to make two such agents interact.

> J, at 24 months, is offered several toy figures, among them a lion and a girl. He picks up the lion, makes it roar at and then approach the girl. "Get you, get you, RRRRRR." He then makes the girl rush away, first off the table and onto the floor, then back to the table, and eventually under the bed.

Whereas six months previously children could feed or diaper a doll, thus finding a symbol for the situational role of object or recipient of the action, they could not or did not simultaneously represent the role of the agent—they performed it. At 2 years, at least two situational roles can be represented simultaneously.

During this same period, there is evidence for the transition from one-word utterances to several-word sentences indicative of the emergence of semantic case-based grammars (Chafe, 1970; Fillmore, 1968). In fact, it is a period marked by the active use and the playful exploration of just the kinds of distinctions between situational roles that such a grammar encodes clearly. Here is a sample of monologue that will serve as an illustration:

> J at 22 months, is playing with a truck and several musical instruments, on his back porch.
> J beats on a drum and says "Tinny (his nickname) go boom. Boom, boom, boom." He puts the truck on the drumhead, "Truck boom. Two trucks?" J hunts for a second truck. He finds it and puts it in the back of the first one and rolls them on the drum head. "Two trucks. Trucks boom. Tinny trucks." The trucks roll onto the floor.
> J says "Trucks boom. Tinny boom. Boom trucks. Tinny trucks boom."

With the emergence of the encoding structure based on an understanding of roles, the child's practical knowledge of events and actions in the world—the long-standing knowledge that persons and objects interlock in complex situations—can be more fully captured on a representational plane (Nelson and Gruendel, 1979; Bruner and Sherwood, 1976; Watson and Fischer, 1977). The results of this broad symbolic acquisition are profound. In terms of language development, the application of role-structure understandings to speech permits children to describe their experience, not just in piecemeal strings, but in statements ordered by rules that make meaning intelligible even to people who do not share the same physical and emotional world as the child. In sociodramatic play, a child can take on familiar roles and play them out with a degree of reciprocity. In symbolic play with toys, the props can be given agent status while the child maintains the position of operator or stage-manager. In this case, what is originally a capacity for multiple pretense roles evolves into a capacity to maintain diverse relations to the ongoing pretense. As the voice and activity for the toy, the child is quite fully involved in the make-believe. As the stage-manager, the child is at the "rim" of the pretense. This split perspective on pretense may be an important precursor to division between dialogue and narration critical to later storytelling competence.

As the comment above indicates, although the advent of role-structures initiates a number of symbolic acquisitions, it in no way signals their completion. This can be made clear by looking to the case of language development. Once a child has the rules requisite to forming sentences like those recorded in the monologue above, he or she is involved in using the elements of a particular conventional symbol system, language, for which his or her pragmatically derived understanding of situational roles and the recently constructed knowledge of how to symbolize roles provides only a kind of "first draft" knowledge. Although the bulk of early sentences focus on agent-action, agent-action-object sequences, other types of utterances that provide evidence for additional semantic cases—locative, beneficiary, experiencer—also occur (Brown, 1973; Chafe, 1970, Fillmore, 1968). These cases have no simple or clear origins in the earlier pragmatic role-structures—they are possibilities made available by the structure of language itself (e.g., the distinction between agent and experiencer cases may be rooted in the linguistic difference between transitive and intransitive verbs). It is here that the medium or symbol-system based view of symbolization is highly relevant, even essential. The child as a language-user soon leaves behind utterances derived rather directly from familiar situational roles (e.g., agent, object) moving on to encode roles highlighted or defined by the grammar of language as a symbol system.

This perspective on symbol use may help to reconcile what has been seen as an insolvable debate between two views on the relative contributions of general cognition and system-specific knowledge within the development of symbolic functioning. In the most pronounced instance of this debate, Piaget and his followers seek to find in sensorimotor development the full range of antecedents for linguistic competence. On the opposing side, Chomsky is skeptical of any deep affiliation between these two domains, arguing for the developmental independence of language fron enactive roots. The analysis presented here suggests that the foundations of linguistic competence can be found in the understandings available to presymbolic intelligence. It similarly suggests, however, that once these understandings come into contact with the cultural system of language, the original cognitive structures themselves undergo considerable changes dictated by the structures of the symbol system that is being acquired (Piatelli-Palmarini, 1980).

This discussion delineates a final step in the evolution of role-structures. Having provided a "point-of-entry" and primitive rules for the structuring of symbolic statements, role-structures give way to the more refined and specific "grammars" of particular conventional symbol systems. This process is schematized in Table 4, p. 327.

It is equally important to point out how role-structures serve as a kind of generator or template for a range of symbolic performances other than language and play. Some examples will illustrate how this first encoding structure is available, though unequally effective, across a range of media and symbol systems. For instance, it seems that children, during this period, address the problem of creating similarities largely in enactive terms. One object "becomes" another by being made to act as that second object typically does. When asked to draw a car going fast, children between the ages of 2 and 3 often turn their crayon into the agent of that action, pushing or driving it along the page (Pariser, 1979; Smith, 1972). Early metaphoric performances seem to operate on similar principles. In the course of symbolic play, children of this age frequently transform one object into another, by transferring the actions typical of the second object onto the first. A block can be "made into" a train, if it can be made to fulfill the agent role in ways typical for trains (Winner, 1979; Winner et al., 1979).

The concept of role-structuring as the basic symbolic skill to emerge in the first 2 years effectively organizes much of what is known regarding this early period of symbolic development. As a theoretical construct, role-structuring can account for the observed yoking of symbolic play and language skills pursuant to the appearance of a capacity for internalized representation. Additionally, such a concept effectively predicts the particular skills within play and language that are likely to appear in this first period of symbolization—notably semantic or case grammars for sentences, the imitations of sociodramatic play, and the ability to use toys as actors in the replica-based play. As mentioned earlier, the appearance of a skill like role-structuring might also account for the nature of prelinguistic "metaphors" in which one object can be made to stand for another by assuming the characteristic situational role of that second object. In this way a block can become a telephone if it is the object of being picked up and put to the ear; a spoon can become a person if it is made to act as the agent of typically animate actions. Similarly, early representational drawings make temporary use of role-structuring; a line on the paper can signify a "car going fast" if it acts as the agent moving quickly across a location.

Finally, the hypothesis of role-structuring provides important insights into the limitations of this first phase of symbol use. Although it yields an effective base for simple sentences and play sequences, it lends only temporary solutions to the problems of representation, which are better solved by different approaches to encoding meaning. For instance, representational drawing and construction that conventionally require meaning to be encoded in static rather than enactive and visual rather than situational terms are not acquired until several years later. Also lacking are those forms of symbolization like number and writing that depend on more purely formal part-to-whole relations.

Role-Structures Within A Broader Model for Symbolic Development

It is possible to place the findings concerning role-structure within the context of a broader model for symbolic development, which has emerged from Project Zero. This model posits a sequence of distinct meaning structures, valid across a range of materials and appearing in an ordered sequence between the ages of 1 and 5.

Following role-structures as a ground for a first approach to encoding meaning, a second and distinct approach to representation emerges in the third and fourth years. Particularly visible in the areas of two- and three-dimensional depiction, this ability entails the capacity to notice and make representational use of the salient physical features of objects by re-creating them according to the grammar and conventions of particular symbolic media. A prototypical example of this new attribute mapping is the capacity to make a representational drawing of a face: using a pencil and paper, the child draws a circle, places within it marks that designate facial features and, if asked, provides the appropriate names for each of these features. At about the same time, the child is able to capture in the arrangement of blocks, pieces of clay, or other three-dimensional media, analogous relations among elements that suggest object(s) in the world. And, underscoring that this encoding skill is not restricted to plastic media, an important change also occurs in linguistic renaming: metaphors are no longer based primarily on action (as in the role-structuring phase) but rather on perceptual analogies between realms. A child walking through woods and contemplating the branches of trees will spontaneously and reliably recognize familiar objects or designs from his or her home, the shapes of letters of the alphabet, even face-like configurations (c.f., Winner, 1979; Winner et al., 1979).

What is crucial is that the novel skill is generative. It readily spreads across a range of symbolic systems and can be used versatilely within a single symbol system. Moreover, these skills of symbolization can, on a formal basis, be equated with those already achieved in the areas of symbolic play and language; but in fact they emerge 1 or more years later. This finding strongly suggests that it is more appropriate to think in terms of successive encoding structures that cross media, rather than in terms of a single overarching symbolization skill or succinct medium-specific knowledge.

Although the two first encoding structures have been most carefully studied thus far, two subsequent structures appear and seem strong candidates for inclusion in the eventual scheme of early symbolic development. The first of these structures is a more abstract type of mapping, one of a "digital" or "notational" form. In this case, the child conveys his or her knowledge of the existence of a set of elements, and the relations among them, mapping it into a new medium; but rather than capturing the broad relations among the elements, he or she instead focuses on the number of elements per se, the intervals between them, simple arithmetic operations of adding and subtracting, and other notational facets. Examples of this second form of mapping include the child's ability to place objects into one-to-one correspondence, the ability to construct arrays that presuppose numerical understanding such as a staircase (c.f., Shotwell, 1979), and the capacity to recreate pitch and rhythmic intervals in the musical domain (e.g., a scale). Indeed, it is the apparent co-occurrence of the abilities to build a staircase out of blocks and to sing scales that provides one of the most suggestive lines of evidence in favor of this third kind of symbolization. A final structure, occurring at age 5 or 6, entails the mastery of certain symbolic codes, particularly ones devised by the surrounding culture. Included here is mastery of systems that feature the reading and writing of verbal, numerical, and perhaps musical notations. These systems are introduced by the culture at this time and it is possible that this fact is one of their defining features. The syntactic complexity of these systems may be another common feature.

Yet, it seems more likely that the major feature of symbolization is its "second-order" or "recursive" property; for the first time, a symbol system stands not only for elements in the world (as does picturing or natural language) but rather for other symbols: a written word standing for a spoken word, a written numerical equation for a series of spoken numbers. Once the individual is able to use a symbol system to denote a "first-order" system, the potential exists for an indefinite recursive process, which makes possible the highest forms of numerical and linguistic symbolization. Concomitantly, the child will develop a "meta-symbolic" capacity to reflect upon his or her symbolic activities.

What has been outlined here is a highly stylized portrait of the emergence of a series of basic structures for encoding meaning. Each was treated as if it was a separate entity, whereas the interaction among such competencies within an individual at any given time is much more likely to be the rule. A 5-year-old making a drawing of a person running may make major use of his mapping skills to achieve a graphic rendition of the figure, but the child may resort to older role-structuring skills to depict motion if his or her drawing skills fall short. Equally, in completing the figure, the child may use coding skills to represent information that lines and shapes do not render—to write down a name for the person or to make certain that all the toes and fingers are present. The isolated treatment of the proposed encoding-structures is simply to underscore their separate ontogeneses.

Clearly, it is important to be cautious about drawing such broad conclusions from correlational data taken from so small a sample of children. Work of this kind provides only the necessary "hunches" that must be followed up using quite different methods of inquiry. An important source for testing these hypotheses lies in our cross-sectional work. Given the larger population, treated in a carefully standardized manner, it will be possible to subject the hypothesized linkages to more rigorous testing by probabilistic and factor analysis. But clearly, even strong demonstrations of correlations in these broader studies do not constitute proof of causal relations among behaviors. Crucial further testing can derive from both observational and experimental work with populations where either cultural or disease related factors make for patterns of symbolic development that may differ from those typical of our longitudinal subjects. Finally, transfer-of-training experiments with both normal and disabled populations probably represent the most rigorous tests of picture of very early symbolic developments presented here.

CONCLUSION: STRUCTURE OF EARLY
SYMBOLIZATION IN OTHER POPULATIONS

This proposal for a developmentally ordered series of encoding struc-tures derives from research in progress. Even the most carefully studied of these structures, role-structuring, must still be analyzed in the context of findings from the cross-sectional study, and a detailed and systematic investigation has not yet been undertaken of the later-emerging symbolic structures. Nonetheless, unless initial impressions prove surprisingly deceptive, it seems likely that the final portrait of early symbolization to emerge from the study will bear at least a strong family resemblance to the one introduced here.

Should this portrait prove to be accurate, its implication for theoretical and practical issues needs to be considered. On the theoretical side, the notion of a series of encoding structures seems to revise, or at least supplement, the strong positions outlined above. Neither is it the case that all symbolic competences are integrally tied together; nor can it any longer be maintained that each symbol system has its idiosyncratic nature and rate of development. Rather, it seems likely that a limited number of distinct psychological processes underlie symbolic growth; these processes determine the time at which, and the manner in which, milestones occur in specific symbolic domains.

It may be worth noting that this portrait is not self-evident. It points up resemblances between realms that might have been thought disparate (e.g., sensitivity to perceptual resemblances and metaphoric production; intervalic senses in number and music). At the same time it indicates that putatively singular realms may in fact have to be decomposed into separate families of skills (language exhibiting both role-structuring and attribute-mapping properties).

Yet, even if this view of symbolic development proves valid for the subjects in this study, the present results do not indicate the generality of the model presented here. The particular order of symbolic structures may obtain only in the environments studied here, or, even less palatably, may be an artifact of the kinds of tasks administered, the kinds of operationalizations invoked, or even the kinds of interpretations made. Eventually, it will be crucial to consider this same set of concerns in other cultural settings to determine whether the waves of symbolization have more than parochial applicability.

Populations where symbolic development does not occur with the assurance characteristic of normative growth may provide some of the most useful tests of the accuracy and applicability of the model proposed here for early symbolic development. Concentrating only on the structure suggested for the first phase of symbolization, such populations provide important initial corroborations. It seems, for instance, that mildly retarded children, as well as Down's syndrome children, exhibit the same broad linkages between generative language use and productive symbolic play (Hill and Nicholich, 1979; Hulme and Lunzer, 1966). Even more intriguing is a similar link across the same two symbol systems evident in mildly autistic children (McHale, 1979; Riquet, 1979).

This second finding is particularly significant. At first it seemed that autistic children strongly contradicted the proposed model for symbolization; at a time when they exhibited no observable role-structuring skills, they could sing entire operas (Rimland, 1964) or draw with astonishing accuracy (Selfe, 1977). On closer examination, it now seems that these musical and graphic abilities are akin to the autistic child's echolalic language—staggering reproductions or re-organizations of familiar schemes that exist independent of comparable productive abilities. When such children do break into more genuine representational activity, the first symbolic abilities to appear resemble the role-structure related capacities of younger, normal children (McHale, 1979). Nonetheless, the linkages across play and language evident in retardation, Down's syndrome, and autism are quite broad; it remains to be seen whether the precise relations evident in the longitudinal work reported here will prevail among these populations.

There are still other populations that can provide either correction or corroboration to the proposed model. Congenitally deaf children are a crucial example. If role-structures provide an essential cognitive template for first symbol systems, they should be visible, although probably somewhat altered, in the gesture systems that these children develop. Equally critical are populations with whom transfer-of-training studies and tests of coherence of role-structuring are appropriate. For instance, it will be essential to know whether training symbolic play behaviors in language-delayed children would produce any subsequent advances in their linguistic performance.

If the proposed model stands up to such tests, it could have considerable clinical application. Failure to attain the pragmatic forms of role-structuring at the end of the first year might indicate similar or further delays in the onset of those symbolic forms associated with role-structure knowledge, dramatic play and semantic grammars. Alternatively, it is possible to envision screening procedures that used symbolic play tasks to determine whether a nonspeaking child suffered from a language-specific deficit or a more general difficulty with the cognitive structure underlying early language and play.

These possibilities for prediction and treatment derive from examining the process of language acquisition against the wider background of early symbolic development. Specifically, these possibilities emerge from the proposal that the first use of language as a generative symbol system occurs as one of several manifestations of a major, although initial, understanding about how meaning can be encoded.

This first approach to representation is called role-structuring. Role-structuring refers to a set of understandings about the distinct situational roles that objects and persons can play in events. These understandings originate in the pragmatic coordinations of means with ends evident in early object handling and social interchange. During the second year, these understandings crystallize into highly flexible "pragmatic role-concepts" that provide the cognitive "scaffolding" on which a first wave of effective symbolization is based. Included in this phase are symbolic and dramatic play and semantic grammars, as well as less conventional attempts at other symbolic tasks like drawing and metaphor.

Rather than obscuring or losing the particular nature of language, this model highlights a distinction between the cognitive bases for early sentences and the use of language as a much more articulate and distinctive symbol system. Although role-structures may provide a critical point of entry to language, language as a symbol system offers its users possibilities that are in no way contained within the original concepts of agent, action, object. These possibilities include not only morphemes and syntactic structure, but options like dialect and metaphor.

Although symbolization is not "all talk," talk is a unique form of symbolization.

ACKNOWLEDGMENTS

Neither the conceptualization nor the specific findings would have been possible without the help of co-workers: Jennifer Shotwell, Shelley Rubin, Pat McKernon who saw children, wrote transcripts, and mulled things over; Lyle Davidson, George Forman, George Scarlett, and Sheldon Wagner who listened and made suggestions. The parents and children who have let us come in and out of their lives also deserve acknowledgment.

REFERENCES

Arnheim, R. 1974. Art and Visual Perception. University of California Press, Berkeley.

Barrett, T. 1965. The relation between measures of pre-reading visual discrimination and first grade reading achievement: A view of the literature. Read. Res. Q. 1(1):51–76.

Bates, E. 1976. Language and Context: The Acquisition of Pragmatics. Academic Press, Inc. New York.

Bates, E., Benigni, L., Bretherton, I., Camaioni, L. and Volterra, V. 1979. The Emergence of Symbols: Cognition and Communication in Infancy. Academic Press, Inc. New York.

Bayley, N. 1969. Bayles Scales of Infant Development. The Psychological Corporation. New York.

Biemiller, A. 1970. The development of the use of graphic and contextual information as children learn to read. Read. Res. Q. 6:75–96.

Bloom, L. 1970. Language Development: Form and Function in Emerging Grammars. M.I.T. Press, Cambridge, Mass.

Bloom, L. 1973. One Word at a Time. Mouton. The Hague.

Bower, T. G. R. 1974. Development in Infancy. W. H. Freeman & Co. San Francisco.

Bowerman, M. 1973. Structural relationships in children's utterances: Syntactic or semantic? In T. E. Moore (ed.), Cognitive Development and the Acquisition of Language, pp. 196–213. Academic Press, Inc. New York.

Brown, R. 1973. A First Language: The Early Stages. Harvard University Press, Cambridge, Mass.

Bruner, J. S. 1966. Toward a Theory of Instruction. Harvard University Press, Cambridge, Mass.

Bruner, J. S. 1975. The ontogenesis of speech arts. J. Child Lang. 2:1–19.

Bruner, J. S., and Sherwood, V. 1976. Early rule structure: The case of peek-a-boo. In J. S. Bruner, A. Jolly, and K. Sylva (eds.), Play: Its Role in Evolution and Development. Penguin, London.

Chafe, W. L. 1970. The Meaning and Structure of Language. University of Chicago Press, Chicago.

Chomsky, C. 1972. Stages in language development and reading exposure. Harvard Educ. Rev. 42:1–22.

Chomsky, N. 1957. Syntactic Structures. Mouton, The Hague.

Chomsky, N. 1965. Aspects of a Theory of Syntax. M.I.T. Press, Cambridge, Mass.

Corrigan, R. 1978. Language development as related to stage 6 object permanence development. J. Child Lang. 5:173–196.

Corrigan, R. 1979. Cognitive correlates of language: Differential criteria yield differential results. Child Dev. In press.

Douglas, M. 1975. Implicit Meanings: Essays in Anthropology. Routledge & Kegan Paul Ltd., London.

Feldman, D. H. 197. Map understanding as a possible crystallizer of cognitive structures. American Educ. Res. J. 8:485–503.

Fenson, L., Kagan, J., Kearsley, R., and Zelazo, P. 1976. The developmental progression of manipulative play in the first two years. Child Dev. 47:232–236.

Ferreiro, E. 1977. Vers un theorie genetique de l'apprentissage de la lecture. Schweizerische Zeitschrift fur Psychologie und ihre Anwendungen, 36:109–130.

Fillmore, C. J. 1968. The case for case. In E. Bach, and R. T. Harms (eds.), Universals in Linguistic Theory. Holt, Rinehart & Winston, Inc., New York.

Forman, G. 1980. The child's construction of vacant space. Paper submitted to the Southeastern Conference on Human Development, Old-Town-Alexandria, Virginia.

Freeman, N. H., and Janikoun, R. 1972. Intellectual realism in children's drawings of familiar objects with distinctive features. Child Dev. 43:1116–1121.

Freud, S. 1927. Beyond the Pleasure Principle. Boni and Liveright, N.Y.

Freud, S. 1938. The Interpretation of Dreams. The Modern Library, New York.

Freud, S. 1955. The relation of the poet to day-dreaming. In The Collected Works of Sigmund Freud. Hogarth Press, London.

Furth, H. G. 1969. Piaget and Knowledge. Prentice-Hall, Engelwood Cliffs, N.J.

Gardner, H. 1973. The Arts and Human Development. John Wiley & Sons, New York.

Gardner, H. 1979. Developmental psychology after Piaget. Human Dev. 22:73–80.

Gardner, H., Howard, V., and Perkins, D. 1974. Symbol systems: A philosophical, psychological, and educational investigation. In D. Olson (ed.), Media and Symbols. University of Chicago Press, Chicago.

Garvey, C. 1974. Some properties of social play. Merrill-Palmer Quart. 20:463–480.

Gesell, A. 1940. The First Five Years of Life. Methuen & Co. Ltd., London.

Goldin-Meadow, S., and Feldman, H. 1975. The creation of a communication system: A study of deaf children of hearing parents. Paper presented to the Biennial Conference of the Society for Research in Child Development, Denver.

Golomb, C. 1974. Young Children's Sculpture and Drawing: A Study in Representational Development. Harvard University Press, Cambridge, Mass.

Goodman, N. 1968. Languages of Art. Bobbs-Merrill Company, Inc., Indianapolis.

Goodnow, J. 1977. Children's Drawings. Harvard University Press, Cambridge, Mass.

Greenfield, P. M., and Smith, J. H. 1976. The Structure of Communication in Early Language Development. Academic Press, Inc., New York.

Halliday, M. A. K. 1975. Learning How to Mean: Explorations in the Development of Language. Edward Arnold, London.

Hill, P. M., and Nicolich, L. M. 1979. Pretend play and patterns of cognition in Down's Syndrome children. Unpublished paper, Center for Infancy and Early Childhood, Graduate School of Education, Rutgers University, New Brunswick, N.J.

Hulme, I., and Lunzer, E. A. 1966. Play, language and reasoning in sub-normal children. J. Child Psychol. Psychiatry. 7:107–123.

Inhelder, N., Lezine, I., Sinclair, H., and Stambak, W. 1971. Les debuts de la function symbolique, 'The origin of the symbolic function'. Arch. Psychol. 41:187–243.

Inhelder, B., and Piaget, J. 1958. The Growth of Logical Thinking from Childhood to Adolescence. Basic Books, Inc., New York.

Ives, S. W. 1979. Unpublished researched. Harvard Project Zero.

Karmiloff-Smith, A. 1979. Micro— and macrodevelopmental changes in language acquisition and other representational systems. Cognitive Sci. 3:91–117.

Kellogg, R. 1968. Analyzing Children's Art. National Press Books, Palo Alto, Calif.

Kelly, H., and Meringoff, L. 1979. A comparison of story comprehension in two media. Paper presented at the Annual Convention of the American Psychological Association, New York.

Killen, M., and Uzgiris, I. 1978. Imitation of actions with objects: The role of social meaning. Paper presented at the International Conference on Infant Studies, Providence, R.I.

Kris, E. 1952. Psychoanalytic Explorations in Art. International Universities Press, N.Y.

Kubie, L. 1971. Neurotic distortions of the creative process. Farrar, Straus and Giroux, Inc., N.Y.

Levi-Strauss, C. 1957. Le symbolisme cosmique dans la structure sociale et l'organisation cermonielle des tribus americaines (The cosmic symbolism in the social structure and ceremonial organization of American tribes). Serie Orientale Roma, XIV, Institut pour l'Etude de l'orient et de l'Extreme Orient, Rome, 47–56.

Levi-Strauss, C. 1962. La pensee sauvage. Plon, Paris.

Lezine, I. 1973. The transition from sensorimotor to earliest symbolic function in early development. Early Development. Res. Publ. A.R.N.M.D., 51.

Lowe, M. 1975. Trends in the development of representational play in infants from one to three years–an observational study. J. Child Psychiatry. 16:33–47.

Luquet, G. H. 1917. Les dessins d'un enfant, 'Children's drawing' Alcan, Paris.

Mahler, M., Pine, F., and Bergman, A. 1975. The Psychological Birth of the Human Infant: Symbiosis and Individuation. Basic Books, Inc., New York.

McCarthy, D. 1970. McCarthy Scales of Children's Abilities. The Psychological Corporation, New York.

McDevitt, J. B. 1972. Separation—individuation and object constancy. Paper presented at the New York Psychoanalytic Society.

McHale, S. 1979. Play, language and social development in mildly autistic children. Paper presented at the annual meeting of the American Association for Mental Deficiency.

Meringoff, L. The influence of the medium on children's story apprehension. J. Educ. Psychol. In press.

Miller, J. F., Chapman, R. S., Branston, M., and Reichle, J. 1978. Language comprehension in sensori-motor stages 5 and 6. Paper presented at the Boston University Child Language Forum.

Nelson, K., and Gruendel, J. 1979. From personal episode to social script. Paper presented at the Society for Research in Child Development, San Francisco.

Nicolich, L. 1975. A longitudinal study of representational play in relation to spontaneous imitation and development of multiword utterances: Final report. ERIC Document—PS007 854.

Olson, D. 1970. Cognitive Development. Academic Press, Inc., New York.

Olson, D. 1970. Language and thought: Aspects of a cognitive theory of semantics. Psychol. Rev. 77:257–273.

Pariser, D. 1979. The orthography of disaster: children's drawings of wrecked cars. Technical Report, No. 10, Harvard Project Zero.

Peirce, C. 1932. Collected Papers. C. Hartshorne and P. Weiss (eds.), Harvard University Press, Cambridge, Mass.

Piaget, J. 1954. The Construction of Reality in the Child. Basic Books, Inc., N.Y.

Piaget, J. 1962. Play, Dreams, and Imitation. W. W. Norton, N.Y.

Piaget, J. 1967. The Origins of Intelligence in Children. (orig. English publication, 1952). Norton, N.Y.

Piaget, J. 1965. The Child's Conception of Number. Norton, N.Y.

Piaget, J., and Inhelder, B. 1956. The Child's Conception of Space. Routledge, Kegan, Paul, Ltd., London.

Piatelli-Palmarin, M. (ed.). 1980. On Language and Learning. Harvard University Press, Cambridge, Mass.

Read, C. 1970. Children's perceptions of the sounds of English: Phonology from three to six. Unpublished doctoral dissertation, Harvard University, Cambridge, Mass.

Rimland, B. 1964. Infantile Autism. Appleton-Century-Crofts, New York.

Riquet, C. B. 1979. Symbolic play in autistic, Down's, and normal children of equivalent mental age. Unpublished masters thesis. Concordia University, Montreal.

Rubin, S., and Wolf, D. 1979. The development of maybe: The evolution of social roles into narrative roles. New Directions for Child Dev. 6:15–28.

Salomon, G. 1979. Interaction of Media, Symbols, and Cognition. Jossey-Bass, Inc., San Francisco.

Saxe, G. 1979. Children's counting: The early formation of numerical symbols. New Directions for Child Dev. 3.

Scarlett, G. W., and Wolf, D. 1979. When it's only make-believe: The construction of a boundary between fantasy and reality in storytelling. New Directions for Child Dev. 6:29–40.

Selfe, L. 1977. Nadia. Academic Press, Inc., London.

Shotwell, J. 1979. Counting steps. New Directions for Child Dev. 3:85–96.

Shotwell, J., Wolf, D., and Gardner, H. 1979. Exploring early symbolization: Styles of achievement. In B. Sutton-Smith (ed.), Playing and Learning. Gardner Press, New York.

Smith, N. R. 1972. The origins of graphic symbolization in children 3–5. Unpublished doctoral dissertation, Harvard University, Cambridge, Mass.

Smith, N. R. 1979. How a picture means. New Directions for Child Dev. 3:59–72.

Smith, N. R. 1980. Development and creativity in American art education: A critique.High School J. 63:348–352.

Uzgiris, I., and Hunt, J. McV. 1975. Assessment in Infancy: Ordinal Scales of Psychological Development. University of Illinois Press, Urbana, Ill.

Wagner, S., and Walters, J. The development of number as a symbol system. In H. Berlin (ed.), Developmental Psychology Series. Academic Press, Inc., N.Y. In press.

Wagner, S., Winner, E., Gardner, H., and Cicchetti, D. 1979. Metaphoric mapping in human infants. Paper presented at the Eastern Psychological Association Meetings, Philadelphia.

Watson, M., and Fischer, K. 1977. A developmental sequence of agent use in late infancy. Child Dev. 48:828–836.

Werner, H., and Kaplan, B. 1963. Symbol Formation. John Wiley & Sons, N.Y.

Winner, E. 1979. New names for old things. J. Child Lang. 6:469–491.

Winner, E., McCarthy, M., Kleinman, S., and Gardner, H. 1979. First metaphors. New Directions for Child Dev. 3:29–41.

Winnicott, D. W. 1971. Playing and Reality. Basic Books, Inc., N.Y.

Wolf, D. 1978. Otherhood: The development of an independent agent concept. Unpublished doctoral dissertation, Harvard University, Cambridge, Mass.

Wolf, D. (ed.), 1979. Early symbol use. New Directions for Child Dev. 3, whole.

Wolf, D. 1980. When do children draw: The representation of space in two dimensions. Paper presented to Division 10, American Psychological Association, Montreal.

Wolf, D., and Gardner, H. 1979. Style and sequence in early symbolic play. In N. Smith and M. Franklin (eds.), Symbolic Functioning in Children. Erlbaum. Hillsdale, N.J.

APPENDIX

Table 1. Summary of tasks and behaviors coded in relation to the emergence of event-structuring skill

Type of observation	Frequency of observation	Source for description categories
Social interaction		
reactions to separations	weekly	Mahler et al., 1975;
contrasting intentions		McDevitt, 1972
(in conflicts, teasing, etc.)		
knowing others have different		
capacities, experiences		
Game-playing		
spontaneous	weekly	Garvey, 1974; Bruner
elicited peek-a-boo		and Sherwood, 1976
Symbolic play with people		
spontaneous dramatic play	weekly	Garvey, 1974
role-continuation task*	monthly	
role-switching task*	monthly	
Symbolic play with replicas		
spontaneous play with replicas	weekly	Watson and Fischer,
(dolls, toy animals, etc.)		1977
agent continuation task*	monthly	
agent substitution task*	monthly	
agent/self conflict task*	monthly	
Utterances		
spontaneous	weekly	Brown, 1973;
language elicited over potential inde-	weekly	Fillmore, 1968
pendent agent use (as when child		
plays with dolls)		

* Specifics of these tasks are provided in Table 2.

Table 2. Tasks designed to assess the ability to distinguish roles in symbolic play events

A. *Symbolic Play with Replicas Tasks*

Agent role continuation task: In this task the observer showed a small figure moving through a short, familiar event—for instance, walking down a road of blocks to a small house, knocking, and entering. A number of other props, appropriate for use with the small figure were also present—a car, a bed, another figure. The child was then free to play with the entire set of items. The question was: Would the child exhibit any capacity to continue to use the figure as an agent, and in particular, would the child generate any novel agent-appropriate moves (for instance, making the first figure talk to the second figure)?

Table 2. (*Continued*)

Substitution in the agent-role task: In this task the observer set up a situation in which there were places for multiple agents (for instance, a toy table with six chairs around it). The observer asked the child to pick out "who can sit down and eat dinner" from a box containing six different possibilities. The six different possibilities were made up of six types of items: two recognizable replicas (two different but realistic baby dolls), an animate but not human replica (a toy dog), an abstract replica (a highly stylized figure looking like 日), a possible replica (like a simple chess pawn), an ambiguous block (like a 3-inch cylinder block), a counter-identity item (like a small car). Each time that the child put one item at a place, he or she was then shown a remaining place and asked "Who can sit here?" We were curious at what point children would say that there was nothing appropriate left. Sometimes children would simply set any old figure on a block—"to get rid" of us. To check whether children's initial willingness to set an item at a place was connected to a more broadly-based recognition that the figure could be treated as an independent agent, we asked children to do more things with them. "Show him taking a drink." To avoid training children on a particular situation and set of items, a set of three different situations and items was developed (eating, going to bed and waking up, getting in a car and driving away).

Self/other agent conflict task: In this task, the observer began a game of ball with the child. After several rounds of throwing and catching, the observer introduced a small doll and made it throw the ball to the child. The observer handed the child the doll, saying, "You make *her* play." The observer then threw the ball to the doll. Throughout the duration of the game, we observed whether the child could "set aside" his or her own catching and throwing activity in favor of making the doll do it. Being able to make the doll act continuously as if it were the active partner really entailed the child's maintaining two separate independent roles— that of the active catcher and thrower, as well as that of the "stage-manager" who was making things happen.

B. Symbolic Play with People Tasks

Role continuation task: In this task, the observer "installed" the child in a familiar role, like that of the caregiver, providing appropriate props (e.g., blankets and clothes; dishes and utensils) and making an initial suggestion for beginning the play: "You be the father/mother and I will be a baby. Here are some dishes. Make me some dinner." The point of the task was to assess not only the detail with which the child took on the assigned role but also the extent to which the child acknowledged the dramatic role that the observer had assumed.

Role switching task: In this task, situations like the one described above were established. Following a period of play in the originally assigned roles, the observer then suggested that she and the child trade roles. This trading suggestion was supported nonverbally by changing physical locations and trading the props associated with each of the roles.

Table 3. Schematization for the development of role-structures across domains

	Domain				
	Social interaction	Games	Symbolic play with persons	Symbolic play with replicas	Utterances
Definition	This refers to the realm of pragmatic interaction with others—in which things are accomplished, information is conveyed, intentions clash and are coordinated.	This refers to playful interactions with other people where there is no goal other than amusement. The activity is often ritualized, imitative, and organized into turns.	This refers to the realm often designated as "dramatic play" in which the child, alone or with others, plays out familiar action. Much attention centers on "who'll be who" and what it is appropriate for each actor to do.	This refers to the realm of symbolic or pretense play with small props (where dolls, animals, even blocks play out the roles of the actors in the pretended action).	This refers to meaningful utterances on the part of the child. The particular focus falls on those portions of the event, especially roles of the various actors, the child can capture linguistically.
Stage I (9 months–1;1)	*Use of others as tools/ means* C recognizes and uses distinctive, asymmetrical situational roles—as when C directs mother's attention to a music box he wants to make play by holding it out, vocalizing at her; but C acts only from his own perspective, never showing her what to do. *Use of others as human means* C uses other as means to end but now behavior shows C's greater aware-	*Static imitation games* C alternates taking turns with partner, but the turns are simply imitations rather than dis-	*Simple visible imitation of others* C imitates father making a scarey face.	Conventional schemes for replicas C imitates, first directly, then in deferred formats, schemes typi-	*Vocalization to achieve joint focus of attention* C develops uses for invented or conventional words: "bird" = to be

ness of the *human* parts of interaction—C at piano wants more music so moves father's hands into position, pressing down the father's fingers.

tinct; there is no variety in the way C fulfills his part; C is the passive member of the interchange.

lifted up to window.

cally applied to person and animal replicas—for instance: hugging, kissing.

Replica status for small props

C independently demonstrates that he regards replicas as similar to animate beings; C will point out familiar facial features on replicas and apply words like "sleeping" to them.

Patient status for props

C can use a prop as a recipient of actions, at first very conventionally putting to bed, feeding; slowly the range expands to giving rides, brushing hair; begins with very familiar, beloved dolls and extends to novel instances. If C shown prop acting agent-role, C, in continuing to handle the prop, transforms it to the recipient rather than performer of act (out of agent, into patient status).

Holophrases

(a) single word utterances that pick out the current locus of action; C says "dada" when he hears father coming; "Raggy," as she feeds her doll. C cannot distinguish linguistically between and/or coordinate mention of more than one role, so names most salient role only.

Stage II
(1;2–1;8)

Two-part games

a) *strict alternation games*

C alternates taking turns; now as a partner; C does not simply imitate, but makes his own moves; moves rarely vary from turn to turn; there is no capacity for role-switching.

Equivalence between self and other

a) *mapping for features*

C establishes a similarity between self and other—as in a shared feature possession (C points to eye on observer, walks over to his father and pats his eye, tries to find his own eye).

b) *mapping for actions*

C establishes a similarity between self and other in action—as when C is lying down on the floor in sleeping posture and pulls his father down into that same position.

Table 3. (Continued)

		Domain		
Social interaction	Games	Symbolic play with persons	Symbolic play with replicas	Utterances
Conversations C is offering information from his/her perspective and answering others' questions informatively.	*c) varied alternation games* C now fulfills his part in a game more generatively, varying what he does in a turn; C may also initiate games and take the role of the game-leader—as when in imitation-based games, C takes the responsibility for being the model and changing what it is his partner is to imitate.	*Deferred imitations of others* a) *imitations of object-use* C imitates the actions of another person without an immediate model, but imitation is triggered by the presence of an object that the other uses in a particular manner; imitation is no more elaborate than the brief or maybe the repeated use of this particular object; C cannot expand the imitation past object-use, toward "being" in that person's role—as when C slings mother's pocketbook over her shoulder and parades, but performs no further depictions of mother.	*Replicas become human equivalents* C often applies actions typically enacted on self to replicas—as in scolding, changing diapers, etc. *Replica becomes child's equivalent* C gets hurt, points to tear on doll's face, calling it "Raggy's boo boo." C will take medicine if doll does; these behaviors are strongest with transitional objects.	*Names to distinguish between persons*— "mama," "dada," etc. C often invents an all-purpose word e.g., ("ba") used to refer to others for whom he lacks proper name. C develops a way of referring to self.

Stage III
(1;9–2;0)

*Two-part games with distinct roles**
C is now capable of switching between roles in simple, familiar games like hide-and-seek or follow-the-leader.

b) imitations of salient behaviors
C imitates the actions of another without an immediate model. Now the imitation expands to include "being" in that person's role, at least briefly; this occurs either for very familiar events or striking ones; C performs a shopping trip, which includes details typical of parent's behavior as in buying specific items, saying "no candy"; or, as when C, having watched another child cry on leaving play-group and protest being put in a car-seat, repeats the sequence herself (playfully) when it is her own turn to leave.

Role-switching within simple dramatic play events
C can play out simple events, first taking one role, relative to his partner, then switching off; as when C plays

Child-replica interactions
relative to the replica in the child role, C takes up the role of the care-giver/parent—as when C holds doll up to the window so it "can see"; or as in changing the doll, washes, and cleans the doll's bottom, talking to doll all the while.

Replicas in agent-role
C can now use prop as if it were the agent (was patient exclusively up to now): this means C can distinguish the prop's actor role from own "stage-manager"

Holophrases
(b) single-word utterances in which C productively combines environmental elements with single words in a way that suggests increased ability to coordinate situational roles—as when C holds out truck to his father saying "fix."

*Descriptive strings**
utterances that pick out the different situations of participants in events through stringing together single words; as in "down . . . down . . . up" to describe

Table 3. (Continued)

	Domain			
Social interaction	Games	Symbolic play with persons	Symbolic play with replicas	Utterances
		first at photographing his parent, then plays at being photographed by his parent.	role''—denoting a capacity to handle two roles at once in symbolic play with replicas—so long as C occupies one of the roles; limits are evident when C tries to replay story with two prop roles as two props playing same role over.	that two other persons are seated, while C is up on the table. *2-word utterances* early grammatical combinations that include: possession as in "Daddy coat," location as in "Ball down," agent-action as in "Get cookie." Utterances combining roles around the central action (as in agent-object combinations) appear later and more rarely. *2-word utterances combining roles* C capable of distinguishing clearly between several events and roles in utterances. "Daddy fix trucks." (agent-action-object)

Key—C = child
* = based on fewer than 4 subjects

Table 4.   Major phases in the development from nonsymbolic foundations to specific symbol systems

The specific example: Language	A general model
I. Pragmatic Role Knowledge Based on considerable prior learning, a set of pragmatic abilities to analyze whole events into their constituent elements emerges between 9 and 13 months.	I. Nonsymbolic Cognitive Understandings
II. The Appearance of Role-Structures A. Between 14 and 20 months, these pragmatic abilities cease to be simply practical (e.g., activated only in the service of immediate motivations in actual situations) and become proto-symbolic (e.g., children attempt to signify actors and actions rather than simply imitating or re-presenting them.) The earliest attempts at symbolic encoding of roles occur in the format of deferred imitations of salient human actions. Subsequently, toys can be used, at least passively, to signify *individual* actors or situational roles. B. Between 20 and 24 months, the ability to coordinate the representation of *several* co-occurring situational roles emerges concurrently in both language and symbolic play. It spills over into other signification efforts like drawing and object-based "metaphors" but there it yields unconventional and often "illegible" symbols.	II. The Appearance of an Intermediate Encoding Structure
III. The Emergence of Language as a Specific Symbol System Through much of a symbol-user's life, increasingly system-specific skills develop. In the case of language, grammatical morphemes, transformational rules, subtleties of clause structure appear, presumably through the interaction of original encoding structures and models of mature performance.	III. The Construction of Specific Symbol Systems

chapter

10

Early Psycholinguistic Acquisition

Summary Chapter

Jon F. Miller

Waisman Center on Mental Retardation and Human Development
University of Wisconsin–Madison
Madison, Wisconsin

The two chapters in this section deal with the important relationships between language and cognitive constructs. They are directed toward discovering how the specific domains relate and the way these relationships may change over time. This chapter considers how the conceptual organization and outcomes presented by Wolf and Gardner and by Ingram affect the study of language-disordered populations. Particularly important are the hypotheses about developmental mechanisms and control variables that can be manipulated in early intervention programs.

WOLF AND GARDNER

The Wolf and Gardner chapter presents an alternative conceptionalization of the mental abilities presumed to be related to language/communication performance. The goal of their research program is to discover the links between these multiple domains of symbolization through the developmental period. They hypothesize that the domains emerge at different points in development with each having a distinct rate of acquisition.

The conceptualization presented in this chapter is intriguing for at least two reasons. First, in the research literature dealing with children who have deficits specifically in language, frequent appeal is made to general symbolic deficits as a causal construct. If general symbolic deficits are to be studied systematically and documented, the conceptualization presented by Wolf and Gardner seems to be a promising avenue to begin to unravel areas and levels of symbolic performance.

Second, in the area of learning disabilities many clinicians and teachers claim to have identified children with specific cognitive deficits, particularly in the area of spatial notions. Usually Piagetian tasks of spatial knowledge or understanding have been used as the basis for claiming specific cognitive deficits. These tasks include drawing, which is the primary task used by Wolf and Gardner in operationalizing symbolization of spatial notions. The ways in which spatial knowledge as a symbolic activity relates to learning, reading, and general language performance in children require careful study. The existence of specific cognitive deficits needs to be documented, and the impact of such deficits on language/communication performance over time should be included. Any attempt to differentiate general versus specific symbolic deficits will require a conceptual framework in order to segment these areas of performance for further study. The conceptualization presented in this chapter seems to be a productive beginning.

As the work of Wolf and Gardner progresses, the data resulting from specific studies will help us to begin considering some important questions relative to symbolization in general.

First, if language symbolization refers to all language-like behavior, that is, all language systems, regardless of input or output mode, then similar rates of acquisition would be expected in learning different language systems regardless of medium in Wolf and Gardner terms. We would expect signing systems and verbal language to be learned with equal difficulty if a general language symbolization system exists. Some support for this notion comes from a study by Prinz and Prinz (1979) in which signing and verbal English were shown to develop at the same rate in a bilingual child.

Second, if deficits in general symbolization exist, will they be characterized by deficits in language comprehension and production together or production deficits only? Furthermore, within comprehension or production, will a specific linguistic domain be affected or a number of linguistic domains including syntax, semantics, and pragmatic deficits. The most obvious predicted outcome is that general symbolic deficits would affect both comprehension and production rather than production only. There seem to be contradictory cases of adult aphasic patients with specific deficits in producing representational verbal language where verbal comprehension seems to be intact. Detailed study of patients with Broca's aphasia, however, reveals deficits in sentence comprehension as well—particularly the failure to use heuristic strategies to gain sentence meaning (Zurif and Caramazza, 1978).

A third and later outcome of this line of research may lead to the early identification of children who have suspect performance. In the Appendix of Wolf and Gardner's chapter, a clustering of behaviors emerging between 11 and 12 months that may well provide the basis for developing instruments aimed at early detection of children at risk for communication development is presented.

These are three areas of inquiry that are important in furthering our understanding of the relationship between symbolic process and language performance. The Wolf and Gardner chapter, at a conceptual level, provides a productive framework to view the problem and to construct experimental tests of questions regarding the specific relationships between symbolic processes and language performance.

INGRAM

In contrast with the Wolf and Gardner chapter, Ingram presents a specific piece of research that has significant implications for those of us dealing with disordered populations. Ingram addresses the cognition-language relationship with longitudinal data on three children in the sensorimotor period of development. With a large data base he used detailed analysis procedures to discover the extent to which the language and other nonverbal mental abilities are related, specifically exploring cognitive requirements necessary for the emergence of syntax.

If we look at the general ways in which the cognition hypothesis has been expressed, we find three general views currently, two of which have been delineated by Cromer (1974, 1976). The first of these is the strong form: cognitive development is both necessary and sufficient for language to develop. A second is the weak form: cognitive development is necessary but not sufficient for language to develop. Third and more recently is the correlational view, in which the two co-occur in time but slight advances or delays in linguistic development may occur relative to cognitive development at various points in time. This last view has emerged from the work of Bates et al. (1977) and is supported by a recent study of language comprehension in the second year of life by Miller et al., (1980).

In general, Ingram's study supports the correlational form of the cognition hypothesis. His careful examination of individual performance reveals that two of the three subjects passed into sensorimotor Stage 6 prior to the onset of syntax evidence by two-word productions. The third subject, K, produced two-word combinations while still in sensorimotor Stage 5. Sensorimotor stage, across the six domains of mental abilities, cannot be considered prerequisite to syntactic development in any generalized way, but may be related to the expression of semantic or meaning relationships.

The finding that productive syntactic development is not systematically related to stage of sensorimotor development is also supported by the Miller et al. (1980) comprehension study. Some children in the latter part of the second year of life evidence the ability to comprehend two-word constructions in sensorimotor Stage 5, indicating that achieving sensorimotor Stage 6 is not necessary or sufficient to comprehension of multiple lexical items in an utterance.

The most intriguing outcome of Ingram's work, both theoretically and clinically, is his detailed analysis of K's syntactic performance. Although her multiword utterances were productive, produced with rules, he concluded that "Cognitive limitations appeared to restrict the use and content of language, but not its syntactic processing (p. 27)." He then proposes that K evidenced specific syntactic mechanisms for the development of a grammar that are not causally linked to cognitive advances. Ingram's emphasis on criteria for productivity, based on syntactic grammars, is central to his apparent demonstration of independent syntactic mechanisms in K. As a result of his detailed analysis he proposes K's pattern of syntactic development may not be unique when compared to that of his other subjects and that of the subjects of other investigations that had similar syntactic analysis.

This line of argument has important implications for early intervention. If K's syntactic mechanisms for the development of grammar are 1) not causally linked to cognitive advancement and 2) not unique, then what mechanisms can be proposed to account for her rapid rate of syntactic acquisition? Ingram poses two possible mechanisms, both of which may be considered environmental. Given that the basis of intervention is environmental manipulation, these potential mechanisms deserve mention.

Ingram points out that K differed from the other two subjects in two ways. First, linguistic input was judged to be very frequent and consistent in terms of types introduced, evidenced by the number of discourse routines documented in the data. K evidenced devices to respond to questions and to maintain discourse initiated by her mother. In addition, K used interactional terms, *Hi, OOH, TaTa,* to initiate discourse with her mother. It seems that the frequency and consistency of the initiation of verbal routines and the consistent responding to K's utterances within discourse routines provided increased opportunity to learn new words and phrases.

Discourse routines provide joint focus on topic, a set of expectations, consistent utterances to be discriminated, responses that can be consistently modeled and reinforced, leading to increased frequency of initiations and responses. Careful examination of early mother-child interactions reveals frequent and consistent discourse routines centered around routine activities like meal times and baths (see Chapter 6, this volume). Pursuing discourse strategies as a basic approach to intervention will require careful study of mothers' initiation and response styles to determine the specific contingencies fostering development.

Ingram points out a second dimension on which K differed from the other two subjects, that is, her ability to imitate. The role of imitation in verbal learning has a long and varied history. It has been considered both basic and necessary for learning in behavioral intervention programs as well as marking variations in individual learning style. Germane to K's advanced status however, is the role of her high frequency of imitation in her rapid syntactic acquisition. We could argue that her high frequency of imitation is a result of her mother's input style, consistently reinforcing imitative response. Alternately, we could argue that her imitative style is causal in her advanced syntactic status. Clearly imitation remains an important topic for intervention research.

Ingram's discussion and specification of productivity is a very important construct for us because it provides the means to explore the systematic organization of children's productive language. This leads us to an innovative methodological step that he has introduced with his chapter. It is not sufficient to take a transcript of the child's free speech and calculate status from frequencies of lexical realizations of grammatical structures or general status measures like mean length of utterance. We can explore the child's abilities much further if we analyze the transcript carefully for productivity as discussed in Ingram's chapter. In this process, the distinction between productive and unproductive constructions can be drawn. Unproductive or absent forms can then be examined in detail through structuring elicitation techniques in specific contexts. These data can then be used to "fill in the gaps" of the speech sample, to complete the picture of the child's syntactic system. This methodological advance will lead to a more complete data base from which to discover whether the child does have a systematic organization to his or her grammatical system.

The application of the work demonstrating the relationship between cognition and language has real implications for work with retarded populations. In our own clinic, we have examined 82 children that have been evaluated with cognitive tasks, both standardized measures of intelligence and nonstandard Piagetian measures of mental abilities, and multiple domains of language performance including comprehension of vocabulary and syntax, production of syntax, semantics, phonology, and pragmatics when possible (Miller, Chapman and Bedrosian, 1978). These children are multiply handicapped children, ranging in chronological age (CA) from 6 months to 18 years, functioning conceptually from Stage 4 of sensorimotor development to the late preoperational period. When we examined carefully the relationship between language and cognitive performance, using mental age as a general construct of mental abilities measured across a number of domains, we find that 80% of the children in our sample exhibit language performance that is consistent with their mental age status. Upon careful examination of individual children, only eight children evidenced language in advance of mental age. All eight showed advances in comprehension of vocabulary, which is consistent with Rondal's (1978) findings. Three, however, did evidence advances in syntax. The proper explanation for this outcome is uncertain. Obviously it supports the correlational view of the relationship between mental age and performance on multiple linguistic domains in the same way Ingram's subject supports this view for normal children. More importantly, further study of these eight subjects, like Ingram's K, offers great potential for revealing causal factors in language development that have significant implications for early intervention strategies.

The practical significance of the correlational view of the cognition hypothesis is the value of mental age over chronological age in determining whether the child has a problem in acquiring language at an appropriate rate. The data to date clearly support MA as the general pacesetter for language acquisition. As a result, we cannot judge performance status as deficit unless we have measures of nonverbal mental age. The alternative, chronological age, leads us to conclude that all retarded children have language deficits that can be remediated to CA level.

The clinical data, then, employing multiple procedures testing a variety of linguistic constructs support the careful basic research with normal children. Ingram's detailed study has demonstrated the value of exploring children whose performance seems unusual or difficult to explain. The identification and study of children like K and similar children in clinical populations is vital to promoting our understanding of causal mechanisms responsible for language development and, alternatively, language delay or disorders.

Although a general version of the cognition hypothesis can be supported, Ingram's chapter begins to unravel the specific questions of which cognitive constructs and mental abilities are related to which linguistic constructs and performance over time. Clearly, this relationship changes through the developmental period and our ability to understand it certainly will have significant impact on clinical science.

As we begin to discuss intervention, we should also consider the basic problems in quantification of language behavior that are basic to getting children into programs and monitoring performance within treatment consistently and systematically.

REFERENCES

Bates, E., Benigni, L., Bretherton, I., Camaioni, L. and Volterra, V. 1977. Cognition and Communication From 9–13 Months: A Correlational Study. Program on cognitive and perceptual factors on human development. Report No. 12 Institute for the Study of Intellectual Behavior. University of Colorado, Boulder, Col.

Cromer, R. 1974. The Development of Language and Cognition: The Cognition Hypothesis. *In* D. Foss (ed.), New Perspectives in Child Development. Penguin, Baltimore.

Cromer, R. 1976. The cognitive hypothesis of language acquisition and its implications for child language deficiency. *In* D. Morehead and A. Morehead (eds.), Normal and Deficient Child Language. University Park Press, Baltimore.

Miller, J., Chapman, R., and Bedrosian, J. 1978. The relationship between etiology, cognitive development and communicative performance. New Zealand Speech Therapists' J. 33:2–17.

Miller, J., Chapman, R., Branston, M., and Reichle, J. 1980. Language comprehension in sensorimotor Stages V and VI. J. Speech Hear. Res. 23(2) 284–311.

Prinz, P., and Prinz, E. 1979. Acquisition of ASL and Spoken English in a Hearing Child of a Deaf Mother and a Hearing Father. Paper presented at the Stanford Child Language Research Forum, Stanford University, April.

Rondal, J. 1978. Maternal speech to normal and Down's syndrome children matched for mean utterance length. *In* C. E. Meyers (ed.), Quality of Life in Severely and Profoundly Mentally Retarded People: Research Foundations for Improvement. American Association on Mental Deficiency, Washington, D.C.

Zurif, E., and Caramazza, A. Comprehension, memory, and levels of representation: A perspective for aphasia. *In* J. Kavanagh and W. Strange (eds.), Speech and Language in the Laboratory, School, and Clinic. pp. 337–387. MIT Press, Cambridge.

Section IV

Decision and Implementation Procedures

chapter
11

Early Intervention

Design and Evaluation

Gerard Kysela

Alex Hillyard

Linda McDonald

Julie Ahlsten-Taylor

The Center for the Study of Mental Retardation and
The Department of Educational Psychology
The University of Alberta
Edmonton, Alberta
Canada

contents

An increasing number of intervention strategies for infants and young children during the last 5 years have been directed toward the prevention or attenuation of intellectual handicaps and developmental delays. The designs and evaluation procedures have been sufficiently diverse as to preclude the description of generic principles of instruction as a basis for successful intervention approaches. Glaser (1976) emphasized the importance of developing a psychology of instruction as a link between the conceptual basis of program development and evaluation, on the one hand, and the practice of education on the other. Thus, Glaser recapitulated issues raised by Dewey (1900) many years earlier.

The description of an intervention system incorporating our present knowledge of learning principles and concepts of child development and handicapping conditions as a basis for program development constitutes the beginning steps in this developing science of instruction. The Early Education Project described in this chapter develops these linkages for a broadly applicable intervention system of assessment and teaching. The goal was the design of an *effective* intervention system for developmentally delayed infants and toddlers. The evaluation of the system's applicability when used by parents and teachers attempting to attenuate developmental delay and foster more typical development constituted a fundamental dimension of effectiveness.

INTERVENTION RATIONALE

A major objective of the Early Education Project (Kysela et al., 1979) was to develop a systematic early intervention program for moderately/severely handicapped children. This section provides 1) a brief description of two intervention models within the Early Education Program, 2) four requirements that were necessary to accommodate the two models, and 3) a rationale for the direct and incidental teaching procedures used within the two intervention models.

Two Intervention Models: A Brief Description

The Early Education Project accommodated two intervention models. Each model had its own service delivery system. The *home-based* program provided services for developmentally delayed children from birth to 2½ years of age. Two home specialists provided parent-training and program assistance to the parents. The home specialists did not work with the children directly, but with the parents who were the primary teaching agents. The *school-based* program provided services

This project was funded by Alberta Education, Planning and Research Branch and Early Childhood Services Branch through the Centre for the Study of Mental Retardation.

for developmentally delayed children from 2½ to 6 years of age. Two teachers and two developmental assistants instructed these children in an elementary school setting.

Requirements of the Two Intervention Models

A key requirement of the models was a home- and school-based program rather than an institution-based program. Procedures and methods had to be found that were appropriate to the child's natural environment. Although this consideration limited the complexity and applicability of the intervention process, it was assumed that home and school-based programs had greater ecological validity than institution-based programs (Brooks and Baumeister, 1977; Hanson, 1976).

A second requirement was a systematic approach to early intervention. Teachers and parents were provided with a program containing consistent, replicable methods with built-in safeguards and guidelines for implementation. In addition, this approach used data collection to monitor and evaluate child development and program effectiveness. Data collection also served as an evaluation method for improving parent and teacher instructional skills and isolating program deficiencies.

An intervention approach should result in generalizable parent teaching skills for new behaviors in addition to producing generalized child responses. This third requirement was the most difficult to program and evaluate.

A fourth feature of this program involved the development of teaching methods for children with moderate/severe handicaps. Children with moderate/severe handicaps have deficiencies in the psychological processes of attention, memory, and transferability of learned skills (Robinson and Robinson, 1965). A systematic teaching format and environment was developed to overcome these deficiencies. The intervention approach required instructional mechanisms that attenuated these problems associated with learning. These requirements were considered when designing the direct and incidental teaching methods.

Rationale: Direct and Incidental Teaching Models

A general consideration when developing direct and incidental teaching methods was their functional use. To be functional these teaching procedures had to have general applicability for both school and parent teaching. The conceptual basis of these models stemmed from the experimental and applied behavior analysis research conducted within an operant learning framework. The following sections provide the logical and empirical support for both the functional and conceptual bases of these testing and teaching methods.

A Functional Basis   The four requirements previously identified required a systematic test-teach model for several reasons. Because of the severe degree of retardation and the cumulative effect of developmental delay starting at birth, a systematic intervention system was required rather than a less-structured, uncontrolled method. Also, assessment and teaching needed to be closely correlated to ensure a high degree of assessment validity in terms of its implications for teaching. Third, a data-based method for monitoring the child's performance was required to determine when criterion was attained or when to revise programs and procedures.

The testing and teaching procedures developed by Martin et al. (1975) provided a framework for a test-teach method that satisfied a number of these requirements. These procedures were developed for para-professionals in a large institution for teaching a number of self-help skills (Martin et al., 1975). Thus, it was assumed that lay persons (e.g., parents) and teachers could use the model if provided with an adequate training program.

The procedures Martin et al. (1975) proposed included five levels of instruction. The levels of instruction progressed from full manual guidance of the child through a response sequence, fading to gestures, then to a final level of spontaneous responding to instructions or naturally occurring environmental cues. The Martin et al. methods were modified by using cumulative presentation of prompts (Table 1). For example, at the minimum guidance level (Level 2), a verbal cue from Level 4 and a gesture or model from Level 3 followed the instruction (Level 5) and preceded the minimum guidance of the child's response. This procedural modification facilitated the gradual transfer from level to level and enhanced the likelihood of these additional cues functioning as mediators of the correct response (Reese, 1972).

The teaching procedures developed by Martin et al. also included a criterion-referenced assessment method that incorporated the five levels of guidance and prompting, thus closely linking the testing and teaching processes (Anderson and Faust, 1973). This assessment system was used with the teaching curriculum to provide the initial information of a child's skills and knowledge. The Martin et al. (1975) teaching procedures included a data collection system to monitor children's progress in a particular program.

The Martin et al. approach also included procedures to correct the child's errors. After erring, the child would return to the previous teaching level, reach criterion, and then proceed to the next level. This procedure ensured that the parent or teacher had an option for continuing the teaching process if the child made an error. The parent was also precluded from continuing indefinitely at the same instructional

Table 1.   Comparison of Martin et al. (1975) teaching levels and the direct teaching model

Teaching levels	Martin et al.	Direct teaching
Level 1	Instruction Physical guidance-maximum	Instruction Model* Verbal prompt Physical prompt Physical guidance-maximum
Level 2	Instruction Physical guidance-minimum	Instruction Model* Verbal prompt Physical prompt Physical guidance-minimum
Level 3	Instruction Physical prompt	Instruction Model* Verbal prompt Physical prompt
Level 4	Instruction Verbal prompt	Instruction Model* Verbal prompt
Level 5	Instruction	Instruction Model*

* May or may not be included, depending upon terminal objective of program.

level if the child made errors. Previously, this problem reduced effective teaching if parents or teachers did not have an alternative to follow when errors were made.

The incidental teaching method was developed to complement the direct teaching procedures. Directly-taught skills were generalized to new settings, novel stimulus material and individuals through the incidental teaching model. In addition, the incidental method increased parental opportunities for teaching their children. A review of the work of Hart and Risley (1975) and Hart and Rogers-Warren (1978) as well as a post hoc analysis of the first 6 months of intervention with the Early Education Project indicated the need for a complementary method that could provide greater responsiveness to the multitude of potential teaching instances in a child's natural environment. The first 6 months of teaching produced extensive progress in language and cognitive development (Kysela et al., 1979) which is discussed on pages 365–370. The children frequently lacked generalization to other persons or settings when informal probes were conducted.

Hart and her colleagues (Hart and Risely, 1975; Hart and Rogers-Warren, 1978) suggested a second method that could be used to expand or generalize a child's language repertoire during child-initiated contacts. Hart and Rogers-Warren (1978) expanded this concept as a milieu teaching approach lying on a continuum between one-to-one direct teaching and the natural environment. The incidental teaching method adopted by the Early Education Project provided parents and teachers with the means of generalizing directly taught language skills during either child-initiated or parent/teacher-initiated interactions. In addition, this method provided a means of teaching the child new concepts and skills in a variety of naturally occurring situations. The incidental method was readily adapted to home and school-based implementation for which parents and teachers had previously developed skills using specific instructions, verbal cues, physical cues and prompts, and guidance. Thus, the incidental teaching method could be combined with the direct method for parent/teacher use. The combination of the two procedures facilitated generalization of language skills in both the home and school-based programs and provided a functional basis of intervention.

A Conceptual Basis   Glaser (1976) identified four essential components for designing an instructional environment: "1) the *analysis* of competence (the state of knowledge and skill) to be achieved; 2) *description* of the initial state with which learning begins; 3) *conditions* that can be implemented to bring about change from the initial state of the learner to the state described as the competence; and 4) *assessment procedures* for determining the immediate and long-range outcomes of the conditions that are put into effect to implement change from the initial state of competence to further development" (Glaser, 1976, emphasis added). These components closely parallel Bijou's (1976) description of characteristics essential for optimal early intervention programs. Table 2 presents the parallels between Glaser's components, Bijou's components, and the characteristics of the early intervention system developed in the Early Education Project (Kysela et al., 1979). The design of the direct test-teach method, the incidental teaching model, and the curriculum operationalized each of these components to optimize instruction and learning for moderate/severely handicapped children.

In order to analyze and establish a child's level of behavioral competence, the teaching curriculum was constructed and organized as an initial series of targets and objectives. A criterion referenced assessment format (Snelbecker, 1974) was used to determine initial skill level of the children within the curriculum.

The use of skill assessment employing the criterion-referenced assessment ensured a clear description of the initial competence level of the learner. As mentioned above, this criterion-referenced assessment was used because of its direct bearing on the measurement of competency (Anderson and Faust, 1973; Snelbecker, 1974). The direct

Table 2.   Comparison of components of instructional design by Glaser, Bijou, and the Early Education Project

Glaser	Bijou	Early Education Project
Analysis of competence to be achieved	Specify goals of teaching and learning in observable terms	Behaviorally based teaching curriculum
Description of initial state when learning begins	Begin teaching at child's level of competence	Criterion-referenced assessment to identify initial point for teaching
Conditions implemented to change from initial state to state of competence	Arrange teaching to facilitate learning Use practices to generalize elaborate, and maintain behaviors	Use of Direct Teaching Model, Incidental Teaching Model, and Structured Programs for teaching
Assessment procedures to measure immediate and long-range outcomes of conditions from initial to competent state	Monitor learning progress and make changes to advance learning	Systematic data collection during learning, review, and maintenance to monitor progress

relationship of this testing procedure to the teaching model was a second significant factor in choosing this approach (c.f., Baine, 1977). The results of the assessment procedure provide specific data regarding the starting point of instruction.

The specification of conditions employed to bring about a change from the initial state of assessment to the state of competence on the concept/skill were prescribed clearly in both the direct and incidental methods. In the direct method, the antecedent and consequent determinants of change were based upon the instructional procedures developed by Engelmann (Becker, Engelmann, and Thomas, 1975) and are presented in Figure 1. The first part of these instructional procedures, the attention component, has been demonstrated to be an important factor in mentally retarded children's difficulty in learning (Zeaman and House, 1963; Fisher and Zeaman, 1973). The functional influence of antecedent and consequent events upon the children's observed behavior change was the key process in this teaching procedure (Skinner, 1953, 1968).

The initial component of the direct teaching model was designed to build up the infant's attentiveness to discriminative cues being presented by parents and to continue to maintain this attentiveness as they learned new skills and concepts. Persistent attentiveness was gained by shifting to partial reinforcement of attentiveness once the infant reliably responded during continuous reinforcement (Ferster and Skinner, 1957). A remedial procedure using increasing prompting and guidance was introduced (Becker et al., 1975) if the child did not attend to the attention signal when presented.

Second, direct teaching began at the initial assessment level, frequently Level 1 with maximum guidance, and gradually shifted up through the teaching levels as the child responded correctly. The use of maximum (hands on) and minimum (one finger) guidance has been demonstrated to be effective in assisting mentally retarded persons in attaining new skills (Martin et al., 1975; Kazden and Erickson, 1975). This procedure is similar in topography to physical shaping methods, which also have been successful in teaching children new skills (Martin and Treffry, 1970; Horner, 1971; O'Brien, Bugle, and Azrin, 1972). In addition, for Levels 3 and 4, the use of physical prompts and verbal prompts to establish and maintain the children's responding has also been supported by numerous research studies (Becker et al., 1975; Cowart, Carnine, and Becker, 1973; Martin et al., 1975; Siegel and Rosenshine, 1973). Using an observational prompt or model to foster imitative learning at Level 3 has been documented by Bandura (1977) as a successful instructional strategy for early development. Thus, there is extensive support for the use of these antecedent events as the components of the direct teaching method.

During the shift from level to level, the parent/teacher gradually *faded* the guidance or prompts employed (depending upon which teaching level was being used) until the child continued to respond at the next highest level of the sequence. This procedure of fading antecedent prompting cues was found effective for training skills, concepts, and discriminations by a number of investigators (Sidman and Stoddard, 1966; Engelmann, 1969; Schreibman, 1975). These procedures have been associated with rapid learning and fewer errors when employed with mentally retarded children.

The use of consequences for a child's responses included positive reinforcement in the form of praise, consumables, naturally occurring

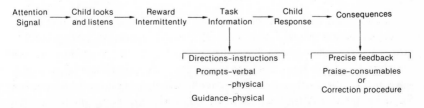

Figure 1.   Component model for instruction.

consequences, physical contact, and precise feedback. Considerable research evidence has strongly supported the importance of continuous and intermittent consequent determinants increasing and maintaining behavior change (Skinner, 1953; see Sulzer-Azaroff and Mayer, 1977 for a thorough review of reinforcement practices in the classroom). The empirical data obtained provided an ongoing measure of the acquisition and maintenance of a skill or concept. This was an empirical means of evaluating the consequent's effectiveness.

Because the same prompts, guidance, shaping and fading procedures, and consequent determinants including extensive social regulation (Bruner, 1975) were incorporated into the incidental teaching model, the same empirical evidence previously reviewed supported the basic components.

For incidental teaching, the resultant naturalistic consequences of many teaching situations and the social regulation function of the child's behavior have been established as important dimensions of early infant acquisition of language by both Bandura (1977) and Bruner (1975).

To increase generalization by the child to other persons, places, and stimuli, the incidental method could be used by the parent or teacher in a wide variety of situations as well as by other persons. This aspect of the model was specifically intended to facilitate generalization of the newly acquired skills and concepts to a broad variety of situations and stimulus events (Stokes and Baer, 1977).

Parents were taught to structure situations in which the child could spontaneously manage his or her environment by using appropriate language or gestures. This natural interplay between parent/child is proposed as a critical mechanism of the developing language repertoire of the child (Bruner, 1975; Hart and Risley, 1975). Thus, spontaneous language usage by the infants could be increased.

The combination of the direct teaching model for specific instruction on new skills/concepts and the incidental teaching model enhanced the application and generalization of this new knowledge.

THE DIRECT INSTRUCTION MODEL

The direct teaching procedures provided the basic framework of instruction for parents and teachers. They used the direct method of this model to teach children skills in the areas of language, cognition, motor development, self-help, and socialization. The descriptions below define the specific procedures of the five teaching levels. Level 5 included the appropriate instructions or other naturally occurring discriminative stimuli which occasioned the occurrence of a specific behavior or class of behaviors. Level 4 included the instructions and verbal prompts that were repeated instructions, and other verbal events intended to help initiate the behavior or focus the child's attention upon salient characteristics of the material.

Level 3 included the instructions and verbal prompts from Level 4 with the addition of physical prompts or an imitative model. (In all conditions, the additional prompts followed the instruction after a 1–2 second delay; this allowed for the occurrence of a spontaneous response before the presentation of additional prompts or cues.) Physical prompts included gestures or signals that provided information to the child regarding relevant stimulus attributes or information regarding when and where to respond. Imitative models were either parent/ teacher or child responses (by another child) that the learner could subsequently imitate. These imitative models were faded out prior to Level 4 unless the instruction included a model as an implicit component, for example, vocal imitation training.

Level 2 included the use of instructions and prompts from Levels 3 and 4 as well as minimum physical guidance. Minimum guidance was defined as parent or teacher-initiated behavior of physical contact with the child; the degree of physical contact involved assisting the child with one finger for a maximum of 5 seconds. In some programs, however, the response pattern was, by its nature, longer; in these cases, Level 2 guidance lasted several seconds longer than the typical 5-second period. Listed below is an example of the teaching levels to clarify the component sequence for any given trial.

Level 1

Teacher Behavior	Scoring Categories
Say eat	Instruction model
You say it Danny "eat"	Verbal prompt
Gestures to own mouth while saying this	Physical prompt
Use both hands to form child's mouth	Physical guidance—Level 1

Note: In the foregoing example the word eat is scored as a model because the teacher is emitting the sound she wants the child to imitate. If the teacher used one finger on the child's mouth to produce the sound, this would have been an example of Level 2 teaching.

Level 3

Teacher Behavior	Scoring Categories
Say eat	Instruction model
Danny say "eat"	Verbal prompt model
Points to the child while saying this	Physical support

Note: "Danny say" is scored as a verbal prompt because it is a verbal directive following the instruction, directing the child to engage in a specified behavior. In this instance the verbal prompt is an expanded instruction because the teacher includes the child's name. The physical prompt is pointing to the child indicating he should respond.

Level 4

Teacher Behavior	Scoring Categories
Say "eat"	Instruction model
Say "eat"	Verbal prompt model

Note: In this example the verbal prompt is a repetition of the initial instruction.

Level 5

Teacher Behavior	Scoring Categories
Say "eat"	Instruction model

Level 1 included the use of prompts from Levels 3 and 4 and maximum physical guidance; maximum physical guidance was defined as anything more than Level 2 including full hands-on guidance or leading through for a period of 5 seconds. The crucial difference between Level 1 and Level 2 involved the very limited actual physical management of Level 2, which mainly served as the initial impetus of the response; whereas, maximum guidance involved leading through the response pattern by the parent. Level 1 guidance typically functioned as a shaping procedure in that sometimes the child's response gradually approximated the desired form through the use of maximum guidance.

Within a series of several trials at a particular level, the parent/ teacher gradually reduced or faded the amount of guidance or the strength of the prompt for that level. The transition between each of the trials at a particular level was similar to the transition from the last trial of one level to the first trial of the next level. This procedure ensured a minimal amount of disruption while making the transition to lesser amounts of prompting or guidance. At the same time, the child's dependence upon the parent for assistance was reduced. This gradual reduction of prompting ensured success by the learners.

The criterion for shifting from one level to another was three consecutive correct responses at a given teaching level. If the child exhibited an error at any particular level, the parent/teacher would drop back to the previous level of instruction and continue teaching until three consecutive correct responses were obtained. On the other hand, if the child responded spontaneously after the instruction was given and before the additional prompting and guidance, this was noted; following five consecutive instances of this type the child was moved from that step to the next. This procedure allowed for skipping through steps of a program if the child responded to the instructions without requiring prompting and guidance.

THE INCIDENTAL INSTRUCTION MODEL

The incidental teaching model was designed to inform the child, to generalize a skill or concept, and to increase the persons/situations to which the child responds. The incidental procedure was readily employed by teachers, parents, and other family members to help the child use language more efficiently. Modifications to the procedure outlined by Hart and Risely (1975) included the development of parent/teacher-initiated situations for incidental teaching. Figure 2 presents the general model used for both child-initiated and parent-initiated incidental teaching situations. This procedure could accommodate both parent/teacher-initiated situations involving verbal and nonverbal behaviors by the child and child-initiated situations.

Parent/Teacher Initiated Situation

There were two types of parent/teacher-initiated situations for incidental teaching opportunities. In the first, the parent/teacher was trying to prompt a motoric response from the child in reply to a verbal instruction. A second type involved an attempt by the parent or teacher to occasion a verbal response (or gesture) from the child appropriate to the stimulus context. The major difference between these two teaching situations in terms of the model involved the inclusion of Level 4 verbal prompting, that is, when a verbal response was desired. Here, the parent/teacher moved from Level 5 to Level 4 if the child did not respond to the instruction.

Juice time, for example, was used by the parent or teacher to elicit a verbal response from a child. (Figure 2 provides the guidelines for these procedures.) The parent presented a juice glass to the child and said "What *you* want?" (Level 5). If the child responded, "Want juice," the parent complied. If, however, there was no response, the parent moved to Level 4, presenting a verbal prompt and repeating the instruction, for example, "Say, want juice. What you want?" Again, if the child answered, the parent complied. If the child still did not respond, the parent shifted down to Level 3 using a physical prompt and the instruction, for example, pointing to the juice and saying, "What you want?" If the child still was unresponsive, the parent used hands-on guidance and the instruction to shape the child's verbal or

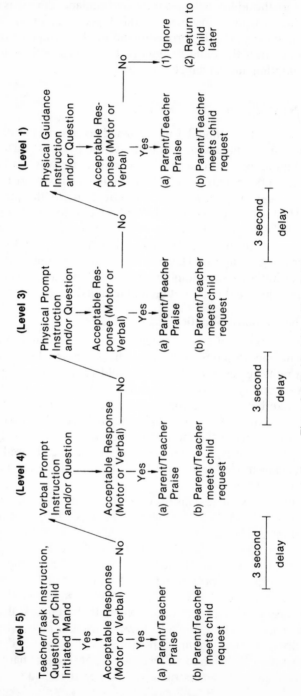

Figure 2.   Incidental teaching model.

gestural response, if appropriate to the child's skill level or conceptual level of learning.

When prompting a motor response the parent might request the child to push a car with the instruction "Push car." If the child did not respond, the parent would present a physical prompt (Level 3) and repeat the instruction, for example, pointing to the car and saying "Push car." The parent would not include Level 4 verbal prompts for the motor response "Push car." If there was still no response, the parent would use maximum physical guidance (Level 1) and the instruction, for example, placing her hands on the child's and assisting simultaneously saying, "Push car." If the child still made no response, the parent moved away and returned later to repeat the procedures if appropriate.

Child-Initiated Situation

A child-initiated situation meant that the child indicated either through verbalization or gesture that he or she required assistance in the completion of a task or in attaining an object. The major consideration in this situation was that the child approached the parent as opposed to the parent arranging the child's environment. In this situation the parent assisted the child only if the child emitted an appropriate verbalization or gestures. If the request from the child was not acceptable, the parent presented a question, for example, "What want" (Level 5). If the child did not respond, the parent followed the same prompting system used in the above example until an acceptable response was given by the child. Following a correct response, the parent/teacher elaborated the child's utterances with verbal feedback.

PROGRAM FORMAT

The final component of the conditions employed to facilitate change toward competencies being taught included the use of a consistent instructional program format by both parents and teachers. Some of the initial programs were obtained from standard sources (Anderson, Hodson, and Willard, 1976; Fredericks et al., 1976) and were written by the teaching staff of the home and school program. The format of these programs included the following components:

Behavioral objectives stating the terminal objective the child must attain for mastery of the skill or concept and completion of the program.
The sequence of steps appropriate to teach the objective were derived from a task analysis of the objective in terms of simple to complex

behaviors leading to the terminal objective, conditions in which the behavior is taught, and the shifting standards of performance and product necessary for mastery.

A procedural section that outlined how to implement the direct teaching model in relation to the specific objective.

Review and maintenance components that were implemented following attainment of criterion to ensure generalization and maintenance of the behaviors over time.

PARENT AND STAFF TRAINING

Staff of the Early Education Project were trained as either home-based teachers or school-based personnel. A series of ten staff training units provided the teachers with the specific assessment method, direct and incidental teaching procedures, a program writing format and a data collection system. These procedures and models were then implemented by the trained staff in either the home-based or school setting.

In the home setting, the teacher's initial role was to train the parents in the procedures and methods of the program. This ensured that the parent in the home became the primary teacher for the child. Home-teachers began working with a family by initiating the assessment of the child and starting a three-step parent-training program. The first step of parent training began with an overview of the teaching formats and an explanation of how assessment indicates where to begin instruction. Parents were given a behavioral objective assessed at Level 5. An objective assessed at Level 5 was not taught but placed on a maintenance program. The home teachers instructed the parents in the use of the maintenance program and data collection procedure. This program was then left with the parent for 1 week and was reviewed by the home teacher the following week before beginning step two of the training program.

The second step in parent training required teaching an objective that had been assessed at Level 3. This step practiced using verbal and physical prompts (Levels 3 and 4). The parents were taught how to fade the amount of prompting from trial to trial. The specific data-recording procedure was also introduced and used at this stage. If the child attained Level 5 mastery during this phase, the behavior would be reviewed and maintained as in the first step of the training program.

The final step required the parent to implement a teaching program for an objective assessed at Levels 1 or 2 requiring the use of minimum and maximum guidance. This step incorporated a cumulative review of the previous steps. Thus, the parent used the teaching levels that incorporated verbal and physical prompts and physical guidance. Following the development of these teaching skills parents could implement a program at any teaching level, move their child through the program, maintain the skill or concept after mastery, and record the child's performance on the data sheets for monitoring learning. After they mastered these teaching procedures, the parents were also taught the incidental teaching method.

In contrast, the school-based teachers and developmental assistants provided direct instructional programming and teaching for the school-based program. Parents with children in the school program assisted in maintenance and generalization of new concepts and skills from school to home. The parents were instructed by the teachers to carry out teaching programs at home in an attempt to ensure greater generalization of learned skills between home and school. In addition, school parents assisted the teachers as weekly volunteers.

After the formal parent training in the home program, the home teacher began regular weekly or bi-weekly visits; these visits clarified problems for parents, introduced new programs, and ensured accurate teaching. School-based teachers attended weekly inservice meetings. During these times, teaching procedures were evaluated, revised, and clarified. A formal monitoring system, the Behavior Analysis System (Hillyard, Kysela, and Davis, 1976), was devised and was used to evaluate the parents' and teachers' reliable implementation of the teaching model. This system also increased the accuracy of the parent and teacher skills with the direct teaching method.

INSTRUCTIONAL ENVIRONMENTS

The early intervention process began at home—with the parents. Data were presented, however, for children from both the home-based program implemented by in-home specialists and a school-based program implemented by the trained teaching staff. In each situation, the teaching models and programs were similar. Major differences in the two programs were the children's ages, the home versus classroom environments, and the teaching agents. The classroom was in a regular elementary school in Edmonton, Alberta. Two groups of toddlers attended half-day sessions 4 or 5 days per week. During this time, direct and incidental teaching activities were structured and conducted depending upon the child's skills and knowledge. Table 3 is an example of a weekly schedule for the classroom program. The children received daily individual language sessions. While one teacher and a volunteer conducted group activities, the other teacher conducted individual language training sessions. One day a week was devoted to maintenance checks for learned skills and probes for higher level skills.

Table 3. Weekly schedule for the classroom

	Monday	(Volunteer)	Tuesday	(Volunteer)	Wednesday	(Volunteer)	Thursday	(Volunteer)	Friday	(Volunteer)
9:00–9:15	Undressing Incidental teaching	Juice Art prep	Undressing Incidental teaching	Juice Get book	Undressing Incidental teaching	Juice Art prep	Undressing Incidental teaching	Juice Get book		Juice prep
9:15–9:25	Cognition writing	Set-up house	Cognition writing	Set-up store	Cognition writing	Set-up house	Cognition writing	Set-up store		Set-up house
9:25–9:35	Motor exercises	Snack prep	Motor exercises	Join games	Motor exercises	Snack prep	Motor exercises	Join games		Snack prep
9:35–9:45	Story corner	Sit with group	Story corner	Sit with group	Story corner	Sit with group	Story corner	Sit with group		Sit with group
9:45–10:00	Cognition matching	Large blocks	Cognition lacing	Snack prep	Cognition matching	Large blocks	Cognition lacing	Snack prep		Large blocks
10:00–10:10	Juice and snack	Coffee	Juice and snack	Coffee	Juice and snack	Coffee	Juice and snack	Coffee		Coffee
10:10–10:20	Art	Help with art	Music	Help with music	Art	Help with art	Music	Help with music		Help with art
10:20–10:30	Toileting	Lotto	Toileting	Sorting	Toileting	Bending animals	Toileting	Sorting		Tracing
10:30–10:45	Washing		Washing		Washing		Washing			
10:45–10:55	Cognition cutting and stacking	House	Cognition puzzles and operations	Store	Cognition cutting and stacking	House	Cognition puzzles and operations	Store		House
10:55–11:05	Self-help fasteners	Sand/water play	Body parts	Sand/water play	Self-help fasteners	Sand/water play	Body parts	Sand/water play		Peg board
11:05–11:15	Self-help fasteners	Sand/water play	Self-help	Sand/water play	Self-help fasteners	Sand/water play	Self-help	Sand/water play		Peg board
11:15–11:25	Guided play	Sit with group	Guided play	Sit with group	Guided play	Sit with group	Guided play	Sit with group		Sit with group
11:25–11:30	Dressing	Dressing	Dressing	Dressing		Dressing				

The Friday column spanning cell reads: Probes and Maintenance

DESCRIPTION OF CHILDREN

In the home program, 22 children between the ages of birth and 2½ years of age were involved in the early intervention. Table 4 lists their sex, birthdate, and residential location. An indication of the population's skills in walking, dressing, toileting, and speech patterns as of June, 1976 is also included in the table. All but three of the 22 children had Down's syndrome. Serious medical problems existed for 64% of the children. Most of the children were between 3 months and 1½ years of age when intervention was initiated (mean age—13.5 months). In addition, most of the children did not crawl or walk, used very little expressive language or receptive language, and lacked basic self-help skills such as dressing and toileting.

The descriptions of the eight children in the toddler classroom program (under age 3 at the project's initiation) are presented in Table 5. This table shows that several of the toddlers were walking, few had adequate language skills, few had basic self-help skills, and cognitive development was significantly delayed. All of the children in this group had Down's syndrome. Three of the children had serious medical complications.

DIRECT TEACHING RESULTS

In order to demonstrate the effectiveness of the direct teaching methods on children's language skills, a review of the data obtained from these language programs is presented.

Daily individual language sessions were conducted in both the home and school settings. The parent/teacher recorded trial-by-trial results during each session. Results were obtained on total trials to criterion, total errors to criterion, review, and maintenance.

The language programs were developed from the work of Guess, Sailor, and Baer (1976), Striefel (1974), and Bricker and Bricker (1970). Modifications to the imitation sequence followed from the work of Kent (1976) and Stremel-Campbell, Cantrell, and Halle (1976). The resulting sequence included both expressive and receptive language skills. Table 6 presents the terminal objectives and performance criteria for both receptive and expressive early-language sequences. Expressive and receptive language skills in Table 6 were assessed separately; the child began each sequence independently at the point indicated from initial assessment.

Expressive Language Programs

Beginning with the first program in the sequence (Attention), the child was assessed until he or she failed to reach criterion on a language

Table 4. Description of home program children

Sex	Date of birth	Residence	Day program	Medical problems (elaborate)	Ambulatory	Dressing skills	Toilet training	Speech
M	12/19/75	Home	EEP	Gastrointestinal	No	No	No	No
F	6/29/75	Institution	EEP	Heart	No	No	No	No
M	3/31/75	Home	EEP	Heart	Yes	No	No	No
F	12/31/74	Institution	EEP	Heart	No	No	No	No
M	8/9/74	Home	EEP	Heart	No	No	No	No
M	3/27/75	Home	EEP	Respiratory	No	No	No	No
F	3/6/77	Home	EEP	Heart disorders	No	No	No	No
M	1/22/75	Home	EEP	Respiratory	No	No	No	No
F	4/2/75	Home	EEP	Heart	No	No	No	No
F	4/29/75	Home (foster)	EEP	No*	No	No	No	No
M	6/2/74	Home	EEP	No*	No	No	No	No
M	1/13/75	Home	EEP	Heart	Yes	No	No	No
M	7/25/76	Home	EEP	No	No	No	No	No
F	3/20/76	Home	EEP	No	No	No	No	No
F	1/9/75	Home	EEP	Hypothyroid*	No	No	No	No
F	4/8/76	Home	EEP	Heart	No	No	No	No
F	6/13/75	Home	EEP	No	No	No	No	No
M	12/28/74	Institution	EEP	Congenital heart disorder	No	No	No	No
M	1/15/76	Home	EEP	No*	No	No	No	No
M	2/18/77	Home	EEP	Congenital heart disorder	No	No	No	No
M	1/21/76	Home	EEP	No	No	No	No	No
M	8/16/76	Home	EEP	No	No	No	No	No

* These children did not have Down's syndrome.

Table 5. Description of school program children

Sex	Date of birth	Residence	Day program	Medical problems (elaborate)	Ambulatory	Dressing skills	Toilet training	Speech
M	7/11/73	Institution	EEP	No	Yes	Some	Partial	Some
M	9/17/73	Home	EEP	No	Yes	Some	Partial	Some
M	10/5/73	Institution	EEP	Heart	Yes	Some	Partial	Some
F	11/23/73	Foster home	EEP	No	No	Some	Partial	Some
F	2/8/74	Home	EEP	Heart/Lung	Yes	Some	Partial	Some
M	2/9/74	Home	EEP	Heart disorder	No	Some	Partial	Some
M	3/25/74	Home	EEP	No	Yes	Some	Partial	Some
M	5/20/73	Home	EEP	No	Yes	Some	Yes	Some

Table 6. Language program sequence

	Expressive language		Receptive language
Attention	The child will look at teacher's (parent's) face within 5 seconds of the instruction "(Child's name), look" or "Look at me (child's name). Criterion: 3 consecutive correct.	Responds to name:	The child will indicate by a change in body movement, eye movement or motion that he or she recognizes his or her own name within 5 seconds of the parent (teacher) calling the child's name. Criterion: 3 consecutive correct.
Motor/action imitation	The child will imitate a motor action within 5 seconds of the instruction, "Do this," plus the model. Criterion: 3 consecutive correct.	One-concept instructions	The child will respond appropriately within 5 seconds of an instruction such as "Give" or "Bye bye." Criterion: 3 consecutive correct.
Sound imitation	The child will imitate sound within 5 seconds of the instruction, "Say (sound)." Criterion: 3 consecutive correct.	Object identification	The child will point to an object within 5 seconds of the instruction, "Show (object)" in the presence of 3 distractor items. Criterion: 80% or more correct in a session of 32 trials or 12 correct in a row.
Word imitation	The child will imitate a word within 5 seconds of the instruction, "Say (word)." Criterion: 3 consecutive correct.	Operations	The child will execute each of the operations (put in, put on, take off, take out, push, pull, open, close) within 5 seconds of the instruction. No distractor items are present. Criterion: 3 consecutive correct.
Labeling	The child will label an object within 5 seconds of the parent (teacher) holding up an object and asking "What's that?" Criterion: 80% or more correct in a session of 32 trials or 12 correct in a row. (Guess, Sailor, and Baer, 1976.)	Operations with distractors	The child will execute each of the operations above with 1 distractor present. Criterion: 3 consecutive correct.

objective. At this point the teaching program began. The direct instruction procedure was used to teach all expressive language programs up to Labeling. These programs prepared the children for entry into the functional speech and language program developed by Guess et al. (1976). (Labeling is the first step in this functional language program.)

For the first 8 months of the program, the language training sequence was taught as follows: 1) gross motor imitation (e.g., tap table, touch head) 2) fine motor imitation (e.g., stick out tongue, blow) 3) sound imitation (e.g., mm, oh) 4) word imitation (e.g., cat, boat). Teachers and parents used the five direct instructional levels described above to teach gross motor, fine motor, and sound imitation. Word imitation was taught using the direct instructional levels three through five. Children learned two items concurrently during language sessions. When a child reached criterion on an item, it was replaced by another item until the child reached criterion on four imitative responses. The child then progressed to the next program. The child entered the functional language program (Guess et al., 1976) at Step 1 after meeting criterion on the word imitation program.

Each time a child reached criterion on an imitative response, that response was reviewed once a day for 5 days. After review, the behavior was placed on maintenance check once a week for 5 weeks. Two untaught items were probed each day to monitor the spontaneous emergence of imitation if this occurred. (Labeling responses reaching criterion during a session were not placed on review or maintenance because the words reaching criterion in this step were used in subsequent steps of the program (Guess et al., 1976).)

After the first 8 months of teaching, the motor and sound imitation programs were changed. The results of current research in language intervention (e.g., Stremel-Campbell et al., 1976) and frustrations with motor imitation training prompted three conclusions. First, children should be started on sound and word imitation as soon as possible rather than spending an inordinate amount of time on motor imitation alone. Second, language training should be as functional as possible. If motor imitation is a necessary step in a language intervention program for a particular child, that child can be taught to imitate putting on a hat rather than being taught to imitate tapping a table; the first motor behavior being more useful to the child in the natural environment. Word imitation training was made more functional by holding up the appropriate object when the child was learning to imitate the name for the object (Carpenter, 1976). Third, recent research investigations (Stremel-Campbell et al., 1976; Bricker, 1972) suggested that manual sign language could facilitate acquisition of basic language functions as word imitation or word-object associations.

With the above three points in mind, a revised imitation training sequence was formulated. The new imitation training sequence was: 1) action/sound imitation, 2) sound/word imitation, 3) word imitation. Each program is described in detail below.

Action/Sound Imitation This program taught imitation of both sounds and functional actions, (e.g., turning a crank on a jack-in-the-box; putting a penny in a bank) in a randomly alternating sequence. Learned actions were replaced by new unlearned actions. When the child reached criterion on one sound, two randomly alternating sounds were then taught. At this point in training, action imitation training was discontinued. During action imitation, the child was given the object used on the trail for a brief period of play. This procedure allowed the parent (teacher) to incidentally teach a receptive language concept saying, "Give (object)" when she wanted the object back. The direct teaching procedures (Levels 1–5) taught the action and sound imitations. The child advanced to the next program in the sequence after criterion was reached on two sounds.

Sound/Word Imitation This component of the new imitation sequence consisted of teaching one sound and one word on randomly alternating trials. Sounds were replaced with new sounds as the child reached criterion. Sound imitation training was identical to the Action/Sound Imitation procedures. When criterion was reached for one word, sound imitation was discontinued and the child began training on two randomly alternating words. During word imitation training, the appropriate object was always present and was given to the child as an activity reinforcer if the word was correctly imitated or approximated. Approximations to words were initially accepted as correct. A shaping procedure was employed until the child could eventually articulate either a word with all phonemes present and in order or an acceptable approximation. An approximation to a word was considered correct only if it was consistently used in the presence of a particular model and could be distinguished from other approximations to words already in the child's repertoire (Whitehurst, 1977). The child advanced to the next program after reaching criterion on two words or approximations of two words.

Word Imitation This program was procedurally similar to the word imitation segment of the previous program. At the time of implementation of ɪne new sequence, an investigation of the differential effects of three methods of teaching word imitation was initiated (McDonald, 1977).

The three methods of imitation training were: 1) use of an imitation cue alone, for example, "Say (word)," 2) use of an imitation cue with physical and verbal prompts that were faded over training (Levels 3,

4, and 5 of the direct teaching procedures), 3) use of an imitation cue paired with the appropriate manual sign taken from *Talk to the Deaf* (Riekhoff, 1963). The results of this comparison indicated that imitation training was no more rapid with manual signs or prompts as additional cues. In accordance with the results of this study, further imitative word training was conducted with the appropriate object present but no additional cues. Words were taught in a randomly alternating sequence in pairs until the child reached criterion, on the imitation of 16 nouns. At this point the child moved into the first step of the functional language program (Guess et al., 1976). Objects used during Step 1 were the same 16 objects on which the child had reached criterion during word imitation.

Receptive Language Programs

Children in the home program received receptive language training on one or more programs before they received expressive language training. In the school program receptive training occurred along with the expressive language programs. The programs in this area included learning to respond to one's name, following one-concept instructions, object identification (Step 2 of Guess et al., 1976), operations, and operations with distractors (see Table 6 for a description of objectives and criteria).

For the four programs, respond to one's name, one concept instructions, operations, and operations with distractors, parents and teachers used the direct teaching method. The object identification program, essentially Step 2 of the Guess et al. (1976) program, was taught after the procedures of the Guess et al. program. In the home, however, this objective was split into several simple steps leading to the terminal objective. The five levels of prompting and guidance were employed for these preceding steps. In the school program, the object identification program was typically taught in a one-to-one teaching situation whereas the operations programs and one concept instruction programs were taught in small groups of three to five children.

TEACHING RESULTS

Home Program

Results of the children's performance were available for several dependent measures from both the home and school program. The home program childrens' progress through the six expressive language programs and the five receptive language programs is summarized in Table 7. There were 21 infants involved in the various teaching programs

Table 7. Language programs—home data

	Mean age of entry (months)	N	Behaviors	Trials to criterion	Standard deviation	Mean total errors	Mean days to criterion	Mean % correct on review
Expressive language								
Attention program	18.5	2	2	21.0	15.6	6.5	10.5	
Motor imitation	15.0	5	42	64.0	80.7	14.3	10.0	
Action imitation	15.2	10	23	85.8	70.0	25.6	13.3	
Sound imitation	15.2	10	25	64.5	51.8			
Word imitation	18.1	5	13	95.1	196.3	61.9	20.5	
Labeling								
Receptive language								
Responds to name	5.8	6	6	139.0	119.0	24.0	20.8	
One concept instruction	13.0	8	17	101.1	87.1	22.8	17.0	
Object identification	14.3	3	33	46.2	72.5	7.9	10.9	
Operations	12.2	12	46	114.8	110.0	22.2	13.5	92.9
Operations with distractors	14.2	4	15	48.8	46.0	9.3	9.5	86.8

with an average age of 13.5 months at the beginning of teaching (standard deviation of 7.9 months). There was a wide range in ages because of the older age of the initial children relative to the very young infants who began the program at later dates. These data reveal the extensive number of linguistic skills and concepts acquired at such young ages.

In the expressive language area, two children attained criterion on attention training very rapidly in 21 trials. The early motor imitation and action imitation programs required 10 teaching days each (64.0 and 85.8 trials to criterion, respectively). Reliable sound imitation was established for 10 children after only 13 days of training (64.5 mean trials to criterion). In each of these programs, the low mean error rates (6.5, 14.3, and 25.6, respectively) attest to the generally positive characteristics of the teaching process. Finally, word imitation was established for five children after 20.5 teaching days (95.1 mean trials to criterion). The high standard deviation (196.3) indicates the extensive range of performance for this skill. For these children the results indicate the ability to acquire imitative responding at a very early age.

With respect to receptive language skills, six children learned to respond to their own name in 20.8 teaching days, and eight children responded to one-concept instructions reliably after 17.0 days of instructions (101.1 mean trials to criterion). The low error rates (24.0 and 22.8 total errors to criterion) again demonstrate the positive nature of the teaching system. For object identification, three children learned this one-word receptive language skill in ten teaching days (46.2 mean trials to criterion) with 7.9 average errors to criterion. The more complex generalizable operations (motor actions such as "put in") that were verbally occasioned resulted in very rapid learning; without distractors, 12 children acquired the operations in 13.5 teaching days (114.8 mean trials to criterion) and four children went on to learn these operations with three distractor items in 9.5 days (48.8 mean trials to criterion). This savings on the operations with distractor programs suggested a positive transfer effect between these two programs although more research is required to verify this phenomenon.

These findings reflect the rapid rate at which the children acquired the skills, and that parents were very effective teaching agents in all of these programs. Parents not only taught their infants these skills and concepts, but they did so very rapidly and with relatively low error rates. Each week the home teacher probed in an attempt to attain the same level of response with the child as the parent recorded. These reliability checks ensured that the child exhibited these behaviors with a person other than a family member. A final point regarding the operations and operations with distractors program involved the review data (92.9% and 86.8% correct). These findings demonstrated that not only were the infants between 2 and 16 months of age able to acquire complex linguistic and cognitive concepts but that they also retained these concepts over several days and weeks of follow-up evaluation. These findings indicate the presence of capable long-term memory processes for these children.

School Program

School program data for the toddler's progress in the language area are summarized in Table 8. Of the eight children who were in the toddler classrooms, varying numbers proceeded through the programs because of individual differences in learning rates.

The expressive language programs were all taught in a one-to-one teaching situation in a separate area of the classroom to avoid distractions. The children's average age on entering the programs was 28.4 months (standard deviation of 4.8 months). The five children who required attention training achieved criterion in 6.8 teaching days (125.4 mean trials to criterion). This represented a very rapid rate of learning to attend to an adult. The early motor imitation sequence was taught to eight children for 52 specific motor acts in an average of 8.4 teaching days (50.6 mean trials to criterion); this rate is contrasted with the six children learning 29 functional motor actions in the latter program in 2.24 mean days (12.2 mean trials to criterion). This difference represents a significant savings effect for the revised actions program compared to the motor imitation sequence initially employed. In these cases the very low error rates for motor and action imitation was rather significant (5.4 and 0.6 mean total errors, respectively); this finding was possibly attributable to the effects of extensive prompting and guidance used in the direct teaching procedure.

The seven children who learned sound imitation attained criterion in 10.3 days (50.2 mean trials to criterion) and exhibited a high rate of retention with an average of 80.7% correct on review trials. For word imitation, eight children reliably imitated words in an average of 4.5 teaching days (31.9 mean trials to criterion). The trials to criterion for word imitation was lower than for sound imitation (31.9 versus 50.2, respectively) and the total errors to criterion was greater for words compared to sounds (22.7 versus 16.8, respectively). This difference possibly was attributable to the positive process of the direct teaching method used for sound imitation compared to the different instructional procedure used in word imitation, which did not employ prompts and guidance.

Regarding the labeling program (Step 1 of Guess et al., 1976), five children acquired a total of 24 words in an average of 2.9 teaching days

Table 8. Language programs—school data

Program	Mean age of entry (months)	Number of children	Mean baseline (%)	Number of behaviors	Mean trials to criterion	Mean total errors	Mean days to criterion	Mean % correction review
Expressive								
Attending	24.2	5	50	5	125.4	15.4	6.8	100
Motor imitation	26.4	8		52	50.6	5.4	8.4	93.9
Action imitation	26.3	6		29	12.2	.6	2.24	95.6
Sound imitation	25.6	7		15	50.2	15.8	10.3	80.7
Word imitation	26.4	8	0	73	31.9	22.7	4.5	90.1
Labeling	26.4	5	39	17*	81.5*		2.9*	
Receptive								
Object identification	26.5	2	61	4*	46.0*		1.3*	94.5
Operations	27.2	6	49	27	33.8	4.9	7.2	
Operations with distractors	29.0	2	40	4	19.5*	1.5	7.8	

* Date represents a word pair rather than a single word.

per word pair (81.5 mean trials to criterion). This rate seemed to be rather rapid for children in this young age range (26.4 months).

The receptive language programs were taught in small groups of three to five children except for the object identification program (Step 2, Guess et al., 1976), which was taught in a one-to-one situation in a separate area of the classroom. As Table 8 indicates, two children completed the object identification program in 1.3 average teaching days (46.0 mean trials to criterion per object pair). This step was acquired very rapidly possibly because most of the objects had been used in the labeling step of the Guess et al. (1976) program before this step. The six children attaining criterion on operations did so in 7.2 mean teaching days (33.8 mean trials to criterion) with a high degree of retention at an average of 94.5% correct items on review. With distractors, two children attained criterion in 7.8 mean teaching days (19.5 mean trials to criterion). An interesting comparison between the home and school groups on these two programs revealed the school group acquired these two skills (33.8 and 19.5 mean trials to criterion) more rapidly than the home group (114.8 and 48.4 mean trials to criterion), perhaps as a result of the age differences between the two groups. Both groups exhibited a substantial savings, however, when the distractor items were added. This suggests the influence of positive transfer from the operations program.

The review data, all above 80% for these programs, indicated the high degree of retention of these skills and concepts by the children. Overall, these results demonstrated the high rate of acquisition the children exhibited in mastering previously absent skills and concepts. The generally low error rates seem to be a result of the direct teaching method's use of extensive prompting and guidance. In both the home and school programs, children exhibiting moderate to severe degrees of mental retardation acquired complex language skills with a rapid rate of learning and very few errors. Thus, through the use of the structured teaching process new learning can be expeditiously arranged for severely handicapped learners at a very young age.

DESCRIPTION OF THE BEHAVIOR ANALYSIS SYSTEM (BAS)

The early intervention approach included parent training of teaching techniques in the home and staff training in assessment, teaching, and program writing for school personnel. Boone and Prescott (1972) and Butler (1974) developed self-monitoring analysis systems useful for videotape analysis of one-to-one language therapy. They stressed the importance of self-monitoring for clinicians during initial training and as a periodic feedback device for therapy analysis. The early intervention approach required a similar system to monitor and evaluate the parents' and teachers' use of the direct teaching model.

The BAS (Hillyard et al., 1976) was designed for this purpose. This system was used for the observation of teaching activities and for providing consistent feedback to the parents/teachers regarding their teaching skills.

Instrument and Procedure

The BAS is a behaviorally based observation system designed to monitor the interaction between the parent/teacher and child during direct teaching situations. It was developed to evaluate parent/teacher implementations of direct teaching programs in all developmental areas. Two observation modes monitor and analyze teaching interactions. In the first mode, the rater analyzed a teaching episode from a videotape of parent/teacher performance during direct teaching. The second mode included in situ observations of the direct teaching episode. Raters were trained for one week to use the rating system. The criterion for interrater reliability was 85% or greater agreement between two raters during training. This criterion was satisfied for all trained raters, suggesting that the device was relatively easy to use and yielded reliable interobserver agreement.

The observational unit for the BAS was an individual teaching trial. Structurally, the observational unit consisted of a teacher/child/ teacher or parent/child/parent behavior sequence. A trial began with an attending signal or an instruction and ended when the teacher/parent scored the trial. The behaviors of the parent/teacher and the child during this sequence were scored using the BAS categories. The three categories shown in Figure 3 were designated as parent/teacher antecedent conditions (categories a–f), student responses (categories g–h) and parent/teacher dispensed consequences (categories i–m). The behavior of the child while the parent/teacher was teaching or dispensing consequences was not scored. Similarly, the behavior of the parent/ teacher while the child was responding and any "between trial" behaviors were not scored.

The initial assumption was that close adherence to the direct teaching model would result in accelerated child behavior change. Feedback to the parent/teacher was always centered on increasing the procedural accuracy of the direct teaching method. The BAS became a method for assessing procedural reliability of parent/teacher adherence to the specific model of instruction.

There were a number of scoring and observational rules that described the teaching interaction between the parent/teacher and child. Scoring rules indicated how a parent/teacher deviated from the model.

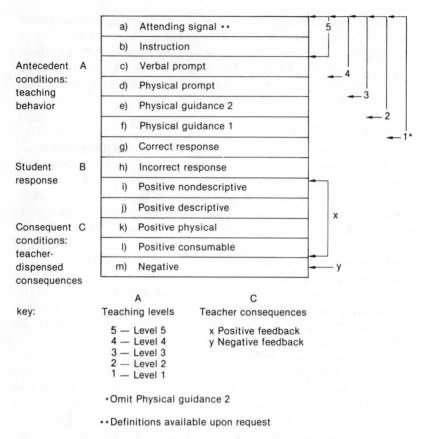

Figure 3.   The system of categories used in observation.

Within category A (antecedent teaching behaviors), errors made by parents/teachers included timing errors, omission errors, and inclusion errors. For example, the parent may have dropped out the verbal and physical prompts before employing guidance when teaching at Level 1.

In Category B (student responses) the child's correct or incorrect response to task instructions was monitored. A correct response was a student-initiated or parent/teacher assisted behavior that was compatible with the preceding instruction(s). Errors in this category included resistance by the child to parent/teacher "physical guidance" at Level 1. "No response" by the child was also scored as an incorrect response.

In Category C, (parent/teacher dispensed consequences) parent/teacher responses to incorrect or correct child responses were recorded. A correct response by parent/teacher to a correct child re-sponse was positive descriptive feedback. Omission and timing errors were scored in this category; this emphasized the importance of rein-forcing a child immediately after a correct response is given. For ex-ample, a timing delay could occur when dispensing consequences, both for correct and incorrect responses.

In the home program, videotaped segments analyzed with the BAS were used by the home teacher to provide feedback to the parent regarding correct and incorrect implementation of the teaching model and recording procedures. The following example illustrates how the BAS was used to evaluate and monitor parent teaching with one family. Figure 4 presents behavioral data of a child progressing through an operations program (put in) with mother as the primary teacher. Mother and child were videotaped once a week for 6 weeks. Each videotape segment consisted of a complete teaching session of approximately 10 minutes.

The first 3 weeks of teaching were analyzed with the BAS. The analysis of teaching during this period revealed considerable proce-dural errors. In the attending component, the mother was initiating 45% of the attending signals correctly. Her procedural errors consisted of inappropriate use of the hand signal to draw the child's attention to herself or task material and inappropriate use of the remedial procedure to facilitate the child's attending when not attending.

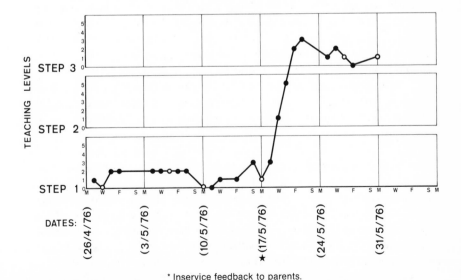

* Inservice feedback to parents.

Figure 4.   Behavioral data of a child progressing through an operations programs.

During antecedent instructions at teaching Levels 1 and 2, the mother was observed to be procedurally correct on 50% of all teaching trials. The major procedural error observed was no verbal or physical prompts. The parent was giving the initial instruction (put in) using guidance directly, without including additional verbal or physical prompts. The concern was that this could hinder the shift to the next teaching level. The child would therefore be exposed to mediators previously not seen. This can disrupt the rate of progress through the levels or inhibit movement from one level to another. Time errors were noticed when the parent was allowing too much time to elapse between components at Levels 1 and 2. The suggested presentation rate was not more than a 1-second delay between the components. On the basis of the BAS analysis an inservice that consisted of showing the parent on videotape the procedurally correct and incorrect aspects of her teaching procedure was provided.

Following the inservice during weeks 4–6 (shown in Figure 4), parent instruction for the attending was procedurally correct 55% of the time, and Levels 1 and 2 were procedurally correct 87% of the time. There was an increase during weeks 4–6 in the accuracy of parent instructional procedures and correct child responses.

The most noticeable and exciting change was in the child's performance on the "put in" program after the inservice. Before the inservice he was having difficulty moving beyond Level 2. After the inservice he quickly moved through Levels 3–5 and through two more steps in the program. One explanation for this was the increased use of verbal and physical prompts by the parent at Levels 1 and 2. These prompts were used at Level 3, and verbal prompts were used at Level 4. The prompts increased the rate of learning and the transition from Levels 1 and 2 to Levels 3, 4, and 5.

Additional research and observation of parent teaching for purposes of inservice feedback to the parents and general research in the area of paraprofessional training is currently being conducted.

School Program

The BAS in the school program monitored teacher performance using the three different instructional procedures for imitation training. Reliability measures (or, more accurately, proficiency measures) were taken by trained observers using a videotape system and the BAS. With the use of the video system, each of the teachers was scored on the accuracy with which procedures were carried out as specified in three teaching methods. The three methods of imitation training consisted of a model with the instruction (imitation alone), a model with the instruction and a sign from American Sign Language (imitation with sign) and the use of the three levels of prompting starting at Level 3 and moving to Level 5 (imitation plus prompts). Proficiency data taken on the independent measures using the BAS indicated that the teachers were procedurally correct in 96.5% of the observed trials for the imitation alone condition, in 86.5% of the observed trials for the imitation plus prompts condition and in 89.5% of the observed trials for imitation plus signs condition.

There was no noticeable difference in child imitative behavior resulting from these three different procedures. The BAS analysis suggested that each procedure was carried out at an acceptable level of procedural reliability.

The BAS was a very useful tool for initial training and monitoring procedural reliability for parent/teacher direct teaching. There are generally three things that can affect performance as he or she progresses through a program:

1. Accuracy of teacher implementation of the program
2. Difficulty of the program
3. Consequent conditions or reinforcing events

Often a child's difficulty with a program is reflected in a low rate of performance. The parent/teacher must decide where the problem is and remedy it. The BAS was very useful for deciding which changes needed to be made. These results indicated to the parents or teachers how accurately a program was being implemented. If the level of accuracy was below a set standard or criterion, then the lack of child change could be because of poor program implementation. If the procedure implementations were reliable and there was still no behavior change, the program content or task analysis may need revision.

NORMATIVE EVALUATION

A description of children's growth compared to typical child development was obtained through the use of normative standardized assessments. Tjossem (1976) stated that "the balanced use of research and evaluation is essential to the development of effective early intervention programs" (p. 25). The normative data presented in this chapter was an attempt to attain the balanced evaluation suggested using normal development as the benchmark for comparison.

Haring (1977) suggested that there are two types of evaluation. First, broad-based evaluations are designed to monitor children's overall progress in one or more areas of development. Second, fine-grained evaluations are designed for a more detailed analysis of children's behavior change in specific instructional programs. The fine-grained evaluation was presented in a section above on children's performance in the specific language programs. This section presents the broad-based evaluation for three test periods during the first 12 to 14 months of the Early Education Project.

Haring (1977) suggested that there are three requirements for a broad-based evaluation. First, it should be scheduled on a monthly, quarterly, or semi-annual basis and not require more than a few hours for any child. Second, instruments should allow for repeated assessments at several intervals. Third, the assessments should measure a child's full range of development during the entire length of the program. This type of assessment acts as a "levelling device" (Haring, 1977) to observe the overall effect of the program as well as the specific emphasis in curriculum content areas. Subsequent decisions can be made concerning program changes if a curriculum content area is lagging. The normative assessment of the children in the Early Education Project served two functions. First, it provided a general evaluation of program impact on development and second it allowed for an evaluation of specific curriculum emphasis.

Evaluation Format and Instruments

During the first 18 months of the project, a broad-based assessment was undertaken with each child enrolled. The instruments employed included the Bayley Scales of Infant Development (Bayley, 1969) the Stanford-Binet Intelligence Scale when appropriate (Terman and Merrill, 1960), and the Reynell Developmental Language Scales (Reynell, 1969). Each child was assessed up to three times over approximately 6- to 9-month intervals with either the Bayley Scales or the Stanford-Binet and the Reynell Language Scale. Data was thus available for two, three, and in a few cases four assessment periods, depending upon the child's date of entry into the project.

All assessments were conducted by trained psychologists or special education teachers specifically instructed and trained in the use of these instruments. Because the children between birth and 2½ years were in the home program, the assessors became familiar with them and their environment in order to create optimal conditions for testing. Baine (1977) suggested that unless care is taken to create an optimal testing environment, the results may not reflect a child's typical performance, but rather a reaction to the examiner or the assessment situation. Standardized procedures were closely followed with limited parental involvement except where such involvement was specified by the testing manual. The same precautions were taken for the children in the school program. These assessments required an average of 2 hours each and were conducted on a one-to-one basis in a separate testing room.

Results

The data obtained from these normative tests is presented for mental development first (the Bayley Scales-Mental Development and the Stanford-Binet Scales) and for expressive language and receptive verbal comprehension second (Reynell Language Scales). The results are reported for both the total group and for home and school-based programs separately. The data are reported in developmental ratios rather than intelligence quotients or language age quotients. This procedure was necessary because many children scored below the available norms for the instruments. This developmental ratio is similar to that employed by Brassell (1977) and was obtained by dividing the child's mental or language age corresponding to the number of items passed on the test by their chronological age at the time of assessment. A mental development ratio was obtained for each testing and consisted of a ratio of mental age (determined from the number of items passed on the Bayley Scales or the Stanford-Binet Scales) to chronological age at the time of testing. Similarly an expressive language ratio and a verbal comprehension ratio were obtained by dividing the equivalent by the expressive language age equivalent or the receptive-comprehension age equivalent by the child's chronological age at the time of assessment. When comparing the children across the testing periods, the ratio allowed for the numerical control of chronological age changes.

The data were analyzed for changes across the three testing periods employing a one-way analysis of variance procedure for repeated measures. A Newman-Keuls comparison of ordered means was employed to test for mean differences when a significant main effect was obtained with the analysis of variance. Many children entered the program after it began and, as a result, were only assessed twice over their first 6 to 8 months in the program. These children were combined with all children for a comparison between Test 1 and Test 2. A correlated t-test was computed to evaluate changes between the two test times. A Kruskal-Wallis Test was employed for post-hoc comparisons when the number of subjects was very small (H-test).

Mental Development

The normative mental development assessment was administered three times over a period of the first 12 to 14 months of the Early Education Project. The data yielded mental age equivalents based on the number of items on the test. Table 9 presents the means and standard deviations

Table 9.   Means and standard deviations for chronological age, mental age equivalents, and mental development ratios across three testing periods

	Test	CA	MA	Ratio
Home program	1	13.5	7.3	0.59
Means		(21)*		
	2	20.7	13.7	0.69
		(21)		
	3	26.0	16.8	0.67
		(10)		
Standard deviations	1	7.9	4.9	0.21
	2	7.5	4.8	0.16
	3	5.2	3.0	0.12
School program	1	28.4	11.9	0.46
Means		(8)		
	2	34.4	18.2	0.53
		(8)		
	3	38.8	21.5	0.55
		(8)		
Standard deviations	1	4.8	3.9	0.14
	2	4.3	5.0	0.12
	3	4.0	5.4	0.12

* Number of subjects in each cell.

for the data for both home- and school-based groups of children. The children who began the intervention at different times were only assessed twice, thereby resulting in fewer scores in Test 3 period. In Figure 5 is a graph of the mental age ratio scores for both home and school groups. The analysis of variance for the home program revealed a significant difference across test periods (F = 4.68, df = 2,18, pc.05). The test of ordered means indicated a significant difference between Test 1 and Test 2. The analysis for the school program yielded a marginally significant overall effect for test periods (F = 3.03; df = 2,14; p<.10) suggesting increased mental development.

The results suggested a significant increase in mental age ratios across the home subjects over the first six months of the program with a maintenance of this elevated level of performance 6–8 months later at the third test period. The home-based children exhibited more rapid gains in the early segment of the program and the school-based children only exhibited a trend in this direction. A post hoc comparison of ordered means (for the school program) revealed a significant difference between Test 1 and Test 3 (p<.05). This suggests a slightly delayed effect on accelerated mental development.

Language Development

The Reynell Developmental Language Scale yielded separate perform-ance measures of the children's expressive language skills and verbal comprehension (receptive) skills. The data are presented separately for these two.

Expressive Language   The expressive language section of the Rey-nell Language Scales described the child's use of productive language in a direct assessment context. Table 10 presents the means and stand-ard deviations for the expressive language age equivalents and the expressive language ratios. Graphs of these ratios are presented in Figure 6. The analysis of variance for the home program group indi-cated no significant differences between test periods. The analysis of variance across test periods for the school group yielded a significant main effect (F = 10.81; df = 2,12; p<.001). The Newman-Keuls comparisons indicated a significant difference between Test 1 and 2 and Tests 1 and 3, but Tests 2 and 3 did not differ significantly.

Although the home analysis revealed no significant differences across the test periods, the results from the school program indicated a significant linear trend in terms of increased expressive language ratios. The home-program children exhibited a significantly higher in-

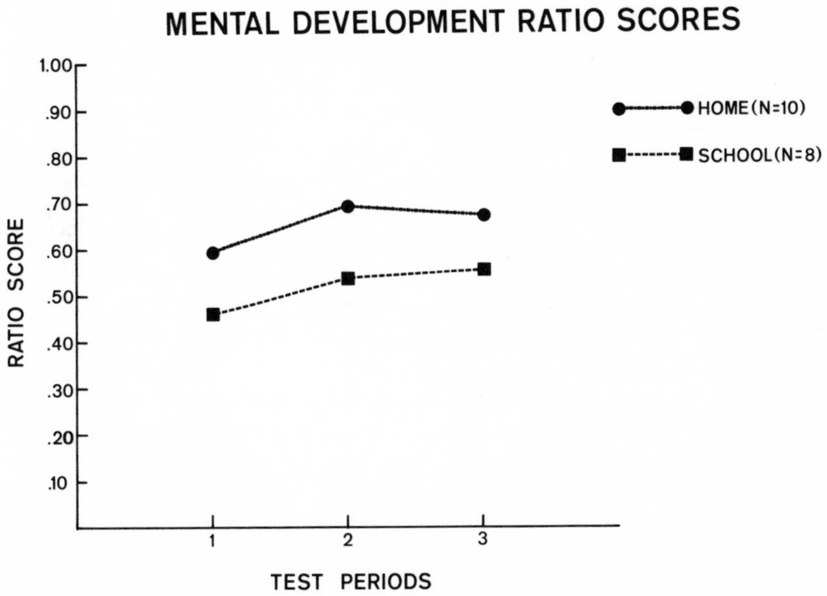

Figure 5.   Mental development ratio scores.

Table 10. Means and standard deviations for expressive language age equivalents and expressive ratios for home and school programs

	Test	EA	Ratio
Home program	1	7.5	0.59
Means		(15)	
	2	12.0	0.56
		(15)	
	3	15.4	0.58
		(10)	
Standard deviations	1	5.6	0.28
	2	6.4	0.22
	3	3.5	0.12
School program	1	7.7	0.26
Means		(7)	
	2	12.8	0.38
		(7)	
	3	18.4	0.47
		(7)	
Standard deviations	1	1.7	0.05
	2	4.1	0.10
	3	5.0	0.15

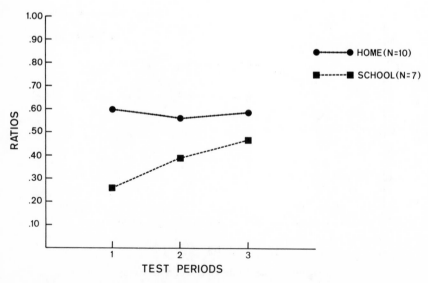

Figure 6. Expressive language age ratios.

itial expressive ratio, as assessed by a Kruskal-Wallis Test ($\bar{x}_H$ = 0.59, x_S = 0.26, H = 8.15; p<.01) when compared to the school program. This initially higher level was maintained during the course of the home program. The school program children did show a significant linear gain across the three test periods, however, the level of development did not reach a level similar to that of the home program children.

Verbal Comprehension   The second section of the Reynell Developmental Language Scale provided data regarding the children's verbal comprehension. The results for the home and school programs are presented in Table 11. The data are portrayed in graphs in Figure 7 for each program. Although the overall analysis for the home program children was not significant, a t-test between Test 1 and Test 2 yielded a significant effect (t = 2.124, df = 14, p<.05).

In the school program, the main effect for verbal comprehension ratios across testings was significant (F = 6.697; df = 2,12; p<.01). The Newman-Keuls comparisons yielded a significant difference between Test 1 and Test 2 as well as between Test 1 and Test 3. Tests 2 and 3 did not differ from each other.

The positive linear trend was found most significant between Test 1 and Test 2 for gains in verbal comprehension for both groups. Al-

Table 11.   Means and standard deviations for verbal comprehension age equivalents and comprehension age ratios for home and school program

	Test	Verbal comprehension	Ratios
Home program Means	1	6.1 (15)	0.44
	2	12.9 (15)	0.60
	3	15.9 (9)	0.62
Standard deviations	1	6.6	0.37
	2	6.7	0.17
	3	4.5	0.18
School program Means	1	8.4 (7)	0.30
	2	13.4 (7)	0.40
	3	19.9 (7)	0.49
Standard deviations	1	1.9	0.08
	2	6.4	0.16
	3	6.2	0.15

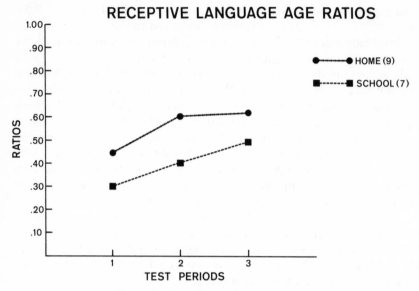

Figure 7.   Receptive language age ratios.

though the change between Test 2 and Test 3 was not significant, the increasing trend remained and the initial gains were maintained.

Summary of Normative Results

For the home program, the age equivalent ratio scores yielded significant increases across the three assessment periods for mental development. The data indicated the greatest gains between Test 1 and Test 2 during the first 7 months of the project with a maintenance of these gains over the next 7-month period. The school program also showed significant changes in expressive language development across the three testing periods.

The home program children, although not exhibiting a significant increase in expressive language ratios, maintained a high level of expressive ratios between Test 1 and Test 3. This initial level of expressive language for the home program children was significantly higher at Test 1 relative to the school children. The general implication of these results was a reversal of the expected cumulative deficit that would normally be exhibited by moderate/severely handicapped children. The accelerated rate of development exhibited for mental development and receptive language skills was contrary to the expected downward trend described by Cornwall and Birch (1969) for moderately handicapped persons.

Because only 10 of the infants had begun the action/sound and word imitation training and because the group exhibited a higher level of development initially in expressive language, it is not surprising that increases in expressive language were limited. Improvements in the early sequence of the expressive language curriculum were also explored in an attempt to accelerate the children's early development in this area.

A post hoc comparison of some significance is the performance of the home program group at Test 3 with the school program group at Test 1. At these times the children in both groups were approximately the same chronological age. The mental development ratio of the home program group was 0.67 compared to 0.46 for the school group ($H = 8.02$; df $= 1$, $p<.01$). The expressive language ratio for the home program group was 0.58 compared to 0.26 for the school group ($H = 12.10$; df $= 1$, $p<.01$). The verbal comprehension ratio for the home group was 0.62 and the school group was 0.30 ($H = 8.32$; df $= 1$; $p<.01$). These comparisons revealed the extensive gains and maintenance the home program children made when reaching the same chronological age as the school program children were before they began the project. That is, this post hoc comparison reveals the low level of growth the school program children exhibited prior to program entry as well as the high level of development attained by the children in the home program at the same chronological age level after 12–15 months in the program.

SUMMARY

A basis for program design and evaluation was presented incorporating characteristics of a generic instructional model useful for the presentation of comprehensive early intervention. The results of this project have yielded data regarding three characteristics of the early intervention. First, the effects of the direct teaching process upon children's ability to learn new skills and concepts indicated substantial gains in the areas of expressive and receptive language. In the home program, the children were acquiring basic imitation skills and receptive comprehension of instructions and operations. In the school program, besides rapid learning of vocal imitation, several children moved into expressive labeling and receptive object identification as well as responding to instructions and learning operations before age 3. The behavioral data demonstrated the rapid increases in skills and knowledge that were attained by moderately to severely handicapped children.

Second, by using the standardized normative assessments, the children's rate of achieving developmental milestones increased significantly during the first 6–8 months of the project and was maintained at this high rate of development during the subsequent 6–8 month period. This accelerated rate occurred in mental development and in both areas of language development for the school program and in mental development for the children in the home program. The increased rate of development occurred at a time when an accumulating deficit would typically be predicted for moderate/severely handicapped children. This trend of increasing rates of development reversed the expected cumulative deficits.

Third, the use of the Behavior Analysis System provided initial evaluation and ongoing monitoring of program implementation. This analysis system ensured the accurate implementation of the direct teaching method and the incidental teaching procedures. The reliability of program implementation was enhanced and the parents and teachers increased the level of accuracy and consistency of their teaching skills.

Limitations

Two limitations of the project should be mentioned. First, the project did not have a control group of children with which to compare the participating children's growth and development. Although extensive changes occurred in the rate of development in both groups, and seem to be due to early intervention and contrary to expected cumulative deficiencies, a true experimental demonstration of this fact was not possible without a control group.

Second, the children exhibited some degree of developmental delay from mild to severe, although most of the children in this program had Down's syndrome and also had other handicapping conditions. The inclusion of a more heterogeneous sample of children would have expanded the applicability of these findings to a broader range of developmentally delayed children. The generalization of this intervention approach to children with severe and profound handicapping conditions remains to be investigated.

ACKNOWLEDGMENTS

Our thanks are expressed to the children and parents in the Early Education Project and the staff of the Project and Mayfield Elementary School for their support and tireless efforts. In addition, we thank Maria Carey, Ph.D., Alberta Social Services and Community Health for her continuing support and Stephen T. Carey, Ph.D., for his valuable comments and critique of the original paper, and Irving Hastings, Alberta Education and Early Childhood Services.

REFERENCES

Anderson, D. R., Hodson, G. D., and Willard, J. G. 1976. Instructional Programming for the Handicapped Student. Charles C Thomas, Springfield, Ill.

Anderson, R. C. and Faust, G. W. 1973. Educational Psychology: The Science of Instruction and Learning. Dodd, Mead, and Co., Toronto.

Baine, D. 1977. Task analysis and vocational habilitation of the trainable mentally retarded. Conference proceedings of the WIRTC 1st National Research Conference on Mental Retardation, Edmonton.

Bandura, A. 1977. Social Learning Theory. Prentice-Hall, Englewood Cliffs, N.J.

Bayley, N. 1969. Bayley Scales of Infant Development. The Psychological Corporation, New York.

Becker, W. C., Engelmann, S. E., and Thomas, D. R. 1975. Teaching 1: Classroom mangagement. Science Research Associates, Palo Alto.

Bijou, S. W. 1976. Child Development: The Basic Stage of Early Childhood. Prentice Hall, Engelwood Cliffs, N.J.

Boone, D. R. and Prescott, T. E. 1972. Content and sequence analysis of speech and hearing therapy. J. Am. Speech Hear. Assoc. 14:50–62.

Brassell, W. R. 1977. Intervention with handicapped infants: Correlates of progress. Ment. Retard. 15:18–22.

Bricker, D. 1972. Imitative sign training as a facilitator of word-object association with low functioning children. Am. J. Ment. Defic. 77:509–516.

Bricker, W. A. and Bricker, D. D. 1970. A program of language training for the severely language handicapped child. Except. Child. 37:101–111.

Bricker, W. A. and Bricker, D. D. 1976. The infant, toddler, and pre-school research and intervention project. In T. D. Tjossem (Ed.), Intervention Strategies for High-risk Infants and Young Children, pp. 545–572, University Park Press, Baltimore.

Bronfenbrenner, U. 1974. A report on longitudinal evaluations of pre-school programs. Vol. 2 "Is early intervention effective?" DHEW Publication No. (OHD) 74–25, Washington, D.C.

Brooks, P. H. and Baumeister, A. A. 1977. A plea for consideration of ecological validity in the experimental psychology of mental retardation: A guest editorial. Am. J. Ment. Defic. 81:407–416.

Bruner, J. S. 1975. The ontogenesis of speech acts. J. Child Lang. 3:1–19.

Butler, K. W. 1974. Videotaped self-confrontation. Language, Speech, and Hearing Services in Schools. 5:162–170.

Carpenter, J. 1976. An experimental comparison of acquisition rates of motor imitation items with and without manipulable consequences in a group setting. Unpublished manuscript, Kansas Neurological Institute, Topeka, Kansas.

Cornwall, A. C. and Birch, H. G. 1969. Psychological and social development in home-reared children with Down's Syndrome. Am. J. Ment. Defic. 74:341.

Cowart, J., Carnine, D. W., and Becker, W. C. 1973. The effects of signals on attending, responding, and following in-direct instruction. Unpublished manuscript (mimeo). Eugene, Oregon: University of Oregon.

Dewey, J. 1900. Psychology and social practice. Psychol. Rev. 7:105–124.

Engelmann, S. 1969. Preventing Failure in the Primary Grades. Science Research Associates, Chicago.

Ferster, C. S., and Skinner, B. F. 1957. Schedules of Reinforcement. Appleton-Century-Crofts, New York.

Fisher, M. A., and Zeaman, D. 1973. An attention-retention theory of retardate discrimination learning. In N. R. Ellis (ed.), International Review of Research in Mental Retardation. Vol. 7, pp. 171–257, Academic Press, New York.

Fredericks, H. D., Riggs, C., Furey, T., Grove, D., Moore, W., McDonnel, J., Jordon, E., Hanson, W., Baldwin, V., and Wadlow, M. 1976. The Teaching Research Curriculum for Moderately and Severely Handicapped. Charles C Thomas, Springfield, Ill.

Glaser, R. 1976. Components of a psychology of instruction: Toward a science of design. Review of Educational Research. 46:1–24.

Guess, D., Sailor, W., and Baer, D. M. 1976. Functional speech and language training for the severely handicapped. Part 1. H. and H. Enterprises, Lawrence, Kansas.

Hanson, M. J. 1976. Evaluation of training procedures used in a parent implemented intervention program for Down's Syndrome infants. American Association for Education of Severely/Profoundly Handicapped Review. 1:36–52.

Haring, N. G. 1977. Assessment, Evaluation Management: An Introduction to a National Topical Conference on Appraisal of the Severely Handicapped. In N. Haring (ed.), Developing Effective Individual Education Programs for Severely Handicapped Children and Youth. 724, S., Roosevelt, Special Press, Columbus, Ohio.

Hart, B., and Risley, T. R. 1975. Incidental teaching of language in the preschool. J. Appl. Behav. Anal. 8:411–420.

Hart, B. and Rogers-Warren, A. G. 1978. A milieu approach to teaching language. In R. L. Schiefelbusch (ed.), Language Intervention Strategies. University Park Press, Baltimore.

Hillyard, A., Kysela, G. M., and Davis, T. 1976. The behavior analysis system. Unpublished manuscript, The University of Alberta.

Horner, R. D. 1971. Establishing use of crutches by a mentally retarded Spina Bifida child. J. Appl. Behav. Anal. 4:183–189.

Karnes, M. B., Teska, J. A., and Hodgins, A. S. 1970. The successful implementation of a highly specific pre-school instructional program by paraprofessional teachers. J. Special Educ. 4:69–80.

Kazden, H. E. and Erickson, L. M. 1975. Developing responsiveness to instructions in severely and profoundly retarded residents. J. Behav. Therapy Exper. Psychiatry. 6:17–21.

Kent, L. 1976. Language Acquisition Program for the Severely Retarded or Multiply Impaired. Research Press, Champaign, Ill.

Klaus, R. A. and Gray, S. W. 1968. The early training project for disadvantaged children: A report after five years. Monographs of the Society for Research in Child Development. 33: No. 4.

Kysela, G. M., Daly, K., Doxsey-Whitfield, M., Hillyard, A., McDonald, L., McDonald, S., and Taylor, J. 1979. The Early Education Project. In L. A. Hamerlynck (ed.), Behavioral Systems for the Developmentally Disabled: I. School and family environments, pp. 128–171, Bruner/Mazel, Inc., New York.

McDonald, L. 1977. A comparison of three methods of word imitation training with Down's Syndrome children under six years of age. Unpublished master's thesis, the University of Manitoba.

Martin, G., Murrell, M., Nicholson, C., and Tallman, B. 1975. Teaching Basic

Skills to the Severely and Profoundly Retarded. Vopic Press Ltd. Portage la Prairie Manitoba.

Martin, G. L. and Treffry, D. 1970. Treating self-destruction and developing self-care with a severely retarded girl: A case study. Psychological Aspects of Disability. 17:125–131.

O'Brien, F., Bugle, C., and Azrin, N. H. 1972. Training and maintaining a retarded child's proper eating. J. Appl. Behav. Anal. 5:67–72.

Premack D. 1965. Reinforcement theory. In M. R. Jones (ed.), Nebraska Symposium on Motivation. University of Nebraska Press, Lincoln.

Reese, H. W. 1972. Discrimination learning set in children. In L. N. Lipsitt and C. C. Spiker, (eds.), Advances in Child Development and Behavior, pp. 115–146, Academic Press, New York.

Reynell, J. 1969. Reynell Developmental Language Scales, Manual (experimental edition). Published by N.F.E.R. Publishing Co. Ltd., 2 Jenning's Building's, Thomas Avenue, Windsor, Berks, England.

Riekhoff, L. L. 1963. Talk to the deaf. Gospel Publishing House, Springfield, Mo.

Robinson, H. B. and Robinson, N. M. 1965. The Mentally Retarded Child: A Psychological Approach. McGraw-Hill, New York.

Schreibman, L. 1975. Effects of within-stimulus and extra-stimulus prompting on discrimination learning in artistic children. J. Appl. Behav. Anal. 8:91–112.

Shearer, D., Billingsley, J., Feshman, A., Hilliard, J., Johnson, F., and Shearer, M. 1972. The portage guide to early education (Experimental edition). The Portage Project. 412 East Slifer Street, Portage, Wisconsin, 53901.

Sidman, M. and L. T. Stoddard, 1966. Programming perception and learning for retarded children. In N. R. Ellis (ed.), International Review of Research in Mental Retardation. Vol. II. Academic Press, New York.

Siegel, M. A. and Rosenshine, B. 1973. Teacher behavior and student achievement in the Bereiter-Engelmann Follow-Through Program. (ERIC Document Reproduction No. Ed. 076 564). Paper presented at the Annual Meeting of the American Educational Research Association, New Orleans.

Skinner, B. F. 1953. Science and Human Behavior. Macmillan, New York.

Skinner, B. F. 1968. The Technology of Teaching. Appleton-Century-Crofts, New York.

Snelbecker, G. E. 1974. Learning Theory, Instructional Theory, and Psychoeducational Design. McGraw-Hill, New York.

Stokes, T. F., and Baer, D. M. 1977. An implicit technology of generalization. J. Appl. Behav. Anal. 10:349–368.

Stremel-Campbell, K., Cantrell, D., and Halle, J. 1976. Manual signing as a language system and a speech imitator for the non-verbal handicapped student. Education and Training of the Mentally Retarded Monograph.

Striefel, S. 1974. Teaching a Child to Imitate. H. and H. Enterprises. Lawrence, Kansas.

Sulzer-Azaroff, B. and Mayer, G. R. 1977. Applying Behavior Analysis Procedures with Children and Youth. Holt, Rinehart & Winston, Toronto.

Terman, L. M., and Merrill, M. A. 1960. Standford-Binet Intelligence Scale. Houghton-Mifflin, Boston.

Tjossem, T. D. (ed.) 1976. Intervention Strategies for High-risk Infants and Young Children. University Park Press, Baltimore.

Whitehurst, G. 1977. Comprehension, selective imitation, and the CIP hypothesis. Am. J. Speech Hear. 1:23–37.

Winer, B. J. 1962. Statistical Principles in Experimental Design. McGraw-Hill, New York.

Zeaman, D. and House, B. J. 1963. The role of attention in retardate discrimination learning. *In* N. R. Ellis (ed.), Handbook of Mental Deficiency. McGraw-Hill, New York.

chapter 12

Decision Making in Early Augmentative Communication System Use

Howard C. Shane

The Children's Hospital Medical Center
Developmental Evaluation Clinic
Hearing and Speech Division
Boston, Massachusetts

contents

This chapter discusses the assessment aspect of augmentative communication with a focus on early intervention. Early augmentative communication intervention for hearing, severely speech-impaired children is a relatively new concept. Inclusion of this concept in the overall early intervention schema reflects the growing interest in communication methods for persons with limited potential for intelligible speech. This interest is forcing a reconsideration of the traditional concepts concerning communication disorders and the acceptability of using augmentative communication systems.

Several factors have helped change public and professional attitudes. Biomedical engineering advances and improved software have brought technology to the nonspeaking population and improved communication potential. Perhaps the most important influence has been an ideological shift prompted by exposés such as *Christmas in Purgatory* (Blatt and Kaplan, 1966), reinforced by works such as *Normalization* (Wolfensberger, 1972) and continued through the efforts of parents of the handicapped. These efforts have in turn led to federal legislation making public education a right for all persons regardless of handicapping condition. Consequently, there has been a movement toward deinstitutionalization.

Professionals who once worked exclusively with persons with less severe handicaps are now required to integrate more significantly handicapped children into their programs and facilities. For many of these severely handicapped youngsters, speech is not and may never be the optimal means of communication. To offset the inappropriateness, ineffectiveness, or slow progress of traditional speech therapy and yet enhance the nonspeaker's communication, the use of augmentative communication systems is increasing with the anticipated benefit of better assessment and intervention technology. To date that technology has been applied, for the most part, to older nonspeaking persons (Kapisovsky, 1978; Silverman, McNaughton, and Kates, 1978) and even then as a last resort.

The availability of high-risk registers and medical and paramedical specialists, who are more informed about developmental issues, is leading to earlier identification of handicapped persons in general and communication disorders in particular. It is expected that more improved differential assessment will follow when those communicatively disordered children can be further screened in order to predict: 1) those who will not become oral communicators, 2) those whose oral communication will improve following augmentative communication usage, and 3) those whose communication through speech and/or augmen-

This paper was supported through Project 928 from Maternal and Child Health Services, U.S. Department of Health and Human Services.

tative means will depend upon the audience, the context, and/or the nature of the information.

POPULATION AND DEFINITIONS

This chapter focuses on children whose ability to express themselves through speech is severely limited either temporarily or permanently. Furthermore, the reason for their inability to speak is not because of hearing impairment. Some of the terms used to describe the "non-speaking" individual include non-oral, nonverbal, aphonic, and non-vocal. Although persons with acquired conditions are often nonspeaking, this chapter concentrates on communication disorders that are congenitally based.

An augmentative communication system is a system or device that enhances a nonspeaking person's current communicative abilities. Although a device may serve as a substitute or alternative for speech processes, it augments communication transmitted through some other mode like affect or gestures (Vanderheiden and Harris-Vanderheiden, 1976). There are two generic terms used to describe augmentative communication systems; *communication prosthesis* describes those aids and systems that are not a natural part of the communicator's body. Examples of such prostheses include electronic or nonelectronic communication boards. Both the augmentative display (i.e., hardware) and the augmentative content (i.e., software) are part of the communication prosthesis. (See Figure 1.) The second term is *manual systems*. This refers to communication that is expressed through upper extremity movement. Included in this category are gestures (pointing, mime, and pantomime), sign language (including American Sign Language and other pedagogical systems), and fingerspelling. Further discussion on both forms of augmentative systems is included on page 394.

Augmentative systems are often designed to transmit information that typically is expressed through oral speech. Because clinical investigations and experience have provided frequent reports of increased speech following the implementation of an augmentative system (Skelly et al., 1974; Skelly et al., 1975; Rosenbek, Collins, and Wertz, 1976; Reich, 1978; Kates and McNaughton, 1974; Schaeffer et al., 1977; Oxman, Webster, and Konstantareas, 1978; Duncan and Silverman, 1978), professionals can now, with some confidence, consider such procedures as facilitators of oral speech, but there are still unanswered questions in this area. Augmentative systems also enhance speech intelligibility (Beukelman and Yorkston, 1977), and can help organize language through its explicit visual content (McDonald and Schultz, 1973; Davis, 1973; Fitzgerald, 1954; Chapman and Miller, 1979).

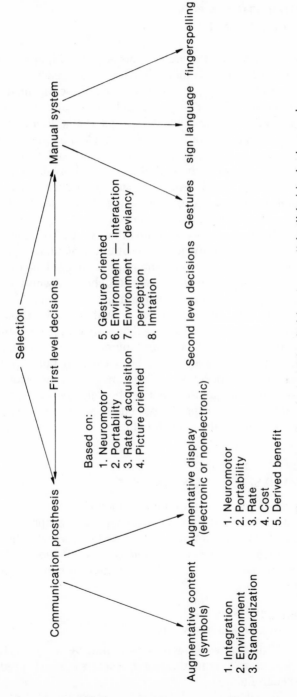

Figure 1. Flow diagram of selection decisions (assume "elect" decision has been made.

EARLY IDENTIFICATION: A FIRST
STEP TOWARD EARLY INTERVENTION

The literature suggests that the greatest proportion of individuals successful with augmentative methods fall into four disability groups.
These include cerebral palsy or, more specifically, congenital dysarthria (Shane, 1980; Vickers, 1974; McDonald and Schultz, 1973; Hagan,
Porter, and Brink, 1973); apraxia of speech (adult literature only)
(Skelly et al., 1974; Skelly et al., 1975; Rosenbek et al., 1976); mental
retardation (Fristoe and Lloyd, in press; Shaffer and Goehl, 1974;
Bricker, 1972); and autism (Schaeffer et al., 1977; Fulwiler and Fouts,
1976; Miller and Miller, 1973). Also, clinical experience suggests that
extreme structural anomalies also underlie oral speech failure whereby
augmentative systems generally prove beneficial.

Early identification of the conditions that most often lead to augmentative system consideration leads to better augmentative programming. In this light, early detection could improve overall augmentative
communication system management. Not all children who are dysarthric, apraxic, mentally retarded, autistic or have gross anomaly of the
oral structure, however, are incapable, or will never be capable, of
producing intelligible speech suggesting that early detection of the condition alone is not sufficient to warrant augmentative communication
programming. Thus, detection should be a concern but it is not so
definitive as to rule out speech as a viable mode of expression. What
is needed, therefore, are factors that go beyond the existence of a
particular condition and are predictive either singly or in some yet
unknown combination of oral speech failure.

CRITERIA FOR DETERMINING
CANDIDATES AND SELECTING SYSTEMS

Decision-making involves determining who needs an augmentative
communication system and then deciding on the appropriate system
for that individual. This section presents those factors that indicate the
need for an augmentative communication system (election) and those
factors influencing the choice of an augmentative communication system (selection).

Factors Indicating the Need for an
Augmentative Communication System

The presence of the following factors may indicate the need for the
use of an augmentative system. Many of the factors are early predictors
of later oral speech failure.

Presence of "High-Risk Condition"   It was suggested earlier that greater use of augmentative communication systems occurs with particular disability groups. The high-risk conditions are: mental retardation, autism, congenital dysarthria, and apraxia of speech. Knowing a high-risk disability exists should itself be a factor that influences the overall decision-making process. Because 100% of the persons within each high-risk group will not necessarily remain nonspeakers, other criteria need to be examined.

Oral Reflex Factors   A strong predictor of oral speech failure is the persistence of obligatory oral reflexes. All humans are born with many protective and life sustaining reflex patterns that over time change and become nonobligatory. When these reflexes extend beyond the normal period of elicitation, concerns regarding the integrity of the child's nervous system arise. The reflexes and corresponding periods of integration are listed in Table 1.

Ingram (1962) stressed that the primitive oral reflexes should not be viewed independently but rather as a complex, reflexively evoked pattern of movement necessary for early feeding. If spontaneous feeding is to occur, an integration of the reflexes beginning with the rooting response and ending with a swallow needs to take place.

Caution must be exercised in both interpretation and elicitation of the reflexes. In examining for reflexes it is necessary to realize that:

1. Elicitation in the same child is variable and is affected by body position, state, method, and time of elicitation.
2. The "normal" period of expression is variable (Mysak, 1963; Ingram, 1962).
3. A gag reflex exists throughout life. In the context of primitive reflex pattern a *hyperactive*, or overactive, gag reflex should be differentiated from the expected or normal gag response.

The presence of primitive and obligatory primitive oral reflex patterns is highly predictive of oral speech failure (Shane and Bashir, 1980; Morris, personal communication). Abnormal retention of prim-

Table 1.   Primitive oral reflexes and normal period of elicitation[a]

Reflex	Time of normal elicitation
Rooting	Birth to 3 months
Suckle/swallow	Birth to 7 months
Bite	Birth to 9 months
Gag (hyperactive)	Birth to 7 months

[a] Data from Radtka (1978), Mysak (1963), and Ingram (1962).

itive oral reflex patterns is considered by Mysak (1963) to directly
interfere with articulatory behavior of children having congenital dysarthria. Mysak stated:

> When attempted articulatory movements also elicit infantile reflexes
> which, for example, cause involuntary jaw deviation, lip movement,
> mouth opening, and tongue protrusion, it may be appreciated how these
> extraneous movements may make adequate articulation more difficult
> (p. 253).

Shane and Bashir (1980) reported that the persistence of primitive
oral reflex patterns are sufficient reason for imposing an augmentative
communication system. This belief stems from clinical experience that
has shown that when primitive oral reflexes are persistent and obligatory, children do not emit sufficient intelligible speech to enable effective communication.

Primitive oral reflexes are a powerful election factor. This factor
is unique because its presence in isolation seems sufficient to lead to
an augmentative communication implementation recommendation. No
other election criteria has such a strong singular influence on decision
making.

Laryngeal Blocking   Another predictor of oral speech failure is the
cessation of voice during vocal efforts, which is known as a laryngeal
block (Palmer, 1949). Morris (1978) stated that in her clinical experience with childhood neuromuscular disorders, the presence of a laryngeal block during voice production attempts seems to be predictive
of failure to develop oral speech. The laryngeal block mentioned by
Morris is synonymous with the "adductor spasm" reported by
McDonald and Chance (1964), and it often characterizes the laryngeal
involvement in children with cerebral palsy. Those authors reported
that the vocal cords are held together (or adducted) with such force
that the child cannot initiate voice production. In some cases laryngeal
adduction spasms occur during sound production, and consequently,
an abrupt termination of voicing occurs. Most likely the onset of laryngeal blocking or spasms does not begin until laryngeal functioning
is integrated into volitional speech production behaviors. This factor
requires further analysis because its predictive value at this point is
based exclusively on clinical observation.

Eating Problems   The presence of, or a history of, early problems
with eating (sucking, swallowing, chewing, or coordination of these
functions) can be an early predictor of later oral speech difficulty or
even failure. Jones (1975), for example, retrospectively studied a group
of children who at an early age had feeding problems. The children
had a mean age of 8 years, and all had speech difficulties. She concluded
that the early food management problems were related to the speech

difficulties existing currently. Ingram (1962) stated that abnormalities in "spontaneous feeding" have the greatest prognostic and diagnostic significance regarding the neurological status of the infant. Mueller (1975) considered "a good feeding pattern essential for future speech" (p. 113).

Eating problems are predictive of oral speech failure because they suggest the presence of neuromotor involvement of the oral structures. Furthermore, in cases where neuromotor involvement is uncertain (particularly in hard-to-test or younger infants), eating behavior, past and present, are suggestive of neuromotor compromise.

Morris (1978) specified that a comprehensive feeding assessment requires a description of sucking, swallowing, and chewing as well as the coordination of these behaviors. Each of these needs to be viewed in terms of normal feeding development in order to determine delayed development as well as deviant or pathological feeding patterns. These patterns are:

Jaw thrusting
Tongue thrusting
Tonic bite reflex
Lip retraction
Tongue retraction
Nasal pharyngeal reflex

Whereas failure to acquire speech milestones often serves as a "red flag" regarding the disturbed status or function of the speech mechanism, eating behavior predates that information. In evaluating nonspeaking infants, the eating behavior can be viewed as a "window" allowing observation of the speech mechanism.

Confirmatory Motor Information   In young or hard-to-test infants the presence of a neuromotor speech disorder (which may preclude adequate speech development) can be difficult to specify. Confirmed neuromotor involvement can help explain speech production deficits and might warrant election of an augmentative communication system.

Feeding history, laryngeal blocks, and oral reflex behavior can be considered confirmatory information factors as can the presence of cerebral palsy or apraxia, vocal production consisting mainly of vowel sounds, undifferentiated or lack of speech sounds, and excessive drooling.

Chronological Age   Some researchers feel that chronological age (CA) influences decision making by serving as a standard with which to compare other factors such as comprehension, production, or cognitive development (Chapman and Miller, 1980). In this light, age tends to affect the relative importance or weight of other factors at different points in time. Silverman et al. (1978) further contend that overall developmental level is more predictive of success (with regard to Blissymbols) than CA alone.

A consideration of the above factors can provide some insight for determining when is the most appropriate or earliest time to formally introduce an augmentative communication system. When oral reflex behavior is used as a criterion, primitive reflex patterns are judged pathological only after they do not disappear within expected time frames. According to Table 1, one needs to wait at least until age 9 months, but a more conservative clinician might wish to extend the normal range to at least age 1. When cognitive criteria are used, 1 year of age also approximates the beginning of Piaget's sensorimotor Stage 5 ability (12–18 months). Age 1 may be an appropriate time to encourage use of gestures or to begin receptive and expressive sign training, but it probably is not an appropriate age for using a communication prosthesis even one made of the most iconic materials. This is more appropriate toward the end of Stage 5 or closer to 18 months of age.

According to Silverman et al. (1978), the youngest child studied, who had formally been introduced to a communication prosthesis containing Blissymbols, was age 2. This writer has introduced a communication prosthesis to children as young as 18 months old, using black and white photographs as the augmentative content. Before 18 months mental age (MA) some success in training pointing (as a request function) to pictorial information has been observed using actual food packages that are commercially available. A frequent answer to questioning of informed caregivers about response patterns in the presence of these three-dimensional containers is a report of awareness (as reflected through behavioral responses). Those containers, in their three-dimensional format, can be attached to a "snack board" having two or three choice selections. The child selects the item (through eye gaze, hand pointing, finger pointing) in order to receive its tangible reward. Gradually the carton is reduced to two dimensions and programming is continued. At this time photographs can usually be used on the board also.

If an augmentative system cannot be introduced formally, one can suspect that its use will be appropriate eventually and can consider developing early prerequisites specific for augmentative system use. Morris (1975) suggested that prerequisite behavior for use of a communication board can begin as early as 5 to 6 months. At an early age the infant can be positioned and guided to reach, point to, or look at objects that are named. As the child develops both motorically and cognitively, the opportunity to select objects through pointing or gaze response can be introduced. Reichle and Yoder (1979) reviewed additional prerequisite communication skills including attending, localizing, eye gazing, and tracking.

The possibility of employing a manual communication system for the hearing nonspeaking child raises a clinically interesting but perhaps unfeasible approach to intervention. It has been reported that for children raised in environments where signing is a natural language, sign acquisition is at least comparable to speech acquisition and, in fact, the process of sign learning may be advanced (Schlesinger and Meadow, 1972; McIntire, 1977). For many hearing impaired youngsters, manual signing is introduced at or near the time the sensory defect is detected with the possibility of providing an effective communication system, allowing symbolic interaction to take place and presumably to maintain normal parent-child interaction (Schlesinger and Meadow, 1972).

The question that arises is can the intervention logic used with hearing impaired youngsters be applied to hearing, nonspeaking children. That is, assuming early detection of the nonspeaking child who had necessary motor skills for signing and persons in the environment agreed to sign, what would be the influence on communication development? The effect of such an intervention remains unstudied.

Numerous problems are inherent to the above suggestion. First, early detection of the condition indicating the probability of limited speech potential is becoming more possible. Determining the predictive factors, however, remains an elusive clinical skill. At this time researchers cannot predict future nonspeakers. The only possibility for this clinical fantasy to be actualized is by introducing early signing to a group of children at risk for oral speech failure with the hopes that those who will become nonspeaking will benefit maximally from the augmentative system at a time considerably earlier than typical intervention time. The adverse effect of introducing an augmentative system to the eventual "talkers" within that group is an unstudied issue.

Chronological age bears additional consideration when discussing an augmentative approach to communication with the family of a potentially nonspeaking child. Although we are becoming increasingly aware of factors predictive of speech failure, such predictions cannot be made with total accuracy. Consequently, statements that set the stage for speech failure by providing families with a "self-fulfilling prophecy" should be avoided.

Cognitive Factors   A critical dimension in candidacy determination (and system selection) is level of cognitive development. Its influence is pervasive because it can have the effect of delaying implementation until prerequisite cognitive levels have been achieved. Several researchers have touched either directly or indirectly on the cognitive prerequisites to augmentative communication system use. Chapman and Miller (1980) related cognitive development to the area of augmentative communication. They contend that Stage 5 sensorimotor intelligence must be attained before an augmentative communication system can be implemented with success. For the Stage 5 child, comprehension and production are tied to items within the immediate situation.

Cognitive requisites to communicative behavior also were examined by Reichle and Yoder (1979). They observed that Stage 5 means-end behavior was necessary for their severely and profoundly retarded subjects to demonstrate intentional communication. Kahn (1975) studied 16 severely and profoundly retarded children between 4 and 8 years old. Half of the subjects had expressive language (defined as ten or more true words and the ability to request) and the control half did not. His results indicated that the subjects using language were functioning at Stage VI (according to the Uzgiris and Hunt, 1975 series) in two of the four areas tested. Seven subjects had Stage VI achievement in all areas investigated.

Curcio (1978) studied sensorimotor intelligence in a group of 12 mute autistic children. This study revealed that differences in performance across means, causality, object permanence, and imitation occurred with object permanence consistently the highest achievement and imitation consistently the lowest. When sensorimotor performance was related to a measure of nonverbal communication, a minimum of Stage 5 achievement in means-ends and causality and Stage 3 imitation tended to be minimal prerequisites for intentional communication.

The cognitive factor also includes the child's ability to perceive pictographic information as representing real objects, events, or persons. According to Smith (1972), picture-pointing tasks are not appropriate until the child is at an 18 month developmental level. This finding is slightly more than a month in advance of the Bayley Scales of Infant Development (Bayley, 1969), where representation of objects through pictures is considered a 19.3 month level skill. Shane (1980) discussed the necessity of and methods for assessing a child's ability to perceive pictorial information in an augmentative communication evaluation. A hierarchy of representational material is offered, based on developmental literature, which extends from models of objects or miniatures at the lower end to more abstract line drawings at the upper end. Photographs and pictures fall between.

In summary, the cognitive factor has a powerful influence on election because this factor can delay implementation when requisite abilities have not been met. Available literature, having a Piagetian orientation, suggests that sensorimotor Stage 5 is necessary to show communication behavior with objects in the immediate present. At Stage 6 the referential context is apparently not as important an issue. How the pictographic information contained on a communication board affects the need for the referent to be available deserves further consideration. In addition, a child's ability to deal with pictorial information, at least at a photograph level, underlies communication prosthesis usage. Presumably, a MA of approximately 18 months is required for this ability. In the event that these prerequisite abilities are not met, the child is not considered a candidate (at that time) for an augmentative communication system. Intervention directed at increasing cognitive ability is suggested.

Comprehension—Production Discrepancy   The child's understanding of language and use of the language system influence both the decision and the type of system to be employed. Here, concern is with the documentation of the child's understanding of the grammar and the state of the child's grammatical production rules. Because of the all too frequent disruption in phonological skills, data pertinent to language production skills cannot always be obtained. Research in the area of augmentative methods for assessing production knowledge is needed. Researchers are often limited by making assumptions about production skills on the basis of comprehension alone. An election criterion applied often to older nonspeaking persons is a discrepancy between comprehension and production. For the purposes of early intervention, however, one should consider intervention before the gap between these functions becomes so large that production is significantly below comprehension. Frustration frequently accompanies this discrepancy. The importance of investigating a production comprehension discrepancy was described by Chapman and Miller (1980).

As noted above, not all children termed *high risk* for an augmentative communication system (i.e., mentally retarded, autistic, dysarthric, apraxic) will be nonspeakers. This suggests that criteria is needed to help with effective decision making within the high risk groups. A careful monitoring of comprehension and production can be one such criterion. Frequent and systematic evaluation of production and comprehension skill levels may reveal continuous widening of the gap, thereby providing evidence to elect an augmentative system.

Imitation   Response to oral therapy is an important aspect of deciding who needs an augmentative communication system. One factor thought to be predictive of improvement in oral speech is a child's ability to imitate. In a program for minimally verbal and echolalic children, Lovaas (1967) found that speech training was ineffective when no vocal imitation skills were present at the beginning of training. Guess, Sailor, and Baer (1978) stated that verbal imitation is the most consistent predictor of success in their functional language program. Vocal imitation training using functional stimuli is a consistent theme throughout this program. It follows that poor vocal imitation skill should be examined carefully in determining candidacy for an augmentative communication system. An initial inability to imitate vocally, however, cannot be the sole criterion for measuring or predicting oral therapy success. For example, Guess et al. (1978) reported that 60% of their children learned to imitate but this required 2 years of training.

Several behavioral researchers contend that before initiating vocal imitation training, motor imitation should be brought under control (Kent, 1974; Baer, Peterson, and Sherman, 1967; Sloane, Johnston, and Harris, 1968). Gross motor imitation is considered less difficult to teach than vocal imitation because gross movements technically require topographically less complicated motor skills and a trainer can physically direct a correct response. Thus, a child who is nonimitative vocally or motorically is less likely to be successful in vocal instruction because, presumably, a person needs to be capable of gross motor imitation before moving on to more complex vocal imitation. Thus, motor imitation ability is examined more as a prediction of ability to teach vocal imitation which in turn is viewed as a predictor in deciding between speech and nonspeech communication intervention.

Previous Intervention A knowledge of previous intervention is important for both the election and selection processes. The occurrence of previous therapy, the nature of that intervention, and the individual's response (and perhaps the rate of response) to that therapy must all be considered. If no previous therapy was tried, then one could decide to delay introduction of an augmentative communication system until an approach has been tried. This seems to be the case with many emotionally based communication handicaps such as elective mutism where oral therapies have been implemented successfully. Furthermore, an individual who currently is capable of speaking, but is nonspeaking for psychogenic reasons, may be provided with an augmentative system. This decision may lead to dependence on the alternative system and in fact not act as a facilitator of speech.

A decision to delay augmentative system implementation may result when previous therapy was inappropriate. In this situation, one may wait for the results of a more optimal intervention. Implicit is the need for the evaluation to judge the adequacy of a myriad of therapy regimes having both a speech and nonspeech orientation.

At times therapy may have been appropriate, growth may have resulted, but the change may not have been sufficient to enable effective communication. For example, children with significant feeding problems who have a neuromuscular basis will experience "prespeech" intervention aimed at decreasing oral-sensory dysfunction, inhibiting pathological oral reflex patterns, and improving oral muscle strength, movement, and tone. Improvement in the use of oral structures for vegetative or eating purposes will frequently result in improvement in the quality, frequency, and type of vocalizations. These positive changes, however, may not be sufficient to enable effective communication through speech. In this case, therapy, although appropriate, does not allow for adequate speech and may suggest an augmentative communication approach in conjunction with prespeech intervention.

Finally, knowledge of previous attempts with an augmentative communication approach might have some bearing on the election process because no improvement may signal a lack of cognitive readiness or motivation for any system or it could be related to teaching methodology, initial system selection, or other factors.

Historical data on the use and effectiveness of augmentative communication systems also influences the selection process. Ineffective augmentative communication attempts can indicate that the system itself, the level of its implementation, or the level of implementation within the system was inappropriate. Thus, a selection issue that might suggest switching between or across systems might be indicated.

In summary, those therapies aimed at oral habilitation should be evaluated for appropriateness and overall effect on the child's communicative growth. Failure in speech therapy, when that therapy is appropriate, is a strong indication that an augmentative communication system might be tried. An investigation of communicative effectiveness of ongoing augmentative communication programming also should be considered. Failure with an augmentative system or slow rate of responding has influence on the selection process.

The Environment Significant persons, including caregivers and other professionals in the child's life, need to be consulted when considering an augmentative communication system. These persons are an election factor because their cooperation determines the success of the augmentative program regardless of the appropriateness of the system. In other words, the best of plans will be to no avail if parents 1) will not allow the program to be carried out and/or 2) will not carry it out themselves. Often, parents seem reluctant to allow augmentative communication programming for two related reasons: 1) they con-

LEVEL I   COGNITIVE FACTORS
At least Stage V sensorimotor intelligence?
At least 18 months mental age; or ability to
recognize at least at photograph level?
YES ──► Go to II
NO ──► Delay

LEVEL II   ORAL REFLEX FACTORS
Persistent (1) Rooting (2) Gag; (3) Bite; (4) Suckle Swallow;
or (5) Jaw Extension Reflex?
YES ──► ELECT   Go to X
NO ──► Continue to III

LEVEL III   LANGUAGE AND MOTOR SPEECH PRODUCTION FACTORS
A. Is there a discrepancy between receptive and expressive skills?
YES ──► Go to III B
NO ──► Go to V
B. Is the discrepancy explained predominantly on the basis of
a motor speech disorder?
YES ──► Go to V
NO ──► Go to III C
UNCERTAIN ──► Go to IV
C. Is the discrepancy explained   predominantly on the basis of
an expressive language disorder?
YES ──► Go to VII
NO ──► Go to VI
UNCERTAIN ──► Go to V

LEVEL IV   MOTOR SPEECH — SOME CONTRIBUTING FACTORS
Presence of neuromuscular involvement affecting postural tone
and or postural stability?
Presence of praxic disturbance?
Vocal production consists primarily of vowel production?
Vocal production consists primarily of undifferentiated sounds?
History of eating problems?
Excessive drooling?
YES ──► Evidence to support motor
speech involvement (Go to V)
NO ──► Evidence against motor
speech involvement (Go to V)

LEVEL V   PRODUCTION — SOME CONTRIBUTING FACTORS
Speech unintelligible except to family and immediate friends?
Predominant mode of communications is through pointing,
gesture, facial–body affect?
Predominance of single word utterances?
Formation associated with inability to speak?
YES ──► (Evidence to ELECT) Go to VII
NO ──► (Evidence to DELAY or REJECT)
Go to VII

Figure 2.   An example of a branching-type decision matrix.

LEVEL VI EMOTIONAL FACTORS
 A. History of precipitous loss of expressive speech?
   YES ➞ Go to VIII
   NO ➞ Go to VI B
 B. Speaks to selected persons or refuses to speak?
   YES ➞ Go to VIII
   NO ➞ Go to V

LEVEL VII CHRONOLOGICAL AGE FACTORS
 A. Chronological age less than 3 years?
   YES ➞ Go to VIII A
 B. Chronological age between 3 and 5 years?
   YES ➞ Go to VIII A
 C. Chronological age greater than 5 years?
   YES ➞ Go to VIII A

LEVEL VIII PREVIOUS THERAPY FACTORS
 A. Has had previous therapy?
   YES ➞ Go to VIII B
   NO ➞ Go to IX, weigh evidence.
    (DELAY with Trial Therapy or
    ELECT) Go to X
 B. Previous therapy appropriate?
   YES ➞ Go to VIII C
   NO ➞ DELAY with Trial Therapy
 C. Therapy progress too slow to enable effective
 communication?
   YES ➞ ELECT ➞ Go to X
   NO ➞ DELAY ➞ continue therapy
 D. Therapy appropriately withheld?
   YES ➞ ELECT ➞ Go to X
   NO ➞ DELAY with Trial Therapy

LEVEL IX PREVIOUS THERAPY — SOME CONTRIBUTING FACTORS
 Able to imitate (with accuracy) speech sounds or words;
 gross motor or oral motor movements?
   YES ➞ (Evidence to delay) Go to VIII
   NO ➞ (Evidence to ELECT) Go to VIII

LEVEL X IMPLEMENTATION FACTORS — ENVIRONMENT
 Family willing to implement (use, allow to be introduced)
 Augmentative Communication System recommendation?
   YES ➞ IMPLEMENT
   NO ➞ COUNSEL

Figure 2. *Continued.*

sciously or unconsciously consider the use of an augmentative system as a prognosis for oral speech failure, 2) they believe that its use will hinder further speech development because of a reliance on a non-oral means. Both of these issues are discussed in this chapter.

 If parents disapprove of a recommendation to elect an augmentative communication system, the professional is obligated by conscience and law to honor that request. Naturally, a review of the decision process that leads to that recommendation might need to be restated through counseling. According to Public Law 94-142, parents of handicapped children are given the right to reject or accept an educational plan. Should that plan suggest that an augmentative communication program be instituted or continued, the parents can reject that segment of the educational plan.

Furthermore, professionals have long recognized the importance of enlisting parental assistance in carrying out intervention programs. It follows that cooperation by caregivers is essential to augmentative communication programming as well. Lack of parental involvement and/or cooperation can be considered synonymous with program failure.

Summary   The factors influencing election decision making have been reviewed. Oral reflex behavior is the only factor considered at this time to be powerful enough, as a single feature, to lead directly to election. Other factors like the presence of cerebral palsy, eating problems, or nature of early speech output are thought to influence decision making by having a confirmatory influence. The presence of these factors provides evidence to adopt a system but as isolated factors or conditions are insufficient to lead to election. The cognitive factor, also powerful within the overall election schema, exerts a somewhat different influence. Because some level of cognitive achievement is necessary to introduce an augmentative communication system, it is viewed as having a prerequisite influence.

Many factors involving both the child and the environment (or family) are involved in the election decision process.[1] An example of a branching-type decision matrix (Shane and Bashir, 1980) containing many of the factors discussed is contained in Figure 2. Although the matrix was not intended specifically for early intervention purposes, it does demonstrate the interaction of many of these factors. It is suggested that the reader test the efficiency of this preliminary decision matrix through usage with nonspeaking children.

SELECTING AN APPROPRIATE
AUGMENTATIVE COMMUNICATION SYSTEM

The process of determining candidacy parallels the process of selecting the most appropriate system for the person. An election decision nat-

---

[1] Many of the election factors described developed as a result of long discussions with Anthony S. Bashir, my colleague at the Children's Hospital Medical Center in Boston. We used those discussions in formulating the branching-type decision matrix that is contained in Figure 2.

urally precedes selection; however, selection would not occur unless election was indicated.

Figure 1 depicts the selection process, which is based on a series of decisions. At the first level of decision making, it is determined whether a manual system or communication prosthesis is better for the client. That decision is made after a review of several factors which are discussed below. Following the review of first-level decision making is a series of subsequent decisions pertaining to both communication prosthesis and manual communication. The factors related to second-level decisions follow the discussion of first-level decision factors.

Another goal of first-level decision making is to match the best augmentative options to a particular child living in a particular environment. Because this is a new area of clinical inquiry, communication system selections seemed to be based more on familiarity with a particular system (Fristoe and Lloyd, 1978) than on a systematic assessment of the child's abilities and disabilities or the needs and desires of the environment.

The significant factors to be considered when selecting a system are neuromotor involvement, portability of system, imitation skill level, rate of acquisition, preference toward pictures, gestural orientation, and environment.

Neuromotor Factors Neuromotor involvement, whether of a neuromuscular or motor-planning basis, influences the election process. During election the presence of neuromotor involvement was considered with respect to its influence on vocal production. The presence of neuromotor impairment also influences selection but in a different manner. Its presence here is more in terms of upper extremity rather than vocal tract involvement.

When a child has neuromuscular involvement, range of motion, rate of movement, strength, and coordination are compromised. These deficits influence the degree to which an individual makes the gross and fine motor movement necessary for execution of gestures, sign language, and fingerspelling. Furthermore, the presence of motor planning deficits involving the upper extremities (limb apraxia) can also influence a child's ability to execute learned individual signs and sign sequences and may also have some bearing on the extent and quality of gestures used spontaneously by the child.

No systematic method for predicting to what extent neuromuscular involvement or severity of motor planning deficits will interfere with the ability to sign is available in the exceptional child literature. Recently, a model for describing normal hand shape acquisition has been proposed (Boyes-Braem, 1973). Nevertheless, some determination of extent of motor involvement of the arm, hands, and fingers needs to be examined when considering a manual versus a communicative prosthetic system.

The degree of neuromuscular involvement is a critical factor in selecting an augmentative system, because a child with severe neuromuscular disability is a less likely candidate for a signing system than a child with mild or no known motor involvement. The "clumsy" child or one with a mild cerebral palsy, however, is the child who presents an even greater diagnostic challenge. This child may have gross motor movements involved in executing gross signs such as "eat" (i.e., cupped hand brought to mouth with fingers pointed toward face) or be able to give a gross approximation to a target for the more motorically complicated signs. In the early stages of programming, these gross approximations may be understood, especially when the child has a repertoire of only 10 to 20 signs. As the number of signs in that child's expressive vocabulary increases, however, comprehension by others may decrease because the approximations of the target lack specificity. When examining potential for signing, one needs to consider the effect increased vocabulary will have on intelligibility of expressive sign due to degree of physical involvement.

Interaction between current and future physical ability and future cognitive and language comprehension ability also needs to be considered. A relationship exists between potential physical skill and potential cognitive skill and language comprehension. A child's expressive communication system should approach language comprehension and cognitive level. The child with extensive knowledge needs a symbolic system that will allow for its expression. Limited physical ability (in this case upper extremity control) could reduce expressive opportunities because expression of extensive information requires sophisticated motor control. For the child with more limited physical, cognitive, and comprehension abilities, a functional but limited sign vocabulary may be affordable through formal signs and/or gestures. Keep in mind, however, that as greater knowledge seeks expression, more refined motor control is necessary. This suggests the importance of a diagnostic talent to predict cognitive and motor potentials—a skill that may require further refinement.[2]

First-level decision making is a process of weighing the advantages and disadvantages of a prosthetic and manual communication systems. But it may not be an either/or situation. For some children, introduction

---

[2] For a review of matching sign system with cognitive level, see Chapman and Miller (1980).

of both systems simultaneously may be appropriate. The decision to teach both formally is usually not recommended because an excessive time commitment and a working knowledge of both systems are required of the instructor. In some cases, one system is introduced intensively while another is encouraged informally. For example, a communication prosthesis is often imposed while the child is simultaneously encouraged to continue gesturing. At times, simultaneous introduction tends to confuse some children and caution is advised.

Portability   With an increase in weight and size of a communication prosthesis, there may be a corresponding decrease in its portability. One disadvantage of a communication prosthesis over a manual system is the need to transport the display. Fristoe and Lloyd (in press) considered systems that require something in addition to the communicator's body in order to express information as an "aided or static" system. Unaided or dynamic systems, on the other hand, are said to allow expression without additional equipment. They recommended that aided systems be reserved for persons whose physical limitations prevent the development of speech or the use of an unaided system. Although portability is a relevant issue in overall selection decisions across the available augmentative communication system options, this singular criteria for system selection seems incomplete at best, given the host of other factors that require consideration at this level.

In the overall decision process the lack of portability of a particular device works to the obvious disadvantage of the user. Inability to use a prosthesis because of a portability compromise deserves the attention of the evaluator. Specifying a manual system only because a child is ambulatory (or will be ambulatory), however, seems to fly in the face of other variables known to influence performance.

Rate of Acquisition   A child's responsiveness to the imposition of an augmentative communication system is another first-level decision factor. Learning or response rate to a prosthetic versus a manual system would need to be monitored whereby the outcome suggests system selection. Oxman et al. (1978), in a similar vein, suggest that response rate to various therapies be used as a "diagnostic device," a method they admit is costly in time and money but often fruitful.

This criteria is now being considered in determining the more appropriate system for children whose motor ability allows use of either system. In exploring acquisition rate between systems we are examining how rapidly the child acquires the referential signs or symbols and how quickly that information is used as a communicative tool. To determine response rate, the instructor should simultaneously introduce information from either system and plot a learning curve. Assuming equivalence of materials and teaching input, one presumably can begin to determine system choice through a child's responsiveness.

A related concept is that of diagnostic teaching. The child's responsiveness to a given system is not only observed in the more structured teaching situation but also in the home and other familiar environments. Here the concept of system selection "ex juvantibis" or selection based on the result of treatment might be a way of substantiating or validating initial system selection decisions.

Picture Oriented   This rather nondescript heading is intended to characterize a number of nonspeaking children. Clinically these children present themselves as having a striking interest in pictorial stimuli of all forms. Parents often report considerable time spent looking through the family photograph album, magazines, catalogues, etc. Sorting and matching pictures for extended periods is common. Some will begin, without instruction, to spontaneously use pictures to describe events and request important items. For example, one child the author knows, would tear pictures from the Sears or Fischer-Price catalogues to specify certain toys or other paraphernalia that he or his sibling had misplaced. He would often pull out the family album and point to photographs of visitors or family members before their arrival. High levels of frustration surrounding communication attempts are frequently observed in picture-directed children. Furthermore, it seems as if frustration motivated the utilization of pictures, which, in turn, ameliorates the problem.

Behavior similar to that described above is strong support, given other support factors, for employing a communication prosthesis containing graphic content. A communication board, if organized properly and tailor-made for the child, greatly enhances communication and helps defuse high frustration levels.

Gesture Oriented   Some nonspeaking children, when unable to establish effective communication through speech, develop extensive gestural means of communication. These nonverbal forms of expression can be quite sophisticated and seem to develop to compensate for ineffectual expression through the more typical oral channel. Myklebust (1954) noted that this phenomenon diagnostically differentiates hearing impaired from other language-disordered children. Goldin-Meadow and Feldman (1975) explored the gestural achievement of four deaf children of hearing parents. None of the children, who ranged in age from 1½ to 4 years, had been exposed to sign language, but they were receiving oral speech training. Emitted gestures were coded in terms of semantic relations as outlined by Bloom (1970) for normal children. Results showed that three phases of gesturing occurred: 1) single-unit gestures that are context-dependent for interpretation were observed, 2) objects and actions were specified into rule-governed two-gesture phrases, and 3) two gestures were combined to specify more than one semantic relation. These results indicate that even with little auditory and no formal visual modality input (i.e., sign language), hearing-impaired children of normal intelligence tend to generate spontaneously a rule bound system to express themselves. The upper limit of this arbitrary system is a problem that has not been studied.

Although research similar to that done by Goldin-Meadow and Feldman (1975) has not systematically explored gestural achievement by hearing nonspeaking children, clinical observation suggests similar behavior. For example, Ferretti, Shane, and Greenwood (1979) studied speech development of a 24-month-old who, because of a malabsorption syndrome, was fed exclusively through intravenous procedures. It was hypothesized that the resulting speech delay was related to a lack of oral stimulation normally provided by oral food management. Observation of her nonverbal communication revealed that a two- and three-step gesture system had emerged—again suggesting that lack of expressive speech or unintelligible speech is compensated for by other communication outlets. Some children with developmental apraxia of speech also use gestures extensively.

For those children who do use gestures, whether as elaborate or as systematic as that reported above, such communicative forms seem to represent a factor favoring the adoption of a manual communication system. Assuming, therefore, that motor skills are sufficient for adequate expression by sign language and possibly fingerspelling, the "gesturally oriented" factor weighs on the side of manual system selection over a communication prosthesis.

Environment-Interaction   The "normalization principle" relates to another selection issue (Wolfensberger, 1972). Normalization is "the utilization of means which are as culturally normative as possible in order to establish, enable, and support behaviors, appearances, and interpretations which are as culturally normative as possible" (p. 28). With regard to first level decisions, integration refers to the degree to which an augmentative communication system can restrict or promote social interaction between the nonspeaking person and the community.

Sign language is the third most used language in the United States (O'Rourke, in Wilbur, 1976, 1979) and is the major symbolic communication channel for a half million deaf and hard of hearing persons. Using number of users as the sole criterion, one might think that the use of a manual system would allow considerable integration for hearing nonspeaking persons. This statement seems untenable because an observation of deaf citizens would support the fact that they tend to form subgroups or a linguistic minority (Charrow and Wilbur, 1975) within the larger community. Furthermore, whether nonspeaking persons using sign language would assimilate into the deaf community is an unstudied issue but one which this writer considers unlikely. If deaf signers form isolated groups because of communication incompatability with the speaking/hearing community, would similar subgroups be formed by nonspeaking persons? Or even worse, would sign language by nonspeaking persons lead to limited community exposure, which seems at odds with the normalization concept?

The use of a communication prosthesis might allow more social interaction. More people can read than can comprehend sign language. Traditional orthography is a common symbol system used on a communication prosthesis. Furthermore, unfamiliar or unusual symbol systems might confuse novel viewers but the ability to write a symbol's meaning over the caricature can eliminate this problem. Also with advances in engineering, input via an unfamiliar symbol can lead to traditional orthographic or even speech (synthetic or prerecorded) output.

Finally, it has been the author's experience in recent years that professionals and parents are requesting communication prostheses for children who are effective manual system communicators. The requests for the second augmentative system have increased apparently because the child is limited in terms of the number of persons with whom he or she can communicate, and it is assumed by the referring agent that a communicative prosthesis would facilitate more interaction. This issue might be likened to the use of written communication by many hearing-impaired persons who carry pencil and paper to augment or allow interaction with nonsigners. The question that arises is whether the communication prosthesis should have been introduced initially. The benefits derived from signing in order to communicate, even with a limited number of individuals, seems to make this a moot point.

Environment-Deviancy Perception   Also contained within the normalization principle is the concept of deviancy (Wolfensberger, 1972). In order to eliminate deviant image or stigmata as much as possible, an atypical person should be as typical as possible in appearance, behavior, and environment (Wolfensberger and Glenn, 1972). Applying this idea to selection decisions, one might assume that communication prostheses that have not had as much public exposure as manual systems may be perceived as more deviant. Only further public exposure to communication prostheses (as well as to manual systems) will decrease the deviancy image and increase their public acceptance.

Imitation   Poor gross and fine motor as well as vocal imitation skills are considered predictive of oral speech failure. Similarly, motor imitation might be considered a prerequisite for and predictive of the ability to perform sequences of learned motor activity such as that needed for signing. A consideration of children seen previously for evaluation (having a multitude of diagnostic labels including apraxia of speech, autism, and mental retardation), as well as recent published evidence has confused more than clarified what once seemed self evident—one cannot sign unless one can imitate.

Autistic and autistic-like children have also been observed clinically and described through research efforts (Oxman et al., 1978; Curcio, 1978; Prior, 1977; DeMeyer et al., 1972) to be poor imitators; yet, they too benefit from sign intervention (Oxman et al., 1978). Because nonimitative or minimally imitative, autistic children learn to communicate manually, despite poor imitative ability, is imitation a legitimate system selection criterion? The poor imitation ability may be more a function of atypical interpersonal style reflected as an inability or unwillingness to relate (Ornitz and Ritvo, 1976; Rutter, 1978) than an actual inability to replicate previously seen motor acts. Oxman et al. (1978) stated that language deficits in autistic children are often ". . . more apparent than real" (p. 293). Similarly, because the imitation deficits may be more apparent than real suggests an artifact inherent to measures of imitative skills in characteristically nonrelating or low-relating children.

In summary, within the boundaries of cognitive achievement, imitation ability should have predictive power for future sign language success. In cases of known or suspected autism, however, performance on imitation tasks may not be useful as a selection criterion. At the very least, imitation per se as a selection criterion leads to the conclusion that if imitation ability is a problem, the instructor charged with teaching signing to a nonimitative child has a formidable task.

Summary of First Level Factors Selection is a complicated process involving a number of personal as well as environmental considerations. Ideally all professionals and significant persons in the child's life should be involved because effective decision making is a team process.

With the exception of extreme neuromotor involvement, no other single factor seems to obligate selection of a manual or a prosthetic system. System selection is best viewed as a matter of considering the factors supporting each of the two available alternatives.

SECOND LEVEL DECISION MAKING— AUGMENTATIVE CONTENT AND DISPLAY AND MANUAL SYSTEMS

Assuming that a first-level decision has been made, second-level decisions concern the specifics of a manual system or a communication prosthesis. Prosthesis decisions at this level explore the display and the content of the prosthetic device. Manual issues relate to sign language options, fingerspelling, and gestural system usage.

Augmentative Content

Decisions regarding the most appropriate augmentative content material are like decisions at other levels, a multifaceted issue. Although a plethora of content materials exists, no symbol system has been designed specifically for nonspeaking persons. Instead, principles and elements of systems designed originally for other purposes are being applied to the nonspeaking. For example, Rebus symbols (Woodcock, Clark, and Davies, 1968), originally designed for reading instruction, and Blissymbols (Bliss, 1965), intended originally as an international language, are now used extensively with nonspeaking persons (Silverman, 1978). Similarly the Roman alphabet and the Initial Teaching Alphabet, used typically as secondary linguistic systems for the nonhandicapped, are now employed with nonspeaking persons (e.g., Shane and Melrose, 1974; Vicker, 1974; McDonald and Schultz, 1973). Other popular augmentative content options include noncommercial idiosyncratic line drawings, pictures, or photographs.

Most current literature concerning available content material has been descriptive in nature (Vicker, 1974; McDonald and Schultz, 1973; Archer, 1977) or has explored the benefits of a particular symbol system approach (Shane and Melrose, 1974; Harris-Vanderheiden et al., 1975; Silverman et al., 1978). The paucity of comparative research across the different symbol system options deters optimal content determination based on clinical success. Rather, suspected cognitive prerequisites for a system (Chapman and Miller, 1980), intuitive or clinical good sense, or system familiarity (Goodman, Wilson, and Bornstein, 1978; Fristoe and Lloyd, 1978) have dominated content selection.

A significant issue in evaluation is the level at which the child can represent the material world through representations. For specific clinical suggestions for determining this information see Shane (1980). For purposes of early intervention, symbols having feature similarity to their referents (iconic or transparent) are more advantageous because these seem to be the first means the young child can use to represent the material world.

In addition to estimating current symbol needs, an orientation toward future symbol use is important. As the nonspeaking child matures cognitively, more arbitrary symbols can be imposed that allow for generalization of content, material, and greater communicative use. For example, Blissymbol content, which contains some relatively iconic material, has a predominance of arbitrary and relational symbols. When meaning is attached to these less transparent symbols, opportunities to combine symbols through prescribed symbol logic is possible.

Interaction   An important measure of effectiveness is whether or not the symbol promotes communicative interaction between the non-speaking child and his teachers, peers, and family. There is little information regarding interactions by nonspeaking children either with handicapped or nonhandicapped partners. Harris (1978) explored patterns of interaction of nonspeaking physically handicapped children and found that interaction consisted mainly of teacher-to-child rather than child-to-child interaction. The results of this study seem typical of informal observation as well.

A number of deterrants to interaction are created by the very nature of an augmentative communication system. For one, the listener in most cases needs to decode visually rather than auditorially. Also, the positioning of many communication prostheses, when laid horizontally across a child's lap, can deter adequate visualization by the communicative partner. Third, the rules of communication encountered in typical interactions are unquestionably altered by the nature of this communicative method. Finally, the symbols themselves seem to create major obstacles to effective communicative interaction.

Frequently a nonspeaking child uses symbols that his or her peers are unable or unprepared to comprehend. Also, it is not unusual to find a nonspeaking preschool child with a reading vocabulary a year or two ahead of his or her nonhandicapped peers. This situation allows the child to express thoughts to teachers, parents, and others capable of reading but severely limits the child's interaction with peers. Furthermore, arbitrary symbols like those contained within Blissymbolics are often difficult to decode without an understanding of the logic behind symbol generation or an ability to read the English equivalent usually written below or above the symbol. Again, interaction is hampered.

Iconic symbols discussed previously as being more appropriate for developmentally younger children may also allow for greater interaction between younger symbol users and nonhandicapped communicative partners because their meaning may be more readily discerned.

The issue of interaction has significant implications for evaluation. Not only must the nonspeaking child's communicative capacity be assessed, but also the needs of the listener should be considered. Because communicative partners are seen as part of the evaluation process, their needs and abilities too must be reviewed.

Environment   The environment (teachers, parents, etc.) have a pervasive influence throughout election and selection. For symbol system selection, teacher/therapist experience with the various augmentative contents should be examined. Whether the teacher/therapist is willing to or has the time to create (e.g., locate, cut, paste, draw, etc.) symbols or desires to subscribe to an established program needs to be considered at this level of decision making.

Standardization   It is important to consider the willingness of instructors to prepare materials for the communication prosthesis and to design teaching strategies, that is, strategies to combine symbols, layout of the materials, and creativity in introducing new information. In this regard, Blissymbols offer the advantage of a network of trained teachers and a mechanism for further inservice training with instructional materials that are readily available. The use of more idiosyncratic content created by teachers and family often is necessitated by some children but at the expense of considerable preparation time.

Augmentative Display

The major issue involved in selecting the augmentative display is whether an electronic or a nonelectronic device should be imposed.[3] That decision should be based on a consideration of factors relating to motor capability, portability, cost, and the overall benefits of electronic technology for a particular child.

Neuromotor   The degree of neuromotor handicap has a pervasive influence on the nonspeaking person's ability to indicate desired content on the display. A significant motor impairment can prevent direct selection of desired information by a hand/finger pointing gesture but may not preclude headpointing or eye gaze selection. Also in cases of extreme upper extremity involvement, eye encoding methods (i.e., Etran) or determination of a reliable muscle gesture that can control a switch that in turn operates an electronic device is needed.

Portability   The more hardware technology involved in a communication system the more likely that portability will be compromised. Vanderheiden (1978), in a resource text of available communication prostheses, implicitly cited the importance of portability by using it to categorize devices; those weighing less than 25 pounds are considered *portable* and those weighing more than 30 pounds are considered *stationary*. In choosing between an electronic versus a nonelectronic device, one must consider whether the device will remain in a single location or whether it will or can be with the child at all times in order to meet all of his or her communicative needs.

Rate of Message Transmission   Normal communicators speak at the rate of 150 to 180 words per minute (Fairbanks, 1960). A proficient

---

[3] For a description of electronic and nonelectronic communication prostheses refer to Vanderheiden (1978).

typist types at a rate of approximately 60 words per minute. Speed of message transmission by persons using communication prostheses has received little research attention to date. Gorden, Walton, and Shane (1979) evaluated an adult with congenital spastic quadriplegia who communicated through direct selection of letters and common words contained on a non-electronic communication board. The results indicated that the subject's fastest rate with a familiar listener (subject's mother) was 15 words per minute. Fastest rate with an unfamiliar listener was five words per minute indicating that his best performance with either listener is grossly below normal rate of expressive speech or typing. Beukelman and Yorkston (1977) examined rate of expression in acquired dysarthric speakers when they pointed either to the first letter of a word and said it simultaneously or spelled the entire word on a letter board. Results indicated an average of 28 words expressed per minute in the first condition and five words per minute in the latter.

The question that arises is whether an electronic system would improve the efficiency of output for the speakers in these investigations. Furthermore, that same question must be asked whenever a child is being evaluated for a communication prosthesis and the evaluator is making second level decisions. That is, will the introduction of an electronic device increase efficiency over the nonelectronic system? This information should be helpful in making the appropriate second level decision.

Cost   In choosing between an electronic versus a nonelectronic device, one needs to remember that because of the high cost of technology commercial aids are expensive. Also, a child's device probably will not serve him or her for an indefinite time. Additional devices or optional equipment likely will be needed.

Third party payment agents have been reluctant in the past to purchase the needed devices. With increased technology, widespread use, and recognition of their importance, greater cooperation with third party payers should develop.

Cost alone should not be a deterrent in securing an electronic device when one is appropriate. Although cost must be considered, this alone should not be the decision-making factor. Rather, a cost-benefit ratio needs to be determined.

Benefit   The benefit of an electronic device should be measured by an improvement factor over a nonelectronic device. A permanent message, for example, may allow interaction to take place at a later time or provide a means to record homework, correspond in writing, or create one's biography. Speech output might also enhance interaction between the child and peers who are unable or unprepared to decode visual symbol content. For the child who does as well with a nonelectronic device, one should opt for that over the more costly, less portable device. The general rule is: introduce an electronic device only if it will contribute significantly to the nonspeaker's communicative ability.

Manual Systems

Selecting between sign systems, determining appropriateness of fingerspelling, and classifying and evaluating gestural performance are all part of second-level decision making.

Sign System   For more than a decade, deaf educators have been debating over the advantages and disadvantages of American Sign Language (ASL) as compared to the pedagogical sign systems.[4] Whether any or all of the sign systems are advantageous to the hearing-impaired child is a controversial topic. With the exception of systematic sign language (Paget, 1951; Paget and Gorman, 1968), each of these signing methods is a modification of ASL. Knowing the principal arguments of that debate should be instructive in clarifying sign system selection for the non hearing-impaired person.

Persons supporting use of ASL in education with the hearing-impaired contend that this system represents a true language and, therefore, one capable of unlimited expressive capability. This determination followed extensive linguistic scrutiny in recent years assessing its qualifications as a language, albeit a visual one. If popularity is any criterion (and ASL being far and above the more common sign language), many persons would continue to share this common language. Modified systems on the other hand, are not used by many deaf citizens as a home language (Wilbur, 1976). That many persons use ASL implies that numerous deaf educators know its principles and can recognize effective teaching strategies.

Whether these trained teachers could or would move into special education and work with nonspeaking children or could influence teachers of hearing nonspeaking persons is not known. If the results of two recent surveys (Fristoe and Lloyd, 1978; Goodman et al., 1978) concerning sign language in special education are any indication, however, little assimilation is occurring. The majority of respondents to the surveys indicated that American Sign Language was the preferred sign system. Further questioning, however, revealed a general lack of sophistication regarding even the basic principles unique to this language (as well as to the other pedagogical systems). For example, many reported using ASL but did not indicate an appreciation of its word-

---

[4] For a comprehensive review of sign language systems, see Wilbur (1976, 1979) and Fristoe and Lloyd (in press).

order differences from that of English. When respondents were questioned further as to why a particular sign system is selected, they indicated their choice was based more on familiarity with a particular system or experience with a client or group of clients than on a systematic review of available options (Fristoe and Lloyd, 1978; Goodman et al., 1978).

Opponents of ASL might argue that the linguistic structure of American Sign Language (being unlike English) has significant educational and social implications for deaf students. Most notably, with word order being dramatically different from that of English, reading achievement and interaction with English speakers can suffer. To counteract the stated negative influence of ASL, Wilbur (1979) reviewed both sides of this argument and suggested that educational and interactional deficits of the hearing impaired are such that linguistic structure changes alone will not eliminate the deficiencies.

In selecting the most appropriate sign language or sign system for hearing, nonspeaking persons, arguments similar to those concerning the hearing impaired are beginning to emerge. Fristoe and Lloyd (in press) suggest that for the mentally retarded person who is a candidate for manual communication, a method that uses English word order seems more appropriate. They contend that for the hearing child with cognitive impairment, auditory information has varying degrees of meaning. Imposing word order other than English may cause more confusion than ease. These authors recognize specifically that a pedagogical system that puts ASL in English word order seems to be the best compromise for the hearing client. They suggest that Signed English (Bornstein et al., 1973) is the preferred system because it is the "simplest" in that it does not initially require morphological makers. In effect, it allows for expansion in use of more sophisticated linguistic forms as the child develops and yet it requires relatively little fingerspelling. Furthermore, this system has a well developed set of available materials that parents and children can utilize.

Gesture Developmental aspects of gesture in disordered persons has been investigated most intensely with the hearing impaired (Goldin-Meadow and Feldman, 1975; Feldman, 1975; Carr, 1971). Gestural impairment has also been investigated in acquired neurological conditions (Guinotti and Lemmo, 1976; Goodglass and Kaplan, 1973), however, developmental or instructional aspects of gestural communication are relatively unexplored in the nonspeaking population although their utility for communication is recognized.

The lack of research reflects an overall scarcity of normative information on gestural development and use (Wood, 1976). Consequently, evaluative efforts regarding gestural communication are generally descriptive statements about form and use with some consideration given to developmental level implied from available normal developmental literature on the subject (e.g., Kaplan, 1978; Bates, 1976; Nelson, 1973).

Although the use of gestures is a viable form of expression, it is nonetheless a restricted expressive mode. In order to use upper extremity movement for unrestricted information exchange that is not heavily dependent on speech or environmental context, a sign language system is required. According to a survey by Fristoe and Lloyd (1978), gestures were a frequent mode of instruction for nonspeaking persons. When gestures are taught as the exclusive expressive form, however, that decision generally reflects a more pessimistic outlook regarding the communication potential of the user because only a limited number of communicative functions can be expressed (Chapman and Miller, 1980).

A more formal gestural system using American Indian Sign Language (Amerind) has been used with glossectomized and apraxic patients (Skelly et al., 1974; Skelly et al., 1975). Amerind has no grammatical structure and is not considered a language. According to Skelly et al. (1974), observers can interpret Amerind with over 80% comprehension without previous instruction suggesting a high degree of iconicity. Fristoe and Lloyd (in press) suggest that instructors considering gestural intervention procedures might use Amerind because it is more formal than idiosyncratic signs and is capable of conveying considerable functional information. A recent study investigated the use of Amerind with the moderately and severely mentally retarded (Duncan and Silverman, 1978). These investigators noted that after a 10-week training program: 1) spontaneous use of Amerind was observed in 27 of the 32 subjects; 2) there were changes in behavior in the form of reduced temper tantrums; and 3) there were increased attempts at spontaneous speech.

Fingerspelling   Fingerspelling is a unified series of 26 distinct hand configurations, each representing one of the 26 letters of the Roman alphabet.

Although fingerspelling is not relevant for nonspeaking children under age 5, it is mentioned here to highlight it as a future consideration for the developing child. Prerequisites for fingerspelling include an ability to spell or break words into their component parts and assign corresponding letters. These abilities generally emerge around the end of kindergarten or the beginning of Grade 1 and will improve with linguistic and cognitive maturation and academic achievement. Also, fingerspelling requires greater manual dexterity than signs or gestures.

SUMMARY

This chapter applies developmental and clinical literature from several disciplines to the evaluation of communication in nonspeaking persons. It is emphasized throughout the chapter that only recently has there been a surge of interest in this clinical area that makes information on the nonspeaking child most incomplete. Early intervention and augmentative communication have not shared the same podium until now, which makes the task of organization and detail formidable.

Personal clinical experiences are used to support several points but what has undergone formal study is distinguished from what is informal observation. It is hoped that this chapter will assist others in clinical management of nonspeaking and potentially nonspeaking children as well as promote a search for more information in this area.

ACKNOWLEDGMENTS

Special thanks to Dr. Anthony Bashir for his assistance especially on the *Election* portion. Thanks also to Dr. Martin Schultz for his support and insights. Finally, the author is grateful to Elyse Gustin for her editorial assistance and encouragement.

REFERENCES

Archer, L. A. 1977. Blissymbolics—A nonverbal communication system. J. Speech Hear. Disord. 42:568–579.

Baer, D., Peterson, R., and Sherman, J. 1967. The development of imitation by reinforcing behavioral similarity to a model. J. Exp. Anal. Behav. 10:405–416.

Bates, E. 1976. Language and Context: The Acquisition of Pragmatics. Academic Press, Inc. N.Y.

Bayley, N. 1969. Bayley Scales of Infant Development. The Psychological Corporation, N.Y.

Beukelman, D. R., and Yorkston, K. 1977. A communication system for the severely dysarthric speaker with an intact language system. J. Speech Hear. Disord. 42:265–270.

Blatt, B., and Kaplan, F. 1966. Christmas in Purgatory: A Photographic Essay on Mental Retardation. Allyn and Bacon, Inc. Boston.

Bliss, C. K. 1965. Semantography. Semantography Publications, Sydney, Australia.

Bloom, L. 1970. Language Development: Form and Function in Emerging Grammers. MIT Press, Cambridge, Mass.

Bornstein, H., Hamilton, L., Kannapell, B., Roy, H., and Saulnier, K. 1973. Basic Pre-School Signed English Dictionary. Gallaudet College, Washington, D.C.

Boyes-Braem, P. 1973. A study of the acquisition of the Dez in American Sign Language. Unpublished masters thesis. University of California, Berkeley, Calif.

Bricker, D. D. 1972. Imitative sign training as a facilitator of word-object association with low-functioning children. American Association of Mental Deficiency. 76:509–516.

Carr, M. 1971. Communicative behavior of three and four year old deaf children. Unpublished doctoral dissertation, Columbia University, N.Y.

Chapman, R., and Miller, J. 1980. Analyzing language and communication in the child. *In* R. L. Schiefelbusch (ed.), Nonspeech Language and Communication, Acquisition and Intervention, pp. 161–196. University Park Press, Baltimore.

Charrow, V. R., and Wilbur, R. B. 1975. The deaf child as a linguistic minority. Language Use and Acquisition, XIV, 353–358.

Curcio, F. 1978. Sensorimotor functioning and communication in mute autistic children. J. Autism Child. Schizo. 3:281–292.

Davis, G. A. 1973. Linguistic and language therapy: The sentence construction board. J. Speech Hear. Disord. 38:205–214.

De Meyer, M. K., Alpern, G. D., Barton, S., Demeyer, W. E., Churchill, D. W., Hington, J. N., Bryson, D. C., Pontius, W., and Kimberlin, C. 1972. Imitation in autistic, early schizophrenic, and non-psychotic subnormal children. J. Autism Child. Schizo. 2:264–287.

Duncan, J. L., and Silverman, F. L. 1978. Impacts of learning American Indian Sign Language on mentally retarded children. A preliminary report. Perceptual and Motor Skills. 44:p. 1138.

Eisenson, J. 1972. Aphasia in Children. Harper and Row, Publishers, N.Y.

Fairbanks, G. 1960. Voice and Articulation Drill Book. Harper and Brothers, N.Y.

Feldman, H. 1975. The development of a lexicon by deaf children of hearing parents or, there's more to language then what meets the ear. Unpublished doctoral dissertation, University of Pennsylvania, College Park, Pennsylvania.

Ferretti, A., Shane, H. C., and Greenwood, W. An investigation of cognitive, speech and language development of an infant with short bowel syndrome: A case study. Unpublished paper.

Fitzgerald, E. 1954. Straight Language for the Deaf. Volta Bureau, Washington, D.C.

Fristoe, M., and Lloyd, L. 1978. A survey of the use of nonspeech systems with the severely communication impaired. Mental Retard. 16:99–103.

Fristoe, M., and Lloyd, L. Nonspeech communication. *In* N. R. Ellis (ed.), Handbook of Mental Deficiency. Earlbaum Associates, N.Y. In Press.

Fulwiler, R. L., and Fouts, R. S. 1976. Acquisition of American Sign Language by a noncommunicating autistic child. J. Autism Child. Schizo. 4:43–51.

Goldin-Meadow, S., and Feldman, H. 1975. The creation of a communication system: A study of deaf children of hearing parents. Sign Lang. Studies. 8:225–234.

Goodglass, H., and Kaplan, E. F. 1973. Disturbance in gesture and pantomime in aphasia. Brain. 86:703–720.

Goodman, L., Wilson, B. S., and Bornstein, H. 1978. Results of a national survey of sign language programs in special education. Mental Retard. 16:104–106.

Gordon, G., Walton, K., and Shane, H. C. 1979. An investigation of comprehension, production and strategies of communication in a nonspeaking adult with congenital spastic quadriplegia. Unpublished paper.

Guess, D., Sailor, W., and Baer, D. 1978. Children with limited language. *In* R. L. Schiefelbusch (ed.), Language Intervention Strategies. University Park Press. Baltimore.

Guess, D., Sailor, W., and Baer, D. 1976. Functional Speech and Language Training for the Severely Handicapped, Part I: Persons and Things. H & H Enterprises, Inc. Lawrence, Ks.

Guinotti, G., and Lemmo, M. A. 1976. Comprehension of symbolic gestures in aphasia. Brain and Language. 3:451–460.

Hagan, C., Porter, W., and Brink, J. 1973. Nonverbal communication: An alternative mode of communication for the child with severe cerebral palsy. J. Speech Hear. Disord. 38:pp. 448, 455.

Harris-Vanderheiden, D. W., Brown, W. P., MacKenzie, P., Beinen, S., and Scheibel, C. 1975. Symbol communication for the mentally handicapped: An Application of Bliss symbols as an alternate communication mode for nonvocal mentally retarded children with motoric involvement. Mental Retard. 13:34–37.

Harris, D. 1978. Description Analysis of Communicative Interaction Processes Involving Non-vocal Severely Physically Handicapped Children. Unpublished doctoral dissertation. University of Wisconsin, Madison, Wis.

Ingram, T. T. S. 1962. Clinical significance of the infantile feeding reflexes. Dev. Med. Child Neurol. 4:159–169.

Jones, M. H. 1975. Habilitative management of communicative disorders in young children. *In* D. B. Tower (ed.), The Nervous System: Human Communication and Its Disorders, Vol. 3. Raven Press, Pubs. N.Y.

Kahn, J. V. 1975. Relationship of Piaget sensorimotor period to language acquisition of profoundly retarded children. Am. J. Mental Defic. 79:640–643.

Kapisovsky, M. M. 1978. The use of sign language with nonverbal, hearing children: A review of the literature. Unpublished masters thesis, Boston University, Boston.

Kaplan, E. 1978. The development of praxis. *In* B. Wolman (ed.), International Encyclopedia of Neurology, Psychiatry, Psychoanalysis and Psychology.

Kates, B., and McNaughton, S. 1974. The First Application of Blissymbolics as a Communication Medium for Nonspeaking Children: History and Development, 1971–1974. Blissymbolics Communication Foundation, Toronto, Ontario, Canada.

Kent, L. R. 1974. Language Acquisition Program for the Retarded or Multiply Impaired. Research Press, Co. Champaign, Ill.

Lovaas, O. I. 1967. A Behavior Therapy Approach to the Treatment of Childhood Schizophrenia. University of Minnesota Press, Minneapolis, Minn.

McDonald, E., and Schultz, A. 1973. Communication boards for cerebral palsied children. J. Speech Hear. Disord. 38:73–88.

McDonald, E. T., and Chance, B. 1964. Cerebral Palsy. Prentice-Hall, Englewood Cliffs, N.J.

McIntire, M. L. 1977. The acquisition of American Sign Language hand configurations. Sign Language Studies. 16:247–266.

Miller, A., and Miller, E. E. 1973. Cognitive development training with elevated boards and sign language. J. Autism Child. Schizo. 3:65–85.

Morris, S. E. 1975. A neurodevelopmental approach to communication boards. *In* S. E. Morris (ed.), Pre-Speech and Language Programming for the Young Child with Cerebral Palsy: A Workshop Training Manual. Evanston, Ill.

Morris, S. E. 1978. Oral-Motor development: Normal and abnormal. *In* J.

Wilson (ed.), Oral Motor Function and Dysfunction in Children. Division of Physical Therapy, Chapel Hill, N.C.

Mueller, H. 1975. Feeding. *In* N. R. Finnie (ed.), Handling the Young Cerebral Palsied Child at Home, pp. 113–132. E. P. Dutton and Co., Inc., N.Y.

Myklebust, H. 1954. Auditory Disorders in Children. Grune and Stratton, N.Y.

Mysak, E. D. 1963. Dysarthria and Oropharyngeal Reflexology: A review. J. Speech Hear. Disord. 28:252–260.

Nelson, K. 1973. Structure and strategy in learning to talk. Monographs of the Society for Research in Child Development. 38:1–2.

Ornitz, E. E., and Ritvo, E. R. 1976. Medical Assessment. *In* E. R. Ritvo (ed.), Autism: Diagnosis, Current Research and Management. Spectrum Publication, Inc., N.Y.

Oxman, J., Webster, C. D., and Konstantareas, M. M. 1978. The perception and processing of information by severely dysfunctional nonverbal children: A rationale for the use of manual communications. Sign Lang. Studies. 21:289–316.

Paget, R. 1951. The New Sign Language. The Welcome Foundation, London.

Paget, R., and Gorman, P. 1968. A Systematic Sign Language. National Institute for the deaf, London.

Palmer, M. D. 1949. Laryngeal blocs in the speech disorders of cerebral palsy. Cent. States Speech J. 1:35–42.

Prior, M. R. 1977. Psycholinguistic disabilities of autistic and retarded children. J. of Mental Defic. Res. 21:37–45.

McDonald and Schultz, 1973, p. 34.

Radtka, S. 1978. Feeding reflexes and nerval control. *In* J. Wilson (ed.), Oral-Motor Function and Dysfunction in Children. Division of Physical Therapy, Chapel Hill, N.C.

Reich, R. 1978. Gestural facilitation of expressive language in moderately/severely retarded preschoolers. Mental Retard. 16:113–117.

Reichle, J. E., and Yoder, D. E. 1979. Communication behavior for the severely and profoundly mentally retarded: Assessment and early stimulation strategies. *In* R. York, and E. Edgar (eds.), Teaching the Severely Handicapped, Vol. IV, pp. 180–218. Special Press, Columbus, Ohio.

Rosenbek, J. C., Collins, M. J., and Wertz, R. T. 1976. Intersystemic for apraxia of speech. *In* R. H. Brookshire (ed.), Clinical Aphasiology: Conference Proceedings, pp. 255–260. BRK Publishers, Minneapolis, Minn.

Rutter, M. 1978. Diagnosis and definitions of childhood autism. J. Autism Child. Schizo. 8:139–161.

Schlesinger, H. S., and Meadow, K. P. 1972. Sound and sign: Childhood Deafness and Mental Health. University of California Press, Berkley

Schaeffer, B., Kollinzas, G., Musil, A., and McDowell, P. 1977. Spontaneous verbal language for autistic children through signed speech. Sign Lang. Studies. 17:287–328.

Shaffer, T., and Goehl, H. 1974. The alinguistic child. Mental Retardation. 4:3–6.

Shane, H. C., and Bashir, A. S. 1980. Election criteria for determining candidacy for an augmentative communication system: Preliminary considerations. J. Speech Hear. Disord. 45:408–414.

Shane, H. C., and Melrose, J. 1974. An electronic conversation board and an accompanying training program for aphonic expressive communication.

Paper presented at the American Speech and Hearing Association Convention. Washington, D.C. 4.

Shane, H. C. 1979. Approaches to assessing people who are nonspeaking. *In* R. L. Schiefelbusch (ed.), Nonspeech Language Intervention, Acquisition and Intervention, pp. 197–224. University Park Press, Baltimore.

Shane, H. C., and Cohen, C. In press. A discussion of interaction strategies and patterns of communication by nonspeaking persons. Lang. Speech Hear. Serv. in Schools.

Silverman, F. H. 1978. Non-vocal communication system: Implications for the neurosciences. TINS, December, 147–148.

Silverman, H., McNaughton, S., and Kates, B. 1978. Handbook of Blissymbolics. Blissymbolics Communication Institute, Toronto. (Distributed by Blissymbolics Communication Institute, 350 Rumsey Road, Toronto, Ontario, Canada M4G 1R8.

Skelly, M., Schinsky, L., Smith, R. W., and Fust, R. S. 1974. American Indian (Amerind) as a facilitator of verbalization for the oral verbal apraxic. J. Speech Hear. Disord. 39:445–456.

Skelly, M., Schinsky, L., Smith, R. W., Donaldson, R. C., and Griffin, J. M. 1975. American Indian sign: A gestural communication system for the speechless. Arch. Physical Med. 56:156–160.

Sloane, H. N., Johnston, M. K., and Harris, F. R. 1968. Remedial procedures for teaching verbal behavior to speech deficient or defective young children. *In* H. N. Sloane, and B. MacAuley (eds.), Operant Procedures in Remedial Speech and Language Training. Houghton Mifflin Co., Boston.

Uzgiris, I. C., and Hunt, J. 1975. Assessment in Infancy. University of Illinois Press, Chicago.

Vanderheiden, G. (ed.). 1978. Non-vocal Communication Resource Book. University Park Press, Baltimore.

Vanderheiden, G., and Vanderheiden, Harris D. 1976. Communication techniques and aides for the nonvocal severely handicapped. *In* L. Lloyd (ed.), Communication Assessment and Intervention Strategies. University Park Press, Baltimore.

Vicker, B. 1974. Nonoral Communication System Project: 1964/1973. Campus Stores Publishers, Iowa City.

Wilbur, R. B. 1976. The linguistics of manual language and manual systems. *In* L. Lloyd (ed.), Communication Assessment and Intervention Strategies. University Park Press, Baltimore.

Wilbur, R. 1979. American Sign Language and Sign Systems. University Park Press, Baltimore.

Wolfensberger, W. 1972. The Principle or Normalization in Human Services. National Institute on Mental Retardation, Downsview, Ontario.

Wolfensberger, W., and Glenn, L. 1972. Program Analysis of Service Systems; Pass 2. National Institute on Mental Retardation, Toronto, Canada.

Wood, B. S. 1976. Children and Communication: Verbal and Nonverbal Language Development. Prentice-Hall, Inc., Englewood, N.J.

Woodcock, R. W., Clark, C. R., and Davies, C. 1968. Peabody Rebus Reading Program. American Guidance Service, Circle Pennsylvania, Minn.

chapter
13

Strategies and Evaluation of Early Intervention

Summary Chapter

James Hogg

Deputy Director
Hester Adrian Research Centre
The University of Manchester
Manchester, England

The focus of the discussion is on the investigation of language acquisition and the processes involved in language development. The central concern is early intervention with children at risk for slow or aberrant communication and language development.

It is understandable that researchers should express reservations about the application of their findings when they see such application as an overextension of existing knowledge. Nevertheless, application is no longer a matter of "whether" but of "how." Early intervention is very much with us in a variety of contexts and on an international scale (Council of Europe, 1975). Conceptually, and in terms of content, early education programs for severely and profoundly retarded preschoolers have been developed during the past decade and are continuing to be developed (Bricker, Seibert and Casuso, 1980).

Some of the issues raised by Kysela and his colleagues and by Shane, and the observations of other participants are closely related. It might lend clarity to group them in three areas of concern:

1. The relation between developmental psychology and early intervention
2. Problems in evaluation of early intervention
3. Some aspects of teaching practices in this field

DEVELOPMENTAL PSYCHOLOGY AND EARLY INTERVENTION

Early intervention projects draw upon the findings of developmental, child and experimental psychology. They do so to develop their curricula and to explain their teaching methods. They do this with varying degrees of sophistication and emphasis, but the diffusion of developmental knowledge into such projects goes on with some apprehension by developmental researchers. Thus Kysela et al. (this volume) regard their early education system as " . . . an attempt to develop the links between principles of child development and learning and a broadly applicable intervention system of assessment and teaching." More explicitly, Shane (this volume) draws on cognitive prerequisites for language to make decisions concerning the adoption of augmentative communication intervention. An important issue is the relationship between language development as studied in the detailed observational and experimental work reported, and the activity of the early educators on whom the onus lies to promote adaptive development in the child at risk for (or exhibiting) delayed language development.

There are several ways this rapprochement has and is being effected. Bricker et al. (1980) argued that one of the main research aims of early intervention projects in which a service research interface has been established should be the exploration of the relation between developmental findings and intervention. This is not a novel suggestion, but it does point out that a priori analysis of the relation can go only so far, and development of the analysis is a practical activity that begins with the dialogue between the developmental researcher and the early educator.

Developmental information per se does not of itself generate a curriculum (Hogg, 1975). It is one source of the whole curriculum that is derived from many inputs. McMasters (1973) showed that how a curriculum is developed depends upon the historical and social conditions that shape our view of education, as well as the way in which we interpret empirical information from many sources.

There is some consensus that language and communication skills should constitute a central part of most curricula for severely and profoundly retarded children, either as short- or long-term aims. Although not all early educators would necessarily concur, this is an assumption that is not often challenged.

We can begin by asking in what form information from developmental studies comes to the early educator. At the most basic level, information on the sequencing of developmentally significant behaviors is provided by developmental assessment tests, and cross-sectional and longitudinal studies of development. In most test-teach models, this information is synthesized in ordinal checklists within specifically defined, though often arbitrarily compartmentalized, domains. In some instances, there is cross-referencing between domains where more than one skill is tapped. More sophisticated hierarchical organization is reflected in the various complex test-teach lattices (Bricker and Bricker, 1973; Kiernan and Jones, 1980).

These developmental frameworks fall short of presenting a comprehensive rapprochement between theory and intervention on at least two grounds. First, if it is believed that development occurs through interaction between the maturing child and his or her environment, such maps of development are relative to some abstract set of generalizations concerning "typical" conditions for development. Second, they actually offer no information concerning processes in the sense intended by Connolly (1975, p. 22) when he refers to " . . . what triggers off the transition from one developmental stage to another." At best, such frameworks are of heuristic value in giving direction to intervention activities. For individual children, further analysis concerning both the *conditions* for learning and *process* influences will be called for.

By conditions is meant the observable, concrete interactions that occur between the child and his or her physical and social environment and the relationship of these interactions to developmental change or its non-occurrence. In addition, we can consider at an abstract level to what extent developmentally significant behavior exhibited within a number of these related ecological systems reflects possible differences in the processes that developmentalists have suggested underlie change in the child's competence. In exploring conditions and processes we go well beyond the type of developmental information reviewed above, and move closer to the central concern of how process information can inform intervention.

Behavioral technology has had such an impact on the field of early education (Kysela, this volume) that an analysis of the conditions for development could take the form of a functional analysis of developmentally significant behavior (Kiernan, 1973). This would characterize regularities in regard to the child's interaction with the physical and social environments and, through appropriate manipulation of these relations, test hypotheses concerning the antecedent and consequent events influencing behavior (Bijou, 1966). Thus, the analysis of conditions would expand and explore areas of behavior defined in the sequential and hierarchical checklists and lattices.

The exploration of processes described in developmental studies would enter into these functional analyses by enabling researchers to focus on fundamental aspects of the behavior as it occurs across several situations. This use of process information may be illustrated with a specific example drawn from the neglected area of motor skill development. The most comprehensive theoretical analyses of motor skill development available have been proposed by Connolly (1973) and Bruner (1970). Their accounts of motor skill development derive in part from the description of motor problem solving described by the Russian worker Bernstein (1967). In applying Bernstein's theory to the question of motor skill development in children, Connolly suggested that skilled performance reflects the smooth and facile integration of well-defined, coherent skill modules. By analogy to computer-functioning, such modules are controlled by subroutines that constitute a motor program underlying the complete behavioral skill sequence. Developmentally, the child moves from less to more smooth sequences of skilled action as the subroutines of the program become better integrated. Furthermore, subroutines can be transferred between programs directed to solving different motor problems. Again, this process of reintegration underlies developmental trends in motor development. These concepts are complemented by a feedback model in which parameters of movement direction and velocity can be corrected as the behavior is being executed. Changes in information processing channel capacity as the child gets older are also postulated (Connolly, 1970).

The child becomes able to deal with more information as a function of both increased biological maturity and the freeing of attention from the need to concentrate entirely on the mastered task.

Evidence for this theory is limited, although several studies support it (Bruner, 1970; Elliott and Connolly, 1973; Moss and Hogg, 1979). Nevertheless, it offers an approach to the development of early intervention that differs from the functional analysis carried out in most test-teach intervention procedures. In terms of characteristic motor curricula teaching, aims may consist of developing superior pincer grip, block stacking, peg placement and so on. All these skills show relatively well-defined developmental trends. If motor skill development is viewed in terms of a Connolly-Bruner framework, however, a focus for teaching and evaluation will begin to look a little different. We may well persist with these typical nursery materials and develop them further. But we shall be concerned not only with children accomplishing such specific tasks, but with the extent to which component skills are used and the extent to which the child integrates and reintegrates them in novel motor problem solutions.

This excursion into the theory of motor skill development is far from exhaustive. This brief account does show how process information might affect our approach to intervention. A behavior modifier's response to this suggestion might be: What you have done is to redefine the target behaviors by moving to a more molecular level of behavior analysis. Within this finer-grain framework, researchers are basically dealing with target behaviors and their generalization across situations, and both task analysis and generalization are well-documented procedures in the repertoire of the behavior technologist. It must first be acknowledged that the education realization of the process information, to be useful to the interventionist, must be exemplified in behavior, and that therefore the armamentarium of the behavior technologist will and should be applicable. Also, by informing the curriculum aims through this analysis of developmental processes, a radically different specification of what is being taught and what the outcome of the intervention is has been proposed. What is sought here is not a simple generalization of a skill (e.g., container behavior with different types of material and in different places), but manifestations of process one would expect to see exemplified in a number of markedly different tasks. To such an end, teaching might concentrate on inducing transferability of skill modules and the necessary concomitant skill module reintegration, with a progressive expansion of the pool of modules and the complexity of their integration.

A major consideration is the relationship between our knowledge of the process of language development and how that relationship might inform intervention strategies. It may be possible to direct a specific intervention strategy at helping a child to produce more auxiliaries or to understand auxiliaries in declarative sentences. As an alternative to direct programming, we might take account of both our understanding of language as a structured system and the internal factors the child brings to bear on the situation. To undertake this, researchers might draw on the work of Newport, Gleitman, and Gleitman (1977) on motherese. What is learned from these studies is that children are more likely to pay attention to certain aspects of the signal, so they are going to pick up those auxiliaries that are in initial positions. The place they are in these positions is in yes/no questions. Where mothers use more yes/no questions, the later use of auxiliaries by the child is positively affected.

The child's paying attention to certain aspects of the signal may not be identical with the output being trained. The structured nature of the language system is also taken into account. Early educators could well treat such a proposal as the occasion for contrasting such a teaching strategy with alternative teaching modes. Here the early intervention system offers the context for a two-way interchange between the developmental researcher and the early educator. Ramey's conference observation on this interchange follows:

> It seems to me that the people who have traditionally been working with developmentally different populations have frequently been construed by the more general academic community as the consumers and later practitioners of ideas that were generated in a more theoretical context. Typically with normal children (first) . . . then it gets translated and applied (to the) handicapped . . . and I think there's some usefulness to that strategy . . . I'm not sure that the reverse channel of communication has been used as well . . . many people interested in normal language don't really know the developmentally deviant literature. . . . there are probably many, many natural experiments that would preclude a great deal, or at least lessen the likelihood, of having to do a great deal of parametric research.''

The scope for the service/research interchange in the area of language intervention is nowhere more soberingly put than in Brinker and Bricker's (1980) conclusion that '' . . . no sequence of language behavior has been empirically validated as the efficient road to language intervention'' (p. 198).

This level of intervention with an analysis of process has not been met. It would be difficult to point to work that goes beyond some of our colleagues in this respect, but for others it would be unrealistic to expect more than the utilization of information on the prerequisites of language development in the service of his elective decision making.

In establishing the two-way exchange between interventionists and developmental psychologists, much thought needs to be given to the structure of research projects and personnel organization. Beyond the confines of relatively infrequent conferences, research compartmentalization tends to restrict interchange.

The prospect of gaining funds for research in which such interchange is possible seems to be increasingly less tractable over the very period during which researchers have become fully aware of the desirability of such an exchange.

A major problem is the inertia in the intervention system that makes it extremely difficult to make sensitive response to new information concerning developmental processes. This inertia is likely to lead to the ossification of sequential checklists, a state reinforced by their retention for administrative convenience and their contribution to mandated Individual Educational Programs. Checklists can bar new information on developmental processes being incorporated into curriculum activities. In this sense, developmental checklists may contribute to positive outcome in terms of administrative evaluation, that is, demonstrating that certain practices have been conducted, but still have no effective outcome in terms of facilitating developmental advancement.

EVALUATION AND EARLY INTERVENTION

In the chapters discussed here, three phases in the sequence of activities leading to evaluation may be noted: 1) Howard Shane reported on an elective and selective decision-making procedure to assist the educator or clinician in assigning children to augmentative communication systems. The procedure described represents an important step forward in taking augmentative communication out of the realm of intuition and, in some cases the realm of prejudice, into a well-conceived framework in which to make informed decisions. The next step in developing the procedure entails evaluation at both stages of decision making—the elective and selective. It would be inappropriate to undertake summative evaluation that involves "elected" children being assigned randomly to oral language and augmentative communication systems, respectively. Such a procedure would fly in the face of clinical judgment in the case of many of the criteria employed. A child with severe damage to the motor apparatus affecting vocal control, for example, would not go to a conventional speech group with any realistic expectation of success in oral communication training. Some form of formative evaluation based on monitoring the consequences of election and the response to the elected system would seem more appropriate;

2) Kysela et al. evaluate specific programs within an applied analysis of behavior framework. At this level, the effectiveness of their procedures is clearly and impressively demonstrated, and their results complement the growing body of work demonstrating the utility of such procedures in early intervention with young, developmentally delayed children; 3) these authors then go beyond specific program evaluation to consider the impact of their total programs on global scores of rate of development. These measures of rate are compared implicitly, and not quantitatively, with a wider literature describing the declining rate of development in developmentally delayed children. This implicit comparison is employed as an alternative to a formal experimental-control group design.

Two issues arise from these potential and actual evaluative strategies. First, there is the question of the evaluative context. Strategies 1 and 2 are both self contained because they do not necessarily take as their ultimate criterion the changed competence of the child in the various overlapping ecologies (home, classroom, neighborhood) in which the child lives. The second relates to the extent to which inferences concerning program effectiveness can be based on developmental and intelligence test performance and the conditions under which such comparisons are valid.

Kysela et al. refer to the concept of ecological validity as a requirement to be met by their intervention models. It is open to question whether their citation of Brooks and Baumeister's (1977) use of this concept actually provides a justification for working with developmentally delayed children outside institutional settings. Brooks and Baumeister's point is that laboratory studies that establish performance/process deficits in retarded persons should also demonstrate that the postulated deficits actually contribute to the person's retarded functioning in the wider environment, that is, that the experimental demonstration is an ecologically valid explanation of retarded behavior. The applicability of this concept to intervention evaluation is somewhat different. Here the intervention would be ecologically valid if the gap between environmental demands and the child's performance was narrowed as a result of the intervention. In this sense, an intervention could be ecologically valid in an institution if this was the child's primary ecology.

One aspect of evaluating Shane's decision matrices is clearly concerned with ecological validity. At the election level he notes the importance to proposed augmentative communication programs of significant persons in the child's environment. Similarly, at the selection level, he refers to the environment-integration issue: " . . . the degree to which an augmentative communication system can restrict or promote social interaction between the nonspeaking person and the community." Similarly, acquisition of specific skills in a restricted learning situation may offer a positive evaluation of a given teaching method, but still not bear upon the wider issue of whether the child is more able to meet the demands of other ecologies so his or her behavior is less retarded. At the preschool level, such ecologies reflect the expectation of parents and educators of young children, and consists of home and classroom environments, as well as transitory settings (transport, holidays, etc.).

Ecological evaluation then should take place across a range of defined ecologies. The need to ensure this entails the systematic use of the generalization technology described by Baer and Stokes (1977). In terms of evaluation technology, the use of observational procedures can play an important role (Sackett, 1978a, 1978b). Howlin et al. (1975) described methods of analyzing the speech of autistic children and their mothers as recorded during normal interactions in home settings. The observational categories and procedures were then used to evaluate the impact of a behaviorally-based language program on the speech of the mothers and the children in the home over a relatively extensive (18-month) period (Howlin, 1979). Here, teaching and evaluation took place within the same ecology. In the work of Brinker and Goldbart (1981), an observational tool aimed at documenting the social and communicative development of preschool severely and profoundly retarded and nonretarded children has evolved within the Anson House Preschool Project, University of Manchester, England. Direct observation parallels individual and small group language teaching and complements specific training evaluation. Some form of ecological evaluation will provide a valuable addition to our understanding of Shane's decision-making system, and the Language Rating System Kysela is developing will complement his carefully documented program assessments.

Such evaluation obviously differs markedly from traditional forms of evaluation that entail pretest and posttest comparisons of global developmental or intelligence tests in an intervention group with appropriate controls. Although the reasons for change often remain unidentified, it is expected that if changes are made in developmentally significant behavior in our curriculum, then changes in test performance will also occur. Ramey, in the conference discussion, summarized the rationale for global tests. He presupposes that Kysela adopted the measurement instruments employed (e.g., the Bayley Scales) because they:

> " . . . would give . . . a generalized picture of the summative effects of your more specific curriculum, and that the curriculum itself, while not teaching this particular test, is being modified to take into account what

the child's capabilities are . . . so that (when) we come back and give this test repeatedly, if this test is in any way a reflection of more generalized abilities that you've built in, then this should capture in a fairly gross and generalized way, as . . . these tests do, some overall instructional effects.

As Ramey indicated, the use of developmental tests may be tests of generalization removed from the main training context. Baer, in the discussion, questioned how far such global testing within a program of the sort developed by Kysela, does constitute evaluation:

If you had meant the main outcome of your program to be a steadily increasing improvement in this developmental ratio score, you would have redesigned your curriculum to aim exactly at that outcome. In fact, you designed your curriculum on some other logic and it seems to me that including a developmental ratio score as part of your outcome is not done in a spirit of evaluation, that is, in the spirit of asking: did we do well or not do well in this curriculum? It seems to me it could have been done simply in the spirit of open curiosity. We designed a curriculum to produce certain kinds of changes in our subjects and we have data saying the extent to which we did and did not do that. What also happened, the question might be . . . to IQ-like scores or DQ-like scores? And the fact that they are not going down when presumably they would have gone down in a control group . . . is the significant fact. But . . . under that logic, this is not the evaluation of your program, it's simply a fact about your program.

In support of this view it is possible to point to specific examples of program outcome. Sebba (1979) developed a behaviorally-based intervention project for profoundly retarded multiply handicapped children. In several instances, selected objectives were met on specific programs. Often, however, there was a failure to detect change in global developmental scores on a standardized test.

It may be argued that with evaluation technology we should cast out nets wide in considering the impact of a program. For example, Rutman (1977) suggested that unanticipated effects might be of considerable importance in describing the impact of a program, and too tight a selection of evaluation instruments might fail to detect such effects. Willems' (1974) concern with the need to document the wider ecological consequences of behavioral intervention also bears on this point. For example, it may not be the aim of an intervention project to encourage parents to establish their own support system among themselves. Such an unanticipated effect, however, is of interest and worth documenting. Given this point, then global test assessments may provide additional information on a broader front than evaluation of specific programs having a part in *documenting*, if not in strict terms *evaluating*, an intervention program. Under what conditions then, can assessment of general development offer additional information of this sort?

At least two uses of developmental/IQ scores can be proposed. First, there is the conventional experimental-control comparison involving a pretest and posttest design, ideally with at least one intermediate assessment. Second, a comparison of intervention group development may be made with some expected norm of development derived from other studies. Within either context a measure of developmental age may be employed, or alternatively a measure of rate of development, that is, a developmental age or a developmental quotient, respectively. The former is based on a comparison with some standard of actual performance relative to normative development and in reality is in no sense an age. The latter is a derived measure in which rate of development is expressed in terms of a ratio of developmental to chronological age.

Kysela et al. selected the indirect comparison of their intervention groups' performance relative to expected trends in development in the retarded population at large, using a measure of rate as the dependent measure. In considering such a comparison, two points need to be remembered. First, Fisher and Zeaman (1970) in their semi-longitudinal study of the development of intelligence, using a standard measure of IQ, show that rate and direction of change in IQ depend upon the chronological age at which the assessment is undertaken. Second, rate and direction of change of IQ in particular CA ranges depend upon the degree of retardation.

Kysela et al. cite Cornwall and Birch's (1969) cross-sectional study of the decline in IQ with increasing CA in Down's syndrome children as a "marker" against which to evaluate changes in rate in development in their own groups. In general, however, the children in these groups are younger than those in Cromwell and Birch's study where the age range explored was 4–17 years. A more apt marker would have been Carr's (1975) study of development in Down's syndrome infants between the ages of 1.5–24 months. Cunningham (1979) replicated and extended Carr's study by undertaking more regular Bayley Scales assessments longitudinally with Down's syndrome infants. Although the results basically confirmed Carr's data, children from his samples tended to perform at a relatively higher level. Carr's and Cunningham's data confirm the point made by Fisher and Zeaman that the developmental quotient declines consistently from 1.5 to 24 months with the most marked drop occurring between 1.5 and 10 months. Thereafter the decline is more gradual, although not necessarily regular. Thus, even within a restricted chronological range, possible developmental rate markers may vary with obvious consequences for evaluative comparisons.

What are these consequences? First, it is inappropriate to pool data from two groups in which anticipated rate of decline of DQ differs. Several of Kysela's home-intervention groups will have fallen in the CA range in which Carr has shown rapid decline in rate of development. Most in the school program will be in a group in which more gradual decline is anticipated. The impact of a given program on the rate of decline among these children is of great interest. For such a comparison to be made, however, the same program should be applied within different CA ranges for any inferences to be drawn concerning their relative effectiveness.

Within the Kysela et al. study, the home and school programs should be considered in their own right rather than through pooled data or through comparisons between them. For each program, an anticipated decline in rate of development has been reversed from Test period 1 to period 2. For the home group this represents a significant rise, although not for the school group (although here there is also no significant drop in rate). Also, between test periods 2 and 3 there is no significant drop in rate of general development. The Period 1–2 change may reflect the initial facilitating impact of intervention independently of its specific (intended) consequences. Cunningham (1979) demonstrated in a study of home-visiting to families of Down's syndrome infants that the early impact on Bayley Mental Scale scores of visiting families (12–18 weeks) produces gains relative to nonvisited families who receive a later intervention (24 weeks), but that by 48 weeks no significant difference is noted and subsequently the boost for the early intervention group washes out. The Kysela et al. data, however, do not show any dramatic decline between periods 2–3. It is possible that even if Ramey's interpretation is correct for Phases 1 to 2, Kysela's group met their relatively strict aim of halting progressive decline in rate of development. It is important to note Ramey's point that even though the change in rate of development between the first and second, and second and third testings may reflect relatively less impact in phase two than phase one, the impacts in the two phases are equally real (i.e., not artifacts) and demand psychological explanation.

A conclusive demonstration that the aim has been met depends upon some direct comparison of rate of change in the intervention group relative to changes over the specific CA ranges as assessed in a contemporary cohort in the wider developmentally delayed population. If control groups cannot be constituted, then expected rate may be derived from studies approximating most closely to the sample characteristics and test instruments to be employed. Carr's (1975) or Cunningham's (1979) studies mentioned earlier seem to offer such a source for comparison with the home group. Such a reference point is at least more concrete than the generalizations drawn from the Cornwall and Birch study.

A further point of considerable importance regarding the use of ratio measures must be noted: Bayley (1969) stated that DQ should not be calculated using the conventional MA/CA × 100 formula and that there are dangers inherent in this approach. When Dicks-Mireaux (1972) employed this formula (on the Gesell test data from Down's syndrome infants) she found an increase in rate of development between 3 and 6 months. Carr (1970), however, showed that the increase is an artifact of calculating DQ = MA/CA × 100. No such increase will be shown where the more appropriate *sigma score method* is used:

$$DQ = 100 \times \frac{x - \bar{x} \times 16}{S.D.}$$

Where × is the child's score, x̄ the mean of the standardized population, and S.D. the population standard deviation. She suggested that ". . . where standard deviations are not available scores should be reported simply in terms of mental age. This would be less misleading than reporting quotients, which may give the impression of describing population levels, but which may in fact not do so accurately." (p. 218). When evaluation of early intervention is based on relative rates of development this point requires careful consideration.

TECHNIQUES OF EARLY INTERVENTION

There is a link between the information used to develop our teaching aims and evaluation of outcome, that is, the teaching procedure employed. It is the obvious failure of severely and profoundly developmentally delayed children to develop at a rate within normal range that leads us to specialized educational intervention. Typically, as Baer and Stokes (1977) noted, such intervention entails specialized training settings *outside* the ecology in which learned behavior is to be practiced. These authors describe several techniques that may be employed to effect the generalization from the training setting to the wider habitat. They also note that the strategy of setting up behavior change processes in the natural ecology may be employed directly, although the lack of skilled personnel may preclude this technique.

Developing new behaviors in the natural ecology has implications beyond the technology of establishing generalization of learned behavior. Except in the case of a small proportion of profoundly retarded children with exceptional sensory and physical handicaps, most severely and profoundly retarded children will already have evolved complex strategies of interaction with their environment. These strategies are of developmental significance, that is, they reflect the level of development achieved by the child during his or her life-span, and represent level of performance in the habitat that is the critical setting for evaluation. In addition, these strategies reflect motivational states in both specific learning situations as shown by Evans and Hogg (1975) and social interactions as demonstrated by Beveridge and Evans (1978). The teacher concerned with the development of new behavior is then mapping new strategies onto existing strategies, the determinants of which are complex. Such mapping can be more effectively achieved by avoiding imposition of adult demands on the child without taking into account his or her natural strategies.

For these reasons, the Kysela et al. rigorous application across children, situations, and curriculum, of Martin et al.'s (1975) teaching sequence is questionable. This can be counter-productive because the need to establish behavioral control in order to implement such a teaching sequence can in some instances become an unnecessarily time consuming activity where more sensitivity to developing the teaching context in line with the child's natural strategies would be more productive. This seems particularly true in setting criteria that demand repetition of an acquired behavior. Although this may be desirable when a behavior is very unstable, or during a period of consolidation, in many cases motivation is lost and occasionally distress is caused.

What is called for is the development of a technology or set of teaching practices that relate new adaptive strategies for the child to existing patterns of interaction that the child exhibits in his or her environment. It is possible that such an approach may offer a rapprochement between the advances created by the relatively recent technology of behavior modification, and some earlier forms of nursery education with their emphasis of free choice by the child and careful arrangement of developmental materials, with teacher as facilitator rather than direct intervener.

REFERENCES

Baer, D. M., and Stokes, T. F. 1977. Discriminating a generalization technology: Recommendations for research in mental retardation. In P. Mittler (ed.), Research to Practice in Mental Retardation: Vol. II, Education and Training. University Park Press. Baltimore.

Bayley, N. 1969. Manual for the Bayley Scales of Infant Development. Psychological Corporation. New York.

Bernstein, N. 1967. The Co-ordination and Regulation of Movements. Pergamon Press. Oxford.

Beveridge, M., and Evans, P. 1978. Classroom interaction: two studies of severely subnormal children. Res. Educ. 19:39–48.

Bijou, S. W. 1966. A functional analysis of retarded development. *In* N. R. Ellis (ed.), International Review of Research in Mental Retardation, Vol. I. Academic Press. London.

Bricker, W. A., and Bricker, D. D. 1973. Behaviour modification programmes. *In* P. Mittler (ed.), Assessment for Learning in the Mentally Handicapped. Churchill Livingstone. Edinburgh and London.

Bricker, D., Seibert, J. M., and Casuso, V. 1980. Early intervention. *In* J. Hogg and P. Mittler (eds.), Advances in Mental Handicap Research, Vol. I. John Wiley & Sons, Inc., New York.

Brinker, R. D., and Bricker, D. 1980. Teaching a first language: Building complex structures from simpler components. *In* J. Hogg and P. Mittler (eds.), Advances in Mental Handicap Research, Vol. I. John Wiley & Sons, Inc., New York.

Brinker, R. P., and Goldbart, J. 1981. The problem of reliability in the study of early communication skills. Br. J. Psychol. 72:27–41.

Brooks, P. K., and Baumeister, A. A. 1977. A plea for consideration of ecological validity in the experimental psychology of mental retardation. Am. J. Ment. Defic. Res. 81:407–416.

Bruner, J. S. 1970. The growth and structure of skill. *In* K. Connolly (ed.), Mechanisms of Motor Skill Development. Academic Press. London.

Carr, J. 1970. Mental and motor development in young mongol children. J. Ment. Defic. Res. 14:205–220.

Carr, J. 1975. Young Children with Down's Syndrome: Their Development, Upbringing, and Effect on Their Families. Butterworths. London.

Connolly, K. 1970. Response speed, temporal sequencing and information processing in children. *In* K. Connolly (ed.), Mechanisms of Motor Skill Development. Academic Press. London.

Connolly, K. 1973. Factors influencing the learning of manual skills by young children. *In* R. A. Hinde and J. Stevenson-Hinde (eds.), Constraints on Learning. Academic Press. London.

Connolly, K. 1975. Behaviour modification and motor control. *In* C. C. Kiernan and F. P. Woodford (eds.), Behaviour Modification with the Severely Retarded. Associated Scientific Publishers. Amsterdam.

Cornwall, A. C., and Birch, H. G. 1969. Psychological and social development in home-reared children with Down's syndrome (mongolism). Am. J. Ment. Defic. 74:341–350.

Council of Europe. 1975. Problems in the evaluation of pre-school education. Documentation Centre for Education in Europe, Strasbourg.

Cunningham, C. C. 1979. Aspects of early development in Down's syndrome infants. Unpublished doctoral thesis, University of Manchester, Manchester.

Dicks-Mireaux, M. J. 1972. Mental development of infants with Down's syndrome. Am. J. Ment. Defic. 77:26–32.

Elliott, J. M., and Connolly, K. 1973. Hierarchical structure in skill development. *In* K. Connolly and J. Bruner (eds.), The Growth of Competence. Academic Press. London.

Evans, P. L. C., and Hogg, J. 1975. Individual differences in the severely retarded child in acquisition, stimulus generalization and extinction in go/no-go discrimination learning. J. Exp. Child Psychol. 20:377–390.

Fisher, M. A., and Zeaman, D. 1970. Growth and decline of retardate intelligence. *In* N. R. Ellis (ed.), International Review of Research in Mental Retardation, Vol. IV. Academic Press. London.

Hogg, J. 1975. Normative development and educational program planning for severely educationally subnormal children. *In* C. C. Kiernan and F. P. Woodford (eds.), Behavior Modification with the Severely Retarded. Associated Scientific Publishers. Amsterdam.

Howlin, P. 1979. Training parents to modify the language of their autistic children: A home based approach. Unpublished doctoral thesis, University of London, London.

Howlin, P., Cantwell, D., Marchant, R., Berger, M., and Rutter, M. 1975. Analysing mothers' speech to young autistic children: a methodological study. J. Abnorm. Child Psychol. 1:317–339.

Kiernan, C. C. 1973. Functional analysis. *In* P. Mittler (ed.), Assessment for Learning in the Mentally Handicapped. Churchill Livingstone, Edinburgh and London.

Kiernan, C. C., and Jones, M. 1980. The Behaviour Assessment Battery for use with the profoundly retarded. *In* J. Hogg and P. Mittler (eds.), Advances in Mental Handicap Research, Vol. I. John Wiley & Sons, Inc., New York.

McMaster, J. McG. 1973. Toward an Educational Theory for the Mentally Handicapped. Edward Arnold. London.

Martin, G., Murrell, M., Nicholson, C., and Tallman, B. 1975. Teaching Basic Skills to the Severely and Profoundly Retarded. Vopic Press. Portage la Prairie, Manitoba.

Moss, S. C., and Hogg, J. 1979. The Development of Hand Function in Mentally Handicapped and Non-handicapped Preschool Children. Paper presented at the 5th International Congress of the International Association for the Scientific Study of Mental Deficiency, August, Jerusalem, Israel.

Newport, E. L., Gleitman, H., and Gleitman, L. R. 1977. Mother, I'd rather do it myself: some effects and non-effects of maternal speech style. *In* C. E. Snow and C. A. Ferguson (eds.), Talking to Children: Language Input and Acquisition. Cambridge University Press. London.

Rutman, L. 1977. Planning an evaluation study. *In* L. Rutman (ed.), Evaluation Research Methods: A Basic Guide. Sage Publications. London.

Sackett, G. P. (ed.). 1978a. Observing Behavior, Volume I: Theory and Applications in Mental Retardation. University Park Press, Baltimore.

Sackett, G. P. (ed.). 1978b. Observing Behavior, Volume II: Data Collection and Analysis Methods. University Park Press, Baltimore.

Sebba, J. 1979. Intervention for Profoundly Retarded Multiply Handicapped (PRMH) Children through Parent Training in a Preschool Setting and at Home. Paper presented at the 5th International Congress of the International Association for the Scientific Study of Mental Deficiency, August, Jerusalem, Israel.

Willems, E. P. 1974. Behavioral technology and behavioral ecology. J. Appl. Behav. Anal. 7:151–165.

Section

V

Intervention Issues and Strategies

chapter
14

Creating Social Environments to Facilitate Language Development

Craig T. Ramey

Joseph J. Sparling

Barbara H. Wasik

Frank Porter Graham Child Development Center
University of North Carolina at Chapel Hill
Chapel Hill, North Carolina

Family background characteristics are the strongest predictor of academic performance after children enter public school (Coleman, 1966). Ramey et al., (1978) indicated that the child's race and mother's level of education at the time of the child's birth significantly predicted the child's IQ, academic achievement, and teacher's opinion of the child as a student in first grade. These results confirm for the present what historically has been presumed—that relative social disadvantage is associated disproportionately with school failure. Psychology, sociology, and education are replete with studies similar to the one cited, showing that various personal and social background characteristics predict differential performance in academic settings. This genre of studies is concerned with the epidemiology of school failure, that is, the identification of children who are likely to need special services to achieve at an acceptable minimal level. What is not clear is why those molar characteristics are so predictive. To the extent that molar variables, such as mother's educational level, are a direct part of a causal chain, then there must be specific parental practices that are different from those of more advantaged parents that directly affect the disadvantaged child. For an agent to be part of a causal chain it must have direct contact with the child. In the Ramey et al. (1978) study the mother's educational level might be, for example, associated with different nutritional habits, different forms or content of teaching, or an abnegation of parental responsibility.

Educational programs for disadvantaged children can be viewed as experiments in which variables that are thought to be causal agents in school performance are systematically manipulated and the consequences of that manipulation observed. The differences between advantaged and disadvantaged families, however, are numerous and pervasive. Educators must presume that some of those differences are merely stylistic preferences and not critical to the process of a child's meeting the minimal educational expectancies for our society. Therefore, the likely causal differences between advantaged and disadvantaged families must be identified and then priorities must be set for research into the manipulable variables within educational settings.

This chapter summarizes recent research and development at the Frank Porter Graham Center into the correlates and causes of school failure. This chapter describes what is known from the research literature about early environmental differences associated with differences in cognitive and linguistic development; it develops the thesis that the mother-child relationship is the typical *final causal pathway* for early cultural transmission, especially the transmission of language; it critically reviews the previous educational intervention projects that were designed to affect high-risk mother-child interactional systems; it describes a current research project designed to affect the high-risk

449

mother-child systems; and it concludes with a sampling of preliminary results from that project.

ENVIRONMENTAL FACTORS DURING INFANCY
ASSOCIATED WITH COGNITIVE AND LINGUISTIC PERFORMANCE

One of the most consistent findings by psychologists has been the predictable relationship between socioeconomic status (SES) and performance on cognitive and linguistic tasks. Lower-class children, as a group, almost invariably demonstrate different intellectual attributes from those of the rest of the general population, and these attributes are relatively undervalued in social desirability by the larger society. The classic works by Galton (1869) and Burt et al. (1934) attributed these differences in intellectual performance to hereditary factors. Beginning with Hunt's (1961) influential book on *Intelligence and Experience*, however, it became academically respectable once again to consider that these social-class differences might have a very strong environmentally determined component. Thus, during the 1960s and 1970s there has been considerable research concerning environmental influences on intelligence, in general, and more recently on language development in particular. Two major questions have guided this research into environmental influences concerning performance by the different social classes. First, investigators have attempted to specify the earliest ages at which social class differences in cognitive and linguistic performance become significant. Second, researchers have tried to identify the psychological mechanisms that are related to the differential developmental outcomes. A brief review of the empirical literature for each of these research areas is presented below.

Intellectual Development and Social Class

If the various social classes begin life with similar physical and mental performance, the age at which they begin to diverge will provide some clues for possible causal mechanisms underlying that divergence. In general, researchers have failed to show social class differences in intelligence during the first year of life using standardized tests of infant development (Knoblock and Pasamanick, 1953; Hindley, 1960; Bayley, 1965; Golden and Birns, 1968; Lewis and Wilson, 1972; Ramey, Farran, and Campbell, 1979). Significant differences in intellectual performance (with lower SES children scoring lower) have been reported during the second year of life (Knoblock and Pasamanick, 1953; Golden and Birns, 1968; Golden et al., 1971; Ramey et al., 1979). There exists a vast literature concerning the school years to indicate major social class differences in intelligence (Hess, 1970).

Item analyses of performance on intelligence tests have been used to identify the particular components of intelligence most strongly associated with social class. From an item analysis of intelligence test results for school-age children reported by Eells et al. (1951), it was concluded that "mean SES differences were largest for verbal items and smallest for picture, geometric-design, and stylized-drawing items" (Hess, 1970, p. 507). A more recent item analysis of the performance of lower-class children at 18 months using the Bayley Mental Development Index and at 24 and 36 months using the Stanford-Binet has been reported by Ramey and Campbell (1977). In comparing an educationally treated preschool group of lower-class children with a control group not receiving systematic preschool education, they found that the control group's lower scores were due to their higher rate of failure on language items. This finding was also supported by the control group's relative inferiority (and below average performance) at 30 months of age on the Verbal Scale of the McCarthy Scales of Children's Abilities. This implication of language as a major component in the relatively lower intellectual performance of lower-class children is consistent with previously reported deficits in the verbal abilities of older children from lower-class families (Deutsch, 1967). If language is, as it seems to be, a major factor, to what do we attribute the linguistic differences and how early do the differences begin?

Mechanisms for Early Language Learning

Language is a social medium and is acquired, at least initially, in social situations. Therefore, the social situations of children must be examined in order to understand the learning of specific languages. Throughout the world virtually all biologically healthy children develop a language system. In this country, however, there are substantial differences in the specific elements of the language that are learned by lower-class children. Furthermore, these differences exist before the children enter public school. Given that preschool-age children typically spend more time with their parents than others, and more typically with mothers than fathers (Rebelsky and Hanks, 1971), the mother-child interactional system becomes a likely candidate for close scrutiny concerning the development of language.

The current research on social class differences in mother-child interactions during the preschool years flow from a now classic study by Hess and Shipman (1965) and from observations by Bernstein (1961) concerning language. Hess and Shipman (1965) demonstrated that middle-class mothers used more efficient teaching strategies than lower-class mothers and that the quality of the mother's teaching strategy was related to the child's level of cognitive functioning. Bernstein

(1961) argued that the speech of lower- and middle-class parents differed in that lower-class mothers used a more "restricted code" in communicating; whereas, middle-class mothers used a more "elaborated code" characterized by greater flexibility.

Bee et al., (1969) extended these findings with 4- and 5-year-olds and reported that middle-class mothers used longer and more complex sentences, more adjectives, and fewer personal referents than lower-class mothers. With the realization that substantial linguistic differences in interactional styles existed by the end of the preschool years, investigators began to identify the earliest ages of those differences. Thus, Lewis and Wilson (1972) studied 12-week-old infants who represented five socioeconomic levels. They reported that although lower- and middle-class mothers vocalized in equal amounts to their infants, the middle-class mothers were more likely to respond to their infant's vocalizations with a vocalization of their own; whereas, lower-class mothers were more likely to touch their infants in response to infant vocalizations. Tulkin and Kagan (1972), working with 10-month-old first-born girls, found that middle-class mothers exceeded working class mothers on every verbal measure they used, including total amount of vocalization and reciprocal vocalizing. Cohen and Beckwith (1975) reported that better educated mothers vocalized more to their infants at 1, 3, and 8 months and that they were more likely than undereducated mothers to address positive comments to their infants.

Observations of 6-month-old infants and their mothers by Ramey and Mills (1977) showed that lower-class mothers talked less to their infants and that their infants vocalized less than their middle-class comparison sample. These results supported an earlier report by Ramey et al. (1975) that showed that lower-class mothers were observed to be less warm and verbally responsive, more punitive, and less involved with their 6-month-old infants than were middle-class mothers.

That verbal responsivity and involvement by mothers with their infants is important to the child's subsequent intellectual status is supported by the results from three prospective longitudinal studies. Clarke-Stewart (1973) investigated the mothering styles of 36 lower-class mothers and their first-born children between 9 and 18 months in a short-term longitudinal study. She found that "the amount of verbal stimulation directed toward the child significantly influenced the child's intellectual development, particularly the ability to comprehend and express language" (p. 92). Clarke-Stewart also stated that, "it was strongly suggested that maternal responsiveness to the child's social signals was enhancing the child's later intellectual and social performance."

Farran and Ramey (1980) observed the social interactions of 60 mother-infant pairs in a semi-naturalistic setting when the infants were 6 months old and again when they were 20 months. Forty-six of the infants were considered at high risk for later school failure because of the social and psychological situations of their families. Half of these lower-class, high-risk infants had been randomly assigned to an early intervention program (see Ramey and Campbell, 1979, for a more complete description of this early intervention program). The final group of 14 infants was a sample drawn from the general population. Principle components analyses of summed durations of specific behaviors yielded a first component at both 6 and 20 months that was labeled *Dyadic Involvement*. At each age, the first component was bipolar and included mother talking, demonstrating toys, and interacting with her infant at the positive end; and mother reading to herself and the child playing alone at the negative end. At 6 months the Dyadic Involvement factor accounted for 35% of the variance in the interactions. The second component at 6 months accounted for 18% of the variance and was primarily vocalization behaviors, with mother talking and child vocalizing at the positive end and child fussing at the negative end. This factor was labeled *Vocalization*. The Vocalization behaviors were subsumed in the Dyadic Involvement component at 20 months and that factor accounted for 35% of the interaction variance. Analyses of variance indicated that the three groups did not differ on Dyadic Involvement at 6 months. At 20 months, the general population sample scored as more involved than the lower-class, high-risk groups. Furthermore, Pearson correlations revealed a positive association ($r = 0.41$) between the Dyadic Involvement factor scores at 20 months and Stanford-Binet performance at 48 months. Thus, interactional differences are small to nonexistent during the first year of life but become greater and significant during the second year. Those differences during the second year are related to intellectual status at 4 years of age.

That maternal behaviors during infancy are linked to later developmental outcome as assessed by Stanford-Binet performance is also supported in a recent study by Ramey (1978). The Home Observation for Measurement of the Environment (Caldwell, Heider, and Kaplan, 1968) was modified to include only dyadic interactional behaviors that were overt in nature and that heavily emphasized the mother's language style toward her infant. The resulting 22 items that were scored as occurring or not occurring during a visit to the infant's home are contained in Table 1. These items are conceptualized as an *Index of Functional Maternal Concern* for the development of infants.

This index was used to observe 36 socioeconomically heterogeneous mother and infant pairs who were not involved in an early in-

Table 1. Index of functional maternal attachment

Item	Yes	No	No information
1. Mother spontaneously vocalizes to child at least twice during the visit (excluding scolding).	—	—	—
2. Mother responds to child's vocalizations with a vocal or verbal response.	—	—	—
3. Mother tells child the name of some object during the visit or says the name of a person or object in a "teaching" style.	—	—	—
4. Mother's speech is distinct, clear, and audible to interviewer.	—	—	—
5. Mother initiates verbal interchanges with the observer—asks questions, makes spontaneous comments.	—	—	—
6. Mother expresses ideas freely and easily and uses statements of appropriate length for conversation (e.g., gives more than brief answers).	—	—	—
7. Mother pemits child occasionally to engage in "messy" types of play.	—	—	—
8. Mother spontaneously praises child's qualities or behavior twice during the visit.	—	—	—
9. When speaking of or to child, mother's voice conveys positive feelings.	—	—	—
10. Mother caresses or kisses child at least once during visit.	—	—	—
11. Mother does not shout at child during the visit.	—	—	—
12. Mother does not express overt annoyance with or hostility toward child.	—	—	—
13. Mother neither slaps nor spanks child during the visit.	—	—	—
14. Mother reports that no more than one instance of physical punishment occurred during the past week.	—	—	—
15. Mother does not scold or criticize or "run down" the child during the visit.	—	—	—
16. Mother does not interfere with child's actions or restrict child's movement more than three times during the visit.	—	—	—
17. Mother tends to keep child within visual range and to look at him often.	—	—	—
18. Mother talks to child while doing her work.	—	—	—
19. Mother consciously encourages developmental advance.	—	—	—
20. Mother invests maturing toys with value via her attention.	—	—	—
21. Mother structures child's play period.	—	—	—
22. Mother provides toys that challenge the child to develop new skills.	—	—	—

tervention program. The infants were observed at 6 and 18 months of age. Significant positive correlations were found between the Index at both 6 and 18 months of age and the mother's education ($r \geq 0.46$) and her intelligence as assessed by a full scale Wechsler Adult Intelligence Scale (WAIS) ($r \geq 0.43$). The relationship between the level of functional maternal concern and the mother's intelligence is also supported by Clarke-Stewart (1973) who reported that a ". . . mother's PPVT (IQ) score and her knowledge about child development were highly correlated with her positive attitude toward children, and with all variables of "optimal care," giving support to the proposition that stimulating and competent maternal behaviors are related to maternal intelligence" (p. 54). Ramey (1978) found a relationship between performance on the Index of Functional Maternal Concern at 6 and at 18 months. This indicated group stability on functional maternal concern through time. Finally, the index at 6 months correlated significantly with 48-month Stanford-Binet performance ($r = 0.33$) and even higher with Binet performance when administered at 18 months ($r = 0.58$).

Summary

Thus, the available literature indicates that the mother-infant interactional system is strongly implicated in the development of a child's intelligence and language. Furthermore, there seems to be a strong relationship between the mother's SES and her style of mothering. Three major issues about the interactional styles of lower-class mothers, however, need to be addressed. First, we must be cautious not to attribute cause based upon a correlational relationship. The studies reviewed in this chapter are descriptive, nonexperimental studies. Thus, from a strictly logical viewpoint, whether the differences in interactional styles are causally related to the child's developmental outcome is unknown.

Second, although mothering styles are related to social class, many lower-class families rear children who are intellectually and socially competent. Therefore, although lowered intellectual and linguistic performance as a function of social class can be somewhat reliably predicted, those equations need to be improved. A more specific subpopulation of high-risk must be identified if our knowledge about the mother-infant interactional system is to benefit disadvantaged families and society.

Third, even if the mother-infant interactional system proves to be a major causal force in the intellectual and linguistic development of children, it is not known if typical lower-class interactional styles could be modified to better serve the development of disadvantaged children.

To date, the mother-infant interaction literature does not contain a single successful manipulative study concerning the modification of mothering styles in groups of lower-class women. In short, it is not known to what extent the final causal pathway for cultural and linguistic transmission during infancy is modifiable by education.

REVIEW OF INFANT INTERVENTION PROGRAMS

Results from the early intervention programs have been described in review articles by Stedman et al. (1972), Bronfenbrenner (1975), and Haskins, Finkelstein, and Stedman (1978).

The major intervention strategies with a day care/school setting (e.g., Robinson and Robinson, 1971) or a more comprehensive ecological approach (e.g., Garber and Heber, 1977; Ramey and Haskins, in press) have all had impressive results demonstrating the effectiveness of early intervention in enhancing language and cognitive development. Both the Milwaukee Project (Heber and Garber, 1975) and the Carolina Abecedarian Project (Ramey et al., 1976) have accumulated longitudinal data that continue to support program effects. These studies, however, did not focus on the mother-child interaction as its major vehicle for developmental change and for that reason are not considered here. The projects discussed in this chapter include only those that took place in the home when the children were between the ages of birth and 3 years. The children were from low income families and thus at risk for sociocultural mental retardation.

The home-centered projects were initiated in the 1960s and continued into the 70s. These programs shared the belief that planned educational activities could enhance the child's language and cognitive development. Individuals who interacted with the child included professionals, paraprofessionals and parents. When the parent was the primary adult interacting with the child, a parent education component was in effect in which the parent (always the mother in actuality) was instructed in ways to deal with her child.

With one exception (Schaefer and Aaronson) all the major home intervention programs trained the mother to provide planned activities for her child. Schaefer and Aaronson (1972) provided child-centered tutoring for biologically normal lower-class children from 1½ to 3 years of age. Approximately 1 hour of direct tutoring was provided each week. When the program was terminated at age 3, there was a 16 point difference in favor of experimental children compared to control children. The two groups did not differ in their performance on the Stanford Achievement Test after completing the first grade. Because of these nonsignificant long term effects, Schaefer and Aaronson analyzed the mother-child interaction to compare behavior during the tutoring session with the child's IQ level at the end of the intervention phase. The authors concluded that of major importance to the child's early intellectual development was "maternal positive involvement, interest in the child's education, and verbal expressiveness with the child" (p. 427). Schaefer has subsequently emphasized the need for intervention programs focusing on the family rather than the child.

Three other programs initiated in the 1960s involved parents, specifically the mother, in intervention programs for children at risk for sociocultural mental retardation. These programs are the Verbal Interaction Project under the direction of Phyllis Levenstein, an Experimental Program for Disadvantaged Mothers developed by Merle Karnes, and the Parent Education Program originated by Ira Gordon.

The Verbal Interaction Project designed by Levenstein (1970) focused on training the mother to interact with her child. The children were drawn from a suburban New York community when they were 2 years old. The program itself seems almost deceptively simple. A home visitor called a "Toy Demonstrator" went into the homes and showed the mother how to use various materials and techniques in her play with the child. In her initial experiment (Levenstein, 1970) the Toy Demonstrators were trained social case workers. In her later studies (Madden, Levenstein, and Levenstein, 1976) the Toy Demonstrators were nonprofessionals, and many were from low-income families themselves. The materials the Toy Demonstrator brought into the home were designed to stimulate verbal interaction. The materials were commercially available toys and books that were chosen for their stimulus properties and were introduced in order of increasing complexity.

The children initially had IQ scores in the low 80s. At the end of the first year the mean IQ of the experimental group was 101; the mean IQ of the control group was 89. The experimental group was divided in the second year into groups that received either the full program, an abbreviated version, or the toys without further tutoring. By the end of the first grade, the experimental groups were still superior to the control children and their scores varied directly with the intensity of the program.

For the importance of this program, and possibly to account for the long term gains, one must look beyond the curriculum materials or home visitor to note that the focus was on the mother-child interaction. Indeed, the role of the Toy Demonstrator was not merely to show how to use the curriculum materials but rather to enhance the mother-child relationship recognizing the primary role of the mother in the child's education. By enhancing this relationship, the possibility of continued positive and constructive mother-child interactions is provided. This should contribute to the child's cognitive and social development once the formal intervention phase ends.

Another major intervention effort in which the mother was trained to work with her child was conducted by Karnes and her colleagues. The mothers were from low-income backgrounds. The infants at the beginning of the study had a mean chronological age (CA) of 20 months, ranging from 13 to 27 months. The mothers, viewed as the primary agents of intervention, met in weekly meetings where they were instructed in how to use a sequential education program to stimulate cognitive and verbal development.

During the first year of intervention the 20 mothers met in groups of 10 over a 7-month period and covered both child- and mother-centered activities. The educational curriculum for the children centered on the use of toys to facilitate the intellectual and language development of the child. The mother-centered activities were based on the assumption that interactions in the groups would bring about positive attitude change.

In the second year, 15 of the original 20 mothers continued the group meetings for 8 months. Additional child-centered activities appropriate for the older child were introduced. During the group meetings, topics on community involvement were introduced along with principles of teaching.

On standardized IQ measures taken at the end of the program, the mean IQ of the experimental group was 106, and of the control group, 90. Karnes cautioned that these results could be transitory and might not be maintained later in school. She suggested that to obtain more stable gains those intervention efforts implemented through the mother should be planned to affect the child's total environment on a sustained basis (Karnes et al., 1970).

Another series of home intervention programs was initiated in 1966 under the direction of Ira Gordon. In each intervention situation the mother was instructed in the use of learning activities by a home visitor. The basic study was designed to determine the effectiveness of instructional home visits. A paraprofessional trained as a home visitor demonstrated materials that were designed to foster cognitive and language development in the child. The mother was then to use these materials with her child. The families were all low income and most were black. Comparison groups included families who received home visits that were not educationally oriented. During the second year the experimental design was altered to allow a comparison of a Piaget-based, language curriculum with a curriculum developed by paraprofessionals. Also, half of the original experimental group was randomly assigned as a new control group. During the third year, the children, who were then 2 years old, had a group experience added to their home visitation program. The children attended groups with four other children for two 2-hour periods each week. During this third year, half of the children were again randomly assigned to an experimental or to a control group and new families were also added.

The design for these 3 years resulted in seven treatment groups and one control group that were followed up in a longitudinal effort over several years. All phases of the program ended when the children were 3 years old. A follow-up study of the IQ scores through age 6 showed that children who had been in the program for 2 consecutive years or for 3 years were performing consistently at a higher level than the control children on the Stanford-Binet (Gordon and Guinagh, 1974). Perhaps even more important is an analysis of the achievement of the children as defined by achievement scores at grade level when in the second, third, or fourth grades. This analysis showed significant differences between the children in the longitudinal treatment groups (those with 2 or 3 years of intervention) and the control group. There were also significant differences in the number of children assigned to special education classes with only 6% of the longitudinal treatment group assigned compared to over 33% of the control group (Guinagh and Gordon, 1976).

Even more impressive results were obtained when the children were examined at age 10. Children who were in the study for either 2 consecutive years or for 3 years obtained significantly higher WISC-R scores than the control group. The analysis also revealed that 71.5% of the children who had been in the study for 3 years scored above IQ 85, and only 25% of the control children did. Confirming the data reported in 1976, the results at age 10 also showed significant differences between the longitudinal treatment groups and the control groups on the number of children assigned to special education classes (Gordon and Guinagh, 1978).

These last three studies have in common a strong component of parent education and parent involvement. Conclusions from all three studies have revealed the critical role of the parent and especially that of the mother. Yet, presently, there is a lack of evidence supporting either that there were specific observable changes in the mothers as a function of the program or that changes in the mother have a causative relationship to the child's behavior. The introduction of curriculum materials designed to enhance children's language and cognitive development can be effective, whether presented by the mother or by another adult. In all these programs the focus has been on having the adult gain competence in teaching the children.

This view of the parents' role is now seen as somewhat limited and one that does not result in easy generalities across other areas of development or one that allows the parent to plan constructively for the child in those months and years ahead when a specific set of curriculum materials is no longer available. During the past few years, almost every major investigator of programs for children at risk have acknowledged and stressed the need to go beyond the development of the child's curriculum materials and to focus more broadly on an adult curriculum. The need for this move from a focus on the child's curriculum to a focus on the adult's curriculum in the service of the child was stated recently by O'Keefe, National Director of the Home Start Training Centers and the Child and Family Resource Program:

> If we were planning Home Start all over again, we would have helped home visitors obtain adult education skills very early in the program because the focus of Home Start is an adult—a parent (1977, p. 9).

This view helped us to recognize the adult as learner and to develop a curriculum incorporating elements that facilitate adult learning, and processes that might provide skills for the adult to continue using as an effective parent after the termination of an intervention program. With this major objective in mind, the Carolina Approach to Responsive Education (Project CARE) was developed.

PROJECT CARE

Objectives

In 1978, Project CARE was designed to investigate issues in preventing socioculturally caused developmental retardation. Basically the project has three major objectives:
1. To develop and evaluate a parent curriculum that can be used in conjunction with day care or independently
2. To discover the psychological process through which the parent or caregiver "carries" the intervention
3. To describe the relationships among treatment programs and psychological, biological and family attributes during the first 5 years of the child's life.

Subjects

Twenty-four families identified by the High Risk Inventory (Ramey and Smith, 1977) were assigned in October, 1978, to one of three treatment groups: a home visitation group ($N = 12$), a home visitation plus day care group ($N = 6$), and a control group ($N = 6$). Additional families seeking day care from a general population also were included and randomly assigned to the second and third groups. A second cohort of families was identified and assigned in a similar pattern in the fall of 1979.

CONCEPTUAL FRAMEWORK FOR THE PARENT CURRICULUM

Project CARE's program development is based on the traditional conceptualization of curriculum as a union of the characteristics of the subject matter, the society, and the learner (Tyler, 1950). The contribution of each of these sources to the Project CARE curriculum is discussed below.

Curriculum Input from Parent Education

Although there has been increasing activity in developing parent education (Odell, 1974; Bronfenbrenner, 1975), the process of parent education is not well documented in the literature. In the absence of a comprehensive theory of parent education, Project CARE posits a central concept, a functional attachment or concern, as the organizing theme for the first 3 years of the child's life. During infancy, the primary developmental task of the mother-child dyad is the mutual establishment of functional attachment. Functional attachment is at the positive end of a continuum of dyadic interchange. Its polar opposite is functional abuse, and midway on the continuum is functional neglect. This continuum is a hypothetical construct that is similar to Erikson's (1950) idea of basic trust and of Bowlby's (1958) and Ainsworth's (1973) theories concerning the child's attachment to his or her mother. It differs from these, however, by emphasizing the dyadic and reciprocal nature of the attachment bond, that is, the attachment of both the child to the parent and of the parent to the child. The term *functional* is important in this hypothetical continuum because emphasis is on the observable consequences of interaction of one member of the dyad upon the other, rather than upon an inferred hypothetical state within either or both members of the dyad.

Functional attachment, evidenced by the parent toward the child, is stimulated through the parent curriculum. This attachment is assessed through observation of specific caregiving arrangements and behaviors that are observed either in preparation for the child's presence or actually in the child's presence. The broadest objectives for functional attachment are solving problems and communication. Functional attachment is described by the terms *plan, show*, and *change*. These are the working concept labels used in the parent curriculum. The labels are purposefully kept in simple, straightforward language. The depth of these concepts, however, is illustrated by their subcomponents listed in Figure 1.

This approach focuses on the actions of the adult and tries to sensitize the adult to the significance of his or her interactive role in the parent/child dyad. This approach does not primarily emphasize

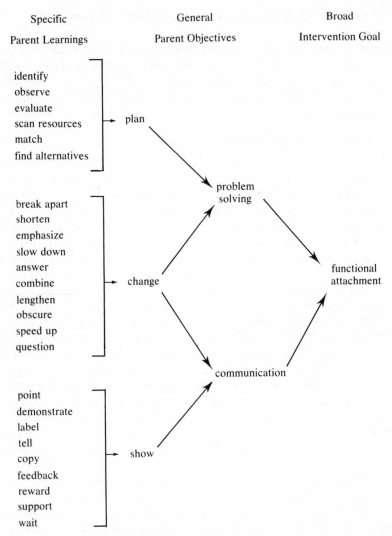

Figure 1.   Hierarchy of goals in parent curriculum.

whether the child's language abilities, creative abilities, or motor abilities, etc., are being stimulated but rather tries to increase the adult's awareness of adult behaviors that may gently and playfully stimulate these or other child processes or outcomes.

Curriculum Input from Society

A national survey of 1,500 parents (Sparling et al., 1978) supplemented by an ongoing dialogue with a local parent-advisory committee provides the basic inputs from the society into the curriculum. These two sources (however imperfect) provide a distal and proximal view of parental values, problems, and needs in contemporary society. This input provides no guidance on the level of abstractions such as functional attachment but it does reveal details of practical application and content in daily parenting. Not only does the societal input identify the needed curriculum content, it assigns varying values to particular aspects. For example, the empirically derived content factors in order of primacy from the national survey are as follows:

1. Promoting health
2. Community resources
3. Family coping
4. Promoting learning and development
5. Social-emotional development
6. Continuing child development
7. Non-traditional parenthood   (Sparling et al., 1978, p. 68)

Thus, the values and needs emphasized by society take the curriculum somewhat afield from the direct interaction of the parent/child dyad by including elements of health, community, and family. This emphasis does not negate the curricular focus on the direct parent/child interaction, but suggests parent needs that must be supported if this focus is to be successful. A summary of additional survey results indicates other useful information available from this source:

The top three interests of parents show that they hold a balanced, whole-child view: "Build your child's self-confidence," "The sick child: what to do," and "Prepare your child for learning."

Parents clearly see themselves in a facilitative and skillful role vis a vis their young children. Their top interests contain phrases such as "what to do . . . , prepare your child . . . , games to enhance . . . , help. . ."

Younger mothers have a cluster of topics of particular interest to them including: the sick child, spoiling, baby's bath, prematurity, babysitter.

Some titles represent particularly strong concerns of the high risk (poverty level, minority) parents, e.g., "Raising a family as a single parent" and "The challenge of being a teenage parent."

The six most frequently reported problems are the parents' concern about helping the baby develop his or her full potential, time alone for the mother, finding a babysitter, the child's crying, household safety, and the demanding child (Sparling et al., 1978).

Curriculum Input from the Parent

Information about the learner is the third source of any curriculum development plan. Three factors internal to the parent as learner and one situational factor are hypothesized to bear direct relationships to the strength of functional attachment, and therefore must be considered in the parent education curriculum. The first three factors are: 1) parental attitudes; 2) parental knowledge; and, 3) parental skills. The fourth factor is opportunity to exercise parental skills.

Attitudes   The attitude of parents, especially motivation to care for children, is one of the most basic qualities of the parent as learner. This motivation may be a product either of altruism or of self interest. The basic nature of the motive is not important. It is important that there is a positive interest in the care of the child. The curriculum must attend to attitudes and motivation before succeeding on higher levels with the learner.

Knowledge   Effective parenting must include some general knowledge about developmental sequence and pace. Expectations that are too high will lead to dissatisfaction and disappointment with the child's progress. Expectations that are minimal or below the child's actual capabilities will result in developmental delay because of a lack of appropriate stimulation.

Skills   Assuming that the parent is aware of developmental sequence and pace, it is necessary to determine if the parent possesses the specific skills for actively encouraging the child's development. These skills include specific modes of social interaction and the arrangement of the child's caregiving environment so that it is developmentally enhancing. Examples of such arrangements would include provisions for the child's safety, provisions for the child's exploration, provisions for basic care arrangements such as hygiene and feeding.

Skills, knowledge, and attitudes are conceived to operate in a bidirectional manner upon functional attachment. Positive expression of these qualities will promote functional attachment; whereas, possession of negative attitudes, little knowledge or relatively few skills will direct the dyad toward functional neglect or actual abuse.

Opportunity   Even though attitudes, knowledge, and skills may be high in any given primary caregiver, such prerequisites for functional attachment are useless if there is no opportunity to exercise those parental skills. At present, there is no information about the optimal level of opportunity for skill engagement concerning the developmental progression of the child. It is clear, however, that this area is one that merits research. Factors that may influence the opportunity for the exercise of parental skills include such things as employment of the mother, the presence of a spouse or helpmate in the home, the presence of other siblings both older and younger, and a variety of other more indirect influences. Although it may not be possible for the curriculum to react to these influences, they must be taken into account and responded to when possible.

Using input from the subject matter, the society, and the learner, the curriculum development team creates small units of experience, each with a brief written guide. Oral and written evaluation on the clarity and usefulness of these materials from the Family Educator and parents is used to revise and improve the materials on a cyclical basis.

THE INTERVENTION PROCEDURE—HOME VISITATION

There are two experimental groups in Project CARE that receive intervention through home visitation. One of these groups also receives day care for its children. The day care is essentially the same as that of the Abecedarian Project (Ramey et al., 1977). The group that receives visitation is described in this section.

Visits typically begin before the infant is 12 weeks old and occur about every 1½ weeks. Visitations occur in the home or some other convenient place, such as the grandmother's home or the child's day care center.

Home Visitation

There is no typical routine for the visits. Generally they last about 1 hour and begin with a few minutes of informal visiting. The Family Educator presents information that he or she feels the parents need or that the parents requested. Frequently the information is a new learning activity or game for the mother to do with her child. A game is chosen to increase the child's development and to develop the parents' skill in one of the elements of the parent curriculum such as problem solving, communication, planning, showing or changing. The readiness of the child is considered by the mother and Family Educator. Materials are found in the home for use in the game, and the game is demonstrated by the visitor. Sometimes materials are prepared in advance and given to the mother or they are prepared by the mother and Family Educator together. Informal questions are encouraged by the visitor while she talks about the materials and observes the parent trying the game. The focus is always on the parent whether at the level of attitude, knowledge, or skill. The Family Educator often reviews earlier games in order to observe the parent's progress and skill and to answer questions which the parent might have about the child's progress. Occasionally, the visitor may have to delay discussing the information he or she had planned to present and simply support the parent in the attempt to solve more immediate problems. When a common interest arises, parents may be invited to a group meeting for exchange of information.

Staff Development

The Family Educators are experienced with children through day care or other social services training, but they are not certified teachers. They receive continuing inservice training and, in the process, make suggestions that are used in the parent curriculum.

Staff development sessions occur each week. These sessions not only involve issues of home visiting, record keeping and general instructional procedures, but they also provide an opportunity for the visitor to have input into the curriculum development process.

Modeling, demonstration, discussion, role-playing, and video feedback (all found to be useful in the Abecedarian and Florida Projects) are used to refine the visitor's skills in carrying out curriculum activities, in recognizing and performing the basic parenting/teaching strategies, and in communicating more effectively with parents.

Parent Advisory Council

A parent's council (with rotating membership) enables parents to share in the ongoing decisions, needs, and problems of Project CARE. The staff benefits from parents' insights and parents benefit from exposure to the various needs and concerns of the program staff and the research organization.

EVALUATION STRATEGIES

Evaluation and research within Project CARE can be classified within the following six broad areas:

1. Physical development
2. Intellectual development of the children
3. Parent/child interaction styles
4. Parent skill and knowledge
5. Attitudes of parents
6. Quality of the home environment

The most crucial issue concerning parent-centered early intervention is whether mother-child interactions can be altered within high-risk samples. If mother-child interactions are the final causal pathway for cultural transmission during infancy, then the malleability of that system is critical for family-oriented education. To investigate this issue semi-naturalistic observations of mothers and their 6-month-old infants were conducted. The subjects were 10 of the 12 dyads from the parent education group. (Because the random assignment to groups resulted in a pair of twins in the parent education group, results from only one of the twins are reported here, otherwise, that mother would be represented twice in the data set.) Another child was not observed because he was not yet 6 months old. The control group was composed of five of the high-risk children who had been randomly assigned from this cohort to that condition. Again, one child was not observed because he was not 6 months of age. To bring the control group to an N of 10 and, therefore, equal to the size of the parent education group, five infants were randomly chosen from a previous control group cohort that had been admitted using the same high-risk criteria (Ramey and Smith, 1977). Those five infants had been randomly assigned to the control group instead of a day care experimental group (Ramey and Campbell, 1977). Thus, although five of the present control group infants had not had the opportunity to be assigned to the parent education group, their random assignment to a similar control group and their random selection from a larger pool of that control group was thought to be sufficiently experimentally rigorous to allow a comparison of the effects of parent education on mother-infant interactions.

Observations of the interactions were made for 20 minutes in a situation described by Ramey et al. (1979). Mother and child dyads were observed and videotaped in a room containing a couch, chair, small table and lamp, books, toys, and current magazines. A behavioral scoring system developed by Farran and Haskins (1977) and modified by Burchinal (1978) was used to score mother-infant interactions.

The Procedure. The observational session began with the mother and the infant being escorted into the living room by the experimenter. The mothers were told that the experimenters were interested in different aspects of the child's play and that the session was to be videotaped for later analysis.

The coding of the sessions involved observing the duration and frequency of the interactions. These were obtained by viewing videotapes of the observations and recording the sequences using electronic digital recorders ("Datamyte" by Electro General). The coding was designed so that mother and infant behaviors could be coded separately into the following modes of behavior: 1) independent or mutual play with toys and books, 2) interactive behaviors such as showing/giving of toys, 3) proximity, 4) initiations of major activities, and 5) caregiving. (For a greater elaboration of the codes, see Appendix A.)

Table 2 contains the means and standard deviations of interaction session behaviors. Results from the interaction sessions indicated that mothers in the parent education group spent less time away from their infants ($t_{18} = 2.27$, p < 0.036) and more time holding them ($t_{18} = 2.48$,

Table 2.   Means and *SD*s of mother-child interaction behaviors[a]

	Behavior	Home education (N = 10)		Control (N = 10)	
		Mean	SD	Mean	SD
1.	Mutual play (frequency)	20.0	8.7	10.0	7.5
2.	Mutual play (total duration, sec.)	458.7	144.5	180.6	142.7
3.	Mother joins child's play (frequency)	9.7	7.4	3.2	3.2
4.	Duration of play once mother joins (sec.)	189.3	149.5	48.3	62.6
5.	Mother far from child (total duration, sec.)	23.8	48.2	223.2	274.0
6.	Mother holds child (total duration, sec.)	453.4	285.8	180.8	196.9
7.	Mother reads alone (total duration, sec.)	28.7	58.1	329.5	345.0
8.	Infant involved in no activity (total duration, sec.)	143.7	118.6	280.7	161.8
9.	Infant playing alone (mean length, sec.)	12.2	4.4	21.1	10.9

[a] Each of these nine behaviors are significantly ($p < 0.05$) different between the Home Education and Central groups by t-test comparisons.

$p < 0.023$) than did control group mothers. An important finding is that mothers and infants in the parent education group were involved more frequently in mutual play ($t_{18} = 2.75$, $p < 0.001$) than control dyads.

Mothers in the control group spent more time reading to themselves ($t_{18} = 2.72$, $p < 0.014$) and had infants who spent more time either playing alone ($t_{18} = 2.39$, $p < 0.027$) or not involved in any discernible activity ($t_{18} = 2.16$, $p < 0.045$). This apparent greater involvement by mothers in the parent education group seems to be mediated primarily by their greater frequency of joining an ongoing child activity ($t_{18} = 2.54$, $p < 0.020$) and staying with that activity longer ($t_{18} = 2.75$, $p < 0.013$).

These results conform well to the construct of *Dyadic Involvement* isolated earlier at 6 months of age by Farran and Ramey (in press) and was shown to be related to the child's developmental status as assessed by IQ performance at 4 years of age. Thus, these results are particularly encouraging concerning the positive modifiability of the early mother-infant interactional system among high-risk dyads—a system that previously was thought to be the typical final causal pathway for cultural transmission and particularly for language development.

It must be stressed that the authors regard these data analyses as preliminary and that a great deal of caution must be exercised in their interpretation. The sample is small and we await long term outcomes that have established validity such as increased intelligence and achievement in the parent education group. The theoretical point about the modifiability of mothering, however, seems reasonable to assume, at least during early infancy. The main tasks that lie before us are to create theoretically defensible curricula for the mothers as their children grow older and to assess more finely the child's developmental progress and the mother's role in that progress.

REFERENCES

Ainsworth, M. D. 1973. The development of the infant-mother attachment. *In* B. Caldwell and H. Ricciuti (eds.), Review Of Child Development Research, Vol. III. University of Chicago Press, Chicago.

Bakeman, R. 1976. Untangling the streams of behavior: Sequential analyses of observational data. Presented at the Conference on Application of Observational-Ethological Methods to the Study of Mental Retardation, June, Lake Wilderness, Washington.

Bayley, N. 1965. Comparisons of mental and motor test scores for ages 1–15 months by sex, birth order, race, geographical location and education of parents. Child Dev. 36:379–441.

Bee, H. L., VanEgeren, L. F., Streissguth, A. P., Nyman, B. A., and Leckie, M. S. 1969. Social class differences in maternal teaching strategies and speech patterns. Dev. Psychol. 1:726–734.

Bernstein, B. 1961. Social class and linguistic development: A theory of social learning. *In* A. H. Halsey, J. Floud, and C. A. Anderson (eds.), Economy Education and Society, pp. 288–314. Free Press, New York.

Bowlby, J. 1958. The nature of a child's tie to his mother. Int. J. Psychoanal. 39:350–373.

Bronfenbrenner, U. 1975. Is early intervention effective? *In* M. Guttentag and E. L. Struening (eds.), Handbook of Evaluation Research, Vol. 2. Sage Publications, Beverly Hills.

Burchinal, P. 1978. The contingent relationships of mother and infant behaviors in dyadic interactions. Unpublished thesis, University of North Carolina.

Burt, C., Jones, E., Miller, E., and Moodie, W. 1934. How the Mind Works. Appleton-Century-Crofts, New York.

Caldwell, B., Heider, J., and Kaplan, B. 1968. The inventory of home stimulation. Unpublished manuscript, Syracuse University.

Clarke-Stewart, K. A. 1973. Interactions between mothers and their young children: Characteristics and consequences. Monogr. Soc. Res. Child Dev. 38:6–7.

Cohen, S. E., and Beckwith, L. 1975. Maternal language input in infancy. Presented at the annual meeting of the American Psychological Association, August, Chicago.

Coleman, J. S. 1966. Equality of educational opportunity. U.S. Government Printing Office, Washington, D.C. (Monograph produced under a grant from the U.S. Office of Education).

Deutsch, M. 1967. The Disadvantaged Child. Basic Books, New York.

Eells, N. W., Davis, A., Havighurst, R., Herrick, V., and Lyler, R. 1951. Intelligence and Cultural Differences. University of Chicago Press, Chicago.

Erikson, E. H. 1950. Childhood and Society. W. W. Norton & Company, New York.

Farran, D. C. and Haskins, R. 1977. Reciprocal control in social interactions of mothers and three year old children. Chapel Hill, North Carolina: Frank

Porter Graham Child Development Center. (ERIC Document Reproduction Service No. ED 139511).

Farran, D. C., and Ramey, C. T. 1980. Social class differences in dyadic involvement during infancy. Child Dev.

Galton, F. 1869. Hereditary Genius: An Inquiry into its Laws and Consequences. MacMillan Publishing Company, London.

Golden, M., and Birns, B. 1968. Social class and cognitive development in infancy. Merrill-Palmer Quarterly. 14:139–149.

Gordon, I. J., and Guinagh, B. J. 1974. A home learning center approach to early stimulation. Final report to the National Institute of Mental Health Project No. R01 MH 16037-01. Institute for Development of Human Resources, University of Florida, Gainesville. Published in JSAS Catalog of Selected Documents in Psychology. 1978. 8:6 (Ms. No. 1634)

Guinagh, B. J., and Gordon, I. J. 1976. School performance as a function of early stimulation. Final report to the Office of Child Development, Grant No. NIH-HEW-OCD-09-C-638. University of Florida, Gainesville. Institute for Development of Human Resources. (ERIC document reproduction service # ED135469) Published in JSAS Catalog of Selected Documents in Psychology. 1978. 8:31. (Ms. No. 1637)

Haskins, R., Finkelstein, N. W. and Stedman, D. J. 1978. Infant-stimulation programs and their effects. Pediatr. Ann. 7(2):123–144.

Heber, R., and Garber, H. 1975. The Milwaukee Project: A study of the use of family intervention to prevent cultural-familial retardation. In B. Friedlander, G. Sterritt, and S. Kirk (eds.), Exceptional Infant, Vol. 1. Brunner/Mazel, New York.

Hess, E. H. 1970. Ethology and developmental psychology. In P. H. Mussen (ed.), Carmichael's Manual of Child Psychology, Vol. 1. John Wiley & Sons, New York.

Hess, R. D., and Shipman, V. C. 1965. Early experience and the socialization of cognitive modes in children. Child Dev. 34:869–886.

Hindley, C. B. 1960. The Griffiths scale of infant development: Scores and predictions from 3 to 18 months. Child Psychol. and Psychiatr. 1:99–112.

Hunt, J. McV. 1961. Intelligence and Experience. Ronald Press, New York.

Karnes, M., Teska, J., Hodgins, A., and Badger, E. 1970. Educational intervention at home by mothers of disadvantaged infants. Child Dev. 41:925.

Knoblock, H., and Pasamanick, B. 1953. Further observation on the behavioral development of Negro children. J. Genet. Psychol. 83:137–157.

Levenstein, P. 1970. Cognitive growth in preschoolers through verbal interaction with mothers. Am. J. Orthopsychiatry. 40:426–432.

Lewis, M., and Wilson, C. D. 1972. Infant development in lower-class American families. Human Dev. 15:112–127.

Madden, J., Levenstein, P. and Levenstein, S. 1976. Longitudinal IQ outcomes of the mother-child home program. Child Dev. 47:1015–1025.

Odell, S. 1974. Training parents in behavior modification: A review. Psychol. Bull. Vol. 8. 7:418–433.

O'Keefe, A. 1977. An overview of the El Paso National Head Start Conference—parents, children and continuity. Head Start Newsletter, pp. 1–16.

Ramey, C. T. 1978. The functional concern of mothers for their infants. Revision of paper presented at the annual meeting of the American Psychological Association, September, Toronto, Canada.

Ramey, C. T., and Campbell, F. A. 1977. The prevention of developmental retardation in high-risk children. *In* P. Mittler (ed.), Research to Practice in Mental Retardation Vol. 1, Care and Intervention. pp. 157–164. University Park Press, Baltimore.

Ramey, C. T., and Campbell, F. A. 1979. Compensatory education for disadvantaged children. School Rev. 87:171–189.

Ramey, C. T., Collier, A. M., Sparling, J. J., Loda, R. A., Campbell, F. A., Ingram, D. L., and Finkelstein, N. W. 1976. The Carolina Abecedarian Project: A longitudinal and multidisciplinary approach to the prevention of developmental retardation. *In* T. Tjossem (ed.), Intervention Strategies for High-Risk Infants and Young Children. pp. 629–665. University Park Press, Baltimore.

Ramey, C. T., Farran, D., and Campbell, F. A. 1979. Predicting IQ from mother-infant interactions. Child Dev. 50:804–814.

Ramey, C. T., and Haskins, R. The causes and treatment of school failure: Insights from the Carolina Abecedarian Project. *In* M. Begab, H. Garber, and H. C. Haywood (eds.), Causes and Prevention of Retarded Development in Psychosocially Disadvantaged Children. University Park Press, Baltimore. In press.

Ramey, C. T., Holmberg, M. C., Sparling, J. J., and Collier, A. M. 1977. An introduction to the Carolina Abecedarian Project. *In* B. M. Caldwell and D. J. Stedman (eds.), Infant Education: A Guide for Helping Handicapped Children in the First Three Years, pp. 101–121. Walker and Co., New York.

Ramey, C. T., and Haskins, R.

Ramey, C. T., Mills, P., Campbell, F., and O'Brien, C. 1975. Infants' home environments: A comparison of high-risk families and families from the general population. Am. J. Ment. Defic. 80:40–42.

Ramey, C. T., and Mills, P. J. 1977. Social and intellectual consequences of day care for high-risk infants. *In* R. Webb (ed.), Social Development in Childhood: Day Care Programs and Research. John Hopkins University Press, Baltimore.

Ramey, C. T., and Smith, B. J. 1977. Assessing the intellectual consequences of early intervention with high-risk infants. Am. J. Ment. Defic. 81:318–324.

Ramey, C. T., Stedman, D. J., Borders-Patterson, A., and Mengel, W. 1978. Predicting school failure from information available at birth. Am. J. Ment. Defic. 82:525–534.

Rebelsky, F., and Hanks, C. 1971. Father's verbal interaction with infants in the first three months of life. Child Dev. 42:63–68.

Robinson, H., and Robinson, N. 1971. Longitudinal development of very young children in a comprehensive day-care program. The first two years. Child Dev. 42:1673–1683.

Schaefer, E. S., and Aaronson, M. 1972. Infant education research project: Implementation and implications of a home tutoring program. *In* R. K. Parker (ed.), The Preschool in Action, pp. 410–430. Allyn and Bacon, Inc., Boston.

Sparling, J., Lowman, B., Lewis, I., and Bartel, B. 1978. What parents say about their information needs. Progress report to ACYF (Administration for Children, Youth and Families).

Stedman, D. J., Anastasiow, N. J., Dokecki, P. R., Gordon, I. J., and Parker, R. K. 1972. How can effective early intervention programs be delivered to potentially retarded children? A report for the Office of the Secretary of the Department of Health, Education and Welfare, Sept.

Stein, J. 1977. Datamyte System Documentation. Unpublished manuscript.

Tyler, R. W. 1950. Basic principles of curriculum and instruction. University of Chicago Press, Chicago.
Tulkin, S., and Kagan, J. 1972. Mother-child interaction in the first year of life. Child Dev. 43:31.

APPENDIX

Reciprocal Control Categories
for Scoring Social Interaction at 6 Months

Dale Farran, Peg Burchinal, and Ron Haskins
Frank Porter Graham Child Development Center

This set of categories was developed to code the social interactions of mothers and children in a 20-minute free play laboratory situation. The categories are divided into primary modes with each mode being divided into smaller units of behavior. Within each mode the *duration* categories are mutually exclusive. Frequency categories within a mode and duration categories across modes (except where noted) may be scored simultaneously. Mother and child are coded separately. The categories were established to be coded from videotapes recording onto an electronic digital recording system (Electro General's Datamyte). After they are coded, the recorded codes must be processed through a series of Datamyte programs. The first cleans the data. The second merges the records of mother and child (the program automatically adds the prefix 1 to all child codes and 0 to all mother codes). The third program provides a frequency count of the duration and frequency of all codes. For further information on the Datamyte software, see Stein (1977).

RECIPROCAL CONTROL CATEGORY SYSTEM

1   Level of Play (Mother)

1-1   Independent Play With Toys   Mother touching, holding toy or actively manipulating toy without regard to infant's behavior.

1-2   Demonstrating Toys   Mother actively manipulating toy in close proximity to infant or at a distance verbally attempting to get child's attention to attend to toy. Child may be visually attending to toy but has not moved in direction of toy. (When infant moves in direction of toy, reaches for or shows active involvement in demonstration, score 1-5 for mutual play). Mother introduces a rhythmical, predictable set of behaviors (e.g., peek-a-boo) in which the infant has not yet shown active involvement.

1-3   Show/Extend/Point to Toy   Brief-duration behaviors that may occur during demonstrations of toy or mutual play. Mother points to a specific toy or a specific aspect of the toy (television screen, picture in book). Mother may hold up a toy for child to see but never actually demonstrate it or attempt to get the child interested. Frequency behavior only.

1-4   Give Toy   Mother places toy within child's reach or actually in child's hands. Frequency behavior only.

1-5   Mutual Play   Infant and mother are both involved with toy either through mutual contact with toy or infant has responded to mother's demonstration with active attempt to reach toy (reaching for, rocking back and forth, visually tracking after having made an attempt to reach toy physically).

Mutual play may be without toys as well: 1) mother and child are engaged in rhythmical, predictable set of behaviors as in a game (peek-a-boo, pat-a-cake), 2) mother and infant are engaged in affectionate interaction, repetitive nuzzling, repetitive verbalizations. For mutual play to be scored without toys, behavior must be somewhat ritualized, not brief affection (as in a single kiss), and both partners must be actively attentive to each other.

1-0   End Play With Toy   Mother no longer has contact with toy. Mother must be out of contact for at least 3 seconds and no longer visually attentive to play in case of 1-5 or 1-2 to score 1-0.

1   Level of Play (Child)

1-1   Non-directed Play With Toys   Child touching, holding toy without attempting to manipulate it. May have toy in hand but not attending to it. Low frequency of occurrence. Child attends visually to toy with moving parts when toy is in arm's reach.

1-2   Directed Play with Toys   Child actively manipulating toy: mouthing, patting, feeling, or actually using toy (i.e., pushing the mower).

1-3   Show/Extend/Point to Toy   Child must clearly point to toy or some aspect of the toy. Unlikely to occur. Patting the toy even in imitation of mother's previous show/extend is not a point.

1-4   Give Toy   Same definition as for mother; will not occur for infants.

1-5   Mutual Play   (See definition for mother).

1-7   Gross Motor Activity   Child exhibits directed motoric activity without toy. Includes crawling, pulling up on mother, bouncing on crib. If it involves mother, mutual play is coded.

1-8   Reaching for Toys   Child has hand extended toward toy that he has not reached. Or child is on hands and feet rocking back and forth in direction of toy or making another type of effort to crawl with toy clearly in visual field.

1-0   End of Play With Toy   Child ceases to have contact with toy for 3 seconds and is not engaged in active attempt to reach toy.

2   Physical Proximity (Mother and Child)

2-1   Far   Mother and child are far enough from each other so that neither could reach out an arm and touch the other. If mother is sitting on couch with infant at her feet such that child could touch her, score near, even though mother cannot reach child.

2-2   Near   Mother and child are sharing same piece of furniture *or* are near enough so that one or other could reach out and touch the other.

2-3   Reaching   Mother or child has arms extended toward the other but is not touching the other. Mother may be attempting to get the child to crawl toward her or to reach to her.

2-4   Hold   Mother has child in arms with child's feet off floor or it can be clearly determined that mother is supporting most of child's weight; child would fall if mother was not holding him.

2-6   Hit   A movement of hand, arm, or foot toward the other in an attempt to make physical contact with force, regardless of whether physical contact is established. Frequency behavior only.

2-7   Kiss/Hug   An affectionate brief interchange. Mother or child gives to other a kiss or a hug. Frequency behavior only.

3   Books (Mother and Child)

3-1   Contact   Scored whenever subject is in contact with book or magazine, whether open or closed.

3-2   Read Alone   Book is open. Subject is looking at book and reading (or talking about book) to self while the other is involved in a different behavior.

3-3   Read Together   Both partners are near to and looking at the same book. One may be pointing to pictures or talking about book but there is no reading of the text aloud.

3-4   Read Aloud   Subject reads text of book aloud to the other. There must be clear indication that his reading is intended to be heard by the other. (e.g., "Listen, mommy," or "Mommy, I'm going to read now.")

3-0   Terminate   All involvement (reading or contact) with book ended. If mother or child closes book but continues to hold it or have it in lap, score 3-1.

4   Initiation of Activity (Mother and Child)

4-1   Begins New Activity—Independently Initiated   Scored at the beginning of each new activity that was not suggested by the other or a join of an ongoing activity. If child has been actively exploring one toy and then turns to another, score 4-1. 4-1 for mother may be a new activity she is attempting to get child to do (i.e., coupled with a 1-2 for demonstrate), or may be entirely unrelated to child, as in reading.

4-2   Suggests New Activity   Subject verbally or nonverbally suggests that the other begin an activity different from the one in which he is engaged. If subject has herself been involved in the activity prior to suggesting it to the other, score 4-3, not 4-2.

4-2 may occur in conjunction with any of the other 4 categories. It must always precede a 4-5. It will come at the beginning of 1-2 in addition to the 4-1 (i.e., the mother's picking up a toy and demonstrating it to the infant would be scored 4-1, 1-2, 4-2). Frequency only.

4-3   Suggest Other Join Play   Subject engaged in directed activity and suggests verbally or nonverbally that other join the play. Unlikely to occur. Frequency behavior only.

4-4   Join   The other is engaged in some activity and the subject enters into the activity by playing with the same material. Subject must actively begin to interact in same activity or with same materials; if subject merely moves closer in order to observe other's activity, she is scored 4-7 (passive interact).

4-5   Accept   Subject begins to do activity suggested by the other (i.e., after mother begins to demonstrate toy, child begins to move toward toy). Lags between accept and suggest may be great, as long as no other activity interrupts the ongoing one.

4-6   Reject Other's Suggestions For Major Activity

4-7   Passively Participate   Subject observes what the other is doing without participating. Subject must be attending to other's activity: visually oriented, leaning forward, actively aware of other's activity. Child may be watching mother demonstrate toy without having made a move toward it. When he makes the move, score 4-5.

4-0   No Clear Activity   Subject stands or sits without looking at the other actively or engaging in any manipulation of objects.

5   Modification of Behavior

5-1   Attempts to Modify Other's Behavior   One verbally or nonverbally indicates a suggestion that the other alter his physical behavior (i.e., "come here," "Mommy, look"). Does not include verbal interactions that are a request for verbal information (i.e., "What color is that?" "What's this?"). Frequency only.

5-2   Complies   One does whatever other told him or her to do. (Mother does "look," etc., when requested). Does not include looks. Frequency only.

5-3 *Rejects* One actively refuses to do whatever has been suggested, by either continuing activity if the other has told him or her to stop, verbally refusing, etc. Does not include ignoring requests by other. Frequency only.

7 Caregiving

7-1 *Mother caregiving* Any routine care giving activity: feeding, diapering, cleaning, adjusting clothes, Mother only.

7-2 *Child Caregiving* The mother's caregiving of her infant is the sole activity on the infant's part.

7-0 *Caregiving Ceases*

chapter
15

Issues in
Early Language
Intervention

Diane D. Bricker

Laurel Carlson

Center on Human Development
University of Oregon
Eugene, Oregon

The study of early communicative behavior has at least two important consequences: 1) knowledge about the young child is expanded and 2) information is provided that can assist in the development of effective training strategies for children with deficient language skills. Although there has been some progress over the past 10 years in helping children with language disorders acquire a variety of communication skills, there are still significant deficiencies in designing effective training programs. This is especially true for children with the most serious communication problems. Progress is being made as we become more adept at fostering the development of alternative communication systems, but many complex problems need to be solved before reaching the goal of providing every child with some form of communication.

During the past 5 years, three important concepts have emerged concerning communication in young children. First, it seems that a basic continuity exists between prelinguistic communicative behavior and language acquisition. To begin studying or intervening when a child is at the stage of one- or two-word utterances is to ignore the origins of language and results in a serious loss of instructional time. Second, communication skills do not develop in a vacuum or as a linear process. Rather, it seems that language is acquired as an integral interactive part of the young child's developing systems. Third, environmental contexts and feedback significantly affect the acquisition of language behaviors. These three assumptions: the usefulness of early intervention, the viewing of language as interactive with and dependent upon other behavioral systems, and the importance of environmental context provide the theme for this chapter. Specifically, many issues concerning language acquisition and training are reviewed. These issues can be divided into two major areas: early development and language intervention. In this context, "early" refers to those years of development in a child's life before age 2; therefore, the first part of this chapter discusses some of the issues in early development that are pertinent to language. The second part discusses proposed strategies for language intervention.

ISSUES IN EARLY DEVELOPMENT

As Miller et al. (1980) suggest, the development of language is based on the convergence of cognitive, affective, and linguistic processes. We stress the importance of convergence that occurs early in the child's life. That is not to say that children beyond the preschool years (or even adults) may not learn language skills, but the acquisition of those skills may follow a different sequence, focus on different content or come under different environmental controls. Surely, such factors as expanding experience, changing social expectations, and shifting motivational systems have the potential for affecting language development differentially in the older versus the younger child. This chapter is directed toward a discussion of the development of early processes in the young child and their implication for early language intervention.

Although there have always been educators and psychologists interested in early development, recently there has been a dramatic increase in the study of the human infant (e.g., Lewis and Rosenblum, 1978; Kagan, Kearsley, and Zelazo, 1978). The literature suggests a growing consensus that development proceeds in hierarchical patterns that may be separate processes or domains of behavior but are so interrelated in the young child as to be functionally inseparable (Decarie, 1978). A second position found in this literature is the interactive nature of the infant with his or her environment. There are substantial indications that the effects of the child on his or her environment and the environment on the child are not unidirectional but rather, bidirectional (Lewis and Lee-Painter, 1974) or reciprocally interactive (Snow, 1977).

These two issues in early development are discussed in this section. The later section discusses their implications for early language intervention. It may be useful and functional to view early language intervention from the perspective of the interrelated nature of early development and the interactive effect between the child and his or her social environment.

INTERRELATED NATURE OF EARLY DEVELOPMENT

A number of investigators have indicated that sensorimotor and affective development are interrelated (Decarie, 1978; Saarni, 1978). Others have suggested a similar relationship between sensorimotor and early language behavior, although the nature of this relationship is still unclear (Miller et al., 1980; Bricker and Bricker, 1974; Cromer, 1976). This argument seems to suggest that affective and linguistic development might then also be intertwined. When infants coo to their mother, the behavior could be classified as social (reflecting the baby's emotional state) and prelinguistic (uttering sounds). The tracing of early development in the sensorimotor, affective, and prelinguistic domains should assist in the evaluation, or at least the appreciation, of their interrelated nature in regard to the development of the speech act.

> . . . it is eminently worth studying what might be called the prerequisites necessary for learning a language or for progressing in the mastery of that language. At the most general level, we may say that to master a language a child must acquire a complex set of broadly transferable or generative skills—perceptual, motor, conceptual, social, and linguistic (Bruner, 1975a, p. 256).

Sensorimotor Development

According to Piaget (1970), the infant is born with a set of reflexive behaviors that are automatically triggered by either internal states or environmental stimuli. As the infant exercises these reflexes, their form changes to simple volitional responses that are maintained by the environmental changes they produce. Through subsequent interaction with both people and objects, these simple responses or action schemes (i.e., tracking, reaching, mouthing) become modified and elaborated into more complex and coordinated schemes (i.e., hand-eye coordination) or levels of organization.

The basis for cognitive development is described by Piaget (1970) as the inevitable succession of states of disequilibrium that are produced as a natural consequence of encountering new environmental objects and events (both physical and social) for which no repertoire is available. Through continuous interaction with the environment, the child constructs a variety of adaptations that constitute the basis for development. Kohlberg (1970) characterized these changes in terms of five criteria:

1. The change is irreversible.
2. The change is general over a field of responses and situations.
3. The change is a change in shape, pattern, or quality of response.
4. The change is sequential; it occurs in invariant steps.
5. The change is hierarchial.

In the sensorimotor period, these adjustments toward equilibrium form the basis for expanding the reflexive behavior of the newborn. This is true both in terms of the number and the characteristics of stimuli that evoke reflexive forms of behavior. When a particular reflexive behavior produces a consequence that is interesting to the infant, the rate of that behavior will increase. Increases that are directly attributable to reflexively produced behavior are called primary circular reactions (Stage II) or the level of undifferentiated actions (Uzgiris, 1976). That is, the infant develops a number of different action schemes but does not use these schemes in a differentiated manner. For example, the infant may attempt to suck any object placed in the mouth. In Piaget's system, observational learning is unimportant compared with learning that is a consequence of direct interaction with environmental objects or events during the first months of life.[1]

---

[1] Although most infants explore their environment through active manipulation, a number of investigators have reported the acquisition of specific sensorimotor behaviors by limbless and sensory impaired young children (Fraiberg, 1975; Kopp and Shaperman, 1973; Decarie, 1978). Such findings have led to the questioning of and disagreement with Piaget's position on observational learning (Kagan, 1971).

As a result of environmental interactions, the infant begins to learn which objects (e.g., a toy mobile) produce which consequences (e.g., movement) in response to specific forms of behavior (e.g., kicking). Thus, the infant learns to discriminate among objects and events in terms of what Piaget calls secondary circular reactions (or Stage 3). The beginning of differential responding based on feedback from the environment forms the basis for the infant's primitive sensorimotor knowledge about the social and physical environment. The interaction and subsequent adaptation of the infant must not be too redundant with previous objects or events nor so novel that the child cannot assimilate them into his or her current cognitive organization. In fact, if objects or events are too different (novel), then the infant may show distress or fear. This discrepancy between the child's current cognitive structure and the location of a particular environmental stimulus along a continuum of familiarity to the child is called the problem of the match and has been described by Hunt (1961). As Kohlberg (1970) suggested, "some moderate or optional degree of discrepancy constitutes the most effective experience for structural change in the organism" (p. 7). In early infancy, assimilative novelties are contained in discrepancies between physical stimuli. As the infant develops, discrepancies in cognitive dimensions trigger the assimilation of new structures (Kagan et al., 1978).

The development of secondary circular reactions is followed by the construction of more complex systems, which Piaget described as the stage of coordinating secondary schemes, or Stage 4. For example, a child may learn to push a chair around the room as one secondary circular reaction and to climb up and down from the chair as another secondary circular reaction. When he or she pushes the chair to the table and then climbs on it to get a cookie, however, the child is coordinating secondary circular reactions and thereby beginning to separate means from goals.

The separation of means and goals usually coincides with a differentiation of self from others. At this point the child moves into the stage of tertiary circular reactions, or Stage 5. This stage occurs between 12 and 18 months of age and is the basis for exploratory behavior. As children increase the number of secondary circular reactions in their repertoire, and coordination among such organization increases, they satiate on known events and may actively search for the unknown in order to test existing repertoires.

The final stage of the sensorimotor period, Stage 6, is often called invention of new means through mental combinations. This stage is exemplified by the ability of the 18- to 24-month-old child to deal with practical here and now problems through the use of various schemes that have become differentiated as means to a variety of ends. At this stage, children have developed a repertoire of movements and have discriminated relationships that allow them to overcome barriers, to use sticks and strings to obtain objects that are out of reach, to open new containers through exploratory manipulations, and to use chairs in order to reach desired objects. Perhaps the hallmark of this period is the child's ability to anticipate events based on environmental cues and to regulate and organize behavior based on his or her prediction of successive happenings (Uzgiris, 1976).

Although there are arguments counter to Piagetian stage-theory, even critics acknowledge the existence of ". . . some sort of coherence or system in cognitive growth" (Brown and Desforges, 1977, p. 12). This chapter views the notion of stages as a broadly conceived descriptive term suggesting an overall qualitatively distinct organization rather than clear cut categorical boundaries. In this sense the authors have found Uzgiris' (1976) reformulation of sensorimotor stages into levels of organization or functioning to be more useful. The successive levels of organization a child "constructs" can be viewed as natural outgrowths of his or her previous interactions with the surroundings. Such constructions or organizations serve as the basis for developmental change and should constitute a major curriculum focus for early interventionists.

Affective Development

Studying affective behavior and its development has been a more elusive, complex task than exploring the genesis of more cognitive forms of behavior. The affective domain of behavior refers to those responses that have to do with feelings or emotions that produce physiological change in the organism. In general, there are two basic models for explaining the development of affective behavior: the biological model and the socialization model (Lewis and Rosenblum, 1978). The biological model suggests that certain conditions produce specific emotional responses that are unlearned. That is, the approach of an unfamiliar adult automatically triggers fear in an infant. In contrast, the socialization model suggests that relationships between internal states (e.g., increased heart rate) and surface behavior (e.g., look of fear) are learned. "Thus, the emotional state or experience is a consequence of the social environments' responses to the child's behavior in a specific context" (Lewis and Rosenblum, 1978, p. 6). It is possible that the development of affective behavior is a result of a combination of elements from both models. There may be some unlearned, biological emotional responses to specific environmental conditions (Harlow and Mears, 1978), but equally probable is that more complex meaning-laden affective behavior is learned through interaction with the environment.

The infant's first indications of affective behavior are responses to the human face and voice. These responses take many forms such as quieting, becoming alert or attempting to keep the face or voice in the perceptual field. In the early stages of development, the infant smiles when presented with a pleasant situation (e.g., caregiver's attention, observation of an interesting object), and indicates stress when exposed to an aversive or excessively novel stimulus. Emde et al. (1978) suggested the organization of the central nervous system is such that around 3 months of age, three dimensions of emotional expression can be reliably discriminated in the infant. These dimensions are:

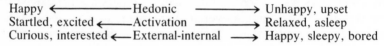

Happy ←——————Hedonic   ——————→ Unhappy, upset
Startled, excited ←——Activation ——————→ Relaxed, asleep
Curious, interested ←——External-internal ——→ Happy, sleepy, bored

On the other hand, Emde et al. (1978) suggested that developmentally more complex "categories of emotional expression, characterized by discrete messages, undergo an epigenesis continuing through the first postnatal year and beyond. Cognitive development plays an increasingly important role in this epigenesis, and the study of its integration with ongoing motoric components of expression offer an exciting challenge" (Emde et al., 1978, p. 145).

As the infant develops, he or she discriminates social smiling and shows affective anticipation of common events. Once the child becomes facile at discriminating mother and familiar persons from others, wariness and fear of strangers or different situations may emerge. The range of the child's social responses and emotions is expanded, and the child becomes more adept at discriminating different social contexts. As the infant learns to both discriminate and produce a variety of social/emotional responses that are dependent upon both internal states and external conditions, he or she is also acquiring other social/affective behaviors of potential importance to the development of language.

As mentioned above, affective behavior seems to be interrelated to cognitive systems. Kagan et al. (1978) described the growth function of one aspect of affective behavior, separation distress. Research suggests that crying or inhibition of play following maternal departure is infrequent before 8 months of age. From 9 to 18 months, infants characteristically show distress, but after 18 months this behavior declines. Kagan et al. (1978) suggested that the upswing in distress observed between 9 and 18 months may be attributable to the infant's improved memory capacity. When the mother departs, the 10-month-old is capable of detecting the incongruence between the scheme for his or her mother and the now empty environment. The third trend of the growth function, in which distress accompanying maternal departure diminishes, seems to coincide with the infant's enhanced ability to retain structures of past experiences and concurrently generate anticipations of the future.

Early Language Development

It is difficult to separate prelinguistic behavior from sensorimotor and/ or affective behaviors in young children. Perhaps it is in the area of language that the interrelated nature of early development is most obvious. Language does not develop in a vacuum or as an isolated form of behavior. Language depends upon the acquisition of other complex skills such as sensorimotor intelligence, motor coordination, and social behavior. A child acquires many skills before emitting the first words. Investigators such as Piaget and Inhelder (1969), Sinclair deZwart (1969), and Bricker and Bricker (1974) pointed out the potential importance of earlier forms of behavior for language development. Thus, the infant's early interaction with his or her environment (e.g., sucking, tracking, grasping) may provide a foundation for later language development.

It could be said that prelinguistic development begins with the initial vocal behavior produced by infants. These vocal responses are varied and often of a nonspeech nature. The infants seem to be learning to operate their sound production mechanism, and at this stage often vocalize noises and sounds that an adult has difficulty imitating (Irwin and Chen, 1946). Between 3 and 4 months, infants generally develop enough control over their vocal mechanism to produce sounds that more closely approximate those made by other members of their language community. During the next phase of phonological development (the babbling phase), most babies learn to reproduce sounds in a reduplicated manner. Oller et al. (1976) investigated phonological development in the normal infant and reported the following developmental progression.

Age	Characteristic Vocalization
0–1 month	Vocalic in nature
2–3 months	Vocalic coos and goos
4–6 months	Vowels, raspberries, squeals, marginal babbling
7–10 months	Reduplicated babbling
11–14 months	Variegated babbling and gibberish

According to deVilliers and deVilliers (1978), two factors influence this phonologic progression in infants: "the progressive maturation of the child, allowing increased control over the vocal apparatus, and the reaction to his vocalization by the adults around him . . ." (p. 37).

Acquisition of vowels and consonants from the child's language milieu provides him or her with the surface elements of language. When surface elements are combined, following the phonological rules of the language, functional or meaningful sound units or phonemes are produced.

Babbling or early phonological responses seem to enable most children to acquire several critical skills. First, the child learns to develop more precise control over his articulation. Second, the environment generally responds favorably to the child's babbling, thus shaping his or her behavior to more closely approximate the language milieu. For example, "mama" is one of the first consistent sound patterns emitted by many babies. In most cases its origin may be traceable to the fact that this speech sound sequence is more apt to attract the mother's attention than other sound combinations. The mother's responsiveness to these particular sounds probably leads to the child's more frequent and consistent use of them. This transaction is considered one of the initial instances when verbal behavior is used to manipulate the child's environment. Consequently, it is believed that babbling is important in the language acquisition process.

Listening to a young child who has no words but produces long sound sequences is interesting. Although the child produces only unintelligible utterances, the child's inflectional pattern may still approximate the adult pattern at a primitive level. The force, quality, and pitch of vocal behavior are called prosodic features, and acquisition of early prosody coincides developmentally with the acquisition of speech sounds (Reese and Lipsitt, 1970). Generally, prosodic features can be described as the "melody" of language, and the words as "lyrics." Both Menyuk (1964) and Ruder and Smith (1974) suggested that the production of prosodic features is so basic that they precede children's acquisition of their first words.

The development of early production skills is important, but equally important are the infant's speech perception skills and the comprehension of meaningful sound units. Speech sounds are particularly salient to the infant; however, it is not always clear which acoustic features the infant uses to differentiate between environmental sounds. Furthermore, there is controversy about the role of learning in speech sound perception (Eilers, 1978). Moving from speech sound perception to phonemic discrimination apparently is a more difficult task. In any event, discrimination of meaningful units of speech is reported to occur later in infancy (Eilers, 1978). Apparently, early word or phrase comprehension is enhanced by numerous extralinguistic cues available to the infant. For example, a young child may be able to indicate the location of the family pet when asked to do so in the presence of the animal in the usual setting. Cues provided by familiar environmental stimuli and settings are in addition to facial, gestural, postural, or intonational elements. The sociolinguistic context assists the young child in the arduous task of comprehending his or her language (Nelson, 1978).

Before babies utter their first word, they probably already are responding to many familiar words or simple phrases spoken by the adults in their environment. Miller et al. (1980) reported that comprehension of various lexical items follows a consistent pattern of acquisition. The general pattern of comprehension exhibited by their subjects was as follows: person names, object names, action verbs, possession, absent objects, action-object, agent-action, agent-action-object, yes-no question. The reliable emergence of this pattern across their subjects suggests a number of explanations: the early environments of these youngsters may have been similar, certain elements of the environment may have general saliency for most children, or some lexical items are simply easier to acquire than others. Probably each of these explanations has some validity and contributes to the development of early comprehension skills.

Before the development of first words, most infants can effectively communicate a variety of functions and/or intentions to the listener. A variety of systems have been generated to describe this period of transition from prelinguistic to linguistic production. Nelson (1978) discussed the descriptive analyses proposed by Bates, Dore, and Halliday, and concluded, in accord with Bruner (1975b), that fewer problems will result when viewing early production from a functional rather than an intentional perspective. It seems likely that attempting to classify a child's utterances on the basis of use may be less inferential than trying to interpret the child's communicative intent. In Nelson's view, Halliday's procedure for classifying early child utterances into functional categories is:

> . . . the most completely worked out functional analysis of the child's first language, and it connects at least, in principle with the acquisition of intonational patterns, vocabulary, grammar, and even dialogue. It has illuminated the many different functions that the child's first communicative acts can serve at the same time that it has distinguished two general classes of functions in both child and adult language (Nelson, 1978, p. 460).

Halliday (1975) identified a number of linguistic functions expressed through early vocal productions:

Classification	Functions
1. Instrumental	Demand, request
2. Regulatory	Control
3. Interactional	Social
4. Personal	Personal descriptions
5. Heuristic	Explanatory
6. Imaginative	Pretend
7. Informative	Sharing of information

The first four of these seem prelinguistically as "forms used consistently to express a meaning but not part of the conventional language system" (Nelson, 1978), and continue with the onset of single word speech. As the child begins using words in standard form, one word expresses one specific function. The child also expands the uses of the language system as he or she begin expressing imaginative and heuristic functions. Therefore, the origins of many communicative functions can be traced to a combination of vocalizations, gestures, and intonational patterns at the preverbal level.

As previously indicated, production of first words is generally considered to mark the first stage of linguistic development. deVilliers and deVilliers (1978) suggested two criteria as the defining characteristics of early words:

1. recognizable phonetic approximation to adult form and
2. fairly consistent use of a particular word in the presence of specific persons, objects or situations.

The production of early linguistic forms has received much attention from the field yet is still a controversial issue (Creelman, 1966; Reese and Lipsitt, 1970; Palermo, 1971; Dore, 1975; deVilliers and deVilliers, 1978).

A number of investigators examined the stage of one-word utterances or single word production from a holophrastic position. Dore (1975) argued for viewing a child's one-word utterances as primitive speech acts. These utterances are composed of three components: the surface elements or phonological units of the word, the communicative intent or function of the utterance (as in Halliday), and the referential meaning carried by the utterance.

There are other developmental processes (e.g., affective, sensorimotor, and prelinguistic) that may serve as precursors to the particular elements of one-word productions. The interrelated nature of early developmental processes can be most clearly seen in the production of early words. In viewing early word production as speech acts, the pragmatic function of the child's word can be emphasized. That is, when the child says "car," the function as well as the referential meaning must be interpreted by the listener.

Of interest is the fact that the sequence of early word comprehension reported by Miller et al. (1980) resembles the production sequence of single words suggested by deVilliers and deVilliers (1978).

Comprehension Sequence	Production Sequence
Person name	Proper names
Object name	Common names
Action verbs	Simple verbs, adjectives
Possession	Relational words
Absent objects	Deitic expressions

The sequence of early word production indicates that young children tend to focus their linguistic attention on those aspects of the environment that hold the greatest saliency for them—that is, young children talk about what they see and do (Bloom, 1970; Greenfield and Smith, 1976; Nelson, 1973; Bowerman, 1976). Both overextension and underextension of word meaning have been reported in the early productions of young children (Bowerman, 1976), and yet no consistent pattern has been found, suggesting that word meaning acquisition may begin as a rather idiosyncratic undertaking by children (Nelson, 1978). Attention to salient aspects of the environment elicits words from the child that are either in his or her repertoire or provided by an adult. The element or characteristic of the person, object or event the child focuses on will, in part, determine how the word will be used subsequently and to which items or events the child will attach the word. Furthermore, the types of lexical items used initially by children also vary. For example, Greenfield and Smith (1976) reported that the two children in their study initially tended to predominantly use either entity words or relational words. Nelson (1973) found that children were either expressive or referential, which coincided with the aspect of the environment their mothers stressed.

Because labels for persons, objects, actions, and events are arbitrary, childrens' word acquisition is dependent upon which label a parent chooses to provide the child. It has been suggested that parents provide labels "at an intermediate level of generality" (deVilliers and deVilliers, 1978). When indicating a cat to a young child, an "intermediate" term such as kitty or cat is offered rather than Siamese or animal. Such a strategy, if found to occur reliably across parents or caregivers, implies that semantic understanding for the child must be expanded downward to the more specific (e.g., Siamese) and upward to the more general (e.g., animal). Variability exists in the specific words children initially acquire; however, comprehension and production expansions and limitations are necessary if the child is to progress beyond the stage of primitive communication.

Between 18 and 24 months, most toddlers begin sequencing words (Prutting, 1979). Producing two-word utterances is the initial stage of grammatical or syntactic development. Sequencing words assumes that the child has developed a rudimentary organizational system that functions by using rules. These rules convey the child's early meanings and help him or her to be understood by others. Bellugi (1972) and others have argued convincingly that young children produce sentences on the basis of generative rules. Children learn that words are sequenced according to systematic patterns rather than randomly strung together. Many of the two-word utterances produced by young children can be classified as representing a variety of semantic relations although far fewer than adults are capable of producing. Brown (1973) reported that for children whose mean length of utterance (MLU) is between 1.0 to 2.0 words, the following semantic relations can describe the majority of their utterances:

Agent-action
Action-object
Agent-object
Action-locative
Entity-locative
Entity-attributive
Demonstration-entity

With the addition of more formal linguistic elements to these basic semantic relations, the further development of the phonologic system, the assimilation of more complex pragmatic functions, and the acquisition of syntactic rules, the child's linguistic competence is gradually expanded until an almost infinite variety of appropriate sentences can be both comprehended and generated.

Summary

This section provides an overview of how infants acquire early sensorimotor, affective, and language behavior. In particular, the developmental structure of early prelinguistic and linguistic behavior is emphasized. The tracings of early development in the sensorimotor, affective, and language domains illustrate the probable overlap and interaction between specific responses and entire domains of behavior. If one accepts the position of the interrelated nature of early development, it may be productive to acknowledge the reciprocal interactive nature of development and organize both research and intervention efforts with this perspective in mind.

RELATIONSHIP BETWEEN THE CHILD AND HIS ENVIRONMENT

A second issue in early development is the interplay between the infant and his or her environment. Several years ago, the predominant theoretical position regarding environment-child interaction was unidirectional—that is, investigators primarily examined the effect the environment had on the infant or young child and not the child's effect on the environment (Bell, 1974). For example, in a series of influential investigations (e.g., Bowlby, 1973; Dennis, 1973), the depressing effect of institutional environments on young children was suggested. This research was unidimensional in that the investigators focused on what they thought were the effects of inconsistent caregiving or mothering for the young child.[2] These investigators did not emphasize the effect of the child on the environment. Another group of investigations concentrated on specific infant responses that could be controlled or manipulated by environmental feedback. For example, Rheingold, Gerwirtz, and Ross (1959), found that vocalizations can be affected by social consequences provided by the caregiver. Although such investigations demonstrated that environmental manipulations can control affective forms of behavior, the focus was unidirectional in that the investigators examined only the effect of the caregiver's behavior on the child's responses.

Although an interactionist model has been a part of many theories of cognitive development, the interactionist position did not have much influence on viewing the relationship between the child and the child's social and/or linguistic environment until the early 1970s. Many investigators (e.g., Lewis and Rosenblum, 1974) began considering the child-caregiver relationship as one in which both participants affected the behavior of the other. That is, there seemed to be a reciprocal exchange governed by each participant's response to the other. The caregiver responds to a baby's crying by comforting the infant who, in turn, becomes quiet and may coo to the adult. The adult may then smile at the infant, which elicits a smile from the baby. A pattern of social interaction governed by the participants' responses to each other can be seen. This circular feedback system can be viewed as a simple interaction model; however, Lewis and Lee-Painter (1974) discussed in detail the problems associated with the position that the child-caregiver interaction is a simple interactive system. Rather, they suggest a complex model in which both the child and caregiver are actively

---

[2] A number of investigators (e.g., White and Held, 1967; Dennis and Najarian, 1963) suggested that the reactions of infants that Bowlby and his colleagues observed could have been attributed to the lack of any appropriate environmental stimulation rather than caused primarily by maternal deprivation.

involved and "significantly influence each other." Figure 1 is a simple schematic representation of a more complex interactive model. This model is composed of a number of elements. First, the large arrows occurring at the interaction junctures between the child and environmental elements suggest an impact following behavioral exchanges that travels in at least three directions: the child affects the environmental element (point B); the environmental element affects the child (point A); and the nature of such interactions affect future interactions between the child and in particular the child's social environment (point 1). The latter effect is indicated by the downward arrow. Subsequent interactions (for example at interactions 2 and 3) are influenced by previous interactions. Environmental feedback continues to influence the child as illustrated by arrows D and F, and likewise the child affects the environment as indicated by arrows C and E. Clearly, such interactional chains are significant for the child in relation to his or her social and linguistic development.

The reciprocal nature of parent-child interactions assumes an underlying time-sequence frame. That is, one partner's response generally precedes the other's. The timing or "synchrony" of the mother's

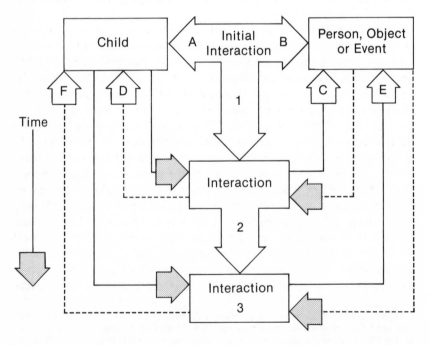

Figure 1.   Model of child-environment interaction.

or the caregiver's response to the baby seems to have the potential for seriously affecting the quality of their relationship even during the very early phases of development (Osofsky, 1976). Synchrony of responding refers to the parents' ability (and to a lesser extent the child's capacity) to monitor the state, mood or needs of the child and to respond in a facilitating manner according to the child's needs. For example, if a baby is thrashing and crying vigorously, a synchronous move on the part of the parent is to respond with behaviors that are soothing to the infant; therefore the parent might lift the child/children, rock them, and talk quietly to them. If the baby were awake and alert, an appropriate response might be to offer some form of stimulation the baby might find interesting, for example, showing the baby a bright colored toy, tickling the toes or returning coos and gurgles. Such synchronous responding to infants and young children takes the form of "doing what comes naturally" to most parents. Fortunately, most babies and their parents arrive at a reasonable balance in their reciprocal responses; however, a number of investigators (Brazelton, Koslowski, and Main, 1974; Bell, 1974; Denenberg and Thoman, 1976) noted that some babies exceed the ability of their caregivers to cope or respond in a synchronous manner. The development of an asynchronous relationship can result from having a difficult-to-manage child (e.g., an autistic child) or a caregiver with little sensitivity to the state or needs of the child. In examining caregiver's sensitivity, Brazelton et al. (1974) reported the differential effects produced by mothers on two similarly tense, over-reactive infants. The mother who was able to modulate or synchronize her behavior to the infant helped the baby become more responsive; in the other case, the infant learned to escape his mother's increased stimulation by tuning her out. These two parallel cases demonstrate that a mother's behavior "must not only be reinforcing and contingent upon the infant's behavior, but that it must meet more basic 'needs' of the infant in being aware of his capacity to receive and utilize stimuli" (Brazelton et al., 1974).

Although the quality of the early parent-child interaction is probably more dependent upon the sensitivity of the adult, asynchrony in the relationship can be produced by the infant as well. Denenberg and Thoman (1976) discussed a case in which the infant's irritable and unresponsive behavior made it extremely difficult for a mother to respond appropriately. An investigation of the state or mood changes of this infant revealed that this baby shifted states significantly more often than other infants of comparable age. This baby's erratic behavior apparently made it difficult for the mother to modulate her responses appropriately and the amount of time the mother spent with her infant was observed to gradually decrease over time. Decreasing the amount of interaction between the child and his parent may eventually lead to an even more ineffectual relationship.

MOTHER-INFANT INTERACTION

Bruner (1975a) made the assumption that the coordination of sensory, motor, conceptual, and social learnings is prerequisite to language development. Beginning in early infancy, mothers help their babies focus on the salient features of cognitive, social, and linguistic environmental stimuli. By engaging in an "implicit pedagogy" (Bruner 1975a) in their everyday interactions with their babies, mothers are instrumental in teaching them transferable skills that may be classified as precursors of language proper.

It is possible to look at the form and function of socially determined or mother determined salience. This one-way analysis risks distortion of the reciprocally interactive nature of the mother-infant relationship. What must be kept in mind is that the dyad is a mutually interactive communicative system benefitting from two-way inputs and joint regulation and control. For example, mothers can frequently be observed following the visual line of regard of their infants, and according to Bruner (1975a), infants often follow their mother's visual focus from about 4 months of age. This suggests a joint determination of selective attention. In an observational study, Sylvester-Bradley and Trevarthen (1978) examined the relationship between changes in a mother's baby talk and her infant's behavior between 8 and 20 weeks. The mother's production of baby talk was found to be a function of her infant's lowered sociability. Furthermore, only when the baby talk decreased did the infant smile once again. Sylvester-Bradley and Trevarthen (1978) characterized baby talk as one component of a social behavior complex in which a mother assumes a playful receptive role with her young infant constantly mirroring the child's moods, facial expressions, and actions. Verbal mirroring is used by the mother for selecting and categorizing salient features of the baby's sphere, and "appears to be sometimes a substitute for and sometimes a projection of a nonverbal interactive process into the verbal sphere" (p. 87).

During the preverbal stage of language development, mothers often talk to their babies. Child-addressed speech or "motherese" differs from adult addressed speech in terms of rate, pitch, and intonation. Mothers typically simplify the structure of the message lexically and shorten it syntactically (Nelson, 1978; Chapman, this volume). There are two approaches for examining the functional rationale for motherese. The first is the particular communicative mode that mother-child speech represents, and the second is the communicative function served by mother speech. Snow (1977) maintained that babies learn their roles as conversational partners by participating with their mothers in preverbal communicative exchanges. She characterizes mother-infant interactions as "conversations" in which the child learns to function in give-and-take dialogue. By consistently initiating and maintaining the conversational model, the mother is unwittingly highlighting the salient aspects of the basic communicative partnership. In addition, the child is being reinforced for taking turns, a skill with applications in the social domain.

Mother-infant conversations serve a variety of important communicative functions. The development of reference, meaning that a vocalization or gesture represents something in the extralinguistic environment, is crucial if the baby is to differentiate among objects and refer to one object in particular. Mothers shape early reference by using gestural and vocal procedures to get their babies to attend to a salient object or event. Mothers use indicating strategies to build the rudiments of reference by marking the target object in different ways, for example, by touching, waving or shaking it. If an infant's attention deviates from the mother's intended target, she can reestablish it by indicating. As a result, the child acquires a generative skill for tuning into another's attentional focus. Mutual referencing frees the infant from an exclusively egocentric perspective.

Mothers have been observed to carry this marking process a step further by first focusing their infants' attention on a particular object, and then directing their infants' activity in order to acquire the object (Bruner, 1975a). For example, the salient action events required to capture an object partially hidden by a barrier are exaggerated or marked for the infant. In effect, the mothers are tutoring their babies to perform simple goal-directed behavior with respect to physical objects.

Early synchrony of child and caregiver behavior may provide the basis for shaping the expression and comprehension of communicative intent, or in Bruner's term, "communicative function," into the repertoire of the infant. Underlying the role of speaker and listener in a communicative interaction are sequenced synchronized responses between partners. Children apparently learn the basic roles necessary for communication through the mother's systematic, although "natural," arrangements of the environment. That is, mothers create "transactional" situations in which they provide ". . . an interpretation to which the infant 'speaker' can conform, dissent, or which he can attempt to modify. . . ." (Bruner, 1975a, p. 267).

This section has emphasized the importance of viewing early development from an interactionist's position. The investigation of language acquisition apart from its context has resulted in the drawing of imperfect conclusions (Bloom, 1970). To study language development without concern for the reciprocal effect between the child and, in particular, the child's linguistic-social environment will generate at best incomplete findings and at worst, misleading information.

EARLY LANGUAGE INTERVENTION

The first part of this chapter offers a foundation for developing a program of language intervention for young handicapped infants and children who have not acquired communicative skills. Although the premise of the interrelated nature of early developmental processes and the reciprocal interactive nature of the child with the environment have been implicit in previous intervention efforts, the continuing synthesis of information provided by the handicapped child has emphasized the need to make these biases explicit in the intervention approach. The next section of this chapter focuses on the implications of these two positions; specifically, on the content, context, and structure of early language intervention. The final section addresses evaluation issues pertinent to intervention.

The language intervention approach we had advocated for a number of years is a combination of developmental and behavioral approaches. The content of instruction is based on theories and studies of language acquisition and sensorimotor development, and the instructional strategies are derived from the principles of operant learning. This position over the years has managed to create critics in both camps. Recently, however, there seems to be an increasing number of interventionists who suggest similar approaches (MacDonald, 1978). Our current model has evolved from experimenting with a variety of different approaches which, as described below, were not as successful as we had imagined.

Our initial foray into language began with involvement in a project that examined the effects of general linguistic training on groups of institutionally based and community-based retarded children (Sievers and Essa, 1961). The findings of this study were equivocal, implying that there was a need for more structure in the training approach. For the next several years, the effectiveness of different language training techniques was tested with institutionalized retarded children in controlled laboratory situations (Bricker and Bricker, 1969; Bricker and Bricker, 1970; Bricker, 1972). Although we were successful in improving the language skills of many subjects, we observed two additional outcomes concerning the language behavior developed in such controlled training environments: the devastating effect of institutional living on our subjects and the lack of transfer of learned language skills to other environments (e.g., cottage living). These findings prompted a shift from older institutionalized children to developing community-based educational intervention programs for younger handicapped children (Bricker and Bricker, 1971). Working with a preschool handicapped population required a variety of changes in our approach to language training. In particular, we were influenced by a student of Piaget's, Gisela Chatalanat, who convinced us of the need for the young child to have an understanding of his physical world before teaching a representational system such as language. Subsequently, our language intervention was broadened to include training of early sensorimotor behaviors (e.g., action schemes and socially influenced schemes) as precursors to linguistic training (Bricker and Bricker, 1974). During our early involvement in community-based intervention, we depended primarily on a one-to-one tutor training regime which used relatively inflexible arrangements of antecedent events and copious use of tangible rewards (Bricker, Vincent-Smith, and Bricker, 1970; Vincent-Smith, Bricker, and Bricker, 1974). The young subjects taught us two important lessons. First, skills acquired in the tutorial system failed to generalize to other facets of the child's daily living activities. Second, the youngsters became bored and disinterested with the repetitious nature of the training. These observations prompted a number of changes. The teaching of language and sensorimotor skills was emphasized throughout the child's day rather than in brief training sessions. Parents and teachers were encouraged to seize any opportunity for developing communication skills. In particular, the value of using the child's own initiation as an ideal strategy for eliciting target behaviors was suggested. Finally, the content of the training program was broadened and refined to include other responses (e.g., appropriate use of objects, early word recognition in context) that many young handicapped children did not acquire without assistance (Bricker and Dennison, 1978).

The modest success of this program, and the continuing flow of data and new perspectives offered by the field, suggests that further modifications of these language training efforts may yield more productive outcomes.

Theoretical Framework for Language Intervention

"The purpose of language is communication" (Bruner, 1975a). One can lose sight of this among the flurry of models, structures, and analyses detailing the intricacies of child language. Yet for all the esoteric activity, the interventionists' goal must be to assist handicapped children in acquiring the most functional communication skills possible. To reach this goal, intervention programs need direction and regulation by some broad underlying theoretical framework or orientation.

> An underlying theoretical framework should provide cohesiveness and consistency to the program by directing the decision-making process at a number of levels which include: 1) the determination of short-term and long-term objectives and priority areas for the child's educational program, 2) the selection of strategies for facilitating acquisition of the established objectives, 3) the selection of appropriate evaluation instruments to assess initial levels of development and monitor change, and 4) the construction, adaptation, or modification of training materials and curricula (Bricker, Seibert and Casuso, 1980, p. 233–234).

Such a developmental-interactive approach is based on the following assumptions:

Early developmental processes are so intimately related as to render them often inseparable for educational or training purposes.

The child engages in ongoing reciprocal activities that continually influence intervention efforts.

Behavior changes from simple to complex forms following general but consistent guidelines providing a set of behavioral targets for intervention.

Disequilibrium produced by changing environmental demands is necessary for building new adaptive responses.

It was argued above that sensorimotor, affective, and early language behavior are closely related and often inseparable. This premise has implications for intervention programs. Most importantly, it suggests than an intervention approach with young children might be most logically and effectively formulated by the coordination of training targets across related domains of behavior rather than by developing isolated training that focuses on single behavioral domains (Brinker and Bricker, 1980). An analysis of the young child's behavioral repertoire in the area of language, sensorimotor, and affective domains can yield useful information for designing an intervention program that affects all three areas of behavior. For example, teaching toddlers to shake their heads affirmatively 1) increases their communicative repertoire, 2) enables them to express their emotional state with more sophistication, and 3) equips them with a convenient response mode for learning conceptual material presented by their teacher.

It is believed that many interventionists proceed in this fashion implicitly. There are still teachers, however, who compartmentalize their instructions, and thus fail to encourage and reinforce language production outside the intervention session. There are situations when the teacher should focus on the development of a specific response, but organizing and coordinating intervention across related domains makes logical if not empirical sense.

A second theoretical premise for intervention is the assertion that development is the result of a complex interactional process between organism (organismic structure) and environmental input (Piaget, 1970). This interactional process between structure and environment refers to the adaptations that the infant must make to develop into a mature organism. Neither maturational nor environmental variables can account for development; rather, one must consider the interaction between the child and the environment. The functioning of a healthy young infant reflects an organismic structure of organized reflexes such as sucking, grasping, vocalizing, and looking. By interacting with a demanding environment, infants modify those basic reflex structures that gradually shift from involuntary to voluntary activation and allow them to explore their environment. Such modifications result in more flexible and generalizable responses which in time are reorganized into more complex structures. The organism-environment interactions allow the infants to gradually build a more sophisticated knowledge of the world by selecting information and fitting it to their current structured organization or understanding. As discussed above, a similar interactive system exists between the child and his or her social environment, in particular the caregiver, during the earliest stages of development. The interactional process between the child and the caregivers accounts for, in part, the shaping of socially acceptable affective response forms into the child's repertoire. Without appropriate feedback, the child may not develop social behaviors such as smiling, eye contact, and gazing, or establish joint referents and joint actions that seem to provide the basis for more advanced communicative exchanges. The importance of interactional or transactional processes for intervention must be emphasized.

The general description of normal development during infancy addresses the third premise of our theoretical framework. It is believed that developmental hierarchies, composed of a series of sequentially acquired behaviors (e.g., from head to trunk to limb control) currently provide the best criteria for establishing objectives. These data provide general maps of emerging behavior during the first years of life that can specify a framework for determining appropriate long-term objectives and for determining the most desirable sequence for the program.

The developmental-interactive framework also suggests appropriate immediate intervention priorities. As discussed above, sensitivity to relationships among domains of behavior can help the interventionist select targets that are both appropriate within and across domains. For example, many early social and self-help skills require a level of understanding of objects in terms of their social functions (e.g., a spoon is for eating, shoes are to wear). To understand these functions, the child must have passed the stage where objects are only sucked, banged or dropped. The child must attend to and discriminate the unique physical properties of objects before he or she can begin to understand their social significance.

Although subject to criticism (Guess, Sailor, and Baer, 1974), the use of logical sequences of development to select patterns of intervention targets for young handicapped children seems justified until more functionally effective strategies emerge. (See Brinker and Bricker, 1980, for a further discussion.)

The fourth premise of this framework emphasizes the use of strategies that provide experience that conflicts with the child's current level of understanding or organization—in other words, the problem of the match (Hunt, 1961). An important Piagetian principle of "moderate novelty" or just tolerable disequilibrium is critical in the process of development or adaptation (Kagan et al., 1978). Adaptation occurs as a function of the assimilation of new environmental inputs which in turn permit accommodation of these inputs to existing schemes or structures. The effectiveness of this system is influenced by the amount of discrepancy between the novel or more difficult environmental information acquired and the current schemes available to the child. If the degree of discrepancy is too great, adaptation does not occur, possibly because of a paucity of external/internal cues pointing to a common linkage between the new circumstances and the existing schemes (Hunt, 1961). Similarly, if the degree of discrepancy is too small, the child's interest is not maintained and the process of adapting to this environmental situation is terminated (Bricker, Ruder, and Vincent, 1976).

The interventionist's task is to create a balance between asking too much or asking too little from the child. Arranging the environment to create a minimal discrepancy between the child's current skill level and the next level of acquisition is a hallmark of effective intervention. Unfortunately, few methods for operationalizing this concept now exist, although initiation of the process has begun (Cantrell, 1974).

The framework described above provides both orientation and direction for programs of language intervention. Although it is acknowledged that such assumptions are difficult to test empirically, their articulation is necessary in order to highlight more specific issues including the content, context, structure, and evaluation of intervention.

Content, Context, and Structure of Intervention

A broad approach to language intervention should be used with young handicapped children. Such an approach includes attention to the development of social/affective and sensorimotor behavior when developing a program for young language-delayed children. To organize information from these domains of behavior into a cohesive, useful training package is an ambitious undertaking and one that is far from completed (Prutting, 1979). Nonetheless, some tentative formulations have been initiated and are offered below.

Content

While developing the content for language intervention, we have not deviated from relying on normal acquisition patterns except to become more eclectic in our approach. The development of social/affective forms of behavior deserve explicit attention. The guidance offered by normal developmental patterns in the formulation of intervention programs is useful, although we share the reservations of Guess, Sailor and Baer (1977) about the applicability of the normal model of development when dealing with the more severely handicapped and/or older handicapped individuals.

> . . . children being taught language later in their lives no longer represent the same collection of abilities and deficits that normal children experience as they acquire language . . . (Guess et al., 1977, p. 360).

It is important to consider how the use of developmental information is advocated in language intervention for young handicapped children. There are at least two important issues concerning the use of normal developmental data to provide the content of intervention: deviations in the developmental hierarchy or sequences, and the level of specificity of the hierarchies. If one uses developmental data to generate a series of training steps that are highly specific, then the applicability and appropriateness across groups of children, particularly handicapped children, is questionable. If, however, one moves to a more molar level of analysis, the developmental sequences generated are useful in presenting a series of "bench marks" or targets that are appropriate to include in the repertoires of most handicapped children. Such developmental sequences or logical sequences, as Baer (1973) described them, can illuminate training in three ways. First, viewing sequences of relevant domains of behavior (e.g., affective, sensorimotor, language) may assist the interventionist in noting points of overlap that can be used to enhance the efficiency of training. Second, the progression of responses from simple to more complex, whether linear or branching, should suggest a sequence of training that has a probability of being more effective than armchair selections (Kagan et al., 1978). Third, the interventionist can have the perspective of an entire behavioral domain rather than isolated response packages. Developers of language intervention programs operate from a relatively complete, broad base of understanding about the form and function of language. Unfortunately, many practitioners using these programs lack such breadth and consequently can only view language from the often limited perspective detailed by the program. Providing interventionists with a more global picture of language helps the practitioner focus on short-term objectives, as well as the long-term communicative needs of the child. Teachers who understand the communicative functions of language may move away from selecting unimportant targets to choosing more functional and useful responses (Bloom and Lahey, 1978).

> Data from normal language acquisition can be useful in developing a language training program. However, to rely exclusively on the normal language development model as the basis for remedial language training may eventually be shown to be inefficient. Unfortunately, few other models on which to structure a language training program currently exist (Bricker, Ruder, and Vincent, 1976, p. 303)

Our knowledge of the field suggests the continuing validity of those statements. The most appropriate content source for language programs for young handicapped children comes from data on normal acquisition. Those data have increased considerably of late and knowledge of both normal and deviant language behavior continues to increase (McLean and Snyder-McLean, 1978; Morehead and Morehead, 1976). Our strategy is to continue to modify our training content to reflect these changes and maintain our reliance on normal developmental processes until objective evidence persuades us otherwise.

Context

Following completion of the influential project on classification of exceptional children, Hobbs (1978) concluded that the most effective forms of intervention include all important aspects of the child's ecosystem. If we are to be successful in our habilitation efforts, we must broaden our scope to include all significant elements of the child's life. It was suggested earlier in this chapter that it is important to analyze language acquisition from an interactive position—that is, there is a reciprocal feedback system operating between the child and, in particular, his or her social environment. This position argues for the inclusion of primary caregivers and other family members as necessary participants in the intervention effort with handicapped infants and young children.

Broadening the context of language intervention to include caregiver's and all aspects of the child's social milieu has been cogently presented by Mahoney (1975) using an ethological model.

> The ethological approach would develop an intervention program based upon the principle that language evolves from the social interaction and nonverbal communication system which exist between language-learning children and their primary language models (Mahoney, 1975, p. 145).

The important notion in this position is that language evolves from the early forms of nonverbal communication through synchronous interaction with the primary caregivers (Snow, 1977). Development of more complex language behavior is the result of gradual shifts in the model's behavior that elicit shifts in the child's behavior (Bruner, 1975b). The form and frequency of communicative activity or exchange provided by the primary models is important. As a number of investigators have reported, the language development of children is significantly related to the communicative environment provided by primary caregivers (Nelson, 1973; Tizard, 1974).

The interaction model and supporting data suggest three practical implications for the context of language training. First, family members need to be part of the intervention team. Providing appropriate language models and communicative exchanges throughout the handicapped child's day will be dependent upon the skills of the individuals with whom the child has the most contact. The interventionist must be prepared to assist parents in acquiring the necessary skills to become effective change agents with their child. To limit the context of intervention to only professional staff defies logic from two perspectives. First, the primary caregiver, usually the mother, is the one individual with whom the infant spends the most time. If the mother does not know how to arrange the environment and respond to the infant, this reduces the number of reciprocal interactions that can foster the development of appropriate communicative behavior. Second, the primary caregiver through bonding and attachment is usually the infant's most salient social reinforcer. To ignore this relationship is to abbreviate the use of a powerful reinforcing consequence to build communicative skills.

Intervention should include training not only across people but across environments as well. By including all settings as potential training environments, one increases the likelihood of expanding the child's language functions and helps assure the generalization of already acquired skills.

There are many programs in which language intervention is conceived of and executed as two daily 30 minute training sessions. The remainder of the day, which could be so effectively used to build language skills, is ignored. A more effective format superimposes the language instruction over the many daily training activities and events. For example, diapering time can be an ideal situation for encouraging vocalizations while child and caregiver are face to face. Likewise, feeding activities can be designed to foster social exchange.

Implementation Guidelines

Educators cannot afford the luxury of waiting for complete experimental validation of a theory before developing intervention strategies. Some theory is better than none; it at least allows the possibility of validation or the generation of data that will suggest viable alternatives. Therefore, this section focuses on the application of the ideas and conceptual positions presented earlier.

The continuity of behavioral development and early responses or processes are the bases for more complex levels of behavioral organization. Again as pointed out by Pick (1978), "We assume and believe that there is continuity of development . . . (but) our present measures provide meager evidence for our assumptions" (p. 107). Nonetheless, it is efficient and effective to provide a structured intervention program at the point the infant or young child's behavioral repertoire is delayed or deviant. For many children, particularly those with genetic or organic disturbances, the point of detection can be during the first year of life.

A program should focus its habilitation efforts across a number of behavioral domains. We have found few children with problems that influence only one area of behavior, although this may be a function of the more severely handicapped infants and children with whom we work. At the very least, the interventionist needs to be alert to the possibility that a youngster with a language delay may have other behavioral deficiencies that call for remediation as well.

The family needs to be included in the intervention team whenever possible. It may be unnecessary to emphasize this point because most early intervention programs now include the parents. The concern, however, is the nature of that inclusion. Rather than tokenism, family members should become at least equal partners with the professional staff in the education of their handicapped infant. For example, with delayed infants, key aspects of the parent-child interaction can become a focus for educational programming. In effect, the "implicit pedagogy" observed in interactional studies of nondelayed infants and their mothers could be made explicit by training parents to intervene during everyday exchanges with their infants.

Our one overriding concern in the development of an intervention program is that the form and function of training be child-imposed rather than adult-imposed. We are not suggesting a laissez faire environment in which the child has complete freedom. Rather, we agree with John Dewey that the teacher/parent input be oriented toward training activities that are functional for the child. Furthermore, it should be relevant to his or her level of development and whenever possible make use of the child's motivational system. For example, one could approach the training of object permanence by placing a small child in front of a table and covering objects that are assumed to be reinforcing to the child. One could use opportunities, however, that occur frequently throughout the child's day for a more "natural" displacement of interesting objects. For example, placing a napkin over a cracker at snack time or putting a desired object behind a barrier.

Interventionists, whether parents or teachers, should limit the use of adult-imposed timelines and tasks.

> Our most effective mothers do not devote the bulk of their day to rearing their children. What they seem to do, often without knowing exactly why, is to perform excellently the functions of the designer and consultant. By that, we mean they design a physical world, mainly in the home, that is beautifully suited to nurturing the burgeoning curiosity of the one- to three-year-old. These mothers rarely spend five, ten or twenty minutes specifically teaching their one- or two-year-olds, but they get an enormous amount of teaching in 'on the fly,' and this is usually at the child's initiation. Although they do volunteer comments opportunistically, they usually act in response to overtures by the child (White, 1971, p. 87, cited in Cazden 1974, p. 214).

Frequently, a young child will vainly try to communicate with a teacher who stops the child in order to begin the language session! Of course it is not being suggested that teachers be limited only to teaching on the fly, because it is not always possible to rely on the occurrence of natural events to teach specific concepts. With a little creativity on the part of parents and interventionists, however, a number of situations occur that can be structured to enhance both the acquisition and generalization of responses. A child-focused orientation is less applicable to the severely handicapped who may have an extremely limited response repertoire and who may be almost entirely dependent upon others to arrange the environment and deliver consequences.

A structured curricular approach to intervention that is infinitely modifiable is advocated. Rather than developing curricula that provide daily lesson plans, we have tried to specify the general content and skills of a specific domain and the probable sequence in which that content or skill is most readily acquired. We do not dispute the claim that some children will acquire responses in an atypical fashion; nevertheless, we believe that most children follow a relatively predictable route in the acquisition of more and more complex behavior. Knowing the route and when to modify it is essential to effective teaching.

After determining the instructional content, the next step is implementation. The first task is determining the level at which to begin intervention in a particular domain. Underlying this and other instructional strategies is the interventionist's ability to selectively attend to the important environmental and organismic variables. To establish the child's developmental level in a certain area, one must examine a child's behavior in relation to a developmental or skill continuum. Once the child's general level of functioning is determined, the interventionist should specify what the child can and cannot do. Once this is accomplished, the next training target can be determined. It is important to define the selected targets carefully. Without a precise definition, staff may disagree about the conditions under which the response should occur or whether the response has even occurred.

Instructional Strategies

During intervention a variety of instructional strategies should be available. A general underlying strategy is the establishment of contingencies between antecedent events, target responses, and consequent events. Most training can be viewed from a tri-part equation A—B—C in which A equals the antecedent event, B equals the behavior, and C equals the consequence. The curriculum should include the arrangement of the environment and specify the target response. Consequences, of course, can be determined by noting which environmental events in general accelerate or decelerate a particular child's behavior.

The training tasks should be selected to encourage the development of a target objective. The goal is for the child to acquire general strategies and/or concepts that can be used across different settings, people, and objects. Learning the label "cup" only for small white cups is not nearly as useful as being able to label all cylindrical containers with handles as a cup, regardless of size, color, texture or location. Selecting tasks that have multiple targets is important to efficient training. In particular, it is often appropriate to superimpose language activities on the training of other skills. Using appropriate words, the interventionist can label an activity or the child's actions. Playground activities can encourage the child to communicate what he or she wants to do (e.g., to swing or slide). Finally, tasks should be selected, when possible, that are functionally reinforcing for the child.

That is, some aspect of the training activity should be designed to be inherently interesting to the child. In some cases, this might be accomplished simply by placing interesting toys on low tables for a child who needs practice in pulling to a standing position.

In other cases, development of functional reinforcers may require a major act of creative insight by the teacher. Similarly, a generative teacher is sensitive to the fact that many aspects of a child's "natural" environment can be used to shape his or her behavior toward the desired target response.

Problems in Evaluating Intervention Effects

Information available on the effects of various language intervention programs, or intervention programs in general is scarce. Many serious difficulties have contributed to this state of affairs (Bricker, Seibert, and Scott, in press; Bricker, 1978).

Two major problems can occur when selecting a target population. First, there is a high probability that families who seek intervention for their young handicapped child are different from other families. This introduces a possible bias which could influence the success of a particular program. If the child progresses toward the acquisition of language skills, at least two interactive causal explanations are possible: the intervention program and/or the parent's input. That is, the parents' concern for the child would guarantee the success of any reasonable intervention approach. In order to isolate the source of the effect, a control group is necessary, but this possibility introduces a second problem. Current legislative and legal trends make the establishment of a nonintervention control almost impossible. Comparison of different intervention approaches is more acceptable than the use of a noninterventional control, although this introduces the problem of group assignment. Random assignment to groups as done by Ramey and Campbell, 1979; and Heber and Garber (1975) may be precluded for a number of reasons such as geographic location, parental preference, personnel or equatability of intervention programs (e.g., home based vs. center based in which amount of intervention time is clearly unequal). Trying to equate experimental groups by matching selected variables presents the dilemma of deciding on which variables to match. Generally, the population of handicapped infants is small, and matching on inappropriate variables may distort the experimental results by exaggerating random fluctuation in the data.

Other evaluation problems concern the parameters of the intervention process. There are only a few investigations where comparisons of different approaches were made and detailed information about the intervention procedures was provided (Weikart, 1972; Miller and

Dryer, 1975). The more common situation is for investigators to de-scribe their programs in general terms. Moreover, procedures rarely ensure that specific interventions were in fact implemented. Under-standing the form and content of the intervention and determining with any precision which of the many programmatic variables account for the success of the program is therefore impossible.

Another difficulty affecting intervention evaluation is the selection of outcome measures. The outcome measure most often chosen to assess the effects of intervention is the IQ. Yet the use of the stand-ardized intelligence test as the single outcome measure for most in-tervention efforts is questionable because the scores do not provide educationally useful information (White and Haring, 1978). Keogh and Kopp (1978) suggested that the pervasive use of weak and inconclusive outcome measures might also be a function of weak nondevelopmen-tally based theoretical constructs and assessment techniques at the entry stages of programming. It is more useful to select outcome meas-ures that are directly related to the objectives of the intervention efforts (Scott, 1978). By clearly stating antecedent and outcome develop-mental events through assessment and specification of objectives, an objective evaluation of program outcomes is facilitated (Escalona, 1974). An assessment-linked intervention model can provide the most accurate evaluation of a child's progress in targeted domains of behavior.

When assessment, objectives specification, and intervention de-sign have been completed, progress toward the achievement of those objectives by the infant or young child must be measured. Unfortu-nately, the development of appropriate measurement strategies for monitoring progress has been slow. As argued elsewhere, a number of criteria should be met in using the evaluation-linked intervention instrument (Bricker et al., in press):

1. The evaluation instrument should reflect the curriculum content of the intervention effort.
2. The evaluation instrument should be flexible enough to be used with a wide range of handicapped infants.
3. The performance criteria should indicate whether the child has a particular skill and more importantly whether the skill is functional.
4. The expectancies or rates of acquisition for subpopulations of handicapped children should be specified.

Each of these criteria is discussed below in reference to the evaluation of language intervention efforts.

If the target of the intervention program is to improve an infant's language skills, then the evaluation instrument needs to focus on the acquisition of those behaviors. Development of language, sensorimo-tor, and affective behavior in the infant, however, are inseparable.

Thus, intervention *and* evaluation should monitor progress in each of these areas. Progress has been made in examining sensorimotor development (see, for example, Uzgiris and Hunt, 1975) but useful instrumentation for assessing the development of early language and affective behavior still needs to be developed. Each child cannot be unique; generalizability across subpopulations with specified behavioral repertoires and handicapped conditions must be a goal.

If we are interested in using a measurement system with a variety of handicapped infants and young children, then the evaluation instruments used must have built-in flexibility. Although an instrument must be flexible in its application, standardized administration procedures and response criteria are necessary to meet validity and reliability requirements. Using periodic samples of the child's language is an appropriate flexible method to monitor progress if the conditions under which the sample is acquired are relatively standard across samples.

Acquiring specific responses under controlled conditions can be an important first step in the language acquisition process. The adaptive use, however, of a response across a variety of settings under different conditions is crucial if a child's communication is to be effective. Evaluation instruments must include mechanisms to determine how functional an acquired language skill is to the child, and whether it can be applied to other situations. More effective intervention programs are partly dependent upon the establishment of "bench marks" or developmental expectancies for subpopulations of handicapped children. Without the establishment of such bench marks, one has no idea whether the progress demonsrated by a specific child is on-target given his or her handicapping conditions, is better than would be expected, or is significantly slower than was predicted. Language evaluation should accumulate information that can be used to develop growth curves for subpopulations of handicapped infants and young children. Such curves can help determine which of the various content procedures used in language intervention produce the greatest gains in specific groups of children.

This discussion highlights the gap between our current evaluation methods of language intervention and what is needed. The intent of this section of the chapter was to point out some of the problems that need to be eliminated and to suggest possible alternatives for better evaluation of the outcomes of early language intervention.

SUMMARY

Recently, new theories about the complex processes involved in early linguistic behavior have been steadily evolving from a plethora of research investigations in early child language and developmental psychology. These developments provide important implications for program developers and interventionists involved in fostering the development of critical language skills in handicapped infants and young children. In planning instruction for very young language-delayed children, our perspectives must be broadened in at least three directions. First, the significance of the period antecedent to the acquisition of formal language needs to be reckoned with in view of the evidence for a basic continuity between prelinguistic and linguistic communication. This emphasis implies that we should extend downward the age for beginning our language intervention efforts. Second, from very early in life the course of language development is integrally related to concomitantly developing cognitive and affective systems. Language interventionists need to learn to recognize and exploit this convergence. Third, the important roles that environmental contexts and complex interactive feedback networks play in the acquisition of child language needs to be acknowledged and capitalized on by language interventionists.

Having devoted considerable attention to discussing the key conceptual bases underlying our approach to language intervention, we then cast this framework in the form of a set of guiding principles to aid language interventionists in program design and implementation.

REFERENCES

Baer, D. 1973. The control of developmental process: Why wait? In J. R. Nesselroads, and H. W. Reese (eds.), Life-span developmental psychology: Methodological issues. Academic Press, Inc., N.Y.

Bell, R. 1974. Contributions of human infants to caregiving and social interaction. In M. Lewis and L. Rosenblum (eds.), The Effect of the Infant on its Caregiver. John Wiley & Sons, Inc., N.Y.

Bellugi, U. 1972. Development of language in the normal child. In J. E. McLean, D. E. Yoder, and R. L. Schiefelbusch (eds.), Language Intervention with the Retarded. University Park Press, Baltimore.

Bloom, L. 1970. Language Development: Form and Function in Emerging Grammars. M.I.T. Press, Cambridge, Mass.

Bloom, L., and Lahey, M. 1978. Language Development and Language Disorders. John Wiley & Sons, N.Y.

Bowerman, M. 1976. Semantic factors in the acquisition of rules for word use and sentence construction. In D. Morehead and A. Morehead (eds.), Normal and Deficient Child Language. University Park Press, Baltimore.

Bowlby, J. 1973. Attachment and Loss: Separation, Anxiety, and Anger. Basic Books, Inc., N.Y.

Brazelton, B., Koslowski, B., and Main, M. 1974. The origins of reciprocity: The early mother-infant interaction. In M. Lewis and L. Rosenblum (eds.), The Effect of the Infant on its Caregiver. John Wiley & Sons, N.Y.

Bricker, D. 1972. Imitation sign training as a facilitator of word-object association with low-functioning children. Am. J. Mental Defic. 76:509–516.

Bricker, D. 1978. Early intervention: The criteria of success. Allied Health and Behavioral Sciences, 1:567–582.

Bricker, W., and Bricker, D. 1969. A programmed approach to operant audiometry for low-functioning children. J. Speech Hear. Disord. 34:312–320.

Bricker, W., and Bricker, D. 1974. An early language training strategy. In R. Schiefelbusch and L. Lloyd (eds.), Language Perspectives: Acquisition, Retardation and Intervention. University Park Press, Baltimore.

Bricker, D., and Bricker, W. 1971. Toddler research and intervention project report: Year 1. IMRID Behavioral Science Monograph No. 20. Institute on Mental Retardation and Intellectual Development, George Peabody College.

Bricker, D., and Dennison, L. 1978. Training prerequisites to verbal behavior. In M. Snell (ed.), Systematic Instruction of the Moderately, Severely and Profoundly Handicapped. C. Merrill, Columbus, Ohio.

Bricker, D., Ruder, K., and Vincent, L. 1976. An intervention strategy for language-deficient children. In N. Haring and R. Schiefelbusch (eds.), Teaching Special Children. McGraw-Hill Book Company. N.Y.

Bricker, D., Seibert, J., and Casuso, V. 1980. Early intervention. In J. Hogg and P. Mittler (eds.), Advances in Mental Handicap Research. John Wiley & Sons, London.

Bricker, D., Seibert, J., and Scott, K. Early intervention: History, current status and the problem of evaluation. In D. Doleys, T. Vaughan and M. Cantrell (eds.), Interdisciplinary assessment and treatment of Developmental Problems. Spectrum, Inc., New York.

Bricker, W., Vincent-Smith, L., and Bricker, D. 1970. Receptive vocabulary in severely retarded children. Am. J. Mental Defic. 74:599–607.

Bricker, W., and Bricker, D. 1970. A program of language training for the severely handicapped child. Except. Child. 37:101–111.

Brinker, R., and Bricker, D. 1980. Teaching a first language: Building complex structures from simpler components. In J. Hogg and P. Mittler (eds.), Advances in Mental Handicap Research. John Wiley & Sons., London.

Brown, G. and Desforges, C. 1977. Piagetian psychology and education: Time for revision. Br. J. Educ. Psychol. 47:7–17.

Brown, R. 1973. A First Language. Harvard University Press, Cambridge, Mass.

Bruner, J. 1974–75a. From communication to language—A psychological perspective. Cognition. 3:255–287.

Bruner, J. 1975b. The ontogenesis of speech acts. J. Child Lang. 2:1–19.

Cantrell, M. 1974. Maladaptive behavior as a function of skill/demand discrepancies: An empirical investigation of the competence model. unpublished doctoral dissertation, Peabody College.

Cazden, C. 1974. Two paradoxes in the acquisition of language structure and function. In K. Connolly and J. Bruner (eds.), The Growth of Competence. Academic Press, Inc. N.Y.

Creelman, M. 1966. The Experimental Investigation of Meaning. Springer Publishing Co., N.Y.

Cromer, R. 1976. Cognitive hypothesis of language acquisition and its implications for child language deficiency. In D. Morehead and A. Morehead (eds.), Normal and Deficient Child Language. University Park Press, Baltimore.

Decarie, T. 1978. Affect development and cognition in a piagetian context. *In* M. Lewis and L. Rosenblum (eds.), The Development of Affect. Plenum Publishing Corp., N.Y.

Dennenberg, V., and Thoman, E. 1976. From animal to infant research. *In* T. Tjossem (ed.), Intervention Strategies for High Risk Infants and Young Children. University Park Press, Baltimore.

Dennis, W. 1973. Children of the Creche. Appleton-Century-Crofts, N.Y.

Dennis, W., and Najarian, P. 1963. Development under environmental handicap. *In* W. Dennis (ed.), Reading in Child Psychology. Prentice-Hall, Englewood Cliffs, N.J.

deVilliers, J., and deVilliers, P. 1978. Language Acquisition. Harvard University Press, Cambridge, Mass.

Dore, J. 1975. Holophrases, speech acts and language universals. J. Child Lang. 2:1–19.

Eilers, R. 1978. Discussion summary: development of phonology. *In* F. Minifie and L. Lloyd (eds.), Communicative and Cognitive Abilities-Early Behavioral Assessment. University Park Press, Baltimore.

Emde, R., Kligman, D., Reich, J., and Wade, T. 1978. Emotional expression in infancy: I. initial studies of social signaling and an emergent model. *In* M. Lewis and L. Rosenblum (eds.), Development of Affect. Plenum Publishing Corp., N.Y.

Escalona, S. 1974. Intervention programs for children at psychiatric risk: the contribution of child psychiatry and developmental theory. *In* E. Anthony and C. Koupernik (eds.), The Child and His Family. John Wiley & Sons., N.Y.

Fraiberg, 1977. Insights From the Blind. Basic Books, New York.

Gouin-Decarie, T. 1969. A study of the mental and emotional development of thalidomide child. *In* B. M. Foss (ed.), Determinants of Infant Behavior IV. Methuen & Co., London.

Greenfield, P., and Smith, J. 1976. Structure and Communication in Early Language Development. Academic Press, Inc., N.Y.

Guess, D., Sailor, W., and Baer, D. 1977. A behavioral-remedial approach to language training for the severely handicapped. *In* E. Sontag (ed.), Educational Programming for the Severely and Profoundly Handicapped. CEC, Reston, VA.

Guess, D., Sailor, W., and Baer, D. 1974. To teach language to retarded children. *In* R. Schiefelbusch and L. Lloyd (eds.), Language Perspectives: Acquisition, Retardation, and Intervention. University Park Press, Baltimore.

Halliday, M. 1975. Learning How to Mean. Elsevier North Holland, New York.

Harlow, H., and Mears, C. 1978. The nature of complex, unlearned responses. *In* M. Lewis and L. Rosenblum (eds.), Development of Affect. Plenum Publishing Corp., N.Y.

Heber, R., and Garber, H. 1975. The Milwaukee Project: A study of the use of family intervention to prevent cultural-familial mental retardation. *In* B. Friedlander, G. Sterritt and G. Kirk (eds.), Exceptional Infant: Assessment and Intervention, Vol. III. Brunner/Mazel, N.Y.

Hobbs, N. 1978. Classification options. Except. Child. 44:494–497.

Hunt, J. McV. 1961. Intelligence and Experience. Ronald Press, N.Y.

Irwin, O., and Chen, H. 1946. Infant speech: Vowel and consonant frequency. J. Speech Disord. 11:123–125.

Kagan, J. 1971. Change and Continuity in Infancy. John Wiley & Sons, N.Y.

Kagan, J., Kearsley, R., and Zelazo, P. 1978. Infancy: Its Place in Human Development. Harvard University Press, Cambridge, Mass.

Keogh, B., and Kopp, C. 1978. From assessment to intervention: an elusive bridge. In F. Minifie and L. Lloyd (eds.), Communicative and Cognitive Abilities-Early Behavioral Assessment. University Park Press, Baltimore.

Kohlberg, L. 1970. The concepts of developmental psychology as the central guide to education: Examples from cognitive, moral, and psychological education. In M. Reynolds (ed.), Psychology and the Process of Schooling in the Next Decade: Alternative Conceptions. Leadership Training Institute/Special Education, University of Minnesota, Minneapolis, Minn.

Kopp, C., and Shaperman, J. 1973. Cognitive development in the absence of object manipulation during infancy. Developmental Psychology. 9:430.

Lewis, M., and Lee-Painter, S. 1974. An interactional approach to the mother-infant dyad. In M. Lewis and L. Rosenblum (eds.), The Effect of the Infant on its Caregiver. John Wiley & Sons, N.Y.

Lewis, M., and Rosenblum, L. (eds.). 1974. The Effects of the Infant on its Caregiver. John Wiley & Sons, N.Y.

Lewis, M., and Rosenblum, L. 1978. Development of Affect. Plenum Publishing Corp., N.Y.

MacDonald, J. 1978. Environmental Language Inventory: A Semantic-Based Assessment and Treatment Model for Generalized Communication. Charles Merrill Publishing Co., Ohio.

Mahoney, G. 1975. Ethological approach to delayed language acquisition. Am. J. Mental Defic. 80(2):139–148.

McLean, J., and Snyder-McLean, L. 1978. A Transactional Approach to Early Language Training. Charles Merrill Publishing Co., Ohio.

Menyuk, P. 1964. Comparison of grammar of children with functionally deviant and normal speech. J. Speech Hear. Res. 7:190–121.

Miller, J., Chapman, R., Branston, M., and Reichle, J. 1980. Language comprehension in sensorimotor stages 5 and 6. J. Speech Hear. Res.

Miller, L., and Dryer, J. 1975. Four preschool programs: Their dimensions and effects. Monographs of the Society for Research in Child Development. 40:5–6, (Serial No. 162).

Morehead, D., and Morehead, A. 1976. Normal and Deficient Child Language. University Park Press, Baltimore.

Nelson, K. 1978. Early speech in its communicative context. In F. Minifie and L. Lloyd (eds.), Communicative and Cognitive Abilities-Early Behavioral Assessment. University Park Press, Baltimore.

Nelson, K. 1973. Structure and strategy in learning to talk. Monographs of the Society for Research in Child Development. 38(1–2), (Serial No. 149).

Oller, D., Wieman, L., Doyle, W., and Ross, C. 1976. Infant babbling and speech. J. Child Lang. 3:1–12.

Osofsky, J. 1976. Neonatal characteristics and mother-infant interaction in two observational situations. Child Dev. 47: 1138–1147.

Palermo, D. 1971. On learning to talk: Are principles derived from the learning laboratory applicable? In D. Slobin (ed.), The Ontogenesis of Grammar. Academic Press, Inc., N.Y.

Piaget, J. 1970. Piaget's theory. In P. Mussen (ed.), Carmichael's Manual of Child Psychology, Vol. I. John Wiley & Sons., N.Y.

Piaget, J., and Inhelder, B. 1969. Psychology of the Child. Basic Books, Inc., N.Y.

Pick, A. 1978. Discussion summary: Early Assessment. In F. Minifie and L. Lloyd (eds.), Communicative and Cognitive Abilities-Early Behavioral Assessment. University Park Press, Baltimore.

Prutting, C. 1979. Process: the action of moving forward progressively from one point to another on the way to completion. 1979. J. Speech Hear. Res. 44:3–23.

Ramey, C., and Campbell, F. 1979. Supplemental preschool education for disadvantaged children. School Review. 87:171–189.

Reese, H. and Lipsitt, L. 1970. Experimental Child Psychology. Academic Press, Inc., New York.

Rheingold, H., Gerwirtz, J., and Ross, H. 1959. Social conditioning of vocalizations in the infant. J. Comp. Physiol. Psychol. 52:68–73.

Ruder, K., and Smith, M. 1974. Issues in language training. In R. Schiefelbusch and L. Lloyd (eds.), Language Perspectives: Acquisition, Retardation, and Intervention. University Park Press, Baltimore.

Saarni, C. 1978. Cognitive and communicative features of emotional experience, or do you show what you think you feel? In M. Lewis and L. Rosenblum (eds.), The Development of Affect. Plenum Publishing Corp., New York.

Scott, K. 1978. The rationale and methodological considerations underlying early cognitive behavioral assessment. In F. Minifie and L. Lloyd (eds.), Communicative and Cognitive Abilities-Early Behavioral Assessment. University Park Press, Baltimore.

Sievers, D., and Essa, S. 1961. Language development in institutionalized and community mentally retarded children. Am. J. Mental Defic. 66:13–420.

Sinclair deZwart, H. 1969. Developing psycholinguistics. In D. Elkind and J. Flavell (eds.), Studies in Cognitive Development. Oxford University Press, New York.

Snow, C. 1977. The development of conversation. J. Child Lang. 4:1–22.

Sylvester-Bradley, B., and Trevarthen, C. 1978. Baby talk as an adaptation to the infant's communication. In N. Waterson and C. Snow (eds.), Development of Communication. John Wiley & Sons., New York.

Tizard, B. 1974. Do social relationships affect language development. In K. Connolly and J. Brunner (eds.), The Growth of Competence. Academic Press, Inc., New York.

Uzgiris, I. 1976. Organization of sensorimotor intelligence. In M. Lewis, (ed.), Origins of Intelligence: Infancy and Early Childhood. Plenum Publishing Corp., New York.

Uzgiris, I., and Hunt, J. McV. 1975. Assessment in Infancy. University of Illinois Press, Urbana, Ill.

Vincent-Smith, L., Bricker, D., and Bricker, W. 1974. Acquisition of receptive vocabulary in the toddler-age child. Child Dev. 45:189–193.

Weikart, D. 1972. Relationship of curriculum, teaching, and learning in preschool education. In J. Stanley (ed.), Preschool Programs for the Disadvantaged: Five Experimental Approaches to Early Childhood Education. Johns Hopkins Press, Baltimore.

White, B., and Held, R. 1967. Experience in early human development, Part II, plasticity of sensori-motor development in the human infant. In J. Hellmuth (ed.), Exceptional Infant, Vol. I, the Normal Infant. Straub and Hell-muth, Seattle.

White, O., and Haring, N. 1978. Evaluating educational programs serving the severely and profoundly handicapped. *In* N. Haring and D. Bricker (eds.), Teaching the Severely Handicapped, Vol. III. Special Press, Columbus.

chapter 16

A Strategy for Stimulating Infant Learning

William Fowler

Graduate School of Education
Harvard University
Cambridge, Massachusetts

contents

SCIENCE AND CULTURE IN COGNITIVE DEVELOPMENT

Norms for the quality and rate of cognitive development are, in most cultures, generally well below the biological potentials for the human species. This assumption serves as a central working hypothesis guiding these investigations on the effects of early cognitive stimulation on development, and in particular the author's recent studies focusing on language.

For most of human history and prehistory, stimulation has apparently not been an item on a planned agenda for rearing children. Stimulation has been largely an unplanned byproduct of culturally prescribed experiences anchored in the work routines and rituals of life in tribal and rural settings (Fowler and Fowler, 1978; Kagan and Klein, 1973; Mead, 1970). Much of cognitive socialization has typically occurred through the extensive opportunities offered young children to observe and imitate older peers and adults in the daily activities of a close-knit community setting. Infancy, particularly, has been a period marked more by a concern for nurturance and pacification than attention to cognitive development through exploratory play, object manipulation, and focus on language. Even today among broad populations of most societies, television, day care, and popular literature on the importance of early experience have made small inroads on this prevalent folk pattern.

Historically, the developmental outcomes for these widespread cultural practices have been in harmony with the tasks each culture gives its members as adults. But what may have been traditionally effective socialization in rural settings for millennia is often quite dissonant for coping with the demands of schooling and adequate adult participation in the urban maze and increasingly complex technology of contemporary society.

Implicit in any critique of a folk model for child rearing is the presupposition of a consciously planned approach as an alternative, a scientific model of rationally selected and empirically tested principles. Although the present state of the art cannot claim to identify even all of the primary factors, let alone their implementation in proper proportions and arrangements over time, we are not without a few theoretical and practical clues.

Recognizing that neither cultural practice nor intervention have been at all times and in all places the same, certain characteristics that typically distinguish planned intervention strategies from historically common cultural practices as ideal types may be outlined as follows:

Models for Cognitive Socialization[1]

Folk Models	Planned Intervention
Social Structure and Authority	
Community based organization and culturally traditional forms and rules	Agency based Scientific and professional knowledge
Family operated	Professionally operated
Informal rules	Formal rules
Causal Framework	
Cultural prescription	Scientific theory and empirical testing
Intuitive arrangements: a mixture of practical science, cultural myth and chance	Rational and conscious selection and organization of means to ends
Community sanctions; person oriented	Agency Sanctions Problem and task oriented
Role Commitment and Training	
Permanent responsibility	Temporary responsibility
Culturally prescribed status and roles	Professionally assigned and achieved roles
Person oriented—unpaid	Job oriented—paid
Observation and imitation, informal, irregular	Formal education, apprenticeship guidance
Time Perspective	
Unplanned	Planned
Indefinite—unfolding	Defined time segments—arranged regard to relations of past, present and future
Socially developmentally defined and integrated	Program and cognitively developmentally defined
Curriculum	
Culturally-familially prescribed developmental tasks	Agency—professional role prescriptions of developmental learning objectives
Intuitively derived norms and goals	Scientifically derived (theory and empirical test) norms and objectives
Subjectively defined processes and products	Objectively defined processes and products
Holistic: combined social, affective and cognitive	Selective: Predominantly cognitive but variable; analytic even when comprehensive

---

[1] Much of the framework for this duality derives from the German sociologists, Tonnies (1940) and Weber (1947), and the American anthropologist, Redfield (1947).

Models for Cognitive Socialization (*Continued*)

Folk Models	Planned Intervention
Methods	
Intuitive—personal decision making regulated by cultural practice and personal interpretation	Objectively defined decision making Rational—empirical problem solving and experimentation
Trial and error	Goal and task oriented: systematic achievement oriented, means-end, and normatively defined
Person-role oriented: unsystematic, contradictory, normatively defined	Diagnostic precision

What most distinguishes the two general approaches is the emphasis on the scientific "attitude" in planned intervention, what Weber (1947), the German sociologist, termed the rational regulation of means to ends that characterizes the organized institutions of complex societies. It is this concern for the rational versus the culturally traditional and intuitive from which most other differences flow. What is also striking is the variety of possibilities for control, for regulating developmental outcomes that planned intervention offers compared with the uncertainty and variability implicit in folk practice. It is not that the folk model, particularly among the highly educated middle classes of today's developed societies, does not frequently take on many of the stimulating and rational features of systematic intervention (Chapman, this volume; Messer, 1978; Snow and Ferguson, 1977) and in fact many techniques employed in planned strategies are traceable to folk wisdom (see Whiting, 1974). It is rather that planned strategies are more likely to use a systematically derived body of knowledge as a means of selecting and implementing stimulation strategies likely to optimize development. Presumably, it is this potential for determining desirable outcomes, which the rational manipulation of methods offers, that is responsible for the growing appeal of planning in recent years. But what is further evident is that not all of the differences necessarily weigh on the side of formal intervention. The temporal constraints, task orientation and job boundaries to which the role of the professional is tied all threaten to lose sight of the person, the needs of both the child and the family, which may undermine the apparent gains.

A STRATEGY FOR EARLY STIMULATION

The inventory above serves as an introduction to the presentation of a systematic strategy (Fowler, 1965b, 1970, 1980) that has guided the author's work on early language and other forms of cognitive stimulation with infants and preschoolers from a broad range of social class and ethnic backgrounds. It serves as a set of guidelines of possibilities to consider and problems to handle in evaluating the effectiveness of a strategy, both logically and empirically. I shall outline the salient features of the approach in general form, discussing their application to various forms of learning, particularly language, along the way. Selected findings from recent infant investigations, some of which are still in progress, are summarized.

The general framework for the strategy necessarily takes on most of the characteristics listed for planned intervention in the outline above. It is first of all planned and systematic, with all that entails in defining and implementing ordered ways of influencing the course of children's development. Second, it is professionally mediated, meaning that professionals design the program and transmit the techniques through written guides or personal guidance to parents or teachers. But, although formal and systematic in conception, the strategy is adaptive and clinical in form; that is, both child stimulation and care-giver guidance are constructed and modified according to the developing styles of the child and caregivers in the home or day care setting. The program is not fixed in advance, but general principles are applied and adapted according to need. This cultural-familial adaptive approach is intended to enhance and strengthen the commitment inherent in the folk model to the children's development over both the short and long term. Finally, as indicated above, it is assumed that any attention to cognitive stimulation for a culture or population group, particularly stimulation based on careful planning, can be expected to produce cognitive outcomes for development that surpass norms for the population groups concerned. Because few families or institutions in any culture use stimulation strategies commensurate with children's biological potential, there is almost always room for improvement. Even special attention without much thought—the "Hawthorne effect"—contains cognitive stimulation and incentive to learning that result in some change (Stedman, 1969).

No one knows much about the cognitive potentials for any population of children. All our information is standardized across whole populations whose development, at least for the preschool period, must largely reflect the effects of folk models of cognitive socialization. About all we do know is that there is considerable variation around those norms, consistent correlations with parent education, social class, family size, birth order, and other social and psychological factors (Hess, 1970), and that the collected early intervention studies of recent decades have regularly raised children's skills above the norms for their group—at least in the short term (Bronfenbrenner, 1975; Horowitz and Paden, 1973) and, to some degree, probably over the long term (Brown, 1978).

Strategies mediated through guiding parents to stimulate their children seem more likely to result in longer term, continuing effects (Bronfenbrenner, 1975; Brown, 1978; Ramey, Sparling, and Wasik, this volume). In the realm of language, however, few studies have selectively assessed the cumulative effects of planned strategies on language or other aspects of cognitive development (Chapman, this volume; Fowler and Swenson, in press; Horowitz and Paden, 1973).

Filling in the broad outlines of this strategic stimulation framework are detailed dimensions designed to harmonize child-environmental interactions and magnify long-term developmental effects. These dimensions fall into clusters relating to distinct problem areas affecting learning and development. First, there are many dimensions that affect development. On the other hand, the setting, types of activity, and similar situational conditions probably influence the child's immediate response more than development over the long run. Closely related, and even more critical, are the modes of interactions employed, with respect to interpersonal relations and cognitive transactions. Underlying this framework of interaction are the assumptions held for how learning takes place. What caregivers do builds in, implicitly or explicitly, a theoretical model for what mechanisms induce cognitive change. In taking account of these different domains, this author has attempted to devise a comprehensive strategy on developmental ecology, in which the matrix of circumstances affecting function and change are balanced with the cumulative aspects of learning, that is long-term developmental learning.

DEVELOPMENTAL DIMENSIONS

Timing

Among the many dimensions of stimulation that could conceivably influence development, certain ones like timing, duration, intensity and sequence are among the most important. Protracted delay of stimulation beyond cultural norms and developmentally optimal (if not critical) periods may lead to intellectual retardation. Greatly increased earliness of timing may be premature, however, leading to failure and a sense of incompetence rather than precocity. The course followed here is to advance the timing of stimulation over norms by various periods according to the concepts employed, on the assumption that norms index outcomes that must necessarily be preceded by experience. The general assumption is that enriched early experience establishes a foundation of cognition systems and styles at threshold levels for processing subsequent stimulation in more efficient forms. In the case of first-language learning, programs have generally been timed to begin at less than 6 months, at least 2 months in advance of the norms for first words for superior development (McCarthy, 1954) and from 4 to 8 months over population norms, depending on which IQ measure is used (Bayley, 1969; Griffiths, 1954, 1970). In light of these considerations, it is difficult to grasp why language stimulation programs have typically been delayed past infancy. In her classic study on identical twins, for example, Strayer (1930) waited until about 19 months to begin training, a point at which the twins had already attained the word-learning stage, and most of the research on early intervention for disadvantaged children, which typically stresses language, has begun after age 2 (Bronfenbrenner, 1975).

Duration

At first glance, duration seems similarly easy to define in its implications. Stimulation presumably needs to continue to a point at which substantial progress in an area can be observed. But what is substantial progress? Perhaps certain threshold achievements, once attained through externally mediated stimulation, in fact establish cognitive styles and motivation that propel the child to seek and process further stimulation on his or her own. Generally, regular language intervention is continued for about 6 months or to 12 months of age, but it seems that a more operational criterion may be until vocabulary accumulation has proceeded beyond the point of easy accurate counting (about 50 words) or even the point at which the shift to beginning (two-word) sentence construction commences, both of which often arrive in infants between 12 and 16 months. At these points, there is generally sufficient grasp of syntactical differentiation and sufficiently accelerated rates of learning that professional intervention becomes less necessary. Undergirding the continuous gains, however, is perhaps also parent competence and interest, developed through intervention, that maintains the accelerated developmental process. Declines or leveling tend to appear in less educated families but follow-up samples are still small and evidence is confounded with measurement and cultural factors (as in Italian and Chinese families).

Intensity

Intensity is integral to the approach followed in this research. It is distinct from planning and systematic methods as such in that parents are encouraged to engage the child in language learning and play in all of the ordinary routines and relations of parenting and to set up others for the purpose. In programs addressed to other types of learning or general cognitive stimulation, caregivers, at home or in day care, are similarly encouraged to set up and seek opportunities for constructive stimulation throughout the day, being careful to foster autonomy in periods of free play activity as well. It is assumed that most concept systems, certainly including language, are quite complex, making both intensive and extensive exposure, much practice and many exemplars important prerequisites for high mastery and advanced development.

LEARNING: DEVELOPMENTAL
SEQUENCE, STRUCTURE, AND CUMULATIVE EFFECTS

Sequence brings us to the question of how the organization of concepts affects the focus and order of stimulation, how concepts are structured and the cumulative, developmental aspects of learning. Most areas of knowledge form interdependent bodies, in which individual concepts are part of structurally and functionally interrelated systems. Knowledge about transportation, for example, involves clusters of concepts about movement and transport, loading and unloading different materials and people with various vehicles and mechanisms. The initial cognitions of infancy, too, involve intimately interconnected concepts and rules about the permanence, means-end relations, movement, functions, and other aspects of all kinds of objects in all sorts of conditions. In each case, bits of knowledge fit together in certain ways to make up the structure of the whole, which can only be acquired through extensive exposure to information that piles up cumulatively over substantial periods of time and development. In this sense, duration is obviously also a condition necessary to permit the acquisition of a substantial body of knowledge. Considerations of ordering must be undertaken if only to pace the flow of novel concepts to the rate at which the child can absorb them.

But the critical aspect of the entire acquisition process is developmental learning. Both the child's mind and the bodies of knowledge are each structured systems, to which cognitive stimulation strategies must interrelate equally. This is the problem of the match of which Hunt (1961) has written extensively, and Piaget's developmental mechanisms of assimilation and accommodation take account. On the one hand, categories of knowledge form coherent systems in ways that simpler concepts learned in a program facilitate learning of increasingly complex concepts in the area. On the other hand, mental processes operate as systems that collect, adapt, and store novel and increasingly complex information to and with the ongoing system, in the course of which modes of thought and problem-solving strategies are themselves continually developed and transformed. Thus the two poles—a dynamic internal organization and governance, and an external structure of concept systems, interact continually to make learning a sequential, cumulative process that operates developmentally over long time spans.

In the case of language, its complex, interdependent, hierarchical organization makes sequence and accumulation over time particularly appropriate. Sound units (phonology) are patterned to form words (morphology), which are patterned to form sentences (syntax), and the whole is woven into a fabric of meaning. Given the intricacy of the maze of rules in such a concept system, at the very least, language accumulation takes time (duration). Even with the biological aid of a Language Acquisition Device (LAD), the hypothesized species specific processing blueprint (Chomsky, 1965), normative steps for mastery of just the basics extend from birth to age 3 or 4 and the elaboration that represents fine control over subtleties of expression continues for many years (Brown, 1973; McNeill, 1970; Menyuk, 1964).

It seems especially clear that language stimulation ought to be an ordered process, in which ordering goes beyond that required for controlling the rate of introducing new concepts. Because language is an intricate, organized hierarchy of rules, it should be useful to locate points of entry where concepts can be greatly simplified and introduced a rule or two at a time, gradually building up in complexity until the child has mastered the system. Yet we do not fully know which concepts are invariant in the order in which they must be acquired, say for reasons of complexity and contingency, and which are a matter of custom and culture. Despite the burgeoning of psycholinguistic research, most research on language development observes small samples of children reared according to prevalent folk practices, with no attempt to vary sequences. The evidence shows that nouns generally precede modifiers, for example (Bloom, 1975; Chapman, this volume; Nelson, 1973), and it is logical that concepts of a substance might precede concepts of attributes about the substance. But a few labels applying to qualities (e.g., hot, yellow) also commonly appear concurrently with and even before those naming objects (e.g., stove, paint), as they have in other studies (Fowler and Swenson, 1979), even if they may reflect perceptions of general states rather than specific attributes. Similarly, other observations show that while Jakobson's (Jakobson and Halle, 1956) phonemic contrast order of wide to narrow vowels and frontal to back consonants is generally true in both English (Fowler and Swenson, 1979) and Chinese (Lee, 1978) speaking infants, there are usually exceptions, emerging out of sequence apparently because of frequency of cultural usage, as in the words *cookie* or *juice*. Researchers even have apparently been able to program maternal stimulation to induce the "k" sound in first words, but not the contrasting "ch" sound, which Jakobson seems to say should appear almost concurrently as a polar opposite (unpublished pilot study).

Flexible Sequences: Levels

As a general principle, therefore, the strategy adopted is to program stimulation sequences in terms of what might be termed *levels*. Levels are major stages or broad steps in a sequence for acquiring cognitive mastery of a body of interrelated concepts, such as concepts of transportation, insects, size, number or language. The levels are organized according to the number and intricacy of perceptual characteristics and concepts with which a child may be expected to make steady progress in a given stage of learning. In concept learning, the rate of presenting both perceptual features and concept complexity is graduated according to skill, age (or general development), complexity of material and phase of program. At the simplest or beginning level, usually a limited number of objects (2 or 3) with relatively simple perceptual features in any task or session are focused on, and no more than one or two novel concepts of a concept area. Uniformly colored balls, blocks or poker chips make excellent material for beginning number concept learning, focusing first on the concepts of one and two. Similarly, the first level for learning classification might use miniature object exemplars such as cars versus trucks that are stripped down versions constructed with only one or two perceptually prominent defining criteria (passenger space and seats versus cab and carrier), keeping other irrelevant features less visible.

The next level might embrace several objects with more perceptual variation (e.g., objects of varying shape, color or size for counting; vehicles with more detail) and perhaps two to three novel concepts (one vs. two vs. three; cars, trucks, and buses) with successive levels including further complexity in number and variety of features and in intricacy and number of concepts. Obviously, sequences move along a continuum but in both writing curricula and implementing programs, it is convenient to arrange material in broad steps or levels. Ordering in definite, if broad, steps provides better control of sequence and mastery through defining a body of material to be mastered before jumping ahead and risking failure. Sticking to a body of material that encompasses a variety of exemplars of about the same complexity also provides *flexibility*, stimulating interest through adding more novelty for both teacher and learner, than when learning proceeds in narrow, rigid steps. Because logical sequences are not well researched and laid out in any concept area; because there is typically cross-mental fertilization among areas and continuing input from general experience; and finally because of the self-regulating, adaptive, and inventive character of cognitive systems, few sequences benefit from rigid programming. It is often convenient to range forward and backward across levels to some degree, depending on ability, motivation, and other factors, and of course to vary the pace through levels according to rates of mastery.

Both sequence and flexibility come into focus in this approach to language stimulation. As a general first level for infants under 6 months, or even during the first year or so, it has seemed useful to concentrate on word learning with concrete nouns, centering on small, manipulable and culturally common objects, which Nelson's (1973) studies show are typically the first object labels acquired. But weight also has been given to labeling visible, easily isolable actions, such as point, touch, push, and kiss. As it turns out, the first spontaneous words of all the infants are principally labels of small objects like ball, button, shoe, book, card, cookie, and flower. But the action terms or verbs have been more marked by their absence, only very few like *walk* or *open* making an early appearance. What does appear in their stead are a variety of general process and state terms, such as *down*, *up*, *out*, *bye-bye*, *no*, and *hiya*, which were not necessarily stressed in curricula presented, but are obviously integral to everyday social experience. Few modifiers appeared in the early vocabularies, which may be associated with their difficulty or with the practice of not encouraging parents to focus on modifiers until language production is well launched, after 50 words or so and phrase-making has begun, or both.

So far, it has not been necessary to define more than two major levels in the strategy for language stimulation, and the rules given parents for following these have not been hard and fast. Although the approach has stressed the utility of simplification, and isolating labels in single words, parents have also been encouraged to use words in phrases and simple, concrete sentences, simplifying through stressing a key label at the point the child's attention is focused on the item, either through caregiver pointing (or otherwise dramatizing) or labeling at the point of infant spontaneous interest. Placing word learning in the context of sentences relates components to larger wholes of meaning and syntax, which is assumed to both foster cultural naturalness and expand opportunities for infants to make preliminary inferences, or at least become familiar with additional linguistic rules that can later be the subject of more systematic attention. Actually, however, by the time the ''second level'' is attained, that is when word learning has attained an accelerated rate of several new words or more per day and phrase construction begins, attention to sequence gives way to flexible interchanges. At this stage, modeling and guidance on various syntactical and semantic rules are engaged as they occur in diverse conversational and activity contexts.

Why start with word units before vocalization units? After all, vocalization play between caregiver and infant appears early in the folk practices of most cultures and vocalization of many parts of the spectrum of phonological approximations is integral to the modal prelinguistic experience. Recently more weight has been given to this form of stimulation. But in fact, focusing on whole word units from the beginning, well before evidence of speech or comprehension appears, starts off the language learning process with the problem of combining phonological units into patterns that provide the most basic meaning unit because individual phonemes carry semantic value only in the context of words. There is plenty of exposure to phonemic variety in word stimulation and combining structure with meaning places the stress on what language is really all about. And while an empirical test is needed to compare the effects of strategies focusing and not focusing on vocalization prior to or parallel with whole word stimulation, studies on language stimulation, minimizing vocalization play, have resulted in greatly accelerated rates and higher levels of language mastery.

The question is closely related to the question of phonic versus whole word approaches in learning to read. In a series of studies on early reading (Fowler, 1962, 1965a, 1971b), it was found that a strategy that combines phonic and whole word learning is highly effective. Grapheme-phoneme units are analyzed from and synthesized into whole words, which are also offered in parallel as units, from the start. The program follows a tightly sequenced, step by step strategy as well, although once a few words and their component sound units are mastered, parallel experimentation with combinatory variations is also encouraged. Moreover, after several primers are covered and perhaps a dozen or so grapheme-phoneme units acquired, children frequently begin to puzzle out random words and bits of commercial labels and text on their own—much as children do once the "second level" is attained in our oral language learning programs. As with language learning, empirical comparisons of different approaches to reading are needed at the preschool level. Nevertheless, the data collected over many years on school age children does suggest that some sort of systematic phonological focus is an advantage to all except the brightest children (Chall, 1967). The highly programmed sequence, incorporating analysis of phonological aspects as well as word learning, in other investigations seems to be a failure-proof system. All 3- and 4-year-olds in the program (selected for linguistic and motivational readiness) routinely learn to read. Logically, reading is different from oral language in that it is difficult to bathe the child's perceptual environment in written exemplars the way it can be saturated with aural exemplars. Graphic forms also lack the intonational patterning that integrates phonological learning with oral word learning and semantics.

Monitoring

Before turning to problems of the mechanisms integral to learning itself, which are intrinsic to the general problem of the structure of concept systems and sequential learning, two additional dimensions relating to developmental perspectives deserve comment. The first is monitoring and the second is the question of cognitive focus and differentiation. Monitoring is almost a given in any well-run program. Teachers typically assess progress at regular intervals on some systematic basis even when the material covered follows a series of relatively arbitrary steps with little regard to a gradient of complexity, as most social studies and history courses are organized. Even parents following a folk model are usually conscious of when sounds are first vocalized, first words are comprehended and uttered, and later when the child begins to form sentences. Monitoring is above all devoting attention to or registering awareness of benchmarks along the way. But the point of it all is not simply to register awareness, it is awareness for a *purpose*, grasping the significance of acquisitions that are attained more or less on target and of those which are delayed. Again, even the cultural model suggests to most parents that prolonged delay in the appearance of first words or phrases, the emergence of distorted speech patterns, or the failure of any sounds to appear at all, may index underlying problems of brain injury, learning problems, emotional conflict or deafness. In professional practice, monitoring is sufficiently refined to provide early cues or feedback that anticipate more critical developmental delays or deviance in time to alter methods to bring about a more productive course. It may be recalled, parenthetically, that one of the problems in the classic pre-posttest educational program design, at first widely applied with little modification in the early Head Start type research, was the absence of formative evaluation (Glick, 1968; Zimiles, 1970). Without monitoring teaching-learning processes, it was often not even known whether teachers were following the designed program strategy, let alone whether the children were making progress.

Assessment and monitoring are intimately involved in almost every detail of tightly sequenced programs such as the one mentioned above but caregiver energies are also engaged in tracking progress in language and other cognitive learning programs. These techniques have

worked reasonably well with educated parents on language development (Fowler and Swenson, 1979) and moderately well with caregivers
in ordinary day care centers in various programs (Fowler, 1972, 1978).
Day care workers will keep tabs on frequency of participation and
some general indices of progress and motivation, but educated parents
in the home, once trained, seem to keep more faithful records. Parents
with less than college level backgrounds are usually less skilled or
reliable and more assailed with the problems of coping in daily living.
With educated families, we can obtain good records of most novel
sounds vocalized, many first single word comprehensions and nearly
all initial single and multiword imitations and spontaneous utterances,
including records of successive approximation of increasing phonological fidelity. The process is less reliable once vocabulary and later
phrase and sentence production accelerate. Productions are necessarily
more reliably recorded than comprehensions, especially of sentences,
without staged manipulation of linguistic and referential components
typically missing in natural contexts. Records of frequency and type
of attention to language stimulation are even more variable, probably
partly because the process furnishes little feedback reward for the
extensive recording labor involved. Because of daily accessibility and
familiarity with the child, however, parents are obviously the most
appropriate and least expensive resources to record early language
indices of development. Periodic audiotapes of speech samples have
provided a more elaborate basis for linguistic assessments.

Assessment has been applied to parental and teacher modes of
stimulation as well as a training device, as a means of checking on
program delivery, and as a method of monitoring caregiver competence
and development in interactive stimulation techniques. Quick scoring,
check-off devices for rating teachers in day care or schools in three
major forms of basic child care activity (basic care routines, free play
and organized teaching projects) have proved useful for assessing the
effectiveness of caregivers on relevant dimensions of both cognitive
and language stimulation, as well as on the quality of interpersonal
relations (Fowler, 1978, 1980). A more comprehensive set of seven-
point rating scales has been devised to assess the quality of caregiver
interaction in our language stimulation projects (Fowler, 1975). The
scales also encompass sequential and cumulative aspects of developmental learning as well as situational dimensions of interaction.

Cognitive Focus and Differentiation

The issue of cognitive focus, that is, how broad or narrow the set of
abilities engaged in planned stimulation, raises the chronic question of
how important the role of general intelligence as opposed to specific

abilities is in the development of competencies. Most early intervention programs have been broadly aimed to facilitate general cognitive development, often assumed to be measured by IQ tests (Bronfenbrenner, 1975). But language stimulation has also enjoyed a special place in such programs, both as a skill vital to later school learning and under the assumption that language mediation may be essential to cognitive development in general as Bruner (1973) and others (Luria, 1976; Luria and Yudovich, 1961; Vygotsky, 1962) hold.

Fowler's programs have followed a similar strategy wherever they have been intended to foster cognitive development and abstract thinking appropriate for later coping in academic environments. But other studies focused on specialized competencies, such as gross motor skills (Leithwood and Fowler, 1971; Ogston, in preparation) based on a rationale of cognitive differentiation of abilities (Fowler, 1969, 1971b, 1972b, 1977; Fowler and Leithwood, 1971). The current series of studies on language, moreover, focuses intensively on language, not only in the interest of giving priority to this obviously critical academic skill and with the hypothesis that language mastery can be greatly accelerated and improved, but also as a means of testing the polar hypotheses of potency of language as the agent of all thought as against potentials for cognitive differentiation. It is assumed that parents follow their own cultural-familial model for cognitive socialization in other areas, such as spatial and mathematical skills. Outcomes in these nonprogram areas are thus believed to follow a course normally expected from the families' usual modes of stimulation for those areas, except insofar as either program or newly acquired parent skills generalize, or as other skills are involved in the focused stimulation.

In one sense, the issue is more than whether the focus of cognitive stimulation employed is wide or narrow. To exercise influence on cognitive processes, any stimulation must offer a variety of exemplars for program concepts and address itself to mental manipulation of rules about phenomena; otherwise the process reduces itself to one of rote learning about limited sets of specific objects and ritualized procedures. Thus the strategy with respect to language stimulation is necessarily cognitive in form, and using diverse exemplars and manipulation of language with respect to linguistic and referential rules is fundamental to the approach, as described above. The only residual issue is then how potent and generalized a coding tool verbal language is in mental processing.

The Griffiths Mental Scales (1954, 1970), in which several specialized abilities (language, personal-social, fine and gross motor, and spatial problem solving, along with counting and measurement after age 2) are scaled independently from 0 to 8 years, have provided a simple and useful tool for assessing the degree of intra-individual developmental differentiation. Collectively, the average of the separate scales yields a general measure of intelligence (IQ), which Griffiths terms GQ. As such, they constitute a componential system of assessing cognitive development, although empirically constructed in terms of linear increments of difficulty according to age, with only limited within-scale consideration of logical sequences of cognitive complexity. The choices of the scales themselves as components of cognition and intelligence, like other IQ scales, is also dictated more by empirical tradition than logical organization. They were also standardized some years ago and are less reliable at older ages because of a decrease in the number of items for each year. Despite such limitations, they are admirably scaled, one of the most reliable infant scales (Thomas, 1970) and in fact the only scales that provide continuous, differentiated measures over the first 8 years of life.

Results have shown mixed effects across different studies and among different skills. The degree of generality of advancement versus differentiation has apparently been influenced by differences in program implementation and the closeness of other abilities in symbolic abstraction to verbal language. Details of the pattern are more conveniently discussed below.

MECHANISMS FOR COGNITIVE LEARNING AND DEVELOPMENTAL LEARNING

Mechanisms for learning engage both immediate and long-term developmental aspects of cognitive change. The first concerns cognitive acquisitions emerging through interaction between persons and environments in a given situation or closely linked series of situations. The second concerns ontogenetic changes that take place over time—weeks, months, and years, in which bodies of concepts accumulate and transformations occur in the mental systems with which the person processes information, a process that may be termed developmental learning.

Until the advent of the linguistic revolution launched by Chomsky (1957) and the cognitive structural revolution led by Piaget, classical S-R learning was the predominant model for explaining changes in human functioning. With the exception of Tolman (1932), whose influence did not extend widely beyond his lifetime, mechanisms for mental processes were generally sidestepped or translated into descriptions of relations between the external environment and behaviors of the organism, which were typically framed as responses to environmental contingencies. While problems of memory, thought, and reasoning, planning and anticipation, and the organization of functioning were dealt with, they were difficult to explain in behavioral terms. As a result, m st research on learning assumed a molecular focus that only occasionally came to grips with problems of the acquisition of knowledge or of complex systems like language (e.g., Skinner, 1975; Staats and Staats, 1968).

The structuralism of Chomskyian linguistics and Piagetian cognitive theory made radical breaks with constraints of a behaviorist framework, departures that permitted the most complex and intricate systems of concepts to be considered and conceptualized in terms of mental structures and interaction. But they did so at some cost, the cost of precision in explaining mechanisms for change. Piaget offered concepts of a mental structural equilibrium adaptively modified by interacting process of accommodation to novel material through assimilation to already acquired structures. But questions of how, when, in what proportion, and at what rate change comes about with different concepts are only vaguely defined by his equilibration theory (Sullivan, 1967). Piagetian theory is far more powerful at characterizing the nature of cognitive structures and how they evolve in general terms than in specifying change (learning) mechanisms for acquiring specific concepts under specific conditions. Chomsky (1965), on the other hand, proposed that the intricacy of the rule structure for a system like language was so complex that for an infant to master such a system so rapidly and early in development, the process must be essentially biologically regulated. There must be some species specific, genetically programmed blueprint (LAD) that enables the infant to assimilate the rules of such an abstract system from the intricate examples of adult speech in everyday life.

Short-Term Cognitive Rule Learning

There seems to be an emerging convergence of behavioral learning theory and mentally regulated, structural theory, taking the best of both worlds, combining the objectivity and precision of one with the richness and complexity of the other (e.g., Case, 1978; Gagne, 1968; Klausmeier, Ghatala, and Frayer, 1974; Levin and Allen, 1976; Kuhn, 1978; Mahoney, 1977; Pascual-Leone and Smith, 1969). Fowler's version of this developing synthesis defines change as a behaviorally anchored process of problem solving and learning (Fowler, 1971a, 1972b, 1976, 1977). Mental systems are organized, internally regulated and constantly evolving through continuing transactions with the environment. In any particular transaction or short term series of transactions, the process is one of selectively perceiving and manipulatively interacting with the environment on the basis of concepts and defining rules about the ongoing situation. The process is an active one of hypothesis testing to solve problems, formulating, trying out and reformulating schemes, or plans as Miller, Gallanter and Pribram (1960) term them, which are conceptual pictures of the means and ends of tasks, themselves variously embedded in long-range goals for coping and accomplishment of socially defined roles and purposes.

Human activity always involves arranging and rearranging means and ends for solving problems, in which both learning and cognitive regulation are always integral to some degree, the intensity depending on the novelty of the situation and task. At one extreme, initial exposure to a highly novel symbol system (e.g., a foreign language), a strange environment or a task demanding that familiar elements be arranged in a novel combination, maximize both the amount of learning and the acuteness of cognitive regulation required to make progress in solving the problem, whether learning the language, coping in the strange situation or figuring out how to rearrange familiar elements in novel combinations. As the problem is solved, that is, as the entire task is mastered, both learning and mental regulation diminish in importance, retreating to the periphery of consciousness; performances in well-mastered tasks then gradually become ritualized routines— fluency in language, social rituals in familiar situations and ritualized accomplishment of familiar tasks. Behavior becomes relatively automatic, resting on habit or dynamic stereotypes. Learning and mental governance are regulated to peripheral monitoring processes in reserve for the moment until snags or novel elements or arrangements recall into play concept learning and plan reformulation. These processes have been discussed with respect to motor learning in detail by Fowler (1976), Fowler and Leithwood (1971), and Bruner and Anglin (1973).

But what is the nature of concept learning when it occurs? Its essence is found, not in the physical behavior of organisms, the motor responses of classical learning theory, but in the mental structuring and restructuring of rules about concepts that form the basic fabric of problem solving. Physical activity often contributes to trying out hypotheses in a concrete, sensory motor code, and is essential to performing tasks, but is not always essential to either solving problems or learning (Lenneberg, 1962). Both can and often do occur by mental manipulation alone through the medium of representational codes of language and imagery whose schemes can then be implemented in action.

These mental manipulations may be defined as processes of analyzing problem components, that is, isolating task elements and identifying features of concepts, on the one hand, and synthesizing them into task structures and meaningful conceptual organizations, on the other. The process involves more than identifying and interrelating concrete elements of a task or percept: the process always implicates general rules about concepts. That is, elements and features are abstracted (isolated and interrelated) as general rules about types of tasks and phenomena, which enables the learner to approach similar tasks and phenomena with similar skill. The degree of skill is of course dependent on the broadness of experience and cognitive flexibility with which the rules were first grasped and the degree of similarity of the new task or phenomena.

Although ritualized activities call for little conscious or intense mental manipulation of rules, compared to the acute cognitive manipulations required in problems with novel material, few activities are completely ritualized, and all activity moves forward through analyzing and synthesizing rules about concepts of phenomena, consciously or automatically. To the degree that novelty is involved, whether of novel rules or of novel combinations, both learning and problem solving seem to be implicated. Learning merely stresses the novelty, problem solving the combinations. But in any case, mental processes are rooted in conceptual activities, however automatic familiar performances may become: perceptual features are abstracted and interrelated in tasks according to rules. Rules are the operational aspects of concepts that identify critical features, functions and relations. Single concepts such as chair or adjective, each are identifiable and utilizable according to their particular defining and operating rules. Single concepts in turn typically form part of complex conceptual networks and hierarchical systems in which defining and operating rules are extensively interrelated in vast intricacy. In sum, mental activity consists of cognitively analyzing, interrelating and using various concept systems according to the rules that define their structure and use.

The mental processes of problem solving and learning seem to engage at least three basic forms of concepts and operating rules, which are discussed at length elsewhere (Fowler, 1971a, 1972b, 1977). There is, first, knowledge, or the concepts we develop about the world, both real and imaginary. This is the substantive basis for coping and problem solving in environmental activity. There is, second, the codes we employ to represent concepts and rules of any kind, language, imagery, math, music, and, at the most concrete level, the sensorimotor action codes, or Piaget's schemas which dominate life in infancy but are always the basic code into which we must ultimately translate all mental manipulation and perform tasks. Finally there are the operating concepts of problem solving and learning themselves, the cognitive style concepts or strategies, in particular those of analysis and synthesis, which take on specialized forms according to the nature of the knowledge concepts and codes in a task. All three categories of concepts are needed in some form in every act of learning and problem-solving concepts of what we are working with, concepts for shorthand representation (codes) and concept strategies for operating on the various concepts in tasks.

Developmental Learning Mechanisms

The perspectives for learning and problem solving over time, developmental learning, are seen in the gradual evolution from active cognitive analysis and synthesis of novel material over a series of steps until mastery is attained and tasks become relatively automatic and ritualized. Sequencing may facilitate developmental learning wherever complex systems like language are involved, and quite possibly advance learning with any body of concepts that is novel for the organism, as object permanence is to the neonate. Even where learning takes place through the folk model, and the child must make its own inferences without the aid of well sequenced intervention strategies, the developmental learning process seems to progress through a series of stages or steps that may be conceptualized as follows. The process begins with exploration, centering on probing, identifying significant features of task concepts (analyzing), and formulating crude rules for how they are related (synthesizing). In the case of language learning, the infant (or even the adult in the case of a second language), focuses on phonemes, learning to discriminate the sound cues that distinguish one from another and interrelate them in terms of contrasting labial, voice, and other dimensions (Jacobson and Halle, 1956; McNeill, 1970). Concurrently, the infant may begin to perceive whole words or sentences as meaningless, global units in which aspects of sound cues are differentiated and compared.

There are probably no sharp stage demarcations, rather a series of steps that overlap in various ways. Thus, soon the process of differentiating and interrelating phonemes in consonant-vowel, and slightly later, vowel-consonant combinations in pairs becomes evident. Then syllable strings appear, first repetitions of identical pairs, then gradually varied pairs until the infant sorts out and constructs whole strings that are interrelated by intonation and stress, resembling real speech, but without meaning. At some early point in this analytic-synthetic process with sound patterns, word structures and meaning begin to be differentiated, organized, and soon related to referents, which become gradually more generalized, according to experience, on the basis of both feature and function similarities (Smith, 1978). Very early in the process differentiation and interrelating of words and meaning according to syntax begins. The general process is thus one of gradually differentiating out key elements and interrelating them into patterns according to the rules of language (or whatever other concept system is engaged). Thus, at the phonological level, the child is sorting out phonemes according to rules about position (e.g., frontal-back consonants) and tongue manipulation (e.g., dental-palatal), and openness of aperture (e.g., broad versus narrow vowels) and interrelating them in words according to such rules as order and blending. Word selection and, later, use in syntax are similarly acquired through these analytic-synthesizing processes of various rule relations.

The process of developmental learning may be conceptualized in two forms. On the one hand, we see these evident cognitive apprehensions of rules, in which newly acquired rules open doors to transforming our modes of processing language and meaning. For example, discovery of the rule that a particular pattern of sounds can represent some type of object (a referent), is a cognitive transformation that launches mental activity into a fundamentally different and more abstract code than sensorimotor schemas. Later, discovery of the rule that words can be strung into combinations, phrase, and sentence strings, provides a shift in kind in the new leverage it provides for representing and manipulating complex meaning.

But, on the other hand, we see progress in learning of a more pedestrian kind, the sort of incremental acquisition of new exemplars through applying the newly acquired rule. This process seems to resemble the traditional cumulative learning curve of classical learning studies, in which new units of the same kind are piled up in an accelerating process. Norm gathering in the language studies of the 1930s and 1940s was centered in such processes, in vocabulary acquisition particularly (McCarthy, 1954).

The two processes work interactively and alternately in intimate association. Key elements are isolated and interrelated in patterns according to rules (e.g., phonemic contrasts, morphophonological patterns, meaning, phrase combination, and syntactical differentiation, etc.). As each novel rule is grasped, usually first in crude form, a cognitive transformation occurs that allows rehearsal of first exemplars and extension of the rules to other exemplars, at first slowly, gradually accelerating, to become incremental, cumulative unit learning, until use of the rule(s) involved becomes automatized and ritualized ready for application to everyday problem solving and coping in related tasks.

The process is essentially the same in all concept learning. The child learns the rules defining the features and relations for each concept and interrelations among concepts as a series of transformations. Each set of basic rules is followed by rehearsal and accelerating acquisition of exemplars. The child learns first, for example, rules about needles and evergreen for conifers versus leaves and seasonal shedding for other trees; then, the basic rules defining the respective types lead to becoming familiar with many exemplars of each type. The soundness of grasping basic rules for a concept and system of concepts, as well as the number and variety of exemplars acquired is of course dependent on the depth and scope of exposure, again pointing up the value of systematic intervention.

Ecological Context

It has been said with respect to the general framework that the approach is adaptive and clinical. The strategy is thus ecological in that stimulation by caregivers is embedded in interpersonal relations and interactive with the ongoing attentional processes of the child. But it also means that, wherever feasible, the child is stimulated in a variety of natural settings and activities. Day care and schools are by their nature constructed environments specifically designed for the care and education of children, but most contemporary programs for young children attempt to simulate the flow and activities of cultural-familial patterns in the home, including at times cross-age, family type grouping (Fein and Clarke-Stewart, 1973; Fowler, 1980). In any case, the basic routines of care in eating, dressing, diapering, and similar activities are rooted in the social life of child care in every context.

Language stimulation is especially well suited to permeating the variety of activities in daily life, in both the home and in day care. Language is an extremely flexible tool that comes with the human voice to represent an endless variety of concepts and activities in any context. For this reason, parents have been able to regularly employ language interaction with their infants in a full half dozen different activities: in the basic care routines; in social play of peek-a-boo and finger play; in object play with a variety of miniature replicas on the floor or at a table, particularly feeding tables; in looking at pictures, starting with displays of isolated common objects against a plain background, comparing pictures with similar objects; and finally in general "labeling tours" around the house or on trips outside, to extend the child's language and concept world. As might be expected, parents typically employ language most regularly in the routines of care, followed at some distance by social play, but there are wide individual differences (Fowler and Swenson, 1979). Chinese speaking families, however, tended to use language more in object play and excursions (Lee, 1978).

Many other forms of concept learning fit with equal ease into many daily activities of young children, because exemplars of the concepts they need to learn, such as object characteristics and functions, number, size, length, color, and so on, generally abound in these contexts. And because many of these activities repeat themselves as routines with similar materials and actions a number of times each day, they are ideal for furnishing sufficient repetition and reinforcement to ensure mastery. Both at home and in day care, then, parents and teachers are tutored in methods of engaging children in stimulation in these many care contexts, using the stuff of the activities themselves as the basis for stimulation.

In day care, it has been found convenient to organize concept learning in terms of theme programs, in which a particular set of concepts, such as of shape or transportation, are stressed in several daily activities for a period of 1 or 2 weeks or more. To the extent possible, when research programs have been focused on the institutional experience, such as day care or nursery school, parents have been involved through home guidance to follow similar stimulation activity at home. Paralleling and sometimes separate from the informal introduction of stimulation in natural contexts are special tutoring sessions set up as sequential learning projects with individual children or small groups. In this way, number learning or early reading, for example, are pursued in depth over a period of months, continuing over a second year where program continuity is possible. Organizing learning in special settings and activities provides an additional and often more precise basis for regulating and monitoring the pace and sequence of learning in complex concept learning projects.

Interaction Framework

The interaction framework is both cognitive and affective in form. The attention and motivation of children for learning are engaged through interactive play and active participation. Exemplars of concepts, such as materials varying in length in a project on length concepts or various objects to label in language learning, are presented with a cluster of interesting toys to engage the child in manipulative and sociodramatic play. Exemplars are manipulated and labeled in dramatic or problem solving play by the caregiver at points and in ways to attract the child's attention, or during pauses in her or his play; alternately, and equally as often, the caregiver labels and indicates a relevant exemplar in the course of the child's manipulations in play. In naturally occurring routines and social activities, caregiver—and as the child acquires self care skill, the child's—manipulations are generally those built into the task itself, although various program relevant objects may be introduced from time to time as well. Timing action with the child's attention and the event is important, to facilitate analytic focus and cognitive synthesis of label and referent (whether object, attribute, action or relationship), and of critical aspects and relations among exemplars. A continuing context of play is usually selected as the developmentally appropriate mode young children naturally employ to experiment with the concept world.

At the same time, warmth, flexibility, and adaptation to the children's preferences and styles are encouraged. Social reinforcement is integral to the interactive style, expressed through the caregiver's personalized mode of interrelating and her or his enthusiasm for the task and the child's efforts and progress. More weight is placed on processes than on accomplishment because the latter is generally found to follow when interest in processes is maintained. Where confusion occurs or persists, repeated demonstrations in varied contexts and with different, perhaps simpler exemplars, is ordinarily the remedy, not verbal correction.

Adapting to cultural-familial styles fosters family involvement and helps to preserve the integrity of family and culture. In a group of functionally illiterate, Italian-speaking families, for example, the participation of the extended family of grandmother and older cousins and teenage aunts and uncles was welcomed. In one case, a particularly interested 10-year-old became a mainstay of an infant's language activity. Toy kits and circulating toy and book libraries are invaluable for uneducated and poor families, for reasons of economics, time constraints on working mothers—particularly single parents, and difficulty in preparing and using suitable stimulus materials that educated families will often prepare on their own. In this way, language kits, for example, will be sure to include two or three exemplars of every object to facilitate concept extension over rote labeling.

SELECTED FINDINGS ON INTERVENTION IN INFANCY

The series of studies on which a major body of preliminary findings are presented consists of a set of four pilot studies (Fowler and Swenson, 1979) and three doctoral dissertations (Ogston, in preparation; Roberts, in preparation; Swenson, in preparation) still in progress. Stimulation in all studies has been mediated through guiding parents in weekly to biweekly home visits on methods of language and/or other forms of cognitive developmental stimulation, individually and sometimes in small groups. Findings for all studies are restricted to developmental change patterns in mental test scores on the Griffiths Mental Scales. They provide the basic source of standardized developmental data for all studies and the only results for which data for all studies is presently available. (Limited Binet and WPSSI test data are presented for the pilot studies.)

Subjects

Infants in the pilot studies were all first born (except two Chinese infants) to optimize intervention control and parental motivation. Families ranged from unskilled working class to upper middle class professional, and elementary school through graduate school in parental education. Study I ($N = 3$) and Study IV ($N = 4$) families were all English speaking, Study II families were Italian speaking ($N = 4$) and Study III ($N = 4$) families were Chinese speaking.

Infants in both the Ogston and Swenson studies were all first-born, from English speaking middle class families with at least high school .educated parents and non-Jewish ethnicity—because of the high verbal stimulation characteristic in Jewish culture (Fowler, 1971b). Infants in the Roberts study were of mixed birth order, second generation, Afro-West Indian families with no more than tenth grade parental education. Families in all studies resided in urban or suburban metropolitan environments. All infants were randomly assigned to experimental and control groups in the three dissertation studies and all groups were balanced for sex. There were no pre-posttest controls in the pilot studies.

Intervention Program

Pilot Studies Referentially oriented language stimulation, designed by the author (as described above), embedding focus on language in cognitive activity. Approximate program period: ages 5 to 12 months ($N = 15$). Written guides and kits, provided according to parental education level, along with demonstrations, clinically oriented guidance and verbal instruction. Home visits: weekly to biweekly visits by principal investigator or students. Parent guidance, infant stimulation, and assessment was conducted in the familial language (English, Italian or Chinese), using paraprofessionals or student interpreters as needed.

Ogston Study Group 1 ($N = 6$): Referentially oriented language stimulation as in pilot studies. Program period: ages 3 to 15 months. Home visits: weekly for 2 months, then biweekly to age 15 months plus periodic (every 6 weeks) small group sessions. (The three months language stimulation and control groups for the Ogston and Swenson studies are later to be pooled to increase sample sizes.)

Group 2 ($N = 12$): Gross motor stimulation, following the Levy (1973) infant exercise program. Same age period and pattern of home visiting.

Group 3 ($N = 6$): Controls—culturally normative home rearing; occasional telephone contact to maintain rapport.

Swenson Study   Group 1 (N = 6): Referentially oriented language stimulation, as in pilot studies and Ogston study. Program period: 3 to 17 months. Home visits: weekly for 3 to 4 months, followed by biweekly from age 8 to 17 months.

Group 2 (N = 6): Same program. Program period: 8 to 17 months. Home visits: weekly for 3 to 4 months and biweekly to 17 months. Thus, experimental groups are comparable over 9 months of stimulation.

Group 3 (N = 6): Controls—culturally normative home rearing.

Roberts Study   Group 1 (N = 20): Cognitive stimulation, embracing the same referentially oriented language program, combined with a multiple concept and sensorimotor stimulation program developed by the author (Fowler, 1980). Program period: Divided into two subgroups in which weekly stimulation extended from 3 to 15 months and 15 to 27 months, respectively.

Group 2 (N = 20): Church-based day care center with no special program. Subgroups matched in age with Group 1.

Group 3 (N = 20): Controls—culturally normative home rearing. Subgroups matched in age with Group 1.

Results

Pilot Studies   The pattern of mean pre- posttest and follow-up scores on the Griffiths Scales, along with WPSSI and Binet mean scores at ages 4 and 5, for all children on whom data is available is displayed in Figure 1. It is evident that, although the children show a general rise of around 15 quotient points on most Griffiths scales during the program, very large mean gains (38.1 points) occurred on the hearing and speech (language) scale, compared to all other scales. Over the successive follow-up testings, mean scores tended to rise a few points or level off on nearly all scales, but again mean scores rose 30 to 40 points on the language scale, after a steady period between 12 and 18 months. The only other scale to match the pattern of the language scale was the practical reasoning scale, a math concept scale measuring counting and measurement. Mean scores on the GQ, however, and the performance scale exceeded 140 quotient points (143.3 and 146, respectively) by age 4 for the reduced sample (Study I, N = 3).

While the mean WPSSI verbal and total IQs registered at lower levels (131.7 and 127, respectively), the mean similarities and arithmetic scores, and the mean Binet at age 5 all reached 140 or more (139.7, 147.3, and 141, respectively).

Ogston Study   The comparison of the two differently stimulated language and exercise groups of infants shown in Figure 2 indicates a somewhat different pattern. Mean scores during the 1 year treatment

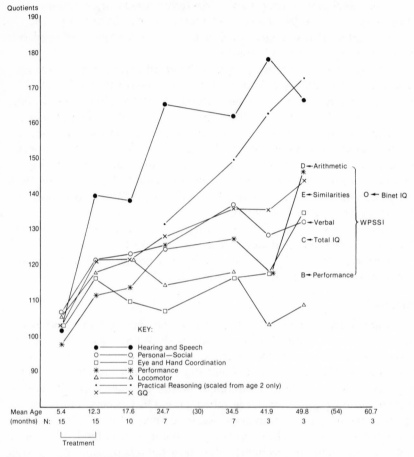

Figure 1. Mean Griffiths Mental Scale scores at pre- and posttests and successive follow-up tests to age 5; mean WPSSI scores at age 4; and mean Binet score at age 5. Pilot studies; cumulative Ns.

period rose enormously for the exercise group on the locomotor scale (39.5 points) compared to mean gains of either the language or the control group, though the latter did gain as much as 19.2 mean points. On the other hand, both the language- and exercise-stimulated groups rose markedly on the language scale (17.8 and 14.9 mean points, respectively), and the controls rose only 6.1 mean points. Both the language- and exercise-stimulated groups also gained substantially on the performance scale (19.7 to 22.9 mean points), compared to a slight mean decline for the controls (5.8 points). Mean changes on the remaining two scales for all groups were small.

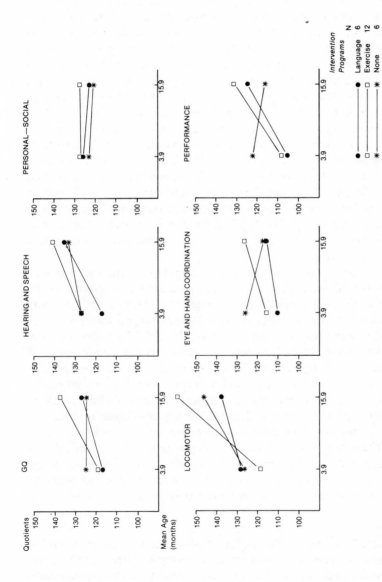

Figure 2. Griffiths Mental Development Scales: Mean pre- and posttest scores for language, exercise, and control groups (Ogston study).

Swenson Study   The incomplete data plotted in Figure 3 for the two language stimulation groups starting at different ages reveals parallel, very large mean overall gains on the hearing and speech scales, parallel substantial mean overall gains on the performance scale, and slight mean rises or fluctuating patterns otherwise. There was, however, also a short initial mean rise of the 3 to 17 months group on the eye and hand coordination scale for the earlier starting group, which was more or less maintained thereafter. It will be noted that the two language stimulation groups made their largest mean language gains over the initial, respective 3 to 8 months and 8 to 13 months language program period (19.7 and 26.9 points, respectively).

The home-reared controls maintained a stable level or rose only slightly overall, except for a substantial mean inital rise of 26.2 quotient points on the hearing and speech scale which, although maintained thereafter, was substantially exceeded by subsequent rises of the two language stimulated groups. The final levels left the 3 to 17 months group separated from the controls by the approximately 20 point mean difference at 16.8 months as they had been at 3.1 months, but the 8 to 17 months group was 20 mean points higher compared to the original spread of about 10 points.

Roberts Study   In this study, both cognitively stimulated groups made substantial mean gains on all scales except the locomotor scale, on which both groups made little change, the older group averaging (GQ) 16 points to the younger group's 10. The largest mean gains for both groups were on the language scale (14 and 18 points), eye and hand coordination (15 and 37 points), and the performance scale (18 points each). Both home reared control groups and the younger day care group, in contrast, made small to large mean declines on nearly all scales, while the older day care group declined slightly on three scales, but rose substantially (from relatively low positions) on two scales (eye and hand coordination, 14 points and personal-social, 12 points). There was also a trend for mean experimental practical reasoning scale (i.e., math) scores to be slightly elevated at posttesting, but these are not recorded because many children were too young to calculate a basal age on the scale (starts only at age 2).

Discussion

The collected findings in this series of investigations on intervention during infancy seem to demonstrate consistently large cognitive developmental effects associated with the strategy of early stimulation employed. Mean language gains during intervention in the four studies, in all of which referentially oriented language stimulation was employed, ranged from a minimum of 16 mean points (Roberts combined

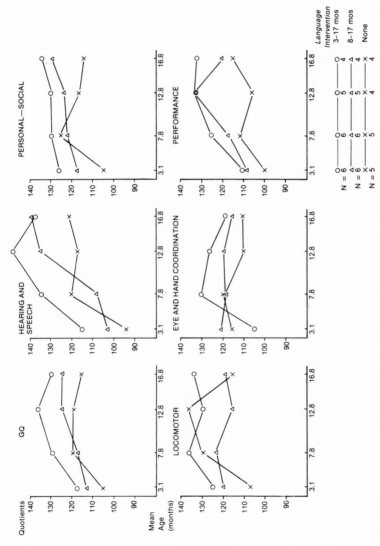

Figure 3. Mean Griffiths Mental Scale scores over four testings for groups varying in age of intervention (3 to 17 months; 8 to 17 months; and control) (Swenson study—Incomplete data).

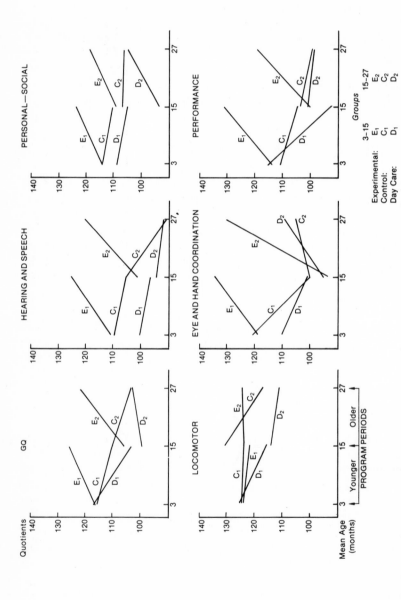

Figure 4.   Mean Griffiths pre- and posttest Mental Scale scores for younger and older experimental, home control and day comparison groups. (Posttest attrition: 2 younger and 1 older control child; 1 each of day care children.) (Roberts study).

groups) through 23 points (Swenson combined groups) to a mean of 40 points in the pilot studies. What is particularly noteworthy is that to date all except 7 of 52 infants (87 percent) exposed to early language stimulation gained at least 6 quotient points on the language scale. Thirty-nine infants (75 percent) gained at least 12 points, 27 (53 percent) gained at least 20, 21 (40 percent) gained at least 30, and 14 (21 percent) gained at least 40 points.

Similar patterns are apparent in the gross motor or exercise stimulation program (Ogston study), which as discussed elsewhere (Fowler, 1976; Fowler and Leithwood, 1971) involves cognitive analytic and synthetic processes of a special form. Among the 12 infants in the gross motor program, every child gained at least 8 points and 10 of the 12 gained 24 to 77 points.

Neither timing (starting age) nor program duration seem to be highly significant factors in affecting language outcomes because both show inconsistent effects. Thus, in the Swenson study, mean gain scores generally favored later (8 months) over earlier (3 months) starting, measured either over the initial 5 months intervention period (26.9 versus 19.7 language quotient points) or over the total period[2] (30.7 versus 23.4 points), despite the slightly longer period of stimulation for the earlier starting group. Earlier starting infants (3 to 15 months) similarly gained less than later starting infants (15 to 27 months) in the Roberts study (14.2 to 18.2 points). In both cases, program duration was fairly constant. On the other hand, early starting infants in the pilot studies ($\bar{x}$ = 5.4 months) gained 40 mean points, more than any group in any of the other studies, the closest being the 8 months starting group in the Swenson study (which gained 30.7 mean points). The language program extended no more than a mean of 7 months in the pilot studies, moreover, less than the 9 to 12 months programs in the other studies.

With respect to the duration of intervention, infants in the pilot studies gained a mean of 40 points (similar for the lower educational background infant subsample) compared to 16 points for the combined lower education background groups in the Roberts study, although intervention lasted 7 months in the former as against 12 months in the latter. Mean language gains were also larger in the Swenson study (23.3 points for the combined groups) than in the Ogston study (17.8 points), despite similar intervention periods. Both gains were closer to the 16

---

[2] N reduced for later periods—see Figure 3. It is true that measured in terms of equivalent periods (3 to 13 versus 8 to 17 months), the earlier starting group rose by 34 points; but this is only slightly more than the later starting group. The 13 to 17 months decline of the earlier group, despite continued stimulation, may in part be the result of the large influence individual problems exercise in small samples.

point Roberts study gain than to the 40 point gain in the pilot studies, despite the shorter 7 months intervention in the latter studies. It would seem that starting intervention any time during the first year or so may be equally effective, depending more perhaps on the quality of intervention. Duration of intervention is apparently similarly variably effective, depending again more on the quality of parent guidance. Assuming some minimum period of a few months and adequate guidance, parents may then be able to effectively maintain the strategy indefinitely. We do have evidence that minimum levels were not as well established and thus gains maintained in some lower education families in the pilot studies. Follow-up measures in the other studies should add to our information on these points.

Both cognitive differentiation and generality or generalization can be found in the collected studies. In all groups when language stimulation was the focus alone, except for its referential cognitive basis (Nelson, 1973), mean language gains substantially exceeded mean gains on competencies measured by most other scales. The noteworthy exceptions were in math (practical reasoning) and nonverbal problem solving (performance) where mean gains and final levels tended to match or approach gains and levels in the language scales in the three studies concerned (pilot, Ogston and Swenson studies). The startling virtually parallel high mean levels attained in math skills in two studies (pilot and Roberts studies) points to a similar abstract symbol basis for language and math. In pilot studies (c.f. Fowler and Swenson, 1979) there was also some spontaneous parent stimulation in math concepts, presumably reinforcing the generalization from language to math. On the other hand, Griffiths considers problem solving the most "concept oriented" of the motor scales, suggesting a greater symbolic involvement, which was reflected in some generalization in these studies, but—it should be noted—not as consistently, apparently, as to math. The high mean score follow-up levels language and arithmetic on the WPSSI verbal measures at age 4 and on the Binet at age 5, although limited to the extremely small Study I pilot sample ($N = 3$), further supports the pattern. Generalization from language stimulation seems to be stronger to highly verbal and abstract symbolic material (Griffiths math, WPSSI arithmetic and similarities scales, and Binet) than to spatial (Griffiths and WPSSI performance) or social (Griffiths personal-social) material.

The reasons for the high mean language gains of the exercise group in the Ogston study are interpreted by Ogston (personal communication) as a result of the almost inevitable intensive use of language in working with infants in baby exercises. Actually, the mean language gain of the exercise group is inflated by the gain of a single infant (83 points). The mean gain without her score is 10.1 points, and 5 of the 12 infants (42 percent) gained fewer than 5 points or declined, suggesting greater irregularity in language outcomes than the systematic program tended to produce.

Completing the picture are the consistently large mean gains on all Griffiths scales except the locomotor scale in the Roberts experimental group, which was exposed to a broadly based program of cognitive stimulation. But it is worth stressing that gains were outstanding in the language, math (i.e., final level) and both fine sensorimotor scales (eye-hand and performance); Roberts stressed language and sensorimotor problem solving above all. The Griffiths scales cannot of course be considered logically well selected and sequenced measures of cognitive differentiation and development, however reliable and well scaled mathematically according to traditional empirical test criteria, but results do seem to demonstrate certain patterns of differentiation and similarity that follow stimulation strategies.

The effect of parent education and social class, which are effectively very similar, and ethnicity or race seem to have been relatively consistent. In the pilot studies infants of lower education parents made large gains paralleling those of infants of higher education parents, through remaining at slightly lower language levels throughout (Fowler and Swenson, 1979). These findings are confounded with communication and test standardization problems for the Italian and Chinese speaking subgroups, however. In the Roberts study, moreover, the 20 infants of West Indian, black immigrants with no more than tenth grade education, made language, fine motor, and performance (and probably math) gains approaching the language and performance gains attained by the language stimulated groups from higher education families in the Ogston and Swenson studies, although remaining at lower levels, as did the lower education background infants in the pilot studies. The gains of both experimental groups in the Roberts study are relatively under-estimated, moreover, because of the consistent mean declines in both control groups and to some extent in the day care groups. Mean posttest score differences between experimental and control groups amounted to from about 15 to 35 points on all scales except the locomotor scale, despite differences of around 5 points or less at pretesting, making gains quite parallel across educational levels. It would thus seem that these language focused early intervention programs produced comparable mean score gains in infants from different educational background groups. Programs seemed to vary slightly in effectiveness as well as in areas effectively stimulated, but more as a function of specific program factors than as a result of factors of social class, ethnic, race or educational level.

The findings of the Roberts study hold important social and educational implications for the socialization of lower education black children. Not only were these infants stimulated to reach well above average levels ($\geq$120) in language and other cognitive skills, but did so in comparison with declining score trends by randomly selected controls. The high gains of the Italian infants from even lower educational backgrounds, although without control comparisons, hold similar implications. The consistency of the positive outcomes in different language communities (Italian and Chinese) have important implications for the preservation of linguistic and cultural diversity, as well as for bilingual education later in development.

All investigators have noted that infants generally continue to gain in language following termination of intervention, although not always immediately. In the only follow-up assessment available to date for the three student dissertations, Ogston reports (personal communication) all three groups (language, gross motor, and controls) reaching the 150 point level on the language scale (149, 153, and 155 points, respectively). The mean 22 point gain of the controls is probably related to her providing detailed information on stimulation strategies at post-testing (15 months), underscoring the flexibility of starting age as a factor. All three students report impressions of later flowering of language expression and richness in various infants. That these may not be merely selectively biased results is suggested by the dramatically high follow-up language gains—evident in *all* of the 7 Ss—appearing at the 24 and 36 months testing in the pilot studies. The continuing high language test scores on the Study I children at ages 4 and 5 is further supportive of this trend. The generally expanding or at least high maintenance trend seems to be a consequence either of parent maintenance of special stimulation or of the children's own self-generated stimulation produced by their early established cognitive learning system, or more possibly a combination of the two. The critical role that language may play in the early establishment of such systems deserves special consideration, given the special weight placed on language stimulation in these studies and the tendency for transfer to other highly symbolic material (especially math).

Given the preliminary data available, there is no place to discuss further such matters as relations between program and developmental sequences among language dimensions or shifts in the form of learning from incremental to cognitive rule transformations. How early, how intense, and how long the stimulation; what variations in form; what follow-through maintenance is necessary; and how much differentiation and generalization may occur from what combinations of cognitive experience all need additional investigation.

What is so dramatically and consistently evident from these data is the general effectiveness of planned infant intervention in several domains with respect to two major outcomes. With due regard to the lack of statistical treatment at this time and the need for follow-up and further study with larger samples by other investigators, in comparison with either baseline test norms or randomly selected controls, reared at home or in day care according to various folk models, planned early stimulation can apparently both substantially accelerate development and greatly elevate mastery levels.

What is also striking is the way in which the systematic, intensified stimulation seems to telescope periods normally required to attain successive benchmarks of development, and at an apparently accelerating rate. Thus, in the pilot studies (Fowler and Swenson, 1979), first words were typically comprehended at 5 to 7 months, first word utterances (4–5) appeared at 8 to 12 months, and first two-word strings appeared at 12 to 14 months, compared to minimum test norms of 8, 14, and 20 months, each successive index increasingly in advance of the preceding one (by at least 1, 2 and 6 months, respectively). Within each type of new dimension, moreover, the time required for learning to move from the cognitive transformational stage to the incremental stage of learning was also markedly accelerated over norms. Thus pilot study infants moved from 2 or 3 new utterances to around 10 words, characteristically, in around 2 months, compared to 8 months for Griffith's test norms, and from two-word phrase constructions to five-word sentence constructions in 7 months, compared with 12 months for Griffith's test norms. If sustained in further investigations, these findings may have many implications for the intellectual development and early education of many socioeconomic and cultural groups, suggesting that their linguistic and other cognitive and skill potentials may often be seriously underdeveloped. Additional findings from combinations of daily monitoring and periodically taped language samples, various measures of language differentiation and complexity earlier reported for the pilot studies (Fowler and Swenson, 1979) and to be reported for the three dissertations seem to support these conclusions.

REFERENCES

Bayley, N. 1969. Bayley Scales of Infant Development (with Infant Behavior Record). The Psychological Corporation, New York.
Bloom, L. 1975. Language development. In F. D. Horowitz (ed.), Review of Child Development Research, Vol. 4. University of Chicago Press, Chicago.
Bronfenbrenner, U. 1975. Is early intervention effective? In B. Z. Friedlander, G. H. Sterrit, and G. E. Kirk (eds.), Exceptional Infant, Vol. 3. Assessment and Intervention. Brunner/Mazel, New York.

Brown, B. (ed.). 1978. Found: Long-term gains from early intervention. AAAS Selected Symposium, No. 8. Westview. Boulder, Colo.

Brown, R. 1973. A First Language. Harvard University Press, Cambridge.

Bruner, J. S., and Anglin, J. M. (ed.). 1973. Beyond the Information Given: Studies in the Psychology of Knowing. W. W. Norton & Co., New York.

Case, R. 1978. Intellectual development from birth to adolescence: A new-Piagetian interpretation. In R. Siegler (ed.), Children's Thinking: What Develops? Lawrence Erlbaum Associates, Hillsdale, NJ.

Chall, J. 1967. Learning to Read: The Great Debate. McGraw-Hill, New York.

Chomsky, N. 1957. Syntactic Structures. Mouton, The Hague.

Chomsky, N. 1965. Aspects of the Theory of Syntax. MIT Press, Cambridge Mass.

Fein, G. G., and Clarke-Stewart, A. 1973. Day Care in Context. John Wiley & Sons, New York.

Fowler, W. 1962. Teaching a two-year-old to read: An experiment in early childhood learning. Genetic Psychology Monographs, 66:181–283.

Fowler, W. 1965a. A study of process and method in three-year-old twins and triplets learning to read. Genetic Psychology Monographs, 72:3–89.

Fowler, W. 1965b. Concept learning in early childhood. Young Children, 21:81–91.

Fowler, W. 1969. The effect of early stimulation: The problem of focus in developmental stimulation. Merrill-Palmer Quarterly, 15:157–170.

Fowler, W. 1970. The patterning of developmental learning processes in the nursery school. In A. Biemiller (ed.), Problems in the Teaching of Young Children. Monograph Series No. 9. Ontario Institute for Studies in Education, Toronto.

Fowler, W. 1971a. A developmental learning strategy for early reading in a laboratory nursery school. Interchange, 2:106–125.

Fowler, W. 1971b. Cognitive baselines in early childhood: Developmental learning and differentiation of competence rule systems. In J. Hellmuth (ed.), Cognitive Studies, Vol. 2, Deficits in Cognition. Brunner/Mazel, New York.

Fowler, W. 1972a. A developmental learning approach to infant care in a group setting. Merrill-Palmer Quarterly, 18:145–175.

Fowler, W. 1972b. The development of competence and deficit and some Canadian perspectives. In T. J. Ryan (ed.), Poverty and the Child. McGraw-Hill Ryerson, Toronto.

Fowler, W. 1974. Language: Developmental stimulation program. Ontario Institute for Studies in Education. Unpublished manuscript. Toronto.

Fowler, W. 1975. Caregiver-Infant Language Interaction Scales. Ontario Institute for Studies in Education. Unpublished. Toronto.

Fowler, W. 1976. The role of cognitive learning in motor development. In Final Report of the State of the Art Research Review and Conference on the Psychomotor Development in Preschool Handicapped Children for the Bureau of Education for the Handicapped, Office of Education, Department of Health, Education and Welfare, Contract N. 300-75-0225. Milwaukee, Wisconsin: Vasquez Associates.

Fowler, W. 1977. Sequence and styles in cognitive development. In F. Weizmann and C. Uzgiris (eds.), The Structuring of Experience. Plenum Publishing Corp., New York.

Fowler, W. 1978. Day care and its effects on early development: A study of group and home care in multi-ethnic working class, families. Ontario Institute for Studies in Education, Toronto.

Fowler, W. 1980. Infant and child care: An approach to education in group settings (Vol. 1). Curriculum and Assessment Guides (Vol. 2). Allyn & Bacon, Boston.

Fowler, W., and Fowler, J. 1978. Competence development in a tribal society. Ontario Institute for Studies in Education. Unpublished Manuscript. Toronto.

Fowler, W., and Keithwood, L. 1971. Cognition and movement: theoretical, pedagogical and measurement considerations. Perceptual and Motor Skills, 32:523–532.

Fowler, W., and Swenson, A. 1979. The influence of early language stimulation on development: four studies. Genetic Psychology Monographs, 100:73–109.

Gagne, R. M. 1968. Contributions of learning to human development. Psychol. Rev. 75:177–191.

Glick, J. 1968. Some problems in the evaluation of preschool intervention programs. In R. Hess and R. Bear (eds.), Early Education: Current Theory, Research, and Action. Aldine Publishing Company, Chicago.

Griffiths, R. 1954. The Ability of Babies. University of London Press, London.

Griffiths, R. 1970. The Abilties of Young Children. Child Development Research Centre, London.

Hess, R. D. 1970. Social class and ethnic influences on socialization. In P. H. Mussen (ed.), Carmichael's Manual of Child Psychology (3rd Edition), Vol. II. John Wiley & Sons, New York.

Horowitz, F. D., and Paden, L. Y. 1973. The effectiveness of environmental intervention programs. In B. M. Caldwell and H. N. Ricciuti (eds.), Review of Child Development Research, Vol. 3. University of Chicago Press, Chicago.

Hunt, J. M. V. 1961. Intelligence and Experience. Ronald, New York.

Jakobson, R., and Halle, M. 1956. Fundamentals of Language. Mouton, The Hague.

Kagan, J., and Klein, R. E. 1973. Cross-cultural perspectives on early development. Am. Psychologist, 28:947–961.

Klausmeier, J. J., Ghatala, E. S., and Frayer, D. A. 1974. Conceptual Learning and Development. Academic Press, New York.

Kuhn, D. 1978. Mechanisms of cognitive and social development: One psychology or two? Human Dev. 21:92–118.

Lawton, M. S. 1977. The development of analytic-integrative cognitive styles in young children. Unpublished doctoral dissertation, University of Toronto.

Lee, P. 1978. Early Chinese language stimulation of Chinese infants. Unpublished master's thesis. University of Toronto.

Leithwood, K. A., and Fowler, W. 1971. Complex motor learning in four-year-olds. Child Dev. 42:781–792.

Lenneberg, E. H. 1962. Understanding language without ability to speak: A case study. J. Abnorm. Soc. Psychol. 65:419–425.

Levin, J. R., and Allen, V. L. (eds.). 1976. Cognitive Learning in Children: Theories and Strategies. Academic Press, New York.

Levy, J. 1973. Exercises for Your Baby. Collins, London.

Luria, A. R. 1976. Cognitive Development: Its Cultural and Social Foundations. Harvard University Press, Cambridge, Mass.

Luria, A. R., and Yudovitch, F. I. 1961. The Role of Speech in the Regulation of Normal and Abnormal Behavior. Liveright, New York.

McCarthy, D. 1954. Language development in children. In L. Carmichael (ed.), Manual of Child Psychology (2nd Edition), 492–630, John Wiley & Sons, New York.

McNeill, D. 1970. The development of language. In P. A. Mussen (ed.), Carmichael's Manual of Child Psychology (3rd Edition), Vol. 1. John Wiley & Sons, New York.

Mahoney, M. J. 1977. Reflections on the cognitive-learning trend in psychotherapy. Am. Psychologist, 82:5–13.

Mead, H. 1970. Culture and Commitment: A Study of the Generation Gap. Doubleday & Co., Inc., New York.

Menyuk, P. 1964. Syntactic rules used by children from preschool through first grade. Child Dev. 35:533–546.

Messer, D. J. 1978. The integration of referential speech with joint play. Child Dev. 49:781–787.

Miller, G. A., Galanter, E., and Pribram, K. H. 1960. Plans and the Structure of Behavior. Holt, Rinehart & Winston, New York.

Nelson, K. 1973. Structure and strategy in learning to talk. Monographs of the Society for Research in Child Development, 38 (Whole No. 149).

Ogston, K. The comparative effects of two forms of developmental stimulation on infant competencies. University of Toronto doctoral dissertation. In preparation.

Pascual-Leone, J., and Smith, J. 1969. The encoding and decoding of symbols by children: A new experimental paradigm and a neo-Piagetian model. J. Exper. Child Psychol. 8:328–355.

Redfield, R. 1947. The folk society. Am. J. Sociology, pp. 293–308.

Roberts, G. Maternal influences on cognitive and language development in the first year of life: A program of infant education for West Indian immigrant parents. University of Toronto doctoral dissertation. In preparation.

Skinner, B. F. 1957. Verbal Behavior. Appleton-Century-Crofts, New York.

Smith, M. D. 1978. The acquisition of word meaning: An introduction. Child Dev. 49:950–952.

Snow, C. E., and Ferguson, C. A. 1977. Talking to Children: Language Input and Acquisition. Cambridge University Press, Cambridge, Mass.

Staats, A. W. 1968. Learning, Language and Cognition. Holt, Rinehart & Winston, New York.

Stedman, D. J. 1969. Cited in J. McVicker Hunt, The Challenge of Incompetence and Poverty, p. 225. University of Illinois Press, Urbana.

Strayer, L. C. 1930. Language and growth: The relative efficacy of early and deferred vocabulary training, studied by the method of co-twin control. Genetic Psychology Monograph. 8:215–317.

Sullivan, E. V. 1967. Piaget and the School Curriculum: A Critical Appraisal. Bulletin No. 2. Ontario Institute for Studies in Education, Toronto.

Swenson, A. Parent-administered language program: A comparison of two starting ages. University of Toronto doctoral dissertation. In preparation.

Thomas, H. 1970. Psychological assessment instruments for use with human infants. Merrill-Palmer Quarterly, 16:179–223.

Tonnies, F. 1940. Fundamental Concepts of Sociology (Gemeinschaft and Gesellschaft), Translated and edited by C. P. Loomis. American Book Company, New York.

Vygotsky, L. S. 1962. Thought and Language. MIT Press, Cambridge, Mass.
Weber, M. 1947. The Theory of Social and Economic Organization. Translated by A. M. Henderson and T. Parsons. Oxford University Press, New York.
Whiting, B. B. 1974. Folk wisdom and child-rearing. Merrill-Palmer Quarterly, 20:9–19.
Zimiles, H. 1970. Has evaluation failed compensatory education? *In* J. Hellmuth (ed.), Disadvantaged Child, Vol. 3, Compensatory Education: A National Debate. Brunner/Mazel, New York.

chapter

17

The Nature of
Intervention Research

Summary Chapter

Donald M. Baer

Department of Human Development and Family Life
The University of Kansas
Lawrence, Kansas

The basic research questions to ask about any intervention are Did it work? and, if the answer is yes, the second is Why did it work? But underlying these two initial research questions is a more basic question that often is not a research question: Why intervene? The role of these three questions in the interventions becoming typical in the case of handicapped children may be clarified, perhaps, by considering as counterpoint a very much lighter intervention into a much less serious case in the early nineteenth century: the case of Thomas Babington Macaulay, the English historian, essayist, and statesman. An apocryphal story asserts that Macauley was mute during the first 4 years of his life despite the concerned efforts of his parents to stimulate him to speak. During his 4th year, when he happened to be present at a tea party held by his mother, a guest accidentally spilled very hot tea on him. As she was mopping him off, asking fearfully if he was all right, he spoke his first words: "Thank you, Madam, the agony has abated somewhat." He continued in that style, obviously; and the literature of history demonstrates that his long-term maintenance was excellent.[1]

To discuss this counterpoint at all, the three introductory questions should be applied to it: Why intervene in this case? Did this intervention work? If it did, why did it work?

Why intervene in this case? Because

I. It would be better for Macaulay, and for any child, to be able to speak.

II. By intervening into the case of a remarkably mute child, something may be discovered about the conditions that can produce speech. If all of the conditions that *can* produce speech are known, then

    A. Eventually researchers should be able to find in them the conditions that *do* produce speech in the normal case, and that would be worth knowing. Then the conditions that at least can produce speech should be collected as fast as possible. As this is being done,

    B. Researchers should be able to find in them conditions that are both practical and generally effective for remarkably mute children, and so develop a therapeutic training program for such cases.

III. Otherwise, England would not have had one of its statesmen and scholarship would not have had one of its histories of England.

---

[1] I often deal with silent children, designing interventions that might produce speech by them. Occasionally, when progress seems minimal, I remember the technique of Macaulay's case. But it is always clear to me that the Advisory Committee on Human Experimentation at the University of Kansas would never countenance the intervention unless the tea were at most lukewarm, and that would so strongly depart from what I suspect to be the essence of the intervention that I doubt the cost effectiveness of attempting its modern-day replication.

Did the intervention work? First, it should be noted that the true function of the story is not to be believed, but simply to be heard; it is a better metaphor than a fact. Taking it as metaphor, note that the intervention was not an experiment, but an accident. Still, accidents do occasionally constitute competent experiments, and so any accident, even a metaphorical one, may repay at least brief evaluation. But in this case, evaluation instantly reveals that, in the language of behavior-analytic research design, this was merely an AB design. AB designs are incompetent to establish that any behavior change was an effect of the intervention (B) that preceded it (even if the intervention was aimed at it, rather than spilled on it). AB designs can as easily testify to coincidences between ineffective interventions and behavior changes that were about to happen anyway, as to cause-and-effect. Furthermore, it is doubtful that the A condition of this study—Macaulay's first 4 years—was accurately measured, and was a true case of zero productive speech. It is clear that the B condition of this case— Macaulay's years after childhood—were characterized by elegant, meaningful, and prolific speech (and writing). Thus, it is doubtful that there was a behavior *change* at all, and if there was, that this was the effective intervention that produced it.

Why did the intervention work? Assuming a metaphor in which the intervention described was indeed functional in producing a radical change in Macaulay's productive speech, then a series of uncertainties arises immediately, even in metaphor:

1. Did it have to be tea? Would coffee do? With or without sugar? With or without cream?
2. Did it have to be hot? And if so, would any sudden painful event have served the same function?
3. Was this simply the first event in Macaulay's life truly worthy of comment?
4. Was this simply the first moment in Macaulay's life when someone who had asked him a question then paused long enough to allow an answer?
5. Was this simply the first moment in Macaulay's life when his English standards of courtesy demanded that he answer? Was the fact that the inquiry came from a lady who obviously was in great personal distress a key element?
6. Were 4 years of maturity (apart from productive language development) a necessary prerequisite?
7. Was the presence of an audience important? Was the character of the audience important?
8. Was it significant that the person to be answered was not from Macaulay's immediate family?

9. Would the intervention have worked as well if the subject had not
    been of the personality type that (in maturity) finds the characters
    of causation in the characters of persons rather than in other social
    forces? Or of the personality type that (in maturity) cannot tolerate
    ambiguity?[2] (A 4-year-old with those characteristics might well
    conclude that someone who had spilled very hot tea on you once
    would do so again, especially if you did not seem to be under good
    instructional control, one aspect of which is answering questions
    addressed to you.)

Why should these questions be answered? If there was reason to
intervene in this case, and if indeed this was the intervention that
accomplished the outcome justified by that reason, then almost certainly researchers will want to intervene again in similar cases. To
intervene again effectively, what it was about this intervention that
made it effective must be understood; otherwise, future efforts may
be ineffective. On the other hand, if the only problem was that young
Macaulay was not talking, then none of these questions needs answering, because young Macaulay, post tea, talked very well. With the
problem gone, there is only academic reason for wanting to know why
it has gone. True, a pessimistic pragmatist might suspect that young
Macaulay would stop talking in the near future, and require restarting;
in that case, it might be important to know the essence of the first
intervention responsible for its apparent success. But a quick estimate
of cost-effectiveness suggests strongly that it would be expensive in
many ways to analyze the essence of the intervention in Macaulay's
case, and that it would not be worth doing until it was clear that the
analysis was necessary. Someone dedicated primarily to young Macaulay (like a senior Macaulay) might argue against this conclusion,
but surely most persons would prefer to invest the resources in more
generally useful efforts.

What is meant by "more generally useful efforts" is likely to be
one or both of two possibilities mentioned above. One is the better
understanding of important natural behavioral processes, such as language acquisition; the other is the development of a therapeutic or
educational technique to remedy some important problem that many
children encounter, such as language delay. The first motivation usually implies a venture called "basic" research; the second, "intervention," or "applied" research. Basic research is done in laboratories
with volunteers not at risk for anything worse than a few hours
of boredom, whereas intervention is done with those who seriously

---

[2] Bartlett (1939) quotes William Lamb (Viscount Melbourne) and William Wind-
ham: "I wish I were as sure of anything as Macaulay is of everything" (pp. 332 and
398).

need it and will benefit by it. But some basic behavioral processes, like language acquisition, do not enter laboratories easily: they are too formidable, meaning that they presumably need too long or too intense conditions to be translated into laboratories, and/or that they are too important to the individual who is to serve as the subject. Thus, such basic processes, at first glance, seem to avoid experimental analysis, and in consequence are relegated to merely observational, naturalistic methods of study. Unfortunately, nonexperimental research methods rarely are able to establish cause-and-effect mechanisms (cf. Bijou and Baer, 1960), and so, eventually, curiosity about cause-and-effect mechanisms in those processes leads (often reluctantly) to an examination of the possibilities of intervention research. In intervention research, children who have failed to develop language in a satisfactory manner, and who seem clearly at risk of continuing to fail in this respect, with all its attendant disadvantages, are tinkered with: they have very, very little to lose in such research, and something exceptionally important to (perhaps) gain.[3] The conditions under which they fail to develop speech satisfactorily are not so mysterious: they are the conditions under which the children presently live. The question is What conditions might be added to those, or replace some of those, such that they would then begin to acquire speech much more satisfactorily? Thus, intervention suggests the possibility of a more satisfying cause-and-effect analysis than merely observational research could.

The basic motivation of intervention researchers, however, often is not simply to investigate basic, natural behavioral processes (under the only circumstances in which experimental research is possible with these particular problems); it is also to develop remedial technique for the solution of a problem. In the terms of this example, it is not only to clarify the nature of normal language acquisition, but also to make a process of better language acquisition in an already abnormal case. Basic theorists, reluctantly considering some language intervention research, often ask skeptically whether the techniques used effectively

---

[3] A serious balancing of potential risks and benefits is of course mandatory in all research, and most especially in applied research; and the balancing is to be done not only by the researcher but also by the subjects, the subject's parents or guardians or advocates, and all other interested social agencies. Yet, when nonresearchers examine the actual process of applied research—of intervention—that might be applied to *their* children, they most often seem disappointed. They usually cannot see anything that looks like a risk, and often cannot see anything that looks like even a process: where are the machines, the wires, the flashing lights, the meters, the computers, that science fiction has taught them are the essence of intervention? Is there nothing more than some teachers, some lesson plans, and an observer with a pencil, a clipboard, and a stopwatch? Can just that really fix the child's problem? At the very least, we should display a Datamyte; otherwise, the compulsive solemnity with which we secure informed consent must seem puzzling—or, sometimes, even suspicious.

in such research could possibly be the ones that operate in the normal child acquiring language in the normal environment. The applied researcher who designed the intervention might have asked that question too, but often cared much more about whether these processes would work well, were practical, and were cost-effective; their naturalness was a side issue (and sometimes a non-issue). In stereotype, a basic researcher will analyze the intervention into Macaulay's case at great length, largely because it is so puzzling. Nothing about it suggests that it should have worked; thus, if it did, and if something is to be learned from it, about natural behavioral processes such as language acquisition then it will require very deep analysis indeed. But in stereotype, an applied researcher obedient to only the pragmatics of problem-solving will not need a deep analysis. Instead, that researcher will require a demonstration that this (admittedly odd) intervention did indeed work, and then will want to know whether it typically will work in similar and even not so similar cases of language absence or delay. The Macaulay example at this point loses usefulness for this discussion, not so much because it is untrue as because, even if it were true, it was not an intervention *designed* by either a basic or an applied researcher—it was an accident.

Stereotypic basic researchers doing interventions as a last resort with which to answer a basic behavioral question usually design their intervention to embody some process that they have reason to suspect operates in the normal case. Because they cannot ethically experiment with the normal case, they try the process quite ethically in the abnormal case, where it can hardly do harm, might do good, and also might answer the basic question. Stereotypic applied researchers doing interventions in order to solve a behavioral problem design their intervention to embody some process that they have reason to suspect is effective in accomplishing the behavior changes necessary to the problem's solution. Indeed, applied researchers, intent on solving a behavioral problem, usually design interventions that involve a number of processes, all of which might well be expected to contribute to the problem's solution. In that context, it is interesting to consider the intervention research described in this volume. Examination shows that it is neither stereotypic basic research nor stereotypic applied research (suggesting once again that the distinctions often supposed to separate stereotypic basic and applied research have little reality in the actual behavior of at least some researchers—cf. Baer, 1978).

It is clear that Kysela, Ramey, and Fowler and their colleagues (this volume) all were interested in clarifying basic behavioral problems, and not simply as a means to a basic end: these researchers wanted those problems remediated, and meant to remediate them by their own efforts. Had they stumbled into a remediation that made no basic sense, they still would have derived a great deal of satisfaction from their work—and they soon would have been engaged in some further research to clarify why a remediation that made no sense in terms of current knowledge and theory worked anyway. Although the conditional probability of such "clarifying" efforts by such researchers is high, its absolute probability is low. These interventions were not stumbled into; they were designed and derived from basic behavioral principle and its technology. Thus, it is no surprise to these intervention researchers that their interventions work: they were expected to work.

What may be a surprise is that an intervention worked as well as it did or as poorly as it did. It seems characteristic of current intervention research that it can aim only approximately at its target. It is expected that the outcome will be in the direction of success (remediation), but that it will require some parametric adjustments before it can go very far in that direction. The principles on which it is based say that it ought to work—qualitatively. The technology on which it is based says that those principles work best—quantitatively—when they are adjusted to the individual case. So far, experience with that technology rather strongly indicates that adjustment of that sort is always possible, often can be extremely successful, but is still very difficult to predict in advance. Thus, it is done on a cut-and-try basis much more often, and much more quickly, than by finding and reading a battery of diagnostic correlates. Intervention researchers, then, expect to succeed modestly in their first tries, and also expect that if they are allowed (funded for) any further tries, they might then adjust the details of their intervention to accomplish something appreciably better than modest success. It is wryly interesting to note that their first tries are much more likely to be funded than are the subsequent adjustments of the modestly successful first tries. Those who fund research seem to consider first tries dramatically uncertain (whereas those who program the first tries know, almost to the point of boredom, that they almost surely will succeed somewhat: can 100 years of experimentally valid principle and 20 years of its experimentally valid technology be useless?) And those who fund first tries, as if there were something to be learned from them, then seem to consider subsequent adjustments of first tries "derivative" almost to the point of boredom (whereas those who program the first tries see that the excitement and the true contribution to a socially useful behavioral technology will come from the second and later tries, wherein the crucial adjustments might be discovered and the great benefit possible in the intervention might finally be approximated.[4]

---

[4] Is there a society somewhere with a National Institute of Intervention Adjustments? Perhaps not: A society might need an NIIA to learn enough to create an NIIA.

Kysela et al. (this volume) all fit this description. Kysela's team has built an intervention very strongly on the principles of operant behavior and on the technology of behavior modification, and a good deal of their research design is exactly from that paradigm. Ramey's team clearly has heard of the same principles and the same technology, but their language is eclectic, and their research design is traditional, conventional, and uncontroversial, and certainly appropriate to what is at the moment (which is a first try) an actuarial question: does this intervention work better than a comparison condition, on the average? Fowler's team knows the same basic behavioral science, talks about it more broadly and with greater attention to possible cognitive processes, and is again conventional (and appropriate) in its experimental design. What is important in these characterizations are their commonalities. Their devotion to proof, behavioral principle, technology, and technique are similar, and their terminology, which varies, is almost trivial for the purpose of designing a first-try intervention. Thus, verbal competition among paradigms (operant, cognitive, whatever) is irrelevant. If one approach is to do better than another in the long run, it will be only in the long run, when adjustments to parameters are being made. If one paradigm knows more about adjustable parameters than another, at that point (on second and later tries) it will be reasonable and fruitful to look for differences between paradigms. But on first tries, any paradigm derived from basic behavioral principle, technology, and technique should accomplish some modest success, and differences among those modest successes will represent luck rather than systematic superiority. Thus, this volume very reasonably presents these three first-try interventions as much more alike than different, and that is exactly correct.

One of the main commonalities is their devotion to proof. Even though intervention research typically is done with near certainty that it will succeed to some degree, nevertheless it is done in an experimental design that is capable of showing whether it did indeed succeed—whether it did better than chance, or better than some alternative condition that was not of the same quality of intervention. Such designs are for audiences not so nearly certain that this intervention will succeed to some degree, and—more important—for the researchers themselves, who hope to adjust their first tries into much more successful second, third, and later tries, and therefore need to know just how much better they did than the alternative, on this first try. The fundamental question is not only Did we do better than the alternative? but also How well did we do, considering how well we need to do? An experimental design is necessary to show us how well we did, and to show us and others that we did *something*. (There is always that slim chance that this intervention has its parameters so maladjusted, by bad luck, that it will accomplish nothing, or worse than nothing, with its present sample.)

Thus, intervention researchers, like stereotypic basic researchers, know basic behavioral science, trust it to work, and prove that it works anyway. And they, like stereotypic applied researchers, want it to work in solving an important social problem, and anticipate its true excitement in its later adjustment more than in its first try. What is exquisitely paradoxical about them, perhaps, is their willingness to contradict key elements of both of those stereotypes at the same time as they conform to the ones noted above. They will deliberately confound an otherwise competent experiment by applying not one remedial technique as the experimental intervention, but a number of them simultaneously, so that the probability of a successful intervention is maximized, but with the result that the separate contributions of each possible contributor to that success cannot be discerned in the final outcome; and they will explicitly calculate or estimate the conditions under which it will be worthwhile to do the second-and-later-tries adjustments that are the essence (in Aristotelian logic, the final cause) of applied research and its finest flowering as a discipline, knowing that most often that calculation or estimation will indicate against the second-and-later tries.

Consider Kysela's team's program as an example. Its target is language skill. It properly analyzes language skill into a logically organized collection of specific language skills. Examination of its coherent curriculum, however, will show that these skills are not independent of each other—they overlap. Each has its own small curriculum, but as the skills overlap, so do the small curricula. Thus, several small curricula, sometimes many small curricula, contribute to the development of each language skill. In the interests of generalized stimulus control over the developing language skills, experimental interventions aimed at them are programmed in both clinic and home settings. The home-based interventions are somewhat different from the clinic-based interventions, but both sets are aimed at largely identical language skills. Much of the intervention consists of straightforward operant conditioning (often referred to as teaching), but some of it—especially in the home setting—consists of a variant called "incidental teaching."

Incidental teaching refers to a family of teaching techniques, the essential core of which is their reliance on natural incidents occurring in the life of the student, in which a lesson can be taught with special force just because the student is specially motivated to learn just that lesson at just that time. For example, when a language-deficient child at play indicates that a certain out-of-reach toy is desired, an alert teacher can seize upon that "incident" to begin to secure the toy for the child, but also to insist on an appropriate language response by the child before the toy is finally handed over. At this moment, the child presumably wants the toy more than anything else that might be used as a reinforcer. If the child learns to label that toy for the teacher, and secures the toy in consequence, the child will have learned the label under the most powerful reinforcement available at that moment, and also will have learned the label that was maximally functional in that child's life at that moment. By contrast, it would seem, massed training trials on labels of objects that the teacher has chosen (or the curriculum has chosen), rather than the child, should have less immediate function for the child, and the reinforcer offered for their correct performance is likely to be less powerful than the reinforcer that can be offered appropriate to a natural "incident." This is not to say that nonincidental teaching is ineffective, of course; it is merely a logical argument to the conclusion that incidental teaching could often be more effective than nonincidental teaching. The prevalence of incidental-teaching techniques in the interventions described by Kysela et al. and their colleagues suggests that many intervention researchers have begun to appreciate this logic. Nevertheless, it is reasonable to note that it is, so far, only a logic: the extensive research that can show under what conditions any member of the family of incidental teaching methods is more, or less, effective than any member of the family of nonincidental teaching methods, remains undone. Furthermore, at the level of logic, a number of disadvantages can be discerned. The incidental teacher, for example, needs to be very skillful, exceptionally flexible, and quick; otherwise, "incidents" pass away into lost opportunities appreciated as such only in retrospect. Furthermore, incidental teaching seems most suitable for more competent, and less suitable for less competent students. For example, profoundly retarded persons, it seems, have very few incidents: their abilities and their typical institutional environments have interacted to stereotype, homogenize, and diminish their behavior—there is little that they seem to want at any moment, and little that they seem to do. When incidents are rare, incidental teaching must be slow. Such persons can have incidents thrust upon them in massed trials by a teacher, of course, and in that format, they have even learned the core language curriculum on which some of the Kysela team's program was based. But that would hardly have been considered as incidental teaching; it would have been considered as very nearly the opposite, as the term is used today. Indeed, if the development of verbal labels were attempted for a profoundly retarded person by completely incidental methods, working through the sequential prerequisites of attention and imitation prior to the incidental modeling of just those labels of most significance in the student's immediate environment, the first label mastered would probably be "deathbed."

When Kysela and his colleagues report some degree of success in establishing the language skills of their curriculum, to what can we attribute that success? To one, some, or all of their multitudinous small curricula? To the validity of the overall logic that generated those individual curricula? To the use of operant techniques? To the clinic instruction? To the home instruction? To the use of two instructional settings? To the use of two (and sometimes more) teachers? To incidental teaching? To home-based incidental teaching? Intervention researchers usually answer that all of these components have been shown to be effective for some purpose in one or more prior experimental applications; it is their cumulative effects that are sought in this intervention, and so they are "packaged" together in the intervention for just that purpose.

Given a package of techniques, and the knowledge that the package works modestly well, it is of course possible in subsequent research to analyze the package: to ask which of its components contributes how much to its final overall outcome, or, more simply, to ask whether each of its components contributes anything to its overall outcome. Note, however, that a component may contribute simply on the basis of what it is; or a component may contribute only because of the presence of a specific other component (or specific other components). In that context, then, note the combinatorial arithmetic of package components.

A package of merely three components–call them A, B, and C— may be effective because of any one of seven possibilities. It is possible that all three components—ABC—are needed for the effective outcome. But perhaps one of them is useless, and is present only because of the designer's superstitions about effective intervention techniques. There are three ways in which that could happen: it is AB that is effective, or AC, or BC. Finally, it is possible that only one of the three components is working effectively. Again, there are three ways in which that could be the case: A, or B, or C. Thus, there are seven combinations of three components to compare with one another, to see how the package works: ABC, AB, AC, BC, A, B, and C. The research that would make the necessary analysis then would have to compare seven conditions, perhaps by comparing the outcomes of seven large, well matched groups, or perhaps by applying all seven conditions repeatedly at different times to all of its subjects. The difficulty and the cost of comparing simply the package, ABC, to a comparison condition, must be multiplied seven-fold to do such research.[5] Then consider the arithmetic for a four-component package, which shows that there are 14 combinations to compare, if the package is to be analyzed; or for a five-component package, which yields 30 combinations. (Listed here are the 30 for sceptics to count: ABCDE, ABCD, ABCE, BCDE, ACDE, ABDE, ABC, ABD, ABE, ACD, ACE, ADE, BCD, BCE, CDE, AB, AC, AD, AE, BC, BD, BE, CD, CE, DE, A, B, C, D, and E.) If the simplest experimental intervention research is difficult to fund and difficult to execute, then seven-fold more difficult research is extraordinarily unlikely, and 30-fold more difficult research is sociologically incredible.

Examination of the components of the interventions described in this volume will show immediately that there are many more enumerable, analyzable components to each of them than five. Indeed, a consideration simply of the technique of incidental teaching, now so common to interventions, shows that the label refers to a quite large family of techniques, each member of which has parameters that may be adjusted for more or less effectiveness—as does the family of teaching techniques not called incidental teaching. Thus, a research analysis of the difference between incidental and nonincidental teaching techniques, if it is to be at all comprehensive, is itself sociologically incredible. This is not to say that occasional studies will not emerge, comparing some idiosyncratically chosen variant of incidental teaching to some equally idiosyncratic representative of nonincidental teaching; nor does it deny the probability that when such studies appear, they will be interpreted as showing the superiority of one entire family to the other (or, if the means do not differ, the equivalence of the families). It is only to say that the research was capricious and the interpretation arbitrary. To restate the same thesis in a simpler context, consider the possibility of comparing two different drugs in the relief of pain. No one would long consider comparing an arbitrary dosage of one drug to an arbitrary dosage of the other; the only meaningful comparison is between the complete dosage-response curve of one and the complete dosage-response curve of the other. This is obvious to us because the strong effects of differences in dosage are obvious to us. Unfortunately, in social intervention research, it is not quite so obvious that an intervention is composed of many "drugs," let alone that each "drug" comes in a range of "dosages" that control its effectiveness

---

[5] Indeed, I suggest that the multiplier is more than seven: that rather than gaining the advantages of mass production, one encounters instead exponentially rising difficulties. The justification for this belief is grounded mainly in The Law of Large Numbers and in past experience, but its detailed explanation is best left for another discussion.

very strongly. Nevertheless, experience shows consistently that this analogy is the correct one.

The sociological incredibility of analytic research to untangle the separate effects of the components of packages is identical to the sociological incredibility of the research necessary to compare one package from a certain theoretical orientation to another package from a different theoretical orientation. If it is arbitrary to compare someone's pet version of incidental teaching techniques derived from operant theory and someone else's pet version of nonincidental teaching techniques derived from operant theory, then it is equally arbitrary to compare someone's pet form of intervention derived from operant theory to someone else's pet form of intervention derived from Piagetian theory. What is needed first is the complete analogue of the dosage-response curve for each intervention: that is, a full understanding of how to adjust the parameters of each intervention so that it operates at its optimum effectiveness. With that in hand, a meaningful comparison of one intervention, at its best, to another, at its best, can be made; until then, comparison is meaningless. But getting to that point is as incredibly expensive as analyzing the components of a package; indeed, it is very nearly the same as analyzing the components of a package.

There is a further complication, one very pertinent to the character of much intervention research. One point in analyzing a package is to know if it could operate just as well without some of its components; each component, after all, is to some degree expensive to apply. Then each component can, in principle, be evaluated in terms of the contribution that it makes to the intervention's total effectiveness, relative to its cost of maintenance as part of the intervention. It may be that some components cost "more" than their contribution to the intervention's effectiveness is "worth." "More" and "worth" require quotation marks because both are metaphors in this context: it is not yet agreed upon, nor is it likely ever to be totally agreed upon, exactly how to measure the worth of an intervention that remediates some form and degree of human misery, so as to balance it against the cost of applying the intervention. Yet despite the absence of such a metric, many citizens of many societies apparently feel that there is some point at which the solution to a certain degree of misery costs more than they are willing to help pay. (They often make exactly this point in school bond elections, for example.)

Just as citizens may feel that a certain degree of effectiveness is not worth its cost of implementation, intervention researchers may feel that a certain degree of knowledge is not worth its cost of gathering. In particular, when they have produced interventions that work modestly well, or perhaps a little better than modestly well, they may contemplate the adjustments to that intervention's parameters that are the next logical order of business, note their cost (i.e., their sociological incredibility), and conclude either that 1) no agency will fund the research necessary to accomplish that adjustment, or even if funded, 2) they themselves are not willing to invest the time and effort necessary to accomplish that adjustment, or 3) both.

Any additional bit of science is worth whatever price it costs. Among scientists, that is a widely held if implicit value. Its possible contradiction by the concept of cost-effectiveness ratios is one that is learned from intervention researchers: they are the researchers who of course confront it most explicitly. Every researcher knows about costs; intervention researchers also know about the effectiveness–ineffectiveness continuum. Having your nose rubbed constantly in both cost and the effectiveness–ineffectiveness continuum is no doubt conducive to considering their ratio, and then acting on it.

Thus, this volume presents intervention research done in a research paradigm, yet deliberately designed to represent what any experimentalist will recognize as a confounded experiment; and it presents work that is implicitly aimed at subsequent refinement through adjustment of its parameters once the first try has shown some worthwhile effectiveness, yet is explicitly submitted to cost-effectiveness judgments that usually prohibit that technological refinement. It is clearly not quite basic research, and not quite applied, according to our frequent stereotypes about them; it is instead simply intervention research. That is the way that intervention research goes, and is likely to, indefinitely into the future.

REFERENCES

Baer, D. M. 1978. On the relation between basic and applied research: No need to discuss relation until you locate two parties. *In* T. A. Brigham and A. C. Catania (eds.), Handbook of Applied Behavior Analysis. Irvington, New York.

Bartlett, J. *Familiar Quotations*. 1939. Eleventh Edition (C. Morley, Editor). Little, Brown & Company, Boston.

Bijou, S. W., and Baer, D. M. 1960. The laboratory-experimental study of child behavior. *In* P. H. Mussen (ed.), Handbook of Research Methods in Child Development. John Wiley & Sons, New York.

chapter

18

Major Themes—
An Epilogue

Diane D. Bricker

Center on Human Development
University of Oregon
Eugene, Oregon

Richard L. Schiefelbusch

Bureau of Child Research
University of Kansas
Lawrence, Kansas

contents

The substance and excitement for this volume evolved from a conference entitled Early Language: Development and Intervention, held in Sturbridge, Massachusetts on May 23–25, 1979. The purpose of the conference was to provide substantive contributions toward the understanding of early language acquisition and intervention. Of particular interest was the development of an integrated state of the art publication that could be used to improve current and future intervention efforts with infants and young children having language and communication problems.

The editors were interested in making relevant areas of investigation applicable to early language intervention efforts. Every chapter in this volume contains material that has relevancy for the interventionist. Kagan remarked:

> Careful empirical work on a delimited aspect of nature occasionally provides a fresh view of a much larger mural. Whether the object of study be peas, fruit flies, horseshoe crabs, or infants, nature occasionally hides a prize deep within one of her possessions. If one is sufficiently gentle, careful, and persistent, she allows it to be possessed (p. 18, 1979).

Progress is built upon the discovery of new information and relationships that lead to the subsequent formulation of new strategies or perspectives. This volume contains just such information. Interventionists in search of effective means to assist handicapped and at risk infants and young children should find much of value in this book.

The goal of this chapter is to highlight the trends and ideas presented in this volume that have the greatest direct and immediate relevance for the future planning, designing, and executing of intervention programs for the communicatively handicapped infant or young child.

MAJOR THEMES

Continuity

The notion of the continuity or the discontinuity of behavior is a recurring theme in the psychological literature, and investigators focusing on early language acquisition seem to be increasingly intrigued by the possible roots of formal linguistic structures and preoperational behavior. The continuity debate will likely not be concluded for some time; yet the progression of this debate is leading to a useful clarification of the possible relationship between early and subsequent forms of behavior.

An almost inescapable conclusion of intervention efforts focusing on at-risk and handicapped infants is that early experience is important to the organism's subsequent development and adaptability. Such a conclusion does not suggest in any way that early experience is either the necessary or sufficient condition to produce a well adjusted adult. On the contrary, it is known that certain genetic disorders or organic damage may preclude any hope of a particular infant obtaining any semblance of normal behavior—no matter the quality of the environmental intervention. In addition, the exposure to a suitable early environment does not protect the child against future adverse situations.

A number of investigators have moved the continuity debate into the area of language by studying the emergence of behaviors before the occurrence of first words. In particular, Thoman (this volume) suggested the critical nature of early affective behavior as an organizing structure for the development of communication. Equally important to the continuity debate is the work of other investigators such as Bruner (1975) and Freedle and Lewis (1977), who have suggested the importance of early social-communicative behaviors as a possible foundation for subsequent language behavior.

Although the notion of continuity is supported in the sense that representational behaviors, it is believed, evolve from a combination or interaction of early forms of social, affective, sensorimotor, and communicative behaviors, one could also support the importance of early behaviors from an alternative perspective. Communication could be viewed in the context of a game that is played according to a set of rules. To play the game the infant/child must learn the rules and under what conditions to apply those rules. It is probably possible, given a relatively intact nervous system, that a child could acquire these rules at any time; however, it is likely that the earlier the rules are acquired, and the more opportunity the child has to practice, the better he or she will be able to play the game, that is, to communicate.

Both arguments suggest that the early developmental period is important to the acquisition of more complex skills. This position takes on increasing importance when the focus becomes a handicapped population. By definition these infants are not acquiring the behaviors essential for maximum adaptability. Whether one prefers to look at the deficit from a continuity perspective or a learning/practice perspective, it seems apparent that a restructuring of the environment is necessary to assist these babies in acquiring early communicative skills.

The Communicative Transaction

The information presented in this volume by Fowler, Ramey et al., Bricker and Carlson, Ingram, Thoman, and Chapman should erase most doubts about the reciprocal effect between the infant and his or her social environment. The description by Chapman of mothers' communication with their young children lends urgency to the intervention efforts described by Ramey et al. and Kysela et al. Although researchers are not yet able to establish discrete causal relationships, it seems clear that the linguistic climate provided the infant—generally by the mother—may determine much of the child's facility with his or her language. Those mothers who do not "naturally" slow down, reduce, emphasize, and repeat messages may be making language acquisition difficult for the young child.

In addition to the importance of the content and delivery style of the primary caregiver, there are two other critical elements in the transactional nature of language: the child's responses and the reciprocal nature of a communicative exchange. The form, content, and use of a child's utterance provides the listener essential information about his or her prelinguistic or linguistic competence, or performance.

The infant who smiles, coos, babbles, and subsequently produces words not only is practicing a number of skills but also is eliciting useful feedback from the environment. Most adult speakers tend to gear their linguistic input to the child's responses, apparently knowing intuitively that it is necessary for communication to occur. There seems little doubt that the quality of the child's responses decidedly affects the communicative transaction.

The final element of a communicative transaction is the manner in which the mother's message and the child's message cause change in each other. The responsive mother or caregiver apparently attends to what she interprets the intent of the preverbal child's message to be. The infant who leans toward an object and vocalizes may elicit from the alert mother the retrieval of the object accompanied by an appropriate message, "Oh, you want the book." It seems possible that the sensitive reading by the mother of the infant's early social-communicative gestures, and subsequent early vocalization is instrumental in the development of language. Many investigators have described mother-infant sequences in which joint attention is established (e.g., a point), followed by the child's gesture/vocalization (e.g., doggie), to which the mother provides subsequent feedback (e.g., that's right that's a doggie). The replication of similar sequences has been observed in a population of Down's syndrome infants involved in a longitudinal study at the University of Oregon; it suggests that such "teaching" sequences may occur "naturally" across many mother-infant dyads.

For the infant whose development is significantly delayed, more care may be necessary in creating and maintaining a "healthy" transactional pattern between caregiver and child. Instances in which an infant's erratic behavior may tax the ability of the caregiver to interpret the baby's needs may lead to mutual extinction (Dennenberg and Thoman 1976; Brazelton, Koslowski, and Main, 1974). Of equal concern is the parent who, for whatever reason, is insensitive to the child's early social-communicative behaviors and does not provide the infant with appropriate feedback for acquiring subsequent linguistic behavior. Communicative competence is built on assimilating the speaker-listener roles. The roots of these roles seem to reside in the early transactions between baby and caregiver. The more effective the transactions, the more effective a communicator the infant may become. A primary goal of the interventionist is to detect problems in the caregiver-infant social-communicative transactions and provide assistance in improving them as necessary.

Communicative "Intent" or Function

One of the prevalent targets for discussion in the recent literature has been the notion of communicative intent of the infant or young child. The infant who makes eye contact with the adult, vocalizes, and points toward an object is producing a chain of behaviors that requires some form of guessing or interpretation by the adult. Such prelinguistic gestural and vocal behavior—often called protoimperatives and protodeclaratives—is open to rich interpretation in terms of the infant's communicative intent. That is, given the infant's behavior in a specific context, assignments of meaning to the vocal/gestural response are attempted by the adult. Based on the infant's subsequent response, the adult's interpretation can often be classified as correct (e.g., baby smiles and plays with the object provided) or in error (e.g., baby refuses object and continues to gesture and vocalize). Primary caregivers often become adept at interpreting the infant's communicative intent.

Although the notion of communicative intent seems a useful construct, it may suggest more specific direction and meaning to an infant's behavior than is actually present. In fact, one cannot be sure of an infant's communicative intent or even if the infant *has* a communicative intent, except by definition. It may be equally plausible to describe an infant's early gestural/vocal behavior as random responses that come to be paired with the presentation of "fun" stimuli. The adult's consistent interpretation of the infant's nondiscriminating responses may help the infant to learn that a vocalization and a point produces an object. Investigators such as Nelson (1978) discussed the problems of assigning communicative intent to infants and young children. As an alternative construct, the notion of communicative function has been introduced. Rather than focusing on the child's supposed intent, the focus is on the effect the child's communicative behavior has on the environment—that is, what has been the function or impact of the infant's vocal/gestural behavior.

The introduction of the notion of communicative function into the realm of the interventionist is most important. Many language inter-

vention programs developed in the 1970s established a set of procedures to elicit specific response forms (see for example, Stremel, 1972;
Bricker, Ruder, and Vincent, 1976; Guess, Sailor, and Baer, 1977;
Kent, 1974; Gray and Ryan, 1973) rather than developing the child's
existing communicative behavior. Few programs suggested attention
to the gestural/vocal production that might serve some communicative
function for the child. In fact few suggested that the language training
include activities that might be of interest to the child. Rather, the
intent seemed to be upon assisting children in acquiring those words
and phrase structures that most closely approximated the goals that
were often established without concern for the child's needs and environmental demands.

The concept of communicative intent or communicative function
can re-orient the interventionist to a potentially more effective approach to language training. For communication to be useful—that is,
for verbal behavior to function in a communicative sense—it should
assist the child in his or her daily environmental transactions. The
children should learn the words and structures that allow them to
acquire desired objects, situations or people, to direct people's activities, to allow social interactions, and to offer and receive desired
information. Adults should not impose desires upon the child, rather
they should assist the child in acquiring the necessary language responses for facilitating the child's functional or intentional
communication.

Adopting this position does not preclude the careful structuring
of language intervention procedures. There is still a need for the operationalizing of objectives, detailing descriptions of intervention procedures, and the monitoring of progress through systematic data collection. The major shift is in the selection of content that more closely
approximates the child's needs.

Communicative Context

Recent approaches to language intervention involve an ecological perspective. There is a move away from intervention efforts that conduct
language training under a tutorial model in which the child's communicative needs are neglected, and no effort is made to include the
significant caregivers in the intervention program. The reiteration of
the need for an ecologically sound approach seems unnecessary; however, it may be useful to examine in more detail how infants spend
their day and what implication that has for communicative training.

Most infants spend a substantial amount of time in activities generally labeled as *play*, and fortunately there has been a resurgence of
interest in infant behaviors labeled as play. Although most of us can

reliably point to behaviors that are classified as play, the development of a useful formal definition still eludes the field. This may be, in part, because many investigators believe the term *play* does not reflect the import of an infant's activity. *Play* tends to connote frivolous activities dissociated from learning or the modification of existing behavioral repertoires. On the contrary, so-called play activities for the infant may assist him or her in acquiring new response forms and modifying existing behavior.

> In particular, experiences gained in the context of imitation and play may teach generativity of action structures and the value of mirroring a puzzling event (Uzgiris, this volume).

Uzgiris and others suggest that those behaviors typically classified as play may be instrumental in the infant's growth and development, in both the context of object and social interaction and as a means for providing early forms of communication.

The interventionist who views "play time" as an opportunity for a break from the rigors of instruction may be overlooking a valuable teaching vehicle for the handicapped infant. The exploration of new relationships (e.g., the truck can go around the chair as well as under the chair), the practicing of old skills under different circumstances (e.g., cover the doll with a Kleenex rather than a blanket), the imitation of social ritual games as early communicative exchanges (e.g., peek-a-boo) should be viewed as important mechanisms for the acquisition of behaviors that develop into increasingly more flexible and useful repertoires.

It is important to recognize the need to conduct intervention efforts across environments, people, and activities and that communicative exchanges go beyond verbal channels. In addition to emphasizing the importance of play and imitative behaviors, or in the broader sense, the entire area of sensorimotor behavior in the development of language, is the need to recognize the role exerted by extralinguistic cues in communicative exchanges. Clearly the reception and production of affective responses are essential in many communicative transactions.

Besides broadening the intervention content and context to include play and attention to extralinguistic features, the interventionist should be prepared to explore alternative communication channels with the young child who cannot or does not acquire verbal communication skills. The most important goal of intervention is the establishment of communicative behavior; the form of that behavior is secondary. Of course, the interventionist should always attempt to select the language system that will make the child most adaptable and therefore, if at all possible, oral language is always the first choice. Unfortunately, many

children may n   ꞉n an intelligible manner
and therefore, an alternative or augmentative channel must be selected.
Shane (this volume) offered a useful strategy for choosing among nonverbal approaches.

The view of language for the infant has been broadened into the
more pervasive concept of communication. In the 1970s, researchers
shifted the focus from examining the development of a symbolic system
at the one-word stage to studying the earliest forms of social, affective,
and sensorimotor responses both as elements of communicative exchanges and as possible precursors to more formal linguistic behaviors.

Intervention

Although the strategies lack refinement, there seems to be ample evidence that many infants at risk for language delays or disorders can
be detected early in life and that effective programs can be prescribed
for them. Perhaps the single most important assumption in this volume
is that the early years are important for the development of representational systems and that if problems arise, some form of assistance
should be forthcoming. If there is disagreement, it lies in the form and
function of intervention. It is interesting to note that most researchers
of early childhood problems are not reluctant to offer informal suggestions as to how mothers or other caregivers might most effectively
respond to an infant. At the same time they may be reluctant to rec-
ommend *early* intervention. This reluctance may indicate a miscon-
ception about what is meant by *intervention*. In considering an intervention strategy to help a child at risk, the possibility of an informal
suggestion to the parent may be a form of intervention or a first step
in intervention. In any event, the style of the intervention should be
similar to the modes used by a mother naturally, but keyed, of course,
to the special needs of the child. Arbitrary, insensitive entries into the
life space of the infant and the family should be avoided.

Nevertheless, careful assessments of infant development, parent
education, and prescriptions for infant stimulation can be sensitively
and creatively introduced. Also, environments can be created jointly
by mothers and the infant interventionist to provide additional specialized stimulation beyond that available or likely to occur in the home
environment.

Most language intervention efforts are undertaken after professional referral and expert assessments have indicated that the child is
at risk for the development of speech and language. The most immediate threat to the child's developmental growth, however, may be in
the area of socialization, specifically, communicative interactions. This
is true for the young child who may be a candidate for an augmentative

system of communication (Shane, this volume) as well as for the child with whom there is the intention of preventing or attenuating intellectual handicaps and developmental delays (Kysela et al., this volume).

Fowler provided an analysis of both folk models and planned professional interventions. In effect, he summarized and characterized socially approved arrangements for intervention. Professionally planned interventions of the kind discussed in this book are based upon the assumption of planned outcomes that are sought during a period of temporary responsibility. The short-term nature of most professional efforts suggests that parental involvement, as a prominent feature of the intervention strategy, is highly desirable. Parental responsibility for long-term care and stimulation likely provides a continuity of efforts for virtually all of the desirable conditions described in previous sections. The emphasis upon caregiver involvement is utilized by each of the intervention plans described in this book. The designs call for the maintenance of the program through continuing sequences of development. Ultimately, the professional worker is always accountable to the parent, who has the long range responsibility for the child.

SUMMARY

It is hoped that the remarks in this final chapter reflect the enormous growth in the understanding of the development of communicative competence in the infant. The infant and his or her ability to both give and receive information has not changed; rather, our perceptions of the sophistication with which the infant communicates and the marvelous "natural" instruction provided by the mother has expanded significantly.

In our excitement to include new information and refocus our efforts, it is well to heed Cromer's (this volume) concern about losing sight of those behaviors such as syntax that were and continue to be crucial to our understanding of language. The trick is to consider the relevant parameters and then to create an appropriate balance among the necessary components. This volume provides a reconceptualization of the areas critical to the understanding of early language development and intervention. It is hoped that the contributions have meshed into a useful balance.

Throughout this book there have been numerous references to the competencies of the infant. For instance, the infant is characterized by Thoman as an active participant in the social milieu from the first day of life. Trehub's research references show the infant to be "good" at speech perception during the early weeks of life. Likewise, Cromer details the infant's epigenetic capabilities for learning formal structures of language. One gathers that the human infant not only is equipped to learn a language but also probably has certain "back up" systems that make learning rather certain under normal environmental circumstances. There are probably redundant capabilities for many, if not most, of the learning processes.

Why then, do some children fail to learn a functional language? Obviously, this is a rhetorical, rather than a scientific question. Nevertheless, the question may be useful if it leads us to study the deficits and delays in the language acquisition of children, as Cromer, Shane, and Kysela et al. have done. Likewise, it is a useful question if we consider the possibilities of teaching a language to a child who has not learned language in the usual way and in the usual contexts. One position taken by some language researchers is that if the epigenetic language capabilities are impaired, the child may learn to communicate, but will retain a deficient potential for language acquisition regardless of the intensity of the training. Another position is that early intervention can often prevent and/or attenuate the early risk conditions. These and other controversies about language acquisition and intervention have not been answered. They require further research. One obvious purpose of this volume is to encourage scientific efforts dedicated to this end. Another purpose is to detail and interpret the relevant information that is now available and thereby use fully the knowledge that we do have. Remarkable progress has been and is being made in early language intervention. The translation and refinement of such understanding into successively more effective intervention approaches is the challenge that lies ahead.

REFERENCES

Brazelton, B., Koslowski, B., and Main, M. 1974. The origins of reciprocity: The early mother-infant interaction. In M. Lewis and L. Rosenblum (eds.), The Effect of the Infant on its Caregiver. John Wiley & Sons, New York.

Bricker, D. D., Ruder, K. F., and Vincent, L. 1976. An intervention strategy for language-deficient children. In N. G. Haring and R. L. Schiefelbusch (eds.), Teaching Special Children. McGraw-Hill, New York.

Bruner, J. 1975. The ontogenesis of speech acts. J. Child Lang. 2: 1–19.

Denenberg, V., and Thoman, E. 1976. From animal to infant research. In T. Tjossem (ed.), Intervention Strategies for High Risk Infants and Young Children. University Park Press, Baltimore.

Freedle, R., and Lewis, M. 1977. Prelinguistic conversations. In M. Lewis and L. Rosenblum (eds.), Interaction, Conversation, and the Development of Language. John Wiley & Sons, New York.

Gray, B., and Ryan, B. 1973. A Language Program for the Nonlanguage Child. Research Press, Champaign, Ill.

Guess, D., Sailor, W., and Baer, D. 1977. A behavioral-remedial approach to language training for the severely handicapped. In E. Sontag (ed.), Educational Programming for the Severely and Profoundly Handicapped. CEC, Reston, Va.

Kagan, J. 1979. Overview: Perspectives on human infancy. *In* J. Osofsky (ed.), Handbook of Infant Development. John Wiley & Sons, New York.

Kent, L. 1974. Language Acquisition Program for the Retarded or Multiply Impaired. Research Press, Champaign, Ill.

Nelson, K. 1978. Early speech in its communicative context. *In* F. Minifie and L. Lloyd (eds.), Communicative and Cognitive Abilities-Early Behavioral Assessment. University Park Press, Baltimore.

Stremel, K. 1972. Language training: a program for retarded children. Mental Retardation. 10:47–49.